THE WORLD'S CLASSICS

THE BERTRAMS

ANTHONY TROLLOPE (1815–82), the son of a failing London barrister, was brought up an awkward and unhappy youth amidst debt and privation. His mother maintained the family by writing, but Anthony's own first novel did not appear until 1847, when he had at length established a successful Civil Service career in the Post Office, from which he retired in 1867. After a slow start, he achieved fame, with 47 novels and some 16 other books, and sales sometimes topping 100,000. He was acclaimed an unsurpassed portraitist of the lives of the professional and landed classes, especially in his perennially popular *Chronicles of Barsetshire* (1855–67), and his six brilliant Palliser novels (1864–80). His fascinating *Autobiography* (1883) recounts his successes with an enthusiasm which stems from memories of a miserable youth. Throughout the 1870s he developed new styles of fiction, but was losing critical favour by the time of his death.

GEOFFREY HARVEY is Senior Lecturer in English at the University of Reading, and the author of *The Art of Anthony Trollope*, *The Romantic Tradition in Modern English Poetry*, and *D. H. Lawrence: 'Sons and Lovers': The Critics Debate*. He has edited *Mr Scarborough's Family* for the World's Classics Series.

THE WORLD'S CLASSICS

ANTHONY TROLLOPE

The Bertrams

Edited with an Introduction by

GEOFFREY HARVEY

Oxford New York
OXFORD UNIVERSITY PRESS
1991

Oxford University Press, Walton Street, Oxford OX2 6DP

Oxford New York Toronto
Delhi Bombay Calcutta Madras Karachi
Petaling Jaya Singapore Hong Kong Tokyo
Nairobi Dar es Salaam Cape Town
Melbourne Auckland

and associated companies in
Berlin Ibadan

Oxford is a trade mark of Oxford University Press

First published 1859
First issued as a World's Classics paperback 1991

British Library Cataloguing in Publication Data

Trollope, Anthony, 1815–1882
The Bertrams. – (The world's classics).
I. Title II. Harvey, Geoffrey
823.8 [F]

ISBN 0–19–282645–X

Library of Congress Cataloging in Publication Data

Trollope, Anthony, 1815–1882.
The Bertrams / Anthony Trollope : edited with an introduction by Geoffrey Harvey.
p. cm. (The World's classics)
Includes bibliographical references.
I. Harvey, Geoffrey, 1943– . II. Title. III. Series.
823'.8—dc20 PR5684 B4 1991
90–7387

ISBN 0–19–282645–X

Typeset by Columns of Reading
Printed in Great Britain by
BPCC Hazell Books
Aylesbury, Bucks

CONTENTS

INTRODUCTION

The Bertrams is one of Trollope's more remarkable novels, drawing on his experiences in Egypt and the Holy Land, and has an unusually exotic flavour, particularly for readers familiar only with the English rural world of his Barsetshire series. Although the spring of 1858 found Trollope in Alexandria, negotiating a treaty for the carriage of the British mails through Egypt, characteristically he refused to allow his Post Office duties to interfere with his regular programme of writing, a decision which he later defended sturdily:

> My novels, whether good or bad, have been as good as I could make them. Had I taken three months of idleness between each they would have been no better. Feeling convinced of that, I finished *Doctor Thorne* on one day, and began *The Bertrams* on the next.[1]

Trollope's working diary records that the novel was commenced in Egypt on 1 April, and was continued on his voyage home by way of Malta and Gibraltar, where he inspected the postal service. He worked on it further in England and Ireland; it occupied his private hours during an official visit to Glasgow; and was completed finally on 17 January 1859, while he was investigating problems with the postal system in the West Indies.[2]

Never a reliable critic of his own writing, Trollope did not regard very highly either of the novels that he had been engaged on while in Egypt. He was pleasantly surprised by the success of *Doctor Thorne*, which demonstrated the continuing demand for chronicles of Barsetshire, but he mistakenly blamed the comparatively modest sales of *The Bertrams* on its characterization and plotting. His view of the novel seems to have been coloured by the arduous nature of his professional life, particularly by days spent accompanying letter-carriers on their rounds of Glasgow tenements, and he complained feelingly: 'It was midsummer, and wearier work I never performed. The men would grumble, and then I would think how it would be with them if they had to go home afterwards and write a love-scene.'[3] In fact Trollope greatly underestimated his achievement in *The Bertrams*. Although its initial reception was mixed, the *Examiner* praised Trollope's extension of his fictional territory,[4] the *Saturday Review* declared it the best novel he had yet written,[5] and Tolstoy read it a few years later with profound admiration.[6] Unfortunately its publishing history has been one of neglect. Since the turn of the century, until very recently, no modern edition has been available, and consequently it has been somewhat overlooked.

The Bertrams repays close attention. It reveals more of the scope of Trollope's imagination than many of his novels, possessing a geographical sweep that extends far beyond Barsetshire, London, and Ireland, the settings of his earlier fiction. The symbolic, biblical landscape of the Middle East plays a significant role in the story and is rooted in a vivid evocation of a range of experiences, such as the view of Jerusalem from the Mount of Olives, the bizarre Easter rituals in the Church of the Holy Sepulchre, the claustrophobia and squalor of the pyramids, or the whirling ceremonial dances of the dervishes. Trollope's truth to detail and his ability to convey the atmosphere of place underpin his splendidly satirical treatment of middle-class English pilgrims in their headlong pursuit of vulgar touristic experience; arrogantly blundering into religious services, posturing in native dress, and picnicking on boiled ham among the ancient Jewish tombs in the sacred valley of Jehoshaphat. Trollope also exploits the potential for comedy when young men and women, thrown together on expeditions on horseback across the desert, or on board ship, take advantage of the temporary relaxation of Victorian etiquette.

Writing about the place of *The Bertrams* in his development as a novelist, Trollope reveals that he was 'moved now by a determination to excel, if not in quality, at any rate in quantity'.[7] What this habitual self-deprecation fails to conceal is his ambition to secure a reputation as a serious author. Trollope's absence in the Middle East had given him a fresh perspective on the English social world, and in *The Bertrams* he embarked on an ambitious examination of the dominant mid-Victorian ethos of competition. The cultural malaise which he identifies amounts to a denial of the ideal society that Barsetshire stood for in his imagination, and the relatively generous community of *Doctor Thorne*, represented by the county families of the Duke of Omnium, the Earl de Courcy, and Mr Gresham, has given way in *The Bertrams* to an altogether more complex and sombre world.

Published in 1859, the same year as two books which, in their different ways, symbolize the climate of the period, Charles Darwin's *Origin of Species*, with its bleak theory of the survival of the fittest, and Samuel Smiles's *Self-Help*, a popular celebration of energetic, self-motivated enterprise, *The Bertrams* explores the pervasive influence of the doctrine of individualism, to which these works give powerful expression. Trollope's main theme is introduced in his opening, keynote chapter entitled 'Væ Victis!' ('Woe to the vanquished!') in which he demonstrates how in the University, where fundamental liberal values have traditionally been nurtured, what matters now is not personal development, much less disinterested scholarship, but gaining the first prize.

Trollope records with deepening irony the effect of this climate, primarily through the careers of three Oxford graduates: the brilliant George Bertram, who has flourished in the academic hothouse, and his friends, the charming, ambitious Henry Harcourt, who scales the political heights to become Solicitor-General, and the honest, dogged Arthur Wilkinson, one of the 'vanquished'. While Wilkinson, depressed at having missed a first-class degree and the chance of a college fellowship, takes up the duties of priest in his late father's parish, George Bertram is tempted by the regal, Junoesque beauty of Caroline Waddington to forsake his ideal of service in the Church for romantic love and the dull grind of a career at the bar. And Caroline likewise succumbs to passion at the expense of her settled aim of gaining a place in the social world through marriage to an ambitious man. Yet because neither can accept the compromise implied in their altered choices, their clash of wills and principles results in psychological torment, which Trollope explores with great tact and subtlety. Although muted by understanding and sympathy, his moral judgement emerges clearly. The fittest to survive are not these intelligent and beautiful egoists, unable to negotiate between passion and prudence; or in the case of Henry Harcourt, between his inflated desires and changed political realities; but ordinary people, such as Arthur Wilkinson and Adela Gauntlet, who make limited claims on life, remaining rooted in their humdrum rural community, far from the allure of London and Paris, and who manage to sustain both love and faith.

The Bertrams has its origin partly in Trollope's perception of the growing conflict within an expanding, prosperous Victorian society between traditional, communal values and the new, individualistic ethic. This is focused most sharply in the tense encounters between the graduate, George Bertram, with his optimism and faith, and his hard-faced, rich uncle, a successful London merchant. In spite of their mutual respect and affection, their deep opposition (a mixture of ideology, snobbery, and stiff-necked pride) proves irreconcilable. As a gentleman, George disdains the vulgar tyranny of commerce, while the old man contemptuously dismisses a University education as irrelevant snobbery, and the Church as sheer nonsense. A world in which material success has become the only measure of value, Trollope suggests, has no place for outmoded beliefs, and the spheres of the University and the Church, each a focus of youthful idealism and a source of shared values, are increasingly marginalized as the novel proceeds.

Trollope's examination of this malaise is intimately linked with his treatment of a fundamental dilemma for young men and women, which fascinated him and which he pursued in several later novels, the problem of choosing a partner, a career, and a code by which to live. In George Bertram Trollope offers a peculiarly subtle and modern example. Although an academic hero with the world at his feet, and alive to the attraction of fame and wealth, nevertheless he is radically at odds with the ideology of the age. The terms of his choice are symbolized for him by the alternative paths taken by his friends, Arthur Wilkinson and Henry Harcourt, and his agonized vacillation, ironically on the Mount of Olives, between the Church and the world, demonstrates his essential unfitness for either. And this is his tragedy.

Trollope regarded the ethic of competition as the chief threat not only to individual happiness, but to the fragile ideal of a harmonious society. The insular community of scholars at the University is riven by the annual contest of the final examinations, as college is set against college, each championing its own intellectual gladiator. And in the wider social world the cause of social cohesion is poorly served, in Trollope's view, by an adversarial legal system, which is merely the lackey of commerce and runs contrary to basic principles of justice. However, Trollope discerned an even greater threat posed by the advent of meritocracy, represented by the proposed introduction into the Civil Service of competitive examinations, the subject of several of Trollope's public lectures, and of a satirical attack in *The Three Clerks*. In *The Bertrams* the idea of a 'grand competitive examination' is savagely mocked:

> Let the devil take the hindmost; the three or four hindmost if you will; nay, all but those strong-running horses who can force themselves into noticeable places under the judge's eye. This is the noble shibboleth with which the English youth are now spurred on to deeds of—what shall we say?—money-making activity. (p. 2)

Trollope felt that such divisiveness would undermine what he considered to be a cornerstone of social harmony, the code of the gentleman, which included the obligation of courteous public service, a theme which he returned to in *The Last Chronicle of Barset*.

The novel's underlying concern with social harmony is developed in a beautifully judged comic scene, which serves to reveal the insidiously dehumanizing effect of the spirit of competition, and also establishes links between the public world of the main story and the predominantly private, feminine domain of Littlebath. The satirical connection is made, through Trollope's description of one of the sociable Miss Todd's card-parties, between the ethic of capitalism and the law of the jungle:

> No stockjobber on 'Change could go about his exciting work with more animating eagerness. There were those who scolded, and those who were scolded. Those who sat silent, being great of mind, and those who, being weak, could not restrain their notes of triumph or their notes of woe; but they were all of them as animated and intense as a tiger springing at its prey. (p. 286)

The repressed ferocity of the contest between the whist-players finally results in the comic collapse of decorum, when the infirm and inoffensive Lady Ruth Revoke, reduced to a silent, nodding automaton by her partner's sustained barrage of contempt, confounds Miss Ruff in front of the stunned company by desiring, with quiet intensity, that her tongue should break like glass, before being helped from the room.

As its title implies, *The Bertrams* is a novel about family relationships, but relationships in the process of being warped by the money ethic. The two elderly Bertram brothers, George, a Croesus of the city, and Sir Lionel, a military man in the diplomatic service, worship the twin gods of money and expediency. Separated by years of distrust and dislike, their only connection is the nexus of debt resulting from George's provision of an education for his nephew. And young George finds his dealings with both his estranged father and his manipulative uncle deeply disturbing. Sir Lionel plainly regards him as a source of ready cash and a future means of access to his brother's fortune, while Mr Bertram's secrecy about the existence of his granddaughter and possible heir is symptomatic of his paranoia. Caroline Waddington, the granddaughter, disillusioned with passion, abandons her principles for the social eminence offered by a loveless match with Sir Henry Harcourt, while her husband plans to advance his career with her grandfather's wealth. A further instance of money forcing family relationships awry is provided in a comic key by Arthur Wilkinson's unnatural subservience to his mother, who naïvely believes that she has some claim on his stipend, and his neurotic anxiety about marriage.

The heady entrepreneurial climate of the mid-Victorian years forms the immediate context for Trollope's social criticism in *The Bertrams*. The most topical, and for modern readers the most elusive of his numerous contemporary references, is his allusion to Colonel Waugh, whose pursuit by the police for a massive fraud perpetrated by his London and Eastern Banking Corporation was recorded in *The Times* during 1857 and 1858. Colonel Waugh's criminality, so vividly before the public in the year prior to the publication of *The Bertrams*, represented for Trollope the logical extension of the money culture. He is introduced in terms of personal contrast, for Mr Bertram, Trollope tells us:

> ... was no Colonel Waugh, rich only by means of his rich impudence. It is not destined that he shall fall brilliantly, bringing down with him a world of ruins. He will not levant to Spain or elsewhere. His wealth is of the old-fashioned sort, and will abide at any rate such touch of time as it may encounter in our pages. (p. 54)

However, the contrast between the historical and fictional figures serves to enforce the parallel, for although a model of financial probity and a pillar of the city, Mr Bertram does not escape the morally debilitating effect of wealth. In spite of his several virtues, in Trollope's view, 'he had been a bad man. He had opened his heart to that which should never find admittance to the heart of man. The iron of his wealth had entered into his very soul.' (p. 549) The developing monomania of this giant of commerce, this Faustian figure as Trollope describes him, who has sold his soul for the power of money, and who even on his deathbed summons sufficient energy to resent the doctor's fee, is allowed to emerge gradually and with skilful psychological realism. And in the end his inflexible, inhuman materialism finds its appropriate symbolism in his physical paralysis.

Although *The Bertrams* captures the ethos of the 1850s, its story is set firmly in the preceding decade and reveals the working of a sensitive historical imagination. In order to create for the reader the sense of a real, varied, and dynamic culture, Trollope tactfully employs historical references of considerable range and density. He alludes not only to the great political figures of the 1840s, such as Sir Robert Peel, Lord John Russell, Lord Brougham, and Richard Cobden, shadows moving in the background of the main story, but also to famous racehorses owned by Lord Palmerston, Lord Derby, and Lord George Bentinck, together with their well-known trainers and jockeys. He mentions briefly such varied events as John Henry Newman's involvement in the Tractarian movement at Oxford, the cut-throat economics of the railway mania, the political troubles of Louis Philippe, the citizen king of France, and popular novels of the day, such as Dickens's *Martin Chuzzlewit*.

This use of history is essential to Trollope's purpose. Writing from the perspective of 1858, he seems to have identified the mid-1840s as representing in the Victorian consciousness a symbolic watershed between an allegiance to generally shared values, and the rampant spread of godless materialism. It was a period of great commercial expansion, epitomized by the railway boom, but more significant for Trollope was the dramatic fall of Peel's government over the repeal of the Corn Laws, and in the same year the production by Mary Ann Evans (later George Eliot) of her translation of David Friedrich Strauss's controversial book, *Das Leben Jesu* (*The Life of Jesus*). Trollope evidently saw these as signalling profound changes in feeling and behaviour. In pushing through what was essentially a Whig measure in order to cling to power, the Tory party, according to Trollope, had sacrificed political integrity to expediency. This is why the demise of Peel's government, dragging down with it the fictional Solicitor-General, Sir Henry Harcourt, is a pivotal event in *The Bertrams*. And the breakdown of the principles governing public life is mirrored in personal experience by the threat to long-cherished Christian beliefs posed by the new theology. Bertram's book, 'The Romance of Scripture', which adopts the de-mythologizing rationalism of his historical counterpart, Strauss, causes a great stir and loses him his college fellowship. Such emphasis on theological matters is rare in Trollope, and the clash between the old theology and the new finds stark expression in the serious debate between George Bertram, whose spiritual frustration is fed by his personal sorrow, and Arthur Wilkinson. The rationalist has much the better of the argument, but fails to shake his friend, the vicar's simpler faith. In *The Bertrams* Trollope employs these events in the spheres of politics and theology to symbolize the general collapse of unifying values, and the ushering in of an altogether worse kind of world.

In order to broaden the scope of his social comment, Trollope occasionally brings forward a representative minor figure. One example of this method is his use of Henry Harcourt's mentor, Mr Neversaye Die, a 'rich, quiet, hard-working, old chancery barrister' (p. 197). Although a Tory of the old school, when he understands that Harcourt's sole aim in entering politics is to become Solicitor-General as soon as possible, Mr Die's advice is that he should adopt Liberal policies, yet be sure to support Peel's desire for free trade in corn, which elicits from Trollope the sardonic comment:

> Mr Die himself of course regarded corn-law repeal as an invention of the devil. He had lived long enough to have regarded Catholic emancipation and Parliamentary reform in the same light. Could you have opened his mind, you would probably have found there a settled conviction that the world was slowly coming to an end, that end being brought about by such devilish works as these. But you would also have found a conviction that the Three per Cents would last his time, and that his fear for the future might with safety be thrown forward, so as to appertain to the fourth or fifth, or, perhaps, even to the tenth or twelfth coming generation. Mr Die was not, therefore, personally wretched under his own political creed. (p. 198)

As the label name of Harcourt's legal tutor suggests, elements of the old morality play lie beneath the realistic surface of this novel, and George Bertram's self-appointed adviser, his uncle's elderly man of business, Mr Pritchett, tempts him throughout the novel with the prospect of Mr Bertram's wealth, just as George continues to be drawn by the proximity of the unhappy Caroline Harcourt. Towards the end of the story Mr Pritchett is also pressed into the service of Trollope's satirical scrutiny of the commercial mind. Troubled by his favourite's unnatural refusal to court Mr Bertram for his enormous fortune, in spite of such determined competition from Sir Henry Harcourt, the melancholy Mr Pritchett reproaches George for this neglect at his uncle's funeral, and his unconscious burlesquing of the

Scriptures reveals the different moral world that he inhabits:

> 'Oh, Mr George!' he said, just before they went to the churchyard, 'we are grass of the field, just grass of the field; here today, and gone tomorrow; flourishing in the morning, and cast into the oven before night! It behoves such frail, impotent creatures to look close after their interests—half a million of money! I'm afraid you didn't think enough about it, Mr George.' (p. 557)

Money is inextricably bound up with another increasingly prominent issue among the Victorians, women's desire for self-determination. Caroline Waddington is one of a number of women in Trollope's novels who wish to achieve independence, but find that the opportunity for individual fulfilment is confined to the sphere of marriage. Trapped between a genuine need for selfhood and the traditional woman's role of helpmate, Caroline displays a disturbing element of masochism in her choice of servitude and the suppression of her identity. Harcourt's political circle approves of wives such as Mrs Stistick, who is content to sit through interminable dinners, 'meditating on her children's frocks or her husband's linen' (p. 423). And similarly Caroline Harcourt, although a goddess in the drawing-room of her fine house in Eaton Square, suffers a lack of animation which in Sir Henry's eyes renders her little more than a 'doll' (p. 421). However, her growing hatred of her husband, fuelled by her passion for her former fiancé, and by her fierce pride, leads inevitably to her dramatic abandonment of her sham marriage, and her penitential retreat to the solitude of her uncle's house.

Throughout the novel Caroline is contrasted with the more traditional heroine of Victorian fiction, Adela Gauntlet, who acts to some extent as a moral touchstone, waiting patiently for Arthur Wilkinson to overcome his inhibiting sense of prudence, break free of his mother, and entrust himself to love. In turn the two young women are contrasted with the spinsters, Miss Todd and Miss Baker, in very unromantic Littlebath, where such women are often pursued for their modest incomes by retired diplomats and military men of dubious backgrounds and morals. For Caroline and Adela, the lives of Miss Todd and Miss Baker present the dire alternative to marriage, and form part of the realistic context of their choices. However, these essentially comic characters, who reappear later in *Miss Mackenzie*, are important to Trollope because they manage to offer a generous and positive response to life's drabness. When the doughty Miss Todd is challenged over the playing of cards, by Mr O'Callaghan, a curate among the pious set in Littlebath, she responds with firmness, realism, and wit:

> 'You see you have your excitement in preaching, Mr O'Callaghan. These card-tables are our pulpits; we have got none other. We haven't children, and we haven't husbands; that is, the most of us. And we should be in a lunatic asylum in six weeks if you took away our cards.' (p. 282)

While Trollope does not endorse unreservedly any of the women's solutions to their dilemmas, for even Adela Gauntlet is somewhat passive and prim, he is concerned to stress, in their transactions with society, the necessity of sustaining a strong sense of self-identity.

There is an almost tragic inevitability about the destinies of Trollope's major characters in *The Bertrams*, for they have an inexplicable propensity for making wrong choices, and his imagination is deeply engaged in exploring the consequences: George's abandonment of his career, and the undermining of his spiritual life; Caroline's failed marriage; Harcourt's political fall and despair; and Arthur's neurotic depression. And equally important for the moralist are the rejected alternatives. The worldly match between Caroline and Harcourt is marred by her earlier experience of genuine passion with George. So, too, George's startling recognition of his attraction to Adela is nullified by her prior emotional commitment to Arthur. In Trollope's moral world people have to live with the full knowledge of their choices, and of the perversity of their hearts.

For many readers one of the pleasures of a Trollope novel is the relationship which is established with the narrator, who assumes terms of friendly equality, and also shared values. He functions variously as commentator, psychologist, moralist, and guide to the novel's social world. In particular he is concerned to establish the realistic basis of this story dealing with such contemporary issues. Spurning sensationalism, he wryly contrasts his own tale with the Gothic horror fiction of 'Monk' Lewis and Ann Radcliffe, which depends on the maintaining of suspense, claiming, 'I have no ambition to surprise my reader. Castles with unknown passages are not compatible with my homely muse' (p. 161), before blithely revealing that Caroline Waddington is in truth old Mr Bertram's granddaughter. Another of the narrator's roles is that of a sounding-board for the views implicit in the novel about, for instance, the position of women in society. He comments acerbically on the barbaric custom of incarcerating the ladies after dinner, and offers the whimsical opinion that young ladies nowadays need a handbook on behaviour, so complex has become the etiquette governing courtship. And the humanity and wisdom of his discourse on more serious topics germane to the story, such as the illusions of youth, the pain of growing older, or the essential subjectivity of all our experience, confer on the narrative a further dimension of interest.

Although *The Bertrams* is remarkable in encompassing the examination of mid-Victorian values, psychological enquiry, travelogue, theological debate, satire, and social comedy, Trollope's story is held together by its realism and its coherent development. In its early stages it is organized by the metaphor of the quest, for George Bertram's visit to the Holy Land is primarily a search for a vocation, and this potent metaphor is repeated towards the end of the novel in the experience of Arthur Wilkinson, who like Bertram only discovers his true priorities freed from the constraints of English society, while visiting Egypt for his health. However, as the story broadens out from the quest, Trollope begins to trace an ironic pattern in the lives of his characters, as he charts the interweaving of their individual destinies. Harcourt's splendid success is counterpointed by Bertram's despair and Wilkinson's depression; while Adela's fidelity is rewarded at precisely the time when her friend Caroline's life is in ruins. And as so often in Trollope's novels, this pattern is extended.

The consecutive courtship of Miss Todd and Miss Baker for their money by Sir Lionel Bertram is a parody of the romantic values tested in the main story; and in a similar way George's desultory flirtation with the young widow on the ship returning from Egypt is a comically debased version of his earlier ardent pursuit of Caroline Waddington.

In spite of its moments of comedy and passages of exotic description, *The Bertrams* is a sombre novel about people's blighted lives; about loveless, mercenary marriages and lonely deaths. Lured by the false promise of ambition, the young gradually lose their illusions, while the hearts of the old harden with cynicism. The novel records the tarnishing of romantic love, the fragmentation of family relationships, and the evaporation of religious faith. It is concerned, too, with the more obscure depths of human nature, and the strange perversity that makes people choose for themselves the most damaging course. Trollope locates the cause of these ills in the pervasive doctrines of individualism and materialism. A modern, atomistic society has been created, in which the traditional, communal values of Barsetshire have been swept away.

[1] *An Autobiography*, ed. Michael Sadleir and Frederick Page (Oxford, 1950; reprinted with an Introduction by P. D. Edwards, World's Classics, 1987), p. 122.

[2] See Bodleian MS Don. C.9, and *Autobiography*, p. 125.

[3] *Autobiography*, p. 127.

[4] Donald Smalley, ed., *Anthony Trollope: The Critical Heritage* (Routledge & Kegan Paul, 1969), p. 98.

[5] *Critical Heritage*, p. 96.

[6] See R. H. Super, *The Chronicler of Barsetshire: A Life of Anthony Trollope* (Ann Arbor: University of Michigan Press, 1988), p. 100.

[7] *Autobiography*, p. 122.

NOTE ON THE TEXT

The Bertrams was first published in March 1859 in three volumes by Chapman and Hall, and reduced to a single-volume format in 1860. The present edition is based on an undated reprint by Ward, Lock of this single volume, probably published in the 1880s. This edition has been checked against the first edition of 1859, and obvious errors and inconsistencies in that text have been silently corrected.

SELECT BIBLIOGRAPHY

Discussions of *The Bertrams* may be found in: Ruth apRoberts, *Trollope: Artist and Moralist* (Chatto & Windus, 1971); Bradford A. Booth, *Anthony Trollope: Aspects of His Life and Art* (Edward Hulton, 1958); A. O. J. Cockshut, *Anthony Trollope: A Critical Study* (Collins, 1955); P. D. Edwards, *Anthony Trollope: His Art and Scope* (Brighton, Harvester Press, 1978); James R. Kincaid, *The Novels of Anthony Trollope* (Oxford, Clarendon Press, 1977); Robert M. Polhemus, *The Changing World of Anthony Trollope* (Berkeley and Los Angeles, University of California Press, 1968); Arthur Pollard, *Anthony Trollope* (Routledge & Kegan Paul, 1978); and R. C. Terry, *Anthony Trollope: The Artist in Hiding* (Macmillan, 1977).

The response of contemporary reviewers to Trollope's novels, including *The Bertrams*, is recorded in Donald Smalley (ed.), *Trollope: The Critical Heritage* (Routledge & Kegan Paul, 1969); and examined in David Skilton, *Anthony Trollope and his Contemporaries* (Longman, 1972). R. H. Super's recent biography, *The Chronicler of Barsetshire* (Ann Arbor, University of Michigan Press, 1988), provides background information about the novel, adding to Trollope's own account in *An Autobiography* (1883: World's Classics, 1987).

General studies of Trollope's fiction include: Geoffrey Harvey, *The Art of Anthony Trollope* (Weidenfeld & Nicolson, 1980); Shirley Robin Letwin, *The Gentleman in Trollope: Individuality and Moral Conduct* (Macmillan, 1982); Bill Overton, *The Unofficial Trollope* (Brighton, Harvester Press, 1982); Stephen Wall, *Trollope and Character* (Faber & Faber, 1988); and Andrew Wright, *Anthony Trollope: Dream and Art* (Macmillan, 1983). Also of interest are two collections of essays: Tony Bareham (ed.), *Anthony Trollope* (Vision Press, 1980); and John Halperin (ed.), *Trollope: Centenary Essays* (Macmillan, 1982).

A CHRONOLOGY OF ANTHONY TROLLOPE

VIRTUALLY all Trollope's fiction appeared first in serial form, with book production timed to coincide with the final instalment of the serial. In this chronology the titles are dated as on the title-page of the first book edition. On a very few occasions the book edition appeared in December of the year previous to that indicated on the title-page, so as to catch the Christmas sales.

1815 (24 Apr.) Born at 6 Keppel Street, Bloomsbury, the fourth son of Thomas and Frances Trollope.

1822 To Harrow as a day-boy.

1825 To a private school at Sunbury.

1827 To school at Winchester.

1830 Removed from Winchester and returned to Harrow.

1834 The family move to Bruges.
(Autumn) He accepts a junior clerkship in the General Post Office.

1841 (Aug.) Deputy Postal Surveyor at Banagher, King's County, Ireland.

1843 (Autumn) Begins work on his first novel, *The Macdermots of Ballycloran*.

1844 (11 June) Marries Rose Heseltine.
Transferred to Clonmel, County Tipperary.

1845 Promoted to the office of Surveyor, and transferred to Mallow, County Cork.

1845–7 Famine and epidemic throughout Ireland, especially the south and west with which Trollope was familiar.

1847 *The Macdermots of Ballycloran* published in 3 vols. (Newby).

1848 Rebellion in Ireland, concentrated in Cork and Tipperary.
The Kellys and the O'Kellys; or Landlords and Tenants 3 vols. (Colburn).

1850 Writes *The Noble Jilt* (published 1923).
La Vendée; an Historical Romance 3 vols. (Colburn).

1851 Transferred to England.

1853 Returns to Ireland; completes *The Warden* (the first of the Barsetshire novels) in Belfast.

1854 (Autumn) Leaves Belfast and settles outside Dublin at Donnybrook.

1855 *The Warden* 1 vol. (Longman).

1857 *Barchester Towers* 3 vols. (Longman).
(Sept.) Visits his mother in Florence.

1858 *Doctor Thorne* 3 vols. (Chapman & Hall).
The Three Clerks 3 vols. (Bentley).
(Feb.) Departs for Egypt on Post Office business.
(Mar.) Removes from Egypt to Palestine.
(Apr.-May) Returns via Malta, Gibraltar, and Spain.
(May-July) Visits Scotland and north of England on business.
(Aug.-Oct.) At home in Ireland.
(Nov.) On Post Office business in the West Indies.

1859 *The Bertrams* 3 vols. (Chapman & Hall).
The West Indies and the Spanish Main 1 vol. (Chapman & Hall).
(Sept.) Holiday in the Pyrenees.
(Dec.) Leaves Ireland; settles at Waltham Cross.

1860 *Castle Richmond* 3 vols. (Chapman & Hall).
(Oct.) With his wife he visits his mother and brother in Florence; makes the acquaintance of Kate Field, a beautiful twenty-year-old American with whom he falls in love.

1861 *Framley Parsonage* 3 vols. (Smith, Elder).
Tales of All Countries—first series, 1 vol. (Chapman & Hall).
(Spring) Elected a member of the Garrick Club; some two years later is elected to the committee to fill the vacancy caused by Thackeray's death.
(Aug.) To America on official business.

1862 *Orley Farm* 2 vols. (Chapman & Hall).
North America 2 vols. (Chapman & Hall).
The Struggles of Brown, Jones and Robinson; by One of the Firm 1 vol. (New York, Harper—an American piracy).
(Spring) Returns home from America.

1863 *Rachel Ray* 2 vols. (Chapman & Hall).
Tales of All Countries—second series 1 vol. (Chapman & Hall).
(6 Oct.) Death of his mother, Mrs Frances Trollope.
(Dec.) Death of W. M. Thackeray.

1864 *The Small House at Allington* 2 vols. (Smith, Elder).
Can You Forgive Her? 2 vols. (Chapman & Hall).
(Summer) Elected a member of the Athenaeum Club.

1865 *Miss Mackenzie* 1 vol. (Chapman & Hall).
Hunting Sketches 1 vol. (Chapman & Hall).

1866 *The Belton Estate* 3 vols. (Chapman & Hall).
Travelling Sketches 1 vol. (Chapman & Hall).
Clergymen of the Church of England 1 vol. (Chapman & Hall).

1867 *Nina Balatka* 2 vols. (Blackwood).
The Last Chronicle of Barset 2 vols. (Smith, Elder).
The Claverings 2 vols. (Smith, Elder).
Lotta Schmidt and Other Stories 1 vol. (Strahan).
(1 Sept.) Resigns from the Civil Service.

1868 *Linda Tressel* 2 vols. (Blackwood).
(Mar.) Leaves London for the United States on business involving copyright, in touch again with Kate Field.
(July) Returns from America.
(Nov.) Stands unsuccessfully as Liberal candidate for Beverley, Yorkshire, losing £2,000 in the enterprise.

1869 *Phineas Finn; the Irish Member* 2 vols. (Virtue & Co.).
He Knew He Was Right 2 vols. (Strahan).
Did He Steal It? A Comedy in Three Acts—a version of *The Last Chronicle of Barset* 1 vol. (printed by Virtue & Co.).

1870 *The Vicar of Bullhampton* 1 vol. (Bradbury, Evans).
An Editor's Tales 1 vol. (Strahan).
The Commentaries of Caesar 1 vol. (Blackwood).

1871 *Sir Harry Hotspur of Humblethwaite* 1 vol. (Hurst & Blackett).
Ralph the Heir 3 vols. (Hurst & Blackett).
(Apr.) Gives up house at Waltham Cross.
(May) Sails to Australia to visit his son.
(20 July) Arrives at Melbourne.

1872 *The Golden Lion of Granpere* 1 vol. (Tinsley).
(Jan.-Oct.) Travelling in Australia and New Zealand.
(Apr.) A dramatized (and pirated) version of *Ralph the Heir* produced by Charles Reade.
(Dec.) Returns via the United States, and settles in Montagu Square, London.

1873 *The Eustace Diamonds* 3 vols. (Chapman & Hall).
Australia and New Zealand 2 vols. (Chapman & Hall).

	(Winter) Hunting actively.
1874	*Phineas Redux* 2 vols. (Chapman & Hall). *Lady Anna* 2 vols. (Chapman & Hall). *Harry Heathcote of Gangoil; a Tale of Australian Bush Life* 1 vol. (Sampson Low).
1875	*The Way We Live Now* 2 vols. (Chapman & Hall). (Feb.) Travels to Ceylon via Brindisi and the Suez Canal, once again on the way to Australia. (Mar.-Apr.) In Ceylon. (June) Arrives in Australia. (Aug.-Oct.) Sailing homewards. (Oct.) Begins work on his *Autobiography*.
1876	*The Prime Minister* 4 vols. (Chapman & Hall).
1877	*The American Senator* 3 vols. (Chapman & Hall). *Christmas at Thompson Hall* 1 vol. (New York, Harper). (June) Leaves London for South Africa. (Dec.) Sails for home.
1878	*Is He Popenjoy?* 3 vols. (Chapman & Hall). *South Africa* 2 vols. (Chapman & Hall). *How the 'Mastiffs' Went to Iceland* 1 vol. (Virtue & Co.). (June-July) Travels to Iceland in the yacht 'Mastiff'.
1879	*An Eye for an Eye* 2 vols. (Chapman & Hall). *John Caldigate* 3 vols. (Chapman & Hall). *Cousin Henry* 2 vols. (Chapman & Hall). *Thackeray* 1 vol. (Macmillan).
1880	*The Duke's Children* 3 vols. (Chapman & Hall). (July) Settles at Harting Grange, near Petersfield.
1881	*Dr Wortle's School* 2 vols. (Chapman & Hall). *Ayala's Angel* 3 vols. (Chapman & Hall).
1882	*Why Frau Frohmann Raised Her Prices; and Other Stories* 1 vol. (Isbister). *Kept in the Dark* 2 vols. (Chatto & Windus). *Marion Fay* 3 vols. (Chapman & Hall). *The Fixed Period* 2 vols. (Blackwood). *Palmerston* 1 vol. (Isbister). (May) Visits Ireland to collect material for a new Irish novel. (Aug.) Returns to Ireland a second time. (Sept.) Moves to London for the winter. (6 Dec.) Dies in London.
1883	*Mr Scarborough's Family* 3 vols. (Chatto & Windus).

	The Landleaguers (unfinished) 3 vols. (Chatto & Windus).
	An Autobiography 2 vols. (Blackwood).
1884	*An Old Man's Love* 2 vols. (Blackwood).
1923	*The Noble Jilt* (a play) 1 vol. (Constable).
1927	*London Tradesmen* 1 vol. (Elkin Mathews).
1972	*The New Zealander* 1 vol. (Oxford University Press).

The Bertrams

CONTENTS

THE BERTRAMS

CHAPTER I

VÆ VICTIS!*

THIS is undoubtedly the age of humanity—as far, at least, as England is concerned. A man who beats his wife is shocking to us, and a colonel who cannot manage his soldiers without having them beaten is nearly equally so. We are not very fond of hanging; and some of us go so far as to recoil under any circumstances from taking the blood of life. We perform our operations under chloroform; and it has even been suggested that those schoolmasters who insist on adhering in some sort to the doctrines of Solomon should perform their operations in the same guarded manner. If the disgrace be absolutely necessary, let it be inflicted; but not the bodily pain.

So far as regards the low externals of humanity, this is doubtless a humane age. Let men, women, and children have bread; let them have, if possible, no blows, or, at least, as few as may be; let them also be decently clothed; and let the pestilence be kept out of their way. In venturing to call these low, I have done so in no contemptuous spirit; they are comparatively low if the body be lower than the mind. The humanity of the age is doubtless suited to its material wants, and such wants are those which demand the promptest remedy. But in the inner feelings of men to men, and of one man's mind to another man's mind, is it not an age of extremest cruelty?

There is sympathy for the hungry man; but there is no sympathy for the unsuccessful man who is not hungry. If a fellow mortal be ragged, humanity will subscribe to mend his clothes; but humanity will subscribe nothing to mend his ragged hopes, so long as his outside coat shall be whole and decent.

To him that hath shall be given; and from him that hath not shall be taken even that which he hath.* This is the special text that we delight to follow, and success is the god that we delight to worship. 'Ah! pity me. I have struggled and fallen—struggled so manfully, yet fallen so utterly—help me up this time that I may yet push forward once again!' Who listens to such a plea as this? 'Fallen! do you want bread?' 'Not bread, but a kind heart and a kind hand.' 'My friend, I cannot stay by you; I myself am in a hurry; there is that fiend of a rival there even now gaining a step on me. I beg your pardon; but I will put my foot on your shoulder—only for one moment. *Occupet extremum scabies*.'*

Yes. Let the devil take the hindmost; the three or four hindmost if you will; nay, all but those strong-running horses who can force themselves into noticeable places under the judge's eye. This is the noble shibboleth with which the English youth are now spurred on to deeds of—what shall we say?—money-making activity. Let every place in which a man can hold up his head be the reward of some antagonistic struggle, of some grand competitive examination.* Let us get rid of the fault of past ages. With us, let the race be ever to the swift; the victory always to the strong.* And let us always be racing, so that the swift and strong shall ever be known among us. But what, then, for those who are not swift, not strong? *Væ victis!* Let them go to the wall. They can hew wood probably; or, at any rate, draw water.

Were we to ask Lord Derby, or Lord Palmerston, or to consult the shade of Lord George Bentinck—or to go to those greater authorities on the subject, Mr Scott,* for instance, and the family of the Days*—we should, I believe, be informed that the racehorse requires a very peculiar condition. It is not to be obtained quickly; and, when obtained, will fit the beast for no other than that one purpose of running races. Crucifix was never good at going in a cab; Iliona never took her noble owner down to the House of Parliament; nor has Toxophilite* been useful in Leicestershire.*

But, nevertheless, let all our work be done by race-horses; all, at least, that shall be considered honourable. Let us have strength and speed. And how shall we know who are strong and swift if we do not train our horses to run against each other? But this early racing will hardly produce that humanity of spirit of which we now deplore the want. "The devil take the hindmost" is the very essence of the young man's book of proverbs. The devil assuredly will take all the hindmost. None but the very foremost can enter the present heaven of good things. Therefore, oh my brother, my friend, thou companion of my youth! may the devil take thee; thee quickly, since it needs must be thee or me.

Væ victis—alas! for these hindmost ones; there are so many of them! The skim-milk will always be so much more in quantity than the cream. With us at present cream is required for everything; nothing can be well done now unless it be done by cream of some sort. That milk has been skimmed; the cream has been taken away. No matter; skim it again. There shall be something yet which we will call cream. Competitive examination will produce something that shall look to be strong; that shall be swift, if it be only for a start of twenty yards.

This is the experiment of the present day. Wise men say that when nothing but cream is accepted, all mankind, all boykind rather, will prepare itself for a skimming of some sort; and that the quantity of cream produced will be immense. It is only done as an instigation to education. Much may be said in opposition to this; but nothing shall be said here. It is merely of the cruelty of spirit that is thus engendered that we now speak. Success is the only test of merit. Words have lost their old significance, and to deserve only is not meritorious. *Væ victis!* there are so many of them!

'Thompson,' says Johnson, the young poet, when he has at last succeeded in getting the bosomest of his friends alone into his chamber with him, 'have you happened to look at my Iphigenia* yet?'

Thompson can't say that he has. He has been busy; has had so many water-parties; and then, somehow, he doesn't think that he is very partial to modern poetry on subjects of old mythology. Of course, however, he means to read it—some of these days.

'I wish you would,' says Johnson, tendering a copy of the thin volume. 'I really wish you would; and let me have your candid opinion. The press certainly have not noticed it much, and what they have said has been very lukewarm.'

'I am sorry for that,' says Thompson, looking grave.

'And I did my best with it too. You would hardly believe how hard I worked at it. There is not a line that has not been weighed and written, perhaps, three times over. I do not think I am conceited; but I cannot but believe that there is something in it. The reviewers are so jealous! if a man has not a name, they will give him credit for nothing; and it is so hard to begin.'

'I am sure it is,' says Thompson.

'I don't expect fame; and as for money, of course I don't think of that. But I should like to know that it had been read by one or two persons who could understand it. I have given to it the best of my time, the best of my labour. I cannot but think that there is something in it.' Thus pleads the unsuccessful one for mercy.

And thus answers to him the successful one, with no grain of mercy in his composition:—'My dear Johnson, my maxim is this, that in this world every man gets in the long run exactly what he deserves—'

'Did Milton get what he deserved?'

'These are not the days of Milton. I don't want to hurt your feelings; but old friends as we are, I should not forgive myself if I didn't tell you what I really think. Poetry is all very well; but you can't create a taste for it if it doesn't exist. Nobody that I know of cares a d— for Iphigenia.'

'You think I should change my subject, then?'

'To tell you the truth, I think you should change your trade. This is the third attempt, you know. I dare say they are very good in their way; but if the world liked them, the world would have found it out by this time. "*Vox populi, vox Dei*"*—that is my motto—I don't trust my own judgment; I trust that of the public. If you will take my advice, you will give up Iphigenia and the rest of them. You see you are doing nothing whatever at the bar,' etc. etc.

And thus Johnson is left, without a scrap of comfort, a

word of consolation, a spark of sympathy; and yet he had given to that Iphigenia of his the best that was in him to give. Had his publisher sold ten thousand copies of it, how Thompson would have admired it! how he would have pressed the poet in his arms, and have given him champagne up at Richmond! But who now has sympathy for failure? To fail is to be disgraced. *Væ victis!*

There is something very painful in these races, which we English are always running, to one who has tenderness enough to think of the nine beaten horses instead of the one who has conquered. Look at that list which has just come out after our grand national struggle at Cambridge. How many wranglers* are there? Thirty, shall we say? and it is always glorious to be a wrangler. Out of that thirty there is probably but one who has not failed, who is not called on to submit to the inward grief of having been beaten. The youth who is second, who has thus shown himself to be possessed of a mass of erudition sufficient to crush an ordinary mind to the earth, is ready to eat his heart with true bitterness of spirit. After all his labour, his midnight oil, his many sleepless nights, his deserted pleasures, his racking headaches, Amaryllis abandoned, and Neæra* seen in the arms of another—! After all this, to be beaten by Jones! Had it been Green or Smith he could have borne it. Would it not have been better to do as others had done? He could have been contented to have gone out in the crowd; but there is nothing so base as to be second—and then second to Jones!

Out of the whole lot, Jones alone is contented; and he is told by his physician that he must spend his next two winters at Cairo. The intensity of his application has put his lungs into very serious jeopardy.

It was at Oxford, in the year 184—, that a young man sat in his college-rooms at Balliol a wretched victim to unsuccessful competition. It had been everything to him to come out as a first in classics, and he had dared to dream even of a double first.* But he had failed in both. The lists had just appeared, and he was only a second-class man. Now, a second-class man is not much thought of at Balliol, and he had lost his chance of an immediate fellowship.

But this was perhaps hardly the worst of it. Arthur Wilkinson, for such was this gentleman's name, had hitherto run his race in life alongside a friend and rival named George Bertram; and in almost every phase of life had hitherto been beaten. The same moment that had told Wilkinson of his failure had told him also that Bertram had obtained the place he had so desired. Bertram was the only double-first man of his year.

As these two young men will play the foremost parts in the following pages, I will endeavour to explain, in as few words as possible, who each of them was. As Bertram seems to have been the favourite with fortune, I will begin with him.

His father at the time alluded to was still alive, but his son George had seen but little of him. Sir Lionel Bertram had been a soldier of fortune, which generally, I believe, means a soldier without a fortune, and in that capacity he was still in some sort fighting his country's battles. At the present moment he held a quasi-military position in Persia, where he had been for the last five years, and previously to that he had served in Canada, India, the Cape of Good Hope, and on some special mission at Monte Video. He had, therefore, seen a good deal of the world; but very little of his only child. Mrs Bertram, George's mother, had died early in life, and Mr (afterwards Sir Lionel) Bertram had roamed the world free from all encumbrances.

The Rev Arthur Wilkinson, vicar of Hurst Staple, on the borders of Hampshire and Berkshire, had married a first-cousin of Mrs Bertram's; and when young George Bertram, at the age of nine, was tossing about the world rather in want of a fixed home, Mr Wilkinson undertook to give him that home, and to educate him with his own eldest child till they should both be sent to some school. For three years George Bertram lived at Hurst Staple, and was educated accordingly. During these years he used to go annually for one month to the house of an uncle, who in due time will also be introduced to the reader; and therefore, not unnaturally, this month was regarded by the boy as his holidays.

Now, it may as well be explained in this place that Sir Lionel Bertram, though a very gallant man, and peculiarly well adapted to do business with outlandish people, had never succumbed to a habit of punctuality in pecuniary matters. An arrangement had been perhaps rather named than made, that one hundred and thirty pounds per annum should be paid for young Bertram's needs; and as this was to include pocket-money, clothing, and washing, as well as such trifles as the boy's maintenance and education, perhaps the bargain was not a very hard one as regarded Sir Lionel. The first seventy-five pounds were paid; but after that, up to the end of the second year, Mr Wilkinson had received no more. As he was a poor man, with six children of his own, and little besides his living, he then thought it better to mention the matter to Sir Lionel's brother in London. The balance was instantly paid, and Mr Wilkinson had no further trouble on that head.

Nor had he much trouble on any other head as regarded young Bertram. The lad was perhaps not fit to be sainted, and gave Mrs Wilkinson the usual amount of trouble as regarded his jackets and pantaloons; but, on the whole, he was a good boy, free and generous in his temper, quick in his parts, affectionate in disposition, and full of humour. Those who examined him most closely (among whom, perhaps, Mr Wilkinson was not included) might have observed that he was hardly as steady as he might have been in his likings and dislikings; that he made too little of the tasks which he learnt without trouble; and that, in fact, he was not sufficiently solicitous about anything. He was, however, undoubtedly a lad of great promise, and one of whom any father might have been proud.

He was not a handsome boy, nor did he become a handsome man. His face was too solid, his cheeks too square, and his forehead too heavy; but his eyes, though small, were bright, and his mouth was wonderfully marked by intelligence. When he grew to be a man, he wore no beard, not even the slightest apology for a whisker, and this perhaps added to the apparent heaviness of his face; but he probably best understood his own appearance, for in those days no face bore on it more legible marks of an acute mind.

At the age of twelve, he was sent to Winchester,* and as his holidays were still passed with his uncle, he then ceased to regard Hurst Staple as his home. Twice a year, as he went up to town, he stayed there for a couple of days; but he was soon looked on as a visitor, and the little Wilkinsons no longer regarded him as half a brother in reality and quite a brother in love.

Arthur Wilkinson was very nearly of the same age. He was just older than young Bertram—by three months or so; just sufficiently to give to Wilkinson a feeling of seniority when they first met, and a consciousness that as he was the senior in age, he should be the senior in scholastic lore. But this consciousness Wilkinson was not able to attain; and during all the early years of his life, he was making a vain struggle to be as good a man as his cousin; that is, as good in scholarship, as good in fighting, as good in play, and as good in spirit.

In looks, at any rate, Arthur was superior to George; and much consolation did his mother receive from this conviction. Young Wilkinson was a very handsome lad, and grew up to be a handsome man; but his beauty was of that regular sort which is more pleasing in a boy than in a man. He also was an excellent lad, and no parent could be so thankless as to be other than proud of him. All men said all good things of him, so that Mr Wilkinson could not but be contented. Nevertheless, one would always wish to see one's own son not less bright than one's friend's son.

Arthur Wilkinson was also sent to Winchester. Perhaps it would have been better for the cousins that they should have gone to different schools. The matter, however, had been left to Mr Wilkinson, and as he thought Winchester good for his own son, he naturally thought the same school good for Sir Lionel's son. But Bertram was entered as a commoner,* whereas Wilkinson was in the college. Those who know Winchester will understand, that though, as regarded school business and school hours, they were at the same establishment, they were not together at the much more important hours of eating, sleeping, and playing. They did not cease to be friends, but they did cease to live together as friends generally do live when educated at the same school.

At Winchester they both did fairly well; but Bertram did

much the best. He got the prizes, whereas his cousin did but nearly get them. He went up from class to class above the other; and when the last tussle for pride of place came on at the close of their boyish career, Bertram was the victor. He stood forth to spout out the Latin hexameters,* and to receive the golden medal, while Wilkinson had no other privilege than to sit still and listen to them.

I believe masters but seldom recognize the agony of spirit with which boys endure being beaten in these contests. Boys on such subjects are very reticent; they hardly understand their own feelings enough to speak of them, and are too much accustomed both to ridicule and censure to look anywhere for sympathy. A favourite sister may perhaps be told of the hard struggle and the bitter failure, but not a word is said to any one else. His father, so thinks the boy, is angry at his failure; and even his mother's kisses will hardly be warmed by such a subject. We are too apt to think that if our children eat pudding and make a noise they require no sympathy. A boy may fail at school, and afterwards eat much pudding, and make much noise; but, ah! how his young heart may sigh for some one to grieve with him over his failures!

Wilkinson was unfortunate at school. It was a great object with his father that he should get a scholarship at New College, to which, as all the world knows, his path lay through the college of Winchester. When his time came, he was all but successful—but he was not successful. The vacancies in his year were few in number, only three, and of these two were preoccupied, according to the then rule of the place, by those heaven-born Wykamists, called founder's kin. He was only the second best on the list, and lost the prize.

Bertram, having been a commoner, had had no right to think of New College; but at the time when he was to be removed to Oxford, his uncle gave him to understand that money was a great object to him. His father's mind was still too fully absorbed in the affairs of his country to enable him to think much of his son's expenditure, and his uncle at this period took a fit of disgust on the subject.

'Very well,' said George, 'I will give up Oxford if I cannot do something for myself.'

He went up, however, to Trinity, and became a candidate for a scholarship there. This he obtained, to the great surprise of all the Wilkinsons and of himself. In those days, a lad of eighteen who could get a scholarship at Trinity was considered to be nearly safe in his career. I do not know how far this may be altered now. The uncle, when he heard of his nephew's success, immediately allowed him what would have been amply sufficient for him had he been in possession of no income from his scholarship. Bertram, therefore, had been almost a rich man during his residence at Oxford.

Young Wilkinson, though he lost New College, received a small scholarship from Winchester, and he also was sent by his father to Oxford. To enable him to do this, Mr Wilkinson was forced to make a great struggle. He had five other children—four daughters, and one younger son, and it was with difficulty that he could make up the necessary allowance to carry Arthur through the University. But he did do so, and the disappointed Wykamist went up to Balliol with an income amounting to about half that which his cousin enjoyed.

We need not follow them very accurately through their college careers. They both became prizemen—one by force of intellect, and the other by force of industry. They both went through their little goes and other goes with sufficient zeal, up to that important day on which the great go of all was to be undergone. They both belonged to the same debating society at Oxford, and though they thought very differently on most important subjects, they remained, with some few temporary interruptions, fast friends through their four years of Oxford residence.

There were periods when the Balliol man was considered by his friends to run a better chance of academical success than his brighter cousin at Trinity. Wilkinson worked hard during his three first years, and Bertram did not. The style of mind, too, of the former was the more adapted to win friends at Oxford. In those days the Tracts were new, and read by everybody, and what has since been called Puseyism was in its robust infancy. Wilkinson proclaimed himself, while yet little more than a boy, to be an admirer of poor Froude and a follower of Newman.* Bertram, on the other hand, was unsparing in his ridicule of the 'Remains,'* set himself in full opposition to the Sewells,* and came out as a poet—successfully, as far as the Newdigate* was concerned—in direct opposition to Keble and Faber.*

For three years Wilkinson worked hard and regularly; but the *éclat* attending on his success somewhat injured him. In his fourth year, or, at any rate, in the earlier part of it, he talked more than he read, and gave way too much to the delights of society—too much, at least, for one who was so poor, and to whom work was so necessary. He could not keep his position by dint of genius, as Bertram might do; consequently, though he was held to have taken honours in taking his degree, he missed the high position at which he had aimed; and on the day which enabled him to write himself bachelor of arts, he was in debt to the amount of a couple of hundred pounds, a sum which it was of course utterly out of his power to pay, and nearly as far out of the power of his father.

It had always been Bertram's delight to study in such a manner that men should think he did not study. There was an affectation in this, perhaps not uncommon to men of genius, but which was deleterious to his character—as all affectations are. It was, however, the fact, that during the last year before his examination, he did study hard. There was a set round him at his college among whom he was esteemed as a great man—a little sect of worshippers, who looked for their idol to do great things; and it was a point of honour with them to assist this pretence of his. They gloried in Bertram's idleness; told stories, not quite veracious, of his doings at wine-parties; and proved, to the satisfaction of admiring freshmen, that he thought of nothing but his horse and his boating. He could do without study more than any other man could do with it; and as for that plodding Balliol hero, he might look to be beaten out of the field without an effort.

The Balliol men had been very confident in their hero up to the last half-year; but then they began to doubt. Poor Wilkinson was beaten by his rival out of the field, though, probably, not without an effort. We may say that no man ever gets a double-first in anything without an effort. But be that as it may, Wilkinson was sitting alone, a very unhappy man, in his rooms at Balliol, while Bertram was being fêted to his heart's content at Trinity.

It is a grievous thing to have to write home to one's father, and to say that one has failed when that father has so anxiously longed for success. Arthur Wilkinson would have been a made man for life—made according to the making which both his father and himself at that time thought the most desirable—if his name had but appeared in that first-class list. A double-first his father had not hoped for; but, in resolving not to hope for it, he had consoled himself with thinking that the hopes which he did form were the more certain of success;—and then there would always be that further chance of happiness in store. But now Arthur Wilkinson had to tell his father that he was neither first nor double-first. His degree was very respectable for a man who had not looked for much, for one who had not been talked of in high places; but it was not respectable for Wilkinson of Balliol.

Væ victis! He was indeed unhappy as he sat there alone, meditating how he would frame his letter. There were no telegraphs or telegrams in those days, and it behoved him to write. If he did not, his father would be at Oxford before the next night was over. How should be write? Would it not be better to write to his mother? And then what should he do, or what should he say, about that accursed debt?

His pen and ink and paper were on the table, and he had got into his chair for the purpose. There he had been for some half-hour, but still not a word was written; and his chair had somehow got itself dragged round to the fire. He was thus sitting when he heard a loud knock at his outer door.

'Come; open the door,' said Bertram's voice, 'I know you are there.'

Wilkinson still sat silent. He had not seen Bertram since the lists had come out, and he could hardly make up his mind whether he could speak to him or no.

'I know you're there, and I'll have the door down if you don't open it. There's nobody with me,' shouted the manly voice of his triumphant friend.

Slowly Wilkinson got up and undid the lock. He tried to smile as he opened the door; but the attempt was a failure. However, he could still speak a few words, heavy as his heart was.

'I have to congratulate you,' said he to Bertram, 'and I do it with all my heart.'

There was very little heart in the tone in which this was spoken; but then, what could be expected?

'Thank'ee, old fellow, I'm sure you do. Come, Wilkinson, give us your hand. It's better to have it all out at once. I wish you'd had more luck, and there's an end of it. It's all luck, you know.'

'No, it's not,' said Wilkinson, barely able to suppress the tears.

'Every bit of it. If a chap gets a headache, or a fit of the colic, it's all up with him. Or if he happens to have been loose as to some pet point of the examiners, it's all up with him. Or if he has taken a fad into his head, and had a pet point of his own, it's all up with him then, too, generally. But it will never do, Wilkinson, to boody* over these things. Come, let you and I be seen walking together; you'll get over it best in that way. We'll go over to Parker's, and I'll stand a lunch. We'll find Gerard, and Madden, and Twisleton there. Twisleton's so disgusted at getting a fourth. He says he won't take it, and swears he'll make them let him go out in the ruck.'

'He's got as much as he thought he'd get, at any rate, and therefore he can't be unhappy.'

'Unhappy! who's unhappy? Nonsense, my dear fellow. Shy all that to the dogs. Come, let's go over to Parker's; we shall find Harcourt there. You know he's up, don't you?'

'No; and I had rather not meet him just at present.'

'My dear fellow, you must get over that.'

'That's all very well for you, who have got nothing to get over.'

'And have I never had anything to get over? I'll tell you what it is; I've come here to prevent you from moping, and I don't mean to leave you. So, you see, you may as well come with me at first.'

With some little hesitation, Wilkinson made his friend

understand that he had not yet written home, and that he could not go out till he had done so.

'Then I'll give you ten minutes to write your letter; it can't possibly take you more, not even if you put into it my love to my aunt and cousins.'

'I cannot do it while you are here.'

'Nonsense! gammon! You shall do it while I'm here. I'll not allow you to make yourself a miserable ass all for nothing. Come, write. If it's not written in ten minutes, I'll write it;' and so saying, he took up a play of Aristophanes* wherewith to amuse himself, by way of light reading, after the heavy work of the week.

Poor Wilkinson again drew his chair to the table, but his heart was very heavy. *Væ victis!*

CHAPTER II

BREAKFAST AND LUNCH

WILKINSON took the pen in his hand and bent himself over the paper as though he were going to write; but not an ink-mark fell upon the paper. How should he write it? The task might have been comparatively light to him but for that dreadful debt. Bertram in the meantime tossed over the pages of his book, looking every now and then at his watch; and then turning sharply round, he exclaimed, 'Well!'

'I wish you'd leave me,' said Wilkinson; 'I'd rather be alone.'

'May I be doomed to live and die a don if I do; which style of life, next to that of an English bishop, I look on as the most contemptible in the world. The Queen's royal beef-eaters come next; but that, I think, I could endure, as their state of do-nothingness is not so absolute a quantity. Come; how far have you got? Give me the paper, and I'll write you a letter in no time.'

'Thank you; I'd rather write my own letter.'

'That's just what I want you to do, but you won't;' and then again he turned for two minutes to the 'Frogs.'* 'Well—you see you don't write. Come, we'll both have a try at it, and see who'll have done first. I wonder whether my father is expecting a letter from me? And, so saying, he seized hold of pen and paper and began to write.

'My dearest Father,

'This weary affair is over at last. You will be sorry to hear that the event is not quite so well as it might have been as far as I am concerned. I had intended to be a first, and, lo! I am only a second. If my ambition had been confined to the second class, probably I might have come out a first. I am very sorry for it, chiefly for your sake; but in these days no man can count on the highest honours as a certainty. As I shall be home on Tuesday, I won't say any more. I can't give you any tidings about the fellowships yet. Bertram has had his old luck again. He sends his love to mamma and the girls.

'Your very affectionate son,

'ARTHUR WILKINSON.'

'There, scribble that off; it will do just as well as anything else.'

Poor Wilkinson took the paper, and having read it, to see that it contained no absurdity, mechanically copied the writing. He merely added one phrase, to say that his friend's 'better luck' consisted in his being the only double-first of his year, and one short postscript, which he took good care that Bertram should not see; and then he fastened his letter and sent it to the post.

'Tell mamma not to be very unhappy.' That was the postscript which he added.

That letter was very anxiously expected at the vicarage of Hurst Staple. The father was prepared to be proud of his successful son; and the mother, who had over and over again cautioned him not to overwork himself, was anxious to know that his health was good. She had but little fear as to his success; her fear was that he should come home thin, pale, and wan.

Just at breakfast-time the postman brought the letter, and

the youngest girl running out on to the gravel brought it up to her expectant father.

'It is from Arthur,' said she; 'isn't it, papa? I'm sure I know his handwriting.'

The vicar, with a little nervousness, opened it, and in half a minute the mother knew that all was not right.

'Is he ill?' said she; 'do tell me at once.'

'Ill! no; he's not ill.'

'Well, what is it? He has not lost his degree?'

'He has not been plucked,* papa, has he?' said Sophia.

'Oh, no; he has got his degree—a second in classics!—that's all;' and he threw the letter over to his wife as he went on buttering his toast.

'He'll be home on Tuesday,' said Mary, the eldest girl, looking over her mother's shoulder.

'And so George is a double-first,' said Mrs Wilkinson.

'Yes,' said the vicar, with his mouth full of toast; not evincing any great satisfaction at the success of his late pupil.

When the mother read the short postscript her heart was touched, and she put her handkerchief up to her face.

'Poor Arthur! I am sure it has not been his own fault.'

'Mamma, has George done better than Arthur?' said one of the younger girls. 'George always does do better, I think; doesn't he?'

'He has made himself too sure of it,' said the father, in almost an angry tone. Not that he was angry; he was vexed, rather, as he would be if his wheat crop failed, or his potatoes did not come up properly.

But he felt no sympathy with his son. It never occurred to him to think of the agony with which those few lines had been written; of the wretchedness of the young heart which had hoped so much and failed so greatly; of the misery which the son felt in disappointing the father. He was a good, kind parent, who spent his long days and longer nights in thinking of his family and their welfare; he would, too, have greatly triumphed in the triumph of his son; but it went beyond his power of heart to sympathize with him in his misery.

'Do not seem to be vexed with him when he comes home,' said the mother.

'Vexed with him! You mean angry. Of course I'm not angry. He has done his best, I suppose. It's unlucky, that's all.'

And then the breakfast was continued in silence.

'I don't know what he's to do,' said the father, after awhile; 'he'll have to take a curacy, I suppose.'

'I thought he meant to stop up at Oxford and take pupils,' said Mary.

'I don't know that he can get pupils now. Besides, he'll not have a fellowship to help him.'

'Won't he get a fellowship at all, papa?'

'Very probably not, I should think.' And then the family finished their meal in silence.

It certainly is not pleasant to have one's hopes disappointed; but Mr Wilkinson was hardly just in allowing himself to be so extremely put about by his son's failure in getting the highest honours. Did he remember what other fathers feel when their sons are plucked? or did he reflect that Arthur had, at any rate, done much better than nineteen out of every twenty young men that go up to Oxford? But then Mr Wilkinson had a double cause for grief. Had George Bertram failed also, he might perhaps have borne it better.

As soon as the letter had been written and made up, Wilkinson suffered himself to be led out of the room.

'And now for Parker's,' said Bertram; 'you will be glad to see Harcourt.'

'Indeed, I shall not. Harcourt's all very well; but just at present, I would much rather see nobody.'

'Well, then, he'll be glad to see you; and that will be quite the same thing. Come along.'

Mr Harcourt was a young barrister but lately called to the bar, who had been at Oxford spending his last year when Bertram and Wilkinson were freshmen; and having been at Bertram's college, he had been intimate with both of them. He was now beginning to practise, and men said that he was to rise in the world. In London he was still a very young man; but at Oxford he was held to be one who, from his three years' life in town, had become well versed in the world's ways. He was much in the habit of coming to

Oxford, and when there usually spent a good deal of his time with George Bertram.

And so Wilkinson walked forth into the street arm and arm with his cousin. It was a grievous trial to him; but he had a feeling within him that the sooner the sorrow was encountered the sooner it would be over. They turned into the High Street, and as they went they met crowds of men who knew them both. Of course it was to be expected that Bertram's friends should congratulate him. But this was not the worst; some of them were so ill advised as to condole with Wilkinson.

'Get it over at once,' whispered Bertram to him, 'and then it will be over, now and for ever.'

And then they arrived at Parker's, and there found all those whom Bertram had named, and many others. Mr Parker was, it is believed, a pastrycook by trade; but he very commonly dabbled in more piquant luxuries than jam tarts or Bath buns. Men who knew what was what, and who were willing to pay—or to promise to pay—for their knowledge, were in the habit of breakfasting there, and lunching. Now a breakfast or a lunch at Parker's generally meant champagne.

Harcourt was seated on the table when they got into the back room, and the other men were standing.

'Sound the timbrels, beat the drums;
See the conqu'ring hero comes,'*

he sung out as Bertram entered the room. 'Make way for the double-first—the hero of the age, gentlemen! I am told that they mean to put up an alabaster statue to him in the Common Room at Trinity. However, I will vote for nothing more expensive than marble.'

'Make it in pie-crust,' said Bertram, 'and let Parker be the artist.'

'Yes; and we'll celebrate the installation with champagne and *pâté de foie gras*,' said Twisleton.

'And afterwards devour the object of our idolatry, to show how short-lived is the fame for which we work so hard,' said Madden.

'I should be delighted at such tokens of your regard, gentlemen. Harcourt, you haven't seen Wilkinson.'

Harcourt turned round and shook hands warmly with his other friend. 'Upon my word, I did not see you, Master Wilkinson. You have such a habit of hiding yourself under a bushel that one always misses you. Well; so the great day is over, and the great deed done. It's a bore out of the way, trampled under foot and got rid of; that's my idea of a degree.'

Wilkinson merely smiled; but Harcourt saw at once that he was a deeply-disappointed man. The barrister, however, was too much a man of the world either to congratulate him or condole with him.

'There are fewer firsts this year than there have been for the last nine years,' said Gerard, thinking to soften the asperity of Wilkinson's position.

'That may be because the examiners require more, or because the men had less to give,' said Madden, forgetting all about Wilkinson.

'Why, what noodles you are,' said Bertram, 'not to know that it's all settled by chance at roulette the night before the lists come down! If it's not, it ought to be. The average result would be just as fair. Come, Harcourt, I know that you, with your Temple* experiences, won't drink Oxford wine; but your good-nature will condescend to see the children feeding. Wilkinson, sit opposite there and give Twisleton some of that pie that he was talking of.' And so they sat down to their banquet; and Harcourt, in spite of the refinement which London had doubtless given to his taste, seemed perfectly able to appreciate the flavour of the University vintage.

'Gentlemen, silence for one moment,' said Harcourt, when the graver work of eating began to lull, and men torpidly peeled their pears, and then cut them into shapes instead of eating them. 'It is always said at all the breakfasts I go to—'

'This is not a breakfast,' said Bertram, 'it's a lunch.'

'Well, all the lunches, then; and God bless you. It's always said at these matutinal meals—which, by-the-by, would be the nicest things in the world, only one doesn't know what on earth to do when they're over.'

'It's time to go to dinner then,' said Twisleton.

'That may do for the "*dura ilia*"* of a freshman, but now

that you're a B.A., you'll find that that power fails you greatly. But, for heaven's sake, let me go on with my speech, or you'll not get away either to dinner or to supper. It is commonly declared, I say, that there should be no speaking at these delicious little morning repasts.'

'Do you call that a little repast?' said Madden, who was lying in his chair with a cigar in his mouth, of which he hardly had strength enough left to puff out the smoke.

'I mean no offence to the feed, which, of its kind, has been only too good. If I'm to be allowed to go on, I'll say, that this rule, which is always laid down, is always broken; and therefore I feel no hesitation in breaking it on this occasion. A long speech is a long bore, and a little speech is a little bore; but bores must be endured. We can't do very well without them. Now my bore shall be a very short bore if I'm allowed to make an end of it without interruption.'

'All right, Harcourt,' said Bertram. 'Go ahead; we're only too delighted to hear you. It isn't every day we have a London barrister here.'

'No; and it isn't every day that we have a double-first at old Trinity. Gentlemen, there are, I think, five, six Trinity men here including myself. It will be a point of honour with you to drink health and prosperity to our friend Bertram with all the honours. We have many men of whom we can boast at Trinity; but if I have any insight into character, any power of judging what a man will do'—it must be remembered that Mr Harcourt, though a very young man in London, was by no means a young man at Oxford—'there have been very few before him who have achieved a higher place than will fall to his lot, or whose name will be more in men's mouths than his. There are also here four gentlemen of other colleges; they will not, I am sure, begrudge us our triumph; they are his old friends, and will be as proud of the Oxford man as we are of the Trinity man. Gentlemen, here is prosperity to our friend the double-first, and health to enjoy the fruits of his labour.'

Whereupon the toast was drunk with a great deal of fervour. It was astonishing that ten men should make so much uproar; even Wilkinson, whose heart the wine had just touched sufficiently to raise it a little from the depth to which it had fallen—even he cheered; and Madden, overcoming by degrees his not unnatural repugnance to rise, produced from certain vast depths a double-bass hurrah.

'Bertram,' said he, when the voices and glasses were once more silent, 'you're a credit to your college, and I've a regard for you; so I don't mind running the risk for once. But I must beg that I may not be asked to repeat it.'

Bertram of course returned thanks to his guests with all the mawkish modesty which usually marks such speeches—or, rather, with modesty which would be mawkish were it not so completely a matter of course. And then he sat down; and then, with a face rather heightened in colour, he got upon his legs again.

'In spite of Madden's difficulty of utterance,' said he, 'and his very visible disinclination to move—'

'I'm not going to do any more shouting,' said Madden, 'even though you propose the health of the chancellor, vice-chancellor, and two members.'*

'Not even though he throws the proctors* into the bargain,' said Twisleton.

'You may shout or not, as you like; but at the risk of giving some temporary pain to as good a friend as I have in the world, I will ask you to drink the health of one whom on this occasion fortune has not favoured—I mean my cousin, Arthur Wilkinson. The lists as they come down are, I dare say, made out with tolerable fairness. It is not at any rate for me to grumble at them. But of this I am quite sure, that did there exist some infallible test for finding out the best man, no man's name in this year would have been placed before his. He is not so jovial as the rest of us now, because he has partly failed; but the time will come when he will not fail.' And then Arthur Wilkinson's health was toasted with a somewhat bated enthusiasm, but still with sufficient *éclat* to make every glass in Mr Parker's house ring on its shelf.

Poor Wilkinson's ears tingled when he heard his name pronounced; and he would at the moment have given anything to be allowed to be quiet. But it may be doubted whether he would not have been more hurt had he been left there without any notice. It is very hard to tune oneself aright to a disappointed man. 'I'll break the ice for him, at any rate,' said Bertram to himself. 'When he's used to talk about it, he will suffer less.'

Wilkinson had been accounted a good hand at speaking in the debating society, and though rather more prolix than Bertram, and not quite so vivacious, had been considered almost more than a match for his cousin on account of his superior erudition and more practised delivery; but now his voluble gift of words deserted him. 'He was much obliged to them,' he said; 'though perhaps, on the whole, it was better that men who placed themselves in a mediocre condition should be left to their mediocrity. He had no doubt himself of the justness of the lists. It would be useless for him to say that he had not aspired; all the world'—it was all the world to him—'knew too well that he had aspired. But he had received a lesson which might probably be useful to him for the rest of his life. As for failing, or not failing, that depended on the hopes which a man might form for himself. He trusted that his would henceforth be so moderate in their nature as to admit of a probability of their being realized.' Having uttered these very lugubrious words, and almost succeeded in throwing a wet blanket over the party, he sat down.

'Now, you're not going to do anybody else, are you?' said Madden.

'Only Twisleton, and Gerard, and Hopgood,' answered Bertram; 'and Fortescue looks as if he expected it. Perhaps, however, he'll let us off till the day after tomorrow.'

And then, with a round of milk punch, another cigar apiece, and a little more chat, the party broke up.

Bertram and Harcourt remained together, and Bertram endeavoured to induce Wilkinson to stay with them. He, however, wished to be alone, and got home to his college by himself.

'You always overrated that man,' said Harcourt.

'I think not; but time will show. After all, a good degree is not everything in the world. Who in London cares about senior wranglers and double-firsts? When all is done, I don't see the use of it.'

'Nobody cares much about wranglers and double-firsts;

but these are the men, nevertheless, who get the best of what's going. Wood that will swim in one water will swim in all waters.'

'You'll find Wilkinson will swim yet.'

'That is, he won't sink. I don't say he will. Nine-tenths of the men in the world neither swim nor sink; they just go along with their bows above the wave, but dreadfully waterlogged, barely able to carry the burdens thrown on them; but yet not absolutely sinking; fighting a hard fight for little more than mere bread, and forgetting all other desires in their great desire to get that. When such a man does get bread, he can't be said to sink.'

'Ah! Wilkinson will do more than that.'

'Something more, or something less, as the case may be. But, believe me, he is not the man to make other men fall before him. Industry alone never does that, and certainly not that sort of industry which breaks down once in every six months. But come, Mr Parker's champagne makes my head buzz: let us take a walk up the river; Twisleton's idea of going to dinner requires far too much pluck for me.'

And so they walked out along the towing-path, discussing many things of much importance to them.

> 'There is a tide in the affairs of men
> Which, taken at the flood, leads on to fortune.'*

In nine cases out of ten, this flood-tide comes *but* once in life, and then in early years. A man may have a second or a third chance for decent maintenance, but hardly a second chance for fortune's brighter favours. The horse that is to win the race needs not make all his best running at once; but he that starts badly will rarely do so. When a young man discusses what shall be his future walk in life, he is talking of all that concerns his success as far as this world is concerned. And it is so hard for a youth to know, to make even a fair guess, as to what his own capacities are! The right man is wanted in the right place; but how is a lad of two-and-twenty to surmise what place will be right for him? And yet, if he surmises wrong, he fails in taking his tide at its single flood. How many lawyers are there who should have been soldiers! how many clergymen who should have been lawyers! how many unsuccessful doctors who might have done well on 'Change, or in Capel Court!*

Bertram had an inkling of this; and Harcourt had more than an inkling. His path in life was chosen, and he had much self-confidence that he had chosen it well. He had never doubted much, and since he had once determined had never doubted at all. He had worked hard, and was prepared to work hard; not trusting over much in his own talents, but trusting greatly in his own industry. But Bertram, with double his friend's genius, had, at any rate as yet, but little of his friend's stability. To him the world was all before him where to choose; but he was sadly in want of something that should guide his choice. He had a high, but at the same time a vague ambition. The law, the church, letters, art, and politics all enticed him; but he could not decide of which mistress the blandishments were the sweetest.

'Well, when shall we have you up in London?' said Harcourt.

'In London! I don't know that I shall go to London. I shall go down to Hadley for a few weeks of course'—Bertram's uncle lived at the village of that name, in the close vicinity of Barnet—'but what I shall do then, I don't in the least know.'

'But I know you'll come to London and begin to keep your terms.'

'What, at the Middle Temple?'

'At some Temple or some Inn: of course you won't go where anybody else goes; so probably it will be Gray's Inn.'

'No, I shall probably do a much more commonplace thing; come back here and take orders.'

'Take orders! You! You can no more swallow the thirty-nine articles* than I can eat Twisleton's dinner.'

'A man never knows what he can do till he tries. A great deal of good may be done by a clergyman if he be in earnest and not too much wedded to the Church of England. I should have no doubt about it if the voluntary principle were in vogue.'

'A voluntary fiddlestick!'

'Well, even a voluntary fiddlestick—if it be voluntary and well used.'

'Of course you'll be a barrister. It is what you are cut out for, and what you always intended.'

'It is the most alluring trade going, I own;—but then they are all such rogues. Of course you will be an exception.'

'I shall do at Rome as Romans do—I hope always. My doctrine is, that we have no immutable law of right and wrong.'

'A very comfortable code. I wish I could share it.'

'Well, you will some of these days; indeed, you do now practically. But the subject is too long to talk of here. But as I know you won't go into the church, I expect to see you settled in London before Christmas.'

'What am I to live on, my dear fellow?'

'Like all good nephews, live on your uncle. Besides, you will have your fellowship; live on that, as I do.'

'You have more than your fellowship; and as for my uncle, to tell you the truth, I have no fancy for living on him. I am not quite sure that he doesn't mean me to think that it's charity. However, I shall have the matter out with him now.'

'Have the matter out with him!—and charity! What an ass you are! An uncle is just the same as a father.'

'My uncle is not the same to me as my father.'

'No; and by all accounts it's lucky for you that he is not. Stick to your uncle, my dear fellow, and come up to London. The ball will be at your foot.'

'Did you ever read Marryat's novel, Harcourt?'

'What, "Peter Simple"?'*

'No, that other one:* I think of going out as another Japhet in search of a father. I have a great anxiety to know what mine's like. It's fourteen years now since I saw him.'

'He is at Teheran, isn't he?'

'At Hongkong, I think, just at present; but I might probably catch him at Panama; he has something to do with the isthmus there.'

'You wouldn't have half the chance that Japhet had, and would only lose a great deal of time. Besides, if you talk of means, that would want money.'

They were now walking back towards Oxford, and had

been talking about fifty indifferent subjects, when Bertram again began.

'After all, there's only one decent career for a man in England.'

'And what is the one decent career?'

'Politics and Parliament. It's all very well belonging to a free nation, and ruling oneself, if one can be one of the rulers. Otherwise, as far as I can see, a man will suffer less from the stings of pride under an absolute monarch. There, only one man has beaten you in life; here, some seven hundred and fifty do so,—not to talk of the peers.'

'Yes, but then a fellow has some chance of being one of the seven hundred and fifty.'

'I shall go in for that, I think; only who the deuce will return me? How does a man begin? Shall I send my compliments to the electors of Marylebone, and tell them that I am a very clever fellow?'

'Exactly; only do something first to show that you are so. I mean also to look to that; but I shall be well contented if I find myself in the House in twenty years' time,—or perhaps in thirty.'

'Ah, you mean as a lawyer.'

'How else should a man without property* get into Parliament?'

'That's just what I want to know. But I have no idea, Harcourt, of waiting twenty years before I make my start in life. A man, at any rate, may write a book without any electors.'

'Yes, but not have it read. The author who does any good must be elected by suffrages at least as honestly obtained as those of a member of Parliament.'

CHAPTER III

THE NEW VICAR

POOR Arthur Wilkinson was in a very unhappy frame of mind when he left the party at Parker's; and, indeed, as he went to bed that night he was in a state not to be envied; but, nevertheless, when the end of the week came, he was able to enter the parsonage with a cheerful step, and to receive his mother's embrace with a smiling face. God is good to us, and heals those wounds with a rapidity which seems to us impossible when we look forward, but which is regarded with very insufficient wonder when we look backward.

Before he left Oxford he had seen the head of his college and the tutor; and had also felt himself bound to visit the tradesmen in whose black books he was written down as a debtor. None of these august persons made themselves so dreadful to him as he had expected. The master, indeed, was more than civil—was almost paternally kind, and gave him all manner of hope, which came as balm poured into his sick heart. Though he had failed, his reputation and known acquirements would undoubtedly get him pupils; and then, if he resided, he might probably even yet have a college fellowship, though, no doubt, not quite immediately. The master advised him to take orders, and to remain within the college as long as the rules permitted. If he should get his fellowship, they would all be delighted to have him as one of their body; there could—so thought the master—be no doubt that he might in the meantime maintain himself at the University by his pupils. The tutor was perhaps not quite so encouraging. He was a working man himself, and of a harder temperament than his head. He thought that Wilkinson should have got a first, that he had owed it to his college to do so, and that, having failed to pay his debt, he should not be received with open arms—at any rate just at first. He was therefore cool, but not generous. 'Yes; I am sorry too; it is a pity,' was all he said when Wilkinson expressed his own grief. But even this was not so bad as Arthur had expected, and on the whole he left his college with a lightened heart.

Nor were his creditors very obdurate. They did not smile so sweetly on him as they would have done had his name been bruited down the High Street as that of a successful University pet. Had such been his condition, they would have begged him not to distress their ears by anything so unnecessarily mundane as the mention of his very small account. All that they would have wanted of him would have been the continuation of his favours. As it was, they were very civil. Six months would do very well. Oh! he could not quite undertake to pay it in six months, but would certainly do so by instalments in two years. Two years was a long time, certainly; would not Mr Wilkinson senior prefer some quicker arrangement? Oh! Mr Wilkinson senior could do nothing! Ah! that was unfortunate! And so the arrangement for two years—with interest, of course—was accepted. And thus Mr Wilkinson junior began the swimming-match of life, as so many others do, with a slight millstone round his neck. Well; it may be questioned whether even that is not better than an air-puffed swimming-belt.

When he got home, his mother and sisters hung about him as they always had done, and protected him in some measure from the cold serenity of the vicar. To his father he said little on the subject, and his father said as little to him. They talked, indeed, by the hour as to the future; and Arthur, in spite of his having resolved not to do so, told the whole story of his debts, and of his arrangement for their payment.

'Perhaps I could do something in the spring,' said Mr Wilkinson.

'Indeed, father, you shall do nothing,' said the son. 'I had enough, and should have lived on it; as I did not, I must live the closer now.' And so that matter was settled.

In a very few days Arthur found himself going into society with quite a gay heart. His sisters laughed at him because he would not dance; but he had now made up his mind for the church, and it would, he thought, be well for him to begin to look to those amusements which would be befitting his future sacerdotal life. He practised singing, therefore, fasted on Fridays, and learnt to make chessmen with a lathe.

But though his sisters laughed at him, Adela Gauntlet, the daughter of the neighbouring vicar at West Putford, did not laugh. She so far approved that by degrees she almost gave over dancing herself. Waltzes and polkas she utterly abandoned; and though she did occasionally stand up for a quadrille, she did it in a very lackadaisical way, as though she would have refused that also had she dared to make herself so peculiar. And thus on the whole Arthur Wilkinson enjoyed himself that winter, in spite of his blighted prospects, almost as well as he had on any previous winter that he remembered.

Now and again, as he walked along the little river-bank that ran with so many turnings from Hurst Staple down to West Putford, he would think of his past hopes, and lament that he could talk of them to no one. His father was very good to him; but he was too cold for sympathy. His mother was all affection, and kindly suggested that, perhaps, what had happened was for the best: she kindly suggested this more than once, but her imagination carried her no further. Had she not four daughters, hitherto without husbands, and also, alas! without portions? Was it not enough for her to sympathize with them? As for his sisters—his sisters were well enough—excellent girls; but they were so gay, so light-hearted, so full of fun and laughter, that he could not talk to them of his sorrows. They were never pensive, nor given to that sober sadness which is prone to sympathy. If, indeed, Adela Gauntlet had been his sister—! And so he walked along the river to West Putford.

He had now fully made up his mind to go into the church. While yet thinking of high academical honours, and the brighter paths of ambition, he also had dreamed of the bar. All young men, I believe, do, who have high abilities, a taste for labour, and scanty fortune. Senior wranglers and double-firsts, when not possessed of means for political life, usually find their way to the bar. It is on the bench of judges, not on the bench of bishops, that we must look for them in after-life. Arthur, therefore, had thought of the joys of a Chancery wig,* and had looked forward eagerly to fourteen hours' daily labour in the purlieus of Lincoln's Inn.* But when, like many another, he found himself disappointed in his earliest hopes, he consoled himself by thinking that after all the church was the safer haven. And when he walked down to West Putford there was one there who told him that it was so.

But we cannot follow him too closely in these early days. He did go into the church. He did take pupils at Oxford, and went abroad with two of them in the long vacation. After the lapse of the year, he did get his fellowship; and had by that time, with great exertion, paid half of that moiety of his debt which he had promised to liquidate. This lapse in his purposed performance sat heavy on his clerical conscience; but now that he had his fellowship he would do better.

And so somewhat more than a year passed away, during which he was but little at Hurst Staple, and very little at West Putford. But still he remembered the sweetly-pensive brow that had suited so well with his own feelings; and ever and again, he heard from one of the girls at home, that that little fool, Adela Gauntlet, was as bad as a parson herself, and that now she had gone so far that nothing would induce her to dance at all.

So matters stood when young Wilkinson received at Oxford a letter desiring his instant presence at home. His father had been stricken by paralysis, and the house was in despair. He rushed off, of course, and arrived only in time to see his father alive. Within twenty-four hours after his return he found himself the head of a wailing family, of whom it would be difficult to say whether their wants or their griefs were more heartrending. Mr Wilkinson's life had been insured for six hundred pounds; and that, with one hundred a year which had been settled on the widow, was now the sole means left for the maintenance of her and her five children;—the sole means excepting such aid as Arthur might give.

'Let us thank God that I have got the fellowship,' said he to his mother. 'It is not much, but it will keep us from starving.'

But it was not destined that the Wilkinsons should be reduced even to such poverty as this. The vicarage of Hurst Staple was in the gift of the noble family of Stapledean. The late vicar had been first tutor and then chaplain to the marquis, and the vicarage had been conferred on him by his patron. In late years none of the Wilkinsons had seen anything of the Stapledean family. The marquis, though not an old man, was reported to be very eccentric, and very cross. Though he had a beautiful seat in the neighbourhood—not in the parish of Hurst Staple, but in that of Deans Staple, which adjoins, and which was chiefly his property—he never came to it, but lived at a much less inviting mansion in the north of

Yorkshire. Here he was said to reside quite alone, having been separated from his wife; whereas his children had separated themselves from him. His daughters were married, and his son, Lord Stanmore, might more probably be found under any roof in the country than that of his father.

The living had now to be given away by the marquis, and the Wilkinson family, who of late years had had no communication with him, did not even think of thinking of it. But a fortnight after the funeral, Arthur received a letter with the postmark of Bowes on it, which, on being opened, was found to be from Lord Stapledean, and which very curtly requested his attendance at Bowes Lodge. Now Bowes Lodge was some three hundred miles from Hurst Staple, and a journey thither at the present moment would be both expensive and troublesome. But marquises are usually obeyed; especially when they have livings to give away, and when their orders are given to young clergymen. So Arthur Wilkinson went off to the north of England. It was the middle of March, and the east wind was blowing bitterly. But at twenty-four the east wind does not penetrate deep, the trachea is all but invulnerable, and the left shoulder knows no twinges.

Arthur arrived at the cold, cheerless village of Bowes with a red nose, but with eager hopes. He found a little inn there, but he hardly knew whether to leave his bag or no. Lord Stapledean had said nothing of entertaining him at the Lodge—had only begged him, if it were not too much trouble, to do him the honour of calling on him. He, living on the northern borders of Westmorland, had asked a man in Hampshire to call on him, as though their houses were in adjacent streets; but he had said nothing about a dinner, a bed, or given any of those comfortable hints which seem to betoken hospitality.

'It will do no harm if I put my bag into the gig,'* said Arthur; and so, having wisely provided for contingencies, he started for Bowes Lodge.

Wisely, as regarded probabilities, but quite uselessly as regarded the event! Hardy as he was, that drive in the gig from Bowes did affect him unpleasantly. That Appleby road has few sheltered spots, and when about three miles from Bowes he turned off to the right, the country did not improve. Bowes Lodge he found to be six miles from the village, and when he drove in at the gate he was colder than he had been since he left Hurst Staple.

There was very little that was attractive about the house or grounds. They were dark and sombre, and dull and dingy. The trees were all stunted, and the house, of which half the windows were closed, was green with the effects of damp. It was large enough for the residence of a nobleman of moderate pretensions; but it had about it none of that spruce, clean, well-cared-for appearance which is common to the country-houses of the wealthy in England.

When he descended from the gig he thought that he might as well leave his bag there. The sombre-looking servant in black clothes who opened the door made no inquiry on the subject; and, therefore, he merely told his Jehu* to drive into the yard and wait for further orders.

His lordship was at home, said the sombre, dingy servant, and in half a minute Arthur found himself in the marquis's study and in the marquis's presence, with his nose all red and moist, his feet in an agony of cold, his fingers benumbed, and his teeth chattering. He was barely allowed time to take off his greatcoat, and, as he did so, he felt almost disinclined to part with so good a friend.

'How do you do, Mr Wilkinson?' said the marquis, rising from his chair behind the study table, and putting out the ends of his fingers so as to touch the young clergyman's hand. 'Pray take a seat.' And Arthur seated himself—as, indeed, he had no alternative—on a straight-backed old horsehair-bottomed chair which stood immediately under a tall black book-case. He was miles asunder from the fire; and had he been nearer to it, it would have availed him but little; for the grate was one of those which our grandfathers cleverly invented for transmitting all the heat up the chimney.

The marquis was tall, thin, and grey-haired. He was, in fact, about fifty; but he looked to be at least fifteen years older. It was evident from his face that he was a discontented, moody, unhappy man. He was one who had not used the world over-well; but who was quite self-assured that the world had used him shamefully. He was not without good instincts, and had been just and honest in his dealings—except in those with his wife and children. But he believed in the justness and honesty of no one else, and regarded all men as his enemies—especially those of his own flesh and blood. For the last ten years he had shut himself up, and rarely appeared in the world, unless to make some statement, generally personal to himself, in the House of Lords, or to proffer, in a plaintive whine to his brother peers, some complaint as to his neighbour magistrates, to which no one cared to listen, and which in latter years the newspapers had declined to publish.

Arthur, who had always heard of the marquis as his father's old pupil, was astonished to see before him a man so aged. His father had been only fifty-five when he died, and had appeared to be a hale, strong man. The marquis seemed to be worn out with care and years, and to be one whose death might be yearly expected. His father, however, was gone; but the marquis was destined to undergo yet many more days of misery.

'I was very sorry to hear of your father's sudden death,' said Lord Stapledean, in his cold, thin voice.

'It was very sudden, my lord,' said Arthur, shuddering.

'Ah—yes; he was not a prudent man;—always too fond of strong wine.'

'He was always a temperate man,' said the son, rather disgusted.

'That is, he never got drunk. I dare say not. As a parish clergyman, it was not likely that he should. But he was an imprudent man in his manner of living—very.'

Arthur remained silent, thinking it better to say nothing further on the subject.

'I suppose he has not left his family well provided for?'

'Not very well, my lord. There is something—and I have a fellowship.'

'Something!' said the marquis, with almost a sneer. 'How much is this something?' Whereupon Arthur told his lordship exactly the extent of his mother's means.

'Ah, I thought as much. That is beggary, you know. Your

father was a very imprudent man. And you have a fellowship? I thought you broke down in your degree.' Whereupon Arthur again had to explain the facts of the case.

'Well, well, well. Now, Mr Wilkinson, you must be aware that your family have not the slightest claim upon me.'

'Your lordship is also aware that we have made none.'

'Of course you have not. It would have been very improper on your part, or on your mother's, had you done so—very. People make claims upon me who have been my enemies through life, who have injured me to the utmost of their power, who have never ceased striving to make me wretched. Yes, these very people make claims on me. Here—here is a clergyman asking for this living because he is a friend of Lord Stanmore—because he went up the Pyramids with him, and encouraged him in all manner of stupidity. I'd sooner—well, never mind. I shan't trouble myself to answer this letter.' Now, as it happened that Lord Stanmore was a promising young nobleman, already much thought of in Parliament, and as the clergyman alluded to was known by Arthur to be a gentleman very highly reputed, he considered it best to hold his tongue.

'No one has a claim on me; I allow no one to have such claims. What I want I pay for, and am indebted for nothing. But I must put some one into this living.'

'Yes; your lordship must of course nominate some one.' Wilkinson said so much, as the marquis had stopped, expecting an answer.

'I can only say this: if the clergymen in Hampshire do their duty as badly as they do here, the parish would be better off without a parson.'

'I think my father did his duty well.'

'Perhaps so. He had very little to do; and as it never suited me to reside there, there was never any one to look after him. However, I make no complaint. Here they are intolerable–intolerable, self-sufficient, impertinent upstarts, full of crotchets of their own; and the bishop is a weak, timid fool; as for me, I never go inside a church. I can't; I should be insulted if I did. It has however gone so far now that I shall take permission to bring the matter before the House of Lords.'

What could Wilkinson say? Nothing. So he sat still and tried to drive the cold out of his toes by pressing them against the floor.

'Your father certainly ought to have made some better provision,' continued Lord Stapledean. 'But he has not done so; and it seems to me, that unless something is arranged, your mother and her children will starve. Now, you are a clergyman?'

'Yes, I am in orders.'

'And can hold a living? You distinctly understand that your mother has no claim on me.'

'Surely none has been put forward, Lord Stapledean?'

'I don't say it has; but you may perhaps fancy by what I say that I myself admit that there is a claim. Mind; I do no such thing. Not in the least.'

'I quite understand what you mean.'

'It is well that you should. Under these circumstances, if I had the power, I would put in a curate, and pay over the extra proceeds of the living for your mother's maintenance. But I have no such power.'

Arthur could not but think that it was very well his lordship had no such power. If patrons in general were so privileged, there would be, he thought, but little chance for clergymen.

'As the law stands I cannot do that. But as you are luckily in orders, I can put you in—on this understanding, that you shall regard the income as belonging rather to your mother and to your sisters than to yourself.'

'If your lordship shall see fit to present me to the living, my mother and sisters will of course want nothing that I can give them.'

'Ah—h—h—h, my young friend! but that will not be sufficient for me. I must have a pledge from you—your word as a gentleman and a clergyman, that you take the living on an understanding that the income is to go to your father's widow. Why should I give you five hundred pounds a year? Eh? Tell me that. Why should I nominate a young man like you to such a living? you, whom I never saw in my life? Tell me that.'

Arthur Wilkinson was a man sufficiently meek in spirit, as ordinary meekness goes—the ordinary meekness, that is, of a young clergyman of the Church of England—but he was not quite inclined to put up with this.

'I am obliged, my lord, to say again that I have not asked for so great a favour from you. Indeed, till I received your letter desiring me to come here, I had no other thought of the living than that of vacating the house whenever your nominee should present himself.'

'That's all very well,' said Lord Stapledean; 'but you must be a very unnatural son if on that account you refuse to be the means of providing for your unfortunate mother and sisters.'

'I refuse! why, my lord, I regard it as much my duty to keep my mother and sisters from want as my father did. Whether I am to have this living or no, we shall live together; and whatever I have will be theirs.'

'That's all very well, Mr Wilkinson; but the question I ask you is this: if I make you vicar of Hurst Staple, will you, after deducting a fair stipend for yourself as curate—say one hundred and fifty pounds a year if you will—will you make over the rest of the income to your mother as long as she lives?'

This was a question to which Wilkinson found it very difficult to give a direct answer. He hardly knew whether he would not be guilty of simony* in making such a promise, and he felt that at any rate the arrangement would be an improper one.

'If you knew,' said he at last, 'the terms on which my mother and I live together, you would perceive that such a promise is not needed.'

'I shall not the less think it necessary to exact it. I am putting great trust in you as it is, very great trust; more so perhaps than I am justified in doing.' His lordship here alluded merely to the disposition of the vicarial tithes, and not at all to the care of souls which he was going to put into the young man's hands.

Arthur Wilkinson again sat silent for awhile.

'One would think,' said his lordship, 'that you would be

glad to have the means of securing your mother from beggary. I imagined that you would have been in some measure gratified by my—my—my good intentions towards your family.'

'So I am, my lord; so I am. But I doubt whether I should be justified in giving such a pledge.'

'Justified! you will make me almost doubt, Mr Wilkinson, whether I shall be justified in putting the living into your hands; but, at any rate, I must have an answer.'

'What time can you allow me to consider my answer?'

'What time! It never struck me that you could require time. Well; you can let me have your decision tomorrow morning. Send it me in writing, so that I may have it before ten. The post goes out at twelve. If I do not hear from you before ten, I shall conclude that you have refused my offer.' And so speaking the marquis got up from his chair.

Arthur also got up, and promised that he would send a letter over from Bowes the first thing on the following morning.

'And tell the messenger to wait for an answer,' said his lordship; 'and pray express yourself definitely, so that there may be no doubt.' And then, muttering something as to his hope that the inn was comfortable, and saying that the state of his health prohibited him from entertaining visitors, the marquis again put out his fingers, and Arthur soon found himself in the gig on his journey to Bowes.

He intended returning to town on the following day by the twelve-o'clock mail, of which Lord Stapledean had spoken. But before that he had a difficult task to perform. He had no friend to consult, no one of whom he could ask advice, nothing to rely on but his own head and his own heart. That suggestion as to simony perplexed him. Had he the right, or could he have it, to appropriate the income of the living according to terms laid down by the lay impropriator?* At one time he thought of calling on the old clergyman of the parish and asking him; but then he remembered what the marquis had said of the neighbouring parsons, and felt that he could not well consult one of them on any matter in which his lordship was concerned.

In the evening he considered the matter long and painfully, sitting over a cup of some exquisitely detestable concoction called tea by the Bowesian landlady. 'If he had only left me to myself,' thought Arthur, 'I should do at least as much as that for them. It is for them that I want it; as for myself, I should be more comfortable at Oxford.' And then he thought of West Putford, and Adela Gauntlet. This arrangement of Lord Stapledean's would entirely prevent the possibility of his marrying; but then, the burden of his mother and sisters would prevent that equally under any circumstances.

It would be a great thing for his mother to be left in her old house, among her old friends, in possession of her old income. As regarded money, they would all be sufficiently well provided for. For himself, his fellowship and his prescribed stipend would be more than enough. But there was something in the proposition that was very distasteful to him. He did not begrudge the money to his mother; but he did begrudge her the right of having it from any one but himself.

But yet the matter was of such vital moment. Where else was he to look for a living? From his college in the course of years he might get one; but he could get none that would be equal in value to this of Hurst Staple, and to his fellowship combined. If he should refuse it, all those whom he loved would in truth suffer great privation; and that privation would not be rendered more endurable by the knowledge that such an offer had been refused.

Thus turning the matter over painfully in his mind, he resolved at last to accept the offer of the marquis. The payment after all was to be made to his own mother. The funds of the living were not to be alienated—were not, in truth, to be appropriated otherwise than they would have been had no such conditions as these been insisted on. And how would he be able to endure his mother's poverty if he should throw away on her behalf so comfortable a provision? He determined, therefore, to accept the goods the gods had provided him, clogged though they were with alloy, like so many other gifts of fortune; and accordingly he wrote a letter to Lord Stapledean, in which he stated 'that he would accept the living, subject to the stipulations named—namely, the payment to his mother, during her life, of three hundred and fifty pounds per annum out of the tithes.' To this he received an answer from the marquis, very short and very cold, but nevertheless satisfactory.

The presentation to the living was, in fact, made in his favour, and he returned home to his family laden with good news. The dear old vicarage would still be their own; the trees which they had planted, the flower-beds which they had shaped, the hives which they had put up, would not go into the hands of strangers. And more than this, want no longer stared them in the face. Arthur was welcomed back with a thousand fond caresses, as one is welcomed who bringeth glad tidings. But yet his heart was sad. What should he now say to Adela Gauntlet?

CHAPTER IV

OUR PRIMA DONNA

WHEN Arthur first explained to his mother the terms on which the living had been given to him, she refused to receive the income. No such promise with reference to money matters between mother and son could be binding. Were they not, moreover, one and the same household? Would it not be in the end the same if Arthur should keep the money himself? If it were paid to her, she should only pay it back again; and so on. But the vicar declared that he would adhere strictly to his promised engagement; and the mother soon fell into the way of thinking the arrangement not altogether a bad one. She had received intimation through the lord's man of business of the exact steps which had been taken for the relief of her great pecuniary distress—so the letter was worded—and it was not long before she regarded the income as fairly her own.

We are so apt to be generous in the hot moments of impulse; but so equally apt to be only coldly just, even if coldly just, in the long years of our ordinary existence.

And so the family again settled down; the commenced packings were again unpacked; the preliminary arrangements for living on a very small income were thrown to the winds; the pony that was to have been sold, and which with that object was being fattened up on boiled barley was put on his accustomed rations. The housekeeper's warning was revoked, as was also that of the old gardener. It was astonishing how soon the new vicar seemed to fill the old vicar's shoes in the eyes and minds of the people of Hurst Staple. Had Mr Wilkinson come up from his grave at the end of three months, he would hardly have found that he was missed. A very elegant little tablet had been placed to his memory; and there apparently was an end of him. The widow's cap did make some change in the appearance of the family circle; but it is astonishing how soon we get used even to a widow's cap!

There had of course been visits of condolence between West Putford and Hurst Staple, and the Hurst Staple girls and Adela had been as much, or perhaps more, together than usual. But Arthur's walks along the river had not been frequent. This, however, was not thought of by any one. He had had new duties to assume, and old duties to put off. He had been a fortnight up at Oxford; and when at home, had been calling on all his parishioners. He had been attending to the dilapidations of the vicarage, and rearranging the books in the book-room. The dingy volumes of thirty years since had been made to give way to the new and brighter bindings which he had brought from college.

And therefore no one had remarked that he had but once been at West Putford. But he thought of it himself. He often longed to go thither, and as often feared to do so. When he next went, it must be to tell Adela, not that he loved her, but that such love was forbidden to him.

The family at West Putford consisted only of the vicar and his daughter. Mrs Gauntlet had been long dead, and there had been no other child. A maiden sister of Mr Gauntlet's occasionally visited them, and had, indeed, lived there altogether while Adela's education had required it; but this lady preferred her own lodgings at Littlebath, and Adela, therefore, was in general the sole mistress of the parsonage.

I beg my reader not to imagine that there had been love-passages between Arthur Wilkinson and Adela Gauntlet: nothing of the sort had occurred. They had known and loved each other as children together, and now that they were no longer children, they still knew and loved each other—that was all. It is true that Arthur, when he had wished to talk of his own disappointments, had found a better listener at West Putford than any that he could find at Hurst Staple. It is true that Adela had always been glad to listen to him; that she had had pleasure in cheering his fainting heart, and telling him that the work of a soldier of Christ was worthier of a man than the bickerings of a statesman or the quibbles of a lawyer; that she had gravely, yet withal so sweetly, spoken to him of the comforts of a rural life, and made him almost in love with his own failure. Such passages there had been between them; but Arthur had never taken her hand and sworn that it must be his own, nor had Adela ever blushed while half refusing to give him all he asked.

Why then need he trouble himself about West Putford? Why not let matters rest as they were? Miss Gauntlet would still be his friend; though seeing that she could never be more, it might not be well for him to walk so often along that river. As there had been no love-passages, one would say that nothing else was necessary.

But he could not content himself that this should be so. Adela would think him strange if he should say nothing to her of his future prospects. True, he had spoken no word of love, but had he not looked at her as though it was in his mind to speak such? Was it not incumbent on him to make her understand why he threw from him such golden hopes? And then, as to her, he did not flatter himself that she loved him—at least, not much; but yet it might be well to let her know that she was now at liberty to love any other swain. So at last he once more went his way to West Putford.

Adela Gauntlet was—No; for once I will venture to have a heroine without describing her. Let each reader make what he will of her; fancy her of any outward shape and colour that he please, and endow her with any amount of divine beauty.

But for her inner character, let him take that from me as I go on, if so be that I can succeed in making clear to others that which is clear enough to my own mind's eye. I have called her a heroine; it is the novelist's customary name for his prima donna, and so I use it. But many opera companies have more than one prima donna. There is the donna prima, and if one may so say, the donna primissima. Now Adela Gauntlet is no more than my donna prima. My donna primissima will be another guess sort of lady altogether.

Arthur, as he walked along, communed with himself as to what he was going to say. 'At any rate, she shall know it all; we shall be more comfortable when we meet afterwards. Not that it will make any difference to her;' and then he sighed deeply, and cut at the river rushes with his walking-stick.

He found her as usual alone in the drawing-room, and, as usual, she smiled sweetly when she saw him. Since the day on which he had first gone up to Oxford, she had always called him 'Mr Wilkinson'—so instructed by Aunt Penelope; but in other respects her manner to him was almost that of a sister, only that it was softer, and more gracious.

'I declare, I thought we were never to see you again, Mr Wilkinson.' Ah, Adela! whom did the *we* mean? But is it possible that any girl should live fairly before the world without some little insincerities?

'I have been so occupied, Adela. There is so much to do in taking up a parish. Even though I know all the people so well, there has been so much to do.'

'Yes, yes, I am sure of it. But now that you are settled, I do so hope that you will be comfortable. I saw Mary the other day, and she told me that your mother was quite well again.'

'Yes, she is pretty well. We are all very well now, I think.'

'I do so love that old lord for giving you the living, though they say he is such a Turk. It was such a good thing in him to do; so considerate to everybody.'

'Yes; it has made my mother and the girls comfortable; that, of course, is what I had first to think of.'

'As for yourself, I have no doubt you would have done better at Oxford. But you could have got no home for them like their old home; could you?'

'No, of course not,' said Arthur, answering almost at random, and thinking how best he might explain the sacrifice which he had made without taking too much credit to himself.

'And then, if you had remained up there, you would only have become a musty old don. I don't think you would have been happy, not so happy as in a parish. And when a man is a clergyman'—this she said in a lower and somewhat a solemn voice—'surely he cannot be so well placed as in charge of a parish. Don't you think so, Mr Wilkinson?'

'Certainly. It is the life for which he is intended; for which he should have intended himself.'

'And I am sure it is a happy life: look at papa; I do not know any happier man—only that poor mamma died.'

And upon this hint he spake. 'Yes, your father I am sure has been a happy man, and he is an excellent clergyman.'

'Is he not? even still so active! And he is so glad now to have you near him.'

'I wish I had received my living as he did his; not that it would make any real difference.'

'He got his, you know, from the bishop. But do you dislike being Lord Stapledean's nominee?'

'It would be ungrateful to say that; but I certainly do not like Lord Stapledean. However, I have taken his living, and should not complain.'

'I did not know that there was anything disagreeable.'

'There is this, Adela. I had rather tell you; and I came over today in part to do so: but you will see that the matter is one that should not be talked about;' and he looked down on the floor, poking about on the carpet pattern with his stick, being unable any longer to meet the clear gaze of her soft eye.

'Oh, I am sorry if there is anything to distress you.'

'Not exactly to distress me, perhaps; but I will tell you. When the marquis offered me the living, he did it on the stipulation that I should pay over to my mother three hundred and fifty pounds a year during her life. I doubt whether it was right to accept it on these conditions; but I did so. The living, therefore, is rather hers than mine.'

'Oh, Arthur, how good of you!' In spite of all Aunt

Penelope's lessons, old habits would sometimes get the better of her.

'I don't know; I am afraid that it was not good.'

'Why? I can't understand? Surely it must be good to give up your time, your labour, your hopes'—Adela did not say his heart—'for your mother and sisters' good! Why, how can it be else than good? I think it good, and shall think so.'

'At any rate, Adela, I could not withstand the offer when it was made to me.'

'I am sure you could not.'

'So I am little more than a curate in the parish as far as the income is concerned; with this difference, that I can't change my curacy for a living should a chance offer.'

Adela had never before known him to be solicitous about money for himself, and now she felt that she did not understand him. 'But you have got your fellowship,' said she.

'Yes, I have got my fellowship: oh, as far as that is concerned, I am better off than I could ever have expected to be. But, nevertheless, one feels—feels crippled by such an arrangement. It is quite impossible, you know, for instance, that—that—that I should do a great many things.' His courage failed him as he was about to make the fatal announcement.

'What things?' said Adela, with all the boldness of innocence.

It was necessary that he should say it. 'Why, for instance,' he continued, 'it is quite impossible, though perhaps that does not make much matter; but it is quite impossible—that I should ever marry.' And still looking down upon the ground, he poked sedulously among the patterns with his stick.

'Oh!' said Adela, with a tremor in her voice, and her eye was no longer able to rest upon his face.

There was a pause during which neither of them said a word, or saw each other. As far as Adela was concerned, immediate speech was impossible. She neither cried, nor sighed, nor sobbed, nor became hysterical. She was simply dumb. She could not answer this little announcement of her neighbour's. Heretofore, when he had come to her with his sorrows, she had sympathized with him, and poured balm into his wounds. But she had no balm for him now—and no sympathy. There they sat, mute; he poking the while at the carpet, while she did not even move a limb.

And then it gradually came home to both of them that this utter silence, this prostration of all power of self-management, told to each the secret of the other. Each felt that every moment of prolonged silence committed both of them the deeper. Why should not Adela be able to speak when thus informed of her neighbour's intended celibacy? Why should he sit like a fool before her merely because he had told her that on which he had long decided?

But it was clearly Wilkinson's duty to have disembarrassed the lady as soon as possible. It was almost unmanly in him to be put thus beyond the power of speech or action. But still he poked the carpet and said nothing. It was Adela who first broke that tell-tale silence; and grievous was the effort which it cost her to do so.

'But you will have your mother and sisters with you, Mr Wilkinson; and so, perhaps, you won't mind that.'

'Yes, I shall have them,' said he; and then there was another silence, which seemed about to be equally dangerous and equally difficult. But Adela, who was fully aware of the error which she had already committed, strove hard to save herself from repeating it.

'You will have a family round you; and if, as you say'—but the ground that she approached was so hot that she could not walk on it. She could not get further in that direction, and therefore merely added: 'I am sure I hope you will always be happy.'

At length Arthur shook himself, positively shook himself, as though that were the only mode by which he could collect his faculties; and then getting up from his chair, and standing with his back against the wall, he spoke out as follows:—

'Perhaps, Adela, there was no necessity for me to have mentioned this subject. At least, I am sure there was no necessity. But you have ever been such a friend to me, have so understood my feelings when no one else seemed to do so, that I could not but tell you this as I have told you everything else. I hope I have not annoyed you by doing so.'

'Oh, no; not at all.'

'It does make me a little sad to think that I shall never be my own master.'

'Never, Mr Wilkinson!' Had Arthur but known it, there was balm, there was sympathy in this word. Had his intellect been as sharp as his feelings, he would have known it. But it passed him unperceived, as it had fallen from her unawares: and she said no other word that could encourage him. If he was cold, she at least would be equally so.

'Certainly not during my mother's life; and you know how good ground we have for hoping that her life will be long. And then there are my sisters. My duty to them will be the same as to my mother, even though, as regards them, I may not be tied down as I am with regard to her.'

'We cannot have everything here,' said Adela, trying to smile. 'But I am sure I need not teach you that.'

'No, we cannot have everything.' And Arthur thought that, in spite of the clerical austerity which he was about to assume, he should very much like to have Adela Gauntlet.

'It will make you happy to know that you are making your mother happy, and the dear girls—and—and I have no doubt you will very soon get used to it. Many clergymen, you know, think that they ought not to marry.'

'Yes; but I never made up my mind to that.'

'No, perhaps not; but now perhaps you will think of it more seriously.'

'Indeed, I used to have an idea that a parish clergyman should be a married man. There are so many things which he can do better when he has a woman to assist him who thinks exactly as he thinks.'

'You will have your sisters, you know. Both Mary and Sophia were always active in the parish, and Jane and Fanny have their school.'

'Yes;' and he uttered a gentle sigh as he paused before he answered her. 'But it is not quite the same thing, Adela. I love my sisters dearly; but one always longs to have one heart that shall be entirely one's own.'

And had he come over to tell her this in the same breath with which he informed her that marriage was a privilege quite beyond his reach? What did he think of her, or of what did he imagine that she was made? There was cruelty in it, of which Adela became immediately conscious, and which she could hardly help wishing to resent. He had performed the object of his visit; why did he not leave her? He had made himself thoroughly understood; why did he not go? His former many sweet visits had created hopes which were all but certain. He had said nothing of love; but coming there as he had come, and gazing at her as he had gazed, Adela could not doubt but that she was loved. That was all now set at rest; but why should he remain there, breaking her heart with allusions to his own past tenderness?

'You must put up with the world as you find it, Mr Wilkinson.'

'Oh, yes; of course. But when one has had such happy dreams the waking reality, you know, does make one sad.'

'You are too happy in your friends and your position to be an object of pity. How many clergymen are there of your age who would look upon your lot as almost beyond their ambition! How many men are there with mothers and sisters for whom they cannot provide! How many who have made rash marriages which have led to no happiness! Surely, Mr Wilkinson, with you there is more cause for thankfulness than for complaint!' And thus, as it was necessary that she should say something, she moralized to him—very wisely.

'It is all true,' said he; 'and perhaps it is for the best. I might probably have been made more wretched in another way.'

'Yes; very likely.' Oh, Adela, Adela!

'I begin to know that a man should not be sanguine. I have always hoped for more than I have had a right to expect, and, therefore, I have always been disappointed. It was so at school, and at Oxford, and it is so now: it shows how true it is that a man should not look for his happiness here. Well; good-bye, Adela. I see that you think I am wrong to have any regrets.'

'Useless regrets are always foolish: we laugh at children who cry for what is quite out of their reach.'

'Yes; and you laugh at me. I dare say you are right.'

'No; do not say that, Mr Wilkinson. I have never laughed at you. But—' She did not wish to be actually unkind to him, though he had been so cruel to her.

At last he went. They shook hands with each other in their accustomed manner, but Wilkinson felt that he missed something from her touch, some warmth from the soft pressure, some scintillation of sympathy which such last moments of his visits had usually communicated to him. Yes; there was much to miss.

As he went back along the river his heart was sad within him. He had made up his mind to give up Adela Gauntlet, but he had not made up his mind to discover that she did not care for him—that she was indifferent to his happiness, and unable to sympathize with his feelings. The fact was, that though he had resolved that duty and his circumstances required him to remain single, nevertheless, he had at the bottom of his heart a sort of wish that Adela should be in love with him. He had his wish; but he was not sharp enough to discover that he had it. 'I never thought her unfeeling before,' said he to himself. 'But all the world is alike. Well; as it is, it does not signify; but it might have been that I should have half broken my heart to find her so unfeeling.—More cause for thankfulness than complaint! Yes; that is true of us all. But it was unfriendly, nay unfeminine in her to say so when she must have known how much I was giving up.' And so he walked on complaining; understanding perhaps accurately the wants of his own heart, but being quite in the dark as to the wants of that other heart.

But his grief, his discontent was mild in comparison with hers. She shook hands with him when he went, and endeavoured to say her last word of farewell in her usual tone; nay, for a few minutes after his departure she retained her seat calmly, fearing that he possibly might return; but then, when the door had closed on him, and she had seen him from her window passing across the lawn, then her spirits gave way, and bitterly she made her moan.

What was this that he had said to her? He would not marry because he had his mother and sisters to support. Would not she have helped to support them? Would not she have thrown in her lot with his for better or for worse, let that lot have been ever so poor? And could it be possible that he had not known this—had not read her heart as she had read his? Could it be that he had come there day after day, looking to her for love, and sympathy, and kindness—that sort of kindness which a man demands from no one but her he loves, and which no one can give him unless she loves him? Could it be that he had done this and then thought that it all meant nothing? that the interchange of such feelings had no further signification?

Money! Had she asked about his money in those days when his father still lived, when there was no question of this living belonging to him? She would have waited for him for years had years been necessary, even though they should be counted by tens and tens. Nay, she would have been contented to wait, even though that waiting should never have been rewarded, had he given her the privilege of regarding herself as his. Money! She would have been contented to live on potato-parings could he have been contented to live with her on potatoes.

She had over and over again questioned herself as to her love, and reminded herself that as yet he had said nothing to her to justify it: but as often she had answered herself that with him she could have no doubt. It was impossible that he should so look into her eyes and so speak to her if he did not love her. And so she had resolved to risk all her happiness upon her conviction of his faithfulness. She had so risked it all; and now he came to her, telling her coldly that he could not afford to marry.

He, to tell her of his happy dreams and his waking reality! he who had not the courage to realize the bliss of his dreams when that bliss was within his reach! He, to talk of sympathy, of a woman thinking with him exactly as he thought! he who was so timid of the world that he feared to love lest perchance his supplies of bread and meat should fail him! What could heart wounds signify to him, or hurt feelings? Had he not his arms sound and his head clear? If, having them, he would not venture for his love's sake to meet the world and its burdens, he could hardly have heart enough to know what love really meant.

Flinging herself on her sofa with outstretched arms, thus Adela made her moan; not in these words, for she spake none: but such were the thoughts which ran through her mind as she bewailed all that she had risked and all that she had lost.

'What would I not have done for him!' she suddenly exclaimed aloud, as, rising from the sofa, she stood erect upon the ground, pressing her hand upon her heart. 'Fool that I have been—fool, fool, fool!'

And then, with her hand still close to her side, she walked up and down the room with quick step.

And she had been a fool according to the world's wisdom. Of what use had been Aunt Penelope's teaching, strictly enacting as it did all the nice proprieties of young-lady life, seeing that it had not sufficed to guard her heart against the first comer? Unasked she had given it all away, had poured it out to the last drop of its warm flood; and now she was told that it was not wanted, that the article was one not exactly in the gentleman's walk of life! She might well call herself a fool:—but what was she to call him?

'It is quite impossible, you know, that I should ever marry!' Why had he not asked her whether or no it were possible; if not now, then in ten years' time—if not in ten years, then in twenty? Had he not been as faithless to her, was he not as much man-sworn,* as though a thousand oaths had passed between them? Oaths between lovers are but Cupid's phrases, made to enable them to talk of love. They are the playthings of love, as kisses are. When lovers trust each other they are sweet bonds; but they will never bind those who do not trust. When he had told her that she, and she only, understood his feelings, that she, and she only, knew his moods, and when she had answered him by the encouragement of her soft smile, could it be that more was necessary between them? Ah! yes, Adela, much more! Never know a gentleman's moods, never understand his feelings till, in the plain language of his mother-tongue, he has asked you to be mistress of them.

When her father came in before dinner, she was still pacing up and down the room. But she had not spent the two hours since Arthur had left her in vain sorrow or in vainer anger. She had felt that it behoved her to resolve how she would act, and what she would do; and in those two hours she had resolved. A great misfortune, a stunning blow had fallen on her; but the fault had been with her rather than with him. She would school herself to bear the punishment, to see him occasionally, and bear with him as she would have done had he never taken those walks along the river; she would still love his sisters; still go when needs was to the Hurst Staple parsonage. As for him, she would wish him no evil, rather every good. As for herself, she would check her rebel heart if she could; but, at any rate, she would learn to check the rising blood which would otherwise tell her tale.

'Arthur Wilkinson has been here today, papa,' she was able to say, with composed voice; 'they are quite settled again at the parsonage.'

'Ah! he is a lucky fellow,' said the old vicar; 'he'll be wanting a wife now before the year's out.'

CHAPTER V

THE CHOICE OF A PROFESSION

WE must now go back to our other hero, or, rather, to another of our heroes. Arthur Wilkinson is our melancholy love-lorn tenor, George Bertram our eager, excitable barytone, and Mr Harcourt—Henry Harcourt—our bass, wide awake to the world's good things, impervious to sentimentality, and not over-scrupulous—as is always the case with your true deep-mouthed opera bass.

Our present business is with the excitable barytone, whom we left some year and a half ago in not a very clear state of mind as to the walk in life which would be best suited for his peculiar legs. Harcourt, who was himself a lawyer, recommended the law. Selfish as was the general tone of Harcourt's heart, still he had within him a high, if not a generous feeling, which made him wish to have near him in his coming life a friend of such promise as George Bertram. Bertram might beat him in his career; nay, probably would so do; but, nevertheless, Harcourt wished to see him keeping his terms in London. He was convinced that he should gain more than he should lose by such a friend.

But Bertram's own mind was not so easily made up. His personal possessions in life may be thus catalogued. He had come of a good family; he had received the best education which England could give him; he was quick in speech and ready in thought; he had a double-first degree, and would at once have a fellowship; he had also an uncle who was very rich and occasionally very disagreeable, and a father who was very poor, and of whom he heard all men say that he was one of the most agreeable fellows that ever lived. Such being his stock in trade, how was he to take it to the best market? and what market would be the best?

In thinking over his markets, it must not be supposed that his only object, or his chief object, was the making of money. That was a rock, rather, of which it behoved him to be very careful. The money-making part of every profession was, according to his present views, a necessary incidental evil. To enable a poor man like him to carry on his work some money must be made; for some sorts of work, perhaps for that very sort which he would most willingly choose, much money must be made. But the making of it should never be his triumph. It could be but a disagreeable means to a desirable end. At the age of twenty-two so thought our excitable barytone hero on that point.

Two ends appeared to him to be desirable. But which of the two was the more desirable—that to him was the difficult question. To do good to others, and to have his own name in men's mouths—these were the fitting objects of a man's life. But whether he would attempt the former in order to achieve the latter; or obtain, if he did obtain, the latter by seeking success in the former: on this point his character was not sufficiently fixed, nor his principles sufficiently high to enable him fitly to resolve.

But the necessity of seeing his uncle before he took any actual steps secured him from the necessity of coming to any absolutely immediate decision. He and Harcourt were together for three or four days, and he listened not unmoved to his friend's eloquence in favour of public life in London. Not unmoved, indeed, but always with a spirit of antagonism. When Harcourt told of forensic triumphs, Bertram spoke of the joy of some rustic soul saved to heaven in the quiet nook of a distant parish. When his friend promised to him Parliament and the later glories of the ermine, he sighed after literary fame, to be enjoyed among the beauties of nature. But Harcourt understood all this: he did not wish to convince his friend, but only to lead him.

Mr George Bertram senior was a notable man in the city of London. I am not prepared to say what was his trade, or even whether he had one properly so called. But there was no doubt about his being a moneyed man, and one well thought of on 'Change. At the time of which I write, he was a director of the Bank of England, chairman of a large insurance company, was deep in water, far gone in gas, and an illustrious potentate in railway interests. I imagine that he had neither counting-house, shop, nor ware-rooms: but he was not on that account at a loss whither to direct his steps; and those who knew city ways knew very well where to meet Mr George Bertram senior between the hours of eleven and five.

He was ten years older than his brother, Sir Lionel, and at the time of which I write might be about seventy. He was still unmarried, and in this respect had always been regarded by Sir Lionel as a fountain from whence his own son might fairly expect such waters as were necessary for his present maintenance and future well-being. But Mr George Bertram senior had regarded the matter in a different light. He had paid no shilling on account of his nephew, or on other accounts appertaining to his brother, which he had not scored down as so much debt against Sir Lionel, duly debiting the amount with current interest; and statements of this account were periodically sent to Sir Lionel by Mr Bertram's man of business,—and periodically thrown aside by Sir Lionel, as being of no moment whatsoever.

When Mr Bertram had paid the bill due by his brother to

Mr Wilkinson, there was outstanding some family unsettled claim from which the two brothers might, or might not, obtain some small sums of money. Sir Lionel, when much pressed by the city Crœsus,* had begged him to look to this claim, and pay himself from the funds which would be therefrom accruing. The city Crœsus had done so: a trifle of two or three hundred pounds had fallen to Sir Lionel's lot, and had of course been duly credited to his account. But it went a very little way towards squaring matters, and the old man of business went on sending his half-yearly statements, which became anything but 'small by degrees.'

Mr Bertram had never absolutely told George of this debt, or complained of his not being repaid the advances which he had made; but little hints dropped from him, which were sometimes understood for more than they were worth, and which made the young Oxonian feel that he would rather not be quite so much in his uncle's hands. The old man gave him to understand that he must not look on himself as an heir to wealth, or imagine that another lot was his than that ordinary to mortals—the necessity, namely, of eating his bread in the sweat of his brow.

Old Mr Bertram ordinarily lived at Hadley, a village about a mile beyond Barnet, just on the border of what used to be called Enfield Chase. Here he had an establishment very fit for a quiet old gentleman, but perhaps not quite adequate to his reputed wealth. By my use of the word reputed, the reader must not be led to think that Mr Bertram's money-bags were unreal. They were solid, and true as the coffers of the Bank of England. He was no Colonel Waugh,* rich only by means of his rich impudence. It is not destined that he shall fall brilliantly, bringing down with him a world of ruins. He will not levant to Spain or elsewhere. His wealth is of the old-fashioned sort, and will abide at any rate such touch of time as it may encounter in our pages. But none of the Hadleyites, or, indeed, any other ites—not even, probably, the Bank-of-Englandites, or the City-of-London-Widows'-Fundites—knew very well what his means were; and when, therefore, people at Hadley spoke of his modest household, they were apt to speak of it as being very insufficient for such a millionaire.

Hitherto George had always passed some part of his vacations at Hadley. The amusements there were not of a very exciting nature; but London was close, and even at Hadley there were pretty girls with whom he could walk and flirt, and the means of keeping a horse and a couple of pointers, even if the hunting and shooting were not conveniently to be had.

A few days after the glories of his degree, when his name was still great on the High Street of Oxford, and had even been touched by true fame in a very flattering manner in the columns of the 'Daily Jupiter,'* he came home to Hadley. His uncle never encouraged visits from him in the city, and they met, therefore, for the first time in the old man's drawing-room just before dinner.

'How are you, George?' said the uncle, putting out his hand to his nephew, and then instantly turning round and poking the fire. 'What sort of a journey have you had from Oxford? Yes, these railways make it all easy. Which line do you use? Didcot, eh? That's wrong. You'll have a smash some of these days with one of those Great Western express trains'—Mr Bertram held shares in the opposition line* by which Oxford may be reached, and never omitted an opportunity of doing a little business. 'I'm ready for dinner; I don't know whether you are. You eat lunch, I suppose. John, it's two minutes past the half-hour. Why don't we have dinner?'

Not a word was said about the degree—at least, not then. Indeed Mr Bertram did not think very much about degrees. He had taken no degree himself, except a high degree in wealth, and could not understand that he ought to congratulate a young man of twenty-two as to a successful termination of his school-lessons. He himself at that age had been, if not on 'Change, at any rate seated on the steps of 'Change. He had been then doing a man's work; beginning to harden together the nucleus of that snowball of money which he had since rolled onwards till it had become so huge a lump—destined, probably, to be thawed and to run away into muddy water in some much shorter space of time. He could not blame his nephew: he could not call him idle, as he would have delighted to do had occasion permitted; but he would not condescend to congratulate him on being great in Greek or mighty in abstract mathematics.

'Well, George,' said he, pushing him the bottle as soon as the cloth was gone, 'I suppose you have done with Oxford now?'

'Not quite, sir; I have my fellowship to receive.'

'Some beggarly two hundred pounds a year, I suppose. Not that I mean to say you should not be glad to have it,' he added, thus correcting the impression which his words might otherwise have made. 'As you have been so long getting it, it will be better to have that than nothing. But your fellowship won't make it necessary for you to live at Oxford, will it?'

'Oh, no. But then I may perhaps go into the church.'

'Oh, the church, eh? Well, it is a respectable profession; only men have to work for nothing in it.'

'I wish they did, sir. If we had the voluntary system—'

'You can have that if you like. I know that the Independent ministers—'*

'I should not think of leaving the Church of England on any account.'

'You have decided, then, to be a clergyman?'

'Oh, no; not decided. Indeed, I really think that if a man will work, he may do better at the bar.'

'Very well, indeed—if he have the peculiar kind of talent necessary.'

'But, then, I doubt whether a practising barrister can ever really be an honest man.'

'What?'

'They have such dirty work to do. They spend their days in making out that black is white; or, worse still, that white is black.'

'Pshaw! Have a little more charity, master George, and do not be so over-righteous. Some of the greatest men of your country have been lawyers.'

'But their being great men won't alter the fact; nor will my being charitable. When two clear-headed men take money to advocate the different sides of a case, each cannot think that his side is true.'

'Fiddlestick! But mind, I do not want you to be a lawyer. You must choose for yourself. If you don't like that way of earning your bread, there are others.'

'A man may be a doctor, to be sure; but I have no taste that way.'

'And is that the end of the list?'

'There is literature. But literature, though the grandest occupation in the world for a man's leisure, is, I take it, a slavish profession.'

'Grub Street,* eh? Yes, I should think so. You never heard of commerce, I suppose?'

'Commerce. Yes, I have heard of it. But I doubt whether I have the necessary genius.'

The old man looked at him as though he doubted whether or no he were being laughed at.

'The necessary kind of genius, I mean,' continued George.

'Very likely not. Your genius is adapted to dispersing, perhaps, rather than collecting.'

'I dare say it is, sir.'

'And I suppose you never heard of a man with a—what is it you call your degree? a double-first—going behind a counter. What sort of men are the double-lasts, I wonder!'

'It is they, I rather think, who go behind the counters,' said George, who had no idea of allowing his uncle to have all the raillery on his side.

'Is it, sir? But I rather think they don't come out last when the pudding is to be proved by the eating. Success in life is not to be won by writing Greek verses; not though you write ever so many. A ship-load of them would not fetch you the value of this glass of wine at any market in the world.'

'Commerce is a grand thing,' said George, with an air of conviction.

'It is the proper work for men,' said his uncle, proudly.

'But I have always heard,' replied the nephew, 'that a man in this country has no right to look to commerce as a profession unless he possesses capital.' Mr Bertram, feeling that the tables had been turned against him, finished his glass of wine and poked the fire.

A few days afterwards the same subject was again raised

between them. 'You must choose for yourself, George,' said the old man; 'and you should choose quickly.'

'If I could choose for myself—which I am aware that I cannot do; for circumstances, after all, will have the decision—but, if I could choose, I would go into Parliament.'

'Go where?' said Mr Bertram, who would have thought it as reasonable if his nephew had proposed to take a house in Belgrave Square with the view of earning a livelihood.

'Into Parliament, sir.'

'Is Parliament a profession? I never knew it before.'

'Perhaps not, ordinarily, a money-making profession; nor would I wish to make it so.'

'And what county, or what borough, do you intend to honour by representing it? Perhaps the University will return you.'

'Perhaps it may some of these days.'

'And in the meantime, you mean to live on your fellowship, I suppose?'

'On that and anything else that I can get.'

Mr Bertram sat quiet for some time without speaking, and George also seemed inclined to muse awhile upon the subject. 'George,' said the uncle, at last, 'I think it will be better that we should thoroughly understand each other. You are a good fellow in your way, and I like you well enough. But you must not get into your head any idea that you are to be my heir.'

'No, sir; I won't.'

'Because it would only ruin you. My idea is that a man should make his own way in the world as I made mine. If you were my son, it may be presumed that I should do as other men do, and give you my money. And, most probably, you would make no better use of it than the sons of other men who, like me, have made money. But you are not my son.'

'Quite true, sir; and therefore I shall be saved the danger. At any rate, I shall not be the victim of disappointment.'

'I am very glad to hear it,' said Mr Bertram, who, however, did not give any proof of his gladness, seeing that he evinced some little addition of acerbity in his temper and asperity in his manner. It was hard to have to deal with a nephew with whom he could find so little ground for complaint.

'But I have thought it right to warn you,' he continued. 'You are aware that up to the present moment the expense of your education has been borne by me.'

'No, sir; not my education.'

'Not your education! How, then, has it been borne?'

'I speak of my residence at Oxford. I have had a great many indulgences there, and you have paid for them. The expenses of my education I could have paid myself.' This was fair on George's part. He had not asked his uncle for a liberal allowance, and was hardly open to blame for having taken it.

'I only know I have paid regularly one hundred and fifty pounds a year to your order, and I find from Pritchett'—Pritchett was his man of business—'that I am paying it still.'

'He sent me the last quarter the other day; but I have not touched it.'

'Never mind; let that pass. I don't know what your father's views are about you, and never could find out.'

'I'll ask him. I mean to go and see him.'

'Go and see him! Why, he's at Bagdad.'

'Yes. If I start at once, I shall just catch him there, or perhaps meet him at Damascus.'

'Then you'll be a great fool for your pains—a greater fool almost than I take you to be. What do you expect your father can do for you? My belief is, that if four hundred pounds would take him to heaven, he couldn't make up the money. I don't think he could raise it either in Europe or Asia. I am sure of this; I wouldn't lend it him.'

'In such a case as that, sir, his personal security would go for so little.'

'His personal security has always gone for little. But, as I was saying, I have consented ever since you went to Wilkinson's to allow your father to throw the burden of your expenses on my shoulders. I thought it a pity that you should not have the chance of a decent education. Mind, I claim no gratitude, as I shall expect your father to pay me what I have advanced.'

'How on earth can he do that, sir? But perhaps I can.'

'Can you? very well; then you can settle it with him. But listen to me.'

'Listen to me for a moment, uncle George. I think you are hard on my father, and certainly hard on me. When I went to Wilkinson's, what did I know of who paid the bill?'

'Who says you knew anything, sir?'

'And, counting on from that time, at what period ought I to have begun to know it? When should I have first learnt to feel that I was a burden to any one?'

'Who has talked about a burden?'

'You say I am not to be your heir?'

'Certainly not.'

'I never thought of being your heir. I don't care a straw about being anybody's heir. What you have given freely, I have taken freely. As for my father, if you felt so harshly towards him, why did you let him incur this debt?'

'I was to see you kicked out of Wilkinson's house and starve in the ditch, I suppose? But now, if you can control your fine feelings for one moment, will you listen to me? I have never blamed you in the matter at all, and don't blame you now—at least not yet.'

'I hope you never will—that is about money matters.'

'Now do listen to me. It seems to me that you are quite astray about a profession. You don't like commerce, and what you said the other day about capital is quite true. I count a man a knave who goes into trade without capital. In a small way we might, perhaps, have managed it. But in a very small way you would not have liked it.'

'Neither small nor great, sir.'

'Very well. You need not be afraid that anything very great will be thrust upon you. But it seems to me that what you are most fitted for is a lawyer.'

Young Bertram paused a moment. 'Uncle, I really hardly know. Sometimes I have a strange desire to go into orders.'

'Very strange indeed! But now, if you will listen to me—I have been speaking to Mr Dry. Messrs Dry and Stickatit have done business for me for the last forty years. Now, George, I will advance you three thousand pounds at four per cent.—'

'What should I want with three thousand pounds?'

'You don't suppose you can get into a house like that without money, do you?'

'And be an attorney?' said George, with a look of horror which almost penetrated the thick skin of the old man's feelings. What! had he taken a double-first, been the leading man of his year, spouted at the debating club, and driven himself nearly dizzy with Aristotle for this—for a desk in the office of Messrs Dry and Stickatit, attorneys of old Bucklersbury! No, not for all the uncles! not for any uncle!

'They net four thousand pounds a year,' said Mr Bertram; 'and in process of time you would be the working partner, and have, at any rate, a full half of the business.'

But, no! George was not to be talked into such a scheme as that by the offer of any loan, by the mention of any number of thousands. He positively refused to consider the proposition; and his uncle, with equal positiveness, refused to hold any further converse with him on the subject of a profession. 'Pritchett will pay you your present allowance,' said he, 'for two years longer—that is, if I live.'

'I can do without it, sir,' said George.

'Pritchett will pay that amount for two years,' said the uncle, with great positiveness; 'after that it will be discontinued. And for the next three months I shall be happy to see you here as my guest.'

It will be readily believed that George Bertram did not overstay the three months.

CHAPTER VI

JERUSALEM

BUT there was no quarrel between George Bertram uncle and George Bertram nephew: though in such conversations as they had about business they were not over civil to each other, still they went on together as good friends, at any rate as they ever had been. Indeed, after the last scene which has been reported, the old man became more courteous to his nephew, and before the three months were over was almost cordial.

There was that about George the younger which made the old uncle respect him, despite himself. The London merchant had a thorough contempt for his brother, the soldier of fortune: he had acted as he had done on behalf of that brother's son almost more with the view of showing his contempt, and getting thereby an opportunity for expressing it, than with any fixed idea of doing a kindness. He had counted also on despising the son as he had despised the father; but here he found himself foiled. George had taken all that he had given, as any youth would take what an uncle gave; but he had never asked for more; he had done as well as it was possible for him to do in that line of education which had been tendered to him; and now, though he would not become an attorney or a merchant, was prepared to earn his own bread, and professed that he was able to support himself without further assistance from any one.

Before the three months were over, his uncle had more than once asked him to prolong his visit; but George had made up his mind to leave Hadley. His purpose was to spend three or four months in going out to his father, and then to settle in London. In the meantime, he employed himself with studying the law of nations, and amused his leisure hours with Coke and Blackstone.*

'You'll never find your father,' said Mr Bertram.

'At any rate, I'll try; and if I miss him, I shall see something of the world.'

You'll see more in London in three months than you will there in twelve; and, moreover, you would not lose your time.'

But George was inexorable, and before the three months were over he had started on his trip.

'I beg your pardon, Mr George,' said Mr Pritchett to him the day before he went (his uncle had requested him to call on Pritchett in the city)—'I beg your pardon, Mr George, but if I may be allowed to speak a word or so, I do hope you'll write a line now and then to the old gentleman while you are away.'

Now George had never written a line to his uncle in his life; all his communications as to his journeys and proposed arrivals had, by his uncle's special direction, been made to the housekeeper, and he had no present intention of commencing a correspondence.

'Write to him, Mr Pritchett! No, I don't suppose I shall. I take it, my uncle does not much care for such letters as I should write.'

'Ah! but he would, Mr George. You shouldn't be too quick to take persons by their appearances. It's half a million of money, you know, Mr George; half—a—million—of—money!' And Mr Pritchett put great stress on the numeration of his patron's presumed wealth.

'Half a million, is it? Well, that's a great deal, no doubt; and I fully see the force of your excellent argument. But I fear there is nothing to be done in that line: I'm not born to be the heir to half a million of money; you might see that in my face.'

Mr Pritchett stared at him very hard. 'Well, I can't say that I do, Mr George; but take my word for it, the old gentleman is very fond of you.'

'Very fond! That's a little too strong, isn't it?'

'That is, if he's very fond of anything. Now, he said to me yesterday, "Pritchett," says he, "that boy's going to Bagdad." "What! Mr George?" says I. "Yes," says he; "and to Hong Kong too, I suppose, before he comes back: he's going after his father;" and then he gave one of those bitter looks, you know. "That's a pity," says I, for you know one must humour him. "He is a fool," says your uncle, "and always will be." '

'I'm sure, Mr Pritchett, I'm very much obliged for the trouble you are at in telling me.'

'Oh! I think nothing of the trouble. "And he knows no more about money," says your uncle, "than an ostrich. He can't go to Bagdad out of his allowance." "Of course he can't," said I. "You had better put three hundred pounds to his credit," said the old gentleman; and so, Mr George, I have.'

'I could have done very well without it, Mr Pritchett.'

'Perhaps so; but three hundred pounds never hurt anybody—never, Mr George; and I can tell you this: if you play your cards well, you may be the old gentleman's heir, in spite of all he says to the contrary.'

'At any rate, Mr Pritchett, I'm very much obliged to you:' and so they parted.

'He'll throw that three hundred pounds in my teeth the next time I see him,' said George to himself.

Good as Mr Pritchett's advice undoubtedly was, Bertram did not take it; and his uncle received no line from him during the whole period of his absence. Our hero's search after his father was not quite of so intricate a nature as was supposed by his uncle, nor so difficult as that made by Japhet under similar circumstances. His route was to be by Paris, Marseilles, Malta, Alexandria, Jaffa, Jerusalem, and Damascus, and he had written to Sir Lionel, requesting him to write to either or all of those addresses. Neither in France, nor Malta, nor Egypt did he receive any letters; but in the little town of Jaffa, where he first put his foot on Asiatic soil, a despatch from his father was awaiting him. Sir Lionel was about to leave Persia, and was proceeding to Constantinople on public service; but he would go out of his course to meet his son at Jerusalem.

The tone of Sir Lionel's letter was very unlike that of Mr Bertram's conversation. He heartily congratulated his son on the splendid success of his degree; predicted for him a future career both brilliant and rich; declared that it was the dearest wish of his heart to embrace his son, and spoke of their spending a few weeks together at Jerusalem almost with rapture.

This letter very much delighted George. He had a natural anxiety to think well of his father, and had not altogether believed the evil that had been rather hinted than spoken of him by Mr Bertram. The colonel had certainly not hitherto paid him very much parental attention, and had generally omitted to answer the few letters which George had written to him. But a son is not ill inclined to accept acts of new grace from a father; and there was something so delightful in the tone and manner of Sir Lionel's letter, it was so friendly as well as affectionate, so perfectly devoid of the dull, monotonous, lecture-giving asperity with which ordinary fathers too often season their ordinary epistles, that he was in raptures with his newly-found correspondent.

'I would not miss seeing you for worlds,' wrote Sir Lionel; 'and although I have been ordered to Constantinople with all the *immediate haste* which your civil-service grandees always use in addressing us military slaves, it shall go hard with me but I will steal a fortnight from them in order to pass it with you at Jerusalem. I suppose I shall scarce know you, or you me: but when you see an old gentleman in a military frock,* with a bald head, a hook nose, and a rather short allowance of teeth, you may then be sure that you look upon your father. However, I will be at Z—'s Hotel—I believe they honour the caravansary* with that name—as soon as possible after the 14th.'

His uncle had at any rate been quite wrong in predicting that his father would keep out of his way. So far was this from being the case, that Sir Lionel was going to put himself to considerable inconvenience to meet him. It might be, and no doubt was the case, that Mr Bertram the merchant had put together a great deal more money than Colonel Bertram the soldier; but the putting together of money was no virtue in George's eyes; and if Sir Lionel had not remitted a portion of his pay as regularly as he perhaps should have done, that should not now be counted as a vice. It may perhaps be surmised that had George Bertram suffered much in consequence of his father's negligence in remitting, he might have been disposed to look at the matter in a different light.

He had brought but one servant with him, a dragoman* whom he had picked up at Malta, and with him he started on his ride from the city of oranges. Oranges grow plentifully enough in Spain, in Malta, in Egypt, in Jamaica, and other places, but within five miles of Jaffa nothing else is grown—if we except the hedges of prickly pear which divide the gardens. Orange garden succeeds to orange garden till one finds oneself on the broad open desert that leads away to Jerusalem.

There is something enticing to an Englishman in the idea of riding off through the desert with a pistol girt about his waist, a portmanteau strapped on one horse before him, and an only attendant seated on another behind him. There is a *soupçon* of danger in the journey just sufficient to give it excitement; and then it is so un-English, oriental, and inconvenient; so opposed to the accustomed haste and comfort of a railway; so out of his hitherto beaten way of life, that he is delighted to get into the saddle. But it may be a question whether he is not generally more delighted to get out of it; particularly if that saddle be a Turkish one.

George had heard of Arab horses, and the clouds of dust which rise from their winged feet. When first he got beyond the hedges of the orange gardens, he expected to gallop forth till he found himself beneath the walls of Jerusalem. But he had before him many an hour of tedious labour ere those walls were seen. His pace was about four miles an hour. During the early day he strove frequently to mend it; but as the sun became hot in the heavens, his efforts after speed were gradually reduced, and long before evening he had begun to think that Jerusalem was a myth, his dragoman an impostor, and his Arab steed the sorriest of jades.

'It is the longest journey I ever took in my life,' said George.

'Longest; yes. A top of two mountain more, and two go-down, and then there; yes,' said the dragoman, among whose various accomplishments that of speaking English could hardly be reckoned as the most prominent.

At last the two mountains more and the two go-downs were performed, and George was informed that the wall he saw rising sharp from the rocky ground was Jerusalem. There is something very peculiar in the first appearance of a walled city that has no suburbs or extramural adjuncts. It is like that of a fortress of cards built craftily on a table. With us in England it is always difficult to say where the country ends and where the town begins; and even with the walled towns of the Continent, one rarely comes upon them so as to see the sharp angles of a gray stone wall shining in the sun, as they do in the old pictures of the cities in 'Pilgrim's Progress.'

But so it is with Jerusalem. One rides up to the gate feeling that one is still in the desert; and yet a moment more, with the permission of those very dirty-looking Turkish soldiers at the gate, will place one in the city. One rides up to the gate, and as every one now has a matured opinion as to the taking of casemated batteries* and the inefficiency of granite bastions, one's first idea is how delightfully easy it would be to take Jerusalem. It is at any rate easy enough to enter it, for the dirty Turkish soldiers do not even look at you, and you soon become pleasantly aware that you are beyond the region of passports.

George Bertram had promised himself that the moment in which he first saw Jerusalem should be one of intense mental interest; and when, riding away from the orange gardens at Jaffa, he had endeavoured to urge his Arab steed into that enduring gallop which was to carry him up to the city of the sepulchre, his heart was ready to melt into ecstatic pathos as soon as that gallop should have been achieved. But the time for ecstatic pathos had altogether passed away before he rode in at that portal. He was then swearing vehemently at his floundering jade, and giving up to all the fiends of Tartarus* the accursed saddle which had been specially contrived with the view of lacerating the nether Christian man.

'Where on earth is this d— hotel?' said he, when he and his dragoman and portmanteau had been floundering for about five minutes down a steep, narrow, ill-paved lane, with a half-formed gully in the middle, very slippery with orange-peel and old vegetables, and crowded with the turbans of all the Eastern races. 'Do you call this a street?' After all his sentiment, all his emotions, all his pious resolves, it was thus that our hero entered Jerusalem! But what piety can withstand the wear and tear of twelve hours in a Turkish saddle?

'Is this a street?' said he. It was the main street in Jerusalem. The first, or among the first in grandeur of those sacred ways which he had intended hardly to venture to pass with shoes on his feet. His horse turning a corner as he followed the dragoman again slipped and almost fell. Whereupon Bertram again cursed. But then he was not only tired and sore, but very hungry also. Our finer emotions should always be encouraged with a stomach moderately full.

At last they stopped at a door in a wall, which the dragoman pronounced to be the entrance of Z—'s hotel. In fact they had not yet been full ten minutes within the town; but the streets certainly were not well paved. In five minutes more, George was in his room, strewing sofas and chairs with the contents of his portmanteau, and inquiring with much energy what was the hour fixed for the table d'hôte. He found, with much inward satisfaction, that he had just twenty minutes to prepare himself. At Jerusalem, as elsewhere, these after all are the traveller's first main questions. When is the table d'hôte? Where is the cathedral? At what hour does the train start to-morrow morning? It will be some years yet, but not very many, before the latter question is asked at Jerusalem.

Bertram had arrived about a fortnight before Easter, and the town was already full of pilgrims, congregated for that ceremony, and of English and Americans who had come to look at the pilgrims.

The inn was nearly full, and George, when he entered the public room, heard such a Babel of English voices, and such a clatter of English spoons that he might have fancied himself at the top of the Righi* or in a Rhine steamboat. But the subjects under discussion all savoured of the Holy Land.

'Mrs Rose, we are going to have a picnic on Monday in the Valley of Jehoshaphat; will you and your young ladies join us? We shall send the hampers to the tomb of Zachariah.'

'Thank you, Miss Todd; we should have been so happy; but we have only three days to do Bethlehem, the Dead Sea, and Jericho. We must be off to-morrow.'

'Mamma, I lost my parasol somewhere coming down the Mount of Offence. Those nasty Arab children must have stolen it.'

'They say the people in Siloam are the greatest thieves in Syria; and nobody dares to meddle with them.'

'But I saw it in your hand, my dear, at the Well of Enrogel.'

'What, no potatoes! there were potatoes yesterday. Waiter, waiter; who ever heard of setting people down to dinner without potatoes?'

'Well, I didn't know what to say to it. If that is the tomb of Nicodemus, that seems to settle the question. May I trouble you for the salt?'

'Mr Pott, I won't have anything more to say to you; you have no faith. I believe it all.'

'What, all? from Calvary upstairs in the gallery down to the dark corner where the cock crew?'

'Yes, all, Mr Pott. Why should not a cock crow there as well as anywhere else? It is so beautiful to believe.'

George Bertram found himself seated next to a lady-like well-dressed Englishwoman of the middle age, whom he heard called Miss Baker; and next to her again sat—an angel! whom Miss Baker called Caroline, and whom an odious man sitting on the other side of her called Miss Waddington.

All my readers will probably at different times have made part of a table-d'hôte assemblage; and most of them, especially those who have travelled with small parties, will know how essential it is to one's comfort to get near to pleasant neighbours. The young man's idea of a pleasant neighbour is of course a pretty girl. What the young ladies' idea may be I don't pretend to say. But it certainly does seem to be happily arranged by Providence that the musty fusty people, and the nicy spicy people, and the witty pretty people do severally assemble and get together as they ought to do.

Bertram's next-door neighbour was certainly of the nicy spicy order; but this did not satisfy him. He would have been very well pleased to talk to Miss Baker, had it not been for the close contiguity of Miss Waddington; and even her once-removed vicinity would not have made him unhappy, had not that odious man on her left had so much to say about the village of Emmaus and the Valley of Ajalon.

Now be it known to all men that Caroline Waddington is our donna primissima—the personage of most importance in these pages. It is for her that you are to weep, with her that you are to sympathize, and at her that you are to wonder. I would that I could find it compatible with my duty to introduce her to this circle without any minute details of her bodily and mental charms; but I have already been idle in the case of Adela Gauntlet, and I feel that a donna primissima has claims to description which I cannot get over. Only not exactly now; in a few chapters hence we shall have Miss

Waddington actively engaged upon the scene, and then she shall be described.

It must suffice now to say that she was an orphan; that since her father's death she had lived with her aunt, Miss Baker, chiefly at Littlebath; that Miss Baker had, at her niece's instance, been to Egypt, up the Nile, across the short desert—(short!) having travelled from Cairo to Jerusalem,—and that now, thoroughly sick of the oriental world, she was anxious only to get back to Littlebath; while Caroline, more enthusiastic and much younger, urged her to go on to Damascus, and Lebanon, to Beyrout and Smyrna, and thence home, merely visiting Constantinople and Athens on the way.

Had Bertram heard the terms in which Miss Waddington spoke of the youth who was so great about Ajalon when she and her aunt were in their own room, and also the words in which that aunt spoke of him, perhaps he might have been less provoked.

'Aunt, that Mr M'Gabbery is an ass. I am sure he has ears if one could only see them. I am so tired of him. Don't you think we could get on to Damascus tomorrow?'

'If we did, I have no doubt he'd come too.' Mr M'Gabbery had been one of the party who crossed the desert with them from Cairo.

'Impossible, aunt. The Hunters are ready to start tomorrow, or, if not, the day after, and I know they would not have him.'

'But, my dear, I really am not equal to Damascus. A few more days on a camel—'

'But, aunt, you'll have a horse.'

'That's worse, I'm sure. And, moreover, I've found an old friend, and one that you will like very much.'

'What, that exceedingly ugly young man that sat next to you?'

'Yes. That exceedingly ugly young man I remember as the prettiest baby in the world—not that I think he is ugly. He is, however, no other than the nephew of Mr Bertram.'

'What, papa's Mr Bertram?'

'Yes; your father's Mr Bertram. Therefore, if old Mr Bertram should die, and this young man should be his heir, he would have the charge of all your money. You'd better be gracious to him.'

'How odd! But what is he like?'

'He is one of the cleverest young men of the day. I had heard that he had distinguished himself very much at Oxford; and he certainly is a most agreeable companion.' And so it was arranged between them that they would not start to Damascus as yet, in spite of any evil that Mr M'Gabbery might inflict on them.

On the next morning at breakfast, Bertram managed to separate the aunt from the niece by sitting between them. It was long, however, before Mr M'Gabbery gave up the battle. When he found that an interloper was interfering with his peculiar property, he began to tax his conversational powers to the utmost. He was greater than ever about Ajalon, and propounded some very startling theories with reference to Emmaus. He recalled over and over again the interesting bits of their past journey; how tired they had been at Gaza, where he had worked for the ladies like a slave—how terribly Miss Baker had been frightened in the neighbourhood of Arimathea, where he, Mr M'Gabbery, had specially looked to his pistols with the view of waging war on three or four supposed Bedouins who were seen to be hovering on the hill-sides. But all would not do. Miss Waddington was almost tired of Gaza and Arimathea, and Miss Baker seemed to have a decided preference for London news. So at last Mr M'Gabbery became silent and grand, and betook himself to his associations and a map of Palestine in a corner.

Bertram, when fortified with a night's rest and a good breakfast, was able to recover his high-toned feeling, and, thus armed, proceeded alone to make his first visit to the Church of the Holy Sepulchre. It was a Sunday, the last Sunday in Lent; and he determined to hear mass in the Greek Church, and ascertain for himself how much devotion an English Protestant could experience in the midst of this foreign worship. But one mass was over and another not begun when he reached the building, and he had thus time to follow his dragoman to the various wonders of that very wonderful building.

It is now generally known in England of what the church of the holy places consists; but no one who has not seen it, and none, indeed, who has not seen it at Easter-time, can fully realize all the absurdity which it contains and all the devotion which it occasions. Bertram was first carried to the five different churches which have crowded themselves together under the same roof. The Greeks have by far the best of it. Their shrine is gaudy and glittering, and their temple is large and in some degree imposing. The Latins, whom we call Roman Catholics, are much less handsomely lodged, and their tinsel is by far more dingy. The Greeks, too, possess the hole in which stood—so they say—the cross of Our Saviour; while the Latins are obliged to put up with the sites on which the two thieves were crucified. Then the church of the Armenians, for which you have to descend almost into the bowels of the earth, is still less grand in its pretensions, is more sombre, more dark, more dirty; but it is as the nave of St Peter's when compared to the poor wooden-cased altar of the Abyssinians, or the dark unfurnished gloomy cave in which the Syrian Christians worship, so dark that the eye cannot at first discover its only ornament—a small ill-made figure of the crucified Redeemer.

We who are accustomed to Roman Catholic gorgeousness in Italy and France can hardly at first understand why the Pope here should play so decidedly a second fiddle. But as he is held to be God's vicegerent* among the people of south-western Europe, so is the Russian emperor among the Christians of the East. He, the Russian, is still by far the greatest pope in Jerusalem, and is treated with a much greater respect, a much truer belief than is his brother of Rome, even among Romans.

Five or six times Bertram had attempted to get into the Tabernacle of the Holy Sepulchre; but so great had been the rush of pilgrims, that he had hitherto failed. At last his dragoman espied a lull, and went again to the battle. To get into the little outside chapel, which forms, as it were, a vestibule to the cell of the sepulchre, and from which on Easter Saturday issue the miraculous flames,* was a thing to be achieved by moderate patience. His close contiguity to Candiotes and Copts, to Armenians and Abyssinians was not agreeable to our hero, for the contiguity was very close, and

Christians of these nations are not very cleanly. But this was nothing to the task of entering the sanctum sanctorum. To this there is but one aperture, and that is but four feet high; men entering it go in head foremost, and those retreating come out in the other direction; and as it is impossible that two should pass, and as two or three are always trying to come out, and ten or twelve equally anxious to get in, the struggle to an Englishman is disagreeably warm, though to an Oriental it is probably matter of interesting excitement.

But for his dragoman, Bertram would never have succeeded. He, however, so pulled and hauled these anxious devotees, so thrust in those who endeavoured to come out, and clawed back those who strove to get in, that the passage became for a moment clear, and our hero, having bent low his head, found himself standing with his hand on the marble slab of the tomb.

Those who were there around him seemed to be the outcasts of the world, exactly those whom he would have objected to meet, unarmed, on the roads of Greece or among the hills of Armenia; cut-throat-looking wretches, with close shaven heads, dirty beards, and angry eyes; men clothed in skins, or huge skin-like-looking cloaks, filthy, foul, alive with vermin, reeking with garlic,—abominable to an Englishman. There was about them a certain dignity of demeanour, a natural aptitude to carry themselves with ease, and even a not impure taste for colour among their dirt. But these Christians of the Russian Church hardly appeared to him to be brothers of his own creed.

But he did put his hand on the slab of the tomb; and as he did so, two young Greeks, brothers by blood—Greeks by their creed, though of what actual nation Bertram was quite unable to say—pressed their lips vehemently to the marble. They were dirty, shorn about the head, dangerous-looking, and skin-clothed, as we have described; men very low in the scale of humanity when compared with their fellow-pilgrim; but, nevertheless, they were to him at that moment objects of envy. They believed: so much at any rate was clear to him. By whatever code of morals they might be able to govern their lives, whether by any, or as, alas! might be too likely, by none, at least they possessed a faith. Christ to them was an actual living truth, though they knew how to worship him no better than by thus kissing a stone, which had in fact no closer reference to the Saviour than any other stone they might have kissed in their own country. They believed; and as they reverently pressed their foreheads, lips, and hands to the top and sides and edges of the sepulchre, their faith became ecstatic. It was thus that Bertram would fain have entered that little chapel, thus that he would have felt, thus that he would have acted had he been able. So had he thought to feel—in such an agony of faith had he been minded there to kneel. But he did not kneel at all. He remarked to himself that the place was inordinately close, that his contiguity to his religious neighbours was disagreeable; and then, stooping low his head, not in reverence, but with a view to backing himself out from the small enclosure, with some delay and much precaution, and, to speak truth, with various expressions of anger against those who with their heads continued to push him the way he did not wish to go, he retreated from the chapel. Nor while he was at Jerusalem did he feel sufficient interest in the matter again to enter it. He had done that deed, he had killed that lion, and, ticking it off from his list of celebrities as one celebrity disposed of, he thought but little more about it. Such, we believe, are the visits of most English Christians to the so-called Holy Sepulchre.

And then he killed the other lions there: Calvary up in the gallery; the garden, so called, in which the risen Saviour addressed the women running from the sepulchre; the place where Peter's cock crew; the tomb of Nicodemus—all within the same church, all under the one roof—all at least under what should be a roof, only now it has fallen into ruin, so that these sacred places are open to the rain of heaven, and Greeks and Latins having quarrelled about the repairs, the Turks, now lords of the Holy Sepulchre, have taken the matter into their own hands, and declared that no repairs shall be done by any of them.

And then he attended the Greek mass—at least, he partly believed that he did so, somewhat doubting, for the mass was not said as are those of the Romans, out at an open altar before the people, but in a holy of holies; very holy, it may be imagined, from the manner in which the worshippers rubbed their foreheads against certain gratings, through which a tantalizing glimpse might be had of the fine things that were going on within. Had they but known it, it might all have been seen, holy of holies, head-wagging priest, idle yawning assistant, with legs stretched out, half asleep, mumblement, jumblement and all, from a little back window in a passage opening from that Calvary gallery upstairs. From thence at least did these profane eyes look down and see all the mumblement and jumblement, which after all was little enough; but saw especially the idle clerical apprentice who, had that screen been down, and had he been called on to do his altar work before the public eye, would not have been so nearly asleep, as may perhaps be said of other clerical performers nearer home.

But Bertram's attention was mainly occupied with watching the devotions of a single woman. She was a female of one of those strange nations, decently clad, about thirty years of age, pleasant to the eye were she not so dirty, and had she not that wild look, halfway between the sallow sublime and the dangerously murderous, which seems common to oriental Christians, whether men or women. Heaven might know of what sins she came there to leave the burden: heaven did know, doubtless; but from the length of her manœuvres in quitting herself of their weight, one would say that they were heavy; and yet she went through her task with composed dignity, with an alacrity that was almost joyous, and certainly with no intentional self-abasement.

Entering the church with a quick step, she took up a position as though she had selected a special stone on which to stand. There, with head erect, but bowing between each ceremony, she crossed herself three times; then sinking on her knees, thrice she pressed her forehead to the floor; then rising again, again she crossed herself. Having so done somewhat to the right of the church, but near the altar-screen, she did the same on the corresponding stone towards the left, and then again the same on a stone behind the others, but in the centre. After this she retreated further back, and did three more such worshippings, always choosing her stone with an eye to architectural regularity; then again, getting to the backward, she did three more, thus completing her appointed task, having crossed herself thirty-six times, and pressed her head with twenty-seven pressures upon the floor. And so, having finished, she quickly withdrew. Did any slightest prayer, any idea of praying, any thought of a God giving grace and pardon if only asked to give, once enter that bowing bosom?

'Why do those Turks sit there?' said Bertram, as he left the building. Why, indeed? It was strange to see five or six stately Turks, strict children of the Prophet doubtless, sitting there within the door of this temple dedicated to the Nazarene God, sitting there and looking as though they of all men had the most right so to sit, and were most at home in so sitting; nay, they had a divan there, were drinking coffee there out of little double cups, as is the manner of these people; were not smoking, certainly, as is their manner also in all other places.

'Dem guard de keys,' said the dragoman.

'Guard the keys!'

'Yes, yes; open de lock, and not let de Christian fight.'

So it is. In such manner is proper, fitting, peaceable conduct maintained within the thrice Christian walls of the Church of the Holy Sepulchre.

On his return to the hotel, Bertram accepted an invitation to join Miss Todd's picnic in the Valley of Jehoshaphat, and then towards evening strolled up alone on to the Mount of Olives.

CHAPTER VII

THE MOUNT OF OLIVES

IF there be one place told of in holy writ, the name of which gives rise to more sacred feelings than any other, it is that of the Mount of Olives; and if there be a spot in that land of wondrous memories which does bring home to the believer in Christ some individualized remembrance of his Saviour's earthly pilgrimage, that certainly is it.

There is no doubting there, no question there whether or no the ground on which you tread was not first called 'the mount' by some Byzantine Sophia;* whether tradition respecting it can go back further than Constantine; whether, in real truth, that was the hill over which Jesus walked when he travelled from the house of Lazarus at Bethany to fulfil his mission in the temple. No: let me take any ordinary believing Protestant Christian to that spot, and I will as broadly defy him to doubt there as I will defy him to believe in that filthy church of the holy places.

The garden of Gethsemane near the city, 'over the brook Cedron,'* where he left his disciples resting while he went yonder to pray; the hill-side on which the angel appeared unto him, strengthening him, and whither Judas and the multitude came out to take him; Bethany, the town of Mary and Martha, 'fifteen furlongs from Jerusalem,'* where Lazarus was raised from the dead; the spot from whence he sent for the ass and the ass's colt; the path from thence to the city by which he rode when the multitude 'cried, saying, Hosanna to the son of David'* the same multitude which afterwards came out against him with staves: these places are there, now as they were in his day, very credible—nay, more, impossible not to be believed. These are the true holy places of Jerusalem, places for which Greeks and Latins do not fight, guarded by no sedate, coffee-drinking Turks, open there to all men under the fair heavens, and desolate enough, too, even in these pilgrim weeks, for any one or two who will sit there alone and ponder over the wondrous history of the city that still lies over against him.

But what is the so strong evidence of the actual identity of these places? What is it that makes me so sure that this is the Mount of Olives, and that water-channel there the brook Cedron, and the hamlet on the other side the veritable Bethany? Why is one to be so sure of these, and yet feel such an infinity of doubt as to that village of Emmaus, that valley of Ajalon, that supposed Arimathea, and the rest of them? Nay,

I cannot well say, at any rate not in these light novel pages. Dr Stanley,* with considerable distinctness does say. But go and see: with the ordinary Protestant Christian seeing here will be believing, as seeing over in that church of the holy places most indisputably will be disbelieving.

Hither Bertram strolled, and, seated on the brow of the hill, looked over to Jerusalem till the short twilight of the Syrian evening had left him, and he could no longer discern the wondrous spots on which his eye still rested. Wondrous, indeed! There before him were the walls of Jerusalem, standing up erect from the hill-side—for the city is still all fenced up—stretching from hill to hill in varying but ever continued line: on the left was the Hill of Sion, David's hill, a hill still inhabited, and mainly by Jews. Here is still the Jews' quarters, and the Jews' hospital too, tended by English doctors, nurtured also by English money; and here, too, close to David's Gate, close also to that new huge Armenian convent, shall one, somewhat closely scrutinizing among heaps of rubbish, come upon a colony of lepers. In the town, but not of it, within the walls, but forbidden all ingress to the streets, there they dwell, a race of mournfulest Pariahs.* From father to son, from mother to daughter, dire disease, horrid, polluting, is handed down, a certain legacy, making the body loathsome, and likening the divine face of man to a melancholy ape. Oh! the silent sadness, the inexpressible melancholy of those wan, thoughtless, shapeless, boneless, leaden faces! To them no happy daily labour brings rest and appetite; their lot forbids them work, as it forbids all other blessings. No; on their dunghills outside their cabins there they sit in the sun, the mournfulest sight one might look on, the leper parents with their leper children, beggars by inheritance, paupers, outcasts, mutilated victims,—but still with souls, if they or any round them did but know it.

There also, directly facing him, was the Mount Moriah, also inside the walls, where Solomon built the house of the Lord, 'where the Lord appeared unto David his father, in the place that David had prepared, in the threshing-floor of Ornan the Jebusite.'* For this city, Jerusalem, had, in still more ancient days, before the thought of that temple had come into men's minds, been the city Jebus, a city even then fenced up, and here had been the threshing-floor which Ornan tendered to David without price, but which the king bought for six hundred shekels of gold.

Yes; here before him as he sat was the site of that temple, Solomon's temple, 'exceeding magnificent, of fame and glory throughout all countries,'* of which David had been worthy only to collect the materials. The site! nay, but there were the very stones themselves.

Seen from that hill, the city seems so close that you may lay your hand upon it. Between you and it (you, if ever you should happily come to sit there) lies that valley of Jehoshaphat, in which Miss Todd is going to celebrate her picnic. This is the valley in which the Jews most love to have themselves buried; as there, according to them, is the chosen site of the resurrection: and thus they who painfully journeying thither in their old age, and dying there can there be buried, will have no frightful, moles'-work, underground pilgrimage to detain them when that awful trumpet shall once more summon them to the upper world.

The air, in Syria there, is thin and clear, clouded by no fogs; and the lines of the wall and the minarets of the mosque are distinct and bright and sharp against the sky, as in the evening light one looks across from one hill to the other. The huge stones of the wall now standing, stones which made part of that ancient temple, can be counted, one above another, across the valley. Measured by a rough estimate, some of them may be two-and-twenty feet in length, seven in depth, and five in height, single blocks of hewn rock, cut certainly by no Turkish enterprise, by no mediæval empire, by no Roman labour. It is here, and here only, at the base of the temple, that these huge stones are to be found, at the base of what was the temple, forming part of the wall that now runs along the side of Mount Moriah, but still some forty feet above the ground.

Over them now is the Mosque of Omar—a spot to be desecrated no more by Christian step. On the threshing-floor of Ornan, the children of Mahomet now read the Koran and sing to Allah with monotonous howl. Oh, what a history!

from the treading of the Jebusite oxen down to the first cry of the Mussulman! Yes; no Christian may now enter here, may hardly look into the walled court round the building. But dignified Turks, drinking coffee on their divan within the building, keep the keys of the Christian church—keep also the peace, lest Latin and Greek should too enthusiastically worship their strange gods.

There can be few spots on the world's surface more sacred to any Christian than that on which Bertram sat. Coming up from Bethany, over a spur on the southern side of the Mount of Olives, towards Jerusalem, the traveller, as he rises on the hill, soon catches a sight of the city, and soon again loses it. But going onward along his path, the natural road which convenience would take, he comes at length to the brow of the hill, looking downwards, and there has Mount Sion, Moriah, and the site of the temple full before him. No one travelling such a road could do other than pause at such a spot.

'Twas here that Jesus 'sat upon the mount, over against the temple.'* There is no possibility of mistaking the place. 'And as he went, one of the disciples saith unto him, "Master, see what manner of stones and what buildings are here." And Jesus answering, said unto him, "Seest thou these great buildings? There shall not be left one stone upon another that shall not be thrown down." '* There are the stones, the very stones, thrown down indeed from the temple, but now standing erect as a wall, supporting Omar's mosque.

'And when he was come near, he beheld the city, and wept over it.'* Yes, walk up from Bethany, my reader, and thou, too, shalt behold it, even yet; a matter to be wept over even now. 'Tis hard to sit there and not weep, if a man have any heart within him, any memory of those histories. 'If thou hadst known, even thou, at least in this thy day, the things which belong unto thy peace!'* But thou wouldest not know. And where art thou now, O Jew? And who is it that sittest in thy high place, howling there to Allah most unmusically?

'O Jerusalem, Jerusalem.' Not silently, and in thought only, but with outspoken words and outstretched hands, so then spake our young English friend, sitting there all alone, gazing on the city. What man familiar with that history could be there and not so speak? 'O Jerusalem, Jerusalem, thou that killest the prophets, and stonest them which are sent unto thee, how often would I have gathered thy children together, even as a hen gathereth her chickens under her wings, and ye would not! Behold, your house is left unto you desolate.'*

When talking over the matter with Harcourt at Oxford, and afterwards with his uncle at Hadley, Bertram had expressed a sort of half-formed wish to go into the church; not, indeed, in such a manner as to leave on the minds of either of his counsellors an idea that he would really do so; but this profession of being a parson had been one of those of which he had spoken as being in some sort desirable for himself. Now, as he sat there, looking at the once holy city, it seemed to him to be the only profession in any way desirable. He resolved that he would be a clergyman; thanked his God in that he had brought him there to this spot before it was too late; acknowledged that, doubting as he had done, he had now at length found a Divine counsellor—one whose leading his spirit did not disdain. There he devoted himself to the ministry, declared that he, too, would give what little strength he had towards bringing the scattered chickens of the new house of Israel to that only wing which could give them the warmth of life. He would be one of the smallest, one of the least of those who would fight the good fight; but, though smallest and least, he would do it with what earnestness was in him.

Reader! you may already, perhaps, surmise that George Bertram does not become a clergyman. It is too true. That enthusiasm, strong, true, real as it was, did not last him much longer than his last walk round Jerusalem; at least, did not bide by him till he found himself once more walking on the High Street of Oxford. Very contemptible this, you will say. Yes, contemptible enough, as humanity so often is. Who amongst us have not made such resolves—some resolve of self-devotion, at the sound of the preacher's voice—and forgotten it before our foot was well over the threshold? It is so natural, that wish to do a great thing; so hard, that daily task of bathing in Jordan.

When the bright day had disappeared, all but suddenly, and he could no longer see the minarets of the mosque, Bertram descended the hill. It is but a short walk thence to Jerusalem—thence even into the centre of Jerusalem. But what a walk! To the left is the valley-side—that valley of the Resurrection—covered with tombs—flat, sturdy, short stones, each bearing a semblance, at least, of some short Hebraic epitaph, unmoved through heaven knows how many centuries! apparently immovable; the place, in this respect, being very unlike our more ornamental cemeteries. On his right was the Mount of Olives; a mount still of olives, sprinkled over with olive trees quite sufficiently to make it properly so called, even to this day. Then he passed by the Garden of Gethsemane, now a walled-in garden, in which grow rue and other herbs; in which also, is one fine, aged olive-tree, as to which tradition of course tells wondrous tales. This garden is now in charge of an old Latin monk—a Spaniard, if I remember well—who, at least, has all a Spaniard's courtesy.

It was here, or near to this, just above, on the hill-side, if our topography be reliable, that Jesus asked them whether they could not watch one hour. Bertram, as he passed, did not take the question to himself; but he well might have done so.

Turning round the wall of the garden, on his pathway up to Stephen's Gate, the so-called tomb of the Virgin was on his right hand, with its singular, low, subterranean chapel. A very singular chapel, especially when filled to the very choking with pilgrims from those strange retreats of oriental Christendom, and when the mass is being said—inaudible, indeed, and not to be seen, at the furthest end of that dense, underground crowd, but testified to by the lighting of a thousand tapers, and by the strong desire for some flicker of the holy flame.

And then he ascended to the city, up the steep hill, the side of Mount Moriah, to St Stephen's Gate; and there, on his left, was the entrance to Omar's mosque, guarded by fierce dervishes* against pollution from stray Christian foot. Hence to his hotel every footstep was over ground sacred in some sense, but now desecrated by traditionary falsehoods. Every action of our Saviour's passion has its spot assigned to it; of every noted word the *locale* is given. When once you are again within the walls, all is again unbelievable, fabulous, miraculous; nay, all but blasphemous. Some will say quite so. But, nevertheless, in passing by this way, should you, O reader! ever make such passage, forget not to mount to the top of Pilate's house. It is now a Turkish barrack; whether it ever were Pilate's house, or, rather, whether it stands on what was ever the site of Pilate's house or no. From hence you see down into the court of the mosque, see whatever a Christian can see of that temple's site, and see also across them gloriously to those hills of Jerusalem, Scopus, and the hill of the men of Galilee, and the Mount of Olives, and the Mount of Offence—so called because there 'did Solomon build an high place for Chemosh, the abomination of Moab, on the hill that is before Jerusalem.'*

On his return to his inn, Bertram at once found that there had been an arrival of some importance during his absence. Waiters and boots were all busy—for there are waiters and boots at Jerusalem, much the same as at the 'Saracen's Head,' or 'White Lion;' there is no chambermaid, however, only a chamberman. Colonel Sir Lionel Bertram was there.

CHAPTER VIII

SIR LIONEL BERTRAM

THE personal peculiarities which Sir Lionel had mentioned in his letter to his son as being characteristic of himself were certainly true. He was an old, or, perhaps, rather an elderly gentleman, in a military frock, with a bald head, a hook nose, and a short allowance of teeth. But he was more than this: though elderly he was tall and upright; he was distinguished looking, and, for an old man, handsome in spite of his lost teeth; and though bald as to the top of his head, had yet enough hair to merit considerable attention, and to be the cause of considerable pride. His whiskers, also, and mustache, though iron-grey, were excellent in their way. Had his baldness been of an uglier description, or his want of teeth more disagreeably visible, he probably might not have alluded to them himself. In truth, Sir Lionel was not a little vain of his personal appearance, and thought that in the matter of nose, he was quite equal to the Duke in aristocratic firmness, and superior to Sir Charles Napier* in expression and general design.

But though a vain man, Sir Lionel was too clever to let his vanity show itself in an offensive manner. The 'ars celare artem'* was his forte; and he was able to live before the world as though he never cast a thought on his coat and pantaloons, or ever did more than brush and smooth his iron-grey locks with due attention to cleanliness.

I was going to say that Sir Lionel's appearance was the best thing about him; but in saying so I should belie his manner, with which it was certainly difficult for any one to find fault. It was what the world calls happy, meaning thereby, that so great was the possessor's luck that he was able to make it pleasant to all men, and to all women—for a while. Mrs Bertram—she had not lived to be my lady—had, I believe, not always found it so.

These, joined to a readiness in the use of one or two languages besides his own, were the qualifications which had given Sir Lionel his title, and had caused him to be employed in so many missions in so many countries; and on duty, too, which could not be said to be of a military nature. He never made difficulties or enemies of his own, and could generally smooth down the difficulties and enemies left behind them by others, perhaps of a more sturdy temperament.

But now the catalogue of his virtues is complete. He was not a man of genius, or even a man of talent. He had performed no great service for his country; had neither proposed nor carried through any valuable project of diplomacy; nor had he shown any close insight into the habits and feelings of the people among whom he had lived. But he had been useful as a great oil-jar, from whence oil for the quiescence of troubled waters might ever and anon be forthcoming. Expediency was his god, and he had hitherto worshipped it with a successful devotion.

That he had not been a good husband has been hinted; that he had been a very indifferent father has been made apparent. But at the moment of his meeting with his son, he atoned for all his past sins in this respect by the excellence of his manner; and before the evening was over, George liked his father, who owed him everything and had given him nothing, ten times better than he had ever liked his uncle, who had given him everything though he had owed him nothing.

'It's an odd place for us to have met in at last, is it not, sir?' said George. They were sitting after supper very close together on one of those stationary sofas which are found affixed to the wall in every room in the East, and the son was half holding, half caressing his father's arm. Sir Lionel, to tell the truth, did not much care for such caresses, but under the peculiar circumstances of this present interview he permitted it.

'You see, I'm always in odd places, George.'

'You've been in Jerusalem before?'

'No, never. It's not on the road anywhere, or on any road at all, as one may well see. I never knew such a place to get to. Now there are roads of some sort even about Bagdad.'

'And Damascus?'

'Oh, Damascus is a highway; but nobody comes to Jerusalem except the pilgrims, and those who like to look after the pilgrims. We are just in the thick of them now, I believe.'

'Yes, sir. There are thirteen thousand here. I am sure you'll like the place. I am delighted with it, although I have been here as yet only two days.'

'Perhaps more so than you will be when you have been ten.'

'I don't think it. But it is not the city itself.'

'No; that seems poor and dirty enough.'

'I would not mind the dirt if the place were but true.' Sir Lionel did not quite understand him, but he said nothing. 'It is the country round, the immediate vicinity of Jerusalem that fascinates so wonderfully.'

'Ah! the scenery is good, is it?'

'Well, in one way it is; but I do not mean that. I cannot explain it; but tomorrow you will go to the Mount of Olives with me.'

'Mount of Olives, eh? I'm not very good at climbing up a hill, Master George; you must remember the difference between twenty-three and sixty-three. What is there to see there?'

What was there to see there! This was said in a tone which made George feel rather indisposed to describe, if describe he could, what there was there to be seen. He had quite wit enough to perceive that his father was not enthusiastic about Bible history.

And then they changed the conversation, and began to talk about George Bertram the elder.

'It's eighteen years since I've seen my brother,' said Sir Lionel. 'He was usually cross enough then. I suppose he has hardly improved?'

'I can't exactly call him cross. He has been very kind to me, you know.'

'Kind—well. If you are contented, I am; but, considering that you are his natural heir, I don't think he has done so very much. If he means to be kind, why does he bother me every other month with a long account, of which the postage comes to heaven knows how much?'

'Ah! but, sir, I am not his heir.'

'Not his heir!' said Sir Lionel, with more of sharpness in his tone than was at all usual with him; with a little sharpness also in his eye, as George quickly observed. 'Not his heir—who is his heir then?'

'Ah! that I do not know. Some corporation, perhaps, or some hospital. All I know is, that I am not. That he has told me quite plainly. And he was very right to do so,' added George, after a pause.

Sir Lionel repressed the exclamation of anger against his brother which was in his heart, and had all but risen to his tongue. He had not been wandering for thirty years on foreign missions for nothing. He must find out more of this lad's disposition and feelings before he spoke out plainly before him what he thought. He had intended not only that his son should be the rich uncle's heir, but the rich uncle's adopted child also; so that some portion of that vast wealth might be made use of, certainly by George, perhaps even in some modest degree by himself, without the unnecessary delay of waiting for his brother's death. It would be bad enough to wait, seeing how probable it was that that brother might outlive himself. But now to be told not only that his hopes in this respect were vain, but that the old miser had absolutely repudiated his connection with his nephew! This was almost too much for his diplomatic equanimity. Almost, I say; for in fact he did restrain himself.

'And did he say, George, in so many words that he meant to give you nothing?'

'Yes, very plainly—in so many words. And I told him as plainly, and in as many, that I wanted nothing from him.'

'Was that prudent, my boy?'

'It was the truth, sir. But I must tell you the whole. He offered me a loan of three thousand pounds—'

'Well, you took that?'

'Indeed, no. He offered it on the condition that I should be an attorney.'

'An attorney! and you with a double-first?'

'Ah, he does not much value double-firsts. Of course, I was not going to make myself an attorney.'

'Of course not. But what is he doing about an allowance for you?'

'He has been very liberal. He has given me a hundred and fifty a year—'

'Yes; and sent me the bill of it—with great regularity.'

The son did not remind the father that all regularity in the matter had ended there, and that the bills so sent had never been paid; but he could not help thinking that in justice he might do so.

'But that expense will soon be over; sir, as regards either you or him. The allowance will be discontinued next year.'

'What! he is going to stop even that school-boy's pittance?'

'Why not, sir? I have no claim on him. And as he has not forgotten to tell me so once or twice—'

'He was always a vulgar fellow,' said Sir Lionel. 'How he came to have such a spirit of trade in his very blood, I can't conceive. God knows I have none of it.'

'Nor I either, sir.'

'Well, I hope not. But does he expect you to live upon air? This is bad news, George—very bad.'

'Of course I have always intended to go into a profession. I have never looked at it in the same light as you do. I have always intended to make my own way, and have no doubt that I shall do so. I have quite made up my mind about it now.'

'About what, George?'

'I shall go into orders, and take a college living.'

'Orders!' said Sir Lionel; and he expressed more surprise and almost more disgust at this idea than at that other one respecting the attorney scheme.

'Yes; I have been long doubting; but I think I have made up my mind.'

'Do you mean that you wish to be a parson, and that after taking a double-first?'

'I don't see what the double-first has to do with it, sir. The only objection I have is the system of the establishment. I do not like the established church.'

'Then why go into it?' said Sir Lionel, not at all understanding the nature of his son's objection.

'I love our liturgy, and I like the ritual; but what we want is the voluntary principle. I do not like to put myself in a position which I can, in fact, hold whether I do the duties of it or no. Nor do I wish—'

'Well; I understand very little about all that; but, George, I had hoped something better for you. Now, the army is a beggarly profession unless a man has a private fortune; but, upon my word, I look on the church as the worst of the two. A man *may* be a bishop of course; but I take it he has to eat a deal of dirt first.'

'I don't mean to eat any dirt,' said the son.

'Nor to be a bishop, perhaps,' replied the father.

They were quite unable to understand each other on this subject. In Sir Lionel's view of the matter, a profession was—a profession. The word was understood well enough throughout the known world. It signified a calling by which a gentleman, not born to the inheritance of a gentleman's allowance of good things, might ingeniously obtain the same by some exercise of his abilities. The more of these good things that might be obtained, the better the profession; the easier the labour also, the better the profession; the less restriction that might be laid on a man in his pleasurable enjoyment of the world, the better the profession. This was Sir Lionel's view of a profession, and it must be acknowledged that, though his view was commonplace, it was also common sense; that he looked at the matter as a great many people look at it; and that his ideas were at any rate sufficiently intelligible. But George Bertram's view was different, and much less easy of explanation. He had an idea that in choosing a profession he should consider, not so much how he should get the means of spending his life, but how he should in fact spend it. He would have, in making this choice, to select the pursuit to which he would devote that amount of power and that amount of life which God should allot to him. Fathers and mothers, uncles and aunts, guardians and grandfathers, was not this a singular view for a young man to take in looking at such a subject?

But in truth George was somewhat afflicted by a *tête montée* in this matter. I say afflicted, because, having imagination and ideality to lead him to high views, he had not a sufficient counter-balance in his firmness of character. If his father was too mundane, he was too transcendental. As, for instance, he approved at the present moment, in theory, of the life of a parish clergyman; but could he have commenced the life tomorrow, he would at once have shrunk from its drudgery.

They did not understand each other; perceiving which, Sir Lionel gave up the subject. He was determined not to make himself disagreeable to his son. He, at any rate, intended to make him no allowance, to give him no fortune, and was aware, therefore, that he had no right to interfere otherwise than as his advice might be asked. Nor indeed had he any wish to do so, if he could only instil into the young man's mind a few—not precepts; precepts are harsh and disagreeable—a few comfortable friendly hints as to the tremendous importance of the game which might be played with Mr George Bertram, senior. If he could only do this pleasantly, and without offence to his son, he would attempt nothing further.

He turned the conversation, and they talked agreeably on other matters—of Oxford, of the Wilkinsons, of Harcourt, and by degrees also a little of uncle George.

'What sort of a house does my brother keep at Hadley—eh, George? Dull enough it used to be.'

'Well; it is dull. Not that he is dull himself; I can always talk to my uncle when he will talk to me.'

'Sees no company, I suppose?'

'Not much.'

'Never goes into society?'

'He dines out in London sometimes; and sometimes gives dinners too.'

'What! at taverns?'

'Yes; at Blackwall, or Greenwich, or some of those places. I have been at his dinners, and he never spares anything.'

'He doesn't feel his years, then? He's not infirm? no rheumatism or anything of that sort—strong on his legs, eh?'

'As strong as you are, sir.'

'He's ten years my senior, you know.'

'Yes, I know he is. He's not nearly so young a man as you are; but I really think he is as strong. He's a wonderful man for his years, certainly.'

'I'm delighted to hear it,' said Sir Lionel. A keen judge of character, however, scrutinizing the colonel's face closely, would not then have read much warm delight therein depicted.

'You rather like him on the whole, then—eh, George?'

'Well; I really think I do. I am sure I ought to like him. But—'

'Well, George; speak out. You and I need have no secrets.'

'Secrets, no; I've no secret. My uncle has a way of saying too much himself about what he does for one.'

'Sends in the bill too often—eh, George?'

'If it is to be a bill, let him say so. I for one shall not blame him. There is no reason he should give me anything. But situated as I have been at Oxford, it would have been almost absurd in me to refuse his allowance—'

'Quite absurd.'

'When he knew I was coming out to you, he made Pritchett—you know Pritchett?'

'And his handwriting—very well indeed.'

'He made Pritchett put three hundred pounds to my credit; that was over and above my allowance. Well, I did almost make up my mind to return that; as it is, I have not touched it, and I think I shall repay it.'

'For heaven's sake do no such thing. It would be an offence which he would never forgive.' Sir Lionel did say so much with something of parental energy in his tone and manner.

'Yes, sir; but to be told of it!'

'But he does not ask you to pay it him back again?'

'If he asks you;—is not that the same thing? But you hardly understand me, or him either.'

'I think I understand him, George. I wonder whether they could give us a cup of coffee here?'

'Of course they can:' and George rang the bell.

'Perhaps so: but as far as my experience goes, wherever Englishmen frequent, there the coffee is spoilt. Englishmen, as far as I can see, have a partiality for chicory, but none at all for coffee.'

'What I mean, sir, is this. Connected as I and my uncle are together, seeing that he has all my life—' Here George paused a moment, for what he was about to say might have seemed to imply a censure on his father.

'Paid your school-bills, and all that sort of thing,' filled in Sir Lionel.

'Yes; as he has always done that, it seemed so natural that I should take what he gave me.'

'Quite natural. You could have done nothing else.'

'And now he speaks of it as though—as though—of course I am under an obligation to him—a very deep obligation. I understand that, and should not fret at it. But he thinks of it as though I had been to blame in spending his money. When

I see him next, he'll say something of the same sort about that three hundred pounds. All I can do is to remind him that I did not ask for it, and tell him that he may have it back again.'

'Do nothing of the kind, George,' said Sir Lionel, who regarded as little less than lunacy on his son's part this declared intention to refund money to a rich man. 'I know very well what you mean. It is disagreeable to be reminded of money that you have spent.'

'But I haven't spent it.'

'Well, of money that you have received. But what can you do? It is not your fault. As you truly say, it would be absurd and ungrateful too if you were to decline to take such trifles from your own uncle; especially seeing what he has done for you. It is his manner, and that was always disagreeable; especially in money matters.' And so having given to his son the best advice he had to offer, Sir Lionel sipped his coffee. 'Very bad—very bad, indeed; it always is at these English places. If I could have my own way, I would always keep out of English haunts.' In this respect Sir Lionel had had his own way during the greater portion of his life.

Before they parted for the evening, George communicated to his father the great fact of Miss Todd's picnic as settled for the next day; and Sir Lionel expressed himself as willing to make one of the party if Miss Todd could be induced to extend to him the light of her countenance. On this head young Bertram, though his own acquaintance had certainly been short, thought that he might take on himself to answer. People soon get intimate with each other at such places as Jerusalem. When you have been up the Great Pyramid with a lady, the chances are you know more about her than you would do from a year's acquaintance fostered by a dozen London parties; and a journey up the Nile with a man may be considered quite equal to three years spent together at the same college,—that is, if the fellow-travellers be young. After a certain age, men never become really intimate, let their relations with each other be ever so close.

'There will be a Miss Baker there, sir, who says she knows you; and a Miss Waddington, a very fine girl, who at any rate knows my name.'

'What! Caroline Waddington?'

'Yes, Caroline Waddington.'

'She is a ward of your uncle.'

'So Miss Baker tells me; but I never heard my uncle mention them. Indeed, he never mentions anything.'

'It will be very desirable that you should know Miss Waddington. There is no saying what your uncle may do with his money. Yes, I'll go to the picnic; only I hope the place is not distant.' So that matter was settled.

CHAPTER IX

MISS TODD'S PICNIC

THAT matter of obtaining permission for Sir Lionel to join the picnic was not found difficult of arrangement. Good-looking, pleasant-mannered Sir Lionels, who bear the Queen's commission, and have pleasant military ways with them, are welcome enough at such parties as these, even though they be sixty years of age. When George mentioned the matter to Miss Todd, that lady declared herself delighted. She had heard, she said, of the distinguished arrival at the hotel, but she had been almost afraid to ask such a man as Sir Lionel to join their foolish little party. Then Miss Baker, who in this affair bore the next authority to Miss Todd, declared that she had intended to ask him, taking upon herself the freedom of an old acquaintance; and so that matter was arranged.

The party was not to be a large one. There was Miss Todd, the compounder of it, a maiden lady, fat, fair, and perhaps almost forty; a jolly jovial lady, intent on seeing the world, and indifferent to many of its prejudices and formal restraints. 'If she threw herself in Sir Lionel's way, people would of course say that she wanted to marry him; but she did not care a straw what people said; if she found Sir Lionel agreeable, she would throw herself in his way.' So she told Miss Baker—with perhaps more courage than the occasion required.

Then there were Mrs and Miss Jones. Miss Jones was the young lady who lost her parasol on the Mount of Offence, and so recklessly charged the Arab children of Siloam with the theft. Mr Jones was also in Jerusalem, but could not be persuaded to attend at Miss Todd's behest. He was steadily engaged in antiquarian researches, being minded to bring out to the world some startling new theory as to certain points in Bible chronology and topography. He always went about the city with a trowel and a big set of tablets; and certain among the more enthusiastic of the visitors to Jerusalem had put him down as an infidel.

There were also Mr and Mrs Hunter—a bridegroom and bride, now on their wedding trip; a somewhat fashionable couple, who were both got up with considerable attention as to oriental costume. Mrs Hunter seemed to think a good deal about her trousers, and Mr Hunter's mind was equally taken up with the fact that he had ceased to wear any. They had a knowing way of putting on their turbans, and carried their sashes gracefully; those, however, who had seen Mr Hunter roll himself into his sash, were of opinion that sooner or later he would suffer from vertigo in his head. Miss Baker and her niece had fallen in with these people, and were considered to be of the same party.

There was a clergyman to be there, one Mr Cruse, the gentleman who had been so keenly annoyed at the absence of potatoes from the dinner board. He was travelling in charge of a young gentleman of fortune, a Mr Pott, by whose fond parents the joint expense of the excursion was defrayed. Mr Cruse was a University man, of course; had been educated at Trinity College, Cambridge, and piqued himself much on being far removed from the dangers of Puseyism. He was a man not of a happy frame of mind, and seemed to find that from Dan to Beersheba everything in truth was barren. He was good-looking, unmarried, not without some talent, and seemed to receive from the ladies there assembled more attention than his merits altogether deserved.

Mr M'Gabbery had talked of not going, but had been overpersuaded by the good-natured Miss Todd. He had become almost overwhelmed by the intensity of his feelings in regard to the sacred associations of the place, since George Bertram had contrived to seat himself between Miss Baker and Miss Waddington. Up to that moment, no one had been merrier than he. He had, so he had flattered himself, altogether cut out Mr Cruse in that special quarter, the good graces namely of those two ladies, and had been prepared to take on his own shoulders all the hard work of the picnic. But now things were altered with him; he had some doubts whether the sacredness of the valley would not be desecrated by such a proceeding, and consulted Mr Cruse on the matter. Hitherto these gentlemen had not been close friends; but now they allied themselves as against a common enemy. Mr Cruse did not care much for associations, seemed indeed to think that any special attention to sacred places savoured of idolatry, and professed himself willing to eat his dinner on any of the hills or in any of the valleys round Jerusalem. Fortified with so good an opinion, and relying on the excellence of his purpose, Mr M'Gabbery gave way, and renewed his offers of assistance to Miss Todd.

There was also Mr Pott, Mr Cruse's young charge, the son of a man largely engaged in the linen trade; a youth against whom very little can be alleged. His time at present was chiefly given up to waiting on Miss Jones; and, luckier in this respect than his tutor, Mr Cruse, he had no rival to interfere with his bliss.

Miss Baker and Miss Waddington made up the party. Of the former, little more need be said, and that little should be all in her praise. She was a lady-like, soft-mannered, easy-tempered woman, devoted to her niece, but not strongly addicted to personal exertions on her own part. The fact that she was now at Jerusalem, so far away from her own comfortable drawing-room, sufficiently proved that she *was* devoted to her niece.

And now for Caroline Waddington, our donna primissima. Her qualities, attributes, and virtues must be given more in detail than those of her companions at the picnic, seeing that she is destined to fill a prominent place upon our canvas.

At the time of which we are speaking, she might perhaps be twenty years of age; but her general appearance, her figure, and especially the strong character marked in her face, would have led one to suspect that she was older. She was certainly at that time a beautiful girl—very beautiful, handsome in the outline of her face, graceful and dignified in her mien, nay, sometimes almost majestic—a Juno* rather than a Venus.* But any Paris* who might reject her, awed by the rigour of her dignity, would know at the time that he was wrong in his judgment. She was tall but not so tall as to be unfeminine in her height. Her head stood nobly on her shoulders, giving to her bust that ease and grace of which sculptors are so fond, and of which tight-laced stays are so utterly subversive. Her hair was very dark—not black, but the darkest shade of brown, and was worn in simple rolls on the side of her face. It was very long and very glossy, soft as the richest silk, and gifted apparently with a delightful aptitude to keep itself in order. No stray jagged ends would show themselves if by chance she removed her bonnet, nor did it even look as though it had been prematurely crushed and required to be afresh puffed out by some head-dresser's mechanism. She had the forehead of a Juno; white, broad, and straight; not shining as are some foreheads, which seem as though an insufficient allowance of skin had been vouchsafed for their covering. It was a forehead on which an angel might long to press his lips—if angels have lips, and if, as we have been told, they do occasionally descend from their starry heights to love the daughters of men.*

Nor would an angel with a shade of human passion to his temperament have been contented with her forehead. Her mouth had all the richness of youth, and the full enticing curves and ruby colour of Anglo-Saxon beauty. Caroline Waddington was no pale, passionless goddess; her graces and perfections were human, and in being so were the more dangerous to humanity. Her forehead, we have said, or should have said, was perfect; we dare not affirm quite so much in praise of her mouth; there was sometimes a hardness there, not in the lines of the feature itself, but in the expression which it conveyed, a want of tenderness, perhaps of trust, and too much self-confidence, it may be, for a woman's character. The teeth within it, however, were never excelled by any that ever graced the face of a woman.

Her nose was not quite Grecian; had it been so, her face might have been fairer, but it would certainly have been less expressive. Nor could it be called *retroussé*, but it had the slightest possible tendency in that direction; and the nostrils were more open, more ready to breathe forth flashes of indignation than is ever the case with a truly Grecian nose.

The contour of her face was admirable: nothing could exceed in beauty the lines of her cheeks or the shape and softness of her chin. Those who were fastidious in their requirements might object to them that they bore no dimple; after all, it is only prettiness that requires a dimple: full-blown beauty wants no such adventitious aid.

But her eyes! Miss Waddington's eyes! The eyes are the poet's strongest fortress; it is for their description that he most gathers up his forces and puts forth all his strength. What of her eyes? Well, her eyes were bright enough, large enough, well set in her head. They were clever eyes too—nay, honest eyes also, which is better. But they were not softly feminine eyes. They never hid themselves beneath their soft fringes when too curiously looked into, as a young girl at her window half hides herself behind her curtain. They were bold eyes, I was going to say, but the word would signify too much in their dispraise; daring eyes, I would rather say, courageous, expressive, never shrinking, sometimes also suspicious. They were fit rather for a man than for so beautiful a girl as our Caroline Waddington.

But perhaps the most wonderful grace about her was her walk. 'Vera incessu patuit Dea.'* Alas! how few women can walk! how many are wilfully averse to attempting any such motion! They scuffle, they trip, they trot, they amble, they waddle, they crawl, they drag themselves on painfully, as though the flounces and furbelows around them were a burden too heavy for easy, graceful motion; but, except in Spain, they rarely walk. In this respect our heroine was equal to an Andalusian.

Such and so great were Miss Waddington's outward graces. Some attempt must also be made to tell of those inner stores with which this gallant vessel was freighted; for, after all, the outward bravery is not everything with a woman. It may be that a man in selecting his wife rarely looks for much else;—for that in addition, of course, to money; but though he has looked for little else, some other things do frequently force themselves on his attention soon after the knot is tied; and as Caroline Waddington will appear in these pages as wife as well as maid, as a man's companion as well as his plaything, it may be well to say now something as to her fitness for such occupation.

We will say, then, that she was perhaps even more remarkable for her strength of mind than for her beauty of person. At present, she was a girl of twenty, and hardly knew her own power; but the time was to come when she should know it and should use it. She was possessed of a stubborn, enduring, manly will; capable of conquering much, and not to be conquered easily. She had a mind which, if rightly directed, might achieve great and good things, but of which it might be predicted that it would certainly achieve something, and that if not directed for good, it might not improbably direct itself for evil. It was impossible that she should ever grow into a piece of domestic furniture, contented to adapt itself to such uses as a marital tyrant might think fit to require of it. If destined to fall into good hands, she might become a happy, loving wife; but it was quite as possible that she should be neither happy nor loving.

Like most other girls, she no doubt thought much of what might be her lot in love—thought much of loving, though she had never yet loved. It has been said that her turn of mind was manly; but it must not on that account be imagined that her wishes and aspirations were at present other than feminine. Her heart and feelings were those of a girl, at any rate as yet; but her will and disposition were masculine in their firmness.

For one so young, she had great and dangerous faults of character—great, as being injurious to her happiness; and dangerous, as being likely to grow with her years. Her faults were not young faults. Though true herself, she was suspicious of others; though trustworthy, she was not trustful; and what person who is not trustful ever remains trustworthy? Who can be fit for confidence who cannot himself confide? She was imperious, too, when occasion offered itself to her proud spirit. With her aunt, whom she loved, she was not so. Her she was content to persuade, using a soft voice and a soft eye; but with those whom she could not persuade and wished to rule, her voice was sometimes stern enough, and her eye far from soft.

She was a clever girl, capable of talking well, and possessed of more information than most young ladies of the same age. She had been at an excellent school, if any schools are really excellent for young ladies; but there was, nevertheless, something in her style of thought hardly suitable to the softness of girlhood. She could speak of sacred things with a mocking spirit, the mockery of philosophy rather than of youth; she had little or no enthusiasm, though there was passion enough deep seated in her bosom; she suffered from no transcendentalism; she saw nothing through a halo of poetic inspiration: among the various tints of her atmosphere there was no rose colour; she preferred wit to poetry; and her smile was cynical rather than joyous.

Now I have described my donna primissima, with hardly sufficient detail for my own satisfaction, doubtless with far too much for yours, O my reader! It must be added, however, that she was an orphan; that she lived entirely with her aunt, Miss Baker; that her father had been in early life a sort of partner with Mr George Bertram; that Mr George Bertram was her guardian, though he had hitherto taken but little trouble in looking after her, whatever trouble he may have taken in looking after her money; and that she was possessed of a moderate fortune, say about four thousand pounds.

A picnic undertaken from Jerusalem must in some respects be unlike any picnic elsewhere. Ladies cannot be carried to it in carriages, because at Jerusalem there are no carriages; nor can the provisions be conveyed even in carts, for at Jerusalem there are no carts. The stock of comestibles was therefore packed in hampers on a camel's back, and sent off to the valley by one route, whereas Miss Todd and her friends went on horseback and on donkey-back by another and a longer road.

It may as well be mentioned that Miss Todd was a little ashamed of the magnitude to which her undertaking had attained. Her original plan had merely been this:—that she and a few others should ride through the valleys round the city, and send a basket of sandwiches to meet them at some hungry point on the road. Now there was a *cortège* of eleven persons, exclusive of the groomboys, a boiled ham, sundry chickens, hard-boiled eggs, and champagne. Miss Todd was somewhat ashamed of this. Here, in England, one would hardly inaugurate a picnic to Kensal Green, or the Highgate Cemetery, nor select the tombs of our departed great ones as a shelter under which to draw one's corks. But Miss Todd boasted of high spirits: when this little difficulty had been first suggested to her by Mr M'Gabbery, she had scoffed at it, and had enlarged her circle in a spirit of mild bravado. Then chance had done more for her; and now she was doomed to preside over a large party of revellers immediately over the ashes of James the Just.

None but Englishmen or Englishwomen do such things as this. To other people is wanting sufficient pluck for such enterprises; is wanting also a certain mixture of fun, honest independence, and bad taste. Let us go into some church on the Continent—in Italy, we will say—where the walls of the churches still boast of the great works of the great masters.—Look at that man standing on the very altar-step while the priest is saying his mass; look at his grey shooting-coat, his thick shoes, his wide-awake hat* stuck under one arm, and his stick under the other, while he holds his opera-glass to his eyes. How he shuffles about to get the best point of sight, quite indifferent as to clergy or laity! All that bell-ringing, incense-flinging, and breast-striking is nothing to him: he has paid dearly to be brought thither; he has paid the guide who is kneeling a little behind him; he is going to pay the sacristan who attends him; he is quite ready to pay the priest himself, if the priest would only signify his wish that way; but he has come there to see that fresco, and see it he will: respecting that he will soon know more than either the priest or his worshippers. Perhaps some servant of the church, coming to him with submissive, almost suppliant gesture, begs him to step back just for one moment. The lover of art glares at him with insulted look, and hardly deigns to notice him further: he merely turns his eye to his Murray,* puts his hat down on the altar-step, and goes on studying his subject. All the world—German, Frenchman, Italian, Spaniard—all men of all nations know that that ugly grey shooting-coat must contain an Englishman. He cares for no one. If any one upsets him, he can do much towards righting himself; and if more be wanted, has he not Lord Malmesbury or Lord Clarendon* at his back? But what would this Englishman say if his place of worship were disturbed by some wandering Italian?

It was somewhat in this way with Miss Todd. She knew that what she was about to do was rather absurd, but she had the blood of the Todds warm at her heart. The Todds were a people not easily frightened, and Miss Todd was not going to disgrace her lineage. True, she had not intended to feed twelve people over a Jewish sepulchre, but as the twelve people had assembled, looking to her for food, she was not the woman to send them away fasting: so she gallantly led the way through the gate of Jaffa, Sir Lionel attending her on a donkey.

When once out of town, they turned sharp to the left. Their path lay through the valley of Gihon, through the valley of Hinnom, down among those strange, open sepulchres, deeply excavated in caves on the mountain-sides—sepulchres quite unlike those below in the valley of Jehoshaphat. There they are all covered, each stone marking a grave; but here they lie in open catacombs—in caves at least, of which the entrance is open. The hardy stranger crawling in may lay his hand within the cell—nay, may crawl up into it if he will—in which have mouldered the bones of some former visitor to Jerusalem. For this, so saith tradition, is the field purchased with the reward of iniquity. It was the burying-place for strangers, Aceldama, the field of blood.*

But where be these bones now? for the catacombs are mostly empty. Mr Pott, descending as far as he could into the deepest of them, did at last bring forth a skull and two parts of a back-bone; did present the former with much grace to Miss Jones, who, on beholding it, very nearly fell from off her donkey.

'For shame, Pott!' said Mr Cruse. 'How could you handle anything so disgusting? You are desecrating the grave of some unfortunate Mussulman who has probably died within the last fifty years.' Mr Cruse was always intent on showing that he believed none of the traditions of the country.

'It was quite dreadful of you, Mr Pott,' said Miss Jones; 'quite dreadful! Indeed, I don't know what you would not do. But I am quite sure he was never a Mahomedan.'

'He looked like a Jew, didn't he?' said Pott.

'Oh! I did not see the face; but he was certainly either a Jew or a Christian. Only think. Perhaps those remains have been there for nearly eighteen hundred years. Is it not wonderful? Mamma, it was just here that I lost my parasol.'

Sir Lionel had headed the cavalcade with Miss Todd, but George Bertram was true to his new friends, Miss Baker and Miss Waddington. So also, for a time, were Mr M'Gabbery and Mr Cruse. As the aunt and niece rode beside each other, a great part of this gallant attention fell upon the former. Indeed, the easiest way of addressing the beauty was often found to be through the beauty's aunt; and it may be doubted whether Mr M'Gabbery would not have retreated long since in despair, but for the scintillations of civility which fell to him from Miss Baker's good-humour. He had had the good fortune of some previous days' journeying with them on horseback through the desert, and had found that privilege gave him an inestimable advantage over Mr Cruse. Why should it not also suffice as regarded this new comer? He had held much commune with himself on the subject that morning; had called himself to task for his own pusillanimity, and had then fortified his courage with the old reflection about fair ladies and faint hearts—and also with a glass of brandy. He was therefore disposed to make himself very unpleasant to poor George if occasion should require.

'How delighted you must have been to see your father!' said Miss Baker, who, though her temper would not permit her to be uncivil to Mr M'Gabbery, would readily have dispensed with that gentleman's attendance.

'Indeed I was. I never saw him before, you know.'

'Never saw him, your father, before, Mr Bertram?' said Caroline. 'Why, aunt Mary says that I have seen him.'

'I never saw him to remember him. One doesn't count one's acquaintance before seven or eight years of age.'

'Your memory must be very bad, then,' said Mr M'Gabbery, 'or your childhood's love for your father very slight. I perfectly remember the sweetness of my mother's caresses when I was but three years old. There is nothing, Miss Waddington, to equal the sweetness of a mother's kisses.'

'I never knew them,' said she. 'But I have found an aunt's do nearly as well.'

'A grandmother's are not bad,' said Bertram, looking very grave.

'I can never think of my mother without emotion,' continued Mr M'Gabbery. 'I remember, as though it were yesterday, when I first stood at her knee, with a picture-book on her lap before me. It is the furthest point to which memory carries me—and the sweetest.'

'I can remember back much before that,' said George; 'a great deal before that. Listen to this, Miss Baker. My earliest impression was a hatred of dishonesty.'

'I hope your views have not altered since,' said Caroline.

'Very materially, I fear. But I must tell you about my memory. I was lying once in my cradle—'

'You don't mean to tell me you remember that?' said M'Gabbery.

'Perfectly, as you do the picture-book. Well, there I was lying, Miss Baker, with my little eyes wide open. It is astonishing how much babies see, though people never calculate on their having eyes at all. I was lying on my back, staring at the mantel-piece, on which my mother had left her key-basket.'

'You remember, of course, that it was her key-basket?' said Miss Waddington, with a smile that made M'Gabbery clench his walking-stick in his hand.

'Perfectly; because she always kept her halfpence there also. Well, there was a nursery-girl who used to be about me in those days. I distinctly saw her go to that basket, Miss Baker, and take out a penny; and I then made up my mind that the first use I would make of my coming speech should be to tell my mother. That, I think, is the furthest point to which my memory carries me.'

The ladies laughed heartily, but Mr M'Gabbery frowned bitterly. 'You must have dreamt it,' said he.

'It is just possible,' said George; 'but I don't think it. Come, Miss Waddington, let us have your earliest recollections.'

'Ah! mine will not be interesting. They do not go back at all so far. I think they have reference to bread and butter.'

'I remember being very angry,' said Miss Baker, 'because papa prophesied that I should be an old maid. It was very hard on me, for his prophecy no doubt brought about the fact.'

'But the fact is no fact as yet,' said Mr M'Gabbery, with a smirking gallantry for which he ought to have been kicked.

'I beg your pardon, Mr M'Gabbery,' said Miss Waddington. 'It is quite an established fact. My aunt will never have my consent to marry; and I am sure she will never dream of such a thing without it.'

'And so Mr M'Gabbery's hopes in that direction are all at an end,' said George, who was now able to speak to Caroline without being heard by the others.

'I declare I think he has entertained some such idea, for he never leaves my aunt alone for a minute. He has been very civil, very; but, Mr Bertram, perhaps you know that a very civil man may be a bore.'

'He always is, I think. No man is really liked who is ever ready to run on messages and tie up parcels. It is generally considered that a man knows his own value, and that, if he be willing to do such work, such work is fit for him.'

'You never do anything to oblige, then?'

'Very rarely; at least, not in the little domestic line. If one could have an opportunity of picking a lady out of a fire, or saving her from the clutches of an Italian bravo, or getting her a fortune of twenty thousand pounds, one would be inclined to do it. In such cases, there would be no contempt mixed up with the lady's gratitude. But ladies are never really grateful to a man for turning himself into a flunky.'

'Ah! I like to be attended to all the same.'

'Then there is Mr M'Gabbery. Half a smile will keep him at your feet the whole day.'

Mr M'Gabbery and poor Miss Baker were now walking behind them, side by side. But his felicity in this respect was not at all sufficient for that gentleman. In their long journey from Egypt, he and Miss Waddington had always been within speaking distance; and who was the stranger of today that was thus to come and separate them?

'Miss Waddington,' he cried, 'do you remember when your horse stumbled in the sand at El Arish? Ah! what a pleasant day that was!'

'But you have not recalled it by a very pleasant incident. I was very nearly being thrown out of my saddle.'

'And how we had to wait for our dinner at Gaza till the camels came up?' And Mr M'Gabbery, urging on his horse, brought him up once more abreast with that of Miss Waddington.

'I shall soon have as great a horror of Gaza as Samson had,'* said she, *sotto voce*. 'I almost feel myself already in bonds under Philistian yoke whenever it is mentioned.'

'Talking of recollections, that journey will certainly be among the sunniest of my life's memories,' said Mr M'Gabbery.

'It was sunny, certainly,' said Miss Waddington; for the heat of the desert had been oppressive.

'Ah! and so sweet! That encamping in your own tent; preparing your own meals; having everything, as it were, within yourself. Civilized life has nothing to offer equal to that. A person who has only gone from city to city, or from steamboat to steamboat, knows nothing of oriental life. Does he, Miss Waddington?' This was intended as a blow at Bertram, who had got to Jerusalem without sleeping under canvas.

'What ignorant wretches the natives must be!' said George; 'for they apparently sleep as regularly in their own beds as any stupid Christian in England.'

'I am not sure that even Mr M'Gabbery would admire the tents so much if he had not some Christian comforts along with him.'

'His brandy-flask and dressing-case, for instance,' said George.

'Yes; and his mattress and blankets,' said Caroline.

'His potted meat and preserved soup.'

'And especially his pot to boil his potatoes in.'

'That was Mr Cruse,' said Mr M'Gabbery, quite angrily. 'For myself, I do not care a bit about potatoes.'

'So it was, Mr M'Gabbery; and I beg your pardon. It is Mr Cruse whose soul is among the potatoes. But if I remember right, it was you who were so angry when the milk ran out.' Then Mr M'Gabbery again receded, and talked to Mrs Jones about his associations.

'How thoroughly the Turks and Arabs beat us in point of costume!' said Mrs Hunter to Mr Cruse.

'It will be very hard, at any rate, for any of them to beat you,' said the tutor. 'Since I have been out here, I have seen no one adopt their ways with half as much grace as you do.'

Mrs Hunter looked down well pleased to her ankles, which were covered, and needed to be covered, by no riding-habit. 'I was not thinking so much of myself as of Mr Hunter. Women, you know, Mr Cruse, are nothing in this land.'

'Except when imported from Christendom, Mrs Hunter.'

'But I was speaking of gentlemen's toilets. Don't you think the Turkish dress very becoming? I declare, I shall never bear to see Charles again in a coat and waistcoat and trousers.'

'Nor he you in an ordinary silk gown, puffed out with crinoline.'

'Well, I suppose we must live in the East altogether then. I am sure I should not object. I know one thing—I shall never endure to put a bonnet on my head again. By-the-by, Mr Cruse, who is this Sir Lionel Bertram that has just come? Is he a baronet?'

'Oh dear, no; nothing of that sort, I imagine. I don't quite know who he is; but that young man is his son.'

'They say he's very clever, don't they?'

'He has that sort of boy's cleverness, I dare say, which goes towards taking a good degree.' Mr Cruse himself had not shone very brightly at the University.

'Miss Waddington seems very much smitten with him; don't you think so?'

'Miss Waddington is a beautiful girl; and variable—as beautiful girls sometimes are.'

'Mr Cruse, don't be satirical.'

' "Praise undeserved is satire in disguise," '* said Mr Cruse, not quite understanding, himself, why he made the quotation. But it did exceedingly well. Mrs Hunter smiled sweetly on him, said that he was a dangerous man, and that no one would take him to be a clergyman; upon which Mr Cruse begged that she would spare his character.

And now they had come to the fountain of Enrogel, and having dismounted from their steeds, stood clustering about the low wall which surrounds the little pool of water.

'This, Sir Lionel,' said Miss Todd, acting cicerone, 'is the fountain of Enrogel, which you know so well by name.'

'Ah!' said Sir Lionel. 'It seems rather dirty at present; doesn't it?'

'That is because the water is so low. When there has been much rain, there is quite a flood here. Those little gardens and fields there are the most fertile spot round Jerusalem, because there is so much irrigation here.'

'That's where the Jerusalem artichokes are grown, I suppose.'

'It is a singular fact, that though there are plenty of artichokes, that special plant is unknown,' said Mr M'Gabbery. 'Do you remember, Miss Waddington—'

But Miss Waddington had craftily slipped round the corner of the wall, and was now admiring Mrs Hunter's costume, on the other side of the fountain.

'And that is the village of Siloam,' continued Miss Todd, pointing to a range of cabins, some of which seemed to be cut out of the rock on the hill-side, on her right hand as she looked up towards the valley of Jehoshaphat. 'And that is the pool of Siloam, Sir Lionel; we shall go up there.'

'Ah!' said Sir Lionel again.

'Is it not interesting?' said Miss Todd; and a smiling gleam of satisfaction spread itself across her jovial, ruddy face.

'Very,' said Sir Lionel. 'But don't you find it rather hot?'

'Yes, it is warm. But one gets accustomed to that. I do so

like to find myself among these names which used to torment me so when I was a child. I had all manner of mysterious ideas about the pool of Bethesda and the beautiful gate, about the hill of Sion, and Gehenna, and the brook Cedron. I had a sort of belief that these places were scattered wide over the unknown deserts of Asia; and now, Sir Lionel, I am going to show them all to you in one day.'

'Would they were scattered wider, that the pleasure might last the longer,' said Sir Lionel, taking off his hat as he bowed to Miss Todd, but putting it on again very quickly, as he felt the heat.

'Yes; but the mystery, the beautiful mystery, is all gone,' said Miss Jones. 'I shall never feel again about these places as I used to do.'

'Nor I either, I hope,' said Mr Pott. 'I always used to catch it for scripture geography.'

'Yes, the mystery of your childhood will be gone, Miss Jones,' said Mr M'Gabbery, who, in his present state of hopelessness as regarded Miss Waddington, was ill-naturedly interfering with young Pott. 'The mystery of your childhood will be gone; but another mystery, a more matured mystery, will be created in your imagination. Your associations will henceforth bear a richer tint.'

'I don't know that,' said Miss Jones, who did not approve of being interfered with a bit better than did Mr Pott.

And then they remounted, and the cavalcade moved on. They turned up the rising ground towards the city wall, and leaving on the left the gardens in which Jerusalem artichokes did not grow, they came to the pool of Siloam. Here most of them again descended, and climbed down to the water, which bursts out from its underground channel into a cool, but damp and somewhat dirty ravine.

'You are my guide, Miss Todd, in everything,' said Sir Lionel. 'Is it necessary that I should study scripture geography down in that hole? If you bid me, I'll do it.'

'Well, Sir Lionel, I'll let you off; the more especially as I have been down there myself already, and got dreadfully draggled in doing so. Oh! I declare, there is Miss Waddington in the water.'

Miss Waddington was in the water. Not in such a manner, gentlest of readers, as to occasion the slightest shock to your susceptible nerves; but in such a degree as to be very disagreeable to her boots, and the cause of infinite damage to her stockings. George Bertram had handed her down, and when in the act of turning round to give similar assistance to some other adventurous lady, had left her alone on the slippery stones. Of course any young lady would take advantage of such an unguarded moment to get into some catastrophe.

Alas! and again alas! Unfortunately, Mr M'Gabbery had been the first to descend to the pool. He had calculated, cunningly enough, that in being there, seeing that the space was not very large, the duty must fall to his lot of receiving into his arms any such ladies as chose to come down—Miss Waddington, who was known to be very adventurous, among the number. He was no sooner there, however, than George Bertram jumped in almost upon him, and hitherto he had not an opportunity of touching Miss Waddington's glove. But now it seemed that fortune was to reward him.

'Good heavens!' cried Mr M'Gabbery, as he dashed boldly into the flood, thereby splashing the water well up into Caroline's face. There was not much occasion for this display, for the gentleman could have assisted the lady quite as effectually without even wetting his toes; but common misfortunes do create common sympathies—or at least they should do. Would it not be natural that Miss Waddington and Mr M'Gabbery, when both wet through up to their knees, should hang together in their sufferings, make common cause of it, talk each of what the other felt and understood so well? Nay, might it not be probable that, in obedience to the behests of some wise senior, they might be sent back to the city together;—understand, O reader, that the wall of Jerusalem had never yet been distant from them half a mile—back, we say, together to get dry stockings? To achieve such an object, Mr M'Gabbery would have plunged bodily beneath the wave—had the wave been deep enough to receive his body. As it was, it only just came over the tops of his boots, filling them comfortably with water.

'Oh, Mr M'Gabbery!' exclaimed the ungrateful lady. 'Now you have drowned me altogether.'

'I never saw anything so awkward in my life,' said Mr M'Gabbery, looking up at Bertram with a glance that should have frozen his blood.

'Nor I, either,' said Caroline.

'What had you better do? Pray give me your hand, Miss Waddington. To leave you in such a manner as that! We managed better in the desert, did we not, Miss Waddington? You really must go back to Jerusalem for dry shoes and stockings; you really must. Where is Miss Baker? Give me your hand, Miss Waddington; both hands, you had better.'

So much said Mr M'Gabbery while struggling in the pool of Siloam. But in the meantime, Miss Waddington, turning quickly round, had put out her hand to Bertram, who was standing—and I regret to say all but laughing—on the rock above her: and before Mr M'Gabbery's eloquence was over, she was safely landed among her friends.

'Oh, Mr Bertram,' said she; 'you are a horrid man. I'll never forgive you. Had I trusted myself to poor Mr M'Gabbery, I should have been dry-footed at this moment.' And she shook the water from off her dress, making a damp circle around herself as a Newfoundland dog sometimes does. 'If I served you right, I should make you go to the hotel for a pair of shoes.'

'Do, Miss Waddington; make him go,' said Sir Lionel. 'If he doesn't, I'll go myself.'

'I shall be delighted,' said Mr Cruse; 'my donkey is very quick;' and the clergyman mounted ready to start. 'Only I shouldn't know where to find the things.'

'No, Mr Cruse; and I couldn't tell you. Besides, there is nothing I like so much as wet feet,—except wet strings to my hat, for which latter I have to thank Mr M'Gabbery.'

'I will go, of course,' said M'Gabbery, emerging slowly from the pool. 'Of course it is for me to go; I shall be glad of an opportunity of getting dry boots myself.'

'I am so sorry you have got wet,' said the beauty.

'Oh! it's nothing; I like it. I was not going to see you in the water without coming to you. Pray tell me what I shall fetch. I know all your boxes so well, you know, so I can have no difficulty. Will they be in the one with C. W. on it in brass nails? That was the one which fell off the camel near the Temple of Dagon.' Poor Mr M'Gabbery! that ride through the desert was an oasis in his otherwise somewhat barren life, never to be forgotten.

'I am the sinner, Miss Waddington,' said George, at last, 'and on me let the punishment fall. I will go back to Jerusalem; and in order that you may suffer no inconvenience, I will bring hither all your boxes and all your trunks on the backs of a score of Arab porters.'

'You know you intend to do no such thing,' said she. 'You have already told me your ideas as to waiting upon young ladies.'

There was, however, at last some whispering between Miss Baker and her niece, in which Mr M'Gabbery vainly attempted to join, and the matter ended in one of the grooms being sent into the town, laden with a bunch of keys and a written message for Miss Baker's servant. Before dinner-time, Miss Waddington had comfortably changed her stockings in the upper story of the tomb of St James and Mr M'Gabbery —but Mr M'Gabbery's wet feet did not receive the attention which they deserved.

Passing on from the pool of Siloam, they came to a watercourse at which there was being conducted a considerable washing of clothes. The washerwomen—the term is used as being generic to the trade and not to the sex, for some of the performers were men—were divided into two classes, who worked separately; not so separately but what they talked together, and were on friendly terms; but still there was a division. The upper washerwomen, among whom the men were at work, were Mahomedans; the lower set were Jewesses. As to the men, but little observation was made, except that they seemed expert enough, dabbing their clothes, rubbing in the soap, and then rinsing, very much in the manner of Christians. But it was impossible not to look at the women. The female followers of the Prophet had, as they always have, some pretence of a veil for their face. In the present instance, they held in their teeth a dirty blue calico rag, which passed over their heads, acting also as a shawl. By this contrivance, intended only to last while the Christians were there, they concealed one side of the face and the chin. No one could behold them without wishing that the eclipse had been total. No epithet commonly applied to women in this country could adequately describe their want of comeliness. They kept their faces to their work, and except that they held their rags between their teeth, they gave no sign of knowing that strangers were standing by them.

It was different with the Jewesses. When they were stared at, they stood up boldly and stared again;—and well worth looking at they were. There were three or four of them, young women all, though already mothers, for their children were playing on the grass behind them. Each bore on her head that moon-shaped head-dress which is there the symbol of a Jewess; and no more graceful tiara can a woman wear. It was wonderful that the same land should produce women so different as were these close neighbours. The Mahomedans were ape-like; but the Jewesses were glorious specimens of feminine creation. They were somewhat too bold, perhaps; there was too much daring in their eyes, as, with their naked shoulders and bosoms nearly bare, they met the eyes of the men that were looking at them. But there was nothing immodest in their audacity; it was defiant rather, and scornful.

There was one among them, a girl, perhaps of eighteen, who might have been a sculptor's model, not only for form and figure, but for the expression of her countenance and the beautiful turn of her head and shoulders. She was very unlike the Jewess that is ordinarily pictured to us. She had no beaky nose, no thin face, no sharp, small, black, bright eyes; she was fair, as Esther was fair;* her forehead and face were broad, her eyes large and open; yet she was a Jewess, plainly a Jewess; such a Jewess as are many still to be seen—in Palestine, at least, if not elsewhere.

When they came upon her, she was pressing the dripping water from some large piece of linen, a sheet probably. In doing this she had cunningly placed one end firmly under her foot upon a stone, and then, with her hands raised high above her head, she twisted and retwisted it till the water oozing out fell in heavy drops round her feet. Her arms and neck were bare, as were also her feet; and it was clear that she put forth to her work as much strength as usually falls to the lot of a woman in any country.

She was very fair to look at, but there was about her no feminine softness. Do not laugh, reader, unless you have already stopped to think, and, thinking, have decided that a girl of eighteen, being a washerwoman, must therefore be without feminine softness. I would not myself say that it is so. But here at least there was no feminine softness, no tenderness in the eye, no young shame at being gazed at. She paused for a moment in her work, and gave back to them all the look they gave her; and then, as though they were beneath her notice, she strained once more at her task, and so dropped the linen to the ground.

'If I knew how to set about the bargain, I would take that woman home with me, and mould her to be my wife.' Such was George Bertram's outspoken enthusiasm.

'Moulded wives never answer well,' said Sir Lionel.

'I think he would prefer one that had been dipped,' whispered Miss Todd to the colonel; but her allusion to Miss Waddington's little accident on the water, and to the chandler's wares, was not thoroughly appreciated.

It has been said that the hampers were to be sent to the tomb of Zachariah; but they agreed to dine immediately opposite to that of St James the Less. This is situated in the middle of the valley of Jehoshaphat, in the centre of myriads of Jewish tombs, directly opposite to the wall built with those huge temple stones, not many feet over the then dry watercourse of the brook Cedron. Such was the spot chosen by Miss Todd for her cold chickens and champagne.

Of course they wandered about a little in pairs and trios while these dainties were being prepared for them. This St James's tomb is a little temple built on the side of the rock, singularly graceful. The front towards the city is adorned with two or three Roman pillars, bearing, if I remember rightly, plain capitals. There is, I think, no pediment above them, or any other adjunct of architectural pretension; but the pillars themselves, so unlike anything else there, so unlike any other sepulchral monument that I, at least, have seen, make the tomb very remarkable. That it was built for a tomb is, I suppose, not to be doubted; though for whose ashes it was in fact erected may perhaps be questioned. I am not aware that any claimant has been named as a rival to St James.

The most conspicuous of these monuments is that which tradition allots to Absalom, close to this other which we have just described. It consists of a solid square erection, bearing what, for want of a better name, I must call a spire, with curved sides, the sides curving inwards as they fall from the apex to the base. This spiral roof, too low and dumpy to be properly called a spire, is very strong, built with stones laid in circles flat on each other, the circles becoming smaller as they rise towards the top. Why Absalom should have had such a tomb, who can say? That his bones were buried there, the Jews at least believe; for Jewish fathers, as they walk by with their children, bid their boys each cast a stone there to mark their displeasure at the child who rebelled against his parent. It is now nearly full of such stones.

While Miss Waddington was arranging her toilet within the tomb of St James, her admirers below were not making themselves agreeable to each other. 'It was the awkwardest thing I ever saw,' said Mr Cruse to Mr M'Gabbery, in a low tone, but not so low but what Bertram was intended to hear it.

'Very,' said Mr M'Gabbery. 'Some men are awkward by nature;—seem, indeed, as though they were never intended for ladies' society.'

'And then to do nothing but laugh at the mischief he had caused. That may be the way at Oxford; but we used to flatter ourselves at Cambridge that we had more politeness.'

'Cambridge!' said Bertram, turning round and speaking with the most courteous tone he could command. 'Were you at Cambridge? I thought I had understood that you were educated at St Bees.' Mr Cruse had been at St Bees, but had afterwards gone to the University.

'I was a scholar at St John's, sir,' replied Mr Cruse, with much dignity. 'M'Gabbery, shall we take a stroll across the valley till the ladies are ready?' And so, having sufficiently shown their contempt for the awkward Oxonian, they moved away.

'Two very nice fellows, are they not?' said Bertram to Mr Hunter. 'It's a stroke of good fortune to fall in with such men as that at such a place as this.'

'They're very well in their own way,' said Mr Hunter, who was lying on the grass, and flattering himself that he looked more Turkish than any Turk he had yet seen. 'But they don't seem to me to be quite at home here in the East. Few Englishmen in fact are. Cruse is always wanting boiled vegetables, and M'Gabbery can't eat without a regular knife and fork. Give me a pilau and a bit of bread, and I can make a capital dinner without anything to help me but my own fingers.'

'Cruse isn't a bad kind of coach,' said young Pott. 'He never interferes with a fellow. His only fault is that he's so spooney about women.'

'They're gentlemanlike men,' said Sir Lionel; 'very. One can't expect, you know, that every one should set the Thames on fire.'

'Cruse won't do that, at any rate,' put in Mr Pott.

'But Mr M'Gabbery perhaps may,' suggested George. 'At any rate, he made a little blaze just now at the brook above.' And then the ladies came down, and the business of the day commenced; seeing which, the two injured ones returned to their posts.

'I am very fond of a picnic,' said Sir Lionel, as, seated on a corner of a tombstone, he stretched out his glass towards Miss Todd, who had insisted on being his cupbearer for the occasion; 'excessively fond. I mean the eating and drinking part, of course. There is only one thing I like better; and that is having my dinner under a roof, upon a table, and with a chair to sit on.'

'Oh, you ungrateful man; after all that I am doing for you!'

'I spoke of picnics generally, Miss Todd. Could I always have my nectar filled to me by a goddess, I would be content with no room, but expect to recline on a cloud, and have thunderbolts ready at my right hand.'

'What a beautiful Jupiter* your father would make, Mr Bertram!'

'Yes; and what a happy king of gods with such a Juno as you, Miss Todd!'

'Ha! ha! ha! oh dear, no. I pretend to no *rôle* higher than that of Hebe.* Mr M'Gabbery, may I thank you for a slice of ham? I declare, these tombs are very nice tables, are they not? Only, I suppose it's very improper. Mr Cruse, I'm so sorry that we have no potatoes; but there is salad, I know.'

'Talking of chairs,' said Mr Hunter, 'after all there has been no seat yet invented by man equal to a divan, either for ease, dignity, or grace.' Mr Hunter had long been practising to sit cross-legged, and was now attempting it on the grass for the first time in public. It had at any rate this inconvenient effect, that he was perfectly useless; for, when once seated, he could neither help himself nor any one else.

'The cigar divan is a very nice lounge when one has nothing better to do,' suggested Mr Pott. 'They have capital coffee there.'

'A divan and a sofa are much the same, I suppose,' said George.

But to this Mr Hunter demurred, and explained at some length what were the true essential qualities of a real Turkish divan: long before he had finished, however, George had got up to get a clean plate for Miss Waddington, and in sitting down had turned his back upon the Turk. The unfortunate Turk could not revenge himself, as in his present position any motion was very difficult to him.

Picnic dinners are much the same in all parts of the world, and chickens and salad are devoured at Jerusalem very much in the same way as they are at other places—except, indeed, by a few such proficients in Turkish manners as Mr Hunter. The little Arab children stood around them, expectant of scraps, as I have seen children do also in England; and the conversation, which was dull enough at the commencement of the feast, became more animated when a few corks had flown. As the afternoon wore on, Mr M'Gabbery became almost bellicose under the continual indifference of his lady-love; and had it not been for the better sense of our hero—such better sense may be expected from gentlemen who are successful—something very like a quarrel would have taken place absolutely in the presence of Miss Todd.

Perhaps Miss Waddington was not free from all blame in the matter. It would be unjust to accuse her of flirting, at least, in the objectionable sense of the word. It was not in her nature to flirt. But it was in her nature to please herself without thinking much of the manner in which she did it, and it was in her nature also to be indifferent as to what others thought of her. Though she had never before known George Bertram, there was between them that sort of family knowledge of each other which justified a greater intimacy than between actual strangers. Then, too, he pleased her, while Mr M'Gabbery only bored. She had not yet thought enough about the world's inhabitants to have recognized and adjudicated on the difference between those who talk pleasantly and those who do not; but she felt that she was amused by this young double-first Oxonian, and she had no idea of giving up amusement when it came in her way. Of such amusement, she had hitherto known but little. Miss Baker herself was, perhaps, rather dull. Miss Baker's friends at Littlebath were not very bright; but Caroline had never in her heart accused them of being other than amusing. It is only by knowing his contrast that we recognize a bore when we meet him. It was in this manner that she now began to ascertain that Mr M'Gabbery certainly had bored her. Ascertaining it, she threw him off at once—perhaps without sufficient compunction.

'I'll cut that cock's comb before I have done with him,' said M'Gabbery to his friend Mr Cruse, as they rode up towards St Stephen's gate together, the rest of the cavalcade following them. Sir Lionel had suggested to Miss Todd that they might as well return, somewhat early though it was, seeing that there was cause why that feast of reason and that flow of soul should no longer be continued by them round the yet only half-emptied hampers. So the ladies had climbed up into the tomb and there adjusted their hats, and the gentlemen had seen to the steeds; and the forks had been packed up; and when Mr M'Gabbery made the state of his mind known to

Mr Cruse, they were on their way back to Jerusalem, close to the garden of Gethsemane.

'I'll cut that young cock's comb yet before I have done with him,' repeated Mr M'Gabbery.

Now Mr Cruse, as being a clergyman, was of course not a fighting man. 'I shouldn't take any notice of him,' said he; 'nor, indeed, of her either; I do not think she is worth it.'

'Oh, it isn't about that,' said M'Gabbery. 'They were two women together, and I therefore was inclined to show them some attention. You know how those things go on. From one thing to another it has come to this, that they have depended on me for everything for the last three or four weeks.'

'You haven't paid any money for them, have you?'

'Well, no; I can't exactly say that I have paid money for them. That is to say, they have paid their own bills, and I have not lent them anything. But I dare say you know that a man never travels with ladies in that free and easy way without feeling it in his pocket. One is apt to do twenty things for them which one wouldn't do for oneself; nor they for themselves if they had to pay the piper.'

Now here a very useful moral may be deduced. Ladies, take care how you permit yourselves to fall into intimacies with unknown gentlemen on your travels. It is not pleasant to be spoken of as this man was speaking of Miss Baker and her niece. The truth was, that a more punctilious person in her money dealings than Miss Baker never carried a purse. She had not allowed Mr M'Gabbery so much as to lay out on her behalf a single piastre* for oranges on the road. Nor had he been their sole companion on their journey through the desert. They had come to Jerusalem with a gentleman and his wife: Mr M'Gabbery had been kindly allowed to join them.

'Well, if I were you, I should show them a cold shoulder,' said Mr Cruse; 'and as to that intolerable puppy, I should take no further notice of him, except by cutting him dead.'

Mr M'Gabbery at last promised to follow his friend's advice, and so Miss Todd's picnic came to an end without bloodshed.

CHAPTER X

THE EFFECTS OF MISS TODD'S PICNIC

SIR LIONEL did not participate violently either in his son's disgust at the falsehood of that holy sepulchre church, nor in his enthusiasm as to the Mount of Olives. In the former, he walked about as he had done in many other foreign churches, looked a little to the right and a little to the left, observed that the roof seemed to be rather out of order, declined entering the sanctum sanctorum, and then asked whether there was anything more to be seen. He did not care, he said, about going upstairs into the gallery; and when George suggested that he should descend into the Armenian chapel, he observed that it appeared to be very dark and very crowded. He looked at the Turkish janitors without dismay, and could not at all understand why George should not approve of them.

He was equally cold and equally complaisant on the Mount of Olives. He would willingly have avoided the ascent could he have done so without displeasing his son; but George made a point of it. A donkey was therefore got for him, and he rode up.

'Ah! yes,' said he, 'a very clear view of the city; oh, that was Solomon's temple, was it? And now they have a mosque there, have they? Ah! perhaps the Brahmins will have a turn at it before the world is done. It's a barren sort of hill after all, is it not?'

And then George tried very much in vain to make his father understand why he wished to go into the church.

'By-the-by,' said Sir Lionel—they were then sitting exactly on the spot where George had placed himself before, when he made that grand resolve to give up everything belonging to this world for the sake of being one of Christ's shepherds—'by-the-by, George, for heaven's sake don't throw your uncle over in choosing a profession. I certainly should be sorry to see you become an attorney.'

'I have never thought of it for a moment,' said George.

'Because, with your abilities, and at any rate with your chance of money, I think you would be very much thrown away; but, considering his circumstances and yours, were I you, I would really submit almost to anything.'

'I will not at any rate submit to that,' said George, not very well able to reconcile his father's tone to the spot on which they were sitting.

'Well, it's your own affair, my boy. I have no right to interfere, and shall not attempt to do so; but of course I must be anxious. If you did go into the church, I suppose he'd buy a living for you?'

'Certainly not; I should take a college living.'

'At your age any that you could get would be very small. Ah, George! if I could only put an old head upon young shoulders, what a hand of cards you would have to play! That old man could leave you half a million of money!'

This was certainly not the object with which the son had ascended the mount, and he did not use much eloquence to induce his father to remain long in the place. Sir Lionel got again on his donkey, and they returned to Jerusalem; nor did George ever again talk to him about the Mount of Olives.

And he was not very much more successful with another friend into whose mind he endeavoured to inculcate his own high feelings. He got Miss Baker up to his favourite seat, and with her Miss Waddington; and then, before he had left Jerusalem, he succeeded in inducing the younger lady to ramble thither with him alone.

'I do not know that I think so highly of the church as you do,' said Caroline. 'As far as I have seen them, I cannot find that clergymen are more holy than other men; and yet surely they ought to be so.'

'At any rate, there is more scope for holiness if a man have it in him to be holy. The heart of a clergyman is more likely to be softened than that of a barrister or an attorney.'

'I don't exactly know what you mean by heart-softening, Mr Bertram.'

'I mean—' said Bertram, and then he paused; he was not quite able, with the words at his command, to explain to this girl what it was that he did mean, nor was he sure that she would appreciate him if he did so; and, fond as he still was of his idea of a holy life, perhaps at this moment he was fonder still of her.

'I think that a man should do the best he can for himself in a profession. You have a noble position within your grasp, and if I were you, I certainly would not bury myself in a country parsonage.'

What this girl of twenty said to him had much more weight than the time-honoured precepts of his father; and yet both, doubtless, had their weight. Each blow told somewhat; and the seed too had been sown upon very stony ground.

They sat there some three or four minutes in silence. Bertram was looking over to Mount Moriah, imaging to himself the spot where the tables of the money-changers had been overturned, while Miss Waddington was gazing at the setting sun. She had an eye to see material beauty, and a taste to love it; but it was not given to her to look back and feel those things as to which her lover would fain have spoken to her. The temple in which Jesus had taught was nothing to her.

Yes, he was her lover now, though he had never spoken to her of love, had never acknowledged to himself that he did love her—as so few men ever do acknowledge till the words that they have said make it necessary that they should ask themselves whether those words are true. They sat there for some minutes in silence, but not as lovers sit. The distance between them was safe and respectful. Bertram was stretched upon the ground, with his eyes fixed, not upon her, but on the city opposite; and she sat demurely on a rock, shading herself with her parasol.

'I suppose nothing would induce you to marry a clergyman?' said he at last.

'Why should you suppose that, Mr Bertram?'

'At any rate, not the parson of a country parish. I am led to suppose it by what you said to me yourself just now.'

'I was speaking of you, and not of myself. I say that you have a noble career open to you, and I do not look on the ordinary life of a country parson as a noble career. For myself, I do not see any nobility in store. I do not know that there is any fate more probable for myself than that of becoming a respectable vicaress.'

'And why may not a vicar's career be noble? Is it not as noble to have to deal with the soul as with the body?'

'I judge by what I see. They are generally fond of eating, very cautious about their money, untidy in their own houses, and apt to go to sleep after dinner.'

George turned upon the grass, and for a moment or two ceased to look across into the city. He had not strength of character to laugh at her description and yet to be unmoved by it. He must either resent what she said, or laugh and be ruled by it. He must either tell her that she knew nothing of a clergyman's dearest hopes, or else he must yield to the contempt which her words implied.

'And could you love, honour, and obey such a man as that, yourself, Miss Waddington?' he said at last.

'I suppose such men do have wives who love, honour, and obey them; either who do or do not. I dare say I should do much the same as others.'

'You speak of my future, Miss Waddington, as though it were a subject of interest: but you seem to think nothing of your own.'

'It is useless for a woman to think of her future; she can do so little towards planning it, or bringing about her plans. Besides, I have no right to count on myself as anything out of the ordinary run of women; I have taken no double-first degree in anything.'

'A double-first is no sign of a true heart or true spirit. Many a man born to grovel has taken a double-first.'

'I don't perhaps know what you mean by grovelling, Mr Bertram. I don't like grovellers myself. I like men who can keep their heads up—who, once having them above the water, will never allow them to sink. Some men in every age do win distinction and wealth and high place. These are not grovellers. If I were you I would be one of them.'

'You would not become a clergyman?'

'Certainly not; no more than I would be a shoemaker.'

'Miss Waddington!'

'Well; and what of Miss Waddington? Look at the

clergymen that you know; do they never grovel? You know Mr Wilkinson; he is an excellent man, I am sure, but is he conspicuous for highmindedness, for truth and spirit?' It must be remembered that the elder Mr Wilkinson was at this time still living. 'Are they generally men of wide views and enlightened principles? I do not mean to liken them to shoemakers; but were I you, I should think of the one business as soon as the other.'

'And in my place, what profession would you choose?'

'Ah, that I cannot say. I do not know your circumstances.'

'I must earn my bread, like other sons of Adam.'

'Well, earn it then in such a manner that the eyes of the world shall be upon you; that men and women shall talk of you, and newspapers have your name in their columns. Whatever your profession, let it be a wakeful one; not one that you can follow half asleep.'

Again he paused for awhile, and again sat looking at the rock of the temple. Still he thought of the tables of the money-changers, and the insufficiency of him who had given as much as half to the poor. But even while so thinking, he was tempted to give less than half himself, to set up on his own account a money-changing table in his own temple. He would fain have worshipped at the two shrines together had he been able. But he was not able; so he fell down before that of Mammon.

'You can talk to me in this way, urge me to be ambitious, and yet confess that you could give yourself to one of those drones of whom you speak with such scorn.'

'I speak of no one with scorn; and I am not urging you; and at present am not talking of giving myself to any one. You ask as to the possibility of my ever marrying a clergyman; I say that it is very possible that I may do so some day.'

'Miss Waddington,' said George; and now he had turned his face absolutely from the city, and was looking upwards to the hill; upwards, full into the beauty of her countenance. 'Miss Waddington!'

'Well, Mr Bertram?'

'You speak of me as though I were a being high in the scale of humanity—'

'And so I think of you.'

'Listen for a moment—and of yourself as one comparatively low.'

'No, no, not low; I have too much pride for that; much lower than you, certainly, for I have given no proofs of genius.'

'Well—lower than me. That is what you have said, and I do not believe that you would say so falsely. You would not descend to flatter me?'

'Certainly not; but—'

'Believe equally of me that I would not flatter you. I have told you no falsehood as yet, and I have a right to claim your belief. As you look on me, so do I on you. I look up to you as one whose destiny must be high. To me there is that about you which forbids me to think that your path in the world can ever be other than conspicuous. Your husband, at least, will have to live before the world.'

'I shall not have the slightest objection to his doing so; but that, I think, will depend a great deal more on him than on me.'

Bertram was very anxious to say something which might tend towards the commingling of his destiny with hers. He was hardly yet prepared to swear that he loved her, and to ask her in good set terms to be his wife. But he did not like to leave her without learning whether he had at all touched her heart. He was fully sure now that his own was not whole.

'Come, Mr Bertram,' said she; 'look at the sun, how nearly it is gone. And you know we have no twilight here. Let us go down; my aunt will think that we are lost.'

'One minute, Miss Waddington; one minute, and then we will go. Miss Waddington, if you care enough for me to bid me take up any profession, follow any pursuit, I will obey you. You shall choose for me, if you will.'

She blushed, not deeply, but with a colour sufficiently heightened to make it visible to him, and with a tingling warmth which made her conscious of it herself. She would have given much to keep her countenance, and yet the blush became her greatly. It took away from the premature firmness of her womanly look, and gave her for the moment something of the weakness natural to her age.

'You know that is nonsense: on such a subject you must of course choose for yourself.'

Bertram was standing in the path before her, and she could not well go on till he had made way for her. 'No,' said he; 'thinking as I do of you, feeling as I do regarding you, it is not nonsense. It would be absolutely nonsense if I said so to your aunt, or to Mrs Hunter, or to Miss Jones. I could not be guided by a person who was indifferent to me. But in this matter I will be guided by you if you will consent to guide me.'

'Of course I shall do no such thing.'

'You have no personal wish, then, for my welfare?'

'Yes, I have. Your uncle is my guardian, and I may therefore be allowed to look upon you as a friend of a longer standing than merely of yesterday. I do regard you as a friend, and shall be glad of your success.' Here she paused, and they walked on a few steps together in silence; and then she added, becoming still redder as she did so, but now managing to hide her face from her companion, 'Were I to answer you in the way that you pretend to wish, I should affect either less friendship that I feel, or much more.'

'Much more!' said Bertram, with a shade of despondency in his tone.

'Yes, much more Mr Bertram. Why, what would you have me say?'

'Ah me! I hardly know. Nothing—nothing—I would have you say nothing. You are quite right to say nothing.' And then he walked on again for a hundred yards in silence. 'Nothing, Miss Waddington, nothing; unless, indeed—'

'Mr Bertram;' and as she spoke she put out her hand and gently touched his arm. 'Mr Bertram, stop yourself; think, at any rate, of what you are going to say. It is a pity when such as you speak foolishly.' It was singular to see how much more composed she was than he; how much more able to manage the occasion—and yet her feelings were strong too.

'Nothing; I would have you say nothing—nothing, unless this: that whatever my destiny may be, you will share it with me.'

As he spoke he did not look towards her, but straight

before him down the path. He did not sigh nor look soft. There was indeed not much capability for soft looks in his square and strongly-featured face. He frowned rather, set his teeth together, and walked on faster than before. Caroline did not answer him immediately; and then he repeated his words. 'I do not care for you to say anything now, unless you can say this—that whatever your lot may be, I may share it; whatever mine, that you will share it.'

'Mr Bertram.'

'Well—'

'Now you have spoken foolishly. Do you know that you have spoken foolishly?'

'I have spoken truly. Do you speak as truly. You should be as much above false girlish petty scruples, as you will be and are above falsehood of another kind. You will never tell a man that you love him if you do not.'

'No; certainly, I never will.'

'And do not deny it if it be the truth.'

'But it is not the truth. How long have we known each other, Mr Bertram?'

'Counting by days and hours, some fortnight. But what does that signify? You do not love a man the better always, the longer you know him. Of you, I discern that there is that in you I can love, that would make me happy. I have talent—some sort of talent at least. You have a spirit which would force me to use it. I will not pretend to say that I am suited for you. You must judge that. But I know that you are suited for me. Now I will take any answer that you will give me.'

To tell the truth, Miss Waddington hardly knew what answer to give him. He was one, it seemed, who, having spoken with decision himself, would take any answer as decisive. He was one not to be tampered with, and one also hardly to be rejected without consideration; and certainly not so to be accepted. She had liked him much—very much, considering the little she had known of him. She had even asked herself, half playfully, whether it were not possible that she might learn to love him. He was a gentleman, and that with her was much. He was a man of talent, and that with her was more. He was one whose character and mode of thought she could respect. He was a man whom any woman might probably be able to respect. But Caroline Waddington wanted much more than this in her future lord. She could talk pleasantly of the probability of her marrying a country parson; but she had, in truth, a much wider ambition for herself. She would never marry—such was the creed which was to govern her own life—without love; but she would not allow herself to love where love would interfere with her high hopes. In her catalogue of human blisses love in a cottage was not entered. She was not avaricious; she did not look to money as the summum bonum,*—certainly not to marry for money's sake. But she knew that no figure in the world could be made without means. Her own fortune was small, and she did not even rate her beauty high. Her birth was the birth of a lady, but that was all; her talents had never been tried, but she thought of them more indifferently than they deserved. She felt, therefore, that she had no just ground to hope for much; but she was determined that no folly on her own part should rob her of any chance that fortune might vouchsafe to her.

Under such circumstances what answer should she make to Bertram? Her heart would have bid her not reject him, but she was fearful of her own heart. She dreaded lest she should be betrayed into sacrificing herself to love. Ought prudence now to step in and bid her dismiss a suitor whose youth had as yet achieved nothing, whose own means were very small, with whom, if he were accepted, her marriage must be postponed; who, however, was of great talent, who gave such promise of future distinction? Bertram, when he made his offer, made it from a full heart; but Caroline was able to turn these matters in her mind before she answered him.

She will be called cold-hearted, mercenary, and unfeminine. But when a young girl throws prudence to the winds, and allows herself to love where there is nothing to live on, what then is she called? It seems to me that it is sometimes very hard for young girls to be in the right. They certainly should not be mercenary; they certainly should not marry paupers; they certainly should not allow themselves to become old maids. They should not encumber themselves with early, hopeless loves; nor should they callously resolve to care for nothing but a good income and a good house. There should be some handbook of love, to tell young ladies when they may give way to it without censure. As regards our heroine, however, she probably wanted no such handbook. 'Now I will take any answer you will give me.' Bertram, when he had said that, remained silent, awaiting her reply.

'Mr Bertram,' she said at last, 'I think that you have spoken unwisely; let us agree to forget it. What you have said has come from impulse rather than judgment.'

'Not so, Miss Waddington. I cannot forget it; nor can you. I would not have it again unsaid if I could. When once I learned that I loved you, it became natural to me to tell you so.'

'Such quick speaking is not perhaps natural to me. But as you demand an immediate answer, I must give you one. I have had much pleasure in your society, but I have never thought of loving you. Nor can I love you without thinking of it.'

It would be hard to say what answer Bertram expected; indeed, he had no expectations. He had had no idea of making this offer when he walked up the hill with her. His heart was then turned rather to worship at that other shrine: it had been her own words, her own eloquence in favour of the world's greatness, that had drawn him on. He had previously filled his mind with no expectation; but he had felt an intense desire for success when once he had committed himself to his offer.

And now, as he walked down beside her, he hardly knew what to make of her answer. A man, if he be not absolutely rejected, is generally inclined to think that any answer from a lady may be taken as having in it some glimmer of favour. And ladies know this so well, that they almost regard any reply on their own part, short of an absolute refusal, as an acceptance. If a lady bids a gentleman wait awhile for his answer, he thinks himself quite justified in letting all the world know that she is his own. We all know what a reference to a parent's judgment means. A lady must be very decisive—very, if she means to have her 'no' taken at its full meaning. Now Caroline Waddington had not been very decisive.

Whatever Bertram's thoughts or his hopes might be, he said nothing more on the present occasion. He walked silently down the hill by her side, somewhat moody-looking, but yet not with the hang-dog aspect of a rejected suitor. There was a fire in his eyes and a play upon his countenance which did not tell of hope altogether extinguished. Before they were at the foot of the hill, he had resolved that he would have Caroline Waddington for his wife, let the difficulties in his way be what they might. But then he was ever so keen to resolve; so often beaten from his resolutions!

And Caroline also walked silently down the hill. She knew that she had given an ambiguous answer, and was content to let it remain so. In the silence of her chamber, she would think over this thing and make her calculations. She would inquire into her own mind, and learn whether she could afford to love this man whom she could not but acknowledge to be so lovable. As for asking any one else, seeking counsel in the matter from her aunt, that never for a moment suggested itself to Caroline Waddington.

They had left Miss Baker and Miss Todd at the bottom of the hill. It was a beautiful evening, and those ladies had consented to sit down and rest there while the more enthusiastic and young lovers of the mount ascended to the spot of which Bertram was so fond. But in giving that consent, they had hardly expected that such encroachment would be made on their good-nature. When Caroline and Bertram again found them, the daylight had almost waned away.

CHAPTER XI

VALE VALETE*

MISS BAKER was a little querulous at being left so long sitting with Miss Todd at the corner of the garden wall; but Miss

Todd was never querulous: she was one of those good-humoured persons who never complain, and find some antidote to every ill in life, even in the ill itself. True, she had been kept a couple of hours and more sitting on a stone by the brook Cedron; but then she had acquired the privilege of telling how Mr George Bertram and Miss Caroline Waddington had passed those hours *tête-à-tête* together on the mountain-side.

'Why, Caroline, we thought you were never coming down again,' said Miss Baker.

'It was Mr Bertram's fault, aunt; he is immovable when he gets to a certain rock up there. He has an idea of turning hermit, and constructing a cell for himself in that spot.'

'If I did turn hermit, it should certainly be for the sake of living there,' said he. 'But I fear I want the proper spirit for so holy a life.'

'I hope you have not kept us all this time for nothing: you have had some success, I trust?' said Miss Todd to Bertram, in a laughing whisper. Miss Todd's face was quite joyous as she whispered; but then her face was always joyous.

'I certainly have not done that which I intended to do,' said Bertram, with a mock sententiousness. 'And so far I have been unsuccessful.'

'Then she has rejected him,' said Miss Todd to herself. 'What a fool the girl must be!' but it was a great comfort to Miss Todd that she knew all about it.

That evening their plans were decided on as to leaving Jerusalem—the plans, that is, of those whose fortunes we must follow;—Miss Baker, namely, and her niece; Sir Lionel and his son. Of Miss Todd we may here take our leave for awhile. She did not on this occasion marry Sir Lionel, nor did she even have the satisfaction of knowing that her friends accused her of wishing to do so. Miss Todd had her weak points, but taking her as a whole, and striking the balance between good and bad, I do not care how soon we may meet her again. To her friends also we may bid adieu. Mr M'Gabbery did not die of love. Mr Pott did propose to and was accepted by Miss Jones; but the match was broken off by the parental Potts, who on the occasion nearly frightened poor Mrs Jones out of her life. The Hunters sojourned for awhile on the sides of Lebanon, but did at last return to the discomforts of European life. Mrs Hunter tried the effect of her favourite costume at Tenby, but it was not found to answer. Of Mr Cruse, I can only say that he was dreadfully scolded by Mrs Pott, in that he had allowed her son to fall in love; and that Mr Pott threatened to stop his salary. An attorney's letter, however, settled that.

It must be confessed that Miss Baker had allowed her plans to be altered by the arrival of the Bertrams at Jerusalem; and confessed also that Miss Baker's complaisance in this respect had been brought about by her niece's persuasion. Their original intention had been to go on to Damascus. Then Miss Baker had begged off this further journey, alleging that her clothes as well as her strength were worn out; and Caroline had consented to return home by the shortest route. Then came the temptation of going as far as Beyrout with the Bertrams, and Miss Baker had been enjoined to have herself patched up externally and internally. She was accordingly being patched up; but now things were altered again. Caroline knew that she could not travel with George Bertram without engaging herself to be his wife; or that if she did, their journey would not be a happy one. And she did not wish so to engage herself without further thought. She determined, therefore, that they would fall back upon her aunt's plan, and return home by the easier route, by Jaffa, that is, and Alexandria.

Her altered mind had to be explained, not only to her aunt, but to the Bertrams; and she came to the somewhat singular resolve to explain it in both cases by the simple truth. She would tell her aunt what had happened; and she would make George Bertram understand in a few and as kind words as might be, that under the present circumstances it would be better that they should not be thrown into the very close intercourse necessary for fellow-travellers in the East. She was very prudent, was Miss Waddington; and having freed herself of one lover because she did not like him, she prepared to rid herself of another because she did.

The Bertrams were to leave Jerusalem together in a couple of days' time. George was to go with his father as far as Constantinople, and, having seen something of real Turks in real Turkey, was to return at once to England. After his last visit to the Mount of Olives, he said nothing further about the church as a profession.

That evening Caroline settled it all with her aunt. 'Aunt,' said she, as they sat together brushing their hair before they went to bed, 'you will think me very fanciful; but after all, I believe we had better go back by Alexandria.'

'Oh dear, I shall be so glad, my dear. Jane says that I could not possibly get a travelling dress made here that I could wear.'

'You could get a dress in Damascus, I don't doubt, aunt. But—'

'And I really am not fit for much more riding. I don't like to disappoint you; but if you really wouldn't mind it—'

'Well, I should mind it,—and I should not. But let me tell you. You must not think that I am so very changeable, first pressing you to go one way, and then begging you to go another, without a reason.'

'No; I know you do it for my sake.'

'Not that either, aunt—quite; but do listen. Mr Bertram today made—'

'He has not offered to you, has he?'

'Yes, aunt; that is just what he has done. And, therefore, perhaps it will not be quite so well that we should travel together.'

'But, Caroline, tell me—pray do tell me; what did he say, and what have you said? Oh dear me, this is very sudden.' And Miss Baker sat back in her chair, with her now greyish hair hanging over her shoulders, with her hair-brush still held in one hand, and with the other resting on the toilet-table.

'As for what he said, I may skip that, aunt. It was the old story, I suppose, merely signifying that he wanted me to marry him.'

'Well, well.'

'As you truly say, aunt; it was too sudden. Mr Bertram has a great deal to recommend him; a very great deal; one cannot but like him. He is very clever too.'

'Yes, Caroline; and will be his uncle's heir—doubtless.'

'I know nothing of that; to tell the truth, indeed, I never thought of that. But it would have made no difference.'

'And you refused him.'

'Well, I hardly know. I do know this—that I did more towards refusing him than accepting him; that I must have much more love for any man I do marry than I have for him at present; and that after what has passed, I think we had better not go to Damascus together.'

To this latter proposition aunt Mary fully agreed; and thus it was decided that the extra patching for the longer journey need not be accomplished. Miss Baker would explain the matter to Sir Lionel in her way; and Caroline would do the same to George Bertram in hers. On one other point, also, Miss Baker made up her mind fully; though on this matter she did not think it prudent to make her mind known to her niece. She was very confident that the marriage would take place, and resolved to do all in her power to bring it about. Personally, she was fond of George Bertram; she admired his talents, she liked his father, and felt very favourably inclined towards his uncle's wealth. She finished her toilet therefore in calm happiness. She had an excellent match in view for her niece—and, after all, she would escape that dreadful horse-back journey to Damascus.

During the next day Caroline and George Bertram were not together for a moment—that is, they were not together alone; for they breakfasted and dined at the same table, and he sat between the aunt and her niece as he had done continually since he had been at Jerusalem. Sir Lionel told him in the forenoon that they were not to have the pleasure of the ladies' company on their journey, and rallied him as to the heart-breaking tendency of these tidings. But George showed, in his countenance at least, no symptoms of heart-breaking.

That evening, as they all parted for the night, George did press Miss Waddington's hand more warmly than was usual with him; and, as he did so, he did look into her face for one moment to see what encouragement he might find there. I cannot say that there was no encouragement. The pressure was perhaps not met by any similar warmth on her part, but it was submitted to without any touch of resentment: the love which shot from his eye was not returned to him from hers, but hers were soft beneath his glance, softer than was usual with Caroline Waddington.

But on the next morning they did come together. It was the day before the departure of the Bertrams, and whatever was to be said must be said then. Caroline watched her opportunity, and as soon as breakfast was over—they all breakfasted in the public salon—asked him to come into her aunt's sitting-room. She was quite collected, had fully made up her mind what to say, and was able also to say it without hesitation, and with perfect self-possession. This was more than could be boasted of on the gentleman's behalf.

'You know, Mr Bertram, that we are not going to travel together?'

'Yes; my father told me so yesterday.'

'And you will understand the reason of it, I am sure?'

'Not exactly, Miss Waddington. I cannot say I do understand it. I may have been presumptuous in what I said to you the other day; but I do not see why on that account your aunt should be put to the inconvenience of altering her plans. You fear, I suppose, that I should annoy you; but you might trust me—and still may if you will do so.'

'Now, Mr Bertram, you are hardly so sincere as you asserted yourself to be, and required me to be on the mount. You are yourself quite aware that nobody has thought you presumptuous. I have nothing to complain of, and much to thank you for—independently of the honour you have now done me;—for from you it is an honour. But I cannot say that I love you. It would not be natural that I should do so.'

'Good heavens! not natural. I love you with the whole strength of my heart. Is that unnatural?'

'It is the province of men to take the initiative in such matters,' said Caroline, smiling.

'I know nothing as to man's province, or of woman's province either. By province, you mean custom and conventional rule; and conventional rule means falsehood. I have known you but a week or two, and I love you dearly. You, of course, have known me as long, and are at any rate as capable of loving as I am. There would be nothing unnatural in your loving me—though, indeed, it may be very unlikely that you should do so.'

'Well; I will not contradict you in anything if I can help it, except perhaps as to that last little would-be-proud, petulant protest. But putting out of sight all question of likelihood what ought I to do if I do not love you? What in such a case would you recommend a sister to do? Is it not better that we should not be immediately thrown together, as must so certainly be the case in travelling?'

'Then I am to understand that you positively can never love me?'

'I have not said so: but you press me unfairly, Mr Bertram.'

'Unfairly. No, by heavens! no pressure in such case can be unfair. I would press the truth out from you—the real truth; the truth that so vitally concerns myself. You will not say that you have an aversion to me?'

'Aversion! No, certainly not.'

'Or that you cannot love me? Then why not let us remain together? You argue that you do not yet know me well enough; will not that be the way to know me better?'

'If I were to travel with you now, Mr Bertram, it would be tantamount to accepting you. Your own sense will certainly tell you that. Were I to do so, I should give you the privilege of coming with me as my lover. Forgive me for saying that I cannot give you that privilege. I grieve to hurt your feelings for a day even; but I am sure you will ultimately approve of what I am doing.'

'And are we to meet no more, then?'

'Of course we shall meet again; at least, in all human probability. My guardian is your uncle.'

'I never even knew that till I met you the other day.'

'Because you have always been at school or at college; but you know it now. I, at least, shall look forward to meeting you—and so will my aunt.'

'Yes; as acquaintances. It would be impossible for me to meet you in that way. I hardly think you know or realize what my feelings to you are. I can only meet you to tell you again and again that I love you. You are so cold yourself that you cannot understand my—my—my impetuosity, if you choose to call it so.'

'In three or four months, Mr Bertram, you will be laughing at your own impetuosity—when I perhaps shall be grieving over my own coldness.' These last words she said with a smile in which there was much archness, and perhaps also a little encouragement.

'You will tell me at any rate that I may hope?'

'No; certainly not. You will hope enough for anything you really desire without my telling you. But I will not joke, as I believe that you are serious.'

'Oh, you believe so, do you?'

'Yes; I suppose I must believe so. Your declaration the other day took me very much by surprise. I had no conception that you had any feelings towards me of that sort. I certainly had entertained none such towards you. Love with me cannot be the birth of a moment. I cannot say that I will love merely because I am asked. You would not wish me to be false even in your own favour. We will part now, Mr Bertram; and being apart we shall better learn to know, each of us, how we value the other. On my part I can truly say that I hope we shall meet again—at any rate, as friends.' And then she held out her hand to him.

'Is this to be our farewell?' he said, without at once taking it.

'It shall be if you so please. We shall meet again only at the public table.'

'And you will not tell me that I may hope?'

'I will tell you nothing further, Mr Bertram. You will shake hands with me as with a friend, will you not?'

He then took her hand, and holding it in his own, gazed for a moment into her face. She bore the weight of his eyes with unabashed front. She showed neither anger nor pleasure; neither disdain nor pride; the same sweet smile was still upon her face, somewhat playful, somewhat hopeful, but capable of no definite construction either for making or marring a man's comfort.

'Caroline!' he said at last.

'Good-bye, Mr Bertram. I thoroughly hope you may enjoy your journey.'

'Caroline!'

She essayed to withdraw her hand from his. Feeling this, he raised it to his lips and kissed it, and then left the room. As he closed the door the same smile was on her face.

I hope it will be admitted that Miss Waddington had played her part with skill, and judgment, and good breeding; and not altogether heartlessly either. She had thought much on the subject since George had first thrown himself at her feet, and had concluded, putting the good against the bad, and balancing the affair as accurately as facts would enable her, that the match would be one which she ought to regard as desirable. There were two valid reasons, however, why she should not at once accept his offer. Firstly, he might not know his own mind, and it might be serviceable to him to have the option of renewing his proposal or retreating from it after a few months' trial of his own feelings. And secondly, she hardly knew her own mind. She could not in truth say yet whether she did love him, or whether she did not. She was rather inclined to think she did; but it would be well that she should try the matter before she committed herself.

The statement made by her aunt that George would doubtless be his uncle's heir certainly had its weight with her. It would be wrong in her to engage herself to a man who was without the means of maintaining her in that rank of life in which she had resolved to live; wrong both on his account and on her own. She felt that she could not be a good poor man's wife; it was not the walk of life for which she had destined herself. She had made up her mind on that point too, and having made it up was not weak enough to be driven from her resolve by any little gust of feeling. She did like Bertram—much, very much, better than she had ever liked any other man. He came up in many points to her idea of what a man should be. He was not sufficiently collected, not sufficiently thoughtful, and perhaps almost too enthusiastic: success in life would be easier to a man who put less heart into everything he said and did. But years would teach him much in this respect and she also might perhaps teach him something. She did like Bertram; and what objection could there be to the match, if, as appeared so probable, he was to inherit his uncle's money?

Prudent as she was, she was ready to run some risk in this respect. She did not wish to be a poor man's wife; but neither did she wish to be an idle man's wife. What she did desire was, that her husband should be an earnest, rising, successful man;—one whose name, as she had herself said to Bertram, might be frequent in men's mouths, and daily to be read in the columns of newspapers. She would not marry a fool, even though he were also a Crœsus; she would not marry a fool, even though he were also an earl. In choosing a master, her first necessity was that she should respect him, then that the world should do so also. She could respect talent—talent if needs be alone—but nothing without talent. The world's respect could not be had without wealth. As for love, that was necessary too; but it was only a third necessity.

Such being our heroine's mind about marriage, I make bold to say that she had behaved with skill and judgment, and not altogether heartlessly either.

On the following morning, Sir Lionel and George left Jerusalem together. The colonel had his own servant, as he always had; George was followed by the dragoman, who had now been with him for some time; and each had also an Arab groom. On quitting Jerusalem, Sir Lionel had made no objection to having the entire bill settled by his son.

'Well, George,' he had said with a smile, 'I know you are in ample funds, and I never am. You, moreover, have a milch cow that will not run dry. The government is my cow, and she is apt to be very chary in her supply; she does run dry with uncommon quickness.'

George smiled also, and paid the bill readily, protesting that of course he ought to do so, as Sir Lionel had come there only to see him. The colonel plumed himself at once upon having managed well; but he was greatly mistaken. His calculation in this respect had been made on a false basis. 'George,' he said to himself, 'is a young man; he will think nothing of this: a fellow at his age cares nothing for money.' George did care but little for the money, but he did care about his father; and he understood the ways of the world well enough to know that his father ought to have paid his own bill. He began for the first time to experience something of that feeling which his uncle so often expressed.

They started, too, with somewhat different ideas as to the purport of their route. Sir Lionel wished to get to Constantinople, and was content, for George's sake, to go by Damascus and Beyrout; but George had to visit Ramah, and Gibeon, and Luz; to see the well of the woman of Samaria at Sichem; to climb Mount Carmel, and to sleep at least for a night within its monastery. Mount Tabor also, and Bethsaida, and Capernaum, he must visit; he must bathe in the Sea of Galilee, as he had already bathed in Jordan and the Dead Sea; Gadara he must see, and Gergesa, and Chorazin; and, above all, he must stand with naked feet in Nazareth, and feel within his heart that he was resting on holy ground.

Sir Lionel did not care a straw for Bethsaida or Chorazin—not a straw even for Nazareth. For many reasons he wished to be well with his son. In the first place, a man whose bill is paid for him always makes some concession to the man who pays it. He should do so, at any rate; and on this point Sir Lionel was willing to be just. And then he had ulterior views, which made it very necessary that George should like him. In this respect he had hitherto played his cards well—well, with the exception of that Jerusalem bill. He had made his society very pleasant to his son, had done much towards gaining the young man's heart, and was well inclined to do more—anything, indeed, short of putting himself to real personal inconvenience. We may perhaps add, without doing too much violence to Sir Lionel's established character, that he himself really liked his son.

All this for some days carried him hither and thither, if not with patience, at any rate with perseverance. He went to spots which he was told had a world-wide celebrity, of the names of which he had but a bare distant remembrance, and which he found to be arid, comfortless, and uninteresting. Gibeon he did endure, and Shiloh, and Sichem; Gilgal, also, and Carmel. But there he broke down: he could not, he said, justify to himself to be absent longer from his official duties.

He found that he was near Beyrout: he could ride thither in two days, avoiding Damascus altogether. The cookery at Mount Carmel did not add to his love of the Holy Land. He found himself to be not very well. He laughingly reminded George that there was a difference between twenty-three and sixty; and ended by declining altogether to go backwards towards the Sea of Galilee. If George could only be induced to think that he had seen enough of these regions, his father would be so delighted to have his company direct from Beyrout to Constantinople!

George, however, was inexorable about Nazareth: and so they parted, agreeing that they would meet again at Constantinople. We need not closely follow either on his journey. Sir Lionel, having had everything paid for him up to the moment of their separation, arrived—let us hope with a full purse—at the Bosphorus. George, when left to himself, travelled more slowly, and thought much of these holy places—much also of his love. He could have found it in his heart to rush back, and catch Miss Baker and Caroline at Jaffa. He would have done so as soon as he quitted Nazareth, only that he was ashamed.

About a fortnight after his father's departure, he found himself at Damascus, and in another week, he was stepping on board the packet at Beyrout. When leaving Palestine, that land of such wondrous associations, his feelings were not altogether consolatory. He had at one moment acknowledged what he believed to be a spiritual influence within him, and yielding himself to it, had spoken of devoting his life to a high and holy purpose. He had, indeed, spoken only to himself, and the wound to his pride was therefore the less. But his high and holy purpose had been blown to the winds by a few words from a pair of ruby lips, by one glance of scorn from a pair of bright eyes. And he had so yielded, even though those lips would acknowledge no love for him; though those eyes would not look on him kindly. He could not be proud of his visit to the Holy Land; and yet he felt a longing to linger there. It might be, that if he would return once more to that mount, look once again on Sion and the temple, the spirit might yet get the better of the flesh. But, alas! he had to own to himself that he had now hardly a wish that the spirit should predominate. The things of the world were too bright to be given up. The charms of the flesh were too strong for him. With a sigh, he looked back for the last time from Mount Hermon, stretched out his arms once more towards Jerusalem, said one farewell in his heart as his eye rested for a moment on the distant glassy waters of Galilee, and then set his horse's head towards Damascus.

When a traveller in these railroad days takes leave of Florence, or Vienna, or Munich, or Lucerne, he does so without much of the bitterness of a farewell. The places are now comparatively so near that he expects to see them again, or at any rate, hopes that he may do so. But Jerusalem is still distant from us no Sabbath-day's journey. A man who, having seen it once, takes his leave, then sees it probably for the last time. And a man's heart must be very cold who can think of Palestine exactly as of any other land. It is not therefore surprising that Bertram was rather sad as he rode down the further side of Mount Hermon.

At Constantinople, Sir Lionel and George again met, and our hero spent a pleasant month there with his father. It was still spring, the summer heats had hardly commenced, and George was charmed, if not with the city of the Sultan, at any rate with the scenery around it. Here his father appeared in a new light: they were more intimate with each other than they had been at Jerusalem; they were not now living in ladies' society, and Sir Lionel by degrees threw off what little restraint of governorship, what small amount of parental authority he had hitherto assumed. He seemed anxious to live with his son on terms of perfect equality; began to talk to him rather as young men talk to each other than men of ages so very different, and appeared to court a lack of reverence.

In his ordinary habits of life, and, indeed, in his physical vivacity, Sir Lionel was very young for his time of life. He never pleaded his years in bar of any pleasure, and never pleaded them at all except when desirous of an excuse for escaping something that was disagreeable. There are subjects on which young men talk freely with each other, but on which they hesitate to speak to their elders without restraint. Sir Lionel did his best to banish any such feeling on the part of his son. Of wine and women, of cards and horses, of money comforts and money discomforts, he spoke in a manner which Bertram at first did not like, but which after awhile was not distasteful to him. There is always some compliment implied when an old man unbends before a young one, and it is this which makes the viciousness of old men so dangerous. I do not say that Sir Lionel purposely tempted his son to vice; but he plainly showed that he regarded morality in a man to be as thoroughly the peculiar attribute of a clergyman as a black coat; and that there could be no reason for other men even to pretend to it when there were no women by to be respected and deceived.

Bertram certainly liked his father, and was at ease in his company; but, in spite of this, he was ashamed of him, and was sometimes very sorrowful. He was young, full of vivacity, and without that strength of character which should have withstood the charm of Sir Lionel's manner; but he knew well that he would fain have had in his father feelings of a very different nature, and he could not but acknowledge that the severity of his uncle's tone was deserved.

It had been George's intention to stay a week only at Constantinople, but his father had persuaded him to remain four. He had boasted that when he returned to England he would be in a position to give back to his uncle the three hundred pounds which Pritchett had placed to his account. But he would not now be able to do this: his father lived expensively; and even here, where Sir Lionel was now at home, George paid more than his own share of the expense.

One of their chief subjects of conversation, that, indeed, which Sir Lionel seemed to prefer to any other, was the ultimate disposal of his brother's money. He perceived that George's thoughts on this subject were by far too transcendental, that he was childishly indifferent to his own interests, and that if not brought to a keener sense of his own rights, a stronger feeling as to his position as the only nephew of a very wealthy man, he might let slip through his fingers a magnificent fortune which was absolutely within his reach. So thinking, he detained his son near him for awhile, that he might, if possible, imbue him with some spark of worldly wisdom.

He knew how useless it would be to lecture a young man like George as to the best way in which he could play tuft-hunter to his uncle. From such lectures George would have started away in disgust; but something, Sir Lionel thought, might be done by tact, by *finesse*, and a daily half-scornful badinage, skilfully directed towards the proper subject. By degrees, too, he thought that George did listen to him, that he was learning, that he might be taught to set his eyes greedily on those mountains of wealth. And so Sir Lionel persevered with diligence to the end.

'Say everything that is civil from me to my brother,' said the colonel, the day before George left him.

'Uncle George does not care much for civil speeches,' said the other, laughing.

'No, I know he does not; he'd think more of it if I could send home a remittance by you to pay the bill; eh, George? But as I can't do that, I may as well send a few civil words.' Uncle George's bill had gradually become a source of joke between the father and son. Sir Lionel, at least, was accustomed to mention it in such a way that the junior George could not help laughing; and though at first this had gone against the grain of his feelings, by degrees he had become used to it.

'He expects, I fancy, neither money nor civil words,' said George the younger.

'He will not, on that account, be the less pleased at getting either the one or the other. Don't you believe everything that everybody tells you in his own praise: when a man says that he does not like flattery, and that he puts no value on soft words, do not on that account be deterred from making any civil speeches you may have ready. He will not be a bit stronger than another because he boasts of his strength.'

'I really think you would find it difficult to flatter your brother.'

'Perhaps so; and therefore I should set about it with the more care. But, were I in your shoes, I should not attempt flattery; I should be very submissive rather. He always loved to play the tyrant.'

'And I do not love to play the slave.'

'An only nephew's slavery would probably be of a very mild description.'

'Yes; no harder than sitting on a clerk's stool in a merchant's counting-house for seven or eight hours a day.'

'That would be an unendurable bore as a continuance; but take my word for it, George, if you could bring yourself to do it for six months, by the end of that time you would have the game in your own hands.'

'At any rate, I shall not try it, sir.'

'Well, you are your own master: I can only say that the temptation would be too strong for most men. I have not the slightest doubt that if you would give way to him for six months, two years would see you in Parliament.' Sir Lionel had already ascertained that to sit in the House of Commons was the dearest object of his son's ambition.

On the evening of that day, as they were drinking their coffee and smoking together, Sir Lionel for the first time spoke to his son on another matter. 'George,' said he, 'I don't know whether there was anything in it, but when we were at Jerusalem, I thought you were very sweet on Caroline Waddington.'

George blushed deeply, and affected to laugh.

'She was certainly a very fine girl,' continued his father; 'I think as handsome a girl as I have seen these ten years. What a shoulder and neck she had! When you used to be dragging her up the Mount of Olives, I could not but think there was more in it than mere scripture geography—eh, George?'

George merely laughed, and looked rather like a simpleton.

'If you were not in love with her, I can only say that you ought to have been. I was, I know.'

'Well, sir, I believe she is free as yet; you can try your chance if you have a mind.'

'Ah! I would I could. If I knew Medea's secret,* I would have myself chopped and boiled that I might come out young on her behalf; but, George, I can tell you something about her.'

'Well, sir!'

'I would have told you then, when we were at Jerusalem,

but we were not so well acquainted then as we are now, and I did not like to interfere.'

'It could not be interference from you.'

'Well, but the matter is this: if my brother ever loved any human being—and I am not quite sure he ever did—but if he did, it was that girl's father. Had Waddington lived, he would now have been my age. Your uncle took him early by the hand, and would have made his fortune for him, but the poor fellow died. In my opinion, it would assist your views if your uncle knew that you were going to marry Caroline Waddington.'

George said nothing, but sat sucking the mouth-piece of his pipe-stick and blowing out great clouds of smoke. Sir Lionel said nothing further, but easily changed the conversation. Early on the following morning, Bertram left Constantinople, having received a promise that Sir Lionel would visit him in England as soon as the exigencies of the public service would permit of his doing so.

CHAPTER XII

GEORGE BERTRAM DECIDES IN FAVOUR OF THE BAR

GEORGE BERTRAM did not return directly to England. Since he had been in Turkey, he had made arrangement by letter with his friend Harcourt to meet him in the Tyrol, and to travel home with him through Switzerland. It was about the middle of June when he left Constantinople, and Harcourt was to be at Innspruck on the 5th August. George might therefore well have remained a week or two longer with his father had either of them so wished; but neither of them did wish it. The living at Constantinople was dear, and George's funds would not stand much more of it; and Sir Lionel, free and easy as he was, still felt his son's presence of some impediment—perhaps in the way of his business, perhaps in the way of his pleasures.

From Constantinople Bertram went up across the Balkan to the Danube, and thence through Bucharest into Transylvania, travelling, as in those days was necessary, somewhat by permission of the Russian authorities. He then again struck the Danube at Pesth; remained some little time there; again a week or so at Vienna; from thence he visited Saltzburg, and exactly on the appointed day shook hands with his friend in the hall of the old 'Golden Sun' at Innspruck.

At first, on leaving his father, George was very glad to be once more alone. Men delighted him not; nor women either* at that moment—seeing that his thoughts were running on Caroline Waddington, and that her presence was not to be had. But by the time that he found himself in the Tyrol, he was delighted once more to have a companion. He had of course picked up Englishmen, and been picked up by them at every town he had passed; one always does; some ladies also he had casually encountered—but he had met with no second Caroline. While wandering about the mountains of Transylvania, he had been quite contented to be alone: at Pesth he had not ceased to congratulate himself on his solitude, though sometimes he found the day a little too long for his purpose in doing so; at Vienna he was glad enough to find an old Oxonian; though, even while enjoying the treat, he would occasionally say to himself that, after all, society was only a bore. But by the time he had done the Saltzburg country, he was heartily sick of himself, somewhat sick also of thinking of his love, and fully able to re-echo all that Harcourt had to say in praise of some very fine old wine which that fastidious gentleman caused to be produced for them from the cellars of the 'Golden Sun.'

Innspruck is a beautiful little town. Perhaps no town in Europe can boast a site more exquisitely picturesque. Edinburgh would be equal to it, if it had a river instead of a railroad running through its valley and under its Castle-hill. But we sojourned too long in the Holy Land to permit of our dwelling even for half a chapter in the Tyrol. George, however, and his friend remained there for a fortnight. They went over the Brenner and looked down into Italy; made an excursion to those singular golden-tinted mountains, the

Dolomites, among which live a race of men who speak neither German nor Italian, nor other language known among the hundred dialects of Europe, but a patois left to them from the ancient Latins; they wandered through the valleys of the Inn and its tributaries, and wondered at the odd way of living which still prevails in their picturesque castellated mansions.

For awhile Bertram thought that Harcourt was the best companion in the world. He was agreeable and easy-tempered as his father; and was at the same time an educated man, which his father certainly was not. Harcourt, though he put his happiness in material things perhaps quite as much as did Sir Lionel, required that his material things should be of a high flavour. He was a reading man, addicted, in a certain cynical, carping sort of way, even to poetry, was a critic almost by profession, loved pictures, professed to love scenery, certainly loved to watch and scrutinize the different classes of his brother-men. He was gifted pre-eminently with a lawyer's mind, but it was not a lawyer's mind of a vulgar quality. He, too, loved riches, and looked on success in the world as a man's chief, nay, perhaps his only aim; but for him it was necessary that success should be polished. Sir Lionel wanted money that he might swallow it and consume it, as a shark does its prey; but, like sharks in general, he had always been hungry,—had never had his bellyful of money. Harcourt's desire for money was of a different class. It would not suit him to be in debt to any one. A good balance at his banker's was a thing dear to his soul. He aimed at perfect respectability, and also at perfect independence.

For awhile, therefore, Harcourt's teaching was a great improvement on Sir Lionel's, and was felt to be so. He preached a love of good things; but the good things were to be corollaries only to good work. Sir Lionel's summum bonum would have been an unexpected pocketful of money, three months of idleness in which to spend it, and pleasant companions for the time, who should be at any rate as well provided in pocket as himself. Harcourt would have required something more. The world's respect and esteem were as necessary to him as the world's pleasures.

But nevertheless, after a time, Harcourt's morality offended

Bertram, as Bertram's transcendentalism offended Harcourt. They admired the same view, but they could not look at it through the same coloured glass.

'And so on the whole you liked your governor?' said Harcourt to him one day as they were walking across a mountain-range from one valley to another.

'Yes, indeed.'

'One is apt to be prejudiced in one's father's favour, of course,' said Harcourt. 'That is to say, when one hasn't seen him for twenty years or so. A more common, constant knowledge, perhaps, puts the prejudice the other way.'

'Sir Lionel is undoubtedly a very pleasant man; no one, I fancy, could help liking his society.'

'I understand it all as well as though you had written a book about him. You have none of that great art, Bertram, which teaches a man to use his speech to conceal his thoughts.'

'Why should I wish to conceal my thoughts from you?'

'I know exactly what you mean about your father: he is no martinet in society, even with his son. He assumes to himself no mysterious, unintelligible dignity. He has none of the military Grimgruffenuff about him. He takes things easily, and allows other people to do the same.'

'Exactly.'

'But this was not exactly what you wanted. If he had treated you as though a father and son were necessarily of a different order of beings, had he been a little less familiar, a little colder, perhaps a thought more stern and forbidding in his parental way of pushing the bottle to you, you would have liked him better?'

'No, not have liked him better; I might perhaps have thought it more natural.'

'Just so; you went to look for a papa with a boy's feelings, and the papa, who had not been looking for you at all, took you for a man as you are when he found you.'

'I am sure of this at any rate, that he was delighted to see me.'

'I am sure he was, and proud of you when he did see you. I never supposed but that the gallant colonel had some feelings in his bowels. Have you made any arrangements with him about money?'

'No—none.'

'Said not a word about so mundane a subject?'

'I don't say that; it is only natural that we should have said something. But as to income, he fights his battle, and I fight mine.'

'He should now have a large income from his profession.'

'And large expenses. I suppose there is no dearer place in Europe than Constantinople.'

'All places are dear to an Englishman exactly in comparison as he knows, or does not know, the ways of a place. A Turk, I have no doubt, could live there in a very genteel sort of manner on what you would consider a moderate pittance.'

'I suppose he could.'

'And Sir Lionel by this time should be a Turk in Turkey, a Greek in Greece, or a Persian in Bagdad.'

'Perhaps he is. But I was not. I know I shall be very fairly cleared out by the time I get to London; and yet I had expected to have three hundred pounds untouched there.'

'Such expectations always fall to the ground—always. Every quarter I allow myself exactly what I shall want, and then I double it for emergencies.'

'You are a lucky fellow to have the power to do so.'

'Yes, but then I put my quarterly wants at a *very* low figure; a figure that would be quite unsuitable—quite unintelligible to the nephew of a Crœsus.'

'The nephew of a Crœsus will have to put his quarterly wants at something about fifty pounds, as far as I can see.'

'My dear fellow, when I observe that water bubbles up from a certain spot every winter and every spring, and occasionally in the warm weather too, I never think that it has run altogether dry because it may for a while cease to bubble up under the blazing sun of August. Nature, of whose laws I know so much, tells me that the water will come again.'

'Yes, water will run in its natural course. But when you have been supplied by an artificial pipe, and have cut that off, it is probable that you may run short.'

'In such case I would say, that having a due regard to

prudence, I would not cut off that very convenient artificial pipe.'

'One may pay too dear, Harcourt, even for one's water.'

'As far as I am able to judge, you have had yours without paying for it at all; and if you lose it, it will only be by your own obstinacy. I would I had such an uncle to deal with.'

'I would you had; as for me, I tell you fairly, I do not mean to deal with him at all.'

'I would I had; I should know then that everything was open to me. Now I have everything to do for myself. I do not despair, however. As for you, the ball is at your foot.'

They talked very freely with each other as to their future hopes and future destinies. Harcourt seemed to take it as a settled matter that Bertram should enter himself at the bar, and Bertram did not any longer contradict him. Since he had learnt Miss Waddington's ideas on the subject, he expressed no further desire to go into the church, and had, in fact, nothing serious to say in favour of any of those other professions of which he had sometimes been accustomed to speak. There was nothing but the bar left for him; and therefore when Harcourt at last asked him the question plainly, he said that he supposed that such would be his fate.

But on one subject Bertram did not speak openly to his friend. He said not a word to him about Caroline. Harcourt was in many respects an excellent friend; but he had hardly that softness of heart, or that softness of expression which tempts one man to make another a confidant in an affair of love. If Harcourt had any such affairs himself, he said nothing of them to Bertram, and at the present time Bertram said nothing on the subject to him. He kept that care deep in his own bosom. He had as yet neither spoken a word nor written a word concerning it to any one; and even when his friend had once casually asked whether he had met much in the way of beauty in Jerusalem, he had felt himself to wince as though the subject were too painful to be spoken of.

They reached London about the middle of October, and Harcourt declared that he must immediately put himself again into harness. 'Ten weeks of idleness,' said he, 'is more than a man can well afford who has to look to himself for everything; and I have now given myself eleven.'

'And what are you going to do?'

'Do! work all day and read all night. Take notice of all the dullest cases I can come across, and read the most ponderous volumes that have been written on the delightful subject of law. A sucking barrister who means to earn his bread has something to do—as you will soon know.'

Bertram soon learnt—now for the first time, for Harcourt himself had said nothing on the subject—that his friend's name was already favourably known, and that he had begun that career to which he so steadily looked forward. His ice was already broken: he had been employed as junior counsel in the great case of Pike *v.* Perch; and had distinguished himself not a little by his success in turning white into black.

'Then you had decidedly the worst of it?' said Bertram to him, when the matter was talked over between them.

'Oh, decidedly; but, nevertheless, we pulled through. My opinion all along was that none of the Pikes had a leg to stand upon. There were three of them. But I won't bore you with the case. You'll hear more of it some day, for it will be on again before the lords-justices in the spring.'

'You were Pike's counsel?'

'One of them—the junior. I had most of the fag and none of the honour. That's of course.'

'And you think that Perch ought to have succeeded?'

'Well, talking to you, I really think he ought; but I would not admit that to any one else. Sir Ricketty Giggs led for us, and I know he thought so too at first; though he got so carried away by his own eloquence at last that I believe he changed his mind.'

'Well, if I'd thought that, I wouldn't have held the brief for all the Pikes that ever swam.'

'If a man's case be weak, then, he is to have no advocate? That's your idea of justice.'

'If it be so weak that no one can be got to think it right, of course he should have no advocate.'

'And how are you to know till you have taken the matter up and sifted it? But what you propose is Quixotic in every way. It will not hold water for a moment. You know as well as I do that no barrister would keep a wig on his head who pretended to such a code of morals in his profession. Such a doctrine is a doctrine of puritanism—or purism, which is worse. All this moonshine was very well for you when you talked of being a clergyman, or an author, or a painter. One allows outsiders any amount of nonsense in their criticisms, as a matter of course. But it won't do now, Bertram. If you mean to put your shoulders to the wheel in the only profession which, to my mind, is worthy of an educated man's energies, you must get rid of those cobwebs.'

'Upon my word, Harcourt, when you hit on a subject you like, your eloquence is wonderful. Sir Ricketty Giggs himself could hardly say more to defend his sins of forty years' endurance.'

Harcourt had spoken in earnest. Such milk-and-water, unpractical scruples were disgusting to his very soul. In thinking of them to himself, he would call them unmanly! What! was such a fellow as Bertram, a boy just fresh from college, to animadvert upon and condemn the practice of the whole bar of England? He had, too, a conviction, clearly fixed in his own mind, though he could hardly explain the grounds of it in words, that in the long run the cause of justice would be better served by the present practice of allowing wrong and right to fight on equal terms; by giving to wrong the same privilege that is given to right; by giving to wrong even a wider privilege, seeing that, being in itself necessarily weak, it needs the more protection. He would declare that you were trampling on the fallen if you told him that wrong could be entitled to no privilege, no protection whatever—to no protection, till it was admitted by itself, admitted by all, to be wrong.

Bertram had now to establish himself in London; and he was also, as he thought, under the necessity of seeing two persons, his uncle and Miss Waddington. He could not settle himself well to work before he had done both. One preliminary business he did settle for himself, in order that his uncle, when he saw him, might know that his choice for the bar was made up and past recalling. He selected that great and enduring Chancery barrister, Mr Neversaye Die, as the

Gamaliel* at whose feet he would sit; as the fountain from whence he would draw the coming waters of his own eloquence; as the instructor of his legal infancy and guide of his legal youth. Harcourt was at the Common Law bar, and therefore he recommended the other branch of the profession to his friend. 'The Common Law,' said he, 'may have the most dash about it; but Chancery has the substance.' George, after thinking over the matter for some days, gave it as his opinion that Chancery barristers were rogues of a dye somewhat less black than the others, and that he would select to be a rogue of that colour. The matter was therefore so settled.

His first step, then, was to see his uncle. He told himself—and as he thought, truly—that his doing so was a duty, disagreeable in all respects, to be attended with no pecuniary results, but necessary to be performed. In truth, however, the teaching of Sir Lionel and Harcourt had not been altogether without effect: at this present moment, having just paid to Mr Neversaye Die his first yearly contribution, he was well-nigh penniless; and, after all, if a rich uncle have money to bestow, why should he not bestow it on a nephew? Money, at any rate, was not in itself deleterious. So much George was already prepared to allow.

He therefore called on his uncle in the City. 'Ha! George—what; you're back, are you? Well, come and dine at Hadley tomorrow. I must be at the Bank before three. Good-bye, my boy.'

This was all his uncle said to him at their first meeting. Then he saw Mr Pritchett for a moment.

'Oh, Mr George, I am glad to see you back, sir; very glad indeed, sir. I hear you have been to very foreign parts. I hope you have always found the money right, Mr George?'

Mr George, shaking hands with him, warmly assured him that the money had always been quite right—as long as it lasted.

'A little does not go a long way, I'm sure, in those very foreign parts,' said Mr Pritchett, oracularly. 'But, Mr George, why didn't you write, eh, Mr George?'

'You don't mean to say that my uncle expected to hear from me?'

'He asked very often whether I had any tidings. Ah! Mr George, you don't know an old man's ways yet. It would have been better for you to have been led by me. And so you have seen Mr Lionel—Sir Lionel, I should say now. I hope Sir Lionel is quite well.'

George told him that he had found his father in excellent health, and was going away, when Mr Pritchett asked another question, or rather made another observation. 'And so you saw Miss Waddington, did you, Mr George?'

Bertram felt that there was that in his countenance which might again betray him; but he managed to turn away his face as he said, 'Yes, I did meet her, quite by chance, at Jerusalem.'

'At Jerusalem!' said Mr Pritchett, with such a look of surprise, with such an awe-struck tone, as might have suited some acquaintance of Æneas's,* on hearing that gentleman tell how he had travelled beyond the Styx.* Mr Pritchett was rather fat and wheezy, and the effort made him sigh gently for the next two minutes.

Bertram had put on his hat and was going, when Mr Pritchett, recovering himself, asked yet a further question. 'And what did you think of Miss Waddington, sir?'

'Think of her!' said George.

'A very beautiful young lady; isn't she? and clever, too. I knew her father well, Mr George—very well. Isn't she a very handsome young lady? Ah, well! she hasn't money enough, Mr George; that's the fact; that's the fact. But'—and Mr Pritchett whispered as he continued—'the old gentleman might make it more, Mr George.'

Mr Pritchett had a somewhat melancholy way of speaking of everything. It was more in his tone than in his words. And this tone, which was all but sepulchral, was perhaps owing rather to a short neck and an asthmatic tendency than to any real sorrow or natural lowness of spirits. Those who saw Mr Pritchett often probably remembered this, and counted on it; but with George there was always a graveyard touch about these little interviews. He could not, therefore, but have some melancholy presentiment when he heard Miss Waddington spoken of in such a tone.

On the following day he went down to Hadley, and, as was customary there, found that he was to spend the evening *tête-à-tête* with his uncle. Nothing seemed changed since he had left it: his uncle came in just before dinner, and poked the fire exactly as he had done on the last visit George had paid him after a long absence. 'Come, John, we're three minutes late! why don't we have dinner?' He asked no question—at least, not at first—either about Sir Lionel or about Jerusalem, and seemed resolute to give the traveller none of that *éclat*, to pay to his adventures none of that deferential awe which had been so well expressed by Mr Pritchett in two words.

But Mr Bertram, though he always began so coldly, did usually improve after a few hours. His tone would gradually become less cynical and harsh; his words would come out more freely; and he would appear somewhat less anxious to wound the *amour propre* of his companion.

'Are you much wiser for your travels, George?' he said at last, when John had taken away the dinner, and they were left alone with a bottle of port-wine between them. This, too, was asked in a very cynical tone, but still there was some improvement in the very fact of his deigning to allude to the journey.

'Yes, I think I am rather wiser.'

'Well, I'm glad of that. As you have lost a year in your profession, it is well that you should have gained something. Has your accession of wisdom been very extensive?'

'Somewhat short of Solomon's, sir; but probably quite as much as I should have picked up had I remained in London.'

'That is very probable. I suppose you have not the slightest idea how much it cost you. Indeed, that would be a very vulgar way of looking at it.'

'Thanks to your unexpected kindness, I have not been driven to any very close economy.'

'Ah! that was Pritchett's doing. He seemed afraid that the land would not flow with milk and honey unless your pocket was fairly provided. But of course it's your own affair, George. It is money borrowed; that's all.'

George did not quite understand what this meant, and remained silent; but at one moment it was almost on his tongue to say that it ought at least to be admitted that the borrower had not been very pressing in his application.

'And I suppose you have come back empty?' continued his uncle.

George then explained exactly how he stood with regard to money, saying how he had put himself into the hands of Mr Neversaye Die, how he had taken chambers in the Middle Temple, and how a volume of Blackstone was already lying open in his dingy sitting-room.

'Very well, very well. I have no objection whatever. You will perhaps make nothing at the bar, and certainly never the half what you would have done with Messrs Dry and Stickatit. But that's your affair. The bar is thoroughly respectable. By-the-by, is your father satisfied with it as a profession?' This was the first allusion that Mr Bertram had made to his brother.

'Perfectly so,' said George.

'Because of course you were bound to consult him.' If this was intended for irony, it was so well masked that George was not able to be sure of it.

'I did consult him, sir,' said George, turning red in accordance with that inveterate and stupid habit of his.

'That was right. And did you consult him about another thing? did you ask him what you were to live on till such time as you could earn your own bread?'

In answer to this George was obliged to own that he did not. 'There was no necessity,' said he, 'for he knows that I have my fellowship.'

'Oh! ah! yes; and that of course relieves him of any further cause for anxiety in the matter. I forgot that.'

'Uncle George, you are always very hard on my father; much too hard.'

'Am I?'

'I think you are. As regards his duty to me, if I do not complain, you need not.'

'Oh! that is it, is it? I did think that up to this, his remissness in doing his duty as a father had fallen rather on my shoulders than on yours. But I suppose I have been mistaken; eh?'

'At any rate, if you have to complain, your complaint should be made to him, not to me.'

'But you see I have not time to run across the world to Jerusalem; and were I to do so, the chances are ten to one I should not catch him. If you will ask Pritchett, too, you will find that your father is not the best correspondent in the world. Perhaps he has sent back by you some answer to Pritchett's half-yearly letters?'

'He has sent nothing by me.'

'I'll warrant he has not. But come, George, own the truth. Did he borrow money from you when he saw you? If he did not, he showed a very low opinion of your finances and my liberality.'

George might have declared, without any absolute falseness, that his father had borrowed no money of him. But he had not patience at the present moment to distinguish between what would be false and what not false in defending his father's character. He could not but feel that his father had behaved very shabbily to him, and that Sir Lionel's conduct could not be defended in detail. But he also felt that his uncle was quite unjustifiable in wounding him by such attacks. It was not to him that Mr Bertram should have complained of Sir Lionel's remissness in money matters. He resolved that he would not sit by and hear his father so spoken of; and, therefore, utterly disregardful of what might be the terrible ill effects of his uncle's anger, he thus spoke out in a tone not of the meekest:—

'I will neither defend my father, Mr Bertram; nor will I sit still and hear him so spoken of. How far you may have just ground of complaint against him, I do not know, nor will I inquire. He is my father, and that should protect his name in my presence.'

'Hoity, toity!'

'I will ask you to hear me if you please, sir. I have received very many good offices from you, for which I heartily thank you. I am aware that I owe to you all my education and support up to this time. This debt I fear I can never pay.'

'And therefore, like some other people, you are inclined to resent it.'

'No, by heaven! I would resent nothing said by you to myself; but I will not sit by and hear my father ill spoken of. I will not—no; not for all the money which you could give or leave me. It seems to me that what I spend of your money is added up as a debt against my father—'

'Pray don't imagine, my boy, that that is any burden to him.'

'It is a burden to me, and I will endure it no longer. While at school, I knew nothing of these things, and not much while I was at college. Now I do know something, and feel something. If you please, sir, I will renounce any further assistance from you whatever; and beg, in return, that you will say nothing further to me as to any quarrel there may be between you and Sir Lionel.'

'Quarrel!' said his uncle, getting up and standing with his back to the fire. 'He has not spirit enough to quarrel with me.'

'Well, I have,' said George, who was walking about the room; and from the fire in his eyes, it certainly appeared that he spoke the truth in this respect.

'I know the bitterness of your spirit against your brother,' continued George; 'but your feelings should teach you not to show it before his son.'

Mr Bertram was still standing with his hands in his pockets, leaning against the mantelpiece, with his coat-tails over his arms. He said nothing further at once, but continued to fix his eyes on his nephew, who was now walking backwards and forwards from one end of the room to the other with great vehemence. 'I think,' at last said George, 'that it will be better that I should go back to town. Good-night, sir.'

'You are an ass,' said his uncle.

'Very likely,' said George. 'But asses will kick sometimes.'

'And bray too,' said his uncle.

There was a certain spirit about them both which made it difficult for either altogether to get the better of the other.

'That I may bray no more in your hearing, I will wish you good-night.' And again he held out his hand to the old man.

His uncle took hold of his hand, but he did not go through

the process of shaking it, nor did he at once let it go again. He held it there for a time, looked steadfastly into his nephew's face, and then he dropped it. 'You had better sit down and drink your wine,' he said at last.

'I had rather return to town,' said George stoutly.

'And I had rather you stayed here,' said his uncle, in a tone of voice that for him was good-humoured. 'Come, you need not be in a pet, like a child. Stay where you are now, and if you don't like to come again, why you can stay away.'

As this was said in the manner of a request, George did again sit down. 'It will be foolish to make a fuss about it,' said he to himself; 'and what he says is true. I need not come again, and I will not.' So he sat down and again sipped his wine.

'So you saw Caroline at Jerusalem?' said the old man, after a pause of about twenty minutes.

'Yes, I met her with Miss Baker. But who told you?'

'Who told me? Why, Miss Baker, of course. They were both here for a week after their return.'

'Here in this house?'

'Why shouldn't they be here in this house? Miss Baker is usually here three or four times every year.'

'Is she?' said George, quite startled by the information. Why on earth had Miss Baker not told him of this?

'And what did you think of Caroline?' asked Mr Bertram.

'Think of her?' said George.

'Perhaps you did not think anything about her at all. If so, I shall be delighted to punish her vanity by telling her so. She had thought a great deal about you; or, at any rate, she talked as though she had.'

This surprised George a great deal, and almost made him forgive his uncle the injury he had received. 'Oh, yes, I did think of her,' said he. 'I thought of her a little at least.'

'Oh, a little!'

'Well, I mean as much as one does generally think of people one meets—perhaps rather more than of others. She is very handsome and clever, and what I saw of her I liked.'

'She is a favourite of mine—very much so. Only that you are too young, and have not as yet a shilling to depend on, she might have done for a wife for you.'

And so saying, he drew the candles to him, took up his newspaper, and was very soon fast asleep.

George said nothing further that night to his uncle about Caroline, but he sat longing that the old man might again broach the subject. He was almost angry with himself for not having told his uncle the whole truth; but then he reflected that Caroline had not yet acknowledged that she felt anything like affection for him; and he said to himself, over and over again, that he was sure she would not marry him without loving him for all the rich uncles in Christendom; and yet it was a singular coincidence that he and his uncle should have thought of the same marriage.

The next morning he was again more surprised. On coming down to the breakfast-parlour, he found his uncle there before him, walking up and down the room with his hands behind his back. As soon as George had entered, his uncle stopped his walk, and bade him shut the door.

'George,' said he, 'perhaps you are not very often right, either in what you do or what you say; but last night you were right.'

'Sir!'

'Yes, last night you were right. Whatever may have been your father's conduct, you were right to defend it; and, bad as it has been, I was wrong to speak of it as it deserved before you. I will not do so again.'

'Thank you, sir,' said George, his eyes almost full of tears.

'That is what I suppose the people in the army call an ample apology. Perhaps, however, it may be made a little more ample.'

'Sir, sir,' said George, not quite understanding him; 'pray do not say anything more.'

'No, I won't, for I have got nothing more to say; only this: Pritchett wants to see you. Be with him at three o'clock today.'

At three o'clock Bertram was with Pritchett, and learned from that gentleman, in the most frozen tone of which he was capable, and with sundry little, good-humoured, asthmatic chuckles, that he had been desired to make arrangements for paying to Mr George regularly an income of two hundred a year, to be paid in the way of annuity till Mr Bertram's death, and to be represented by an adequate sum in the funds whenever that much-to-be-lamented event should take place.

'To be sure, sir,' said Pritchett, 'two hundred a year is nothing for you, Mr George; but—'

But two hundred a year was a great deal to George. That morning he had been very much puzzled to think how he was to keep himself going till he might be able to open the small end of the law's golden eggs.

CHAPTER XIII

LITTLEBATH

I ABHOR a mystery. I would fain, were it possible, have my tale run through from its little prologue to the customary marriage in its last chapter, with all the smoothness incidental to ordinary life. I have no ambition to surprise my reader. Castles with unknown passages are not compatible with my homely muse. I would as lief have to do with a giant in my book—a real giant, such as Goliath—as with a murdering monk* with a scowling eye. The age for such delights is, I think, gone. We may say historically of Mrs Radcliffe's time* that there were mysterious sorrows in those days. They are now as much out of date as are the giants.

I would wish that a serene gratification might flow from my pages, unsullied by a single start. Now I am aware that there is that in the last chapter which appears to offend against the spirit of calm recital which I profess. People will begin to think that they are to be kept in the dark as to who is who; that it is intended that their interest in the novel shall depend partly on a guess. I would wish to have no guessing, and therefore I at once proceed to tell all about it.

Miss Caroline Waddington was the grand-daughter of old Mr George Bertram; and was, therefore, speaking with absolute technical propriety, the first-cousin once removed of her lover, young Mr George Bertram—a degree of relationship which happily admits of love and matrimony.

Old Mr Bertram has once or twice been alluded to as a bachelor; and most of those who were best acquainted with him had no doubt of his being so. To you, my reader, is permitted the great privilege of knowing that he was married very early in life. He, doubtless, had his reasons for keeping this matter a secret at the time, and the very early death of his wife saved him from the necessity of much talking about it afterwards. His wife had died in giving birth to a daughter, but the child had survived. There was then living a sister of Mrs Bertram's, who had been married some few years to a Mr Baker, and the infant was received into this family, of which our friend Miss Baker was a child. Miss Baker was therefore a niece, by marriage, of Mr Bertram. In this family, Caroline Bertram was educated, and she and Mary Baker were brought up together as sisters. During this time Mr Bertram did his duty by his daughter as regards money, as far as his means then went, and was known in that family to be her father; but elsewhere he was not so known. The Bakers lived in France, and the fact of his having any such domestic tie was not suspected among his acquaintance in England.

In the course of time his daughter married one Mr Waddington, hardly with the full consent of the Bakers, for Mr Waddington's means were small—but not decidedly in opposition to it; nor had the marriage been opposed by Mr Bertram. He of course was asked to assist in supplying money for the young couple. This he refused to give; but he offered to Mr Waddington occupation by which an income could be earned. Mr Waddington wisely acceded to his views, and, had he lived, would doubtless have lived to become a rich man. He died, however, within four years of his marriage, and it so fell out that his wife did not survive him above a year or two.

Of this marriage, Caroline Waddington, our heroine, was the sole offspring. Mr Waddington's commercial enterprises had not caused him to live in London, though he had been required to be there frequently. Mr Bertram had, therefore, seen more of him than of his own daughter. The infant had been born in the house of the Bakers, and there she was brought up. As an orphan of four years old, she had come under the care of Mary Baker, and under her care she remained. Miss Baker was therefore not in truth her aunt. What was their exact relationship I leave as a calculation to those conversant with the mysteries of genealogy. I believe myself that she was almost as nearly connected with her lover.

When Mr Waddington and his daughter were both dead, Mr Bertram felt himself to be altogether relieved from family ties. He was not yet an old man, being then about fifty-five; but he was a very rich man. It was of course considered that he would provide liberally for his grandchild. But when asked to do so by Miss Baker, he had replied that she was provided for; that he had enabled the child's father to leave behind him four thousand pounds, which for a girl was a provision sufficiently liberal; that he would not give rise to false hopes that she would be his heiress; but that if his niece, Mary Baker, would take the charge of her, he would allow an income for the purpose. This he had done with sufficient liberality.

All that is mysterious has now, I believe, been unravelled, and we may go back to our story. Of Mr Pritchett, we should perhaps say a word. He had been habituated in his sundry money dealings to look on Miss Baker as his patron's niece, and had always called her as such. Indeed, the connection had been so far back that he usually styled her Miss Mary. But he did not know, nor—though he was very suspicious on the matter—did he quite suspect what was the truth as to Miss Waddington. She was niece to his patron's niece; he knew no more than that, excepting, of course, that she was the daughter of Mr Waddington, and that she was mistress in her own right of four thousand pounds.

Mr Pritchett was very anxious about his patron's wealth. Here was Mr Bertram turned seventy years of age—Mr Pritchett himself was sixty-six—and no one knew who was to be his heir. As far as he, Mr Pritchett, was aware, he had no heir. Mr George would naturally be so—so thought Mr Pritchett; and the old man's apparent anxiety respecting his nephew, the habit which he had now given himself for years of paying the cost of that nephew's education, and the income which he now allowed him, all led to such a conclusion. But then the uncle liked so well to lead, and Mr George was so unwilling to be led! Had Waddington lived, he would have been the heir, doubtless. Miss Waddington might still be so, or even Miss Baker. Mr Bertram, in his way, was certainly very fond of Miss Baker. It was thus that Mr Pritchett speculated from day to day. George, however, was always regarded by him as the favourite in the race.

And now at last we may return to our story.

Having seen his uncle, George's next business was to see his lady-love. His was a disposition which would not allow him to remain quiet while his hopes were so doubtful and his heart so racked. Had he been travelling with Miss Baker ever since, and living in daily intercourse with Caroline, it is probable enough that he might by this time have been half-tired of her. But his love had had no such safety-valve, and was now, therefore, bubbling and boiling within his heart in a manner very subversive of legal accuracy and injurious to legal studies.

It was absolutely necessary, he said to himself, that he should know on what ground he stood; absolutely necessary, also, that he should be able to talk to some one on the subject. So he wrote to Miss Baker, saying that he intended to do himself the pleasure of renewing his acquaintance with her at Littlebath, and he determined to see Arthur Wilkinson on his way. These were the days in which Wilkinson was taking pupils at Oxford, the days in which he used to think so much of Adela Gauntlet.

The meeting of the two friends was sufficiently joyous; for such love sorrows as those which oppressed Bertram when sitting in the chambers of Mr Neversaye Die rarely oppress a young man in moments which would otherwise be jovial. And Arthur had at this time gotten over one misery, and not yet fallen into another. He had obtained the fellowship which he had hardly expected, and was commencing the life of a don, with all a don's comforts around him.

'Well, upon my word, I envy you, Arthur; I do, indeed,' said Bertram, looking round his cousin's room at Balliol as they sat down to pass an evening quietly together. 'This was what I always looked forward to, as you did also; you have obtained it, I have forsworn it.'

'Your envy cannot be very envious,' said Wilkinson, laughing, 'as all my bliss is still within your own reach. You have still your rooms at Oriel if you choose to go into them.' For Bertram had been elected to a fellowship at that college.

'Ah! that's easily said; but somehow it couldn't be. I don't know why it is, Arthur; but I have panted to have the privileges of an ordained priest, and yet it is not to be so. I have looked forward to ordination as the highest ambition of a man, but yet I shall never be ordained.'

'Why not, George?'

'It is not my destiny.'

'On such a subject, do not talk such nonsense.'

'Well, at any rate it will not be my lot. I do not mind telling you, Arthur, but there is no one else to whom I could own how weak I am. There have been moments since I have been away in which I have sworn to devote myself to this work, so sworn when every object around me was gifted with some solemn tie which should have made my oath sacred; and yet—'

'Well—and yet? as yet everything is in your own power.'

'No, Arthur, no, it is not so; I am now one of the myrmidons* of that most special of special pleaders, Mr Neversaye Die. I have given myself over to the glories of a horse-hair wig; "whereas" and "heretofore" must now be my gospel; it is my doom to propagate falsehood instead of truth. The struggle is severe at first; there is a little revulsion of feeling; but I shall do it very well after a time; as easily, I have no doubt, as Harcourt does.'

'It is Harcourt who has led you to this.'

'Perhaps so, partly; but no—I wrong myself in that. It has not been Harcourt. I have been talked over; I have weakly allowed myself to be talked out of my own resolve, but it has not been done by Harcourt. I must tell you all: it is for that that I came here.'

And then he told the history of his love; that history which to men of twenty-four and girls of twenty is of such vital importance. A young man when first he loves, and first knows that his love is frequent in the thoughts of the woman he has chosen, feels himself to be separated from all humanity by an amber-tinted cloud—to be enveloped in a mystery of which common mortals know nothing. He shakes his mane as he walks on with rapid step, and regards himself almost as a god.

'And did she object to your taking orders?' asked Wilkinson.

'Object! no, I am nothing to her; nothing on earth. She would not have objected to my being a shoemaker; but she said that she would advise me to think of the one trade as soon as the other.'

'I cannot say that I think she showed either good feeling or good taste,' said Wilkinson, stiffly.

'Ah! my dear fellow, you do not know her. There was no bad taste in it, as she said it. I would defy her to say anything in bad taste. But, Arthur, that does not matter. I have told her that I should go to the bar; and, as a man of honour, I must keep my word to her.'

His cousin had not much inclination to lecture him. Wilkinson himself was now a clergyman; but he had become so mainly because he had failed in obtaining the power of following any other profession. He would have gone to the bar had he been able; and felt himself by no means called to rebuke Bertram for doing what he would fain have done himself.

'But she has not accepted you, you say. Why should she be so unwilling that you should take orders? Her anxiety on your behalf tells a strong tale in your own favour.'

'Ah! you say that because you do not understand her. She was able to give me advice without giving the least shadow of encouragement. Indeed, when she did advise me, I had not even told her that I loved her. But the fact is, I cannot bear this state any longer. I will know the worst at any rate. I wish you could see her, Arthur; you would not wonder that I should be uneasy.'

And so he went on with a lover's customary eloquence till a late hour in the night. Wilkinson was all patience; but about one o'clock he began to yawn, and then they went to bed. Early on the following morning, Bertram started for Littlebath.

The Littlebath world lives mostly in lodgings, and Miss

Baker and Caroline lived there as the world mostly does. There are three sets of persons who resort to Littlebath: there is the heavy fast, and the lighter fast set; there is also the pious set. Of the two fast sets neither is scandalously fast. The pace is never very awful. Of the heavies, it may be said that the gentlemen generally wear their coats padded, are frequently seen standing idle about the parades and terraces, that they always keep a horse, and trot about the roads a good deal when the hounds go out. The ladies are addicted to whist and false hair, but pursue their pleasures with a discreet economy. Of the lighter fast set, assembly balls are the ruling passion; but even in these there is no wild extravagance. The gentlemen of this division keep usually two horses, on the sale of one of which their mind is much bent. They drink plentifully of cherry-brandy on hunting days; but, as a rule, they do not often misbehave themselves. They are very careful not to be caught in marriage, and talk about women much as a crafty knowing salmon might be presumed to talk about anglers. The ladies are given to dancing, of course, and are none of them nearly so old as you might perhaps be led to imagine. They greatly eschew card-playing; but, nevertheless, now and again one of them may be seen to lapse from her sphere and fall into that below, if we may justly say that the votaries of whist are below the worshippers of Terpsichore.* Of the pious set much needs not be said, as their light has never been hid under a bushel. In spite of hunt-clubs and assembly-rooms, they are the predominant power. They live on the fat of the land. They are a strong, unctuous, moral, uncharitable people. The men never cease making money for themselves, nor the women making slippers for their clergymen.

But though the residents at Littlebath are thus separated as a rule into three classes, the classes do not always keep themselves accurately to their divisions. There will be some who own a double allegiance. One set will tread upon another. There will be those who can hardly be placed in either. Miss Baker was among this latter number: on principle, she was an admirer of the great divine on the domestic comfort of whose toes so many fair fingers had employed themselves; but, nevertheless, she was not averse to a rubber in its mildest forms. Caroline did not play whist, but she occasionally gave way to the allurement prevalent among the younger female world of Littlebath.

Miss Baker lived in lodgings, and Bertram therefore went to an hotel. Had she been mistress of the largest house in Littlebath, he would hardly have ventured to propose himself as a guest. The 'Plough,' however, is a good inn, and he deposited himself there. The hunting season at Littlebath had commenced, and Bertram soon found that had he so wished he could with but little trouble have provided himself with a stud* in the coffee room of his hotel.

He had intended to call on Miss Baker on the evening of his arrival; but he had not actually told her that he would do so: and though he walked down to the terrace in which she lived, his courage failed him when he got there, and he would not go in. 'It may be that evening calls are not the thing at Littlebath,' he said to himself; and so he walked back to his hotel.

And on the following day he did not go before two o'clock. The consequence was, that poor Miss Baker and her niece were kept at home in a state of miserable suspense. To them his visit was quite as important as to himself; and by one of them, the elder namely, it was regarded with an anxiety quite as nervous.

When he did call, he was received with all the hospitality due to an old friend. 'Why had he not come to tea the night before? Tea had been kept for him till eleven o'clock. Why, at any rate, had he not come to breakfast? He had been much nicer in Jerusalem,' Miss Baker said.

Bertram answered hardly with the spirit which had marked all that he had said in that far-away land. 'He had been afraid to disturb them so late; and had been unwilling to intrude so early.' Miss Waddington looked up at him from the collar she was working, and began to ask herself whether she really did like him so much.

'Of course you will dine with us,' said Miss Baker. George said he would, but assured her that he had not intended to give so much trouble. Could this be the same man, thought

Caroline, who had snubbed Mr M'Gabbery, and had stood by laughing when she slipped into the water.

All manner of questions were then asked and answered respecting their different journeys. Constantinople was described on one side, and the Tyrol; and on the other the perils of the ride to Jaffa, the discomforts of the Austrian boat to Alexandria, and the manners of the ladies from India with whom Miss Baker and her niece had travelled in their passage from Egypt to Marseilles. Then they said something about uncle George—not that Miss Baker so called him—and Bertram said that he had learnt that Miss Baker had been staying at Hadley.

'Yes,' said she; 'when I am in town, I have always money matters to arrange with Mr Bertram, or rather to have arranged by Mr Pritchett; and I usually stay a day or two at Hadley. On this occasion I was there a week.'

George could not but think that up to the period of their meeting at Jerusalem, Miss Baker had been instructed to be silent about Hadley, but that she was now permitted to speak out openly.

And so they sat and talked for an hour. Caroline had given her aunt strict injunctions not to go out of the room, so as to leave them together during Bertram's first visit. 'Of course it would be quite palpable that you did so for a purpose,' said Caroline.

'And why not?' said Miss Baker innocently.

'Never mind, aunt; but pray do not. I don't wish it.' Miss Baker of course obeyed, as she always did. And so George sat there, talking about anything or nothing, rather lackadaisically, till he got up to take his leave.

'You have not a horse here, I suppose?' said Miss Baker.

'No; but why do you ask? I can get one in ten minutes, no doubt.'

'Because Caroline will be so glad to have some one to ride with her.'

'Nothing will induce aunt Mary to mount a steed since the day she was lifted out of her saddle at Jaffa,' said Caroline.

'Oh, that journey, Mr Bertram! but I am a stronger woman than I ever thought I was to have lived through it.'

It was soon arranged that George should go back to his inn and hire a horse, and that he and Caroline should then ride together. In another hour or so they were cantering up the face of Ridgebury Hill.

But the ride produced very little. Caroline here required her attention, and George did not find it practicable to remain close enough to his love, or long enough close to her, to say what he had to say with that emphasis which he felt that the subject demanded. There was some little tender allusions to feats of horsemanship done in Syria, some mention of the Mount of Olives, of Miss Todd's picnic, and the pool of Siloam, which might, if properly handled, have led to much; but they did lead to nothing: and when George helped Miss Waddington to dismount at Miss Baker's door, that young lady had almost come to the conclusion that he had thought better of his love, and that it would be well that she should think better of hers.

In accordance with our professed attempt at plain speaking, it may be as well explained here that Miss Baker, with a view of sounding her uncle's views and wishes, had observed to him that George had appeared to her to admire Caroline very much. Had the old man remarked, as he might so probably have done, that they were two fools, and would probably become two beggars, Miss Baker would have known that the match would be displeasing to him. But he had not done so. 'Ah!' he said; 'did he? It is singular that they should have met.' Now Miss Baker in her wisdom had taken this as a strong hint that the match would not be displeasing to him.

Miss Baker had clearly been on George's side from the beginning. Perhaps, had she shown a little opposition, Caroline's ardour might have been heightened. As it was, she had professed to doubt. She had nothing to say against George; much might doubtless be said in his favour, but—In fact, Miss Waddington would have been glad to know what were the intentions of Mr George Bertram senior.

'I really wish he had stayed away,' she said to her aunt as they were getting ready for dinner.

'Nonsense, Caroline; why should he have stayed away? Why should you expect him to stay away? Had he stayed away, you would have been the first to grumble. Don't be missish, my dear.'

'Missish! Upon my word, aunt Mary, you are becoming severe. What I mean is, that I don't think he cares so very much for me; and on the whole, I am not—not *quite* sure, whether—well, I won't say anything more; only it does seem to me that you are much more in love with him than I am.'

Bertram came to dinner; and so also did one of the Littlebath curates, a very energetic young man, but who had not yet achieved above one or two pairs of worked slippers and a kettle-holder. Greater things, however, were no doubt in store for him if he would remain true to his mission. Aunt Mary had intended to ask no one; but Caroline had declared that it was out of the question to expect that Mr Bertram should drink his wine by himself.

The whole evening was dull enough, and the work of disenchantment on Caroline's part was nearly accomplished; but Bertram, a few minutes before he went away, as the curate was expatiating to Miss Baker on the excellence of his rector's last sermon, found an occasion to say one word.

'Miss Waddington, if I call tomorrow, early after breakfast, will you see me?' Miss Waddington looked as though there were nothing in the proposition to ruffle her serenity, and said that she would. George's words had been tame enough, but there had been something in the fire of his eye that at last reminded her of Jerusalem.

On the next morning, punctually at ten, his knock was heard at the door. Caroline had at first persisted that her aunt should not absent herself; but even Miss Baker would not obey such an injunction as this.

'How do you expect that the poor young man is to behave?' she had said. 'I do not much care how he behaves,' Caroline had replied. But, nevertheless, she did care.

She was therefore sitting alone when Bertram entered the room. He walked up to her and took her hand, and as he did so he seemed to be altogether a different man from that of yesterday. There was purpose enough in his countenance now, and a purpose, apparently, which he had an intention of pursuing with some energy.

'Miss Waddington,' he said, still holding her hand; 'Caroline! Or am I to apologize for calling you so? or is the privilege to be my own?' and then, still holding her hand, he stood as though expectant of an answer that should settle the affair at once.

'Our connection through your uncle entitles you to the privilege,' said Caroline, smiling, and using a woman's wiles to get out of the difficulty.

'I will take no privilege from you on such a basis. What I have to ask of you must be given on my own account, or on my own refused. Caroline, since we parted in that room in Jerusalem, I have thought seriously of little else than of you. You could not answer me then; you gave me no answer; you did not know your own heart, you said. You must know it now. Absence has taught me much, and it must have taught you something.'

'And what has it taught you?' said she, with her eyes fixed on the ground.

'That the world has but one thing desirable for me, and that I should not take a man's part unless I endeavoured to obtain it. I am here to ask for it. And now, what has absence taught you?'

'Oh, so many things! I cannot repeat my lesson in one word, as you do.'

'Come, Caroline, I look at least for sincerity from you. You are too good, too gracious to indulge a girlish vanity at the cost of a man's suspense.'

Missish and girlish! Miss Waddington felt that it behoved her to look to her character. These were words which had not usually been applied to her.

'Indeed, Mr Bertram, I should think myself unpardonable to keep you in suspense.'

'Then answer me,' said he. He had by this time let go her hand, and was standing at a little distance from her, on the hearth-rug. Never had lady been wooed in a sterner manner; but Caroline almost felt that she liked him the better for it. He had simpered and said his little nothings so like an ordinary gentleman during their ride, that his present brusqueness was quite a relief to her.

But still she did not answer him at once. She essayed to stick her needle into her work, and pricked her finger in lieu of it.

'Come, Caroline; am I wrong in supposing that now at least you must know your own feelings? Or shall I tell you again how dearly, how truly I love you?'

'No!—no!—no!'

'Answer me, then. In honest, plain, Christian sincerity, answer me; as a true woman should answer a true man. Do you love me?'

For a moment there was no answer.

'Well, I will not ask again. I will not torment you.'

'Oh, Mr Bertram! What am I to say? What would you have me say? Do not be so stern with me.'

'Stern!'

'Well, are you not stern?' And coming up close to him, she looked into his face.

'Caroline,' said he, 'will you be my wife?'

'I will.' It was a motion of the lips rather than a spoken word; but, nevertheless, he heard it. Fool that he was not to have heard it before in the beating of her heart; not to have seen it in the tear in her eye; nor to have felt it in the warmth of her hand.

On that afternoon, Miss Waddington's ride was much more energetic, and on that evening Miss Baker did not think it necessary to catch a curate to drink wine with George Bertram. He was made quite at home, and given to understand that he had better leave the dining-room when the ladies did so.

There was much talked over that evening and the next day: the upshot of which was, that no marriage could take place till next summer; that perhaps it might be expedient to postpone it till the summer twelvemonths. To this George put, or would have put, an absolute veto; but Miss Baker only shook her head, and smilingly said that she thought it must be so. Nothing was to be done before Christmas; but as Miss Baker was to be at Hadley very early in January, she undertook to inform Mr Bertram, and gave strong hopes that he would be prevailed on to favour the marriage.

'It can make no difference to my purpose whether he does or no,' said George, very independently.

CHAPTER XIV

WAYS AND MEANS

ON the following day Bertram returned to town. Now that he was a successful lover, and about to take upon himself at some future time the responsible duties of a married man, he became very energetic in the chambers of Mr Die. He could hardly spare a day during the winter for running down to Littlebath, and whenever he did so, he took Coke upon Littleton* down with him. Nor did he work in vain. He never had worked in vain. Facility of acquiring the special knowledge which he sought had ever been one of his gifts. Mr Die was already beginning to prophesy great things; and his friend Harcourt, who occasionally wanted his society, declared that he overdid his labours.

Down at Littlebath they did not quite approve of all this industry. Caroline naturally thought that more of her lover's hours should be devoted to her; and Miss Baker, who looked on Mr Bertram's money as certainly destined either for Caroline or George, considered that he was wasting his time with his fusty books. She had not dared to say much to George on this subject, and he had not taken very well the little that she did say. She could not tell him that Caroline was Mr Bertram's grand-daughter, but she did remind him that he himself was Mr Bertram's nephew, and hinted that though a profession might be very eligible for a young man of such brilliant prospects, it could hardly be necessary for him absolutely to make a slave of himself. To this George had answered, somewhat curtly, that he had no reason to expect anything further from his uncle; and that as he looked forward to maintain himself and his wife by his successful exertions as a barrister, it was absolutely necessary that he should at present work very hard. 'I have lost a whole year,' he said to Miss Baker; 'and nothing but very sharp work can atone for that.'

He never once saw his uncle after his first visit to Littlebath till the next year was far advanced. He felt no desire to see him, and certainly no wish to be the bearer of tidings as to his own engagement. Miss Baker had undertaken to do this, and might do so if she so pleased. As far as he was concerned, he had no idea of asking permission to marry from any one.

'Why should I ask him?' he had once said to Miss Baker. 'I shall marry just the same, whether he permits it or whether he does not.'

This was grievous to the ladies at Littlebath. Very little had been said about money between George and Miss Baker up to this time; nothing had been said between George and Caroline; but the two ladies knew that there could be no marriage till there was an adequate income. The income of the gentleman when stripped of his fellowship would be two hundred pounds a year; that of the lady was about the same. Now Caroline Waddington had no intention whatever of marrying on four hundred pounds a year; and it must be more than three years at the very least before all this profound study would result in golden fees.

Now that the matter was so far settled—settled as Bertram considered it—he did tell Harcourt of his love. 'Harcourt,' said he, one day, 'I have a piece of news which perhaps I ought to tell you. I am engaged to be married.'

'Are you?' said Harcourt, rather too coolly to satisfy his friend's expectation.

'I am not joking.'

'Who ever accused you of joking since you took to the law and Mr Die? I did not give you credit for a joke; not even for so bad a one as that would be. Shall I congratulate or condole with you?'

'Either or neither. Perhaps you had better wait till you see the lady.'

'And when is it to be?'

'Well; in this coming summer, I suppose. That is my wish, at least.'

'And your wish of course will be law. I presume then that I

may be justified in surmising that the lady has some considerable fortune?'

'No, indeed, she has not. Something she has got; about as much, perhaps, as myself. We shall have bread to eat.'

'And occasionally cheese,' said Harcourt, who could not understand that any rising man could marry early, unless in doing so he acquired money.

'And occasionally cheese,' repeated Bertram. 'This is a state of things that would not suit your book, I know.'

'Not exactly,' said Harcourt. 'But men have very different ideas about women. I could do, and have done, and am doing with a small income myself; but a wife is in some respects like a horse. If a gentleman does keep a horse, it should be well groomed.'

'You could not endure a woman who was not always got up in satin and velvet?'

'Not satin and velvet exactly. I do not require a curiously-mounted saddle for my horse. But I don't think I should have much enjoyment with a cheap wife. I like cold mutton and candle-ends myself very well, but I do not love feminine economies. Family washing-bills kept at the lowest, a maid-of-all-work with an allowance in lieu of beer, and a dark morning gown for household work, would not, if I know myself, add fuel to the ardour of my conjugal affection. I love women dearly; I like them to be near me; but then I like them to be nice. When a woman is nasty, she is very nasty.'

Bertram said in his heart that Harcourt was a beast, an animal without a soul, a creature capable of no other joys than those of a material nature; but he kept this opinion at the present moment to himself. Not, however, that he was averse to express himself openly before his friend. He often gave Harcourt to understand that he suspected him of being deficient in the article of a soul; and Harcourt would take the reproach with perfect good-humour, remarking, perhaps, that he might probably find it possible to get on decently without one.

'Is the lady's name a secret?' he asked.

'No; not to you, at least. I believe it is generally considered advisable that these sort of things should not be talked about quite openly till the consummation of them is nigh at hand. I have no wish for any mystery in the matter. Her name is Caroline Waddington.'

'What! a daughter of Sir Augustus?'

'No; nothing to Sir Augustus, that I have heard.'

'She must, then, be one of the General's family?'

'Not that either. Her only relative, that I know, is a Miss Baker.'

'Miss Baker!' said Harcourt; and the tone of his voice was not encouraging.

'Yes, Miss Baker,' said Bertram; and the tone of his voice was hardly conciliatory.

'Oh—ah—yes. I don't exactly think I know her. Miss Baker!'

'It would be odd if you did, for she lives at Littlebath, and hardly ever comes to town. When she does, she stays down at Hadley with my uncle.'

'Oh—h! That's a horse of another colour. I beg your pardon entirely, my dear fellow. Why did you not tell me at first that this is a match of your uncle's making?'

'My uncle's making! It is not a match of my uncle's making.'

'Well, well; one that he approves. I hardly gave you credit for so much prudence. That will be as good as having everything settled exactly as you could wish it.'

'You are giving me a great deal too much credit,' said Bertram, laughing. 'My uncle knows nothing about my marriage and I have not the slightest idea of consulting him. I should think it mean to do so, considering everything.'

'Mean to consult the only relative you have who can do anything for you?'

'Yes. He has told me over and over again that I have no claim on him; and, therefore, I will make none.'

Bertram had said to himself frequently that he cared nothing for this man's judgment in such matters; but, nevertheless, after what had passed, he did desire that Harcourt should see Caroline. He was aware, judging rather from Harcourt's tone than from his words, that that keen-sighted friend of his had but a low opinion of Miss

Waddington; that he thought that she was some ordinary, intriguing girl, who had been baiting a hook for a husband, after the manner which scandal states to be so common among the Littlebathians; and Bertram longed, therefore, to surprise his eyes and astound his intellect with a view of her charms and a near knowledge of her attributes. Nothing should be said of her beauty, and the blaze of it should fall upon him altogether unprepared.

George was right in his feelings in this respect. Harcourt had formed a very false idea of Miss Waddington;—had led himself to imagine that she was second-rate and unattractive. In the first place, he had his own ideas about Littlebath, and conceived that it was not the place in which the highest beauty of England should be looked for; and in the next place, he knew George Bertram, and regarded him as a man peculiarly liable to such dangers as these.

'You must come down with me to Littlebath. When will you give me a day?'

Harcourt demurred, as he did not wish to be called on imperiously to praise a woman of whom he knew he should disapprove, and endeavoured to excuse himself from the journey. But Bertram persisted, and at last it was settled that he would go down.

This did not happen till towards the end of winter. Miss Baker had, as she promised, seen Mr Bertram in the meantime, and the answer returned from the Hadley oracle had, like most oracle-answers, been neither favourable nor unfavourable. Mr Bertram had expressed no great anger at the tale of love that was told him; but neither had he expressed any gratification. 'Well,' he had said, 'it is odd that they should have come together; very odd. He is a clever young man, and I dare say may do well.' Miss Baker had then ventured, but in a very modest way, to ask him his opinion as to the sufficiency of the young people's income. 'They must judge of that themselves,' he had said, rather sharply. 'But I suppose they have no idea of marrying yet. They mean to wait, don't they, till he begins his profession?' To this Miss Baker had made no answer, and nothing further had been said at that meeting.

Early in March, Miss Baker had again seen the great man. She had then ventured to explain to him that George was working very hard.

'Ah! you have his word for that, I suppose,' said the uncle; 'but if so, believe me he will get on at such work as that quicker without a wife than he will with one.'

But at this interview Miss Baker did ask him plainly, as had been agreed beforehand between her and her niece that she should do, whether he would on their marriage make any increase to his granddaughter's fortune.

'She has a liberal, ladylike provision,' said he.

'But they will not have enough to live on,' said Miss Baker.

'They will have a third more, Mary, than I had when I married your aunt. And yet I saved money on my income.'

'But remember how they have been brought up, sir.'

'If they will be fine ladies and gentlemen, they must take the penalties for being so. Fine ladies and gentlemen cannot marry at a moment's notice, as do ploughboys and milkmaids. If they cannot live on a limited income, they must wait.' He did, however, on this occasion go so far as to say, that if they would wait for another twelvemonth, and that if he were then living, he would add two thousand pounds to Caroline's fortune. As to George, he had done as much as he intended to do—certainly for the present. 'George likes his own way,' said the old man, 'and as far as I am concerned, he shall have it. It will be well for him to make his own career in the world; he will be happier so than in spending my money.'

On this occasion Miss Baker was permitted to tell Caroline all the circumstances of her parentage and grandparentage. The same story might now be told to George. But they were both to be cautioned that their relative's displeasure would be incurred by any useless repetition of it. 'And, Mary,' said he, 'do not let them mislead themselves. Do not let them marry with the idea that by so doing they will inherit between them my money. I wish them both to understand that my views are altogether different.'

Miss Baker, when she returned to Littlebath, could not think that she had been successful in her mission; and Caroline immediately declared that any idea of marriage for that year, or even for the next, must now be altogether out of the question. She was very much startled at hearing that Mr Bertram was her mother's father, but did not pretend to any suddenly intense affection for him. 'If that be so,' said she, coldly, 'if George and I are his only near connections, and if he does not disapprove of our marriage, he ought to give us an income on which we can live.' It is astonishing how different are the views of grandfathers and grandchildren on such matters!

Unfortunately there was no unanimity of opinion on this matter, either between the lovers themselves or between them and their aunt. George was of opinion that they should marry immediately on their present income, and trust to Providence and his exertions for a future increase. For one year he would have the income of his fellowship; in two years and a half he would be called; and in the meantime, he could make something by the Magazines. If Caroline was not afraid, he was not.

But Caroline was very much afraid. It had by no means formed part of the project of her life to live in London as a married woman on four hundred pounds a year. 'She knew,' she said to Miss Baker, 'what effect that would have on her husband's affections.' She seemed, indeed, to share some of Harcourt's opinions on the subject, and to have a dislike to feminine economies, or at least to the use of them under the surveillance of a man's eye. As far as she could see, the marriage must be postponed indefinitely—at any rate, till after George should have been called to the bar.

Miss Baker's voice was for a middle course. She suggested that they should wait for Mr Bertram's two thousand pounds and then marry. They would then have an income increased to some extent. They would also show a deference to the old man's views, which would undoubtedly—so Miss Baker thought—have ultimate results of a most beneficial nature. 'After all,' as she remarked more than once to her niece, 'who else is there?'

But the young people were quite as obstinate as the old man. George would make no concession whatever to his uncle. He was ready to marry on love and a small income, and he expected Caroline to show an equal warmth. Caroline would by no means alter her views, or risk the misery of an ill-provided nursery. It had been the one great resolve of her life, that she would not be a poor man's wife. 'She was ready to wait,' she said. 'If she could trust and wait, surely George might do so. A man, with all the world around him, encountered neither the misery nor the risk in waiting that fell to a girl's lot.'

The disputes incidental to these different opinions did not ever take place between George and Caroline. He, from a feeling of chivalry, abstained from discussing money matters with her; and she, from a feeling of prudence, was equally silent with him. Poor Miss Baker was the medium for it all. George of course would press with a lover's ardour for an early day; and Caroline would of course say that an immediate marriage was, she found, impracticable. And then each would refer the other to Miss Baker.

Things went on in this way till the middle of May. Sometimes George was almost angry, and wrote letters that were somewhat savage; sometimes Caroline would be haughty, and then she too could write letters which would tell her mind in good plain set terms. But they were not near enough, or sufficiently often with each other, to quarrel.

So matters went on till May; and then, on one fine May-day, Harcourt and George together took their places in the train for Littlebath.

'I wonder what you'll think of her?' said George. 'Of course you'll tell the truth?'

'Oh, of course,' said Harcourt, with his mind duly made up to praise her.

'You haven't the pluck to find fault with her,' said George; 'you would be afraid not to call her handsome, even if you thought her as ugly as Hecate.'*

'Exactly,' said Harcourt; 'and therefore these little experimentary trips are never of any use.'

CHAPTER XV

MR HARCOURT'S VISIT TO LITTLEBATH

DURING the whole of the winter and spring, George's attention to his work had been unremitting. Mr Die was always prophesying still greater things, and still greater. Once a fortnight, on every other Saturday, Bertram had gone down to Littlebath, but he had always returned to London by the first train on Monday morning, and was always up to his elbows in law, even on that morning, before eleven.

During the whole of this time, he had not once seen his uncle, although Miss Baker had softly endeavoured to talk him into visiting Hadley. 'I never go there without being asked,' he had said. 'It is quite understood between us.'

He had made but one excursion out of London, except those to Littlebath, and that had been to Hurst Staple. Mr Wilkinson had died very suddenly, as has been told, about the end of the winter, and Bertram had of course not been able to see him. Arthur Wilkinson had then been quickly put into the living, and as soon as he had taken up his residence in the parsonage, Bertram had gone down. This visit had been made before the last walk to West Putford; but even then the young barrister had found the young vicar in rather a plaintive mood. Wilkinson, however, had said nothing of his love, and George was too much occupied with talking of his own heart to think much of his cousin's.

Miss Gauntlet—I hope the reader has not altogether forgotten Adela Gauntlet—had also an aunt living at Littlebath, Miss Penelope Gauntlet; and it so happened, that very shortly after that memorable walk and the little scene that took place in the West Putford drawing-room, Adela visited her aunt. Bertram, who had known her well when they were children together, had not yet seen her there; indeed, her arrival had taken place since his last visit; but there she was, staying with Miss Penelope Gauntlet, when he and Harcourt went down to Littlebath together.

Caroline and Adela had for years been friends. Not bosom

friends, perhaps; that is, they did not correspond three times a week, each sending to the other on each occasion three sheets of note paper crossed over on every page from top to bottom. Caroline had certainly no such bosom friend, and perhaps neither had Adela; but they were friends enough to call each other by their Christian names, to lend each other music and patterns, and perhaps to write when they had anything special to say. There had been a sort of quasi-connection between Miss Baker and the elder Miss Gauntlet —a connection of a very faint local character—in years gone by. Miss Baker, by reason of her Bertram relations, had been at Hurst Staple, and Miss Gauntlet had been at West Putford at the same time. They had thus become acquainted, and the acquaintance there had led to a Littlebath friendship. Friendships in Littlebath are not of a very fervid description.

Miss Waddington had now been engaged for six months, and hitherto she had made no confidante. She knew no resident at Littlebath whom she would willingly trust with her heart's secret: her aunt, and her aunt's cognizance of the matter were quite another thing. No one could be more affectionate than aunt Mary, no one more trustworthy, no one more thoroughly devoted to another than she was to her niece. But then she was not only old, but old-fashioned. She was prudent, and Caroline also was prudent; but their prudence was a different kind. There was no dash, no ambition about aunt Mary's prudence. She was rather humdrum, Caroline thought; and, which was worse, though she liked George Bertram, she did not seem to understand his character at all in the same light as that in which Caroline regarded it.

From these circumstances it came to pass that Adela had not been a week at Littlebath before she was made acquainted with the grand secret. She also had a secret of her own; but she did not tell that in return. Secrets such as Caroline's are made to be told; but those other secrets, those which burn up the heart instead of watering it as with a dew from heaven, those secrets for the most part are not made to be told.

'And yet, Adela, I suppose it will never happen.' This had been said on the morning of that Saturday which was to bring down not only Bertram, but Harcourt. Caroline knew well that the London friend, the man of the world, was being brought to inspect her, and was by no means afraid of undergoing the inspection. She was not timid by nature; and though, as has been already said, she was hardly yet conscious of her powers of attracting, she was never ashamed of herself.

'And why not? I think that is nonsense, Caroline. If you really thought that, you would not receive him as you will do, nor his friend neither.'

'I do think it; that is to say, I think it very probable. I cannot explain to you, Adela, all the turns of my mind, or of my heart. I would not for worlds of gold marry a man I did not love.'

'And do not you love Mr Bertram?'

'Yes, I do; at times very, very much; but I fear the time may come when I may love him less. You will not understand me; but the fact is, I should love him better if he were less worthy of my love—if he were more worldly.'

'No, I do not understand that,' said Adela, thinking of her love, and the worldly prudence of him who should have been her lover.

'That is it—you do not understand me; and yet it is not selfishness on my part. I would marry a man in the hope of making him happy.'

'Certainly,' said Adela; 'no girl should marry unless she have reasonable hope that she can do that.'

'He would wish me to go to him now, at once; when we have no sufficient income to support us.'

'Four hundred a year!' said Adela, reproachfully.

'What would four hundred a year do in London? Were I to consent, in a year or two he would be sick of me. He would be a wretched man, unless, indeed, his law-courts and his club kept him from being wretched;—his home would not do so.'

Adela silently compared the matter with her own affairs: her ideas were so absolutely different. 'If he could have contented himself to live upon potatoes,' she had once thought to herself, 'I could have contented myself to live on the parings.' She said nothing of this however to Caroline. Their dispositions she knew were different. After all, it may be that Miss Waddington had a truer knowledge of human nature.

'No, I shall not consent; I will not consent to be the cause of his misery and poverty; and then he will be angry with me, and we shall quarrel. He can be very stern, Adela; very.'

'He is impetuous; but however angry he may be, he forgives immediately. He never bears malice,' said Adela, remembering her early dealings with the boy-friend of her girlhood.

'He can be very stern now. I know it will come to our quarrelling; and when he finds that he cannot have his own way, that I cannot yield to him, his proud heart will revolt from me; I know it will.'

Adela could only say that were she in her friend's place she would not think so much about income; but her gentle speech, the eloquence of which had an inward, rather than an outward tendency, had no effect on Caroline. If Bertram could not persuade her, it certainly was not probable that Adela Gauntlet should do so.

Messrs Harcourt and Bertram reached Littlebath quite safely. Harcourt was to dine with the ladies in Montpellier Terrace—it was in Montpellier Terrace that Miss Baker lived—and as some sort of party was necessary for his honour, the curate was again invited, as were also the two Miss Gauntlets.

'You'll go on first, I suppose?' said Harcourt, when they had secured their rooms at the 'Plough,' and were preparing to dress. Bertram was well known at the 'Plough' now, and there was not a boots or chambermaid about the house who did not know why he came to Littlebath.

'Oh, no,' said Bertram, 'I'll wait for you.'

'I didn't know; I thought there might be some lovers' privileges to be exercised, for which the eyes of the world might be inconvenient.'

'They shall be postponed on your behalf, my dear fellow.' And so the two went off together.

They found Miss Baker in her drawing-room, and with her Adela and aunt Penelope.

'And where is Caroline?' said George, when the introductions had been duly performed. He had to make a little effort to say this in a voice that should signify that he was at home there, but which should not savour too much of the lover. On the whole, he succeeded pretty well.

'Why, to tell the truth,' said Miss Baker, laughing, 'she is doing duty at this moment as head-butler in the dining-room. If you feel any vocation that way, you may go and help her.'

'Well, I am a fairish good hand at drawing a cork,' said Bertram, as he left the room.

'So the lovers' privileges are all arranged for,' thought Harcourt to himself.

When Bertram entered the dining-room, the butler's duties seemed to be complete; at any rate, Miss Waddington was not engaged in their performance. She was leaning on the mantelpiece, and was apparently engaged in contemplating a bouquet of flowers which Bertram had contrived to send to the house since his arrival at Littlebath. It was no wonder that the boots should know all about it.

Let us agree to say nothing about the lovers' privileges. Caroline Waddington was not a girl to be very liberal of such favours, and on the occasion in question she was not more liberal than usual.

'Is Mr Harcourt here?' said she.

'Yes, of course he is. He is upstairs.'

'And I am to go up to be looked at. How vain you men are of your playthings! Not that you have anything in this respect of which you ought to be vain.'

'But a great deal of which I ought to be, and am, very proud. I am proud of you, Caroline; proud at this moment that my friend should see how beautiful is the girl that loves me.'

'Tush!' said Caroline, putting the back of her nosegay up to his mouth. 'What delightful nonsense you can talk. But come, your London friend won't much appreciate my excellence if I keep him waiting for his dinner.' And so they went upstairs.

But Caroline, though she laughed at her lover for showing her off, had not failed to make the best of herself. She was sufficiently anxious that Bertram should be proud of her, should have cause to be proud of her; and she seemed to be aware that if she could satisfy Mr Harcourt's fastidious judgment, she might probably hope to pass as approved of among his other friends. She determined, therefore, to look her best as she walked into the drawing-room; and she did look her best.

'Mr Harcourt, my niece, Miss Waddington,' said Miss Baker. Harcourt, as he rose and bowed, was lost in wonder.

Bertram fell immediately into conversation with Miss Penelope Gauntlet, but even while listening to her enthusiasm as to Arthur Wilkinson's luck in getting the living of Hurst Staple, and her praise of Lord Stapledean, he contrived to keep an eye on his friend Harcourt. 'Yes, indeed, quite fortunate; wasn't it?' But as he thus spoke, his very soul within him was rejoicing at his own triumph. He had said nothing about Caroline personally; he had refrained his tongue, and now he had his reward.

We have said that Harcourt was lost in wonder, and such was literally the case. He had taught himself to believe that Caroline Waddington was some tall, sharp-nosed dowdy; with bright eyes, probably, and even teeth; with a simpering, would-be-witty smile, and full of little quick answers such as might suit well for the assembly-rooms at Littlebath. When he heard that she was engaged in seeing that the sherry-bottles were duly decanted, the standard of her value did not at all rise in his estimation. Candle-ends and cold mutton would doubtless be her forte, an economical washing-bill her strong point.

So was he thinking, much distressed in mind—for, to do him justice, he was as anxious on behalf of Bertram as it was in his nature to be anxious for any one—when a Juno entered the room. She did not swim in, or fly in, or glide in, but walked in, as women should walk if they properly understood their parts. She walked in as though she were mistress of her own soul, and afraid to meet no pair of eyes which any human being could bend upon her. He had intended in his good-nature to patronize her; but that other question instantly occurred to him—would she patronize him? Bertram he had known long and intimately, and held him therefore somewhat cheap in many respects, as we are all accustomed to hold our dearest friends. But now, at once he rose in his estimation a hundred per cent. What might not be expected of a man whom such a woman would acknowledge that she loved?

A Juno had entered the room; for her beauty, as we have said before, was that rather of the queen of the gods. George immediately acknowledged to himself that he had never before seen her look so grandly beautiful. Her charms have been related, and that relation shall not be repeated; but when first seen by Harcourt, their power was more thoroughly acknowledged by him, much more thoroughly than they had been by her lover when he had first met her. Then, however, she had been sitting at dinner between her aunt and Mr M'Gabbery, quite unconscious that any one was arriving whose existence could be of importance to her.

There was no time for conversation then. The surprise arising from her entrance had, on Harcourt's part, hardly subsided, when the servant announced dinner, and he was called on to give his arm to Miss Baker.

'I hope you approve your friend's choice,' said that lady, smiling.

'Miss Waddington is certainly the most lovely girl I ever beheld,' replied he, with enthusiasm.

The Rev. Mr Meek handed down Miss Penelope Gauntlet, and Bertram followed with the two girls, happy and high-spirited. He first tendered his arm to Adela, who positively refused it; then to Caroline, who was equally determined. Then, putting a hand behind the waist of each of them, he pushed them through the door before him. There are certainly some privileges which an accepted lover may take in a house, and no one but an accepted lover.

George took his seat at the bottom of the table, as though he were quite at home; and Harcourt, happy sinner! found himself seated between Adela and Caroline. He was not good enough for such bliss. But had his virtues been ever so shining, how could they have availed him? Neither of his neighbours had a portion of a heart left to call her own.

But he was able to perceive that Caroline was not only

beautiful. She talked to him almost exclusively, for she had capriciously seated herself away from her lover, and next to her aunt. 'Adela,' she had whispered, going downstairs, 'I shall look to you to talk to George all the evening, for I mean to make a new conquest.'

Bertram was delighted. It was hardly in him to be jealous, even had there been a shadow of cause. As it was, his love was doing exactly that which he wished her to do. She was vindicating his choice to the man whose judgment on the matter was most vitally essential to him.

When the ladies left the dining-room, both Bertram and Harcourt heartily wished that Miss Baker had not been so scrupulously hospitable. They hardly knew what to do with Mr Meek. Mr Meek remarked that Miss Baker was a very nice person, that Miss Waddington was a charming person, that Miss Penelope Gauntlet was a very nice person indeed, and that Miss Adela was a very sweet person; and then it seemed that all conversation was at an end. 'Eh! what! none especially; that is to say, the Middle Temple.' Such had been Harcourt's reply to Mr Meek's inquiry as to what London congregation he frequented; and then the three gentlemen seemed to be much occupied with their wine and biscuits. This invitation to Mr Meek had certainly been a mistake on Miss Baker's part.

But the misery did not last long. Of the first occasion on which Mr Meek's glass was seen to be well empty, George took advantage. 'If you don't take any more wine, Mr Meek, we may as well go upstairs; eh, Harcourt?' and he looked suppliantly at his friend.

'Oh, I never take any more wine, you know. I'm an anchorite on such occasions as these.' And so they went into the drawing-room, long before Miss Baker had her coffee ready for them.

'You see a good deal of Arthur now, I suppose?' said Bertram, addressing Adela.

'Yes; that is, not a very great deal. He has been busy since he took up the parish. But I see Mary frequently.'

'Do you think Arthur likes it? He seemed to me to be hardly so much gratified as I should have thought he would have been. The living is a good one, and the marquis was certainly good-natured about it.'

'Oh, yes, he was,' said Adela.

'It will be a long time, I know, before I earn five hundred pounds a year. Do you know, he never wrote about it as though he thought he'd been lucky in getting it.'

'Didn't he?'

'Never; and I thought he was melancholy and out of spirits when I saw him the other day. He ought to marry; that's the fact. A young clergyman with a living should always get a wife.'

'You are like the fox that lost its tail,' said Adela, trying hard to show that she joined in the conversation without an effort.

'Ah! but the case is very different. There can be no doubt that Arthur ought to lose his tail. His position in the world is one which especially requires him to lose it.'

'He has his mother and sisters, you know.'

'Oh, mother and sisters! Mother and sisters are all very well, or not very well, as the case may be; but the vicar of a parish should be a married man. If you can't get a wife for him down there in Hampshire, I shall have him up to London, and look one out for him there. Pray take the matter in hand when you go home, Miss Gauntlet.'

Adela smiled, and did not blush; nor did she say that she quite agreed with him that the vicar of a parish should be a married man.

'Well, I shan't ask any questions,' said Bertram, as soon as he and Harcourt were in the street, 'or allow you to offer any opinion; because, as we have both agreed, you have not pluck enough to give it impartially.' Bertram as he said this could hardly preserve himself from a slight tone of triumph.

'She is simply the most lovely woman that my eyes ever beheld,' said Harcourt.

'Tush! can't you make it a little more out of the common way than that? But, Harcourt, without joke, you need not trouble yourself. I did want you to see her; but I don't care twopence as to your liking her. I shall think much more of your wife liking her—if you ever have a wife.'

'Bertram, upon my word, I never was less in a mood to joke.'

'That is saying very little, for you are always in a mood to joke.' Bertram understood it all; saw clearly what impression Miss Waddington had made, and for the moment was supremely happy.

'How ever you had the courage to propose yourself and your two hundred pounds a year to such a woman as that!'

'Ha! ha! ha! Why, Harcourt, you are not at all like yourself. If you admire her so much, I shall beg you not to come to Littlebath any more.'

'Perhaps I had better not. But, Bertram, I beg to congratulate you most heartily. There is this against your future happiness—'

'What?'

'Why, you will never be known as Mr George Bertram; but always as Mrs George Bertram's husband. With such a bride-elect as that, you cannot expect to stand on your own bottom. If you can count on being lord chancellor, or secretary of state, you may do so; otherwise, you'll always be known as an appendage.'

'Oh, I'll put up with that misery.'

This visit of inspection had been very successful, and George went to bed in the highest spirits. In the highest spirits also he walked to church with Harcourt, and there met the two ladies. There was something especially rapturous in the touch of his fingers as he shook hands with Caroline when the service was over; and Miss Baker declared that he looked almost handsome when he went home with them to lunch.

But that afternoon his bliss was destined to receive something of a check. It was imperative that Harcourt should be in town early on the Monday morning, and therefore it had been settled that they should return by the latest train that Sunday evening. They would just be able to dine with Miss Baker, and do this afterwards. Harcourt had, of course, been anxious to be allowed to return alone; but Bertram had declined to appear to be too much in love to leave his mistress, and had persisted that he would accompany him.

This having been so decided, he had been invited to a little conference at Miss Baker's, to be holden upstairs in her private little sitting-room before dinner. He had had one or two chats with Miss Baker in that same room before now, and therefore did not think so much of the invitation; but on this occasion he also found Caroline there. He felt at once that he was to be encounterd with opposition.

Miss Baker opened the battle. 'George,' said she, 'Caroline has made me promise to speak to you before you go up to town. Won't you sit down?'

'Upon my word,' said he, seating himself on a sofa next to Caroline; 'I hardly know what to say to it. You look so formal both of you. If I am to be condemned, my lord, I hope you'll give me a long day.'

'That's just it,' said Miss Baker; 'it must be a long day, I'm afraid, George.'

'What do you mean?'

'Why this; we think the marriage must be put off till after you have been called. You are both young you know.'

'Nonsense!' said George, rather too imperiously for a lover.

'Nay, but George, it is not nonsense,' said Caroline, in her sweetest voice, almost imploringly. 'Don't be impetuous; don't be angry with us. It is for your sake we say so.'

'For my sake!'

'Yes, for your sake; for your sake;' and she put his hand inside her arm, and almost pressed it to her bosom. 'For your sake, certainly, George; you of whom we are so much bound to think.'

'Then for my own sake I disdain any such solicitude. I know the world, at any rate, as well as either of you—'

'Ah! I am not sure of that,' said Caroline.

'And I know well, that our joint income should be ample for the next four or five years. You will have to give up your horse—'

'I should think nothing of that, George; nothing.'

'And that is all. How many thousand married couples are there, do you suppose, in London, who are now living on less than what our income will be?'

'Many thousands, doubtless. But very few, probably not

one, so living happily, when the husband has been brought up in such a manner as has been Master George Bertram.'

'Caroline, my belief is, that you know nothing about it. Some of your would-be-grand friends here in Littlebath have been frightening you on the score of income.'

'I have no friend in Littlebath to whom I would condescend to speak on such a matter, except aunt Mary.' Caroline's tone as she said this showed some slight offence; but not more than she had a right to show.

'And what do you say, aunt Mary?'

'Well, I really agree with Caroline; I really do.'

'Ah, she has talked you over.' This was true.

'And what is the date, Miss Waddington, that you are now kind enough to name for our wedding-day?' asked George, in a tone half of anger and half of banter. To Caroline's ear, the anger seemed to predominate.

'The day after you shall have been called to the bar, Mr Bertram. That is, if the press of two such great events together will not be too much for you.'

'Of course you know that that is putting it off for nearly three years?'

'For more than two, I believe, certainly.'

'And you can talk quite coolly about such a delay as that?'

'Not quite coolly, George; but, at any rate, with a fixed purpose.'

'And am not I then to have a fixed purpose also?'

'Certainly, dearest, you can. You can say, if you are cruel enough, that it shall be postponed for two years again after that. Or you can say, if you will do so, that under such circumstances you will not marry me at all. We have each got what you lawyers call a veto. Now, George, I put my veto upon poverty for you, and discomfort, and an untidy house, and the perils of a complaining, fretful wife. If I can ever assist you to be happy and prosperous, and elate before the world, I will try my best to do so; but I will not come to you like a clog round your neck, to impede all your efforts in your first struggle at rising. If I can wait, George, surely you can? An unfulfilled engagement can be no impediment to a man, whatever it may be to a girl.'

It may have been perceived by this time that Miss Waddington was not a person easy to be talked over. On this occasion, Bertram failed altogether in moving her. Even though at one moment aunt Mary had almost yielded to him, Caroline remained steady as a rock. None of his eloquence—and he was very eloquent on the occasion—changed her at all. She became soft in her tone, and affectionate, almost caressing in her manner; but nothing would induce her to go from her point. Bertram got on a very high horse, and spoke of the engagement as being thus practically broken off. She did not become angry or declare that she took him at his word; but with a low voice she said that she was aware that her determination gave him an option in the matter. He would certainly be justified in so resolving; nay, might do so without the slightest stain upon his faith. She herself would not violate the truth by saying that such a decision would give her pleasure; that it would—would—' Here for the first time she became rather agitated, and before she could finish, George was at her feet, swearing that he could not, would not live without her; that she knew that he could not, and would not do so.

And so the little conference ended. George had certainly gained nothing. Caroline had gained this, that she had made known her resolution, and had, nevertheless, not lost her lover. To all the expressions of her determination not to marry till George should be a barrister, aunt Mary had added a little clause—that such decision might at any moment be changed by some new act of liberality on the part of uncle Bertram. In aunt Mary's mind, the rich uncle, the rich grandfather, was still the god that was to come down upon the stage* and relieve them from their great difficulty.

As George returned to town with his friend, his love was not quite so triumphant as it had been that morning on his road to church.

CHAPTER XVI

THE NEW MEMBER FOR THE BATTERSEA HAMLETS

I MUST now ask my readers to pass over two years with me. It is a terrible gap in a story; but in these days the unities are not much considered, and a hiatus which would formerly have been regarded as a fault utterly fatal is now no more than a slight impropriety.

But something must be told of the occurrences of these two years. In the first place, no marriage had taken place—that is, among our personages; nor had their ranks been thinned by any death. In our retrospective view we will give the *pas* to Mr Harcourt, for he had taken the greatest stride in winning that world's success, which is the goal of all our ambition. He had gone on and prospered greatly; and nowadays all men at the bar said all manner of good things of him. He was already in Parliament as the honourable member for the Battersea Hamlets, and was not only there, but listened to when it suited him to speak. But when he did speak, he spoke only as a lawyer. He never allowed himself to be enticed away from his own profession by the meretricious allurements of general politics. On points of law reform, he had an energetic opinion; on matters connected with justice, he had ideas which were very much his own—or which at least were stated in language which was so; being a denizen of the common law, he was loud against the delays and cost of Chancery, and was supposed to have supplied the legal details of a very telling tale* which was written about this time with the object of upsetting the lord chancellor as then constituted.

But though he worked as a member only in legal matters, of course he was always ready to support his party with his vote in all matters. His party! here had been his great difficulty on first entering the House of Commons. What should be his party?

He had worked hard as a lawyer. In so doing no party had been necessary to him. Honest hard work—honest, that is, as regarded the work itself, if not always as regarded the object.

Honest hard work, and some cunning in the method of his eloquence, had at first sufficed him. He was not called upon to have, or at any rate to state, any marked political tenets. But no man can rise to great note as a lawyer without a party. Opulence without note would by no means have sufficed with Mr Harcourt.

When, therefore, he found it expedient in the course of his profession to go into Parliament, and with this object presented himself to the inhabitants of the Battersea Hamlets, it was necessary that he should adopt a party. At that time the political watchword of the day was the repeal of the corn laws.* Now the electors of the Battersea Hamlets required especially to know whether Mr Harcourt was or was not for free trade in corn.

To tell the truth, he did not care two straws about corn. He cared only for law—for that and what was to be got by it. It was necessary that he should assume some care for corn—learn a good deal about it, perhaps, so as to be able, if called on, to talk on the subject by the hour at a stretch; but it was not a matter on which he was personally solicitous a fortnight or so before he began his canvass.

The Conservatives were at that time in, and were declared foes to free trade in corn. They were committed to the maintenance of a duty on imported wheat—if any men were ever politically committed to anything. Indeed, it had latterly been their great shibboleth—latterly; that is, since their other great shibboleths had been cut from under their feet.

At that time men had not learnt thoroughly by experience, as now they have, that no reform, no innovation—experience almost justifies us in saying no revolution—stinks so foully in the nostrils of an English Tory politician as to be absolutely irreconcilable to him. When taken in the refreshing waters of office any such pill can be swallowed. This is now a fact recognized in politics; and it is a great point gained in favour of that party that their power of deglutition should be so recognized. Let the people want what they will, Jew senators, cheap corn, vote by ballot, no property qualification,* or anything else, the Tories will carry it for them if the Whigs cannot. A poor Whig premier has none but the Liberals to back him; but a reforming Tory will be backed by all the world—except those few whom his own dishonesty will personally have disgusted.

But at that time—some twelve or fifteen years since—all this was not a part of the political A B C; and Harcourt had much doubt in his own mind as to the party which ought to be blessed with his adherence. Lord chancellorships and lord chief-justiceships, though not enjoyed till middle life, or, indeed, till the evening of a lawyer's days, must, in fact, be won or lost in the heyday of his career. One false step in his political novitiate may cost him everything. A man when known as a recognized Whig may fight battle after battle with mercenary electors, sit yawning year after year till twelve o'clock, ready to attack on every point the tactics of his honourable and learned friend on the Treasury seats, and yet see junior after junior rise to the bench before him—and all because at starting he decided wrongly as to his party.

If Harcourt had predilections, they were with the Whigs; but he was not weak enough to let any predilection be a burden to his interests. Where was the best opening for him? The Tories—I still prefer the name, as being without definite meaning; the direct falsehood implied in the title of Conservative amounts almost to a libel—the Tories* were in; but from the fact of being in, were always liable to be turned out. Then, too, they were of course provided with attorneys and solicitors-general, lords-advocate and legal hangers-on of every sort. The coming chances might be better with the Whigs.

Under these circumstances, he went to his old friend Mr Die, Mr Neversaye Die, the rich, quiet, hard-working, old chancery barrister, to whose fostering care he had some time since recommended his friend Bertram. Every one has some quiet, old, family, confidential friend; a man given to silence, but of undoubted knowledge of the world, whose experience is vast, and who, though he has not risen in the world himself, is always the man to help others to do so. Every one has such a friend as this, and Mr Neversaye Die was Harcourt's friend. Mr Die himself was supposed to be a Tory, quite of the old school, a Lord Eldon* Tory; but Harcourt knew that this would in no way bias his judgment. The mind of a barrister who has been for fifty years practising in court will never be biassed by his predilections.

Mr Die soon understood the whole matter. His young friend Harcourt was going into Parliament with the special object of becoming a solicitor-general as soon as possible. He could so become by means only of two moving powers. He must be solicitor-general either to the Whigs or to the Tories. To which he should be so was a question mainly indifferent to Mr Harcourt himself, and also to Mr Die in framing his advice.

Mr Die himself of course regarded corn-law repeal as an invention of the devil. He had lived long enough to have regarded Catholic emancipation and Parliamentary reform* in the same light. Could you have opened his mind, you would probably have found there a settled conviction that the world was slowly coming to an end, that end being brought about by such devilish works as these. But you would also have found a conviction that the Three per Cents would last his time, and that his fear for the future might with safety be thrown forward, so as to appertain to the fourth or fifth, or, perhaps, even to the tenth or twelfth coming generation. Mr Die was not, therefore, personally wretched under his own political creed.

'I should be inclined to support the government if I were going into Parliament as a young man,' said Mr Die.

'There are nine seniors of mine in the House who now do so.' By seniors, Mr Harcourt alluded to his seniors at the bar.

'Yes; but they like young blood nowadays. I think it's the safest.'

'I shall never carry the Battersea Hamlets unless I pledge myself on this corn-law question.'

'Well,' said Mr Die—'well; a seat is certainly a great thing, and not to be had at any moment. I think I should be inclined to yield to the electors.'

'And commit myself to the repeal of the corn laws?'

'Commit yourself!' said Mr Die, with a gentle smile. 'A public man has to commit himself to many things nowadays. But my opinion is, that—that you may hold the popular opinion about free trade, and be not a whit the less useful to Sir Robert* on that account.'

Mr Harcourt was still a young man, and was, therefore, excusable in not seeing to the depths of Mr Die's wisdom. He certainly did not see to the depth of it; but he had come to his oracle with faith, and wisely resolved to be guided by wisdom so much superior to his own.

'Never bind yourself wantonly to an expiring policy,' said Mr Die. 'The man who does so has surely to unbind himself; and, to say the least of it, that always takes time.'

So Mr Harcourt presented himself to the electors of Battersea Hamlets as a man very anxious in their behalf in all things, but anxious in their behalf above all things for free trade in corn. 'Is it credible, that now, in this year of grace 184—,—' and so on. Such were the eloquent words which he addressed to the electors on this subject, and so taken were they by his enthusiasm that they returned him by a large majority.

Mr Dod,* therefore, in his remarkably useful little parliamentary compendium, put down Mr Harcourt as a Liberal: this he had an opportunity of doing immediately after Mr Harcourt's election: in his next edition, however, he added, 'but supports the general policy of Sir Robert Peel's government.'

Mr Harcourt had altogether managed this little affair so well that, despite his youth, despite also those nine political seniors of his, men began to talk of him as one who might shortly hope to fill high places. He made himself very useful in the House, and did so in a quiet, business-like, unexciting manner, very pleasant to the leading politician of the Treasury bench.

And then there came the Irish famine, and all the bindings of all the Tories were scattered to the winds like feathers. The Irishman's potato-pot ceased to be full, and at once the great territorial magnates of England were convinced that they had clung to the horns of a false altar. They were convinced; or at least had to acknowledge such conviction. The prime minister held short little debates with his underlings—with dukes and marquises, with earls and viscounts; held short debates with them, but allowed to no underling—to no duke, and to no viscount—to have any longer an opinion of his own. The altar had been a false altar: it was enough for them that they were so told. With great wisdom the majority of them considered that this *was* enough; and so the bill for the repeal of the corn laws was brought before the House, and the world knew that it would be carried.

And now there was a great opportunity for Mr Harcourt. He could support the prime minister and merit all manner of legal generalships without any self-unbinding. Alas! such comfort as this can only belong to the young among politicians! Up to this period he had meddled only with law questions. Now was the time for him to come out with that great liberal speech, which should merit the eternal gratitude of the Tory leader. Just at the time at which we recommence our tale he did come out with a very great liberal speech, in which, as an independent member, he vehemently eulogized the daring policy of that great man who, as he said, was brave enough, and wise enough, and good enough to save his country at the expense of his party. Whether there were not men who could have saved their country without betraying their friends—who would have done so had not Sir Robert been ready with his apostasy: who in fact did so by forcing Sir Robert to his apostasy—as to that, Mr Harcourt then said nothing. What might not be expected from the hands of a man so eulogized? of a man who was thus able to keep the votes of the Tories and carry the measures of the Liberals? of a man of whom it might now be predicted that his political power would end only with his political life? We should be going on too fast were we to declare in how few months after this triumph that great political chieftain was driven from the Treasury bench.

Mr Harcourt's name was now mentioned in all clubs and all dining-rooms. He was an acute and successful lawyer, an eloquent debater, and a young man. The world was at his feet, and Mr Die was very proud of him. Mr Die was proud of him, and proud also of his own advice. He said nothing about it even to Harcourt himself, for to Mr Die had been given the gift of reticence; but his old eye twinkled as his wisdom was confessed by the youth at his feet. 'In politics one should always look forward,' he said, as he held up to the light the glass of old port which he was about to sip; 'in real life it is better to look back,—if one has anything to look back at.' Mr Die had something to look back at. He had sixty thousand pounds in the funds.

And now we must say a word of Mr Harcourt, with reference to the other persons of our story. He was still very intimate with Bertram, but he hardly regarded him in the same light as he had done two years before. Bertram had not hitherto justified the expectation of his friends. This must be explained more at length in the next two chapters; but the effect on Harcourt had been that he no longer looked up with reverence to his friend's undoubted talents. He had a lower opinion of him than formerly. Indeed, he himself had risen so quickly that he had left Bertram immeasurably below him, and the difference in their pursuits naturally brought them together less frequently than heretofore.

But if Harcourt was less concerned than he had been with George Bertram junior, he was much more concerned than he had been with George Bertram senior. He had in former days known nothing of the old merchant: now he was, within certain bounds, almost intimate with him; occasionally dined down at Hadley, and frequently consulted him on money matters of deep import.

With Miss Baker, also, and Caroline Waddington, Mr Harcourt was intimate. Between him and Miss Baker there existed a warm friendship, and with Caroline, even, he was on such terms that she often spoke to him as to the deep troubles of her love and engagement. For these were deep troubles, as will be seen also in the coming chapters.

George Bertram had been told by Miss Baker that Caroline was the granddaughter of old Mr Bertram, and George in his confidence with his friend had told him the secret. Indeed, there had been hardly any alternative, for George had been driven to consult his friend more than once as to this delay in his marriage; and who can ever consult a friend with advantage on any subject without telling him all the circumstances?

It was after this that Harcourt and Miss Baker became so intimate. The ladies at Littlebath had many troubles, and during those troubles the famous young barrister was very civil to them. In the latter of those two years that are now gone, circumstances had brought them up to London for a couple of months in the spring; and then they saw much of Mr Harcourt, but nothing of George Bertram, though George was still the affianced husband of Miss Waddington.

CHAPTER XVII

RETROSPECTIVE—FIRST YEAR

GEORGE BERTRAM had returned to town that Sunday after the conference in Miss Baker's little room not in the very best of moods. He had talked glibly enough on his way back, because it had been necessary for him to hide his chagrin: but he had done so in a cynical tone, which had given Harcourt to understand that something was wrong. For some ten days after that there had been no intercourse between him and Littlebath: and then he had written a letter to Caroline, full of argument, full also of tenderness, in which he essayed to move her from her high resolve. He had certainly written strongly, if not well. 'He was working,' he said, 'nearly as hard as a man could work, in order to ensure success for her. Nothing, he was aware, but the idea that he was already justified in looking on her as his wife would have induced him to labour so strictly; and for this he was grateful to her. She had given him this great and necessary incitement; and he therefore thanked God that he had on his shoulders the burden, as well as in his heart the blessing, of such an engagement. But the strain would be too great for him if the burden were to remain present to him daily, while the blessing was to be postponed for so long a time. He had already felt his spirits numbed and his energy weakened. It seemed to him in all his daily work that his great hope had been robbed from him. His dreams told him that he was to be happy, but his waking moments brought him back to disappointment. He knew that he could not endure it, that he could not remain there at his post, diligent as he fain would be, if his reward were to be postponed for so long. As being under a holy engagement to you,' he wrote, perhaps almost too solemnly, 'I have given up that sort of life to which my natural disposition might have led me. Do not suppose that I say this with regret. I rejoice to have done so, rejoice to be so doing; but it is for you that I do it. Should I not look to you for my reward? Granting that there may be risk, shall not I share it? Supposing that there may be suffering, shall not I endure it? And if a man with his best efforts may protect a woman from suffering, I will protect you.' So he had written, and had ended by imploring her to let them be married that autumn.

By return of post he got three lines from her, calling him her dearest, dearest George, and requesting that he would allow her a week to answer his letter at length. It could not be answered without deep thought. This gratified him much, and he wrote another note to her, begging her on no account to hurry herself; that he would wait for her reply with the utmost patience; but again imploring her to be merciful. It was, however, apparent in the tone of his note, apparent at least to Caroline, that he judged the eloquence of his letter to be unanswerable, and that he was already counting on her surrender. This lessened the effect of it on Caroline's heart:—for when first received it had had a strong effect.

On that first morning, when she read it in her bedroom before she went down to breakfast, it certainly had a strong effect on her. She made up her mind that she would say nothing about it to her aunt, at any rate on that day. Her aunt would have advised her to yield at once, and she would have preferred some counsellor of a sterner sort. So she put the letter in her pocket, went down tranquilly to breakfast, and after breakfast wrote the note which we have mentioned.

All that day she thought about it to herself, and all the next day. On the evening of the second day she had all but brought herself to give in. Then came George's note, and the fancied tone of triumph hardened her heart once more. On the evening of that day she was firm to her principles. She had acted hitherto, and would continue to act, according to the course she had laid down for herself.

On the fourth day she was sitting in the drawing-room alone—for her aunt had gone out of Littlebath for the day—when Adela Gauntlet came to call on her. Adela she knew would counsel her to yield, and therefore she would certainly not have gone to Adela for advice. But she was sad at heart; and sitting there with the letter among her threads and needles before her, she gradually found it impossible not to talk of it—to talk of it, and at last to hand it over to be read.

There could be no doubt at all as to the nature of Adela's advice; but Caroline had had no conception of the impetuosity of matured conviction on the subject, of the impassioned eloquence with which that advice would be given. She had been far from thinking that Adela had any such power of passion.

'Well,' said she, as Adela slowly folded the sheet and put it back into its envelope; 'well; what answer shall I make to it?'

'Can you doubt, Caroline?' said Adela, and Miss Gauntlet's eyes shone as Caroline had never before seen them shine.

'Indeed, I do doubt; doubt very much. Not that I ought to doubt. What I knew to be wise a week ago, I know also to be wise now. But one is so weak, and it is so hard to refuse those whom we love.'

'Hard, indeed!' said Adela. 'To my thinking, a woman would have a stone instead of a heart who could refuse such a request as that from a man to whom she has confessed her love.'

'But because you love a man, would you wish to make a beggar of him?'

'We are too much afraid of what we call beggary,' said Adela. 'Beggary, Caroline, with four hundred pounds a year! You had no right to accept a man if you intended to decline to live with him on such an income as that. He should make no request; it should come from him as a demand.'

'A demand? No; his time for demands has not yet come.'

'But it has come if you are true to your word. You should have thought of all this, and no doubt did think of it, before you accepted him. You have no right now to make him wretched.'

'And therefore, I will not make him poor.'

'Poor, poor! How fearfully afraid we are of poverty! Is there nothing worse than poverty, what you call poverty—poverty that cannot have its gowns starched above once a week?' Caroline stared at her, but Adela went on. 'Broken hearts are not half so bad as that; nor daily tears and disappointed hopes, nor dry, dull, dead, listless despondency without one drop of water to refresh it! All that is as nothing to a well-grounded apprehension as to one's larder! Never marry till you are sure that will be full, let the heart be ever so empty.'

'Adela!'

'For others there may be excuse,' she continued, thinking then, as always, of that scene at West Putford, and defending to herself him whom to herself she so often accused; 'but for you there can be none. If you drive him from you now, whatever evil may befall him will lie like a weight of lead upon your heart. If you refuse him now, he is not the man to take it quietly and wait.'

'I can live without him.'

'Yes; it is your pride to say so; and I believe you could live without him. But I think too well of you to believe that you could live happily without him; nor will he be happy without you. You will both be proud, and stony-hearted, and wretched—stony-hearted at least in appearance; not fortunate enough to become so in reality.'

'Why, Adela, one would think that you yourself were the victim of some passion nipped in its bud by a cruel prudence.'

'And so I am.' As she said this she rose from her seat as though she intended, standing there before her companion, to go on with her impassioned warning. But the effect was too much for her; and falling down on her knees, with her face buried in her hands, she rested them on the sofa, and gave way to sobs and tears.

Caroline was of course much shocked, and did what she could to relieve her; but Adela merely begged that she might be left to herself one minute. 'One minute,' she said, plaintively, in a voice so different from that she had used just now; 'one minute and I shall be well again. I have been very foolish, but never say anything about it; never, never, not to any one; promise me, promise me, Caroline. Dear Caroline, you do promise me? No one knows it; no one must know it.'

Caroline did promise; but with a natural curiosity she wanted to know the whole story. Adela, however, would tell her nothing, would say no more about herself. In the agony of her strong feeling she had once pointed to herself as a beacon; but even she herself could not endure to do this again. She would say nothing further about that; but in a more plaintive and softer tone she did not cease to implore her friend not to throw away from her the rich heart which was still within her grasp.

A scene such as this could not but have an effect on Caroline; but it did not ultimately have that which Adela had wished. It was Miss Waddington's doctrine that she should not under any circumstances of life permit herself to be carried away by passion. Why then should she allow Adela's passion to convince her? What were the facts? Of Adela's own case she knew nothing. It might be that she had been cruelly treated. Her friends, her lover, or even she herself might have been in fault. But it would surely be the extreme of folly for her, Caroline Waddington, to allow herself to be actuated by the example of one who had not even shown her of what that example consisted.

The upshot of it all was, that at the end of the week she wrote to George, declaring that, grieved as she was to grieve him, she felt herself obliged to adhere to her former resolution. She also wrote strongly, and perhaps with more force of logic than her lover had done. 'I trust the time will come,' she said, 'when you will acknowledge that I have been right. But of this I am quite sure, that were I now to yield to you, the time would come very quickly when you would acknowledge me to have been wrong; and that you should then think me to have been wrong would kill me. I am not, I know, fitted, either by disposition or education, to be a poor man's wife. I say this with no pride; though if you choose to take it for pride, I cannot help myself. Nor are you fitted to be the husband of a poor wife. Your love and enthusiasm now make you look on want as a slight evil; but have you ever tried want? Since you left school, have you not had everything that money could buy you? Have you ever been called on to deny yourself any reasonable wish? Never, I believe. Nor have I. What right have we then to suppose that we can do that for each other which we have never yet done for ourselves?

'You talk of the misery of waiting. Is it not because you have as yet known no misery? Have not all men to wait who look for success in life?—to work, and wait, and bide their time? Your present work is, I know, too hard. In whatever you do, you have too much enthusiasm. Do not kill yourself by work. For my sake, if I may still plead my own sake, do not do so. You say you have given up that sort of life to which your disposition would have led you. I do not believe your disposition to be bad, and I should be grieved to think that you debar yourself from pleasures that are not bad because you are engaged to me.' There was that in the eagerness of Bertram's protestations on this point which could not but be flattering to any girl; but Caroline, when she thought of it, did not wish to be so flattered. She required less passion in her lover and more judgment. She wanted him to be more awake to the fact that the true meaning of their engagement was this, that they two should join themselves together in their world's battle, in order that together each might fight that battle more successfully than either of them could do apart.

'I write this with great grief,' she continued, 'as I know that what I write will grieve you. But I write it under a conviction that I am doing my duty by you. I am ready, however, to acknowledge that such a delay may not be in consonance with your intentions when you proposed to me. That neither of us have deceived the other wilfully I am quite sure; but it may be that we have misunderstood each other. If so, dear George, let all this be as though it had never been. I do not say this on my own behalf. If you so wish it, I am ready to hold myself as yours, and to wait. Ready, I have said! That is a cold word, and you may supply any other that your heart wishes. But if this waiting be contrary to your wishes, be what you are not willing to endure, then consider the matter as altogether in your own hands. I certainly have no right to bind you to my will; all that I ask in such case is, that your decision shall not be delayed.'

Such was Miss Waddington's letter; a portion of it, at least, for not above the half has been given here. Its effect upon Bertram had not been exhilarating. In his heart he called her cold and heartless, and at first resolved to take her at her word and break off from her. He would willingly have done so as far as she was concerned; but he could not bring himself to do it on his own part. He could not endure to part with her, though he would willingly have punished her by telling her that she had forfeited her claim to him. As it was, he did nothing. For three weeks he neither answered the letter nor went near her, nor gave her any token that he was thinking about her.

Then came a note from Miss Baker, asking him to come to Littlebath. It was good-humoured, playful, almost witty; too much so for Miss Baker's unassisted epistle-craft, and he at once saw that Caroline had dictated it. Her heart at any rate was light. He answered it by one equally good-humoured and playful, and perhaps more witty, addressed of course to Miss Baker, in which he excused himself at present in consequence of the multiplicity of his town engagements. It was June, and he could not get away without making himself guilty of all manner of perjuries; but in August he would certainly take Littlebath on his way to Scotland.

He had intended that every light word should be a dagger in Caroline's bosom; but there was not a pin's prick in the whole of it. Sullen grief on his part would have hurt her. And it would have hurt her had he taken her at her word and annulled their engagement; for she had begun to find that she loved him more than she had thought possible. She had talked in her prudence, and written in her prudence, of giving him up; but when the time came in which she might expect a letter from him, saying that so it should be, her heart did tremble at the postman's knock; she did feel that she had something to fear. But his joyous, clever, laughing answer to her aunt was all that she could wish. Though she loved him, she could wait; though she loved him, she did not wish him to be sad when he was away from her. She had reason and measure in her love; but it was love as she began to find—almost to her own astonishment.

George had alluded not untruly to his own engagements. On the day after he received Caroline's letter he shut up Coke upon Littleton for that term, and shook the dust off his feet on the threshold of Mr Die's chambers. Why should he work? why sit there filling his brain with cobwebs, pouring over old fusty rules couched in obscure languages, and useful only for assisting mankind to cheat each other? He had an object; but that was gone. He had wished to prove to one heart, to one soul, that, young as he was, poor as he was, she need not fear to trust herself to his guardianship. Despite his musty toils, she did fear. Therefore, he would have no more of them. No more of them at any rate then, while the sun was shining so brightly. So he went down to Richmond with Twisleton and Madden, and Hopgood and Fortescue. Heaven knows what they did when they got back to town that night—or, rather, perhaps heaven's enemy. And why not? Caroline did not care whether or no he amused himself as other men do. For her sake he had kept himself from these things. As she was indifferent, why need he care? He cared no longer. There was no more law that term; no more eulogy from gratified Mr Die; but of jovial days at Richmond or elsewhere there were plenty; plenty also of jovial Bacchanalian nights in London. Miss Waddington had been very prudent; but there might perhaps have been a prudence yet more desirable.

He did go down to Littlebath on his way to Scotland, and remained there three days. He made up his mind as he journeyed down to say nothing about their late correspondence to Caroline till she should first speak of it; and as she had come to an exactly similar resolution on her part, and as both adhered to their intentions, it so fell out that nothing in the matter was said by either of them. Caroline was quite satisfied; but not so Bertram. He again said to himself that she was cold and passionless; as cold as she is beautiful, he declared, as he walked home to the 'Plough'. How very many young gentlemen have made the same soliloquy when their mistresses have not been so liberal as they would have had them!

The lovers passed the three days together at Littlebath with apparent satisfaction. They rode together, and walked together, and on one evening danced together; nay, they talked together, and Miss Baker thought that everything was smooth. But Bertram, as he went off to Scotland, said to himself that she was very, very cold, and began to question with himself whether she did really love him.

'Do write to me, and tell me what sport you have,' Caroline had said when he went away. What a subject for a woman to choose for her lover's letters! She never said, 'Write, write often; and always when you write, swear that you love me.' 'Oh, yes, I'll write,' said Bertram, laughing. 'I'll give you a succinct account of every brace.' And send some of them too,' said Miss Baker. 'Certainly,' said George; and so he did.

He was joined with Harcourt and one or two others in this trip to Scotland, and it was then that he told his friend how much he was disturbed by Miss Waddington's obstinacy; and how he doubted, not as to her heart being his, but as to her having a heart to belong to any one. In answer to this, Harcourt gave him pretty nearly the same counsel as she had done. 'Wait, my dear fellow, with a little patience; you'll have lots of time before you for married troubles. What's the use of a man having half-a-score of children round him just when he is beginning to enjoy life? It is that that Miss Waddington thinks about; though, of course, she can't tell you so.'

And then, also—that is to say, on some occasion a little subsequent to the conversation above alluded to—Bertram also told his friend what he knew of Miss Waddington's birth.

'Whew-w-w,' whistled Harcourt; 'is that the case? Well, now I am surprised.'

'It is, indeed.'

'And he has agreed to the marriage?'

'He knows of it, and has not disagreed. Indeed, he made some peddling little offer about money.'

'But what has he said to you about it?'

'Nothing, not a word. I have only seen him once since Christmas, and then I did not speak of it; nor did he.'

Harcourt asked fifty other questions on the matter, all eagerly, as though he considered this newly-learned fact to be of the greatest importance: all of which Bertram answered, till at last he was tired of talking of his uncle.

'I cannot see that it makes any difference,' said he, 'whose granddaughter she is.'

'But it does make the greatest difference. I own that I am surprised now that Miss Waddington should wish to delay the marriage. I thought I understood her feelings and conduct on the matter, and must say that I regarded them as admirable. But I cannot quite understand her now. It certainly seems to me that with such a guarantee as that she needs be afraid of nothing. Whichever of you he selected, it would come to the same thing.'

'Harcourt, if she would marry me tomorrow because by doing so she would make sure of my uncle's money, by heaven, I would not take her! If she will not take me for myself, and what I can do for her, she may let me alone.' Thus majestically spoke Bertram, sitting with his friend on the side of a Scottish mountain, with a flask of brandy and a case of sandwiches between them.

'Then,' said Harcourt, 'you are an ass'; and as he spoke he finished the flask.

Bertram kept his word, and told his lady-love all particulars as to the game he killed; some particulars also he gave her as to scenery, as to his friends, and as to Scotch people. He wrote nice, chatty, amusing letters, such as most people love to get from their friends; but he said little or nothing about love. Once or twice he ventured to tell her of some pretty girl that he met, of some adventure with a laird's daughter; nay, insinuated laughingly that he had not escaped from it quite heart-whole. Caroline answered his letter in the same tone; told him, with excellent comedy, of the leading facts of life in Littlebath; recommended him by all means to go back after the laird's daughter; described the joy of her heart at unexpectedly meeting Mr M'Gabbery in the pump-room, and her subsequent disappointment at hearing that there was now a Mrs M'Gabbery. He had married that Miss Jones, of whom the parental Potts had so strongly disapproved. All this was very nice, very amusing, and very friendly. But Bertram, as a lover, knew that he was not satisfied.

When he had done with the grouse and the laird's daughter he went to Oxford, but he did not then go again to Littlebath. He went to Oxford, and from thence to Arthur Wilkinson's parsonage. Here he saw much of Adela; and consoled himself by talking with her about Caroline. To her he did not conceal his great anger. While he was still writing good-humoured, witty letters to his betrothed, he was saying of her to Adela Gauntlet things harsh—harsher perhaps in that they were true.

'I had devoted myself to her,' he said. 'I was working for her as a galley-slave works, and was contented to do it. I would have borne anything, risked anything, endured anything, if she would have borne it with me. All that I have should have gone to shield her from discomfort. I love her still, Miss Gauntlet; it is perhaps my misery that I love her. But I can never love her now as I should have done had she come to me then.'

'How can I work now?' he said again. 'I shall be called to the bar of course; there is no difficulty in that; and may perhaps earn what will make us decently respectable. But the spirit, the high spirit is gone. She is better pleased that it should be so. She is intolerant of enthusiasm. Is it not a pity, Miss Gauntlet, that we should be so different?'

What could Adela say to him? Every word that he uttered was to her a truth—a weary, melancholy truth; a repetition of that truth which was devouring her own heart. She sympathized with him fully, cordially, ardently. She said no word absolutely in dispraise of Caroline; but she admitted, and at last admitted so often, that, according to her thinking, Caroline was wrong.

'Wrong!' Bertram would shout. 'Can there be a doubt? Can any one with a heart doubt?' Adela said, 'No; no one with a heart could doubt.'

'She has no heart,' said Bertram. 'She is lovely, clever, fascinating, elegant. She has everything a woman should have except a heart—except a heart.' And then, as he turned away his face, Adela could see that he brushed his hand across his eyes.

What could she do but weep too? And is it not known to all men—certainly it is to all women—how dangerous are such tears?

Thus during his stay at Hurst Staple, Bertram was frequently at West Putford. But he observed that Adela was not often at his cousin's vicarage, and that Arthur was very seldom at West Putford. The families, it was clear, were on as good terms as ever. Adela and Mary and Sophia would be together, and old Mr Gauntlet would dine at Hurst Staple, and Arthur would talk about the old rector freely enough. But Bertram rarely saw Adela unless he went to the rectory, and though he dined there with the Wilkinson girls three or four times, Arthur only dined there once.

'Have you and Arthur quarrelled?' said he to Adela one day, laughing as he spoke.

'Oh, no,' said she; but she could not keep down her rebellious colour as she answered him, and Bertram at once took the hint. To her he said nothing further on that matter.

'And why don't you marry, Arthur?' he asked the next morning.

And Arthur also blushed, not thinking then of Adela Gauntlet, but of that pledge which he had given to Lord Stapledean—a pledge of which he had repented every day since he had given it.

And here it may be explained, that as Arthur Wilkinson had repented of that pledge, and had felt more strongly from day to day that it had put him in a false and unworthy position, so did his mother from day to day feel with less force the compunction which she had at first expressed as to receiving her son's income. This had become less and less, and now, perhaps, it could no longer boast of an existence. The arrangement seemed to her to be so essentially a good one, her children were provided for in so convenient and so comfortable a manner, it was so natural that she should regard herself as the mistress of that house, that perhaps no blame is due to her in that this compunction ceased. No blame is now heaped upon her, and the fact is merely stated. She had already learned to regard herself as the legal owner of that ecclesiastical income; and seeing that her son deducted a stipend of one hundred and fifty pounds for merely doing the duty—a curate would have only had the half of that sum, as she sometimes said to herself—and seeing also that he had his fellowship, she had no scruple in making him pay fairly for whatever extra accommodation he received at home—exactly as she would have done had poor dear old Mr Wilkinson not been out of the way. Considering all these comfortable circumstances, poor dear old Mr Wilkinson was perhaps not regretted quite so much as might otherwise have been the case.

Mrs Wilkinson was in the habit of saying many things from day to day in praise of that good Lord Stapledean, who had so generously thought of her and her widowhood. When she did so Arthur would look grim and say nothing, and his mother would know that he was displeased. 'Surely he cannot begrudge us the income,' she had once said to her eldest daughter. 'Oh, no; I am sure he does not,' said Mary; 'but somehow he is not so happy about things as he used to be.' 'Then he must be a very ungrateful boy,' said the mother. Indeed, what more could a young full-fledged vicar want than to have a comfortable house under his mother's apron-string?

'And why don't you marry?' Bertram had asked his cousin. It was odd that Arthur should not marry, seeing that Adela Gauntlet lived so near him, and that Adela was so very, very beautiful.

Up to that day, Bertram had heard nothing of the circumstances under which the living had been given. Then did Wilkinson tell him the story, and ended by saying—'You now see that my marriage is quite out of the question.'

Then Bertram began to think he understood why Adela also remained unmarried, and he began to ask himself whether all the world were as cold-hearted as his Caroline. Could it be that Adela also had refused to venture till her future husband should have a good, comfortable, disposable income of his own? But, if so, she would not have sympathized so warmly with him; and if so, what reason could there by why she and Arthur should not meet each other? Could it then be that Arthur Wilkinson was such a coward?

He said nothing on the matter to either of them, for neither of them had confided to him their sorrows—if they had sorrows. He had no wish to penetrate their secrets. What he had said, and what he had learnt, he had said and learnt by accident. He himself had not their gift of reticence, so he talked of his love occasionally to Arthur, and he talked of it very often to Adela.

And the upshot of his talking to Adela was always this: 'Why, oh why, was not his Caroline more like to her?' Caroline was doubtless the more beautiful, doubtless the more clever, doubtless the more fascinating. But what are beauty and talent and fascination without a heart? He was quite sure that Adela's heart was warm.

He went to Littlebath no more that year. It was well perhaps that he did not. Well or ill as the case may be. Had he done so, he would, in his then state of mind, most assuredly have broken with Miss Waddington. In lieu, however, of accepting Miss Baker's invitation for Christmas, he went to Hadley and spent two or three days there, uncomfortable himself, and making the old man uncomfortable also.

Up to this time he had been completely idle—at any rate, as far as the law was concerned—since the day of his great break-down on the receipt of Miss Waddington's letter. He still kept his Temple chambers, and when the day came round in October, he made another annual payment to Mr Die. On that occasion Mr Die had spoken rather seriously to him; but up to that time his period of idleness had mainly been the period of the long vacation, and Mr Die was willing to suppose that this continued payment was a sign that he intended to settle again to work.

'Will it be impertinent to ask,' his uncle at Hadley had said to him—'will it be impertinent to ask what you and Caroline intend to do?' At this time Mr Bertram was aware that his nephew knew in what relationship they all stood to each other.

'No impertinence at all, sir. But, unfortunately, we have no intentions in common. We are engaged to be married, and I want to keep my engagement.'

'And she wants to break hers. Well, I cannot but say that she is the wiser of the two.'

'I don't know that her wisdom goes quite so far as that. She is content to abide the evil day; only she would postpone it.'

'That is to say, she has some prudence. Are you aware that I have proposed to make a considerable addition to her fortune—to hers, mind—on condition that she would postpone her marriage till next summer?'

'I did hear something about some sum of money—that you had spoken to Miss Baker about it, I believe; but I quite forgot the particulars.'

'You are very indifferent as to money matters, Mr Barrister.'

'I am indifferent as to the money matters of other people, sir. I had no intention of marrying Miss Waddington for her money before I knew that she was your granddaughter; nor have I now that I do know it.'

'For her money! If you marry her for more money than her own fortune, and perhaps a couple of thousands added to it, you are likely to be mistaken.'

'I shall never make any mistake of that kind. As far as I am concerned, you are quite welcome, for me, to keep your two thousand pounds.'

'That's kind of you.'

'I would marry her tomorrow without it, I am not at all sure that I will marry her next year with it. If you exercise any authority over her as her grandfather, I wish you would tell her so, as coming from me.'

'Upon my word you carry it high as a lover.'

'Not too high, I hope, as a man.'

'Well, George, remember this once for all'—and now the old man spoke in a much more serious voice—'I will not interfere at all as her grandfather. Nor will I have it known that I am such. Do you understand that?'

'I understand, sir, that it is not your wish that it should be generally talked of.'

'And I trust that wish has been, and will be, complied with by you.'

This last speech was not put in the form of a question; but

George understood that it was intended to elicit from him a promise for the future and an assurance as to the past.

'I have mentioned the circumstance to one intimate friend with whom I was all but obliged to discuss the matter—'

'Obliged to discuss my private concerns, sir!'

'With one friend, sir; with two, indeed; I think—indeed, I fear I have mentioned it to three.'

'Oh! to three! obliged to discuss your own most private concerns as well as mine with three intimate friends! You are lucky, sir, to have so many intimate friends. As my concerns have been made known to them as well as your own, may I ask who they are?'

George then gave up the three names. They were those of Mr Harcourt, the Rev. Arthur Wilkinson, and Miss Adela Gauntlet. His uncle was very angry. Had he utterly denied the fact of his ever having mentioned the matter to any one, and had it been afterwards discovered that such denial was false, Mr Bertram would not have been by much so angry. The offence and the lie together, but joined with the fear and deference to which the lie would have testified, would be nothing so black as the offence without the lie, and without the fear, and without the deference.

His uncle was very angry, but on that day he said nothing further on the matter; neither on the next day did he; but on the third day, just as George was about to leave Hadley, he said, in his usual bantering tone, 'Don't have any more intimate friends, George, as far as my private matters are concerned.'

'No, sir, I will not,' said George.

It was in consequence of what Mr Bertram had then learnt that he became acquainted with Mr Harcourt. As Mr Harcourt had heard this about his grandchild, he thought it better to see that learned gentleman. He did see him; and, as has been before stated, they became intimate with each other.

And so ended the first of these two years.

CHAPTER XVIII

RETROSPECTIVE—SECOND YEAR

THE next year passed almost more uncomfortably for George Bertram and for the ladies at Littlebath than had the latter months of the last year. Its occurrences can, I hope, be stated less in detail, so that we may get on without too great delay to the incidents of the period which is to be awhile for us the present existing time.

This year was Harcourt's great year. In January and February and March he did great things in Chancery. In April he came into Parliament. In May and June and July he sat on committees. In August he stuck to his work till London was no longer endurable. In the latter part of autumn there was an extraordinary session, during which he worked like a horse. He studied the corn-law question as well as sundry legal reforms all the Christmas week, and in the following spring he came out with his great speech on behalf of Sir Robert Peel. But, nevertheless, he found time to devote to the cares and troubles of Miss Baker and Miss Waddington.

In the spring Bertram paid one or two visits to Littlebath; but it may be doubted whether he made himself altogether agreeable there. He stated broadly that he was doing little or nothing at his profession: he was, he said, engaged on other matters; the great incitement to work, under which he had commenced, had been withdrawn from him; and under these circumstances he was not inclined to devote himself exclusively to studies which certainly were not to his taste. He did not condescend again to ask Caroline to revoke her sentence; he pressed now for no marriage; but he made it quite apparent that all the changes in himself for the worse—and there had been changes for the worse—were owing to her obstinacy.

He was now living a life of dissipation. I do not intend that it should be understood that he utterly gave himself up to pleasures disgraceful in themselves, that he altogether abandoned the reins, and allowed himself to live such a life as is passed by some young men in London. His tastes and appetites were too high for this. He did not sink into a slough of despond. He did not become filthy and vicious, callous and bestial; but he departed very widely astray from those rules which governed him during his first six months in London.

All this was well known at Littlebath; nor did Bertram at all endeavour to conceal the truth. Indeed, it may be said of him, that he never concealed anything. In this especial case he took a pride in letting Caroline know the full extent of the evil she had done.

It was a question with them whether he had not now given up the bar as a profession altogether. He did not say that he had done so, and it was certainly his intention to keep his terms, and to be called; but he had now no longer a legal Gamaliel. Some time in the April of this year, Mr Die had written to him a very kind little note, begging him to call one special morning at the chambers in Stone Buildings, if not very inconvenient to him. Bertram did call, and Mr Die, with many professions of regard and regret, honestly returned to him his money paid for that year's tutelage. 'It had been,' he said, 'a pleasure and a pride to him to have Mr Bertram in his chambers; and would still be so to have him there again. But he could not take a gentleman's money under a false pretence; as it seemed to be no longer Mr Bertram's intention to attend there, he must beg to refund it.' And he did refund it accordingly. This also was made known to the ladies at Littlebath.

He was engaged, he had said, on other matters. This also was true. During the first six months of his anger, he had been content to be idle; but idleness did not suit him, so he sat himself down and wrote a book. He published this book without his name, but he told them at Littlebath of his authorship; and some one also told of it at Oxford. The book—or bookling, for it consisted but of one small demy-octavo volume—was not such as delighted his friends either at Littlebath or at Oxford, or even at those two Hampshire parsonages. At Littlebath it made Miss Baker's hair stand on end, and at Oxford it gave rise to a suggestion in some orthodox quarters that Mr Bertram should be requested to resign his fellowship.

It has been told how, sitting on the Mount of Olives, he had been ready to devote himself to the service of the church to which he belonged. Could his mind have been known at that time, how proud might one have been of him! His mind was not then known; but now, after a lapse of two years, he made it as it were public, and Oriel was by no means proud of him.

The name of his little book was a very awful name. It was called the 'Romance of Scripture.'* He began in his first chapter with an earnest remonstrance against that condemnation which he knew the injustice of the world would pronounce against him. There was nothing in his book, he said, to warrant any man in accusing him of unbelief. Let those who were so inclined to accuse him read and judge. He had called things by their true names, and that doubtless by some would be imputed to him as a sin. But it would be found that he had gone no further in impugning the truth of Scripture than many other writers before him, some of whom had since been rewarded for their writings by high promotion in the church. The bishops' bench was the reward for orthodoxy; but there had been a taste for liberal deans. He had gone no further, he said, than many deans.

It was acknowledged, he went on to say, that all Scripture statements could not now be taken as true to the letter; particularly not as true to the letter as now adopted by Englishmen. It seemed to him that the generality of his countrymen were of opinion that the inspired writers had themselves written in English. It was forgotten that they were Orientals, who wrote in the language natural to them, with the customary grandiloquence of orientalism, with the poetic exaggeration which, in the East, was the breath of life. It was forgotten also that they wrote in ignorance of those natural truths which men had now acquired by experience and induction, and not by revelation. Their truth was the truth of heaven, not the truth of earth. No man thought that the sun in those days did rise and set, moving round the earth, because the prolongation of the day had been described by the sun standing still upon Gibeon.* And then he took the book of Job, and measured that by the light of his own candle—and so on.

The book was undoubtedly clever, and men read it. Women also read it, and began to talk, some of them at least, of the blindness of their mothers who had not had wit to see that these old chronicles were very much as other old chronicles. 'The Romance of Scripture' was to be seen frequently in booksellers' advertisements, and Mr Mudie* told how he always had two thousand copies of it on his shelves. So our friend did something in the world; but what he did do was unfortunately not applauded by his friends.

Harcourt very plainly told him that a man who scribbled never did any good at the bar. The two trades, he said, were not compatible.

'No,' said George, 'I believe not. An author must be nothing if he do not love truth; a barrister must be nothing if he do.' Harcourt was no whit annoyed by the repartee, but having given his warning, went his way to his work.

It was very well known that the 'Romance of Scripture' was Bertram's work, and there was a comfortable row about it at Oxford. The row was all private, of course—as was necessary, the book having been published without the author's name. But much was said, and many letters were written. Bertram, in writing to the friend at Oriel who took up the cudgels in his defence, made three statements. First, that no one at Oxford had a right to suppose that he was the author. Second, that he was the author, and that no one at Oxford had a right to find fault with what he had written. Thirdly, that it was quite a matter of indifference to him who did find fault. To this, however, he added, that he was ready to resign his fellowship tomorrow if the Common-room at Oriel wished to get rid of him.

So the matter rested—for awhile. Those who at this time knew Bertram best were confident enough that his belief was shaken, in spite of the remonstrance so loudly put forth in his first pages. He had intended to be honest in his remonstrance; but it is not every man who exactly knows what he does believe. Every man! Is there, one may almost ask, any man who has such knowledge? We all believe in the resurrection of the body; we say so at least, but what do we believe by it?

Men may be firm believers and yet doubt some Bible statements—doubt the letter of such statements. But men who are firm believers will not be those to put forth their doubts with all their eloquence. Such men, if they devote their time to Scripture history, will not be arrested by the sun's standing on Gibeon. If they speak out at all, they will speak out rather as to all they do believe than as to the little that they doubt. It was soon known to Bertram's world that those who regarded him as a freethinker did him no great injustice.

This and other things made them very unhappy at Littlebath. The very fact of George having written such a book nearly scared Miss Baker out of her wits. She, according to her own lights, would have placed freethinkers in the same category with murderers, regicides, and horrid mysterious sinners who commit crimes too dreadful for women to think of. She would not believe that Bertram was one of these; but it was fearful to think that any one should so call him. Caroline, perhaps, would not so much have minded this flaw in her future husband's faith if it had not been proof of his unsteadiness, of his unfitness for the world's battle. She remembered what he had said to her two years since on the Mount of Olives; and then thought of what he was saying now. Everything with him was impulse and enthusiasm. All judgment was wanting. How should such as he get on in the world? And had she indissolubly linked her lot to that of one who was so incapable of success? No; indissolubly she had not so linked it; not as yet.

One night she opened her mind to her aunt, and spoke very seriously of her position. 'I hardly know what I ought to do,' she said. 'I know how much I owe him; I know how much he has a right to expect from me. And I would pay him all I owe; I would do my duty by him even at the sacrifice of myself if I could plainly see what my duty is.'

'But, Caroline, do you wish to give him up?'

'No, not if I could keep him; keep him as he was. My high hopes are done with; my ambition is over; I no longer look for much. But I would fain know that he still loves me before

I marry him. I would wish to be sure that he means to live with me. In his present mood, how can I know aught of him? how be sure of anything?'

Her aunt, after remaining for some half-hour in consideration, at last and with reluctance gave her advice.

'It all but breaks my heart to say so; but, Caroline, I think I would abandon it: I think I would ask him to release me from my promise.'

It may well be imagined that Miss Waddington was not herself when she declared that her high hopes were done with, that her ambition was over. She was not herself. Anxiety, sorrow, and doubt—doubt as to the man whom she had pledged herself to love, whom she did love—had made her ill, and she was not herself. She had become thin and pale, and was looking old and wan. She sat silent for awhile, leaning with her head on her hand, and made no answer to her aunt's suggestion.

'I really would, Caroline; indeed I would. I know you are not happy as you are.'

'Happy!'

'You are looking wretchedly ill, too. I know all this is wearing you. Take my advice, Caroline, and write to him.'

'There are two reasons against it, aunt; two strong reasons.'

'What reasons, love.'

'In the first place, I love him.' Aunt Mary sighed. She had no other answer but a sigh to give to this. 'And in the next place, I have no right to ask anything of him.'

'Why not, Caroline?'

'He made his request to me, and I refused it. Had I consented to marry him last year, all this would have been different. I intended to do right, and even now I do not think that I was wrong. But I cannot impute fault to him. He does all this in order that I may impute it, and that then he may have his revenge.'

Nothing more was said on the matter at that time, and things went on for awhile again in the same unsatisfactory state.

Early in the summer, Miss Waddington and her aunt went up for a few weeks to London. It had been Miss Baker's habit to spend some days at Hadley about this time of the year. She suggested to Caroline, that instead of her doing so, they should both go for a week or so to London. She thought that the change would be good for her niece, and she thought also, though of this she said nothing, that Caroline would see something of her lover. If he were not to be given up, it would be well—so Miss Baker thought—that this marriage should be delayed no longer. Bertram was determined to prove that marriage was necessary to tame him; he had proved it—at any rate to Miss Baker's satisfaction. There would now be money enough to live on, as uncle Bertram's two thousand pounds had been promised for this summer. On this little scheme Miss Baker went to work.

Caroline made no opposition to the London plan. She said nothing about George in connection with it; but her heart was somewhat softened, and she wished to see him.

Miss Baker therefore wrote up for rooms. She would naturally, one would say, have written to George, but there were now little jealousies and commencements of hot blood even between them. George, though still Caroline's engaged lover, was known to have some bitter feelings, and was believed perhaps by Miss Baker to be more bitter than he really was. So the lodgings were taken without any reference to him. When they reached town they found that he was abroad.

Then Miss Waddington was really angry. They had no right, it is true, to be annoyed in that he was not there to meet them. They had not given him the opportunity. But it did appear to them that, circumstanced as they were, considering the acknowledged engagement between them, he was wrong to leave the country without letting them have a word to say whither he was going or for how long. It was nearly a fortnight since he had written to Caroline, and, for anything they knew, it might be months before she again heard from him.

It was then that they sent for Harcourt, and at this period that they became so intimate with him. Bertram had told him of this foreign trip, but only a day or two before he had taken his departure. It was just at this time that there had been the noise about the 'Romance of Scripture.' Bertram had defended himself in one or two newspapers, had written his defiant letter to his friend at Oxford, and then started to meet his father at Paris. He was going no further, and might be back in a week. This however must be uncertain, as his return would depend on that of Sir Lionel. Sir Lionel intended to come to London with him.

Mr Harcourt was very attentive to them—in spite of his being at that time so useful a public man. He was very attentive to both, being almost as civil to the elder lady as he was to the younger, which, for an Englishman, showed very good breeding. By degrees they both began to regard him with confidence—with sufficient confidence to talk to him of Bertram; with sufficient even to tell him of all their fears. By degrees Caroline would talk to him alone, and when once she permitted herself to do so, she concealed nothing.

Harcourt said not a word against his friend. That friend himself might perhaps have thought that his friend, speaking of him behind his back, might have spoken more warmly in his praise. But it was hard at present to say much that should be true in Bertram's praise. He was not living in a wise or prudent manner; not preparing himself in any way to live as a man should live by the sweat of his brow. Harcourt could not say much in his favour. That Bertram was clever, honest, true, and high-spirited, that Miss Waddington knew; that Miss Baker knew: what they wanted to learn was, that he was making prudent use of these high qualities. Harcourt could not say that he was doing so.

'That he will fall on his legs at last,' said Harcourt once when he was alone with Caroline, 'I do not doubt; with his talent, and his high, honest love of virtue, it is all but impossible that he should throw himself away. But the present moment is of such vital importance! It is so hard to make up for the loss even of twelve months!'

'I am sure it is,' said Caroline; 'but I would not care for that so much if I thought—'

'Thought what, Miss Waddington?'

'That his disposition was not altered. He was so frank, so candid, so—so—so affectionate.'

'It is the manner of men to change in that respect. They become, perhaps, not less affectionate, but less demonstrative.'

To this Miss Waddington answered nothing. It might probably be so. It was singular enough that she, with her ideas, should be complaining to a perfect stranger of an uncaressing, unloving manner in her lover; she who had professed to herself that she lived so little for love! Had George been even kneeling at her knee, her heart would have been stern enough. It was only by feeling a woman's wrong that she found herself endowed with a woman's privilege.

'I do not think that Bertram's heart is changed,' continued Harcourt; 'he is doubtless very angry that his requests to you last summer were not complied with.'

'But how could we have married then, Mr Harcourt? Think what our income would have been; and he as yet without any profession!'

'I am not blaming you. I am not taking his part against you. I only say that he is very angry.'

'But does he bear malice, Mr Harcourt?'

'No, he does not bear malice; men may be angry without bearing malice. He thinks that you have shown a want of confidence in him, and are still showing it.'

'And has he not justified that want of confidence?'

To this Harcourt answered nothing, but he smiled slightly.

'Well, has he not? What could I have done? What ought I to have done? Tell me, Mr Harcourt. It distresses me beyond measure that you should think I have been to blame.'

'I do not think so; far from it, Miss Waddington. Bertram is my dear friend, and I know his fine qualities; but I cannot but own that he justified you in that temporary want of confidence which you now express.'

Mr Harcourt, though a member of Parliament and a learned pundit, was nevertheless a very young man. He was an unmarried man also, and a man not yet engaged to be married. It may be surmised that George Bertram would not have been pleased had he known the sort of conversations that were held between his dear friend and his betrothed bride. And yet Caroline at this period loved him better than ever she had done.

A week or ten days after this three letters arrived from Bertram, one for Caroline, one for Miss Baker, and one for Harcourt. Caroline and her aunt had lingered in London, both doubtless in the hope that Bertram would return. There can be little doubt now that had he returned, and had he been anxious for the marriage, Miss Waddington would have consented. She was becoming ill at ease, dissatisfied, what the world calls heart-broken. Now that she was tried, she found herself not to be so strong in her own resolves. She was not sick from love alone; her position was altogether wretched—though she was engaged, and persisted in adhering to her engagement, she felt and often expressed to her aunt a presentiment that she and Bertram would never be married.

They waited for awhile in the hope that he might return; but instead of himself, there came three letters. Harcourt, it seemed, had written to him, and hence arose these epistles. That to Miss Baker was very civil and friendly. Had that come alone it would have created no complaint. He explained to her that had he expected her visit to London, he would have endeavoured to meet her; that he could not now return, as he had promised to remain awhile with his father. Sir Lionel had been unwell, and the waters of Vichy had been recommended. He was going to Vichy with Sir Lionel, and would not be in London till August. His plans after that were altogether unsettled, but he would not be long in London before he came to Littlebath. Such was his letter to Miss Baker.

To Harcourt he wrote very shortly. He was obliged to him for the interest he took in the welfare of Miss Waddington, and for his attention to Miss Baker. That was nearly all he said. There was not an angry word in the letter; but, nevertheless, his friend was able to deduce from it, short as it was, that Bertram was angry.

But on the head of his betrothed he poured out the vial of his wrath. He had never before scolded her, had never written in an angry tone. Now in very truth he did so. An angry letter, especially if the writer be well loved, is so much fiercer than any angry speech, so much more unendurable! There the words remain, scorching, not to be explained away, not to be atoned for by a kiss, not to be softened down by the word of love that may follow so quickly upon spoken anger. Heaven defend me from angry letters! They should never be written, unless to schoolboys and men at college; and not often to them if they be any way tenderhearted. This at least should be a rule through the letter-writing world: that no angry letter be posted till four-and-twenty hours shall have elapsed since it was written. We all know how absurd is that other rule, that of saying the alphabet when you are angry. Trash! Sit down and write your letter; write it with all the venom in your power; spit out your spleen at the fullest; 'twill do you good; you think you have been injured; say all that you can say with all your poisoned eloquence, and gratify yourself by reading it while your temper is still hot. Then put it in your desk; and, as a matter of course, burn it before breakfast the following morning. Believe me that you will then have a double gratification.

A pleasant letter I hold to be the pleasantest thing that this world has to give. It should be good-humoured; witty it may be, but with a gentle diluted wit. Concocted brilliancy will spoil it altogether. Not long, so that it be tedious in the reading; nor brief, so that the delight suffice not to make itself felt. It should be written specially for the reader, and should apply altogether to him, and not altogether to any other. It should never flatter. Flattery is always odious. But underneath the visible stream of pungent water there may be the slightest undercurrent of eulogy, so that it be not seen, but only understood. Censure it may contain freely, but censure which in arraigning the conduct implies no doubt as to the intellect. It should be legibly written, so that it may be read with comfort; but no more than that. Caligraphy betokens caution, and if it be not light in hand it is nothing. That it be fairly grammatical and not ill spelt the writer owes to his schoolmaster; but this should come of habit, not of care. Then let its page be soiled by no business; one touch of utility will destroy it all.

If you ask for examples, let it be as unlike Walpole* as may be. If you can so write it that Lord Byron might have written it, you will not be very far from high excellence.

But, above all things, see that it be good-humoured.

Bertram's letter to the lady that he loved was by no means one of this sort. In the first place, it was not good-humoured;

it was very far from being so. Had it been so, it would utterly have belied his feelings. Harcourt had so written to him as to make him quite clearly understand that all his sins and—which was much more to him—all his loves had been fully discussed between his friend and Miss Waddington—between his Caroline and another man. To the pride of his heart nothing could be more revolting. It was as though his dearest possession had been ransacked in his absence, and rifled and squandered by the very guardian to whom he had left the key. There had been sore misgivings, sore differences between him and Caroline; but, nevertheless, she had had all his heart. Now, in his absence, she had selected his worldly friend Harcourt, and discussed that possession and its flaws with him! There was that in all this of which he could not write with good-humour. Nevertheless, had he kept his letter to the second morning, it may probably be said that he would have hesitated to send it.

'My dearest Caroline,' it began. Now I put it to all lovers whether, when they wish to please, they ever write in such manner to their sweethearts. Is it not always, 'My own love?' 'Dearest love?' 'My own sweet pet?' But that use of the Christian name, which is so delicious in speaking during the first days of intimacy, does it not always betoken something stern at the beginning of a lover's letter? Ah, it may betoken something very stern! 'My dearest Jane, I am sorry to say it, but I could not approve of the way in which you danced with Major Simkins last night.' 'My dearest Lucy, I was at Kensington garden gate yesterday at four, and remained absolutely till five. You really ought—.' Is not that always the angry lover's tone?

I fear that I must give Bertram's letter entire to make the matter sufficiently clear.

'My dearest Caroline,

'I learn from Mr Harcourt that you and Miss Baker are in town, and I am of course sorry to miss you. Would it not have been better that I should have heard this from yourself?

'Mr Harcourt tells me that you are dissatisfied; and I understand from his letter that you have explained your dissatisfaction very fully to him. It might have been better, I think, that the explanation should have been made to me; or had you chosen to complain, you might have done so to your aunt, or to your grandfather. I cannot think that you were at liberty to complain of me to Mr Harcourt. My wish is, that you have no further conversation with him on our joint concerns. It is not seemly; and, if feminine, is at any rate not ladylike.

'I am driven to defend myself. What is it of which you complain, or have a right to complain? We became engaged more than twelve months since, certainly with no understanding that the matter was to stand over for three years. My understanding was that we were to be married as soon as it might reasonably be arranged. You then took on yourself to order this delay, and kindly offered to give me up as an alternative. I could not force you to marry me; but I loved you too well, and trusted too much in your love to be able to think that that giving up was necessary. Perhaps I was wrong.

'But the period of this wretched interval is at my own disposal. Had you married me, my time would have been yours. It would have been just that you should know how it was spent. Each would then have known so much of the other. But you have chosen that this should not be; and, therefore, I deny your right now to make inquiry. If I have departed from any hopes you had formed, you have no one to blame but yourself.

'You have said that I neglect you. I am ready to marry you tomorrow; I have been ready to do so any day since our engagement. You yourself know how much more than ready I have been. I do not profess to be a very painstaking lover; nay, if you will, the life would bore me, even if in our case the mawkishness of the delay did not do more than bore. At any rate, I will not go through it. I loved and do love you truly. I told you of it truly when I first knew it myself, and urged my suit till I had a definite answer. You accepted me, and now there needs be nothing further till we are married.

'But I insist on this, that I will not have my affairs discussed by you with persons to whom you are a stranger.

'You will see my letter to your aunt. I have told her that I will visit her at Littlebath as soon as I have returned to England.

'Yours ever affectionately,

'G.B.'

This letter was a terrible blow to Caroline. It seemed to her to be almost incredible that she, she, Caroline Waddington, should be forced to receive such a letter as that under any circumstances and from any gentleman. Unseemly, unfeminine, unladylike! These were the epithets her lover used in addressing her. She was told that it bored him to play the lover; that his misconduct was her fault; and then she was accused of mawkishness! He was imperative, too, in laying his orders to her. 'I insist on this!' Was it incumbent on her to comply with his insistings?

Of course she showed the letter to her aunt, whose advice resulted in this—that it would be better that she should pocket the affront silently if she were not prepared to give up the engagement altogether. If she were so prepared, the letter doubtless would give her the opportunity.

And then Mr Harcourt came to her while her anger was yet at the hottest. His manner was so kind, his temper so sweet, his attention so obliging, that she could not but be glad to see him. If George loved her, if he wished to guide her, wished to persuade her, why was not he at her right hand? Mr Harcourt was there instead. It did not bore him, multifold as his duties were, to be near her.

Then she committed the first great fault of which in this history she will be shown as being guilty. She showed her lover's letter to Mr Harcourt. Of course this was not done without some previous converse; till he had found out that she was wretched, and inquired as to her wretchedness; till she had owned that she was ill with sorrow, beside herself, and perplexed in the extreme. Then at last, saying to herself that she cared not now to obey Mr Bertram, she showed the letter to Mr Harcourt.

'It is ungenerous,' said Harcourt.

'It is ungentlemanlike,' said Caroline. 'But it was written in passion, and I shall not notice it.' And so she and Miss Baker went back again to Littlebath.

It was September before Bertram returned, and then Sir Lionel came with him. We have not space to tell much of what had passed between the father and the son; but they reached London apparently on good terms with each other, and Sir Lionel settled himself in a bedroom near to his son's chambers, and near also to his own club. There was, however, this great ground of disagreement between them. Sir Lionel was very anxious that his son should borrow money from Mr Bertram, and George very resolutely declined to do so. It was now clear enough to Sir Lionel that his son could not show his filial disposition by advancing on his own behalf much money to his father, as he was himself by no means in affluent circumstances.

He went down to Littlebath, and took his father with him. The meeting between the lovers was again unloverlike; but nothing could be more affectionate than Sir Lionel. He took Caroline in his arms and kissed her, called her his dear daughter, and praised her beauty. I believe he kissed Miss Baker. Inded, I know that he made an attempt to do so; and I think it not at all improbable that in the overflowing of his affectionate heart, he made some overture of the same kind to the exceedingly pretty parlour-maid who waited upon them. Whatever might be thought of George, Sir Lionel soon became popular there, and his popularity was not decreased when he declared that he would spend the remainder of the autumn, and perhaps the winter, at Littlebath.

He did stay there for the winter. He had a year's furlough, during which he was to remain in England with full pay, and he made it known to the ladies at Littlebath that the chief object of his getting this leave was to be present at the nuptials of dear Caroline and his son. On one occasion he borrowed thirty pounds from Miss Baker; a circumstance which their intimacy, perhaps, made excusable. He happened, however, to mention this little occurrence casually to his son, and George at once repaid that debt, poor as he was at the time.

'You could have that and whatever more you chose merely

for the asking,' said Sir Lionel on that occasion, in a tone almost of reproach.

And so the winter passed away. George, however, was not idle. He fully intended to be called to the bar in the following autumn, and did, to a certain extent, renew his legal studies. He did not return to Mr Die, prevented possibly by the difficulty he would have in preparing the necessary funds. But his great work through the winter and in the early spring was another small volume, which he published in March, and which he called, 'The Fallacies of Early History.'

We need not give any minute criticism on this work. It will suffice to say that the orthodox world declared it to be much more heterodox than the last work. Heterodox, indeed! It was so bad, they said, that there was not the least glimmer of any doxy whatever left about it. The early history of which he spoke was altogether Bible history, and the fallacies to which he alluded were the plainest statements of the book of Genesis. Nay, he had called the whole story of Creation a myth; the whole story as there given: so at least said the rabbis of Oxford, and among them outspoke more loudly than any others the outraged and very learned rabbis of Oriel.

Bertram however denied this. He had, he said, not called anything a myth. There was the printed book, and one might have supposed that it would be easy enough to settle this question. But it was far from being so. The words myth and mythical were used half-a-dozen times, and the rabbis declared that they were applied to the statements of Scripture. Bertram declared that they were applied to the appearance those statements must have as at present put before the English world. Then he said something not complimentary to the translators, and something also very uncivil as to want of intelligence on the part of the Oxford rabbis. The war raged warmly, and was taken up by the metropolitan press, till Bertram became a lion—a lion, however, without a hide, for in the middle of the dispute he felt himself called on to resign his fellowship.

He lost that hide; but he got another in lieu which his friends assured him was of a much warmer texture. His uncle had taken considerable interest in this dispute, alleging all through that the Oxford men were long-eared asses and bigoted monks. It may be presumed that his own orthodoxy was not of a high class. He had never liked George's fellowship, and had always ridiculed the income which he received from it. Directly he heard that it had been resigned, he gave his nephew a thousand pounds. He said nothing about it; he merely told Mr Pritchett to arrange the matter.

Sir Lionel was delighted. As to the question of orthodoxy he was perfectly indifferent. It was nothing to him whether his son called the book of Genesis a myth or a gospel; but he had said much, very much as to the folly of risking his fellowship; and more, a great deal more, as to the madness of throwing it away. But now he was quite ready to own himself wrong, and did do so in the most straightforward manner. After all, what was a fellowship to a man just about to be married?* In his position Bertram had of course been free to speak out. If, indeed, there had been any object in holding to the college, then the expression of such opinions, let alone their publication, would not have been judicious.

As it was, however, nothing could have been more lucky. His son had shown his independence. The rich uncle had shown the warm interest which he still took in his nephew, and Sir Lionel was able to borrow two hundred and fifty pounds, a sum of money which, at the present moment, was very grateful to him. Bertram's triumph was gilded on all sides; for the booksellers had paid him handsomely for his infidel manuscript. Infidelity that can make itself successful will, at any rate, bring an income.

And this brings us to the period at which we may resume our story. One word we must say as to Caroline. During the winter she had seen her lover repeatedly, and had written to him repeatedly. Their engagement, therefore, had by no means been broken. But their meetings were cold, and their letters equally so. She would have married him at once now if he would ask her. But he would not ask her. He was quite willing to marry her if she would herself say that she was willing so far to recede from her former resolutions. But she could not bring herself to do this. Each was too proud to make the first concession to the other, and therefore no concession was made by either.

Sir Lionel once attempted to interfere; but he failed. George gave him to understand that he could manage his own affairs himself. When a son is frequently called on to lend money to his father, and that father is never called on to repay it, the parental authority is apt to grow dull. It had become very dull in this case.

CHAPTER XIX

RICHMOND

IT was in the midst of this noise about Bertram's new book that the scene is presumed to be reopened. He had resigned his fellowship, and pocketed his thousand pounds. Neither of these events had much depressed his spirits, and he appeared now to his friends to be a happy man in spite of his love troubles. At the same time, Harcourt also was sufficiently elate. He had made his great speech with considerable *éclat*, and his sails were full of wind—of wind of a more substantial character than that by which Bertram's vessel was wafted.

And just now Harcourt and Bertram were again much together. A few months since it had appeared to Harcourt that Bertram intended to do nothing in the world, to make no figure. Even now there was but little hope of his doing much as a barrister; but it seemed probable that he might at any rate make himself known as an author. Such triumphs, as Harcourt well knew, were very barren; but still it was well to know men who were in any way triumphant; and therefore the barrister, himself so triumphant, considered it judicious not to drop his friend.

It may be said that Bertram had given up all idea of practising as a barrister. He still intended to go through the form of being called; but his profession was to be that of an author. He had all manner of works in hand: poems, plays, political pamphlets, infidel essays, histories, and a narrative of his travels in the East. He had made up his mind fully that there were in England only two occupations worthy of an

Englishman. A man should be known either as a politician or as an author. It behoved a man to speak out what was in him with some audible voice, so that the world might hear. He might do so either by word of mouth, or by pen and paper; by the former in Parliament, by the latter at his desk. Each form of speech had its own advantage. Fate, which had made Harcourt a member of Parliament, seemed to intend him, Bertram, to be an author.

Harcourt, though overwhelmed by business at this period, took frequent occasion to be with Bertram; and when he was with him alone he always made an effort to talk about Miss Waddington. Bertram was rather shy of the subject. He had never blamed Harcourt for what had taken place while he was absent in Paris, but since that time he had never volunteered to speak of his own engagement.

They were together one fine May evening on the banks of the river at Richmond. George was fond of the place, and whenever Harcourt proposed to spend an evening alone with him, they would go up the river and dine there.

On this occasion Harcourt seemed determined to talk about Miss Waddington. Bertram, who was not in the best possible humour, had shown, one might say plainly enough, that it was a subject on which he did not wish to speak. One might also say that it was a subject as to talking on which the choice certainly ought to have been left to himself. A man who is engaged may often choose to talk to his friend about his engaged bride; but the friend does not usually select the lady as a topic of conversation except in conformity with the Benedick's wishes.

On this occasion, however, Harcourt would talk about Miss Waddington, and Bertram, who had already given one or two short answers, began to feel that his friend was almost impertinent.

They were cracking decayed walnuts and sipping not the very best of wine, and Bertram was expatiating on Sir Robert Peel's enormity in having taken the wind out of the sails of the Whigs,* and rehearsing perhaps a few paragraphs of a new pamphlet that was about to come out, when Harcourt again suddenly turned the conversation.

'By-the-by,' said he, 'I believe there is no day absolutely fixed for your marriage.'

'No,' said Bertram, sharply enough. 'No day has been fixed. Could anything on earth have been more base than the manner in which he had endeavoured to leave Cobden* as a necessary legacy to the new government? Would he have put Cobden into any place in a government of his own?'

'Oh, d— Cobden! One has enough of him in the House,—quite.'

'But I have not that advantage.'

'You shall have, some of these days. I'll make over the Battersea Hamlets to you as soon as I can get a judge's wig on my head. But I'm thinking of other things now. I wonder whether you and Caroline Waddington ever will be man and wife?'

'Probably about the time that you are made a judge.'

'Ha! ha! Well, I hope if you do do it, it will come off before that. But I doubt its coming off at all. Each of you is too proud for the other. Neither of you can forgive what the other has done.'

'What do you mean? But to tell you the truth, Harcourt, I have no great inclination to discuss that matter just at present. If you please, we will leave Miss Waddington alone.'

'What I mean is this,' said the embryo judge, perseveringly, 'that you are too angry with her on account of this enforced delay, and she is too angry with you because you have dared to be angry with her. I do not think you will ever come together.'

Bertram looked full at Harcourt as this was said, and observed that there was not the usual easy, gentlemanlike smile on the barrister's face; and yet the barrister was doing his best to look as usual. The fact was, that Harcourt was playing a game, and playing it with considerable skill, but his performance was not altogether that of a Garrick.* Something might have been read in his face had Bertram been cunning enough to read it. But Bertram was not a cunning man.

Bertram looked full in the other's face. Had he been content to do so and to say nothing, he would have gained his point, and the subject would have been at once dropped.

Harcourt then could have gone no further. But Bertram was now angry, and, being angry, he could not but speak.

'Harcourt, you have interfered once before between me and Miss Waddington—'

'Interfered!'

'Yes, interfered—in what I then thought and still think to have been a very unwarrantable manner.'

'It was a pity you did not tell me of it at the time.'

'It is a pity rather than you should drive me to tell you of it now; but you do so. When I was in Paris, you said to Miss Waddington what you had no right to say.'

'What did I say?'

'Or, rather, she said to you—'

'Ah! that was no fault of mine.'

'But it was a fault of yours. Do you think that I cannot understand? that I cannot see? She would have been silent enough to you but for your encouragement. I do not know that I was ever so vexed as when I received that letter from you. You took upon yourself—'

'I know you were angry, very angry. But that was not my fault. I said nothing but what a friend under such circumstances was bound to say.'

'Well, let the matter drop now; and let Miss Waddington and myself settle our own affairs.'

'I cannot let the matter drop; you have driven me to defend myself, and I must do it as best I may. I know that you were angry, exceedingly angry—'

'Exceedingly angry!' he repeated; 'but that was no fault of mine. When Miss Baker sent for me, I could not but go to her. When I was there, I could not but listen to her. When Caroline told me that she was wretched—'

'Miss Waddington!' shouted Bertram, in a voice that caused the glasses to shake, and made the waiter turn round. And then suddenly recollecting himself, he scowled round the room as he observed that he was noticed.

'Hush, my dear fellow. It shall be Miss Waddington; but not quite so loud. And I beg your pardon, but hearing the lady called by her Christian name so often, both by yourself and Miss Baker, I forgot myself. When she spoke to me of her wretched state, what was I to do? Was I to say, fie! fie! and take my hat and go away?'

'She was very wretched,' he continued, for Bertram merely scowled and said nothing, 'and I could not but sympathize with her. She thought that you had neglected her. It was clear that you had gone abroad without telling her. Was it to be wondered at that she should be unhappy?'

'Her telling you that she was so was inexcusable.'

'At any rate, I am blameless. I myself think that she was also; but that is another question. In what I wrote to you, I did my duty as a friend to both parties. After that, I do confess that I thought your anger too great to allow you ever to stand at the altar with her.'

'You do not mean to say that she showed you my letter?' said Bertram, almost leaping at him.

'Your letter! what letter?'

'You know what letter—my letter from Paris? The letter which I wrote to her in reference to the one I received from you? I desire at once to have an answer from you. Did Caroline show you that letter?'

Harcourt looked very guilty, extremely guilty; but he did not immediately make any reply.

'Harcourt, answer me,' said Bertram, much more coolly. 'I have no feeling of anger now with you. Did Caroline show you that letter?'

'Miss Waddington did show it to me.'

And thus the successful Mr Harcourt had been successful also in this. And now, having narrated this interview in a manner which does not make it redound very much to that gentleman's credit, I must add to the narrative his apology. If even-handed justice were done throughout the world, some apology could be found for most offences. Not that the offences would thus be wiped away, and black become white; but much that is now very black would be reduced to that sombre, uninviting shade of ordinary brown which is so customary to humanity.

Our apology for Mr Harcourt will by no means make his conduct white—will leave it, perhaps of a deeper, dingier brown than that which is quite ordinary among men; nay, will leave it still black, many will say.

Mr Harcourt had seen that which in his opinion proved that Bertram and Miss Waddington could never be happy with each other. He had seen that which in his opinion led to the conclusion that neither of them really wished that this marriage should take place. But he had seen that also which made him believe that both were too proud to ask for a release. Under such circumstances, would he be doing ill if he were to release them? Caroline had so spoken, spoken even to him, that it seemed impossible to him that she could wish for the marriage. Bertram had so written that it seemed equally impossible that he should wish for it. Would it not, therefore, be madness to allow them to marry? He had said as much to Miss Baker, and Miss Baker had agreed with him. 'He cannot love her,' Miss Baker had said, 'or he would not neglect her so shamefully. I am sure he does not love her.'

But there was a man who did love her, who had felt that he could love her from the first moment that he had seen her as an affianced bride: he had not then courted her for himself; for then it was manifest that she both loved and was loved. But now, now that this was altered, was there good cause why he should not covet her now? Mr Harcourt thought that there was no sufficient cause.

And then this man, who was not by nature a vain man, who had not made himself apt at believing that young beauties fell readily in love with him, who had not spent his years in basking in ladies' smiles, imagined that he had some ground to think that Miss Waddington was not averse to him. Oh, how she had looked when that part of Bertram's letter had been read, in which he professed that he would not be bored by any love-duties for his lady! And then, this man had been kind to her; he had shown that such service would be no bore to him. He had been gentle-mannered to her; and she also, she had been gentle to him:—

> 'The woman cannot be of nature's making
> Whom, being kind, her misery makes not kinder.'*

And Caroline was kind; at least so he thought, and heaven knows she was miserable also. And thus hopes rose that never should have risen, and schemes were made which, if not absolutely black, were as near it as any shade of brown may be.

And then there was the fact that Caroline was the granddaughter, and might probably be the heiress, of one of the wealthiest men in the city of London. The consideration of this fact had doubtless its weight also. The lady would at least have six thousand pounds, might have sixty, might have three times sixty. Harcourt would probably have found it inexpedient to give way to any love had there been no money to gild the passion. He was notoriously a man of the world; he pretended to be nothing else; he would have thought that he had made himself ludicrous if he had married for love only. With him it was a source of comfort that the lady's pecuniary advantages allowed him the hope that he might indulge his love. So he did indulge it.

He had trusted for awhile that circumstances would break off this ill-assorted match, and that then he could step in himself without any previous interference in the matter. But the time was running too close; unless something was done, these two poor young creatures would marry, and make themselves wretched for life. Benevolence itself required that he should take the matter in hand. So he did take it in hand, and commenced his operations—not unskilfully, as we have seen.

Such is our apology for Mr Harcourt. A very poor one, the reader will say, turning from that gentleman with disgust. It is a poor one. Were we all turned inside out, as is done with ladies and gentlemen in novels, some of us might find some little difficulty in giving good apologies for ourselves. Our shade of brown would often be very dark.

Bertram sat for awhile silent and motionless at the table, and Harcourt seeing his look of grief, almost repented what he had done. But, after all, he had only told the truth. The letter had been shown to him.

'It is incredible,' said Bertram, 'incredible, incredible!' But, nevertheless, his voice showed plainly enough that the statement to him was not incredible.

'Let it be so,' said Harcourt, who purposely misunderstood him. 'I do not wish you to believe me. Let us leave it so.

Come, it is time for us to go back to town.' But Bertram still sat silent, saying nothing.

Harcourt called the waiter, and paid the bill. He then told Bertram what his share was, and commenced smoothing the silk of his hat preparatory to moving. Bertram took out his purse, gave him the necessary amount of shillings, and then again sat silent and motionless.

'Come, Bertram, there will be only one train after this, and you know what a crowd there is always for that. Let us go.'

But Bertram did not move. 'Harcourt, if you would not mind it,' he said, very gently, 'I would rather go back by myself today. What you have said has put me out. I shall probably walk.'

'Walk to town!'

'Oh, yes; the walk will be nothing. I shall like it. Don't wait for me, there's a good fellow. I'll see you tomorrow, or next day, or before long.'

So Harcourt, shrugging his shoulders, and expressing some surprise at this singular resolve, put his hat on his head and walked off by himself. What his inward reflections were on his journey back to London we will not inquire; but will accompany our other friend in his walk.

Hurriedly as it had been written, he remembered almost every word of that letter from Paris. He knew that it had been severe, and he had sometimes perhaps regretted its severity. But he knew also that the offence had been great. What right had his affianced bride to speak of him to another man? Was it not fit that he should tell her how great was this sin? His ideas on the matter were perhaps too strong, but they certainly are not peculiar. We—speaking for the educated male sex in England—do not like to think that any one should tamper with the ladies whom we love.

But what was this to that which she had since done? To talk of him had been bad, but to show his letters! to show such a letter as that! to show such a letter to such a person! to make such a confidence, and with such a confidant! It could not be that she loved him; it could not be but that she must prefer that other man to him.

As he thought of this, walking on hurriedly towards

London on that soft May night, his bosom swelled, but with anger rather than with sorrow. It must be all over then between them. It could not go on after what he had now been told. She was willing, he presumed, to marry him, having pledged him her word that she would do so; but it was clear that she did not care for him. He would not hold her to her pledge; nor would he take to his bosom one who would have a secret understanding with another man.

'Miss Baker,' he said to himself, 'had treated him badly; she must have known this; why had she not told him? If it were so that Miss Waddington liked another better than him, would it not have been Miss Baker's duty to tell him so? It did not signify however; he had learnt it in time—luckily, luckily, luckily.'

Should he quarrel with Harcourt? What mattered it whether he did or no? or what mattered it what part Harcourt took in the concern? If that which Harcourt had said were true, if Caroline had shown him this letter, he, Bertram, could never forgive that! If so, they must part! And then, if he did not possess her, what mattered who did? Nay, if she loved Harcourt, why should he prevent their coming together? But of this he would make himself fully satisfied; he would know whether the letter had truly been shown. Harcourt was a barrister; and in Bertram's estimation a barrister's word was not always to be taken implicitly.

So he still walked on. But what should he first do? how should he act at once? And then it occurred to him that, according to the ideas generally prevalent in the world on such matters, he would not be held to be justified in repudiating his betrothed merely because she had shown a letter of his to another gentleman. He felt in his own mind that the cause was quite sufficient; that the state of mind which such an act disclosed was clearly not that of a loving, trusting wife. But others might think differently: perhaps Miss Baker might do so; or perhaps Miss Waddington.

But then it was not possible that she could ever wish to marry him after having taken such a course as that. Had he not indeed ample cause to think that she did not wish to marry him? She had put it off to the last possible moment.

She had yielded nothing to his urgent request. In all her intercourse with him she had been cold and unbending. She had had her moments of confidence, but they were not with him; they were with one whom perhaps she liked better. There was no jealousy in this, not jealousy of the usual kind. His self-respect had been injured, and he could not endure that. He hardly now wished that she should love him.

But he would go to Littlebath at once and ask her the question. He would ask her all those questions which were now burning inside his heart. She did not like severe letters, and he would write no more such to her. What further communication might of necessity take place between them should be by word of mouth. So he resolved to go down to Littlebath on the morrow.

And then he reached his chambers, weary and sad at heart. But he was no longer angry. He endeavoured to persuade himself that he was absolutely the reverse of angry. He knelt down and prayed that she might be happy. He swore that he would do anything to make her so. But that anything was not to include any chance of a marriage with himself.

CHAPTER XX

JUNO

IN spite of his philosophy and his prayers, Bertram went to bed not in a very happy state of mind. He was a man essentially of a warm and loving heart. He was exigeant, and perhaps even selfish in his love. Most men are so. But he did love, had loved; and having made up his mind to part from that which he had loved, he could not be happy. He had often lain awake, thinking of her faults to him; but now he lay thinking of his faults to her. It was a pity, he said to himself, that their marriage should have been so delayed; she had acted foolishly in that, certainly; had not known him, had not understood his character, or appreciated his affection; but, nevertheless, he might have borne it better. He felt that he had been stern, almost savage to her; that he had resented her refusal to marry him at once too violently: he threw heavy blame on himself. But through all this, he still felt that they could not now marry. Was it not clear to him that Caroline would be delighted to escape from her engagement if the way to do so were opened to her?

He lost no time in carrying out his plans. By an early train on the following day he went down to Littlebath, and at once went to his father's lodgings. For Sir Lionel, in order that he might be near his dear daughter, was still living in Littlebath. He had entered the second, or lighter fast set, played a good deal at cards, might constantly be seen walking up and down the assembly-rooms, and did something in horseflesh.

George first went to his father's lodgings, and found him still in bed. The lighter fast set at Littlebath do not generally get up early, and Sir Lionel professed that he had not lately been altogether well. Littlebath was fearfully, fearfully cold. It was now May, and he was still obliged to keep a fire. He was in a very good humour however with his son, for the period of the two hundred and fifty pounds' loan was not long passed by. Gratitude for that had not yet given way to desire for more.

'Oh, George! is that you? I am delighted to see you. Going up to the terrace, I suppose? I was with Caroline for a few minutes last night, and I never saw her looking better—never.'

George answered by asking his father where he meant to dine. Sir Lionel was going to dine out. He usually did dine out. He was one of those men who have a knack of getting a succession of gratis dinners; and it must be confessed in his favour—and the admission was generally made in the dining-out world—that Sir Lionel was worth his dinner.

'Then I shall probably return this evening; but I will see you before I go.'

Sir Lionel asked why he would not dine as usual in Montpellier Terrace; but on this subject George at present gave him no answer. He merely said that he thought it very probable that he should do so, and then went away to his work. It was hard work that he had to do, and he thoroughly wished that it was over.

He did not however allow himself a moment to pause. On

the contrary, he walked so quick, that when he found himself in Miss Baker's drawing-room, he was almost out of breath, and partly from that cause, and partly from his agitation, was unable to speak to that lady in his usual unruffled manner.

'Ah, how do you do, Miss Baker? I'm very glad to see you. I have run down today in a great hurry, and I am very anxious to see Caroline. Is she out?'

Miss Baker explained that she was not out; and would be down very shortly.

'I'm glad she's not away, for I am very anxious to see her—very.'

Miss Baker, with her voice also in a tremble, asked if anything was the matter.

'No; nothing the matter. But the truth is, I'm tired of this, Miss Baker, and I want to settle it. I don't know how she may bear it, but it has half killed me.'

Miss Baker looked at him almost aghast, for his manner was energetic and almost wild. Only that he so frequently was wild, she would have feared that something dreadful was about to happen. She had not, however, time to say anything further, for Caroline's step was heard on the stairs.

'Could you let us be alone for ten minutes?' said George. 'But I feel the shame of turning you out of your own drawing-room. Perhaps Caroline will not mind coming down with me into the parlour.'

But Miss Baker of course waived this objection, and as she retreated, the two ladies met just at the drawing-room door. Caroline was about to speak, but was stopped by the expression on her aunt's face. Ladies have little ways of talking to each other, with nods and becks and wreathed smiles, which are quite beyond the reach of men; and in this language aunt Mary did say something as she passed which gave her niece to understand that the coming interview would not consist merely of the delights which are common among lovers. Caroline, therefore, as she entered the room composed her face for solemn things, and walked slowly, and not without some dignity in her mien, into the presence of him who was to be her lord and master.

'We hardly expected you, George,' she said.

His father had been right. She was looking well, very well. Her figure was perhaps not quite so full, nor the colour in her cheek quite so high as when he had first seen her in Jerusalem; but, otherwise, she had never seemed to him more lovely. The little effort she had made to collect herself, to assume a certain majesty in her gait, was becoming to her. So also was her plain morning dress, and the simple braid in which her hair was collected. It might certainly be boasted of Miss Waddington that she was a beauty of the morning rather than of the night; that her complexion was fitted for the sun rather than for gaslight.

He was going to give up all this! And why? That which he saw before him, that which he had so often brought himself to believe, that which at this moment he actually did believe to be as perfect a form of feminine beauty as might be found by any search in England, was as yet his own. And he might keep it as his own. He knew, or thought he knew enough of her to be sure that, let her feelings be what they might, she would not condescend to break her word to him. Doubtless, she would marry him; and that in but a few months hence if only he would marry her! Beautiful as she was, much as she was his own, much as he still loved her, he had come there to reject her! All this flashed through his mind in a moment. He lost no time in idle thoughts.

'Caroline,' he said, stretching out his hand to her—usually when he met her after any absence he had used his hand to draw her nearer to him with more warmth than his present ordinary greeting showed—'Caroline, I have come down to have some talk with you. There is that between us which should be settled.'

'Well, what is it?' she said, with the slightest possible smile.

'I will not, if I can help it, say any word to show that I am angry—'

'But are you angry, George? If so, had you not better show it? Concealment will never sit well on you.'

'I hope not; nor will I conceal anything willingly. It is because I so greatly dislike concealment that I am here.'

'You could not conceal anything if you tried, George. It is useless for you to say that you will not show that you are angry. You are angry, and you do show it. What is it? I hope my present sin is not a very grievous one. By your banishing poor aunt out of the drawing-room, I fear it must be rather bad.'

'I was dining with Mr Harcourt last night, and it escaped him in conversation that you had shown to him the letter which I wrote to you from Paris. Was it so, Caroline? Did you show him that very letter?'

Certainly, no indifferent listener would have said that there was any tone of anger in Bertram's voice; and yet there was that in it which made Miss Waddington feel that the room was swimming round and round her. She turned ruby-red up to her hair. Bertram had never before seen her blush like that; for he had never before seen her covered by shame. Oh! how she had repented showing that letter! How her soul had grieved over it from the very moment that it had passed out of her hand! She had done so in the hotness of her passion. He had written to her sharp stinging, words, which had maddened her. Up to that moment she had never known how sharp, how stinging, how bitter words might be. The world had hitherto been so soft to her! She was there told that she was unfeminine, unladylike! And then, he that was sitting by her was so smooth, so sympathizing, so anxious to please her! In her anger and her sympathy she had shown it; and from that day to this she had repented in the roughness of sackcloth and the bitterness of ashes. It was possible that Caroline Waddington should so sin against a woman's sense of propriety; that, alas! had been proved; but it was impossible that she should so sin and not know that she had sinned, nor feel the shame of it.

She did stand before him red with shame; but at the first moment she made no answer. It was in her heart to kneel at his feet, to kneel in the spirit if not in the body, and ask his pardon; but hitherto she had asked pardon of no human being. There was an effort in the doing of it which she could not at once get over. Had his eyes looked tenderly on her for a moment, had one soft tone fallen from his lips, she would have done it. Down she would have gone and implored his pardon. And who that he had once loved had ever asked aught in vain from George Bertram? Ah, that she had done so! How well they might have loved each other! What joy there might have been!

But there was nothing tender in his eye, no tender tone softened the words which fell from his mouth.

'What!' he said, and in spite of his promise, his voice had never before sounded so stern,—'what! show that letter to another man; show that letter to Mr Harcourt! Is that true, Caroline?'

A child asks pardon from his mother because he is scolded. He wishes to avert her wrath in order that he may escape punishment. So also may a servant of his master, or an inferior of his superior. But when one equal asks pardon of another, it is because he acknowledges and regrets the injury he has done. Such acknowledgment, such regret will seldom be produced by a stern face and a harsh voice. Caroline, as she looked at him and listened to him, did not go down on her knees—not even mentally. Instead of doing so, she remembered her dignity, and wretched as she was at heart, she continued to seat herself without betraying her misery.

'Is that true, Caroline? I will believe the charge against you from no other lips than your own.'

'Yes, George; it is true. I did show your letter to Mr Harcourt.' So stern had he been in his bearing that she could not condescend even to a word of apology.

He had hitherto remained standing; but on hearing this he flung himself into a chair and buried his face in his hands. Even then she might have been softened, and he might have relented, and all might have been well!

'I was very unhappy, George,' she said; 'that letter had made me very unhappy, and I hardly knew where to turn for relief.'

'What!' he said, jumping up and flashing before her in a storm of passion to which his former sternness had been as nothing—'what! my letter made you so unhappy that you were obliged to go to Mr Harcourt for relief! You appealed for sympathy from me to him! from me who am—no, who was, your affianced husband! Had you no idea of the sort of bond that existed between you and me? Did you not know that there were matters in which you could not look for sympathy to such as him without being false, nay, almost worse than false? Have you ever thought what it is to be the one loved object of a man's heart, and to have accepted that love?' She had been on the point of interrupting him, but the softness of these last words interrupted her for a moment.

'Such a letter as that! Do you remember that letter, Caroline?'

'Yes, I remember it; remember it too well; I would not keep it. I would not feel that such words from you were ever by me.'

'You mean that it was harsh?'

'It was cruel.'

'Harsh or cruel, or what you will—I shall not now stop to defend it—it was one which from the very nature of it should have been sacred between us. It was written to you as to one to whom I had a right to write as my future wife.'

'No one could have a right to write such a letter as that.'

'In it, I particularly begged that Mr Harcourt might not be made an arbiter between us. I made a special request that to him, at least, you would not talk of what causes of trouble there might be between us; and yet you selected him as your confidant, read it with him, pored over with him the words which had come hot from my heart, discussed with him my love—my—my—my—Bah! I cannot endure it; had not you yourself told me so, I could not have believed it.'

'George!—'

'Good God! that you should take my letters and read them over with him! Why, Caroline, it admits but of one solution; there is but one reading to the riddle; ask all the world.'

'We sent for him as your friend.'

'Yes, and seem to have soon used him as your own. I have no friend to whom I allow the privilege of going between me and my own heart's love. Yes, you were my own heart's love. I have to get over that complaint now as best I may.'

'I may consider then that all is over between us.'

'Yes; there. You have back your hand. It is again your own

to dispose of to whom you will. Let you have what confidences you will, they will no longer imply falsehood to me.'

'Then, sir, if such be the case, I think you may cease to scold me with such violence.'

'I have long felt that I ought to give you this release; for I have known that you have not thoroughly loved me.'

Miss Waddington was too proud, too conscious of the necessity to maintain her pride at the present moment, to contradict this. But, nevertheless, in her heart she felt that she did love him, that she would fain not give him up, that, in spite of his anger, his bitter railing anger, she would keep him close to her if she only could do so. But now that he spoke of giving her up, she could not speak passionately of her love—she who had never yet shown any passion in her speech to him.

'It has grown on me from day to day; and I have been like a child in clinging to a hope when I should have known that there was no hope. I should have known it when you deferred our marriage for three years.'

'Two years, George.'

'Had it been two years, we should now have been married. I should have known it when I learned that you and he were in such close intimacy in London. But now—I know it now. Now at least it is all over.'

'I can only be sorry that you have so long had so much trouble in the matter.'

'Trouble—trouble! But I will not make a fool of myself. I believe at any rate that you understand me.'

'Oh! perfectly, Mr Bertram.'

But she did not understand him; nor perhaps was it very likely that she should understand him. What he had meant her to understand was this: that in giving her up he was sacrificing only himself, and not her; that he did so in the conviction that she did not care for him; and that he did so on this account, strong as his own love still was, in spite of all her offences. This was what he intended her to understand;—but she did not understand the half of it.

'And I may now go?' said she, rising from her chair. The

blush of shame was over, and mild as her words sounded, she again looked the Juno. 'And I may now go?'

'Now go! yes; I suppose so. That is, I may go. That is what you mean. Well, I suppose I had better go.' Not a moment since he was towering with passion, and his voice, if not loud, had been masterful, determined, and imperious. Now it was low and gentle enough. Even now, could she have been tender to him, he would have relented. But she could not be tender. It was her profession to be a Juno. Though she knew that when he was gone from her her heart would be breaking, she would not bring herself down to use a woman's softness. She could not say that she had been wrong, wrong because distracted by her misery, wrong because he was away from her, wrong because disturbed in her spirits by the depth of the love she felt for him; she could not confess this, and then, taking his hand, promise him that if he would remain close to her she would not so sin again. Ah! if she could have done this, in one moment her head would have been on his shoulder and his arm round her waist; and in twenty minutes more Miss Baker would have been informed, sitting as she now was up in her bedroom, that the wedding-day had been fixed.

But very different news Miss Baker had to hear. Had things turned out so, Miss Waddington would have been a woman and not a goddess. No; great as was the coming penalty, she could not do that. She had been railed at and scolded as never goddess was scolded before. Whatever she threw away, it behoved her to maintain her dignity. She would not bend to a storm that had come blustering over her so uncourteously.

Bertram had now risen to go. 'It would be useless for me to trouble your aunt,' he said. 'Tell her from me that I would not have gone without seeing her had I not wished to spare her pain. Good-bye, Caroline, and may God bless you;' and, so saying, he put out his hand to her.

'Good-bye, Mr Bertram.' She would have said something more, but she feared to trust herself with any word that might have any sound of tenderness. She took his hand, however, and returned the pressure which he gave it.

She looked into his eyes, and saw that they were full of

tears; but still she did not speak. Oh, Caroline Waddington, Caroline Waddington! if it had but been given thee to know, even then, how much of womanhood there was in thy bosom, of warm womanhood, how little of goddess-ship, of cold goddess-ship, it might still have been well with thee! But thou didst not know. Thou hadst gotten there, at any rate, thy Juno's pedestal; and having that, needs was that thou shouldst stand on it.

'God bless you, Caroline; good-bye,' he repeated again, and turned to the door.

'I wish to ask you one question before you go,' she said, as his hand was on the handle of the lock; and she spoke in a voice that was almost goddess-like; that hardly betrayed, but yet that did betray, the human effort. Bertram paused, and again turned to her.

'In your accusation against me just now—'

'I made no accusation, Caroline.'

'You not only made it, Mr Bertram, but I pleaded guilty to it. But in making it you mentioned Mr Harcourt's name. While you were absent in Paris, I did talk with that gentleman on our private affairs, yours and mine. I hope I am believed to have done so because I regarded Mr Harcourt as your friend?'

Bertram did not understand her, and he showed that he did not by his look.

'It is difficult for me to explain myself'—and now she blushed slightly—very slightly. 'What I mean is this; I wish to be acquitted by you of having had recourse to Mr Harcourt on my own account—from any partiality of my own.' She almost rose in height as she stood there before him, uttering these words in all her cold but beautiful dignity. Whatever her sins might have been, he should not accuse her of having dallied with another while her word and her troth had been his. She had been wrong. She could not deny that he had justice on his side—stern, harsh, bare justice—when he came there to her and flung back her love and promises into her teeth. He had the right to do so, and she would not complain. But he should not leave her till he had acquitted her of the vile, missish crime of flirting with another because he was absent. Seeing that he still hardly understood her, she made her speech yet plainer.

'At the risk of being told again that I am unfeminine, I must explain myself. Do you charge me with having allowed Mr Harcourt to speak to me as a lover?'

'No; I make no such charge. Now, I have no right to make any charge on such a matter.'

'No; should Mr Harcourt be my lover now, that is my affair and his, not yours. But had he been so then—You owe it to me to say whether, among other sins, that sin also is charged against me?'

'I have charged and do charge nothing against you, but this —that you have ceased to love me. And that charge will be made nowhere but in my own breast. I am not a jealous man, as I think you might know. What I have said to you here today has not come out of suspicion. I have thought no ill against you, and believe no ill against you beyond that which you have yourself acknowledged. I find that you have ceased to love me, and finding that, I am indifferent to whom your love may be given.' And so saying, he opened the door and went out; nor did he ever again see Miss Waddington at Littlebath.

Some few minutes after he had left the room, Miss Baker entered it. She had heard the sound of the front door, and having made inquiry of the servant, had learned that their visitor had gone. Then she descended to her own drawing-room, and found Caroline sitting upright at the table, as though in grief she despised the adventitious aid and every-day solace of a sofa. There was no tear in her eye, none as yet; but it required no tears to tell her aunt that all was not well. Judging by the face she looked at, aunt Mary was inclined to say that all was as little well as might be.

There was still to be seen there the beauty, and the dignity, and still ever in part the composure of a Juno; but it was such composure a Juno might have shown while she devoted to a third destruction the walls of a thrice-built Troy; of Juno in grief, in jealousy, almost in despair; but of Juno still mindful of her pedestal, still remembering that there she stood a mark for the admiration of gods and men. How long shall this Juno mood serve to sustain her? Ah! how long?

'Has he gone?' said Miss Baker, as she looked at her niece.

'Yes, aunt, he has gone.'

'When will he return?'

'He will not return, aunt. He will not come any more; it is all over at last.'

Miss Baker stood for a moment trembling, and then threw herself upon a seat. She had at least had no celestial gift by which she could compose herself. 'Oh, Caroline!' she exclaimed.

'Yes, aunt Mary; it is all over now.'

'You mean that you have quarrelled?' said she, remembering to her comfort, that there was some old proverb about the quarrels of lovers. Miss Baker had great faith in proverbs.

The reader may find it hard to follow Miss Baker's mind on the subject of this engagement. Some time since she was giving advice that it should be broken off, and now she was *au désespoir* because that result had been reached. She had one of those minds that are prone to veering, and which show by the way they turn, not any volition of their own, but the direction of some external wind, some external volition. Nor can one be angry with, or despise Miss Baker for this weathercock aptitude. She was the least selfish of human beings, the least opinionative, the most good-natured. She had had her hot fits and her cold fits with regard to Bertram; but her hot fits and her cold had all been hot or cold with reference to what she conceived to be her niece's chances of happiness. Latterly, she had fancied that Caroline did love Bertram too well to give him up: and circumstances had led her to believe more strongly than ever that old Mr Bertram wished the marriage, and that the two together, if married, would certainly inherit his wealth. So latterly, during the last month or so, Miss Baker had blown very hot.

'No, there has been no quarrel,' said Caroline, with forced tranquillity of voice and manner. 'No such quarrel as you mean. Do not deceive yourself, dear aunt; it is over now, over for ever.'

'For ever, Caroline!'

'Yes, for ever. That has been said which can never be unsaid. Do not grieve about it'—aunt Mary was now in tears—'it is better so; I am sure it is better. We should not have made each other happy.'

'But three years, Caroline; three years!' said aunt Mary through her tears, thinking of the time that had been so sadly lost. Aunt Mary was widely awake to the fact that three years was a long period in a girl's life, and that to have passed three years as the betrothed of one man and then to leave him was injurious to the matrimonial prospects of a young lady. Miss Baker was full of these little mundane considerations; but then they were never exercised, never had been exercised, on her own behalf.

'Yes, three years!' and Caroline smiled, even through her grief. 'It cannot be helped, aunt. And the rest of it; neither can that be helped. Three years! say thirty, aunt.'

Miss Baker looked at her, not quite understanding. 'And must it be so?' said she.

'Must! oh, yes, indeed it must. It must now, must—must—must.'

Then they both sat silent for awhile. Miss Baker was longing to know the cause of this sudden disruption, but she hesitated at first to inquire. It was not, however, to be borne that the matter should be allowed to remain altogether undiscussed.

'But what is it he has said?' she at last asked. Caroline had never told her aunt that that letter had been shown to Mr Harcourt, and had no intention of telling her so now.

'I could not tell you, aunt, all that passed. It was not what he said more than what I said. At least—no; that is not true. It did arise from what he said; but I would not answer him as he would have me; and so we agreed to part.'

'He wished to have the marriage at once?'

'No. I think he wished no such thing. You may rest assured he wishes no marriage now; none with me, at least. And rest assured of this, too, that I wish none with him. Wish! it is no use wishing. It is now impossible.'

Again there was a silence, and again it was broken by Miss Baker. 'I wonder whether you ever really loved him? Sometimes I have thought you never did.'

'Perhaps not,' said she, musing on her fate.

'If it is never to be, I hope that you did not.'

'It would be to be hoped—to be hoped for me, and to be hoped also for him.'

'Oh, he loved you. There is no doubt of that; no doubt at all of that. If any man ever loved a girl, he loved you.' To this Miss Waddington answered nothing, nor would she just then talk any further with her aunt upon the subject. They were to dine early on that day, as their custom was when they went out in the evening. On this evening they were going to the house—lodgings rather—of an old friend they had not seen for some time. She had arrived a week or two since at Littlebath, and though there had been callings between them, they had not yet succeeded in meeting. When Bertram had arrived it was near their dinner hour, and before he went that hour was already past. Had his manner been as it ordinarily was, he would of course have been asked to join them; but, as we have seen, that had been no moment for such customary civility.

Now, however, they went to dinner, and while seated there, Miss Waddington told her aunt that she did not feel equal to going out that evening. Miss Baker of course said something in opposition to this, but that something was not much. It might easily be understood that a young lady who had just lost her lover was not in a fit state to go to a Littlebath card-party.

And thus early in the evening Caroline contrived to be alone; and then for the first time she attempted to realize all that had come upon her. Hitherto she had had to support herself—herself and her goddess-ship,—first before George Bertram, and then with lighter effort before her aunt. But now that she was alone, she could descend to humanity. Now that she was alone she had so to descend.

Yes; she had lost three years. To a mortal goddess, who possessed her divinity but for a short time, this was much. Her doctrine had been to make the most of the world. She had early resolved not to throw away either herself or her chances. And now that she was three-and-twenty, how had she kept her resolves? how had her doctrine answered with her? She had lived before the world for the last two years as a girl betrothed to a lover—before such of the world as she knew and as knew her; and now her lover was gone: not dismissed by her, but gone! He had rather dismissed her, and that not in the most courteous manner.

But, to do her justice, this was not the grief that burnt most hotly in her heart. She said to herself that it was so, that this was her worst grief; she would fain have felt that it was so; but there was more of humanity in her, of the sweetness of womanly humanity, than she was aware. He had left her, and she knew not how to live without him. That was the thorn that stuck fast in her woman's bosom. She could never again look into those deep, thoughtful eyes; never again feel the pressure of that strong, manly arm; never hear the poetry of that rich voice as she had heard it when he poured words of love and truth into her ear. Bertram had many faults, and while he belonged to her, she had thought of them often enough; but he had many virtues also, and now she could think but of them.

She had said that he was gone, gone for ever. It was easy enough to say that with composed voice to Miss Baker. There is nothing so easy as bravado. The wretch who is to be hung can step lightly while multitudes are looking at him. The woman who is about to give up all that her heart most values can declare out loud that the matter is very indifferent to her. But when the victim of the law is lying in his solitary cell, thinking on his doom, the morning before the executioner comes to him; when the poor girl is sitting alone on her bedside, with her heart all empty,—or rather not empty, only hopeless; it is very difficult then to maintain a spirit of bravado!

Caroline Waddington did try it. She had often said to herself, in months now some time past, that she repented of her engagement. If so, now was the time to congratulate herself that she was free from it. But she could not congratulate herself. While he had entirely belonged to her, she had not known how thoroughly she had loved him. When she had only thought of parting with him, she had believed that it would be easy. But now she found that it was not so easy. It was about as easy for her to pluck his image from her heart as to draw one of her limbs from the socket.

But the limb had to be drawn from the socket. There was no longer any hope that it could be saved. Nay, it had been already given up as far as the expression of the will was concerned, and there was nothing left but to bear the pain.

So she sat down and began to draw out the limb. Oh, my sensitive reader! have you ever performed the process? It is by no means to be done with rose-water appliances and gentle motherly pressure. The whole force of the hospital has to be brought out to perform this operation.

She now discovered, perhaps, for the first time, that she had a strong beating heart, and that she loved this violent, capricious man with every strong pulse of it. There was more about him now that was lovable by such a woman as Caroline Waddington than when he had first spoken of his love on the side of Mount Olivet. Then he had been little more than a boy: a boy indeed with a high feeling, with a poetic nature, and much humour. But these gifts had hardly sufficed to win her heart. Now he had added to these a strong will, a power of command, a capability of speaking out to the world with some sort of voice. After all, power and will are the gifts which a woman most loves in a man.

And now that Caroline had lost her lover, she confessed to herself that she did love him. Love him! Yes! How could she recover him? That was her first thought. She could not recover him in any way. That was her second thought. As to asking him to come back to her; the wrenching of the limb from the socket would be better than that. That, at least, she knew she could not do. And was it possible that he of his own accord should come back to her? No, it was not possible. The man was tender-hearted, and could have been whistled back with the slightest lure while yet they two were standing in the room together. But he was as proud as he was tender. Though there might also be some wrenching to be done within his heart, he would never come back again uninvited.

And thus, while Miss Baker was at her old friend's card-party, Miss Waddington sat in her own bedroom, striving, with bitter tears and violent struggles, to reconcile herself to her loss.

CHAPTER XXI

SIR LIONEL IN TROUBLE

IT has been said that Miss Baker was going to spend the evening with an old friend. I trust that Miss Todd, umquhile of the valley of Jehoshaphat, and now of No 7, Paragon, Littlebath, has not been forgotten; Miss Todd of the free heart and the rosy face.

Yes, Miss Todd had come to Littlebath, and was intent rather on forming a party of Toddites than of joining herself to either of the regular sets. She was perhaps not much given to be pious, and she certainly was but ill inclined to be slow. If fast, however, she chose to be fast in her own line.

But before we have the pleasure of attending at her *soirée*, we must say a word or two of one of the most distinguished of the expected guests. Sir Lionel was to be there.

Now, Sir Lionel had been leading a pleasant life at Littlebath, with one single exception—that he was rather in want of funds. He had capital apartments, four rooms *en suite*, a man-servant, a groom, three horses, and a phaeton,* and no one was more looked up to at Littlebath. Ladies smiled, young men listened, old gentlemen brought out their best wines, and all was delightful. All but this, that the 'res angusta'* did occasionally remind him that he was mortal. Oh, that sordid brother of his, who could have given him thousands on thousands without feeling the loss of them! We have been unable to see much of old Mr Bertram in recapitulating the story of young Mr Bertram's latter doings. But it should have been said, that early in the present year he had not been quite as well as his friends could wish. George had gone to see him once or twice, and so also had his niece Miss Baker, and his granddaughter. He had said but very little to them; but on Miss Baker's mind an impression had been left that it would please him to see the marriage completed.

And at this time likewise his brother, Sir Lionel, had thought it expedient to see him. There had hitherto been no interview between them since Sir Lionel's return. The colonel had found out, and had been duly astonished at finding out, the history of Miss Baker and her niece. That George and Caroline would be the heirs to a great portion of his brother's money he could not doubt; that Miss Baker would have something he thought probable; and then he reflected, that in spite of all that was come and gone, his brother's heart might relent on his death-bed. It might be that he could talk the sick man round; and if that were impracticable, he might at least learn how others stood in his brother's favour. Sir Lionel was not now a young man himself. Ease and a settled life would be good for him. What, if he married Miss Baker!

He first called on Pritchett. Mr Pritchett told him that his brother was better—considerably better. Sir Lionel was in raptures. He had hurried up from Littlebath in an agony. He had heard most distressing accounts. He would, however, go down to Hadley and see his brother.

'I am afraid Mr Bertram is not very much up to company just at present,' wheezed out Mr Pritchett.

'But a brother, you know,' suggested Sir Lionel.

Pritchett knew exactly how the brothers stood with each other; and he himself, though he was very partial to Mr George, had not any warm love for Sir Lionel.

'Oh, yes; a brother is a brother, surely. But, Mr Bertram, you know, sir—'

'You mean,' said Sir Lionel, 'that he is a little vexed about the account.'

'Oh, yes, the account; there is the account, Sir Lionel. If it is to settle that, perhaps I can manage without troubling you to go to Hadley. Not but what settling the account *will* make matters smoother.'

Sir Lionel could get nothing more from Mr Pritchett; but he would not be put off from his intention, and he did go to Hadley. He found his brother sitting up in the dining-room, but he would not have known him. And, indeed, many who had seen him lately might have had some difficulty in recognizing him. He was not only lean and lank, and worn and wan, but he spoke with some difficulty, and on close examination it might be seen that his mouth was twisted as it were from the centre of his face. Since his relatives had seen him he had suffered what is genteelly called a slight threatening of paralysis.

But his mind, if touched at all, had recovered itself; and his spirit was in nowise paralyzed. When Sir Lionel was shown into the room—he had first of all taken the precaution of sending down his card from the hotel, and saying that he would call in half an hour—the old man put out his hand to him, but did not attempt to rise from his chair. It must be remembered that the brothers had not seen each other for more than fifteen years.

Sir Lionel had tutored himself carefully as to what he would say and what do. 'George,' he said, and the old man shrank as he heard the unaccustomed name. 'When I heard that you were ill, I could not but come and see you.'

'Very good of you, Sir Lionel; very good of you,' growled the old man.

'It is fifteen years since we met, and we are both old men now.'

'I am an old man now, and nearly worn out; too old and far gone to have many wants. You are not in that condition, I suppose.'

There was an amount of sarcasm in his voice as he spoke, and in his eye also as he looked at his brother, which made Sir Lionel perfectly understand that his rich relative was not specially anxious to be kind to him.

'Well, we are neither of us quite so far gone as that, I hope—not quite so far gone as that;' and Sir Lionel looked very pleasant. 'But, speaking for myself, I have not many wants now'—nor had he, pleasant old man that he was; only three or four comfortable rooms for himself and his servant; a phaeton and a pair of horses; and another smaller establishment in a secluded quiet street; nothing more than that, including of course all that was excellent in the eating and drinking line—'speaking for myself, I have not many wants now.' And he did look very good-humoured and pleasant as he spoke.

Mr Bertram senior did not look good-humoured or pleasant. There was that in his old eye which was the very opposite to good-humour and pleasantness.

'Ah!' said he. 'Well I am glad of that, for you will be able to do the more for poor George. He will have wants; he is going to take care and trouble on himself. Neither he nor his sweetheart have, I take it, been accustomed to do without wants; and their income will be tight enough—forby what you can do for them.'

The colonel sat and still looked pleasant, but he began to think that it might be as well for him that he was back at Littlebath.

'Poor George! I hope they will be happy. I think they will; my greatest anxiety now is of course for their happiness; and yours is the same, doubtless. It is odd that my child and your child's child should thus come together, is it not?' so spoke the colonel.

Mr Bertram looked at him; looked through him almost, but he said nothing.

'It is odd,' continued Sir Lionel, 'but a very happy circumstance. She is certainly the sweetest girl I ever saw; and George is a lucky fellow.'

'Yes, he is a lucky fellow; he will get more than he has any right to expect. First and last she will have six thousand pounds. I have not heard him say what he means to settle on her; but perhaps he was waiting till you had come home.'

Sir Lionel's forte during his whole official career had been the making pleasant—by the pleasantness that was innate in him—things which appeared to be going in a very unpleasant manner. But how was he to make things pleasant now?

'Well, you see, George has been so much knocked about! There was his fellowship. I think they behaved shabbily enough to him.'

'Fellowship! One hundred and seventy pounds a year and the run of his teeth at feast time, or some such thing as that. A man can't marry on his fellowship very well!'

'Ha! ha! ha! no, he can't exactly do that. On the whole, I think it was quite as well that he threw it up; and so I told him.'

'Did you tell him at the same time what his future income was to be?'

'No, upon my soul I did not; but if all I hear be true, I believe you did. You have been exceedingly generous to him, George—and to me also.'

'Then, Sir Lionel, allow me to tell you that all you hear is not true. Anything at all that you may have heard of that kind, if you have heard anything, is perfectly false. I have said nothing to George about his income, and have nothing to say to him.'

'Well, I may have expressed myself wrongly, and perhaps you did say nothing. I was alluding especially to what you have done.'

'I will tell you exactly what I have done. I thought he showed a high spirit when he threw up his fellowship, and as I had always a great contempt for those Oxford fellows, I sent him a thousand pounds. It was a present, and I hope he will make good use of it.'

'I am sure he will,' said Sir Lionel, who certainly had just cause for such confidence, seeing how large a slice out of the sum had been placed at his own disposal.

'I am sure he will,' said Sir Lionel. 'Indeed, I know that he has.'

'Ah, I'm glad to hear of it; of course you know more about it than I do; of course you are arranging these matters. But that is all he has had from me, and all that he is likely to have.'

If such were to be the treatment of George, of George who was certainly in some respects a favourite, what hope could Sir Lionel have for himself? But it was not so much his brother's words which led him to fear that his brother's money-bags were impregnable to him as his brother's voice and his brother's eye. That eye was never off him, and Sir Lionel did begin to wish that he was at Littlebath.

'I don't know whether George may have formed any hopes,' continued the old man; but here Sir Lionel interrupted him, and not imprudently: if anything was to be said, it should be said now.

'Well, if he has formed hopes, George, you cannot but own that it is natural. He has looked on you as a man without any child of your own, and he has been taught so to look by your treating him almost as though he were your son.'

'You mean that I paid his school debts and his Oxford debts when you forgot to do so,' growled out the elder brother.

'Yes, and that you afterwards gave him an income when he came up to live in London. I hope you do not think that I am ungrateful, George?' and Sir Lionel used his softest and, at the same time, his most expressive tone.

'Grateful! I seldom look for much gratitude. But I shall be glad to know when it may suit you to settle with me. The account has been running on now for a great many years. Probably Pritchett may have sent it you.' And as he spoke Mr Bertram rose from his chair and took an ominous-looking piece of paper from off the mantelpiece.

'Yes, Mr Pritchett is punctuality itself in these matters,' said Sir Lionel, with a gentle laugh, which had not about it all his usual pleasantness.

'You have probably checked it, and can say whether or no it be correct,' said Mr Bertram senior, looking at the paper in his hand.

'Well, I can't say that I have exactly; but I don't in the least doubt the figures, not in the least; Mr Pritchett is always correct, I know.'

'Yes, Mr Pritchett is generally correct. And may I ask, Sir Lionel, what you intend to do in the matter?'

It was necessary now that Sir Lionel should summon up his best courage. He reminded himself that after all his brother was but a feeble old man—impotent in all but money; and as it seemed now clear that no further pecuniary aid was to be expected, why need he fear him on this account? Had it been possible for him to get away without further talk, he would have done so; but this was not possible, so he determined to put a good face on it.

'I suppose you are joking now, George,' said he.

I wish I could describe the tone of voice in which the word joking was repeated by the elder Mr Bertram. It made the military knight jump in his chair, and confess to himself that the word impotent could not be safely applied to his ancient relative.

'Well, I dare say it is a joke,' the old man went on to say. 'If I expect to be paid what I have expended in saving George from being turned loose upon the world without education, I suppose it is a joke. Ha! ha! ha! I never thought of laughing at it before, but now I will. I always heard that you were a joker, Sir Lionel. Ha! ha! ha! I dare say you have laughed at it often enough yourself, eh?'

'What I mean is this, when you took upon yourself George's education and maintenance, you could hardly have intended to have it paid back again by such a poor devil as I am.'

'Oh, I couldn't, couldn't I?'

'At any rate, I don't suppose you did count on having your money back.'

'Well, I must admit this, I did not feel very sure of it; I did think there might be a doubt. But what could I do? I could not let poor Wilkinson ruin himself because you would not pay your debts.'

'I am sorry that you take it up in such a manner,' said the colonel, assuming a tone of injured innocence. 'I came here because I heard that you were ill—'

'Thought I was dying, eh?'

'I did not exactly think that you were dying, George; but I knew that you were very ill, and old feelings came back on me. The feelings of our early youth, George; and I could not be happy without seeing you.'

'Very kind of you, I am sure. You altogether then decline to settle the account, eh?'

'If you desire it, I will—will make arrangements, certainly. You do not want it all at once, I suppose?'

'Oh, no: half in three months, and other half in six will do for me.'

'It would take a great deal more than all my income to do that, I fear.'

'Your professional income: yes, I suppose it would. I fear they don't give you five or six thousand a year for staying at home at Littlebath. But surely you must have saved money; you must have intended to do something for your son?'

'I have looked upon him as provided for by his uncle.'

'Oh!'

'And have therefore been satisfied that he would do well.'

'Now, Sir Lionel, I will tell you how the matter is. I know you will never repay me a shilling of this money, and therefore I shall tell Pritchett not to bother himself with sending you any more accounts.'

'He is a worthy man, and I am sorry he should have had so much trouble.'

'So am I, very; but that's done. He has had the trouble, and I've paid the money; and, as far as George is concerned, I do not begrudge it.'

'You would not if you knew what his sentiments are.'

'I don't care a fig for his sentiments.'

'His feelings of gratitude to you are very strong.'

'No, they are not. He is not in the least grateful to me, nor do I wish him to be so. He is an honest lad, with a high spirit, a good heart, and a bad head. Sometimes I have thought of making him my heir.'

'Ah!' sighed Sir Lionel.

'But I have now firmly made up my mind to do no such thing. He has no knowledge of the worth of money. He does not value money.'

'Oh, there you mistake him: indeed you do.'

'He would do no good with it; and, as regards mine, he won't have it.' Sir Lionel's face again became very doleful.

'But who will have it, George? Whom else have you got to leave it to?'

'When I want to consult you on that subject, I'll send for you; just at present I have no wish to do so. And now, if you please, we'll say no more about money.'

Nothing more was said about money, and very little on any other subject. On what other subject could a pleasant votary of pleasure, such as Sir Lionel, wish to hold conversation with a worn-out old miser from the city? He had regarded his brother as a very full sponge, from which living water might probably be squeezed. But the sponge, it seemed, was no longer squeezed by him in any way. So he left Hadley as quickly as he could and betook himself to Littlebath with a somewhat saddened heart. He consoled himself however, by reflecting that an old man's whims are seldom very enduring, and that George might yet become a participator in the huge prize; if not on his own account, at least on that of his wife.

Sir Lionel returned to Littlebath, resolving that come what might he would not again have personal recourse to his brother. He had tried his diplomatic powers and had failed—failed in that line on being successful in which he so pre-eminently piqued himself. In Ireland it is said of any man who is more than ordinarily persuasive, that he can 'talk the devil out of the liver wing of a turkey!' Sir Lionel had always supposed himself to be gifted with this eloquence; but in that discourse at Hadley, the devil had been too stout for him, and he had gone away without any wing at all—liver or other.

On one point on which he had been very anxious to say a word or two, he had been unable to introduce the slightest hint. He had not dreamt that it would be possible to ask his brother in so many words whether or no Miss Baker would be made a participator in the great prize; but he had imagined that he might have led the way to some conversation which would have shown what were the old man's feelings with reference to that lady. But, as the reader will have perceived, he had not been able to lead the conversation in any way; and he had left Hadley without further light for the guidance of his steps in that matrimonial path in which he had contemplated the expediency of taking a leisurely evening stroll.

The wicked old miser had declared that George should not be his heir; and had also said that which was tantamount to a similar declaration regarding Caroline. She would have six thousand pounds, first and last. Nothing more than a beggarly six thousand pounds, of which two-thirds were already her own without thanks to any one. What a wretched old miser! Who then would have his money? It would hardly be possible that he would leave it all to Miss Baker. And yet he might. It was just possible. Anything was possible with a capricious, miserly old fool like that. What a catch would it be if he, Sir Lionel, could become the heir in so deliciously easy a manner!

But, in all probability, anything the old man might say was exactly the opposite of that which he intended to do.

He probably would leave his money to George—or very probably to Caroline; but most probably he would do something for Miss Baker; something handsome for that soft obedient handmaid who had never disobeyed any of his commands; and, better still, had never drawn upon him for more than her regular allowance.

Such were Sir Lionel's thoughts as he made his way back to Littlebath. Yes; he would make himself acceptable to Miss Baker. That George, old George, was not long for this world was very evident to the colonel. He, troublesome old cross-grained churl that he was, would soon be out of the way. Such being certain—all but certain—could not Sir Lionel manage matters in this way? Could he not engage himself to the lady while his brother was yet alive, and then marry her afterwards—marry her, or perhaps not marry her, as might then become expedient? He was well sure of this, that if she promised to marry him before her acquisition of fortune, such acquisition would not induce her to break off from the match. 'She is too true, too honourable for that,' said Sir Lionel to himself, feeling a warm admiration for the truth of her character, as he resolved how he might himself best back out of such an engagement in the event of its being expedient for him so to do.

So passed his thoughts as he made his way back to Littlebath. And when there he did not allow idleness to mar his schemes. He immediately began to make himself pleasant—more than ordinarily pleasant to Miss Baker. He did not make love to her after the manner of his youth. Had he done so, he would only have frightened the gentle lady. But he was assiduous in his attentions, soft and sweetly flattering in his speech, and friendly, oh, so friendly, in his manner! He called almost every day at Montpellier Terrace. To be sure, there was nothing unnatural in this, for was he not about to become the father of his dear Caroline? But dear to him as his dear Caroline might be, his softest whispers, his most sugared words, were always for her aunt.

He had ever some little proposition to make, some kind family suggestion to put forward. He was a man of the world; they were ladies, delicate, unfit for coping with the world, necessarily ignorant of its naughtier, darker ways; he would do everything for them: and by degrees he did almost everything for Miss Baker.

And so that lady was charmed without knowing it. Let us do her full justice. She had not the remotest idea of opening a flirtation with Sir Lionel Bertram. She had looked on him as the future father-in-law of her own dear child; never as anything more: no idea of becoming Lady Bertram had ever for an instant flashed upon her imagination. But, nevertheless, by degrees the warrior's attentions became pleasant to her.

She had had no youthful adorers, this poor, good Miss Baker; never, at least, since she had been merry as other children are, 'when her little lovers came.' She had advanced to her present nearly mature age without perhaps feeling the want of them. But, nevertheless, even in her bosom was living the usual feminine passion for admiration. She was no 'lusus naturæ,'* but a woman with a heart, and blood in her veins; and not as yet a very old woman either. And therefore, though she had no idea that Sir Lionel was her lover, she had learned to be fond of him.

Her little conversations with Caroline on this subject were delightful. The younger lady was certainly the sharper of the two; and though she had her own concerns to occupy her, she was able to see that something might perhaps be intended. Her liking for Sir Lionel was by no means a strong passion. Something probably had passed between her and George; for George could keep no secret from her. At any rate, she suspected the knight, but she could not say anything to put her aunt on her guard beyond using cold expressions in speaking of her future father. But Miss Baker, who suspected nothing, who expected nothing, could not be too lavish in her praises.

'Caroline,' she would say, 'I do think you are so happy in having such a father-in-law.'

'Oh, certainly,' Caroline had answered. 'But, for myself, I think more of my father-in-law's son.'

'Oh, of course you do; I know that. But Sir Lionel is such a perfect gentleman. Did you ever know a gentleman of his age so attentive to ladies as he is?'

'Well, perhaps not; except one or two old men whom I have seen making love.'

'That's a very different sort of thing, you know—that's absurd. But I must say I think Sir Lionel's behaviour is perfect.' What would she have said of Sir Lionel's behaviour had she known all the secrets of his establishments?

And thus, partly on Sir Lionel's account, Miss Baker began in these days to have perhaps her hottest fit, her strongest wish with reference to her niece's marriage. And then just at this hottest moment came the blow which has been told of in the last chapter.

But Miss Baker, as she prepared herself for Miss Todd's party, would not believe that the matter was hopeless. The quarrels of lovers have ever been the renewal of love, since the day when a verb between two nominative cases first became possessed of the power of agreeing with either of them. There is something in this sweet easiness of agreement which seems to tend to such reconciliations. Miss Baker was too good a grammarian to doubt the fact.

She would probably, under existing circumstances, have stayed at home with her niece, but that she knew she should meet Sir Lionel at Miss Todd's party. She was very anxious to learn whether Sir Lionel had heard of this sad interruption to their harmony; anxious to hear what Sir Lionel would say about it: anxious to concert measures with Sir Lionel for repairing the breach—that is, if Sir Lionel should appear to be cognizant that the breach existed. If she should find that he was not cognizant, she would not tell him; at least she thought she would not. Circumstances must of course govern her conduct to a certain degree when the moment of meeting should arrive. And so Miss Baker went to the party, certainly with a saddened heart, but comforted in some degree by the assurance that she would meet Sir Lionel. 'Dear Sir Lionel, what a thing it is to have a friend!' she said to herself as she stepped into the fly. Yes, indeed, the best thing in the world—the very best. But, dear Miss Baker, it is of all things the most difficult to acquire—and especially difficult for both ladies and gentlemen after forty years of age.

In the meantime, Sir Lionel had been calling on Miss

Todd—had heard a good deal about Miss Todd; and was strong at heart, as a man is strong who has two good strings to his bow.

CHAPTER XXII

MISS TODD'S CARD-PARTY

YES. The great Miss Todd had arrived at Littlebath, and had already been talked about not a little. Being a maiden lady, with no family but her one own maid, she lived in lodgings of course. People at Littlebath, indeed, are much given to lodgings. They are mostly a come-and-go class of beings, to whom the possession of furniture and the responsibilities of householding would be burdensome. But then Miss Todd's lodgings were in the Paragon, and all the world knows how much it costs to secure eligible rooms in the Paragon: two spacious sitting-rooms, for instance, a bedroom, and a closet for one's own maid. And Miss Todd had done this in the very best corner of the Paragon; in that brazen-faced house which looks out of the Paragon right down Montpellier Avenue as regards the front windows, and from the back fully commands the entrance to the railway station. This was Mrs O'Neil's house; and, as Mrs O'Neil herself loudly boasted when Miss Todd came to inspect the premises, she rarely took single ladies, or any ladies that had not handles to their names. Her very last lodger had been Lady McGuffern, the widow of the medical director of the great Indian Eyesore district, as Mrs O'Neil called it. And Lady McGuffern had paid her, oh! ever so much per week: and had always said on every Saturday—'Mrs O'Neil, your terms for such rooms as these are much too low.' It is in such language that the widows of Scotch doctors generally speak of their lodgings when they are paying their weekly bills.

And these rooms Miss Todd had secured. She had, moreover, instantly sent for Mr Wutsanbeans, who keeps those remarkably neat livery stables at the back of the

Paragon, and in ten minutes had concluded her bargain for a private brougham* and private coachman in demi-livery at so much per week. 'And very wide awake she is, is Miss Todd,' said the admiring Mr Wutsanbeans, as he stood among his bandy-legged satellites. And then her name was down at the assembly-rooms, and in the pump-room,* and the book-room, and in the best of sittings in Mr O'Callaghan's fashionable church, in almost less than no time. There were scores of ladies desirous of being promoted from the side walls to the middle avenues in Mr O'Callaghan's church; for, after all, what is the use of a French bonnet when stuck under a side wall? But though all these were desirous, and desirous in vain, Miss Todd at once secured a place where her head was the cynosure of all the eyes of the congregation. Such was Miss Todd's power, and therefore do we call her great.

And in a week's time the sound of her loud but yet pleasant voice, and the step of her heavy but yet active foot, and the glow of her red cherry cheek were as well known on the esplanade as though she were a Littlebathian of two months' standing. Of course she had found friends there, such friends as one always does find at such places—dear delightful people whom she had met some years before for a week at Ems, or sat opposite to once at the hotel table at Harrogate for a fortnight. Miss Todd had a very large circle of such friends; and, to do her justice, we must say that she was always glad to see them, and always treated them well. She was ready to feed them at all times; she was not candid or malicious when backbiting them; she never threw the burden of her pleasures on her friends' shoulders—as ladies at Littlebath will sometimes do. She did not boast either of her purse or her acquaintance; and as long as she was allowed to do exactly what she liked, she generally kept her temper. She had an excellent digestion, and greatly admired the same quality in other people. She did not much care what she said of others, but dearly liked to have mischief spoken of herself. Some one once had said—or very likely no one had said it, but a *soupçon* of a hint had in some way reached her own ears—that she had left Torquay without paying her bills. It was at any rate untrue, but she had sedulously spread the report; and now wherever she ordered goods, she would mysteriously tell the tradesman that he had better inquire about her in Devonshire. She had been seen walking one moonlight night with a young lad at Bangor: the lad was her nephew; but some one had perhaps jested about Miss Todd and her beau, and since that time she was always talking of eloping with her own flesh and blood.

But Miss Todd was not a bad woman. She spent much in feeding those who perhaps were not hungry; but she fed the hungry also: she indulged a good deal in silk brocades; but she bought ginghams as well, and calicos for poor women, and flannel petticoats for motherless girls. She did go to sleep sometimes in church, and would sit at a whist-table till two o'clock of a Sunday morning; but having been selected from a large family by an uncle as his heir, she had divided her good things with brothers and sisters, and nephews and nieces. And so there were some hearts that blessed her, and some friends who loved her with a love other than that of her friends of Littlebath and Ems, of Jerusalem and Harrogate.

And she had loved in her early days, and had been told and had believed that she was loved. But evidence had come to her that her lover was a scamp—a man without morals and without principle; and she had torn herself away from him. And Miss Todd had offered to him money compensation, which the brute had taken; and since that, for his sake, or rather for her love's sake, she had rejected all further matrimonial tenders, and was still Miss Todd; and Miss Todd she intended to remain.

Being such as she was, the world of Littlebath was soon glad to get about her. Those who give suppers at their card-parties are not long in Littlebath in making up the complement of their guests. She had been there now ten days, and had already once or twice mustered a couple of whist-tables; but this affair was to be on a larger scale.

Miss Baker she had not yet seen, nor Miss Waddington. The ladies had called on each other, but had missed fire on both occasions; but with Sir Lionel she had already renewed her intimacy on very affectionate terms. They had been together for perhaps three days at Jerusalem, but then three days at Jerusalem are worth a twelvemonth in such a dull, slow place as London. And Sir Lionel, therefore, and Miss Todd had nearly rushed into each other's arms; and they both, without any intentional falsehood, were talking of each other all over Littlebath as old and confidential friends.

And now for Miss Todd's party. Assist me, my muse. Come down from heaven, O Calliope,* my queen! and aid me to spin with my pen a long discourse. Hark! do you hear? or does some fond delusion mock me? I seem to hear, and seem to be already wandering through those sacred recesses—the drawing-rooms, namely, at Littlebath—which are pervious only to the streams and breezes of good society.

Miss Todd stood at her drawing-room door as her guests were ushered in, not by the greengrocer's assistant, but by the greengrocer himself in person. And she made no quiet little curtsies, whispered no unmeaning welcomes with bated breath. No; as they arrived she seized each Littlebathian by the hand, and shook that hand vigorously. She did so to everyone that came, rejoiced loudly in the coming of each, and bade them all revel in tea and cake with a voice that demanded and received instant obedience.

'Ah, Lady Longspade! this is kind. I am delighted to see you. Do you remember dear Ems, and the dear Kursaal? Ah, me! Well, do take some tea now, Lady Longspade. What, Miss Finesse—well—well—well. I was thinking of Ostend only the other day. You'll find Flounce there with coffee and cake and all that. You remember my woman, Flounce, don't you? Mrs Fuzzybell, you really make me proud. But is not Mr Fuzzybell to be here? Oh, he's behind is he? well—I'm so glad. Ha! ha! ha! A slow coach is he? I'll make him faster. But perhaps you won't trust him to me, I'm such a dangerous creature. I'm always eloping with some one. Who knows but I might go off with Mr Fuzzybell? We were near it you know at the end of that long walk at Malvern—only he seemed too tired—ha! ha! ha! There's tea and cake there, Mrs Fuzzybell. Mr dear Sir Lionel, I am delighted. I declare you are five years younger—we are both five years younger than when we were at Jerusalem.'

And so forth. But Sir Lionel did not pass on to the tea-tables as did the Finesses and the Longspades. He remained close at Miss Todd's elbow, as though his friendship was of a more enduring kind than that of others, as though he were more to Miss Todd than Mrs Fuzzybell, nearer than Miss Ruff who had just been assured at her entrance that the decks should be made ready for action almost at once. A lion-hearted old warrior was Miss Ruff—one who could not stand with patience the modern practice of dallying in the presence of her enemies' guns. She had come there for a rubber of whist—to fight the good fight—to conquer or to die, and her soul longed to be at it. Wait but one moment longer, Miss Ruff, and the greengrocer and I will have done with our usherings, and then the decks shall be cleared.

But we must certainly do the honours for our old friend Miss Baker. Miss Todd, when she saw her, looked as though she would have fallen on her neck and kissed her; but she doubtless remembered that their respective head-dresses might suffer in the encounter.

'At last, dear Miss Baker; at last! I am so delighted; but where is Miss Waddington? where is the bride-elect?' These last words were said in a whisper which was not perhaps quite as plainly audible at the other side of the Paragon as were the generality of Miss Todd's speeches. 'Indisposed! Why is she indisposed? you mean that she has love-letters to write. I know that is what you mean.' And the roar again became a whisper fit for Drury Lane. 'Well, I shall make a point of seeing her tomorrow. Do you remember Jehoshaphat, dear Jehoshaphat?' And then having made her little answers, Miss Baker also passed on, and left Miss Todd in the act of welcoming the Rev. Mr O'Callaghan.

Miss Baker passed on, but she did so slowly. She had to speak to Sir Lionel, who kept his place near Miss Todd's shoulder; and perhaps she had some secret hope—no, not hope; some sort of an anticipation—that her dear friend would give her the benefit of his arm for a few moments. But Sir Lionel did nothing of the kind. He took her hand with his kindest little squeeze, asked with his softest voice after his dear Caroline, and then let her pass on by herself. Miss Baker was a bird easily to be lured to her perch,—or to his. Sir

Lionel felt that he could secure her at any time. Therefore, he determined to attach himself to Miss Todd for the present. And so Miss Baker walked on alone, perhaps a little piqued at being thus slighted.

It was a strange sight to see the Rev. Mr O'Callaghan among that worldly crowd of pleasure-seeking sinners. There were, as we have said, three sets of people at Littlebath. That Miss Todd, with her commanding genius and great power of will, should have got together portions of two of them was hardly to be considered wonderful. Both the fast and heavy set liked good suppers. But it did appear singular to the men and women of both these sets that they should find themselves in the same room with Mr O'Callaghan.

Mr O'Callaghan was not exactly the head and font of piety at Littlebath. It was not on his altars, not on his chiefly, that hecatombs of needlework were offered up. He was only senior curate to the great high-priest, to Dr Snort himself. But though he was but curate, he was more perhaps to Littlebath—to his especial set in Littlebath—than most rectors are to their own people.

Mr O'Callaghan was known to be condescending and mild under the influence of tea and muffins—sweetly so if the cream be plentiful and the muffins soft with butter; but still, as a man and a pastor, he was severe. In season and out of season he was hot in argument against the devil and all his works. He was always fighting the battle with all manner of weapons. He would write letters of killing reproach to persons he had never known, and address them by post to—

'John Jones, Esq.,
The Sabbath-breaker,
5, Paradise Terrace,
Littlebath.'

or—

'Mrs Gambler Smith,
2, Little Paragon,
Littlebath.'

Nothing was too severe for him. One may say that had he not been a clergyman, and therefore of course justified in any interference, he would have been kicked from Littlebath to

London and back again long since. How then did it come to pass that he was seen at Miss Todd's party? The secret lay in Miss Todd's unbounded power. She was not as other Littlebathians. When he unintentionally squeezed her hand, she squeezed his in return with somewhat of a firmer grasp. When, gently whispering, he trusted that she was as well in spirit as in body, she answered aloud—and all the larger Paragon heard her—that she was very well in both, thank God. And then, as her guests pressed in, she passed him on rapidly to the tea and cake, and to such generous supplies of cream as Mrs Flounce, in her piety, might be pleased to vouchsafe to him.

'What, Mr O'Callaghan!' said Sir Lionel into Miss Todd's ear, in a tone of well-bred wonder and triumphant admiration. 'Mr O'Callaghan among the sinners! My dear Miss Todd, how will he like the whist-tables?'

'If he does not like them, he must just do the other thing. If I know anything of Miss Ruff, a whole college of O'Callaghans could not keep her from the devil's books* for five minutes longer. Oh, here is Lady Ruth Revoke; my dear Lady Ruth, I am charmed to see you. When, I wonder, shall we meet again at Baden Baden? Dear Baden Baden! Flounce, green tea for Lady Ruth Revoke.' And so Miss Todd continued to do her duty.

What Miss Todd had said of her friend was quite true. Even then Miss Ruff was standing over a card-table, with an open pack in her hands, quite regardless of Mr O'Callaghan. 'Come, Lady Longspade,' she said, 'we are wasting time sadly. It is ever so much after nine. I know Miss Todd means us to begin. She told me so. Suppose we sit down?'

But Lady Longspade merely muttered something and passed on. In the first place, she was not quite so eager as Miss Ruff; and in the next, Miss Ruff was neither the partner nor the opponent with whom she delighted to co-operate. Lady Longspade liked to play first-fiddle at her own table; but Miss Ruff always played first-fiddle at her table, let the others be whom they might; and she very generally played her tunes altogether 'con spirito.'

Miss Ruff saw how Lady Longspade passed on, but she was

nothing disconcerted. She was used to that, and more than that. 'Highty-tighty!' was all she said. 'Well, Mrs Garded, I think we can manage without her ladyship, can't we?' Mrs Garded said that she thought they might indeed, and stood by the table opposite to Miss Ruff. This was Mrs King Garded, a widow of great Littlebathian repute, to whom as a partner over the green table few objected. She was a careful, silent, painstaking player, one who carefully kept her accounts, and knew well that the monthly balance depended mainly, not on her good, but on her bad hands. She was an old friend, and an old enemy of Miss Ruff's. The two would say very spiteful things to each other, things incredible to persons not accustomed to the card-tables of Littlebath. But, nevertheless, they were always willing to sit together at the same rubber.

To them came up smirking little Mr Fuzzybell. Mr Fuzzybell was not great at whist, nor did he much delight in it; but, nevertheless, he constantly played. He was taken about by his wife to the parties, and then he was always caught and impaled, and generally plucked and skinned before he was sent home again. He never disported at the same table as his wife, who did not care to play either with him or against him; but he was generally caught by some Miss Ruff, or some Mrs King Garded, and duly made use of. The ladies of Littlebath generally liked to have one black coat at the table with them. It saved them from that air of destitution which always, in their own eyes, attaches to four ladies seated at a table together.

'Ah, Mr Fuzzybell,' said Miss Ruff, 'you are the very person we are looking for. Mrs Garded always likes to have you at her table. Sit down, Mr Fuzzybell.' Mr Fuzzybell did as he was told, and sat down.

Just at this moment, as Miss Ruff was looking out with eager eyes for a fourth who would suit her tastes, and had almost succeeded in catching the eye of Miss Finesse—and Miss Finesse was a silent, desirable, correct player—who should walk up to the table and absolutely sit down but that odious old woman, Lady Ruth Revoke! It was Mrs Garded's great sin, in Miss Ruff's eye, that she toadied Lady Ruth to such an extent as to be generally willing to play with her. Now it was notorious in Littlebath that she had never played well, and that she had long since forgotten all she had ever known. The poor old woman had already had some kind of a fit; she was very shaky and infirm, and ghastly to look at, in spite of her paint and ribbons. She was long in arranging her cards, long in playing them; very long in settling her points, when the points went against her, as they generally did. And yet, in spite of all this, Mrs King Garded would encourage her because her father had been Lord Whitechapel!

There was no help for it now. There she was in the chair; and unless Miss Ruff was prepared to give up her table and do something that would be uncommonly rude even for her, the rubber must go on. She was not prepared at any rate to give up her table, so she took up a card to cut for partners. There were two to one in her favour. If fortune would throw her ladyship and Mr Fuzzybell together, there might yet be found in the easiness of their prey some consolation for the slowness of the play.

They cut the cards, and Miss Ruff found herself sitting opposite to Lady Ruth Revoke. It was a pity that she should not have been photographed. 'And now, Mr Fuzzybell,' said Mrs King Garded, triumphantly.

But we must for awhile go to other parts of the room. Lady Longspade, Mrs Fuzzybell, and Miss Finesse soon followed the daring example of Miss Ruff, and seated themselves with some worthy fourth compatriot.

'Did you see Miss Ruff?' said Lady Longspade, whose ears had caught the scornful highty-tighty of the rejected lady. 'She wanted to get me at her table. But no, I thank you. I like my rubber too, and can play it as well as some other people. But it may cost too dear, eh, Mrs Fuzzybell? I have no idea of being scolded by Miss Ruff.'

'No, nor I,' said Mrs Fuzzybell. 'I hate that continual scolding. We are playing only for amusement; and why not play in good temper?'—nevertheless Mrs Fuzzybell had a rough side to her own tongue. 'It is you and I, Miss Finesse. Shillings, I suppose, and—' and then there was a little whispering and a little grinning between Lady Longspade and

Mrs Fuzzybell, the meaning of which was, that as the occasion was rather a special one, they would indulge themselves with half-a-crown on the rubber and sixpence each hand on the odd trick. And so the second table went to work.

And then there was a third, and a fourth, and a fifth. Miss Ruff's example was more potent that Mr O'Callaghan's presence in that assembly. That gentleman began to feel unhappy as there was no longer round him a crowd of listening ladies sufficient to screen from his now uninquiring eyes the delinquencies of the more eager of the sinners. The snorting of the war-horse and the sound of the trumpet had enticed away every martial bosom, and Mr O'Callaghan was left alone in converse with Mrs Flounce.

He turned to Miss Todd, who was now seated near enough to the door to do honour to any late arriving guest, but near enough also to the table to help herself easily to cake. His soul burned within him to utter one anathema against the things that he saw. Miss Todd was still not playing. He might opine that she objected to the practice. Sir Lionel was still at her back: he also might be a brand that had been rescued from the burning. At a little distance sat Miss Baker: he knew that she at any rate was not violently attached to cards. Could he not say something? Could he not lift up his voice, if only for a moment, and speak forth as he so loved to do, as was his wont in the meetings of the saints, his brethren?

He looked at Miss Todd, and he raised his eyes, and he raised his hands, but the courage was not in him to speak. There was about Miss Todd as she stood, or as she sat, a firmness which showed itself even in her rotundity, a vigour in the very rubicundity of her cheek which was apt to quell the spirit of those who would fain have interfered with her. So Mr O'Callaghan, having raised his eyes considerably, and having raised his hands a little, said nothing.

'I fear you do not approve of cards?' said Miss Todd.

'Approve! oh no, how can I approve of them, Miss Todd?'

'Well, I do with all my heart. What are old women like us to do? We haven't eyes to read at night, even if we had minds fit for it. We can't always be saying our prayers. We have nothing to talk about except scandal. It's better than drinking; and we should come to that if we hadn't cards.'

'Oh, Miss Todd!'

'You see you have your excitement in preaching, Mr O'Callaghan. These card-tables are our pulpits; we have got none other. We haven't children, and we haven't husbands; that is, the most of us. And we should be in a lunatic asylum in six weeks if you took away our cards. Now, will you tell me, Mr O'Callaghan, what would you expect Miss Ruff to do if you persuaded her to give up whist?'

'She has the poor with her always, Miss Todd.'

'Yes, she has; the woman that goes about with a clean apron and four borrowed children; and the dumb man with a bit of chalk and no legs, and the very red nose. She has these, to be sure, and a lot more. But suppose she looks after them all the day, she can't be looking after them all the night too. The mind must be unbent sometimes, Mr O'Callaghan.'

'But to play for money, Miss Todd! Is not that gambling?'

'Well, I don't know. I can't say what gambling is. But do you sit down and play for love, Mr O'Callaghan, and see how soon you'll go to sleep. Come, shall we try? I can have a little private bet, just to keep myself awake, with Sir Lionel here.'

But Mr O'Callaghan declined the experiment. So he had another cup of tea and another muffin, and then went his way; regretting sorely in his heart that he could not get up into a high pulpit and preach at them all. However, he consoled himself by 'improving' the occasion on the following Sunday.

For the next fifteen minutes Sir Lionel stood his ground, saying soft nothings to Miss Todd, and then he also became absorbed among the rubbers. He found that Miss Todd was not good at having love made to her in public. She was very willing to be confidential, very willing to receive flattery, attentions, hand-pressings, and the like. But she would make her confidences in her usual joyous, loud voice; and when told that she was looking remarkably well, she would reply that she always did look well at Littlebath, in a tone that could not fail to attract the attention of the whole room. Now Sir Lionel would fain have been a little more quiet in his proceedings, and was forced to put off somewhat of what he had to say till he could find Miss Todd alone on the top of a mountain. 'Twas thus at least that he expressed his thoughts to himself in his chagrin, as he took his place opposite to Mrs Shortpointz, at the seventh and last establishment now formed in the rooms.

The only idlers present were Miss Baker and Miss Todd. Miss Baker was not quite happy in her mind. It was not only that she was depressed about Caroline: her firm belief in the grammatical axiom before alluded to lessened her grief on that score. But the conduct of Sir Lionel made her uncomfortable; and she began to find, without at all understanding why, that she did not like Miss Todd as well as she used to do at Jerusalem. Her heart took Mr O'Callaghan's side in that little debate about the cards; and though Sir Lionel, in leaving Miss Todd, did not come to her, nevertheless the movement was agreeable to her. She was not therefore in her very highest spirits when Miss Todd came and sat close to her on the sofa.

'I am so sorry you should be out,' said Miss Todd. 'But you see, I've had so much to do at the door there, that I couldn't see who was sitting down with you.'

'I'd rather be out,' said Miss Baker. 'I am not quite sure that Mr O'Callaghan is not right.' This was her revenge.

'No; he's not a bit right, my dear. He does—just what the man says in the rhymes—what is it? you know—makes up for his own little peccadilloes by damning yours and mine. I forget how it goes. But there'll be more in by-and-by, and then we'll have another table. Those who come late will be more in your line; not so ready to peck your eyes out if you happen to forget a card. That Miss Ruff is dreadful.' Here an awful note was heard, for the Lady Ruth had just put her thirteenth trump on Miss Ruff's thirteenth heart. What Littlebathian female soul could stand that unmoved?

'Oh, dear! that poor old woman!' continued Miss Todd. 'You know one lives in constant fear of her having a fit. Miss Ruff is horrible. She has a way of looking with that fixed eye of hers that is almost worse than her voice.' The fact was, that Miss Ruff had one glass eye. 'I know she'll be the death of that poor old creature some of these days. Lady Ruth will play, and she hardly knows one card from another. And then Miss Ruff, she will scold. Good heavens! do you hear that?'

'It's just seven minutes since I turned the last trick of the last hand,' Miss Ruff has said scornfully. 'We shall have finished the two rubbers about six in the morning, I take it.'

'Will your ladyship allow me to deal for you?' said Mr Fuzzybell, meaning to be civil.

'I'll allow you to do no such thing,' croaked out Lady Ruth. 'I can deal very well myself; at any rate as well as Miss Ruff. And I'm not the least in a hurry;' and she went on slobbering out the cards, and counting them over and over again, almost as each card fell.

'That's a double and a treble against a single,' said Lady Longspade, cheerfully, from another table; 'six points, and five—the other rubber—makes eleven; and the two half-crowns is sixteen, and seven odd tricks is nineteen and six. Here's sixpence, Mrs Fuzzybell; and now we'll cut again.'

This was dreadful to Miss Ruff. Here had her rival played two rubbers, won them both, pocketed all but a sovereign, and was again at work; while she, she was still painfully toiling through her second game, the first having been scored against her by her partner's fatuity in having trumped her long heart. Was this to be borne with patience? 'Lady Ruth,' she said, emitting fire out of her one eye, 'do you ever mean to have done dealing those cards?'

Lady Ruth did not condescend to make any answer, but recommenced her leisurely counting; and then Miss Ruff uttered that terrific screech which had peculiarly excited Miss Todd's attention.

'I declare I don't like it at all,' said the tender-hearted Miss Baker. 'I think Mr O'Callaghan was quite right.'

'No, my dear, he was quite wrong, for he blamed the use of cards, not the abuse. And after all, what harm comes of it? I don't suppose Miss Ruff will actually kill her. I dare say if we were playing ourselves we shouldn't notice it. Do you play cribbage? Shall we have a little cribbage?' But Miss Baker did not play cribbage; or, at any rate, she said that she did not.

'And do tell me something about dear Caroline,' continued

Miss Todd. 'I am so anxious to see her. But it has been a very long engagement, hasn't it? and there ought to be lots of money, oughtn't there? But I suppose it's all right. You know I was very much in love with young Bertram myself; and made all manner of overtures to him, but quite in vain; ha! ha! ha! I always thought him a very fine fellow, and I think her a very lucky girl. And when is it to be? And, do tell me, is she over head and ears in love with him?'

What was Miss Baker to say to this? She had not the slightest intention of making Miss Todd a confidante in the matter: certainly not now, as that lady was inclined to behave so very improperly with Sir Lionel; and yet she did not know how to answer it.

'I hope it won't be put off much longer,' continued Miss Todd. 'Is any day fixed yet?'

'No; no day is fixed yet,' replied Miss Baker, blushing.

Miss Todd's ear was very quick. 'There is nothing the matter, I trust. Well, I won't ask any questions, nor say a word to anybody. Come, there is a table vacant, and we will cut in.' And then she determined that she would get it all out from Sir Lionel.

The parties at some of the tables were now changed, and Miss Baker and Miss Todd found themselves playing together. Miss Baker, too, loved a gentle little rubber, if she could enjoy it quietly, without fear of being gobbled up by any Ruff or any Longspade; and with Miss Todd she was in this matter quite safe. She might behave as badly as had the Lady Ruth, and Miss Todd would do no worse than laugh at her. Miss Todd did not care about her points, and at her own house would as soon lose as win; so that Miss Baker would have been happy had she not still continued to sigh over her friend's very improper flirtation with Sir Lionel.

And thus things went on for an hour or so. Every now and again a savage yell was heard from some ill-used angry lady, and low growls, prolonged sometimes through a whole game, came from different parts of the room; but nobody took any notice of them; 'twas the manner at Littlebath; and, though a stranger to the place might have thought, on looking at those perturbed faces, and hearing those uncourteous sounds, that there would be a flow of blood—such a flow as angry nails may produce—the denizens of the place knew better. So the rubbers went on with the amount of harmony customary to the place.

But the scene would have been an odd one for a non-playing stranger, had a non-playing stranger been there to watch it. Every person in the room was engaged at whist except Mrs Flounce, who still remained quiescent behind her tea and cakes. It did not happen that the party was made up of a number of exact fours. There were two over; two middle-aged ladies, a maiden and a widow; and they, perhaps more happy than any of the others, certainly more silent, for neither of them had a partner to scold, were hard at work at double-dummy* in a corner.

It was a sight for a stranger! It is generally thought that a sad *ennui* pervades the life of most of those old ladies in England to whom fate has denied the usual cares and burdens of the world, or whose burdens and cares are done and gone. But there was no *ennui* here. No stockjobber on 'Change could go about his exciting work with more animating eagerness. There were those who scolded, and those who were scolded. Those who sat silent, being great of mind, and those who, being weak, could not restrain their notes of triumph or their notes of woe; but they were all of them as animated and intense as a tiger springing at its prey. Watch the gleam of joy that lights up the half-dead, sallow countenance of old Mrs Shortpointz as she finds the ace of trumps at the back of her hand, the very last card. Happy, happy Mrs Shortpointz! Watch the triumph which illumines even the painted cheeks and half-hidden wrinkles of Lady Longspade as she brings in at the end of the hand three winning little clubs, and sees kings and queens fall impotent at their call. Triumphant, successful Lady Longspade! Was Napoleon more triumphant? did a brighter glow of self-satisfied inward power cross his features, when at Ulm he succeeded in separating poor Mack* from all his friends?

Play on, ladies. Let us not begrudge you your amusements. We do not hold with pious Mr O'Callaghan, that the interchange of a few sixpences is a grievous sin. At other hours ye are still soft, charitable, and tender-hearted; tender-hearted as English old ladies are, and should be. But, dear ladies, would it not be well to remember the amenities of life—even at the whist-table?

So things went on for an hour or so, and then Miss Baker and Sir Lionel again found themselves separated from the card-tables, a lonely pair. It had been Sir Lionel's cue this evening to select Miss Todd for his special attentions; but he had found Miss Todd at the present moment to be too much of a public character for his purposes. She had a sort of way of speaking to all her guests at once, which had doubtless on the whole an extremely hilarious effect, but which was not flattering to the *amour propre* of a special admirer. So, *faute de mieux*, Sir Lionel was content to sit down in a corner with Miss Baker. Miss Baker was also content; but she was rather uneasy as to how she should treat the subject of Caroline's quarrel with her lover.

'Of course you saw George today?' she began.

'Yes, I did see him; but that was all. He seemed to be in a tremendous hurry, and said he must be back in town tonight. He's not staying, is he?'

'No; he's not staying.'

'I didn't know: when I saw that dear Caroline was not with you, I thought she might perhaps have better company at home.'

'She was not very well. George went back to London before dinner.'

'Nothing wrong, I hope?'

'Well, no; I hope not. That is—you haven't heard anything about it, have you, Sir Lionel?'

'Heard anything! No, I have heard nothing; what is it?'

It may be presumed that such a conversation as this had not been carried on in a very loud tone; but, nevertheless, low as Miss Baker had spoken, low as Sir Lionel had spoken, it had been too loud. They had chosen their places badly. The table at which Lady Ruth and her party were sitting—we ought rather to say, Miss Ruff and her party—was in one corner of the room, and our friends had placed themselves on a cushioned seat fixed against the wall in this very corner.

Things were still going on badly with Miss Ruff. As Sindbad* carried the old man, and could not shake him off, so did Miss Ruff still carry Lady Ruth Revoke; and the weight was too much for her.

She manfully struggled on, however—womanfully would perhaps be a stronger and more appropriate word. She had to calculate not only how to play her own hand correctly, but she had also to calculate on her partner's probable errors. This was hard work, and required that all around her should be undisturbed and silent. In the midst of a maze of uncontrollable difficulties, the buzz buzz of Miss Baker's voice fell upon her ears, and up she rose from her chair.

'Miss Todd,' she said, and Miss Todd, looking round from a neighbouring table, shone upon her with her rosy face. But all the shining was of no avail.

'Miss Todd, if this is to be a conversazione, we had better make it so at once. But if it's whist, then I must say I never heard so much talking in my life!'

'It's a little of both,' said Miss Todd, not *sotto voce*.

'Oh, very well; now I understand,' said Miss Ruff; and then she resumed her work and went on with her calculations.

Miss Baker and Sir Lionel got up, of course, and going over to the further part of the room continued their conversation. She soon told him all she knew. She had hardly seen George herself, she said. But Caroline had had a long interview with him, and on leaving him had said that all—all now was over.

'I don't know what to make of it,' said Miss Baker, with her handkerchief to her eyes. 'What do you think, Sir Lionel? You know they say that lovers always do quarrel, and always do make it up again.'

'George is a very headstrong fellow,' said Sir Lionel.

'Yes, that is what I have always felt; always. There was no being sure with him. He is so wild, and has such starts.'

'Has this been his doing?'

'Oh, yes, I think so. Not but that Caroline is very spirited too: I suppose somehow it came about between them.'

'He was tired of waiting.'

'That might have been a reason twelve months ago, but there was to be no more delay now; that is, as I understood it.

No, it is not that, Sir Lionel. It makes me very unhappy, I know;' and Miss Baker again used her handkerchief.

'You mustn't distress yourself, my dearest friend,' said Lionel. 'For my sake, don't. Oh, if you knew how it pains me to see you suffering in that way! I think more of you in the matter than even of George; I do indeed.' And Sir Lionel contrived to give a little pinch to the top of one of Miss Baker's fingers—not, however, without being observed by the sharp eyes of his hostess.

'But, Caroline!' sobbed Miss Baker, behind her handkerchief. She was nicely ensconced in the depth of a lounging-chair, so that she could turn her face from the card-tables. It is so sweet to be consoled in one's misery, especially when one really believes that the misery is not incurable. So that on the whole Miss Baker was not unhappy.

'Yes, dear Caroline,' said Sir Lionel; 'of course I can say nothing till I have heard more of the matter. But do you think Caroline really loves him? Sometimes I have thought—'

'So have I, sometimes; that is, I used. But she does love him, Sir Lionel; that is, if I know anything about it.'

'Ah, dearest friend, do you know anything about it? that is the very question I want to ask you. Do you know anything about it? Sometimes I have thought you knew nothing. And then sometimes I have thought, been bold enough to think—' And Sir Lionel looked intently at the handkerchief which covered her face; and Miss Todd looked furtively, ever and anon, at Sir Lionel. 'I declare I think it would do very well,' said Miss Todd to herself good-naturedly.

Miss Baker did not quite understand him, but she felt herself much consoled. Sir Lionel was a remarkably handsome man; as to that she had made up her mind long since: then he was a peculiarly gentlemanlike man, a very friendly man, and a man who exactly suited all her tastes. She had for some weeks past begun to think the day tedious in which she did not see him; and now it was driven in upon her mind that conversation was a much pleasanter occupation than whist; that is, conversation with so highly polished a man as Sir Lionel Bertram. But, nevertheless, she did not quite understand what he meant, nor did she know how she ought to answer it. Why need she answer him at all? Could she not sit here, wiping her eyes softly and comfortably, and listen to what might come next?

'I sometimes think that some women never love,' said Sir Lionel.

'Perhaps they don't,' said Miss Baker.

'And yet in the depth of many a heart there may be a fund of passion.'

'Oh, there may, certainly,' said Miss Baker.

'And in your own, my friend? Is there no such fund there? Are there no hidden depths there unexplored, still fresh, but still, perhaps still to be reached?'

Again Miss Baker found it easiest to lie well back into her chair, and wipe her eyes comfortably. She was not prepared to say much about the depths of her own heart at so very short a notice.

Sir Lionel was again about to speak—and who can say what might have come next, how far those hidden depths might have been tried?—when he was arrested in the midst of his pathos by seeing Mrs Garded and Mr Fuzzybell each rush to a shoulder of Lady Ruth Revoke. The colonel quitted his love for a moment, and hurried to the distant table; while Miss Baker, removing her handkerchief, sat up and gazed at the scene of action.

The quarrelling had been going on unabated, but that had caused little surprise. It is astonishing how soon the ear becomes used to incivilities. They were now accustomed to Miss Ruff's voice, and thought nothing of her exclamations. 'Well, I declare—what, the ten of spades!—ha! ha! ha! well, it is an excellent joke—if you could have obliged me, Lady Ruth, by returning my lead of trumps, we should have been out,' etc. etc. etc. All this and more attracted no attention, and the general pity for Lady Ruth had become dead and passive.

But at last Miss Ruff's tongue went faster and faster, and her words became sharper and sharper. Lady Ruth's countenance became very strange to look at. She bobbed her head about slowly in a manner that frightened Mr Fuzzybell, and ceased to make any remark to her partner. Then Mrs Garded made two direct appeals to Miss Ruff for mercy.

But Miss Ruff could not be merciful. Perhaps on each occasion she refrained for a moment, but it was only for a moment; and Mrs Garded and Mr Fuzzybell ceased to think of their cards, and looked only at the Lady Ruth; and then of a sudden they both rose from their seats, the colonel, as we have said, rushed across the room, and all the players at all the tables put down their cards and stood up in alarm.

Lady Ruth was sitting perfectly still, except that she still bobbed her old head up and down in a strange unearthly manner. She had about ten cards in her hand which she held motionless. Her eyes seemed to be fixed in one continued stare directly on the face of her foe. Her lower jaw had fallen so as to give a monstrous extension to her cadaverous face. There she sat apparently speechless; but still she bobbed her head, and still she held her cards.

It was known at Littlebath that she had suffered from paralysis, and Mrs Garded and Mr Fuzzybell, thinking that she was having or about to have a fit, naturally rushed to her assistance.

'What is the matter with her?' said Miss Ruff. 'Is anything the matter with her?'

Miss Todd was now at the old lady's side. 'Lady Ruth,' said she, 'do you find yourself not well? Shall we go into my room? Sir Lionel, will you help her ladyship?' And between them they raised Lady Ruth from her chair. But she still clutched the cards, still fixed her eyes on Miss Ruff, and still bobbed her head.

'Do you feel yourself ill, Lady Ruth?' said Miss Todd. But her ladyship answered nothing.

It seemed, however, that her ladyship could walk, for with her two supporters she made her way nearly to the door of the room. There she stood, and having succeeded in shaking off Sir Lionel's arm, she turned and faced round upon the company. She continued to bob her head at them all, and then made this little speech, uttering each word very slowly:

'I wish she had a glass tongue as well, because then perhaps she'd break it.' And having so revenged herself, she suffered

Miss Todd to lead her away into the bedroom. It was clear at least that she had no fit, and the company was thankful.

Sir Lionel, seeing how it was, left them at the door of the bedroom, and a few minutes afterwards Miss Todd, Mrs Flounce, and Lady Ruth's own maid succeeded in getting her into a cab. It is believed that after a day or two she was none the worse for what had happened, and that she made rather a boast of having put down Miss Ruff. For the moment, Miss Ruff was rather put down.

When Miss Todd returned to the drawing-room that lady was sitting quite by herself on an ottoman. She was bolt upright, with her hands before her on her lap, striving to look as though she were perfectly indifferent to what had taken place. But there was ever and again a little twitch about her mouth, and an involuntary movement in her eye which betrayed the effort, and showed that for this once Lady Ruth had conquered. Mr Fuzzybell was standing with a frightened look at the fireplace; while Mrs King Garded hung sorrowing over her cards, for when the accident happened she had two by honours in her own hand.

When Miss Todd returned, some few of her guests were at work again; but most of the tables were broken up. 'Poor dear old lady,' said Miss Todd, 'she has gone home none the worse. She is very old, you know, and a dear good creature.'

'A sweet dear creature,' said Mrs Shortpointz, who loved the peerage, and hated Miss Ruff.

'Come,' said Miss Todd, 'Parsnip has got a little supper for us downstairs; shall we go down? Miss Ruff, you and I will go and call on Lady Ruth tomorrow. Sir Lionel, will you give your arm to Lady Longspade? Come, my dear;' and so Miss Todd took Miss Baker under her wing, and they all went down to supper. But Miss Ruff said not another word that night.

'Ha! ha!' said Miss Todd, poking her fan at Miss Baker, 'I see all about it, I assure you; and I quite approve.'

Miss Baker felt very comfortable, but she did not altogether understand her friend's joke.

CHAPTER XXIII

THREE LETTERS

GEORGE BERTRAM, as we have seen, returned to town after his interview with Miss Waddington without seeing his father. Neither to his mind nor to hers was any comfort brought by that grammatical rule in which Miss Baker had found so much consolation. For both of them the separation was now a thing completed. Each knew enough of the other to feel that that other's pride was too high to admit of his or her making any first fresh advancement.

George endeavoured to persuade himself that he was glad of what he had done; but he failed utterly. He had loved her, did love her dearly, and found that he never valued her as he did now. She had behaved shamefully to him. He said that to himself over and over again. But what had that to do with love? He did not love her the less because she had made public his letter, the secrets of his heart, that which should have been as private as the passion of her own bosom. He could not love her less because she talked over these with another man, however much he might feel himself bound to cast her off for doing so. So he shut himself up in his chambers; wrote pages for his new book that were moody, misanthropical, and unbelieving; and on the whole was very unhappy.

Nor was Caroline much better able to bear the shock; though with her there was more propriety of demeanour under the blow, and a better mental control. That was of course, for she was a woman—and being a woman, she had to take care that the world knew nothing of what was going on within her heart.

For two days she remained perfectly calm. She allowed herself no vent whatever for her feelings. She made the breakfast; sat close at her tambour frame, or more frequently close at her book; read aloud to her aunt; went out and made calls; and attended minutely to all the ordinary occupations of her life. Her aunt never once caught her with a tear in her eye, never saw her sitting thoughtful, unoccupied, with her head leaning on her arm. Had she done so, she would have spoken to her about George. As it was, she did not dare to do so. There was during these days, and indeed outwardly for many days afterwards, an iron stubbornness about Caroline which frightened Miss Baker and altogether prevented her from alluding to the possibility of a reconciliation. Nothing could be more gentle, nay, more obedient, than Caroline's manner and way with her aunt at this time: she yielded to her on everything; but her aunt perceived that all utterance as to the one subject which was nearest to both their hearts was effectually forbidden.

Caroline allowed two whole days to pass before she would allow herself to think of what had taken place. She read through half the nights, so as to secure sleep for herself when she lay down. But on the third morning she opened her desk in her own room, and sat down and wrote to Adela Gauntlet.

'Dearest Adela, 'Littlebath, Friday.

'An occurrence has taken place of which I have not yet allowed myself to think, and which I shall first realize and bring home to myself in writing to you; and yet before it happened I had thought of it very often—even talked of it with aunt Mary; and sometimes thought of it and talked of it as though it were almost desirable. I wish I may teach myself so to think of it now.

'All is over between me and Mr Bertram. He came down here on Tuesday and told me so. I do not blame him. Nor can I blame him; not at least for what he has done, though his manner in doing it was very harsh.

'I would tell you all if I could, but it is so hard in a letter. I wish you were here. But no; you would drive me mad by advice which I could not, would not take. Last summer, when I was so unhappy in London, aunt and I had some conversation about our affairs with a person there. Mr Bertram heard of this while he was in Paris. He did not approve of it; and he wrote me, oh! such a letter. I should have thought it impossible for him to have written such words to me. I was mad with grief, and I showed this letter to the same person. There, Adela, I must tell you all. It was Mr Harcourt, George's intimate friend. George particularly begged me in that letter not to talk to him any more; and yet I did this. But I was half frenzied with grief; and why was I to obey one who had no right to command me, and who made his commands so harsh? His request would have been a law to me.

'But I know I was wrong, Adela. I have known it every minute since I showed the letter. I was sure I was wrong, because I could not tell him that I had done so. It made me afraid of him, and I never before was afraid of any one. Well; I did not tell him, and now he has found it out. I would not condescend to ask him how; but I think I know. This at least I know, that he did so in no ignoble way, by no mean little suspicions. He did not seek to discover it. It had come upon him like a great blow, and he came at once to me to learn the truth. I told him the truth, and this has been the end of it.

'Now you know it all; all except his look, his tone, his manner. These I cannot tell you—cannot describe. I seem now to know him better, understand him more thoroughly than ever I did. He is a man for a tender-hearted woman to love to madness. And I—Ah! never mind, dearest; I think—nay, I am sure I can get over it. You never could. Yes; he is a man for a woman to worship; but yet he is so rough, so stern, so harsh in his anger. He does not measure his words at all. I don't think he knows the kind of things he says. And yet the while his heart is so tender, so soft; I could see it all. But he gives one no time to acknowledge it—at least, he gave me none. Were you ever scolded, upbraided, scorned by a man you loved? and did you ever feel that you loved him the better for all his scorn? I felt so. I could so feel, though it was impossible to confess it. But he was wrong there. He should not have upbraided me unless he intended to forgive. I think I have read that it is not kingly for a king to receive a suppliant for pardon unless he intends to forgive. I can understand that. If his mind was made up to condemn me altogether, he should have written and so have convicted me. But in such matters he considers nothing. He acts altogether from the heart.

'I am, however, sure of this, dear Adela, that it is all better as it is. There; with you, I will scorn all falsehood. For once, and, if possible, only for once, the truth shall stand out plainly. I love him as I never, never can love another man. I love him as I never thought to love any man. I feel at this moment as though I could be content to serve him as his menial. For she who is his wife must so serve him—and how long should I be content to do so?

'But yet I wrong him in this. He is most imperious, absolutely imperious—must be altogether master in all things; this is what I mean. But to one who loved him well, and would permit this, he would be the tenderest, gentlest, most loving of masters. He would not permit the wind to blow too harshly on his slave. I have loved him well, but I could not permit this. I could not permit it for a whole lifetime; and therefore it is well that we have parted.

'You will hardly believe this of him, for he seems in general company to be so good-humoured. With people that are indifferent to him, no man is less exacting; but with those near to him in life he never bends, not an inch. It is this that has estranged his uncle from him. But yet how noble, how grand a man he is! To all pecuniary considerations he is absolutely indifferent. A falsehood, even a concealment, is impossible with him. Who that either of us knows is equal to or approaches him in talent? He is brave, generous, simple-hearted beyond all that I have ever known. Who is like him? And yet—. To you, once for all, I say all this. But, Adela, do not take advantage of me. You ought to know that were it not all over, I should not say it.

'I wish that you had been betrothed to him. Oh, how I wish it! You are not worldly, as I am; not stubborn, nor proud of heart. Not that you have not pride, a truer, better pride. You could have brought yourself to submit, to be guided, to be a secondary portion of himself—and then how he would have loved you!

'I have often wondered that he should have thought of me. No two persons were ever less suited for each other. I knew that when I accepted him, foolishly accepted him because I liked him, and now I am rightly punished. But, ah! that he should be punished too! for he is punished. I know he loves me; though I know nothing would now induce him to take me. And I know this also, that nothing—nothing—nothing would induce me to be so taken. Not if he were begging—as he never will beg to any woman. I would be too true to him, too true to what I now know to be his happiness.

'As for me, I dare say I shall marry yet. I have some little money, and that sort of manner which many men think most becoming for the top of their tables and the management of their drawing-rooms. If I do, there shall be no deceit. I certainly shall not marry for love. Indeed, from early years I never thought it possible that I should do so. I have floundered unawares into the pitfall, and now I must flounder out. I have always thought that there was much in the world worth living for besides love. Ambition need not be a closed book for women, unless they choose to close it. I do not see but a statesman's wife may stand nearly as high in the world as the statesman himself. Money, position, rank, are worth the having—at any rate, the world thinks so, or why else do they scramble for them? I will not scramble for them; but if they come in my way, why, I may probably pick them up.

'This will be odious to you. I know it will. A potato-paring and a true heart are your beau-ideal for this world. I am made of viler stuff. I have had the true heart, and see what I have made of it!

'You will answer me, of course. I could find it in my heart to beg you not to do so, only now I could not afford to think that you were cold to me. I know you will write to me; but, pray, pray do not advise me to submit myself to him under the idea that a reconciliation is possible. A reconciliation is not possible, and I will not submit myself to him. I know I speak the truth when I say that our marriage is not to be desired. I acknowledge his merits; I confess his superiority; but these very merits, this great superiority, make it impossible that I should suit him as a wife.

'On that matter I have made up my mind. I will never marry him. I only say this to deter you from wasting your energy in endeavouring to bring us again together. I know very well that I shall not be asked—that his mind is equally firm.

'And now, good-bye. You know all my heart, and, as far as I can tell them, all my feelings. A long letter from you will give me much delight if you will comply with my earnest request.

'This letter has been a very selfish one, for it is all about myself. But you will forgive that now. God bless you.

'Your affectionate friend,

'CAROLINE.

'P.S. I have said nothing to aunt Mary, except to tell her that the match is broken off; and she has kindly—so kindly, abstained from any questions.'

Adela Gauntlet was all alone when she received this letter at West Putford. In these days she generally was all alone. That she should answer it, answer it at once, was of course certain. But how should she answer it? Her mind was soon made up, with many tears, partly for her friend and partly for herself. Caroline's happiness had been, nay, probably still was, in her own hands, and she was going to throw it away. For herself, happiness had never been within her own reach. 'Be his menial servant!' she repeated to herself, as she read and re-read the letter. 'Yes; of course she should if he required it. It would be for her to make him know that she could be something better to him!'

Her judgment was soon formed. She condemned Caroline altogether on Caroline's own showing. In such matters one woman almost always condemns another. She took no notice of the allusion to Bertram's harshness; she almost overlooked the generosity with which her friend had written of the lover who had rejected her. She only saw Caroline's great fault. How could she have brought herself to talk with Mr Harcourt—with a young unmarried man—on such a subject? And, oh! how was it possible that she could have brought herself to show him such a letter? She wrote her answer that same night, as follows:—

'West Putford, Saturday night.

'Dearest Caroline,

'Your letter has made me most unhappy. I almost think that I have suffered more in reading it than you did in writing it. You have made a request to me with which I cannot, will not comply. I can only write to you the truth, as I think it. What else can I write? How can I frame my letter in any other way?

'But I will acknowledge this, that it is useless for me to suggest anything to you as to your own happiness. But there is more than that to be thought of. There is that which you are bound to think of before that. Whether you have broken with Mr Bertram or not, there has been that between you which makes it your duty in this matter to regard his happiness as your first consideration.

'Dearest, dearest Caroline, I fear that you have been wrong throughout in this affair. I do not dread your being angry with me for saying so. In spite of what you say, I know your heart is so warm that you would be angry with me if I blamed him. You were wrong in talking to Mr Harcourt; doubly wrong in showing to him that letter. If so, is it not your business to put that wrong right? to remedy if you can the evil that has come of it?

'I feel quite sure that Mr Bertram loves you with all his heart, and that he is one who will be wretched to his heart's core at losing what he loves. It is nothing to say that it is he who has rejected you. You understand his moods; even I understand them well enough to know in what temper that last visit was made. Answer this to yourself. Had you then asked his pardon, do you not know that he would have given it you with a rapture of joy? Do you not feel that he was then at that moment only too anxious to forgive? And are you, you who have sinned against him, to let him break his heart against a rock, because you are too proud to own to him the fault which you acknowledge to yourself? Is that your return for the love which he has borne you?

'You wish that he had loved me, you say. Do not wish away the sweetest gift which God can give to a woman in this world. It was not possible that I should have loved him. It is quite impossible now that you should not do so.

'Try to think in this affair with severity towards yourself, and ask yourself what justice requires of you. My advice to you is to write to him. Tell him, with frank humility and frank affection, that you ask his pardon for the injury you had done him. Say no more than that. If it shall still please him to consider that the engagement between you is at an end, such an acknowledgment from you will in no way constrain him to violate that resolve. But if he relent—and I know this other "if" will be the true one—the first train that runs will bring him back to you; and he, who I am sure is now wretched, will again be happy; ah! happier than he has been for so long.

'I implore you to do this, not for your own sake, but for his. You have done wrong, and it is he that should be considered. You will think what will be your sufferings if he does not notice your letter; should he not be softened by your humility. But you have no right to think of that. You have done him wrong, and you owe him reparation. You cannot expect that you should do wrong and not suffer.

'I fear I have written savagely. Dear, dear Caroline, come to me here, and I will not talk savagely. I too am not happy. I have not my happiness so much in my own hands as you have. Do come to me. Papa will be delighted to see you. I am sure Miss Baker could spare you for a fortnight. Do, do come to

'Your true friend,

'ADELA.'

There was much of craft in Adela Gauntlet's letter; but if craft could ever be pardonable, then was hers pardonable in this case. She had written as though her sole thought was for Mr Bertram. She had felt that in this way only could she move her friend. In her mind—Adela's mind—it was a settled conviction, firm as rocks, that as Caroline and Mr Bertram loved each other, neither of them could be happy unless they were brought together. How could she best aid in doing this? That had been her main thought, and so thinking she had written this letter, filled to overflowing with womanly craft.

And her craft was nearly successful; but only nearly; that was all. Caroline sat in her solitude and cried over this letter till her eyes were weary with tears. She strove, strove valiantly to take her friend's advice; strove to do so in spite of all her former protestations. She got pen and ink and sat herself down to write the letter of humiliation; but the letter would not be written; it was impossible to her; the words would not form themselves: for two days she strove, and then she abandoned the task as for ever hopeless. And thus this third short epistle must be laid before the reader.

'I cannot do it, Adela. It is not in my nature. You could do it, because you are good, and high, and pure. Do not judge others by yourself. I cannot do it, and will not madden myself by thinking of it again. Good-bye; God bless you. If I could cure your grief I would come to you; but I am not fit. God in his own time will cure yours, because you are so pure. I could not help you, nor you me; I had better, therefore, remain where I am. A thousand thousand kisses. I love you so now, because you and you only know my secret. Oh, if you should not keep it! But I know you will; you are so true.'

This was all. There was no more; no signature. 'May God help them both!' said Adela as she read it.

CHAPTER XXIV

BIDDING HIGH

I HOPE to press all the necessary records of the next three or four months into a few pages. A few pages will be needed in order that we may know how old Mr Bertram behaved when he heard of this rupture between his nephew and his granddaughter.

George, when he found himself back in town, shut himself up in his chambers and went to work upon his manuscript. He, too, recognized the necessity of labour, in order that the sorrow within his heart might thus become dull and deadened.

But it was deep, true sorrow—to him at some periods almost overwhelming: he would get up from his desk during the night, and throwing himself on the sofa, lie there writhing in his agony. While he had known that Caroline was his own, he had borne his love more patiently than does many a man of less intensity of feeling. He had been much absent from her;

had not abridged those periods of absence as he might have done; had, indeed, been but an indifferent lover, if eagerness and *empressement* are necessary to a lover's character. But this had arisen from two causes, and lukewarmness in his love had not been either of them. He had been compelled to feel that he must wait for the fruition of his love; and therefore had waited. And then he had been utterly devoid of any feeling of doubt in her he loved. She had decided that they should wait. And so he had waited as secure away from her as he could have been with her.

But his idea of a woman's love, of the purity and sanctity of her feelings, had been too high. He had left his betrothed to live without him, frequently without seeing him for months, and yet he had thought it utterly impossible that she should hold confidential intercourse with another man. We have seen how things fell out with him. The story need not be repeated. He was shocked, outraged, torn to the heart's core; but he loved as warmly, perhaps more warmly than ever.

What he now expected it is impossible to describe; but during that first fortnight of seclusion in the midst of London, he did half expect, half hope that something would turn up. He waited and waited, still assuring himself that his resolve was inviolable, and that nothing should make him renew his engagement: and yet he hoped for something. There was a weight on his heart which then might have been removed.

But no sign was made. We have seen how Adela, who felt for him, had striven in vain. No sign was made; and at the end of the fortnight he roused himself, shook his mane, and asked himself what he should do.

In the first place, there should be no mystery. There were those among his friends to whom he had felt himself bound to speak of his engagement when it was made, and to them he felt himself bound to communicate the fact now that it was unmade. He wrote accordingly to Arthur Wilkinson; he wrote to Harcourt; and determined to go down to Hadley. He would have written also to his uncle, but he had never done so, and hardly knew how to commence a correspondence.

His letter to Harcourt had been a difficult task to him, but at last it was finished in a very few words. He did not at all refer to what had taken place at Richmond, or allude in any way to the nature of the cause which had produced this sudden disrupture. He merely said that his engagement with Miss Waddington was broken off by mutual consent, and that he thought it best to let his friend know this in order that mistakes and consequent annoyance might be spared. This was very short; but, nevertheless, it required no little effort in its accomplishment.

On the very next day Harcourt came to him at his chambers. This surprised him much. For though he had no intention of absolutely quarrelling with the rising legal luminary, he had taught himself to look upon any renewal of their real intimacy as out of the question. They were sailing on essentially different tacks in their life's voyages. They had become men of different views in everything. Their hours, their habits, their friends, their ways were in all things unlike. And then, moreover, Bertram no longer liked the successful barrister. It may be said that he had learned positively to dislike him. It was not that Harcourt had caused this wound which was tearing his heart to pieces; at least, he thought that it was not that. He declared to himself a dozen times that he did not blame Harcourt. He blamed no one but Caroline—her and himself. Nor was it because the man was so successful. Bertram certainly did not envy him. But the one as he advanced in manhood became worldly, false, laborious, exact, polished, rich, and agreeable among casual acquaintances. The other was the very reverse. He was generous and true; but idle—idle at any rate for any good; he was thoughtful, but cloudy in his thoughts, indifferent as to society, poor, much poorer than he had been as a lad at college, and was by no means gifted with the knack of making pretty conversation for the world at large. Of late, whenever they had met, Harcourt had said something which grated painfully on the other's inner sensibilities, and hence had arisen this dislike.

But the dislike seemed to be all on one side. Harcourt now was a man whose name was frequent in other men's mouths. Great changes were impending in the political world, and

Harcourt was one of the men whom the world regarded as sure to be found swimming on the top of the troubled waters. The people of the Battersea Hamlets were proud of him, the House of Commons listened to him, suitors employed him, and men potent in the Treasury chambers, and men also who hoped to be potent there, courted and flattered him.

All this made him busy; but, nevertheless, he found time to come to his dear friend.

'I am sorry for this; very sorry,' he said, as he put out his hand in a manner that seemed to his friend to be almost patronizing. 'Can nothing be done?'

'Nothing at all,' said Bertram, rather curtly.

'Can I do nothing?' said the cunning legal man.

'Nothing at all,' said Bertram, very curtly.

'Ah, I wish I could. I should be so happy to rearrange matters if it be at all possible.' There are some men who are so specially good at rearranging the domestic disarrangements of others.

'It is an affair,' said Bertram, 'which admits of no interference. Perhaps it is unnecessary that I should have troubled you on the matter at all, for I know that you are very busy; but—'

'My dear fellow—busy, indeed! What business could be more important to me than my friend's happiness?'

'But,' continued George, 'as the affair had been talked over so often between you and me, I thought it right to tell you.'

'Of course—of course; and so nothing can be done? Ah, well! it is very sad, very. But I suppose you know best. She is a charming girl. Perhaps, rather—'

'Harcourt, I had rather not hear a word spoken about her in any way; but certainly not a word in her dispraise.'

'Dispraise! no, certainly not. It would be much easier to praise her. I always admired her very much; very much indeed.'

'Well, there's an end of it.'

'So be it. But I am sorry, very sorry; heartily sorry. You are a little rough now, Bertram. Of course I see that you are so. Every touch goes against the hair with you; every little blow hits you on the raw. I can understand that; and therefore I do not mind your roughness. But we are old friends, you know. Each is perhaps the other's oldest friend; and I don't mean to lose such a friend because you have a shade of the misanthrope on you just now. You'll throw the bile off in another essay, rather more bitter than the last, and then you'll be all right.'

'I'm right enough now, thank you. Only a man can't always be in high spirits. At least, some men cannot.'

'Well, God bless you, old fellow! I know you want me gone; so I'll go now. But never talk to me about my business. I do get through a good deal of business, but it shall never stand between you and me.'

And so the cunning legal man went his way.

And then there remained the journey to Hadley. After that it was his purpose to go abroad again, to go to Paris, and live in dingy lodgings there *au cinquième*, to read French free-thinking books, to study the wild side of politics, to learn if he could, among French theatres and French morals, French freedom of action, and freedom of speech, and freedom of thought—France was a blessed country for freedom in those days, under the paternal monarchy of that paternal monarch, Louis Philippe*—to learn to forget, among these sources of inspiration, all that he had known of the sweets of English life.

But there remained the journey to Hadley. It had always been his custom to go to Mr Pritchett in the city before he went to his uncle's house, and he did so now. Everybody who wished to see Mr Bertram always went to Mr Pritchett first, and Mr Pritchett would usually send some *avant-courier* to warn his patron of the invasion.

'Ah, Mr George,' said Pritchett, wheezing with his most melancholy sigh. 'You shouldn't have left the old gentleman so long, sir. Indeed you shouldn't.'

'But he does not want to see me,' said George.

'Think what a sight of money that is!' continued Pritchett. 'One would really think, Mr George, that you objected to money. There is that gentleman, your particular friend, you know, the member of Parliament. He is down there constantly, paying his respects, as he calls it.'

'What, Mr Harcourt?'

'Yes, Mr Harcourt. And he sends grapes in spring, and turkeys in summer, and green peas in winter.'

'Green peas in winter! they must cost something.'

'Of course they do; sprats to catch big fish with, Mr George. And then the old gentleman has got a new lawyer; some sharp new light of Mr Harcourt's recommending. Oh, Mr George, Mr George! do be careful, do now! Could not you go and buy a few ducks, or pigeons, and take them in a basket? The old gentleman does seem to like that kind of thing, though ten years since he was so different. Half a million of money, Mr George! It's worth a few grapes and turkeys.' And Mr Pritchett shook his head and wrung his hands; for he saw that nothing he said produced any effect.

George went to Hadley at last without ducks or pigeons, grapes or turkeys. He was very much amused however with the perpetual industry of his friend. '*Labor omnia vincit improbus*,'* said he to himself. 'It is possible that Harcourt will find my uncle's blind side at last.'

He found the old gentleman considerably changed. There were, occasionally, flashes of his former, customary, sarcastic pungency; now and again he would rouse himself to be ill-natured, antagonistic, and self-willed. But old-age and illness had sadly told upon him; and he was content for the most part to express his humour by little shrugs, shakes of the head, and an irritable manner he had lately acquired of rubbing his hands quickly together.

'Well, George,' he said, when his nephew shook hands with him and asked after his health.

'I hope you are better than you were, sir. I was sorry to hear that you had been again suffering.'

'Suffer, yes; a man looks to suffer when he gets to my age. He's a fool if he doesn't, at least. Don't trouble yourself to be sorry about it, George.'

'I believe you saw my father not long since?' Bertram said this, not quite knowing how to set the conversation going, so that he might bring in the tidings he had come there to communicate.

'Yes, I did,' said Mr Bertram senior; and his hands went to work as he sat in the armchair.

'Did you find him much altered since you last met? It was a great many years since, I believe?'

'Not in the least altered. Your father will never alter.'

George knew enough of his father's character to understand the point of this; so he changed the subject, and did that which a man who has anything to tell should always do at once; he commenced the telling of it forthwith.

'I have come down here, today, sir, because I think it right to let you know at once that Miss Waddington and I have agreed that our engagement shall be at an end.'

Mr Bertram turned sharp round in his chair. 'What?' said he, 'What?'

'Our engagement is at an end. We are both aware that it is better for us it should be so.'

'What do you mean? Better for you! How can it be better for you? You are two fools.'

'Very likely, sir. We have been two fools; or, at any rate, I have been one.'

Mr Bertram sat still in his chair, silent for a few moments. He still kept rubbing his hands, but in meditation rather than in anger. Though his back reached to the back of his chair, his head was brought forward and leaned almost on his chest. His cheeks had fallen in since George had seen him, and his jaw hung low, and gave a sad, thoughtful look to his face, in which also there was an expression of considerable pain. His nephew saw that what he had said had grieved him, and was sorry for it.

'George,' he said, in a softer voice than had ever been usual with him. 'I wish you to marry Caroline. Go back to her and make it up. Tell her that I wish it, if it be necessary to tell her anything.'

'Ah, sir, I cannot do that. I should not have come to you now if there had been any room for doubt.'

'There must be no room for doubt. This is nonsense; sheer nonsense. I shall send to Mary.' George had never before heard him call Miss Baker by her Christian name.

'It cannot be helped, sir, Miss Baker can do nothing in the

matter now; nor can any one else. We both know that the marriage would not suit us.'

'Not suit you! nonsense. Two babies; two fools! I tell you it will suit you; it will suit me!'

Now had George Bertram junior not been an absolute ass, or a mole rather with no eyesight whatever for things above ground, he would have seen from this that he might not only have got back his love, but have made sure of being his uncle's heir into the bargain. At any rate, there was sufficient in what he said to ensure him a very respectable share of those money-bags. How would Pritchett have rejoiced had he heard the old man speak so! and then how would he have sighed and wheezed when he saw the young man's indifference!

But George would not take the hint. He must have been blind and dull, and dead, and senseless. Who before had ever heard Mr Bertram senior speak out in that way? 'It will suit *me*!' And that from an old bachelor, with uncountable money-bags, to his only nephew! and such a request, too, as it conveyed—that he would again make himself agreeable to a beautiful girl whom he thoroughly loved, and by whom also he was thoroughly loved! But George was an ass, as we have said; and a mole, a blind mole, and a mule, a stiff-necked stubborn mule. He would not yield an inch to his uncle; nor an inch to his own feelings.

'I am sorry to vex you, sir,' he said coldly, 'but it is impossible.'

'Oh, very well,' said the uncle, as he compressed his lips, and moved his hands. 'Very well.' And so they parted.

George went back to town and commenced his preparations for Paris. But on the following day he received the unwonted honour of a visit from Mr Pritchett, and the honour was very pointed; in this wise. Mr Pritchett, not finding him at home, had gone to a neighbouring tavern 'to get a bit of dinner,' as he told the woman at the chambers; and stated, that he should go on calling till he did find Mr George. And in this way, on his third or fourth visit, Mr George was found.

Mr Pritchett was dressed in his best, and was very sad and solemn. 'Mr George,' said he, 'your uncle wishes to see you at Hadley, particular.'

'Why, I was there yesterday.'

'I know you was, Mr George; and that's just it. Your uncle, Mr George, is an old man, and it will be only dutiful you should be with him a good deal now. You'd wish to be a comfort to your uncle in his last days. I know that, Mr George. He's been good to you; and you've your duty to do by him now, Mr George; and you'll do it.' So said Mr Pritchett, having thoroughly argued the matter in his own mind, and resolved, that as Mr George was a wilful young horse, who would not be driven in one kind of bridle, another must be tried with him.

'But has my uncle sent to say that he wants to see me again at once?'

'He has, Mr George; sent to say that he wants to see you again at once, particular.'

There was nothing of course for Mr George to do but to obey, seeing that the order was so particular. On that same evening, therefore, he put his dressing-things into a bag, and again went down to Hadley.

On his first arrival his uncle shook hands with him with much more than ordinary kindness, and even joked with him.

'So Pritchett came to you, did he? and sent you down at a moment's notice? ha! ha! He's a solemn old prig, is Pritchett; but a good servant; a very good servant. When I am gone, he'll have enough to live on; but he'll want some one to say a word to him now and again. Don't forget what I say about him. It's not so easy to find a good servant.'

George declared that he always had had, and would have, a regard for Mr Pritchett; 'though I wish he were not quite so sad.'

'Poor Pritchett! well; yes, he is sad,' said the uncle, laughing; and then George went upstairs to get ready for dinner.

The dinner, considering the house in which it was spread, was quite *recherché*. George said to himself that the fat fowls which he saw must have come from Harcourt's larder. Roast mutton and boiled beef—not together, but one on one day and the other on the next—generally constituted the fare at Mr Bertram's house when he did not sit down to dinner alone. But now there was quite a little banquet. During dinner, he made sundry efforts to be agreeable; pressed his nephew to eat, and drank wine with him in the old-fashioned affectionate manner of past days. 'Your health, George,' he said. 'You'll find that sherry good, I think. It ought to be, if years can make it so.'

It was good; and George was very sorry to find that the good wine had been brought out for him. He felt that something would be required in return, and that he could not give that something.

After dinner, that something was soon asked for. 'George,' said the old man, 'I have been thinking much since you went away the other day about you and Caroline. I have taken it into my stupid old head to wish that you two should be married.'

'Ah, sir!'

'Now listen to me. I do wish it, and what you have said has disturbed me. Now I do believe this of you, that you are an honest lad; and though you are so fond of your own way, I don't think you'd wish to grieve me if you could help it.'

'Not if I could help it, sir; not if I could help it, certainly.'

'You can help it. Now listen to me. An old man has no right to have his fancies unless he chooses to pay for them. I know that well enough. I don't want to ask you why you have quarrelled with Caroline. It's about money, very likely?'

'No, sir, no; not in the least.'

'Well, I don't want to inquire. A small limited income is very likely to lead to misunderstandings. You have at any rate been honest and true to me. You are not a bit like your father.'

'Sir! sir!'

'And, and—I'll tell you what I'll do. Caroline is to have six thousand pounds, isn't she?'

'Pray believe me, sir, that money has nothing whatever to do with this matter.'

'Yes, six,' continued Mr Bertram; 'four of her own, and two from me. Now I'll tell you what I'll do. Let me see. You have two hundred a year: that's settled on you. And you had a thousand pounds the other day. Is that all gone yet?'

'I am in no want of money, uncle; none whatever.'

'No, not as a bachelor; but as a married man you would be. Now do tell me—how much of that thousand pounds did the colonel get out of you?'

'Dear uncle, do remember that he is my father.'

'Well, well; two hundred a year, and two thousand pounds, and one, and Pritchett's account. I'll tell you what, George, I should like to see you comfortable; and if you and Caroline are married before next October, I'll give you—'

'I can't tell you how you pain me, sir.'

'I'll give you—I wonder how much income you think you'll want?'

'None, sir; none. As our marriage is out of the question, we shall want no income. As I am, and am likely to remain unmarried, my present income is sufficient for me.'

'I'll give you—let me see.' And the old miser—for though capable of generosity to a great extent, as he had certainly shown with reference to his nephew's early years, he certainly was a miser—the old miser again recapitulated to himself all that he had already done, and tried to calculate at what smallest figure, at what lowest amount of ready money to be paid down, he could purchase the object which he now desired. 'I'll give you four thousand pounds on the day you are married. There, that will be ten thousand beside your own income, and whatever your profession will bring you.'

'What am I to say, sir? I know how generous you are; but this is not an affair of money.'

'What is it then?'

'We should not be happy together.'

'Not happy together! You shall be happy, I tell you; you will be happy if you have enough to live on. Remember, I may leave you something more than that when I die; that is, I may do so if you please me. You will understand, however, that I make no promise.'

'Dear uncle,' said George, and as he spoke he rose from his seat, and crossing over to his uncle, took the old man's hand in his own. 'You shall be asked for no promise; you shall be asked for nothing. You have been most liberal, most kind to me; too kind, I know, for I have not returned it by that attention which you deserved from me. But, believe me, I cannot do as you ask me. If you will speak to Miss Waddington, she will tell you the same.'

'Miss Waddington; pshaw!'

'Caroline, I mean. It is impossible, sir. And it adds greatly to my own suffering—for I have suffered in all this—that you also should be grieved.'

'Why, you were so much in love with her the other day! Mary told me that you were dying for her.'

'I cannot explain it all. But she—Caroline—doubtless will. However, pray, pray take this for granted: the engagement between us cannot be renewed.'

Old Mr Bertram still kept his nephew's hand, and it seemed as though he liked to hold it. He continued to look up into George's face as though striving to read there something different from the words which he heard, something which might yet give him some consolation. He had said that George was honest, and he believed it, as far as he could believe in honesty. But, nevertheless, he was still meditating at what price he could buy over his nephew to his purpose. After such a struggle as that of his whole lifetime, could he have any other faith but that money were omnipotent? No; this of course, this necessarily was his belief. As to the sufficient quantity—on that point it was possible for him to doubt. His nephew's manner to him was very touching; the tone of his voice, the look of his countenance, the grief which sat on his brow, did touch him. But they touched him in this manner; they made him feel that a few thousands were not sufficient. He had at last a desire at his heart, a family domestic warm desire; and he began to feel that if he was not prepared to give up his desire, he must bid high for its fulfilment.

'George,' said he, 'after all, you and Caroline are the nearest relatives I have; the nearest and the dearest.'

'Caroline is your own child's child, sir.'

'She is but a girl; and it would all go to some spendthrift, whose very name would be different. And, I don't know, but I think I like you better than her. Look here now. According to my present will, nine-tenths of my property will go to build a hospital that shall bear my name. You'll not repeat that to anybody, will you?'

'No, sir; I will not.'

'If you will do as I would have you about this marriage, I'll make a new will, and you and your children shall have—I'll let you say yourself how much you shall have; there—and you shall see the will yourself before the wedding takes place.'

'What can I say to him? what can I say to him?' said George, turning away his face. 'Sir, it is quite impossible. Is not that enough? Money has nothing to do with it; can have nothing to do with it.'

'You don't think I'd deceive you, do you, and make another will afterwards? It shall be a deed of gift if you like, or a settlement—to take effect of course after my death.' On hearing this George turned away his face. 'You shall have half, George; there, by G— you shall have half; settled on you—there—half of it, settled on you.' And then only did the uncle drop his nephew's hand. He dropped it, and closing his eyes, began to meditate on the tremendous sacrifice he had made.

There was something terrible in this to young Bertram. He had almost ceased to think of himself in watching his uncle's struggles. It was dreadful to see how terribly anxious the old man was, and more dreadful still to witness the nature of the thoughts which were running through his mind. He was making lavish tenders of his heaven, his god, his blessings; he was offering to part with his paradise, seeing that nature would soon imperatively demand that he should part with it. But useless as it must soon be to him, he could not bring himself to believe that it was not still all-powerful with others.

'Mr Bertram, it is clearly necessary that we should understand each other,' said George, with a voice that he intended should be firm, but which in truth was stern as well as firm. 'I thought it right to come and tell you that this match was broken off. But seeing that that has once been told, there is no longer room for further conversation on the matter. We have made up our minds to part; and, having done so, I can assure you that money can have no effect upon our resolution.'

'Then you want it all—all!' said the uncle, almost weeping.

'Not all, nor ten times all would move me one inch—not one inch,' said George, in a voice that was now loud, and almost angry.

Mr Bertram turned towards the table, and buried his face in his hands. He did not understand it. He did not know whence came all this opposition. He could not conceive what was the motive power which caused his nephew thus to thwart and throw him over, standing forward as he did with thousands and tens of thousands in his hand. But he knew that his request was refused, and he felt himself degraded and powerless.

'Do not be angry with me, uncle,' said the nephew.

'Go your own way, sir; go your own way,' said the uncle. 'I have done with you. I had thought—but never mind—' and he rang the bell violently. 'Sarah, I will go to bed—are my things ready? Woman, is my room ready, I say?' and then he had himself led off, and George saw him no more that night.

Nor did he see him the next morning; nor for many a long day afterwards. When the morning came, he sent in his love, with a hope that his uncle was better. Sarah, coming out with a long face, told George that his uncle had only muttered between his teeth—'That it was nothing to him'—to his nephew, namely—'whether he were better or worse.' And so having received his last message, he went his way, and returned to town.

CHAPTER XXV

DOES HE KNOW IT YET?

ALMOST immediately after this George Bertram did go to Paris; but before he went he received a letter from Arthur Wilkinson, begging him to go down to Hurst Staple. This was Arthur's answer to the letter in which Bertram had communicated the last news from Littlebath. There were not as many words in the letter as there had been in that from Adela to Caroline; but they were much to the same effect. 'This is an important step, old fellow; very: pray—pray be careful for your own sake and hers. I am not good at letter-writing, as you know; but come down here and talk it over. I have other things of my own I want to talk about. The spare bedroom is empty.' That was nearly the whole of it. In answer to this, Bertram had declared his intention of going to Paris, but had promised to go down to Hurst Staple as soon as he returned home.

At this time the popularity of Louis Philippe was on the wane. The grocers of Paris were becoming sick of their paternal citizen-king, who, in spite of his quiet family costume and citizen-umbrella, seemed to think as much as some other kings of crowds of soldiers, of fortifications, and war taxes; who seemed to think also that free-spoken deputies might be judiciously controlled, that a paternally-royal family might be judiciously enriched, and that a good many of the old crown tenets and maxims might again be judiciously brought to bear upon the commonwealth. Poor grocers! too much prosperity had made them over-nice. When Mr Smith* had been about six months gone from them, how gladly would they have had him back again!

But they are again satisfied. The grocer interest, which on the whole may perhaps be looked on as predominant in Paris, is once more swathed in rose-leaves. The swathings certainly are somewhat tight; and rose-leaves may be twisted till there is no breaking them. But there will still remain the fragrance, the *pot-pourri* odour which is so delectable to ancient housewives, the oily savour of plenteousness. If a king can so devise that chocolate shall be sold—and paid for—what more can a grocer interest need? What more than this, that having sold its daily quantum of chocolate, it shall have a theatre to go to, a spectacle to look at, ices, coffee, and *eau sucrée*! Since the world began to open its young eyes and look about it with any understanding, what else has been desirable? What does a man and a grocer want? *Panem et circenses*,* soup that shall not be too maigre; and a seat at the Porte St Martin that shall not be too dear. Is it not all written in that?

England a nation of shopkeepers? No, let us hope not; not as yet, at any rate. There have been nations to whom the buying and selling of bread and honey—especially of honey—has been everything; lost nations—people deadened, whose souls were ever sleeping, whose mouths only and gastric organs attested that life was in them. There were such people in the latter days of ancient Rome; there were such also in that of Eastern Rome upon the Bosphorus; rich and thriving people, with large mouths and copious bellies, wanting merely the salt of life. But let us hope that no English people will be such as long as the roads are open to Australia, to Canada, and New Zealand.

A young man whose life was to be spent in writing politico-religious pamphlets had much to learn in Paris in those days. Indeed, Paris has ever been a school for such writers since men began to find that something was wrong, even under the reign of the great Dubarry.* Since those days it has been the laboratory of the political alchemist, in which everything hitherto held precious has been reduced to a residuum, in order that from the ashes might be created that great arcanum, a fitting constitution under which thinking men may live contented. The secret had been hardly solved in those latter days of poor Louis Philippe. Much had certainly been done when a citizen-king was thought of and set agoing; but even a citizen-king required to be wound up, and the alchemist was still at his crucibles.

Now, indeed, the work has been finished. The laboratory is closed. The philosopher, his task all done, has retired to his needed rest. Thinking men, even Frenchmen, can live contented. Chocolate is sold—and paid for. And a score and a half of daily theatres are open at the most moderate of prices.

Intent on such things, and on his coming volume, our young broken-hearted philosopher stayed out three months at Paris. We need not follow him very closely in his doings there. His name was already sufficiently known to secure his admittance amongst those learned men who, if they had hitherto established little, had at any rate achieved the doubting of much. While he was here the British Ministry went out of office. Sir Robert, having repealed the corn laws, fell to the ground between two stools, and the number of the 'Daily Jupiter' which gave the first authentic list of the members of the new government, contained, among the few new names that were mentioned, that of Sir Henry Harcourt as Her Majesty's solicitor-general.

At the end of the three months Bertram returned to England, enriched by many new ideas as to the government of mankind in general. His volume was not yet finished. So he packed up his papers in his portmanteau and took them down with him to Hurst Staple. He saw no one as he passed through London. The season was then over, and his friend Sir Henry was refreshing himself with ten days' grouse-shooting after the successful campaign of the last session. But had he been in London, Bertram would not have seen him, for he saw no one. He asked no questions about Caroline, nor any about his uncle. He did not even call on his sincere friend Pritchett. Had he done so, he would have learned that Miss Baker and her niece were both staying at Hadley. He might also have learned other news, which, however, was not long in following him.

He went down to Hurst Staple, merely writing a line the day before he started, to prepare his friend for his advent. But when he reached the vicarage, Arthur Wilkinson was not there. He was at Oxford; but had left word that he was to be summoned home as soon as Bertram arrived. The ladies, however, expected him, and there would have been nothing for him to remark in the state of the quiet household had there not been another visitor in the house. Adela Gauntlet was staying there, and she was dressed in the deepest mourning.

The story was soon told to him. Mr Gauntlet had one morning been found dead in his dressing-room. The good old man had been full of years, and there was nothing frightful in his death but its suddenness. But sudden death is always frightful. Overnight he had been talking to his daughter with his usual quiet, very quiet, mirth; and in the morning she was woke with the news that his spirit had fled. His mirth for this world was over. His worldly duties were done. He had received his daughter's last kiss, had closed for the last time the book which had been his life's guide, had whispered to heaven his last prayer, and his soul was now at rest.

There was nothing in this that the world need regard as mournful. There was no pain, no mental pangs, no dire remorse. But for Adela the suddenness had been very dreadful.

Among her other miseries had been the great misery of having to seek a home. An Englishman's house is his castle. And a rector's parsonage is as much the rector's castle, his own freehold castle, as is the earl's family mansion that of the earl. But it is so with this drawback, that the moment the rector's breath is out of his body, all right and claim to the castle as regards his estate and family cease instantly. If the widow and children remain there one night, they remain there on sufferance.

Adela's new home would now necessarily be with her aunt, Miss Penelope Gauntlet; but it happened most unfortunately that at the moment of her brother's death, Miss Gauntlet was absent with her other relatives in Italy. Nor was her address accurately known. Her party had been at Rome; but it was supposed that they had left the holy city before the end of May: and now, at the end of August, when her presence in England was so necessary, Adela had no more than a faint belief that her aunt was at the baths of Lucca. In the meantime it was absolutely necessary that she should somewhere find a resting-place for herself.

Both Caroline Waddington and Miss Baker wrote to her at once. Unfortunately they were at Hadley; but if Adela would come to them, they would return to Littlebath. They, or at any rate, one of them would do so. There was much that was really generous in this offer, as will be seen when we come in the next page or two to narrate what had lately occurred at Hadley. But Adela already knew what had occurred; and much as she then longed for a home, she knew that she could not allow either of them to go to Littlebath.

Immediately that Mr Gauntlet's death was known at Hurst Staple—and it was known there two hours after Adela knew it herself—Mrs Wilkinson went over to bring her to the vicarage. The reader will know that there were reasons why Adela should be most unwilling to choose that house as her temporary residence. She was most unwilling; and for a day or two, much to Mrs Wilkinson's surprise, she refused to leave West Putford. But it was necessary that she should leave it. She could not remain alone in that house on the day that her father's body was carried to the grave; and so at last she submitted, and allowed herself to be taken over to Hurst Staple.

'It is provoking, dear,' said Mrs Wilkinson to her, 'and I am sure you will think it very uncivil, but Arthur went off to Oxford yesterday. And it was uncivil. I am sure he needs not have gone at this very moment.'

Then Adela felt very grateful to her neighbour, and acknowledged in her heart that he had been kind to her.

'But he must be back on Saturday,' continued the widow, 'for he could get no clergyman to take his duty. Indeed, he has to take the evening service at West Putford as well.'

On the day following this, George Bertram arrived at the vicarage.

His first evening in the house was not very bright. Mrs Wilkinson had never been a bright woman. She had certain motherly good qualities, which had been exerted in George's favour in his earliest years; and on this account she was still able to speak to him in a motherly way. She could talk to him about his breakfasts and dinners, and ask after his buttons and linen, and allude to his bachelor habits. And in such conversation the first evening was chiefly passed. Adela said almost nothing. The Wilkinson girls, who were generally cheerful themselves, were depressed by Adela's sorrow—and depressed also somewhat by what they knew of Bertram's affairs. On this matter Mrs Wilkinson was burning to speak; but she had made up her mind to leave it in silence for one evening. She confined herself, therefore, to the button question, and to certain allusions to her own griefs. It appeared that she was not quite so happy with reference to Arthur as one would have wished her to be. She did not absolutely speak against him; but she said little snubbing things of him, and seemed to think him by no means sufficiently grateful for all the care she took of him.

That night, in the privacy of Adela's own room, something was said about George Bertram. 'I am sure he does not know it yet,' said Sophia.

'Caroline told me she would write to him,' said Adela: 'she would be very wrong not to do so—very wrong.'

'You may be sure he has not heard it,' repeated the other. 'Did you not observe the way he spoke of Mr Harcourt?'

'Sir Henry Harcourt,' said Mary.

'I did not hear it,' said Adela.

'Oh, he did speak of him. He said something about his great good fortune. He never would have spoken in that way had he known it.'

'Do you know,' said Mary, 'I do not think he would have come down here had he heard it—not yet, at least.'

The next morning two letters were laid before George Bertram as they were sitting at breakfast. Then he did know it; then he did learn it, and not till then. It was now the end of August, and in the coming month of November—about the end of November—Sir Henry Harcourt, Her Majesty's solicitor-general, and member for the Battersea Hamlets, was to lead to the hymeneal altar Miss Caroline Waddington, the granddaughter and presumed heiress of the great millionaire, Mr Bertram. Who so high now on the ladder of fortune as the fortunate Sir Henry Harcourt? In love and politics and the realms of Plutus,* he carried all before him. Yes, Sir Henry Harcourt was the coming man. Quidnuncs* at the clubs began to say that he would give up the legal side of politics and devote himself to statesmanship. He would be the very man for a home secretary. Old Bertram, they observed, was known to be dying. Old Bertram, they also observed, had made a distinct promise to Sir Henry and his granddaughter. The marriage was to take place at Hadley, from the old man's house; the old man was delighted with the match, etc. etc. etc.; who so happy, who so great, who so fortunate as Sir Henry Harcourt?

That habit of bringing in letters at the breakfast-table has its good points certainly. It is well that one should have one's letters before the work or pleasure of the day commences: it is well to be able to discuss the different little subjects of mutual interest as they are mentioned. 'Eliza's baby has got her first tooth: it's all right. There's nothing like Daffy's Elixir after all.' 'My dear, the guano will be here today; so the horses will be wanted all the week—remember that.' 'What a bore, papa; for here's a letter to say that Kate Carnabie's coming; and we must go over to the Poldoodles. Frank Poldoodle is quite smitten with Kate.' This is all very convenient; but the plan has its drawbacks. Some letters will be in their nature black and brow-compelling. Tidings will come from time to time at which men cannot smile. There will be news that ruffle the sweetest temper, and at the receipt of which clouds will darken the most kindly face. One would fain receive such letters in private.

Two such letters Bertram received that morning, and read while the eyes of the parsonage breakfast-table were—not fixed on him, but which under such circumstances is much worse—were purposely turned away. He knew well the handwriting of each, and would fain have escaped with them from the room. But this he felt to be cowardly; and so he read them both, sitting there in the family circle. They were from Caroline and Sir Henry. We will give precedence to the lady; but Bertram did not so read them. The lady's letter was the most trying to his nerves, and was therefore taken the last. It can hardly be said that their contents surprised him. When they both came into his hands together, he seemed to feel by intuition what was the news which they contained. That from Caroline was very fairly written. But how many times had it been rewritten before that fair copy was prepared?

'Hadley, August, 184—.

'My dear Mr Bertram,

'I do not know whether I am right in thinking that I ought myself to tell you of the step which I am going to take. If it is unnecessary, I know you will forgive me, and will be certain that I have intended to do what is right. Sir Henry Harcourt has proposed to me, and I have accepted him. I believe we shall be married some time before Christmas.

'We are staying here with grandpapa. I think he approves

of what I am doing; but you know that he is not very communicative. At any rate, I shall be married from this house, and I think that he likes Sir Henry. Aunt Mary is reconciled to all this now.

'I do not know that I need say any more, excepting that I shall always—always hope for your welfare; and be so happy if I can hear of your happiness. I pray you also to forgive me what injuries I may have done you.

'It may be that at some future time we shall meet as friends in London. I hope we may. It is a comfort to me that Sir Henry Harcourt knows exactly all that there has been between us.

'Believe me to be,

'Yours most sincerely,

'CAROLINE WADDINGTON.'

Harcourt's letter was written in faster style, and a more running hand. Solicitors-general have hardly time to stop and pick their words. But though the manner of it was free and easy, it seemed to Bertram that the freedom and easiness were but affected.

'My dear Bertram,

'I hope and trust that the news I have to tell you will be no interruption to our friendship. I am sure that it should not be, seeing that I am doing you no injury. Caroline Waddington and I have agreed to put our fortunes into the same boat. We shall feel much more comfortable on the seas if you will be gracious enough to say, "God save the bark."

'Caroline has of course told me all that has occurred; as, indeed, you had done previously. As far as I am concerned, I must say she has behaved gloriously. I always admired her greatly, as you know; though of course till lately I never thought it possible I should possess what I so much admired.

'Speaking plainly, I think that she will be happier with me than she would have been with you; and that I shall be happier with her than you would have been. We are better adapted to each other. There is a dash of worldliness about us both from which your more ethereal composition is happily free.

'God bless you, old fellow. Pray write a line in answer, saying as much to me. Of course, you will let us see you in London. Caroline wishes it particularly; and so do I.

'I believe I shall be turned off in December. Such a mill-horse as I am cannot choose my time. I am going to Scotland for ten days, and shall then be hard at work till our marriage. I must of course be back when the session commences. We talk of going to Nice, and thence to Genoa.

'The old gentleman is very civil; but there has been no word of money, nor will there be a word. However, thank God, I don't want it.

'Always your sincerest friend,

'HENRY HARCOURT.

'Reform Club—, August, 184—.'

These letters did not take long in the reading. Within five minutes Bertram was spreading the butter on his toast; and within two minutes more he was asking what news there was from Arthur—when would he be home? He had received a great blow, a stunning blow; but he was able to postpone the faintness which would follow it till he should be where no eye could see him.

The breakfast passed away very silently. They all knew what those two letters contained. One of the girls had had them in her hand, and had known the handwriting of one and guessed that of the other. But even without this they would have known. Are not most of our innermost secrets known to all the world?

And then Bertram skulked off—or endeavoured rather to do so; for Mrs Wilkinson detected him in the act, and stopped him. She had said nothing hitherto about his matrimonial or non-matrimonial affairs. She had abstained with wonderful discretion; and she now intended that her discretion should be rewarded.

'George, George,' she said, as he turned from the breakfast-parlour door to the rack in the hall on which his hat was hanging, 'I want you just for a minute.' So George returned into the parlour as the girls passed across the hall into the drawing-room.

'I'm afraid you'll think me unkind because I've said nothing about this sad affair of yours.'

'Not at all, aunt,' he said: though she was no aunt of his, he had always called her so when he had been at Hurst Staple as a child. 'There are some things which had, perhaps, better not be talked about.' Mrs Wilkinson, however, was not the woman to be deterred by such a faint repulse as this.

'Exactly so; except among intimate family friends. But I was very sorry to hear about your breaking off the affair with Caroline Waddington. I was, indeed; very. It would have been so suitable as regards the old gentleman—I know all about that, you know—' and the lady nodded her head, as ladies will do sometimes when they flatter themselves that they know more about such things than their neighbours.

'It was necessary,' said Bertram.

'Necessary—ah, yes: I dare say. I don't in the least mean to blame you, George. I am sure you would not behave badly to any girl—and, from what I have heard, I am quite sure—quite sure it was not your fault. Indeed, I know very well—' and in lieu of finishing her speech, Mrs Wilkinson again nodded her head.

'Nobody was to blame, aunt; nobody, and it is much better to say nothing about it.'

'That is very good of you, George; very. But I always shall say—'

'Dear aunt, pray say nothing. We had thought when we knew little of each other that it would suit us to live together. As we learnt each other's characters more thoroughly, we found that we had been wrong. It was better for us, therefore, to part; and we did part.'

'And so now she is going to be Lady Harcourt?'

'Yes; it seems so.'

'Well, at any rate, we must all say this: she hasn't lost any time. I don't know what Sir Henry may think of it; but it certainly does seem to me—'

'Dear aunt, pray do not talk to me about this. I think Miss Waddington quite right to accept Sir Henry Harcourt. That is, I think her right under the circumstances. He is a rising man, and she will grace any station in which he can place her.

I do not at all blame her, not in the least! it would be monstrous if I did.'

'Oh, of course—we all know that it was you broke off the other match; all the world knows that. But what I want to speak about is this. The old gentleman's money, George! Now Sir Henry of course is looking to that.'

'He has my permission.'

'And of course he will get some of it. That's to be expected—she's his grandchild—of course I know that,' and Mrs Wilkinson again nodded her head. 'But, George, you must look very close after the old gentleman. It won't at all do to let Harcourt cut you out altogether. I do hope you mean to be a good deal down at Hadley. It won't last for long, you know.'

Bertram would not condescend to explain to Mrs Wilkinson that he had no intention of going near his uncle again, and that he was sick of the very name of the old man's money. So he hummed and hawed, and changed the conversation by saying that he should be so glad to see Arthur on his return.

'Yes, I am sure you will. But you'll find Arthur much changed—very much.' And it was clear from the tone of Mrs Wilkinson's voice that she did not think that this change in her son was for the better.

'He is growing older, I suppose; like the rest of us,' said Bertram, attempting to laugh.

'Oh, yes; he's growing older, of course. But people should grow better, George, and more contented; particularly when they have everything about them that they can possibly want.'

'Is not Arthur contented? He should get married then. Look at Adela Gauntlet there!'

'Nonsense, George; pray don't put that into his head. What has he to marry on? And as for Adela, if she has fifteen hundred pounds it will be every farthing. And what's that for a family?'

'But Arthur has a living.'

'Now, George, don't you be talking in that way to him. In one sense he has a living; for, situated as things at present are, of course I cannot hold it in my own hands. But in real truth he has not a living—not of his own. Lord Stapledean, whom I shall always regard as the very first nobleman in the land, and a credit to the whole peerage, expressly gave the living to me.'

'To you, aunt?'

'Yes, expressly to me. And now I fear Arthur is discontented because he knows that I choose to remain mistress of my own house. I have done everything I can to make the house pleasant to him. He has the same study his dear father always had; and he has his own separate horse in the stable, which is more than his father had.'

'But Arthur has his fellowship.'

'And where would his fellowship be if he married Adela Gauntlet? I do hope you'll say something to him to make him more contented. I say nothing about his conduct to me. I don't suppose he means to be undutiful.'

And then Bertram did manage to escape; and taking his hat he walked away along that same river-path which led to West Putford—that same path which Arthur Wilkinson had used to take when he went fishing in those happy early days before promotion had come to him, and the glories of manhood.

But George was not thinking now of Arthur or of Adela. He had enough of sorrow in his own breast to make his mind selfish for the present—Caroline Waddington was to be married! to be married so soon after getting quit of her former bondage; to be married to Henry Harcourt. There was no chance left now, no hope, no possibility that he might regain the rich prize which he had flung away.

And did he wish to regain it? Was it not now clear enough that she had never loved him? In May, while the fruits were filling, they had separated; and now before they were well ripe she had given herself to another! Love him! no, indeed. Was it possible that she should love any man?—that she, who could so redeem herself and so bestow herself, should have any heart, any true feeling of what love is?

And yet this was not the worst of it. Such love as she had to give, had she not given it to this Harcourt even before she had rescued herself from her former lover? Had she not given this man her preference, such preference as she had to give, then, then when she was discussing with him how best to delay her nuptials with her acknowledged suitor? This successful, noisy, pushing, worldly man had won her by his success and his worldliness. The glitter of the gold had caught her; and so she had been unhappy, and had pined, and worn herself with grief till she could break away from her honest truth, and bind herself to the horn of the golden calf.*

'Twas thus that he now thought of her, thus that he spoke of her to himself out loud, now that he could wander alone, with no eye to watch him, no ear to hear him. And yet he loved her with a strong love, with a mad passion such as he had never felt before. Much as he blamed her, thoroughly as he despised her for being so venal; yet he blamed, nay, scorned, himself more vehemently in that he had let this plausible knave with his silken words rob from him the only treasure worth his having. Why had he not toiled? Why had he not made a name for himself? Why had he not built a throne on which his lady-love might sit and shine before the world?

CHAPTER XXVI

HURST STAPLE

THE next three or four days passed by heavily enough, and then Arthur Wilkinson returned. He returned on a Saturday evening; as clergymen always do, so as to be ready for their great day of work. There are no Sabbath-breakers to be compared, in the vehemence of their Sabbath-breaking, to hard-worked parochial clergymen—unless, indeed, it be Sunday-school children, who are forced on that day to learn long dark collects, and stand in dread catechismal row before their spiritual pastors and masters.

In the first evening there was that flow of friendship which always exists for the few first hours of meeting between men who are really fond of each other. And these men were fond of each other; the fonder perhaps because each of them had now cause for sorrow. Very little was said between Arthur and Adela. There was not apparently much to alarm the widow in their mutual manner, or to make her think that Miss Gauntlet was to be put in her place. Adela sat among the other girls, taking even less share in the conversation than they did; and Arthur, though he talked as became the master of the house, talked but little to her.

On the following morning they all went to church, of course. Who has courage to remain away from church when staying at the clergyman's house? No one ever; unless it be the clergyman's wife, or perhaps an independent self-willed daughter. At Hurst Staple, however, on this Sunday they all attended. Adela was in deepest mourning. Her thick black veil was down, so as to hide her tears. The last Sunday she had been at church her father had preached his last sermon.

Bertram, as he entered the door, could not but remember how long it was since he had joined in public worship. Months and months had passed over him since he had allowed himself to be told that the Scriptures moved him in sundry places to acknowledge and confess his sins.* And yet there had been a time when he had earnestly poured forth his frequent prayers to heaven; a time not long removed. It was as yet hardly more than three years since he had sworn within himself on the brow of Olivet to devote himself to the service of his Saviour. Why had that oath been broken? A girl had ridiculed it; a young girl had dissipated all that by the sheen of her beauty, by the sparkle of her eye, by the laughter of her ruddy lip. He had promised himself to his God, but the rustling of silks had betrayed his heart. At her instance, at her first word, that promise had been whistled down the wind.

And to what had this brought him now? As for the bright eyes, and the flashing beauty, and the ruddy lips, they were made over in fee-simple* to another, who was ready to go further than he had gone in seeking this world's vanities. Even the price of his apostasy had vanished from him.

But was this all? was this nearly all? was this as anything to that further misery which had come upon him? Where was his faith now, his true, youthful, ardent faith; the belief of his inner heart; the conviction of a God and a Saviour, which had once been to him the source of joy? Had it all vanished when, under the walls of Jerusalem, over against that very garden of

Gethsemane, he had exchanged the aspirations of his soul for the pressure of a soft white hand.

No one becomes an infidel at once. A man who has really believed does not lose by a sudden blow the firm convictions of his soul. But when the work has been once commenced, when the first step has been taken, the pace becomes frightfully fast. Three years since his belief had been like the ardour of young love, and now what were his feelings? Men said that he was an infidel; but he would himself deny it with a frigid precision, with the stiffest accuracy of language; and then argue that his acknowledgment of a superhuman creative power was not infidelity. He had a God of his own, a cold, passionless, prudent God; the same God, he said, to whom others looked; with this only difference, that when others looked with fanatic enthusiasm, he looked with well-balanced reason. But it was the same God, he said. And as to the Saviour, he had a good deal also to say on that subject; a good deal which might show that he was not so far from others as others thought. And so he would prove that he was no infidel.

But could he thus satisfy himself now that he again heard the psalms of his youth? and remembered as he listened, that he had lost for ever that beauty which had cost him so dear? Did he not now begin to think—to feel perhaps rather than to think—that, after all, the sound of the church bells was cheering, that it was sweet to kneel there where others knelt, sweet to hear the voices of those young children as they uttered together the responses of the service? Was he so much wiser than others that he could venture on his own judgment to set himself apart, and to throw over as useless all that was to others so precious?

Such were his feelings as he sat, and knelt, and stood there—mechanically as it were, remembering the old habits. And then he tried to pray. But praying is by no means the easiest work to which a man can set himself. Kneeling is easy; the repetition of the well-known word is easy; the putting on of some solemnity of mind is perhaps not difficult. But to remember what you are asking, why you are asking, of whom you are asking; to feel sure that you want what you do ask, and that this asking is the best way to get it;—that on the whole is not easy. On this occasion Bertram probably found it utterly beyond his capacity.

He declined to go to afternoon church. This is not held to be *de rigueur* even in a parson's house, unless it be among certain of the strictly low-church clergymen. A very high churchman may ask you to attend at four o'clock of a winter morning, but he will not be grievously offended if, on a Sunday afternoon, you prefer your armchair, and book—probably of sermons; but that is between you and your conscience.

They dined early, and in the evening, Bertram and his host walked out. Hitherto they had had but little opportunity of conversation, and Bertram longed to talk to some one of what was within his breast. On this occasion, however, he failed. Conversation will not always go exactly as one would have it.

'I was glad to see you at church today,' said the parson. 'To tell you the truth, I did not expect it. I hope it was not intended as a compliment to me.'

'I rather fear it was, Arthur.'

'You mean that you went because you did not like to displease us by staying away?'

'Something like it,' said Bertram, affecting to laugh. 'I do not want your mother and sisters, or you either, to regard me as an ogre. In England, at any rate in the country in England, one is an ogre if one doesn't go to church. It does not much matter, I believe, what one does when one is there; so long as one is quiet, and lets the parson have his say.'

'There is nothing so easy as ridicule, especially in matters of religion.'

'Quite true. But then it is again true that it is very hard to laugh at anything that is not in some point ridiculous.'

'And God's worship is ridiculous?'

'No; but any pretence of worshipping God is so. And as it is but a step from the ridiculous to the sublime, and as the true worship of God is probably the highest sublimity to which man can reach; so, perhaps, is he never so absolutely absurd, in such a bathos of the ridiculous, as when he pretends to do so.'

'Every effort must sometimes fall short of success.'

'I'll explain what I mean,' said Bertram, attending more to himself than his companion. 'What idea of man can be so magnificent as that which represents him with his hands closed, and his eyes turned to that heaven with which he holds communion? But imagine the man so placed, and holding no such communion! You will at once have run down the whole gamut of humanity from St Paul to Pecksniff.'*

'But that has nothing to do with belief. It is for the man to take care that he be, if possible, nearer to St Paul than to Pecksniff.'

'No, it has nothing to do with belief; but it is a gauge, the only gauge we have, of what belief a man has. How many of those who were sitting by silently while you preached really believed?'

'All, I hope; all, I trust. I firmly trust that they are all believers; all, including yourself.'

'I wonder whether there was one; one believer in all that which you called on us to say that we believed? one, for instance, who believes in the communion of saints? one who believes in the resurrection of the body?'

'And why should they not believe in the communion of saints? What's the difficulty?'

'Very little, certainly; as their belief goes—what they and you call belief. Rumtunshid gara shushabad gerostophat. That is the shibboleth of some of the Caucasian tribes. Do you believe in Rumtunshid?'

'If you will talk gibberish when talking on such a matter, I had rather change the subject.'

'Now you are unreasonable, and want to have all the gibberish to yourself. That you should have it all to yourself in your own pulpit we accede to you; but out here, on the heath, surely I may have my turn. You do not believe in Rumtunshid? Then why should farmer Buttercup be called on to believe in the communion of the saints? What does he believe about it? Or why should you make little Flora Buttercup tell such a huge fib as to say, that she believes in the resurrection of the body?'

'It is taught her as a necessary lesson, and will be explained to her at the proper age.'

'No; there is no proper age for it. It will never be explained to her. Neither Flora nor her father will ever understand anything about it. But they will always believe it. Am I old enough to understand it? Explain it to me. No one yet has ever attempted to do so; and yet my education was not neglected.'

Wilkinson had too great a fear of his friend's powers of ridicule to venture on an explanation; so he again suggested that they should change the subject.

'That is always the way,' said Bertram. 'I never knew a clergyman who did not want to change the subject when that subject is the one on which he should be ever willing to speak.'

'If there be anything that you deem holy, you would not be willing to hear it ridiculed.'

'There is much that I deem holy, and for that I fear no laughter. I am ready to defy ridicule. But if I talk to you of the asceticism of Stylites,* and tell you that I admire it, and will imitate it, will you not then laugh at me? Of course we ridicule what we think is false. But ridicule will run off truth like water from a duck's back. Come, explain to me this about the resurrection of the body.'

'Yet, in my flesh, shall I see God,'* said Arthur, in a solemn tone.

'But I say, no. It is impossible.'

'Nothing is impossible with God.'*

'Yes; it is impossible that his own great laws should change. It is impossible that they should remain, and yet not remain. Your body—that which we all call our body—that which Flora Buttercup believes to be her body (for in this matter she does believe) will turn itself, through the prolific chemistry of nature, into various productive gases by which other bodies will be formed. With which body will you see Christ? with that which you now carry, or that you will carry when you die? For, of course, every atom of your body changes.'

'It little matters which. It is sufficient for me to believe as the Scriptures teach me.'

'Yes; if one could believe. A Jew, when he drags his dying limbs to the valley of Jehoshaphat, he can believe. He, in his darkness, knows nothing of these laws of nature. But we will go to people who are not in darkness. If I ask your mother what she means when she says—"Not by confusion of Substance; but by unity of Person,"* what will she answer me?'

'It is a subject which it will take her some time to explain.'

'Yes, I think so; and me some time longer to understand.'

Wilkinson was determined not to be led into argument, and so he remained silent. Bertram was also silent for awhile, and they walked on, each content with his own thoughts. But yet not content. Wilkinson would have been contented to be let alone; to have his mind, and faith, and hopes left in the repose which nature and education had prepared for them. But it was not so with Bertram. He was angry with himself for not believing, and angry with others that they did believe. They went on in this way for some ten minutes, and then Bertram began again.

'Ah, that I could believe! If it were a thing to come at, as a man wishes, who would doubt? But you, you, the priest, the teacher of the people, you, who should make it all so easy, you will make it so difficult, so impossible. Belief, at any rate, should be easy, though practice may be hard.'

'You should look to the Bible, not to us.'

'Yes; it is there that is our stumbling-block. A book is given to us, not over well translated from various languages, part of which is history hyperbolically told—for all Eastern language is hyperbolical; part of which is prophecy, the very meaning of which is lost to us by the loss of those things which are intended to be imaged out; and part of which is thanksgiving uttered in the language of men who knew nothing, and could understand nothing of those rules by which we are to be governed.'

'You are talking of the Old Testament?'

'It is given to us as one whole. Then we have the story of a mystery which is above, or, at least, beyond the utmost stretch of man's comprehension; and the very purport of which is opposed to all our ideas of justice. In the jurisprudence of heaven can that be just which here, on earth, is manifestly unjust?'

'Is your faith in God so weak then, and your reliance on yourself so firm, that you can believe nothing beyond your own comprehension?'

'I believe much that I do not understand. I believe the distance of the earth from the sun. I believe that the seed of a man is carried in a woman, and then brought forth to light, a living being. I do not understand the principle of this wondrous growth. But yet I believe it, and know that it is from God. But I cannot believe that evil is good. I cannot believe that man placed here by God shall receive or not receive future happiness as he may chance to agree or not to agree with certain doctors* who, somewhere about the fourth century, or perhaps later, had themselves so much difficulty in coming to any agreement on the disputed subject.'

'I think, Bertram, that you are going into matters which you know are not vital to faith in the Christian religion.'

'What is vital, and what is not? If I could only learn that! But you always argue in a circle. I am to have faith because of the Bible; but I am to take the Bible through faith. Whence is the spring of my faith to come? where shall I find the fountainhead?'

'In prayer to God.'

'But can I pray without faith? Did any man ever kneel before a log, and ask the log that he might believe in the log? Had he no faith in the log, could it be possible that he should be seen there kneeling before it?'

'Has the Bible then for you no intrinsic evidence of its truth?'

'Yes, most irrefragable evidence; evidence that no thinking man can possibly reject. Christ's teaching, the words that I have there as coming from his mouth are irresistible evidence of his fitness to teach. But you will permit me to use no such evidence. I must take it all, from the beginning of my career, before I can look into its intrinsic truth. And it must be all true to me: the sun standing still upon Gibeon no less than the divine wisdom which showed that Cæsar's tribute* should be paid to Cæsar.'

'If every man and every child is to select, how shall we ever have a creed? and if no creed, how shall we have a church?'

'And if no church, how then parsons? Follow it on, and it comes to that. But, in truth, you require too much; and so you get—nothing. Your flocks do not believe, do not pray, do not listen to you. They are not in earnest. In earnest! Heavens! if a man could believe all this, could be in earnest about it, how possibly could he care for other things? But no; you pride yourselves on faith; but you have no faith. There is no such thing left. In these days men do not know what faith is.'

In the evening, when the ladies had gone to their rooms, they were again together; and Bertram thought that he would speak of Caroline. But he was again foiled. There had been some little bickering on the part of Mrs Wilkinson. She had been querulous, and had not cared to hide it, though George and Adela were sitting there as guests. This had made her son unhappy, and he now spoke of it.

'I am sorry you should hear my mother speak in that way, George. I hope I am not harsh to her. I try to refrain from answering her. But unless I go back to my round jackets, and take my food from her hand like a child, I cannot please her.'

'Perhaps you are too careful to please her. I think you should let her know that, to a certain extent, you must be master in your own house.'

'Ah! I have given that up long since. She has an idea that the house is hers. I do not care to thwart her in that. Perhaps I should have done it at first; but it is too late now. Tonight she was angry with me because I would not read a sermon.'

'And why then didn't you?'

'I have preached two today.' And the young clergyman yawned somewhat wearily. 'She used to read them herself. I did put a stop to that.'

'Why so? why not let her read them?'

'The girls used to go to sleep, always—and then the servants slept also. I don't think she has a good voice for sermons. But I am sure of this, George—she has never forgiven me.'

'And never will.'

'Sometimes, I almost think she would wish to take my place in the pulpit.'

'The wish is not at all unnatural, my dear fellow.'

'The truth is, that Lord Stapledean's message to her and his conduct about the living, has quite upset her. I cannot blame Lord Stapledean. What he did was certainly kind. But I do blame myself. I never should have accepted the living on those terms—never, never. I knew it when I did it, and I have never since ceased to repent it.' And so saying he got up and walked quickly about the room. 'Would you believe it now; my mother takes upon herself to tell me in what way I should read the absolution; and feels herself injured because I do not comply?'

'I can tell you but of one remedy, Arthur; but I can tell you of one.'

'What remedy?'

'Take a wife to yourself; one who will not mind in what way you read the absolution to her.'

'A wife!' said Wilkinson, and he uttered a long sigh as he continued his walk.

'Yes, a wife; why not? People say that a country clergyman should never be without a wife; and as for myself, I firmly think that they are right.'

'Every curate is to marry, then?'

'But you are not a curate.'

'I should only have the income of a curate. And where should I put a wife? The house is full of women already. Who would come to such a house as this?'

'There is Adela; would not she come if you asked her?'

'Adela!' said the young vicar. And now his walk had brought him to the further end of the table; and there he remained for a minute or two. 'Adela!'

'Yes, Adela,' said Bertram.

'What a life my mother would lead her! She is fond of her now; very. But in that case I know that she would hate her.'

'If I were you, I would make my wife the mistress of my house, not my mother.'

'Ah! you do not understand, George.'

'But perhaps you do not like Adela—perhaps you could not teach yourself to love her?'

'Perhaps not,' said Wilkinson. 'And perhaps she could not teach herself to like me. But, ah! that is out of the question.'

'There is nothing between you and Adela then?' asked Bertram.

'Oh, no; nothing.'

'On your honour, nothing?'

'Nothing at all. It is quite out of the question. My marrying, indeed!'

And then they took their bedroom candlesticks and went to their own rooms.

CHAPTER XXVII

THE WOUNDED DOE

IT was a weary, melancholy household just then, that of Hurst Staple, and one may almost wonder that Bertram should have remained there; but still he did remain. He had been there a fortnight, when he learnt that in three days' time Adela was to go to Littlebath. She was to go down with Miss Baker; and was to remain there with her, or with Miss Todd if Miss Baker should go back to Hadley, till her own aunt should have returned.

'I don't know why you should be in such a hurry to get to Littlebath,' said Mrs Wilkinson. 'We have been very glad to have you; and I hope we have shown it.' As Arthur had evinced no symptoms of making love to Miss Gauntlet, the good lady had been satisfied, and now she felt somewhat slighted that her hospitality was not more valued.

But Adela explained in her own soft manner that it would be better for her to leave that neighbourhood; that her heart was sore there; that her sorrow for her father would be lighter if she were away. What hypocrites women are! Even Ophelia in her madness would pretend that she raved for her murdered father, when it was patent to all the world that she was mad for love for Hamlet. And now Adela must leave Hurst Staple because, forsooth, her poor old father lay buried at West Putford. Would not ten words have quieted that ghost for ever? But then, what is the use of a lady's speech but to conceal her thoughts?

Bertram had spoken to Arthur about Caroline's marriage, but he had as yet said no word on the subject to any one else. Mrs Wilkinson had tried him once or twice, but in vain. He could not bare his bosom to Mrs Wilkinson.

'So you are going, Adela?' he said the morning he had heard the news. They had all called her Adela in that house, and he had learned to do as others did. These intimacies will sometimes grow up in five days, though an acquaintance of twenty years will often not produce them.

'Yes, Mr Bertram. I have been a great trouble to them here, and it is time that I should be gone.'

' "Welcome the coming, speed the parting guest."* Had I a house, I should endeavour to act on that principle. I would never endeavour to keep a person who wished to go. But we shall all regret you. And then, Littlebath is not the place for you. You will never be happy at Littlebath.'

'Why not?'

'Oh, it is a wretched place; full of horse-jockeys and hags—of card-tables and false hair.'

'I shall have nothing to do with the card-tables, and I hope not with the false hair—nor yet much, I suppose, with the horse-jockeys.'

'There will still remain the worst of the four curses.'

'Mr Bertram, how can you be so evil-minded? I have had many happy days at Littlebath.' And then she paused, for she remembered that her happy days there had all been passed with Caroline Waddington.

'Yes, and I also have had happy days there,' said he; 'very happy. And I am sure of this—that they would have been happy still but for the influence of that wretched place.'

Adela could make no answer to this at the moment, so she went on hemming at her collar. Then, after a pause, she said, 'I hope it will have no evil influence on me.'

'I hope not—I hope not. But you are beyond such

influences. It seems to me, if I may say so, that you are beyond all influences.'

'Yes; as a fool is,' she said, laughing.

'No; but as a rock is. I will not say as ice, for ice will always melt.'

'And do I never melt, Mr Bertram? Has that which has made you so unhappy not moved me? Do you think that I can love Caroline as I do, and not grieve, and weep, and groan in the spirit? I do grieve; I have wept for it. I am not stone.'

And in this also there had been some craft. She had been as it were forced to guard the thoughts of her own heart; and had, therefore, turned the river of the conversation right through the heart of her companion.

'For whom do you weep? for which of us do you weep?' he asked.

'For both; that, having so much to enjoy, you should between you have thrown it all away.'

'She will be happy. That at any rate is a consolation to me. Though you will hardly believe that.'

'I hope she will. I hope she will. But, oh! Mr Bertram, it is so fearful a risk. What—what if she should not be? What if she shall find, when the time will be too late for finding anything—what if she shall then find that she cannot love him?'

'Love him!' said the other with a sneer. 'You do not know her. What need is there for love?'

'Ah; do not be harsh to her; do not you be harsh to her.'

'Harsh, no; I will not be harsh to her. I will be all kindness. And being kind, I ask what need is there for love? Looking at it in any light, of course she cannot love him.'

'Cannot love him! why not?'

'How is it possible? Had she loved me, could she have shaken off one lover and taken up another in two months? And if she never loved me; if for three years she could go on, never loving me—then what reason is there to think she should want such excitement now?'

'But you—could you love her, and yet cast her from you?'

'Yes; I could do it. I did do it—and were it to do again, it should be done again. I did love her. If I know what love is, if

I can at all understand it, I did love her with all my heart. And yet—I will not say I cast her off; it would be unmanly as well as false: but I let her go.'

'Ah! you did more than that, Mr Bertram.'

'I gave her back her troth; and she accepted it;—as it was her duty to do, seeing that her wishes were then changed. I did no more than that.'

'Women, Mr Bertram, well know that when married they sometimes bear a sharp word. But the sharp word before marriage; that is very hard to be borne.'

'I measure my words—But why should I defend myself? Of course your verdict will be on your friend's side. I should hate you if it were not so. But, oh! Adela, if I have sinned, I have been punished. I have been punished heavily. Indeed, indeed, I have been punished.' And sitting down, he bowed himself on the table, and hid his face within his hands.

This was in the drawing-room, and before Adela could venture to speak to him again, one of the girls came into the room.

'Adela,' said she, 'we are waiting for you to go down to the school.'

'I am coming directly,' said Adela, jumping up, and still hoping that Mary would go on, so as to leave her one moment alone with Bertram. But Mary showed no sign of moving without her friend. Instead of doing so, she asked her cousin whether he had a headache?

'Not at all,' said he, looking up; 'but I am half asleep. This Hurst Staple is a sleepy place, I think. Where's Arthur?'

'He's in the study.'

'Well, I'll go into the study also. One can always sleep there without being disturbed.'

'You're very civil, master George.' And then Adela followed her friend down to the school.

But she could not rest while the matter stood in this way. She felt that she had been both harsh and unjust to Bertram. She knew that the fault had been with Caroline; and yet she had allowed herself to speak of it as though he, and he only, had been to blame. She felt, moreover, an inexpressible tenderness for his sorrow. When he declared how cruel was his punishment, she could willingly have given him the sympathy of her tears. For were not their cases in many points the same?

She was determined to see him again before she went, and to tell him that she acquitted him;—that she knew the greater fault was not with him. This in itself would not comfort him; but she would endeavour so to put it that he might draw comfort from it.

'I must see you for a moment alone, before I go,' she said to him that evening in the drawing-room. 'I go very early on Thursday morning. When can I speak to you? You are never up early, I know.'

'But I will be tomorrow. Will you be afraid to come out with me before breakfast?'

'Oh no! she would not be at all afraid,' she said: and so the appointment was made.

'I know you'll think me very foolish for giving this trouble,' she began, in rather a confused way, 'and making so much about nothing.'

'No man thinks there is much ado about nothing when the ado is about himself,' said Bertram, laughing.

'Well, but I know it is foolish. But I was unjust to you yesterday, and I could not leave you without confessing it.'

'How unjust, Adela?'

'I said you had cast Caroline off.'

'Ah, no! I certainly did not do that.'

'She wrote to me, and told me everything. She wrote very truly, I know; and she did not say a word—not a word against you.'

'Did she not? Well—no—I know she would not. And remember this, Adela: I do not say a word against her. Do tell her, not from me, you know, but of your own observation, that I do not say one word against her. I only say she did not love me.'

'Ah! Mr Bertram.'

'That is all; and that is true. Adela, I have not much to give; but I would give it all—all—everything to have her back—to have her back as I used to think her. But if I could have her now—as I know her now—by raising this hand, I would not take her. But this imputes no blame to her. She tried to love me, but she could not.'

'Ah! she did love you.'

'Never!' He almost shouted as he said this; and as he did so, he stood across his companion's path. 'Never! She never loved me. I know it now. What poor vile wretches we are! It is this I think that most torments me.'

And then they walked on. Adela had come there expressly to speak to him, but now she was almost afraid to speak. Her heart had been full of what it would utter, but now all utterance seemed to have left her. She had intended to console, but she did not dare to attempt it. There was a depth, almost a sublimity about his grief which kept her silent.

'Oh! Adela,' he said, 'if you knew what it is to have an empty heart—or rather a heart not empty—that would fain be empty that you might again refill it. Dear Adela!' And he put out his hand to take her own. She hardly knew why, but she let him take her hand. 'Dear Adela; have you never sighed for the comfort of an empty heart? You probe my wounds to the bottom; may I not search your own?'

She did not answer him. Was it possible that she should answer such a question? Her eyes became suffused with tears, and she was unable to raise them from the ground. She could not recall her hand—not at that moment. She had come there to lecture him, to talk to him, to comfort him; and now she was unable to say a word. Did he know the secret of her heart; that secret which once and but once had involuntarily broken from out her lips? Had Caroline told him? Had she been so false to friendship—as false to friendship as she had been to love?

'Adela! Adela! I would that we had met earlier in our lives. Yes, you and I.' These last words he added after she had quickly rescued her hand from his grasp. Very quickly she withdrew it now. As quickly she lifted up her face, all covered as it was with tears, and endured the full weight of his gaze. What! was it possible that he knew how she had loved, and thought that her love had been for him!

'Yes, you and I,' he continued. 'Even though your eyes flash upon me so sternly. You mean to say that had it been ever so early, that prize would have been impossible for me. Speak out, Adela. That is what you mean?'

'Yes; it would have been impossible; impossible every way; impossible, that is, on both sides.'

'Then you have not that empty heart, Adela? What else should make it impossible?'

'Mr Bertram, when I came here, I had no wish, no intention to talk about myself.'

'Why not of yourself as well as of me? I say again, I would we had both met earlier. It might have been that I should have been saved from this shipwreck. I will speak openly to you, Adela. Why not?' he added, seeing that she shrank from him, and seemed as though she would move on quickly—away from his words.

'Mr Bertram, do not say that which it will be useless for you to have said.'

'It shall not be useless. You are my friend, and friends should understand each other. You know how I have loved Caroline. You believe that I have loved her, do you not?'

'Oh, yes; I do believe that.'

'Well, you may; that, at any rate is true. I have loved her. She will now be that man's property, and I must love her no longer.'

'No; not with that sort of love.'

'That sort! Are there two sorts on which a man may run the changes, as he may from one room to another? I must wipe her out of my mind—out of my heart—or burn her out. I would not wish to love anything that he possesses.'

'No!' said she, 'not his wife.'

'Wife! she will never be his wife. She will never be bone of his bone, and flesh of his flesh, as I would have made her. It will be but a partnership between them, to be dissolved when they have made the most of their world's trading.'

'If you love her, Mr Bertram, do not be so bitter in speaking of her.'

'Bitter! I tell you that I think her quite right in what she does. If a woman cannot love, what better can she do than trade upon her beauty? But, there; let her go; I did not wish to speak of her.'

'I was very wrong in asking you to walk with me this morning.'

'No, Adela, not wrong; but very, very right. There, well, I will not ask you for your hand again, though it was but in friendship.'

'In friendship I will give it you,' and she stretched out her hand to him. It was ungloved, and very white and fair; a prettier hand than even Caroline could boast.

'I must not take it. I must not lie to you, Adela. I am brokenhearted. I have loved; I have loved that woman with all my heart, with my very soul, with the utmost strength of my whole being—and now it has come to this. If I know what a broken heart means, I have it here. But yet—yet—yet—Oh, Adela! I would fain try yet once again. I can do nothing for myself; nothing. If the world were there at my feet, wealth, power, glory, to be had for the stooping, I would not stoop to pick them, if I could not share them with—a friend. Adela, it is so sad to be alone.'

'Yes, it is sad. Is not sadness the lot of many of us?'

'Yes; but nature bids us seek a cure when a cure is possible.'

'I do not know what you wish me to understand, Mr Bertram?'

'Yes, Adela, you do; I think you do. I think I am honest and open. At any rate, I strive to be so. I think you do understand me.'

'If I do, then the cure which you seek is impossible.'

'Ah!'

'Is impossible.'

'You are not angry with me?'

'Angry; no, not angry.'

'And do not be angry now, if I speak openly again. I thought—I thought. But I fear that I shall pain you.'

'I do not care for pain if any good can come of it.'

'I thought that you also had been wounded. In the woods, the stricken harts lie down together and lick each other's wounds while the herd roams far away from them.'

'Is it so? Why do we hear then "of the poor sequestered

stag, left and abandoned of his velvet friend?"* No, Mr Bertram, grief, I fear, must still be solitary.'

'And so, unendurable.'

'God still tempers the wind to the shorn lamb,* now as he has ever done. But there is no sudden cure for these evils. The time will come when all this will be remembered, not without sorrow, but with a calm, quiet mourning that will be endurable; when your heart, now not broken as you say, but tortured, will be able to receive other images. But that time cannot come at once. Nor, I think, is it well that we should wish it. Those who have courage to love should have courage to suffer.'

'Yes, yes, yes. But if the courage be wanting? if one have it not? One cannot have such courage for the asking.'

'The first weight of the blow will stun the sufferer. I know that, Mr Bertram. But that dull, dead, deathly feeling will wear off at last. You have but to work; to read, to write, to study. In that respect, you men are more fortunate than we are. You have that which must occupy your thoughts.'

'And you, Adela—?'

'Do not speak of me. If you are generous, you will not do so. If I have in any way seemed to speak of myself, it is because you have made it unavoidable. What God has given me to bear is bearable;—though I would that he could have spared my poor father.' And, so saying, Adela at last gave way to tears. On that subject she might be allowed to weep.

Bertram said nothing to disturb her till they were near the house, and then he again held out his hand to her. 'As a true friend; I hope as a dear friend. Is it not so?' said he.

'Yes,' she answered, in her lowest voice, 'as a dear friend. But remember that I expect a friend's generosity and a friend's forbearance.' And so she made her way back to her own room, and appeared at breakfast in her usual sober guise, but with eyes that told no tales.

On the next morning she took her departure. The nearest station on the railway by which she was to go to Littlebath was distant about twelve miles, and it was proposed that she should be sent thither in Mrs Wilkinson's phaëton. This, indeed, except the farm-yard cart, was the only vehicle which belonged to the parsonage, and was a low four-wheeled carriage, not very well contrived for the accommodation of two moderate-sized people in front, and of two immoderately small people on the hind seat. Mrs Wilkinson habitually drove it herself, with one of her daughters beside her, and with two others—those two whose legs had been found by measurement to be the shortest—in durance vile* behind; but when so packed, it was clear to all men that the capacity of the phaëton was exhausted. Now the first arrangement proposed was, that Arthur should drive the phaëton, and that Sophy should accompany Adela to the station. But Sophy, in so arranging, had forgotten that her friend had a bag, a trunk, and a bonnet-box, the presence of which at Littlebath would be indispensable; and, therefore, at the last moment, when the phaëton came to the door with the luggage fastened on the hinder seat, it was discovered for the first time that Sophy must be left behind.

Arthur Wilkinson would willingly have given up his position, and George Bertram would willingly have taken it. Adela also would have been well pleased at such a change. But though all would have been pleased, it could not be effected. The vicar could not very well proclaim that, as his sister was not to accompany him and shield him, he would not act as charioteer to Miss Gauntlet; nor could the lady object to be driven by her host. So at last they started from the vicarage door with many farewell kisses, and a large packet of sandwiches. Who is it that consumes the large packets of sandwiches with which parting guests are always laden? I imagine that station-masters' dogs are mainly fed upon them.

The first half-mile was occupied, on Wilkinson's part, in little would-be efforts to make his companion more comfortable. He shifted himself about into the furthest corner so as to give her more room; he pulled his cloak out from under her, and put it over her knees to guard her from the dust; and recommended her three times to put up her parasol. Then he had a word or two to say to the neighbours; but that only lasted as long as he was in his own parish. Then he came to a hill which gave him an opportunity of walking; and on getting in again he occupied half a minute in taking out his watch, and assuring Adela that she would not be too late for the train.

But when all this was done, the necessity for conversation still remained. They had hardly been together—thrown for conversation on each other as they now were—since that day when Arthur had walked over for the last time to West Putford. Reader, do you remember it? Hardly; for have not all the fortunes and misfortunes of our more prominent hero intervened since that chapter was before you?

'I hope you will find yourself comfortable at Littlebath,' he said at last.

'Oh, yes; that is, I shall be when my aunt comes home. I shall be at home then, you know.'

'But that will be some time?'

'I fear so; and I dread greatly going to this Miss Todd, whom I have never seen. But you see, dear Miss Baker must go back to Hadley soon, and Miss Todd has certainly been very good-natured in offering to take me.'

Then there was another silence, which lasted for about half a mile.

'My mother would have been very glad if you would have stayed at the parsonage till your aunt's return; and so would my sisters—and so should I.'

'You are all very kind—too kind,' said Adela.

Then came another pause, perhaps for a quarter of a mile, but it was up-hill work, and the quarter of a mile passed by very slowly.

'It seems so odd that you should go away from us, whom you have known so long, to stay with Miss Todd, whom you never have even seen.'

'I think change of scene will be good for me, Mr Wilkinson.'

'Well, perhaps so.' And then the other quarter of a mile made away with itself. 'Come, get along, Dumpling.' This was said to the fat steed; for they had now risen to level ground.

'Our house, I know, must be very stupid for you. It is much changed from what it was; is it not?'

'Oh, I don't know.'

'Yes, it is. There is neither the same spirit, nor the same good-will. We miss my father greatly.'

'Ah, yes. I can feel for you there. It is a loss; a great loss.'

'I sometimes think it unfortunate that my mother should have remained at the vicarage after my father's death.'

'You have been very good to her, I know.'

'I have done my best, Adela.' It was the first time she had distinctly heard him call her by her Christian name since she had come to stay with them. 'But I have failed. She is not happy there; nor, indeed, for that matter, am I.'

'A man should be happy when he does his duty.'

'We none of us do that so thoroughly as to require no other source of happiness. Go on, Dumpling, and do your duty.'

'I see that you are very careful in doing yours.'

'Perhaps you will hardly believe me, but I wish Lord Stapledean had never given me the living.'

'Well; it is difficult to believe that. Think what it has been for your sisters.'

'I know we should have been very poor, but we should not have starved. I had my fellowship, and I could have taken pupils. I am sure we should have been happier. And then—'

'And then—well?' said Adela; and as she spoke, her heart was not quite at rest within her breast.

'Then I should have been free. Since I took that living, I have been a slave.' Again he paused a moment, and whipped the horse; but it was only now for a moment that he was silent. 'Yes, a slave. Do you not see what a life I live? I could be content to sacrifice myself to my mother if the sacrifice were understood. But you see how it is with her. Nothing that I can do will satisfy her; and yet for her I have sacrificed everything—everything.'

'A sacrifice is no sacrifice if it be agreeable. The sacrifice consists in its being painful.'

'Well, I suppose so. I say that to myself so often. It is the only consolation I have.'

'Not that I think your home should be made uncomfortable to you. There is no reason why it should be. At least, I should think not.' She spoke with little spasmodic efforts, which however, did not betray themselves to her companion, who seemed to her to be almost more engaged with Dumpling than with the conversation. It certainly had been through no wish of hers that they were thus talking of his household concerns; but as they were speaking of them, she was forced into a certain amount of hypocrisy. It was a subject on which she could not speak openly.

There was then another hill to be walked up, and Adela thought there would be no more of it. The matter had come up by accident, and would now, probably, drop away. But no. Whether by design, or from chance, or because no other topic presented itself, Arthur went back to the subject, and did so now in a manner that was peculiarly startling to Miss Gauntlet.

'Do you remember my calling once at West Putford, soon after I got the living? It is a long time ago now, and I don't suppose you do remember it.'

'Yes, I do; very well.'

'And do you remember what I told you then?'

'What was it?' said Adela. It clearly is the duty of a young lady on very many occasions to be somewhat hypocritical.

'If there be any man to whose happiness marriage is more necessary than to that of another, it is a country clergyman.'

'Yes, I can believe that. That is, if there be not ladies of his own family living with him.'

'I do not know that that makes any difference.'

'Oh, yes; it must make a difference. I think that a man must be very wretched who has no one to look after his house.'

'And is that your idea of the excellence of a wife? I should have expected something higher from you, Adela. I suppose you think, then, that if a man have his linen looked after, and his dinner cooked, that is sufficient.' Poor Adela! It must be acknowledged that this was hard on her.

'No, I do not think that sufficient.'

'It would seem so from what you say.'

'Then what I said belied my thoughts. It seems to me, Mr Wilkinson, since you drive me to speak out, that the matter is very much in your own hands. You are certainly a free agent. You know better than I can tell you what your duty to your mother and sisters requires. Circumstances have made them dependent on you, and you certainly are not the man to disacknowledge the burden.'

'Certainly not.'

'No, certainly not. But, having made up my mind to that, I would not, were I you, allow myself to be a slave.'

'But what can I do?'

'You mean that you would be a poor man were you—were you to give up your fellowship and at the same time take upon yourself other cares as well. Do as other poor men do.'

'I know no other man situated as I am.'

'But you know men who are much worse situated as regards their worldly means. Were you to give your mother the half of your income, you would still, I presume, be richer than Mr Young.' Mr Young was the curate of a neighbouring parish, who had lately married on his curacy.

It will be said by my critics, especially by my female critics, that in saying this, Adela went a long way towards teaching Mr Wilkinson the way to woo. Indeed she brought that accusation against herself, and not lightly. But she was, as she herself had expressed it, driven in the cause of truth to say what she had said. Nor did she, in her heart of hearts, believe that Mr Wilkinson had any thought of her in saying what she did say. Her mind on that matter had been long made up. She knew herself to be 'the poor sequestered stag, left and abandoned by his velvet friend.' She had no feeling in the matter which amounted to the slightest hope. He had asked her for her counsel, and she had given him the only counsel which she honestly could give.

Therefore, bear lightly on her, O my critics. Bear lightly on her especially, my critics feminine. To the worst of your wrath and scorn I willingly subject the other lovers with whom my tale is burthened.

'Yes, I should be better off than Young,' said Wilkinson, as though he were speaking to himself. 'But that is not the point. I do not know that I have ever looked at it exactly in that light. There is the house, the parsonage I mean. It is full of women'—'twas thus irreverently that he spoke of his mother and sisters—'what other woman would come among them?'

'Oh, that is the treasure for which you have to search'—this she said laughingly. The bitterness of the day was over with her; or at least it then seemed so. She was not even thinking of herself when she said this.

'Would you come to such a house, Adela? You, you yourself?'

'You mean to ask whether, if, as regards other circumstances, I was minded to marry, I would then be deterred by a mother-in-law and sister-in-law?'

'Yes, just so,' said Wilkinson, timidly.

'Well, that would depend much upon how well I might like the gentleman; something also upon how much I might like the ladies.'

'A man's wife should always be mistress in his own house.'

'Oh yes, of course.'

'And my mother is determined to be mistress in that house.'

'Well, I will not recommend you to rebel against your mother. Is that the station, Mr Wilkinson?'

'Yes—that's the station. Dear me, we have forty minutes to wait yet!'

'Don't mind me, Mr Wilkinson. I shall not in the least dislike waiting by myself.'

'Of course, I shall see you off. Dumpling won't run away; you may be sure of that. There is very little of the runaway class to be found at Hurst Staple Parsonage; except you, Adela.'

'You don't call me a runaway, I hope?'

'You run away from us just when we are beginning to feel the comfort of your being with us. There, he won't catch cold now;' and so having thrown a rug over Dumpling's back, he followed Adela into the station.

I don't know anything so tedious as waiting at a second-class station for a train. There is the ladies' waiting-room, into which gentlemen may not go, and the gentlemen's waiting-room, in which the porters generally smoke, and the refreshment room, with its dirty counter covered with dirtier cakes. And there is the platform, which you walk up and down till you are tired. You go to the ticket-window half a dozen times for your ticket, having been warned by the company's bills that you must be prepared to start at least ten minutes before the train is due. But the man inside knows better, and does not open the little hole to which you have to stoop your head till two minutes before the time named for your departure. Then there are five fat farmers, three old women, and a butcher at the aperture, and not finding yourself equal to struggling among them for a place, you make up your mind to be left behind. At last, however, you do get your ticket just as the train comes up; but hearing that exciting sound, you nervously cram your change into your pocket without counting it, and afterwards feel quite convinced that you have lost a shilling in the transaction.

'Twas somewhat in this way that the forty minutes were passed by Wilkinson and Adela. Nothing of any moment was spoken between them till he took her hand for the last time. 'Adela,' he then whispered to her, 'I shall think much of what you have said to me, very much. I do so wish you were not leaving us. I wonder whether you would be surprised if I were to write to you?' But the train was gone before she had time to answer.

Two days afterwards, Bertram also left them. 'Arthur,' he said, as he took leave of the vicar, 'if I, who have made such a mess of it myself, may give advice on such a subject, I would not leave Adela Gauntlet long at Littlebath if I were you.'

CHAPTER XXVIII

THE SOLICITOR-GENERAL IN LOVE

CAROLINE WADDINGTON was at Hadley when she received and accepted the proposal made to her by Sir Henry Harcourt. It may be conceived that the affair was arranged without any very great amount of romance. Sir Henry indeed was willing, in a hurried manner, to throw himself at the lady's feet, to swear by her fair hand that he loved her as man never yet had loved, and to go to work in the fashion usually most approved by young ladies. In a hurried manner, I say; for just at this moment he was being made solicitor-general, and had almost too many irons in the fire to permit of a prolonged dallying. But Caroline would have none of it, either hurried or not hurried. Whatever might be the case with Sir Henry, she had gone through that phase of life, and now declared to herself that she did not want any more of it.

Sir Henry did not find the task of gaining his bride very difficult. He had succeeded in establishing a sort of intimacy with old Mr Bertram, and it appeared that permission to run down to Hadley and run back again had already been accorded to him before Miss Baker and Caroline arrived there. He never slept, though he sometimes dined in the house; but he had always something to talk about when an excuse for going to Hadley was required. Mr Bertram had asked him something about some investment, and he had found out this something; or he wanted to ask Mr Bertram's advice on some question as to his political career. At this period he was, or professed to be, very much guided in his public life by Mr Bertram's opinion.

And thus he fell in with Caroline. On the first occasion of his doing so, he contrived to whisper to her his deep sympathy with her sorrow; on his second visit, he spoke more of himself and less of Bertram; on his third, he alluded only to her own virtues; on his fourth, he asked her to be Lady Harcourt. She told him that she would be Lady Harcourt; and, as far as she was concerned, there was an end of it for the present.

Then Sir Henry proposed that the day should be named. On this subject also he found her ready to accommodate him. She had no coy scruples as to the time. He suggested that it should be before Christmas. Very well; let it be before Christmas. Christmas is a cold time for marrying; but this was to be a cold marriage. Christmas, however, for the fortunate is made warm with pudding, ale, and spiced beef. They intended to be among the fortunate, the fortunate in place, and money, and rank; and they would, as best they might, make themselves warm with the best pudding, ale, and spiced beef which the world could afford them.

Sir Henry was alive to the delight of being the possessor of so many charms, and was somewhat chagrined that for the present he was so cruelly debarred from any part of his legitimate enjoyment. Though he was a solicitor-general, he could have been content to sit for ten minutes with his arm round Caroline's waist; and—in spite of the energy with which he was preparing a bill for the regulation of County Courts, as to which he knew that he should have that terrible demigod, Lord Boanerges,* down upon his shoulders—still he would fain have stolen a kiss or two. But Caroline's waist and Caroline's kisses were to be his only after Christmas; and to be his only as payment accorded for her new rank, and for her fine new house in Eaton Square.

How is it that girls are so potent to refuse such favours at one time, and so impotent in preventing their exaction at another? Sir Henry, we may say, had every right to demand some trifling payment in advance; but he could not get a doit. Should we be violating secrecy too much if we suggested that George Bertram had had some slight partial success even when he had no such positive claim—some success which had of course been in direct opposition to the lady's will?

Miss Baker had now gone back to Littlebath, either to receive Adela Gauntlet, or because she knew that she should be more comfortable in her own rooms than in her uncle's dismal house—or perhaps because Sir Lionel was there. She had, however, gone back, and Caroline remained mistress for the time of her grandfather's household.

The old man now seemed to have dropped all mystery in the matter. He generally, indeed, spoke of Caroline as Miss Waddington; but he heard her talked of as his granddaughter without expressing anger, and with Sir Henry he himself so spoke of her. He appeared to be quite reconciled to the marriage. In spite of all his entreaties to George, all his attempted bribery, his broken-hearted sorrow when he failed, he seemed to be now content. Indeed, he had made no opposition to the match. When Caroline had freely spoken to him about it, he made some little snappish remark as to the fickleness of women; but he at the same time signified that he would not object.

Why should he? Sir Henry Harcourt was in every respect a good match for his granddaughter. He had often been angry with George Bertram because George had not prospered in the world. Sir Henry had prospered signally—would probably prosper much more signally. Might it not be safely predicated of a man who was solicitor-general before he was thirty, that he would be lord-chancellor or lord chief-justice, or at any rate some very bigwig indeed before he was fifty? So of course Mr Bertram did not object.

But he had not signified his acquiescence in any very cordial way. Rich old men, when they wish to be cordial on such occasions, have but one way of evincing cordiality. It is not by a pressure of the hand, by a kind word, by an approving glance. Their embrace conveys no satisfaction: their warmest words, if unsupported, are very cold. An old man, if he intends to be cordial on such an occasion, must speak of *thousands of pounds*. 'My dear young fellow, I approve altogether. She shall have *twenty thousand pounds* the day she becomes yours.' Then is the hand shaken with true fervour; then is real cordiality expressed and felt. 'What a dear old man grandpapa is! Is there any one like him? Dear old duck! He is going to be so generous to Harry.'

But Mr Bertram said nothing about twenty thousand pounds, nothing about ten, nothing about money at all till he was spoken to on the subject. It was Sir Henry's special object not to be pressing on this point, to show that he was marrying Caroline without any sordid views, and that his admiration for Mr Bertram had no bearing at all on that gentleman's cash-box. He did certainly make little feints at Mr Pritchett; but Mr Pritchett merely wheezed and said nothing. Mr Pritchett was not fond of the Harcourt interest; and seemed to care but little for Miss Caroline, now that she had transferred her affections.

But it was essentially necessary that Sir Henry Harcourt should know what was to be done. If he were to have nothing, it was necessary that he should know that. He had certainly counted on having something, and on having something immediately. He was a thoroughly hard-working man of business, but yet he was not an economical man. A man who lives before the world in London, and lives chiefly among men of fortune, can hardly be economical. He had not therefore any large sum of money in hand. He was certainly in receipt of a large income, but then his expenses were large. He had taken and now had to furnish an expensive house in Eaton Square, and a few thousand pounds in ready money was almost indispensable to him.

One Friday—this was after his return to town from the ten days' grouse-shooting, and occurred at the time when he was most busy with the County Courts—he wrote to Caroline to say that he would go down to Hadley on Saturday afternoon, stay there over the Sunday, and return to town on the Monday morning; that is to say, he would do so if perfectly agreeable to Mr Bertram.

He went down, and found everything prepared for him that was suitable for a solicitor-general. They did not put before him merely roast mutton or boiled beef. He was not put to sleep in the back bedroom without a carpet. Such treatment had been good enough for George Bertram; but for the solicitor-general all the glories of Hadley were put forth. He slept in the best bedroom, which was damp enough no doubt, seeing that it was not used above twice in the year; and went through at dinner a whole course of *entrées*, such as *entrées* usually are in the suburban districts. This was naturally gratifying to him as a solicitor-general, and fortified him for the struggle he was to make.

He had some hope that he should have a *tête-à-tête* with Caroline on the Saturday evening. But neither fate nor love would favour him. He came down just before dinner, and there was clearly no time then: infirm as the old man was, he sat at the dinner-table; and though Sir Henry was solicitor-general, there was no second room, no withdrawing-room prepared for his reception.

'Grandpapa does not like moving,' said Caroline, as she got up to leave the room after dinner; 'so perhaps, Sir Henry, you will allow me to come down to tea here? We always sit here of an evening.'

'I never could bear to live in two rooms,' said the old man. 'When one is just warm and comfortable, one has to go out into all the draughts of the house. That's the fashion, I know. But I hope you'll excuse me, Sir Henry, for not liking it.'

Sir Henry of course did excuse him. There was nothing he himself liked so much as sitting cosy over a dining-room fire.

In about an hour Caroline did come down again; and in another hour, before the old man went, she again vanished for the night. Sir Henry had made up his mind not to speak to Mr Bertram about money that evening; so he also soon followed Caroline, and sat down to work upon the County Courts in his own bedroom.

On the next morning Sir Henry and Caroline went to church. All the Hadleyians of course knew of the engagement, and were delighted to have an opportunity of staring at the two turtle-doves. A solicitor-general in love is a sight to behold; and the clergyman had certainly no right to be angry if the attention paid to his sermon was something less fixed than usual. Before dinner, there was luncheon; and then Sir Henry asked his betrothed if she would take a walk with him. 'Oh, certainly, she would be delighted.' Her church-going bonnet was still on, and she was quite ready. Sir Henry also was ready; but as he left the room he stooped over Mr Bertram's chair and whispered to him, 'Could I speak a few words before dinner, sir; on business? I know I ought to apologize, this being Sunday.'

'Oh, I don't care about Sunday,' said the stubborn-minded old man. 'I shall be here till I go to bed, I suppose, if you want me.'

And then they started on their walk. Oh, those lovers' rambles! A man as he grows old can perhaps teach himself to regret but few of the sweets which he is compelled to leave behind him. He can learn to disregard most of his youth's pleasures, and to live contented though he has outlived them. The polka and the waltz were once joyous; but he sees now that the work was warm, and that one was often compelled to perform it in company for which one did not care. Those picnics too were nice; but it may be a question whether a good dinner at his own dinner-table is not nicer. Though fat and over forty he may still ride to hounds, and as for boating and cricketing, after all they were but boy's play. For those things one's soul does not sigh. But ah! those lovers' walks, those loving lovers' rambles. Tom Moore* is usually somewhat sugary and mawkish; but in so much he was right. If there be an Elysium on earth, it is this. They are done and over for us, O my compatriots. Never again, unless we are destined to rejoin our houris in heaven, and to saunter over fields of asphodel* in another and a greener youth—never again shall those joys be ours! And what can ever equal them? 'Twas then, between sweet hedgerows, under green oaks, with our feet rustling on the crisp leaves, that the world's cold reserve was first thrown off, and we found that those we loved were not goddesses made of buckram and brocade, but human beings like ourselves, with blood in their veins, and hearts in their bosoms—veritable children of Adam like ourselves.

'Gin a body meet a body comin' through the rye.'* Ah, how delicious were those meetings. How convinced we were that there was no necessity for loud alarm! How fervently we agreed with the poet! My friends, born together with me in the consulship of Lord Liverpool,* all that is done and over for us. We shall never 'gang that gait' again.

There is a melancholy in this that will tinge our thoughts, let us draw ever so strongly on our philosophy. We can still walk with our wives;—and that is pleasant too, very—of course. But there was more animation in it when we walked with the same ladies under other names. Nay, sweet spouse, mother of dear bairns, who hast so well done thy duty; but this was so, let thy brows be knit never so angrily. That lord of thine has been indifferently good to thee, and thou to him hast been more than good. Uphill together have ye walked peacably labouring; and now arm-in-arm ye shall go down the gradual slope which ends below there in the green churchyard. 'Tis good and salutary to walk thus. But for the full cup of joy, for the brimming spring-tide of human bliss, oh, give me back—! Well, well, well; it is nonsense; I know it; but may not a man dream now and again in his evening nap and yet do no harm?

*Vixi puellis nuper idoneus, et militavi.** How well Horace knew all about it! but that hanging up of the gittern*—. One would fain have put it off, had falling hairs, and marriage-vows, and obesity have permitted it. Nay, is it not so, old friend of the grizzled beard? Dost thou not envy that smirk young knave with his five lustrums,* though it goes hard with him to purchase his kid-gloves? He dines for one-and-twopence at an eating-house; but what cares Maria where he dines? He rambles through the rye with his empty pockets, and at the turn of the field-path Maria will be there to meet him. Envy him not; thou hast had thy walk: but lend him rather that thirty shillings that he asks of thee. So shall Maria's heart be glad as she accepts his golden brooch.

But for our friend Sir Henry every joy was present. Youth and wealth and love were all his, and his all together. He was but eight-and-twenty, was a member of Parliament, solicitor-general, owner of a house in Eaton Square, and possessor of as much well-trained beauty as was to be found at that time within the magic circle of any circumambient crinoline within the bills of mortality.* Was it not sweet for him to wander through the rye? Had he not fallen upon an Elysium, a very paradise of earthly joys? Was not his spring-tide at the full flood?

And so they started on their walk. It was the first that they had ever taken together. What Sir Henry may have done before in that line this history says not. A man who is solicitor-general at eight-and-twenty can hardly have had time for much. But the practice which he perhaps wanted, Caroline had had. There had been walks as well as rides at Littlebath; and walks also, though perhaps of doubtful joy, amidst those graves below the walls of Jerusalem.

And so they started. There is—or perhaps we should say was; for time and railways, and straggling new suburban villas, may now have destroyed it all; but there is, or was, a pretty woodland lane, running from the back of Hadley church, through the last remnants of what once was Enfield Chase. How many lovers' feet have crushed the leaves that used to lie in autumn along that pretty lane! Well, well; there shall not be another word in that strain. I speak solely now of the time here present to Sir Henry; all former days and former roamings there shall be clean forgotten. The solicitor-general now thither wends his way, and love and beauty attend upon his feet. See how he opens the gate that stands by the churchyard paling? Does it stand there yet, I wonder? Well, well; we will say it does.

'It is a beautiful day for a walk,' said Sir Henry.

'Yes, very beautiful,' said Caroline.

'There is nothing I am so fond of as a long walk,' said the gentleman.

'It is very nice,' said the lady. 'But I do not know that I care for going very far today. I am not quite strong at present.'

'Not strong?' And the solicitor-general put on a look of deep alarm.

'Oh, there is nothing the matter with me; but I am not quite strong for walking. I am out of practice; and my boots are not quite of the right sort.'

'They don't hurt you, I hope?'

'Oh, no; they don't actually hurt me. They'll do very well for today.' And then there was a short pause and they got on the green grass which runs away into the chase in front of the parsonage windows. I wonder whether wickets are ever standing there now on the summer afternoons!

They were soon as much alone—or nearly so—as lovers might wish to be; quite enough so for Caroline. Some curious eyes were still peeping, no doubt, to see how the great lawyer looked when he was walking with the girl of his heart; to see how the rich miser's granddaughter looked when she was walking with the man of her heart. And perhaps some voices were whispering that she had changed her lover; for in these rural seclusions everything is known by everybody. But neither the peepers nor the whisperers interfered with the contentment of the fortunate pair.

'I hope you are happy, Caroline?' said Sir Henry, as he gently squeezed the hand that was so gently laid upon his arm.

'Happy! oh yes—I am happy. I don't believe, you know, in a great deal of very ecstatic happiness. I never did.'

'But I hope you are rationally happy—not discontented—at any rate, not regretful? I hope that you believe that I shall do my best, my very best, to make you happy?'

'Oh, yes; I quite believe that. We must each think of the other's comfort. After all, that I take it is the great thing in married life.'

'I don't expect you to be passionately in love with me—not as yet, Caroline.'

'No. Let neither of us expect that, Sir Henry. Passionate love, I take it, rarely lasts long, and is very troublesome while it does last. Mutual esteem is very much more valuable.'

'But, Caroline, I would have you believe in my love.'

'Oh, yes; I do believe in it. Why else should you wish to marry me? I think too well of myself to feel it strange that you should love me. But love with you, and with me also for the future, will be subordinate to other passions.'

Sir Henry did not altogether like that reference to the past which was conveyed in the word future; but, however, he bore it without wincing.

'You know so thoroughly the history of the last three years,' she continued, 'that it would be impossible for me to deceive you if I could. But, if I know myself, under no circumstances would I have done so. I have loved once, and no good has come of it. It was contrary to my nature to do so—to love in that mad, passionate, self-sacrificing manner. But yet I did. I think I may say with certainty that I never shall be so foolish again.'

'You have suffered lately, Caroline; and as the sore still smarts, you hardly yet know what happiness may be in store for you.'

'Yes; I have suffered,' and he felt from the touch on his arm that her whole body shuddered.

He walked on in silence for awhile considering within himself. Why should he marry this girl, rejected of her former lover, who now hung upon his arm? He was now at the very fullest tide of his prosperity; he had everything to offer which mothers wish for their daughters, and which daughters wish for themselves. He had income, rank, name, youth, and talent. Why should he fling his rich treasures at the feet of a proud minx who in taking them swore that she could not love him? Would it not be better for him to recede? A word he well knew would do it; for her pride was true pride. He felt in his heart that it was not assumed. He had only to say that he was not contented with this cold lack of love, and she would simply desire him to lead her back to her home and leave her there. It would be easy enough for him to get his head from out the noose.

But it was this very easiness, perhaps, which made him hesitate. She knew her own price, and was not at all anxious to dispose of herself a cheap bargain. If you, sir, have a horse to sell, never appear anxious for the sale. That rule is well understood among those who deal in horses. If you, madam, have a daughter to sell, it will be well for you also to remember this. Or, my young friend, if you have yourself to sell, the same rule holds good. But it is hard to put an old head on young shoulders. Hard as the task is, however, it would seem to have been effected as regards Caroline Waddington.

And then Sir Henry looked at her. Not exactly with his present eyesight as then at that moment existing; for seeing that she was walking by his side, he could not take the comprehensive view which his taste and mind required. But he looked at her searchingly with the eyesight of his memory, and found that she exactly tallied with what his judgment demanded. That she was very beautiful, no man had ever doubted. That she was now in the full pride of her beauty was to him certain. And then her beauty was of that goddess class which seems for so long a period to set years at defiance. It was produced by no girlish softness, by no perishable mixture of white and red; it was not born of a sparkling eye, and a ripe lip, and a cherry cheek. To her face belonged lines of contour, severe, lovely, and of ineradicable grace. It was not when she smiled and laughed that she most pleased. She did not charm only when she spoke; though, indeed, the expression of her speaking face was perfect. But she had the beauty of a marble bust. It would not be easy even for Sir Henry Harcourt, even for a young solicitor-general, to find a face more beautiful with which to adorn his drawing-room.

And then she had that air of fashion, that look of being able to look down the unfashionable, which was so much in the eyes of Sir Henry; though in those of George Bertram it had been almost a demerit. With Caroline, as with many women, this was an appearance rather than a reality. She had not moved much among high people; she had not taught herself to despise those of her own class, the women of Littlebath, the Todds and the Adela Gauntlets; but she looked as though she would be able to do so. And it was fitting she should have such a look if ever she were to be the wife of a solicitor-general.

And then Sir Henry thought of Mr Bertram's coffers. Ah! if he could only be let into that secret. It might be easy to come to a decision. That the old man had quarrelled with his nephew, he was well aware. That George, in his pig-headed folly, would make no overtures towards a reconciliation; of that also he was sure. Was it not probable that at any rate a great portion of that almost fabulous wealth would go to the man's granddaughter? There was doubtless risk; but then one must run some risk in everything. It might be, if he could play his cards wisely, that he would get it all—that he would be placed in a position to make even the solicitor-generalship beneath his notice.

And so, in spite of Caroline's coldness, he resolved to persevere.

Having thus made up his mind, he turned the conversation to another subject.

'You liked the house on the whole; did you?' Caroline during the past week had been up to see the new house in Eaton Square.

'Oh, yes; very much. Nothing could be nicer. Only I am afraid it's expensive.' This was a subject on which Caroline could talk to him.

'Not particularly,' said Sir Henry. 'Of course one can't get a house in London for nothing. I shall have rather a bargain of that if I can pay the money down. The great thing is whether you like it.'

'I was charmed with it. I never saw prettier drawing-rooms—never. And the bedrooms for a London house are so large and airy.'

'Did you go into the dining-room?'

'Oh, yes; I went in.'

'There's room for four-and-twenty, is there not?'

'Well, I don't know. I can't give an opinion about that. You could have three times that number at supper.'

'I'm not thinking about suppers; but I'm sure you could. Kitchen's convenient, eh?'

'Very—so at least aunt Mary said.'

'And now about the furniture. You can give me two or three days in town, can't you?'

'Oh, yes; if you require it. But I would trust your taste in all those matters.'

'My taste! I have neither taste nor time. If you won't mind going to—'

And so the conversation went on for another fifteen minutes, and then they were at home. Caroline's boots had begun to tease her, and their walk, therefore, had not been prolonged to a great distance.

Ah me! again I say, how pleasant, how delightful were those lovers' walks!

Then Caroline went up to her bedroom, and Sir Henry sat himself down near Mr Bertram's chair in the dining-room.

'I wanted to speak to you, sir,' said he, rushing at once into the midst of his subject, 'about Caroline's settlement. It is time that all that should be arranged. I would have made my lawyer see Pritchett; but I don't know that Pritchett has any authority to act for you in such matters.'

'Act for me! Pritchett has no authority to act—nor have I either.' This little renunciation of his granddaughter's affairs was no more than Sir Henry expected. He was, therefore, neither surprised nor disgusted.

'Well! I only want to know who has the authority. I don't anticipate any great difficulty. Caroline's fortune is not very large; but of course it must be settled. Six thousand pounds, I believe.'

'Four, Sir Henry. That is, if I am rightly informed.'

'Four, is it? I was told six—I think by George Bertram in former days. I should of course prefer six; but if it be only four, why we must make the best of it.'

'She has only four of her own,' said the old man, somewhat mollified.

'Have you any objection to my telling you what I would propose to do?'

'No objection in life, Sir Henry.'

'My income is large; but I want a little ready money at present to conclude the purchase of my house, and to furnish it. Would you object to the four thousand pounds being paid into my hands, if I insure my life for six for her benefit? Were her fortune larger, I should of course propose that my insurance should be heavier.'

Sir Henry was so very reasonable that Mr Bertram by degrees thawed. He would make his granddaughter's fortune six thousand as he had always intended. This should be settled on her, the income of course going to her husband. He should insure his life for four thousand more on her behalf; and Mr Bertram would lend Sir Henry three thousand for his furniture.

Sir Henry agreed to this, saying to himself that such a loan from Mr Bertram was equal to a gift. Mr Bertram himself seemed to look at it in a different light. 'Mind, Sir Henry, I shall expect the interest to the day. I will only charge you four per cent. And it must be made a bond debt.'

'Oh, certainly,' said Sir Henry.

And so the affair of the settlement was arranged.

CHAPTER XXIX

MRS LEAKE OF RISSBURY

ADELA GAUNTLET reached Littlebath without any adventures, and at the station she met Miss Baker ready to take her and her boxes in charge. She soon learned what was to be her fate for that autumn. It was imperatively necessary that Miss Baker should go up to town in a week or two. 'There are such hundreds of things to be done about furniture and all that, you know,' said Miss Baker, looking rather grand as she spoke of her niece's great match; and yet doing so with the least possible amount of intentional pride or vanity. Adela, of course, acknowledged that there must be hundreds of things, and expressed her deepest regret that she should be so much in the way. Perhaps she almost wished that she had remained at Hurst Staple.

'Not at all in the way, my dear,' said Miss Baker; 'I shall be back again in a week at the furthest, and Miss Todd will be delighted to have you for that time. Indeed, she would be very much disappointed now, and offended too, if you did not go. But all the same, I would not leave you, only that Sir Henry insists that Caroline should choose all the things herself; and of course he has not time to go with her—and then the responsibility is so great. Why I suppose she will have to lay out about two thousand pounds!'

'But what sort of a person is Miss Todd?' asked Adela.

'Oh, an extremely nice person; you'll like her amazingly—so lively, so good-natured, so generous; and very clever too. Perhaps, for her age, she's a little too fond—'

'Too fond of what? You were going to say dress, I suppose.'

'No, indeed. I can't say that there's anything to blame her for in that. She dresses very handsomely, but always plain. No; what I was going to say is, that perhaps for a woman of her age—she is a little too fond of gentlemen's attention.'

'Caroline told me that she was the most confirmed old maid she knew—an old maid who gloried in being an old maid.'

'I don't know about that, my dear; but if a certain gentleman were to ask her, I don't think she'd glory in it much longer. But she's a very nice person, and you'll like her very much.'

Miss Baker did go up to town, leaving Adela to Miss Todd's hospitality. She did go up, but in doing so resolved to return as soon as possible. Sir Lionel was now in the Paragon nearly every other day. To be sure, he did generally call in Montpellier Terrace on the alternate days. But then there was a reason for that. They had to talk about George and Caroline. What possible reason could there be for his going to the Paragon?

Adela was rather frightened when she found herself left at Miss Todd's lodgings; though that lady's manner to her was not such as need have inspired much awe.

'Now, my dear,' she said, 'don't mind me in the least. Do just whatever you like. If I only knew what you did like, you should have it if I could get it. What are you fond of now? Shall I ask some young people here tonight?'

'Oh, no, Miss Todd; not for me. I have never been much in society, and certainly do not wish for it at present.'

'Well, society is not a bad thing. You don't play cards, I suppose?'

'I don't know one card from another.'

'You'd just suit Mr O'Callaghan then. Are you fond of young clergymen? There's one here might just suit you. All the young ladies are dying for him.'

'Then pray don't let me interfere with them, Miss Todd.'

'Perhaps you like officers better. There are heaps of them here. I don't know where they come from, and they never seem to have anything to do. The young ladies, however—those who don't run after Mr O'Callaghan—seem to think them very nice.'

'Oh, Miss Todd, I don't want clergymen or officers.'

'Don't you? Well then, we'll get some novels from the circulating library. At three o'clock I always drive out, and we'll go to the pastrycook's. Oh, I declare, here's Sir Lionel Bertram, as usual. You know Sir Lionel, don't you?'

Adela said that she had met Sir Lionel at Miss Baker's.

'What a pity that match should have gone off, isn't it? I mean dear Miss Waddington. But though that match is off, another may come on. I for one should be very happy. You don't know anything about it I see. I'll tell you some of these days. How do, Sir Lionel? You mustn't stay long, because Miss Gauntlet and I are going out. Or I'll tell you what. You shall take care of us. It's a beautiful day; and if Miss Gauntlet likes, we'll walk instead of having the fly.'* Miss Todd never aped grandeur, and always called her private carriage a fly, because it had only one horse.

Sir Lionel, having made his salutations to Miss Gauntlet, declared that he should be most happy to be trusted with their custody through the streets of Littlebath.

'But we can't walk, either, Miss Gauntlet, today, because I must call on old Mrs Leake, at Rissbury. I quite forgot Mrs Leake. So you see, Sir Lionel, we shan't want you after all.'

Sir Lionel declared that this last decision made him quite miserable.

'You'll be recovered by dinner-time, I don't doubt,' said Miss Todd. 'And now I'll go upstairs and put my bonnet on. As Miss Gauntlet has got hers, you can stay and talk to her.'

'Charming creature, Miss Todd; isn't she?' said Sir Lionel, before the door was well closed. 'Such freshness of character, so much bonhomie—a little odd sometimes.' These last words were not added till Miss Todd's footsteps, heavier than Camilla's, were heard well up the stairs.

'She seems to be a very good-natured person. I never saw her before today.'

'Did you not? We knew her very intimately in the Holy Land'—as if any land ever was or could be holy to Sir Lionel and such as he. 'That is, George and I and Caroline. Of course, you know all about that Miss Waddington?'

Adela signified to him that she did know the circumstances to which he alluded.

'It is very sad, is it not? and then the connection between them being so near; and their being the joint-heirs to such an enormous property! I know the people here take Caroline's part, and say that she has been hardly used. But I cannot say that I blame George; I cannot, indeed.'

'It is one of those cases in which no one should be blamed.'

'Exactly—that is just what I say. My advice to George was this. Don't let money influence your conduct in any way. Thank God, there's enough of that for all of us! What you have to think of is her happiness and your own. That's what I said; and I do believe he took my advice. I don't think he had any sordid views with reference to Caroline's fortune.'

'I am sure he had not.'

'Oh, no, never. What Sir Henry's views may be, I don't pretend to know. People here do say that he has been ingratiating himself with my brother for some time past. He has my leave, Miss Gauntlet. I am an old man, old enough to be your father'—the well-preserved old beau might have said grandfather—'and my experience of life is this, that money is never worth the trouble that men take to get it. They say my brother is fond of it; if so, I think he has made a mistake in life—a great mistake.'

All this sounded very nice, but even to Adela's inexperienced ears it was not like the ring of genuine silver. After all, mock virtue imposes on but few people. The man of the world is personally known for such; as also are known the cruel, the griping, the avaricious, the unjust. That which enables the avaricious and the unjust to pass scatheless through the world is not the ignorance of the world as to their sins, but the indifference of the world whether they be sinful or no.

'And now, Sir Lionel, you may just put us into the fly, and then we won't keep you any longer,' said Miss Todd, as she re-entered the room with her bonnet and shawl.

Mrs Leake, who lived at Rissbury, was a deaf old lady, not very popular among other old ladies at Littlebath. All the world, of course, knows that the village of Rissbury is hardly more than a suburb of Littlebath, being distant from the High Street not above a mile and a half. It will be remembered that the second milestone on Hinchcombe Road is altogether beyond the village, just as you begin to ascend the hill near the turnpike.

Mrs Leake was not very popular, seeing that though her ear was excessively dull, her tongue was peculiarly acute. She had the repute of saying the most biting things of any lady in Littlebath—and many of the ladies of Littlebath were apt to say biting things. Then Mrs Leake did not play cards, nor did she give suppers, nor add much in any way to the happiness of the other ladies, her compatriots. But she lived in rather a grand house of her own, whereas others lived in lodgings; she kept a carriage with a pair of horses, whereas others kept flies; and she had some mysterious acquaintance with the county-ocracy which went a long way with the ladies of Littlebath: though what good it ever did to Mrs Leake herself was never very apparent.

It is a terrible bore to have to talk to people who use speaking-trumpets, and who are so fidgety themselves that they won't use their speaking-trumpets properly. Miss Todd greatly dreaded the speaking-trumpet; she did not usually care one straw for Mrs Leake's tongue, nor much for her carriage and horses, or county standing; but the Littlebath world called on Mrs Leake; and Miss Todd being at Rome did as Romans do.

'I'll take her for five minutes,' said Miss Todd, as driving through the village of Rissbury, she finished her description of the lady; 'and then do you take her up for five more; and then I'll go on again; and then we'll go away.' Adela agreed, though with a heavy heart; for what subject of conversation could she find on which to dilate to Mrs Leake through a speaking-trumpet for five minutes?

'Miss who?' said Mrs Leake, putting her trumpet down from her ear that she might stare the better at Adela. 'Oh, Miss Gaunt—very well—I hope you'll like Littlebath, Miss Gaunt.'

'Miss Gaunt-let!' shouted Miss Todd, with a voice that would have broken the trumpet into shivers had it not been made of the very best metal.

'Never hollo, my dear. When you do that I can't hear at all. It only makes a noise like a dog barking. You'll find the young men about Littlebath very good-natured, Miss Gaunt. They are rather empty-headed—but I think young ladies generally like them all the better for that.'

Adela felt herself called on to make no answer to this, as it was not her turn at the trumpet.

'What news have you heard lately, Mrs Leake?' asked Miss Todd. The great thing was to make Mrs Leake talk instead of having to talk to her.

'Amuse! No, I don't think they do amuse any one very much. But then that's not their line. I suppose they can dance, most of them; and those who've got any money may do for husbands—as the world goes. We mustn't be too particular; must we, Miss Gaunt?'

'Miss Gaunt—let,' whispered Miss Todd into the trumpet, separating the sounds well, so that they should not clash on the unsusceptible tympanum of her friend's ear.

'Let, let, let! I think I can hear anybody almost better than I can you, Miss Todd. I don't know how it is, but I never can hear the people out of the town as well as I can my own set. It's habit, I take it.'

'They're used to deaf people in the country, I suppose,' said Miss Todd, who, with all her good-nature, didn't choose to be over much put upon.

'Ah, I can't hear you,' said Mrs Leake. She had, however, heard this. 'But I want you to tell me something about this Caroline Waddington. Isn't it true she's got another lover already?'

'Oh, quite true; she's going to be married.'

'Wants to be married. Yes, I don't doubt she wants to be married. That's what they all want, only some are not able to manage it. Ha! ha! ha! I beg your pardon, Miss Gaunt; but we old women must have our joke about the young ones; mustn't we, Miss Todd?' Mrs Leake, be it noticed, was past seventy, whereas our dear Miss Todd was only just forty-four.

'Miss Gauntlet can tell you all about Miss Waddington,' said Miss Todd, in her very plainest voice. 'They are very great friends, and correspond with each other.' So Miss Todd handed over the spout of the trumpet.

'She was corresponding with another! I dare say she was; with half a dozen at once. Do you know anything about it, Miss Gaunt?'

Poor Adela! what was she to say or do? Her hand absolutely trembled as she put it lightly to the instrument. Thrice she bent her head down before she was able to say anything, and thrice she lifted it up in despair.

'Is it the lady or the gentleman that is a friend of yours, my dear? or which of the gentlemen? I hope she has not robbed you of a beau.'

'Miss Waddington is a very dear friend of mine, ma'am.'

'Oh; she is, is she?'

'And I know Mr Bertram also.'

'Is he a dear friend too? Well, I suppose he's disengaged now. But they tell me he's got nothing, eh?'

'I really don't know.'

'It's very hard to know; very. I don't much admire such jilts myself, but—'

'Miss Waddington did not jilt him, madam.'

'Then he jilted her. That's just what I want to come at. I'm very much obliged to you, my dear. I see you can tell me all about it. It was about money, wasn't it?'

'No,' shouted Adela, with an energy that quite surprised herself. 'Money had nothing to do with it.'

'I did not say you had anything to do with it. But don't take up that habit of holloing from Miss Todd. I suppose the truth was that he found out what he wasn't meant to find out. Men shouldn't be too inquisitive; should they, Miss Todd? You are quite right, Miss Gaunt, don't have anything to do with it; it's a bad affair.'

'I think you are very much mistaken, madam,' said Adela, again shouting. But it was all thrown away. 'I can't hear a word when you hollo in that way, not a word,' said Mrs Leake. And then Adela, with an imploring look at Miss Todd, relinquished her seat.

Miss Todd rose with the usual little speech about leave-taking. She had, as we have seen, intended to have gone in for a second innings herself, but all hope of winning the game against Mrs Leake was over; even her courage was nearly upset; so making a little whisper to Adela, she held out her hand to the old lady, and prepared to depart.

'Dear me, you are in a great hurry to go,' said Mrs Leake.

'Yes; we are rather in a hurry this morning,' said Miss Todd, neglectful of the trumpet, 'we have so many people to see.'

'Well, good-bye; I'm very much obliged to you for coming, and Miss Todd'—and here Mrs Leake affected to whisper; but her whisper would have been audible to a dozen, had a dozen been there—'I mustn't forget to wish you joy about Sir Lionel. Good morning to you, Miss Gaunt,' and then Mrs Leake dropt an old-fashioned gracious curtsy.

To say that Miss Todd blushed would be to belie the general rosiness of that lady's complexion. She was all blush always. Over her face colour of the highest was always flying. It was not only that her cheeks carried a settled brilliant tint, but at every smile—and Miss Todd was ever smiling—this tint would suffuse her forehead and her neck; at every peal of laughter—and her peals of laughter were innumerable—it would become brighter and brighter, coming and going, or rather ever coming fresh and never going, till the reflection from her countenance would illumine the whole room, and light up the faces of all around her. But now she almost blushed black. She had delighted hitherto in all the little bits of libellous tittle-tattle to which her position as a young old maid had given rise, and had affected always to assist their propagation; but there was a poison about this old female snake, a sting in the tongue of this old adder, which reached even her.

'The old fool!' said Miss Todd, by no means *sotto voce*.

Mrs Leake heard her though the speaking-trumpet was not in action. 'No, no, no,' she said, in her most good-natured voice, 'I don't think he's such a fool at all. Of course he is old, and in want of an income, no doubt. But then he's a knight you know, my dear, and a colonel;' and then the two ladies, waiting for no further courtesies, went back to their fly.

Miss Todd had quite regained her good-humour by the time she was seated. 'Well,' said she, 'what do you think of my friend, Mrs Leake?'

'What makes her so very spiteful?' asked Adela.

'Why, you see, my dear, she'd be nothing if she wasn't spiteful. It's her fate. She's very old, and she lives there by herself, and she doesn't go out much, and she has nothing to amuse her. If she didn't do that, she couldn't do anything. I rather like it myself.'

'Well, I can't say I like it,' said Adela; and then they sat silent for a time, Miss Todd the while reflecting whether she would, in any way, defend herself from that imputation about Sir Lionel.

'But you see what sort of a woman she is, Miss Gauntlet; and, of course, you must not believe a word that she says.'

'How very dreadful!'

'Oh; it does not mean anything. I call all those white lies. Nobody notices them. But what she said about Sir Lionel, you know—'

'I really shall not think of anything she said.'

'But I must explain to you,' said Miss Todd, in whose mind, in spite of her blushing, a certain amount of pleasure was mixed with the displeasure which Mrs Leake's scandal had caused her. For at this moment Sir Lionel was not a little thought of at Littlebath, and among the Lucretias* there assembled, there was many a one who would have felt but small regret in abandoning her maiden meditations at the instance of Sir Lionel Bertram.

'But I must explain to you. Sir Lionel does come to see me very often; and I should think there was something in it—or, rather, I shouldn't be surprised at others thinking so—only that I am quite sure that he's thinking of somebody else.'

'Is he?' asked Adela, perhaps not with a great deal of animation.

'Yes; and I'll tell you who that somebody else is. Mind, I shouldn't say anything about it if I wasn't sure; that is, almost sure; for one never can be quite sure about anything.'

'Then I don't think one ought to talk about people.'

'Oh, that's all very well. But then, at such a place as Littlebath, one would have to hold one's tongue altogether. I let people talk of me, and so I talk about them. One can't live without it, my dear. But I don't say things like Mrs Leake.'

'I'm sure you don't.'

'But now about Sir Lionel; can't you guess who it is?'

'How should I, Miss Todd? I don't know a person in Littlebath except you and Miss Baker.'

'There; now you have guessed it; I knew you would. Don't say I told you.'

'Miss Baker marry Sir Lionel!'

'Yes, Miss Baker marry Sir Lionel! and why not? Why shouldn't she? and why shouldn't he? I think it would be very wise. I think those sort of marriages often make people very happy.'

'Do you think he loves her?' said Adela, whose ideas of marriage were of a very primitive description.

'Well, I don't see why he shouldn't; that is, in a sort of a way. He won't write poetry about her eyebrows, if you mean that. But I think he'd like her to keep his house for him; and now that Caroline is going away, I think she'd like to have some one to live with. She's not born to be a solitary wild beast as I am.'

Adela was surprised, but she had nothing to say. She was aware of no reason which it suited her to allege why Miss Baker should not marry Sir Lionel Bertram. Had she been asked before, she would have said that Miss Baker seemed settled in her maiden life; and that she was but little likely to be moved by the civil speeches of an old military beau. But silence was perhaps the more prudent, and, therefore, she said nothing.

Her fortnight with Miss Todd passed without much inconvenience to her. She had to sit out one or two card-parties; and to resist, at last with peremptory decision, her host's attempts to take her elsewhere. But Miss Todd was so truly kind, so generous, so fond of making others happy, that she won upon Adela at last, and they parted excellent friends.

'I am so fond of Miss Baker,' Miss Todd said, on the last morning; 'and I do so truly hope she'll be happy; but don't you say a word about what I was saying. Only you watch if it isn't true. You'll see quite as much of Sir Lionel there as you have here:' and so they parted, and Adela was transferred over to Montpellier Terrace.

There had been some probability that Caroline would return to Littlebath with her aunt; but such was not the case. The autumn was advancing to its close. It was now November, and hardly a month remained before that—may we say happy day?—on which Miss Waddington was to become Lady Harcourt. There was, as Miss Baker said, so much to do, and so little time to do it! It had therefore been decided that Caroline should not return to Littlebath.

'And you have come back only on my account?' said Adela.

'Not at all; I should have come back any way, for many reasons. I like to see Mr Bertram from time to time, especially now that he has acknowledged Caroline; but it would kill me to stay long at that house. Did you see much of Sir Lionel while you were at Miss Todd's?'

'Yes, a good deal,' said Adela, who could hardly keep from smiling as she answered the question.

'He is always there, I believe. My idea is, that they mean to make a match of it. It is, indeed.'

'Oh, no; I don't think that.'

'Don't you now? Well, you have been in the house, and must have seen a great deal. But what else can bring him there so much?'

'Miss Todd says he's always talking about you.'

'About me; what nonsense!' And Miss Baker went up to her room rather better pleased than she had been.

Caroline, as will be remembered, had written to Adela with the tidings of her new engagement. Adela had answered that letter affectionately, but shortly; wishing her friend every happiness, and saying what little in the cheerful vein she could allow herself to say on such an occasion. The very shortness of her letter had conveyed condemnation, but that Adela could not help.

Caroline had expected condemnation. She knew that she would be condemned, either by words or by the lack of them; it was nearly equal to her by which. Her mind was in that state, that having half condemned herself, she would have given anything for a cordial acquittal from one she loved and valued. But she did not expect it from Adela, and she did not receive it.

She carried herself with a brave face, however. To her grandfather, to Miss Baker, and to her betrothed, she showed no sign of sorrow, no sign of repentance; but though there was, perhaps, no repentance in her heart, there was much sorrow and much remorse, and she could not keep herself wholly silent.

She wrote again to Adela, almost imploring her for pity. We need not give the whole letter, but a portion of it will show how the poor girl's mind was at work. 'I know you have judged me, and found me guilty,' she said. 'I can tell that from the tone of your letter, though you were generous enough to endeavour to deceive me. But you have condemned me because you do not know me. I feel sure that what I am doing is prudent, and, I think I may say, right. Had I refused Sir Henry's offer, or some other such offer—and any offer to me would have been, and must have been open to the same objections—what should I have done? what would have been my career? I am not now speaking of happiness. But of what use could I have been to any one?

'You will say that I do not love Sir Henry. I have told him that in the usual acceptation of the word, I do not love him. But I esteem his high qualities; and I shall marry him with the full intention of doing my duty, of sacrificing myself to him if needs be, of being useful in the position in which he will place me. What better can I do than this? You can do better, Adela. I know you will do better. To have loved, and married for love the poorest gentleman on God's earth would be to have done better. But I cannot do that now. The power of doing that has been taken from me. The question with me was, whether I should be useful as a wife, or useless as an unmarried woman? For useless I should have been, and petulant, and wretched. Employment, work, duty, will now save me from that. Dear Adela, try to look at it in this way if it be possible. Do not throw me over without an attempt. Do not be unmerciful. * * * At any rate,' she ended her letter by saying—'At any rate you will come to me in London in the early, early spring. Say that you will do so, or I shall think that you mean to abandon me altogether!'

Adela answered this as sweetly and as delicately as she could. Natures, she said, were different, and it would be presumptuous in her to set herself up as judge on her friend's conduct. She would abstain from doing so, and would pray to God that Caroline and Sir Henry might be happy together. And as to going to London in the spring, she would do so if her aunt Penelope's plans would allow of it. She must of course be governed by her aunt Penelope, who was now hurrying home from Italy on purpose to give her a home.

Nothing further occurred this year at Littlebath sufficiently memorable to need relation, unless it be necessary further to relate Miss Baker's nervous apprehensions respecting Sir Lionel. She was, in truth, so innocent that she would have revealed every day to her young friend the inmost secrets of her heart, if she had had secrets. But, in truth, she had none. She was desperately jealous of Miss Todd, but she herself knew not why. She asked all manner of questions as to his going and coming, but she never asked herself why she was so anxious about it. She was in a twitter of sentimental restlessness, but she did not understand the cause of her own uneasiness. On the days that Sir Lionel came to her, she was happy, and in good spirits; when, however, he went to Miss Todd, she was fretful. Sometimes she would rally him on his admiration for her rival, but she did it with a bad grace. Wit, repartee, and sarcasm were by no means her forte. She could not have stood up for five minutes against deaf old Mrs Leake; and when she tried her hand on Sir Lionel, her failure was piteous. It merely amounted to a gentle rebuke to him for going to the Paragon instead of coming to Montpellier Terrace. Adela saw it all, and saw also that Sir Lionel was in no way sincere. But what could she do, or what could she say?

'I hope Miss Todd was quite well yesterday, Sir Lionel?' Miss Baker would say.

'I don't think there was much the matter with her,' Sir Lionel would answer. 'She was talking a great deal about you while I was with her.'

'About me; he! he! he! I'm sure you had something better than me to talk of.'

'There could be nothing better,' the gallant colonel would say.

'Oh, couldn't there? and when is it to be? Adela here is most anxious to know.'

'How can you say so, Miss Baker? You know I am not anxious at all.'

'Well, if you're not, I am. I hope we shall be asked—ha! ha! ha!'

And why did not Sir Lionel make up his mind and put an end, in one way or the other, to the torment of this poor lady? Many reasons guided him in his high policy. In the first place, he could not make himself certain whether Miss Todd would accept him or refuse him. Her money was by far the safer; her fortune was assured; what she possessed, Sir Lionel already knew to a fraction.

But Miss Baker, he was sure, would accept him; and having accepted him, would be amenable to all his little reasons in life, obedient, conformable, and, in money matters, manageable. Miss Todd, on the other hand, might, nay, certainly would have a will of her own. He would sooner have taken Miss Baker with half the money.

But then would Miss Baker have half the money? If that stupid old man at Hadley would only go, and tell the only tale with which it was now possible that he should interest the world, then Sir Lionel would know how to act. At any rate, he would wait till after the solicitor-general's marriage. It might appear on that occasion whether or no Sir Henry was to be regarded as the old man's heir in all things. If so, Sir Lionel would be prepared to run all matrimonial risks, and present Miss Todd to the world as Lady Bertram.

CHAPTER XXX

MARRIAGE-BELLS

AND now came the day of execution. 'A long day, my lord, a long day,' screams the unfortunate culprit from the dock when about to undergo the heaviest sentence of the law. But the convicted wretch is a coward by his profession. Caroline Waddington was no coward. Having made up her mind to a long martyrdom, she would not condescend to ask for one short month of grace.

'I don't like to press you unfairly,' Sir Henry had said, 'but you know how I am situated with regard to business.'

'It shall be as you wish,' Caroline had said. And so the day had been settled; a day hardly more than six months distant from that on which she had half permitted the last embrace from her now forfeited, but not forgotten lover.

Duty was now her watchword to herself. For the last six weeks she had been employed—nay, more than employed—hard at work—doing the best she could for her future husband's happiness and welfare. She had given orders with as much composure as a woman might do who had been the mistress of her lord's purse and bosom for the last six years. Tradesmen, conscious of the coming event, had had their little delicacies and made their little hints. But she had thrown all these to the wind. She had spoken of Sir Henry as Sir Henry, and of herself as being now Miss Waddington, but soon about to be Lady Harcourt, with a studied openness. She had looked to carriages and broughams—and horses also under Sir Henry's protection—as though these things were dear to her soul. But they were not dear, though in her heart she tried to teach herself that they were so. For many a long year—many at least in her still scanty list of years—she had been telling herself that these things were dear; that these were the prizes for which men strive and women too; that the wise and prudent gained them; and that she too would be wise and prudent, that she too would gain them. She had gained them; and before she had essayed to enjoy them, they turned into dust before her eyes, into ashes between her teeth.

Gilding and tinsel were no longer bright to her, silks and velvet were no longer soft. The splendour of her drawing-room, the richness of her draperies, the luxurious comfort of the chamber that was prepared for her, gave her no delight. She acquiesced in these things because her lord desired that they should be there, and she intended that her lord should be among the rich ones of the earth. But not for one moment did she feel that trumpery joy which comes from an elated spirit.

Her lord! there was the misery; there was the great rock against which she feared that the timbers of her bark would go in pieces. If she could only have the three first years done and over. If she could only jump at once to that time in which habit would have made her fate endurable! Her lord! Who was her lord truly? Had she not in her heart another lord, whom her whole soul would worship, despite her body's efforts?

And then she began to fear for her beauty; not for her own sake; not with that sort of sorrow which must attend the waning roses of those ladies who, in early years, have trusted too much to their loveliness. No; it was for the sake of him to whom she had sold her beauty. She would fain perform her part of that bargain. She would fain give him on his marriage-day all that had been intended in his purchase. If, having accepted him, she allowed herself to pine and fade away because she was to be his, would she not in fact be robbing him? Would not that be unjust? All that she could give him he should have.

But neither did Sir Henry see any change, nor did Mr Bertram, nor those others who were round her. Indeed, hers was not a beauty that would fade in such manner. When she saw her own eyes heavy with suppressed wretchedness, she feared for herself. But her power over herself was great, and that look was gone as soon as others were with her.

But her worst sufferings were at night. She would wake from her short slumbers, and see him, him always before her; that him who in the essence of things was still her lord, the master of her woman's mind, the lord of her woman's soul. To screen her eyes from that sight, she would turn her moistened face to the pillow; but her eyeballs would flash in the darkness, and she would still see him there, there before her. She would see him as he stood beside her with manly bashfulness, when on the side of Olivet he first told her that he loved her. She would see him as he had sometimes sat in his sweetest moods, in that drawing-room at Littlebath, talking to her with rapid utterance, with sweet but energetic utterance, saying words which she did not always fully understand, but which she felt to be full of wit, full of learning, full of truth. Ah, how proud she had been of him then—so proud of him, though she would never say so! And then she would see him, as he came to her on that fatal day, boiling in his wrath, speaking such words as had never before reached her ears; words, however, of which so many had been tinged by an inexpressible tenderness.

Then she would turn herself in her bed, and, by a strong effort of her will, she would for awhile throw off such thoughts. She would count over to herself the chairs and tables she had ordered, the cups and china bowls which were to decorate her room, till sleep would come again—but in sleep she would still dream of him. Ah, that there might have been no waking from such dreams!

But in the morning she would come down to breakfast with no trouble on her outward brow. She was minutely particular in her dress, even when no one but her grandfather was to see the effects of her toilet. Her hair was scrupulously neat, her dresses were rich and in the newest fashion. Her future career was to be that of Lady Harcourt, a leader of ton; and she was determined to commence her new duties with a good grace.

And so from week to week, and day to day, she prepared herself for the sacrifice.

Miss Baker of course returned to Hadley a day or two before the ceremony. The recent death of old Mr Gauntlet was Adela's excuse for not being present. Had there been no such excuse, she would have been forced to act a bridesmaid's part. It was much better for both of them that she had not to perform the task.

Bridesmaids were chosen in London—eight of them. These were not special friends of Caroline's; indeed, it had not been her instinct to attach to herself special friends. Circumstances had created friendship between her and Adela, unlike in all things as they were to each other. But other bosom-friends Caroline had not; nor had she felt the want of them.

This was perhaps well for her now. It would have driven her to madness if among the bevy of attendant nymphs there had been any to whom it would have been necessary for her to open her heart—to open it, or to pretend to open it. Much she could do; much sne was now doing; much she was prepared to do. But she could not have spoken with missish rapture of her coming happiness; nor could she, to any ears, have laid bare the secrets of her bosom.

So eight young ladies were had from London. Two were second-cousins by her father's side; one, who was very full of the universal joy that was to follow this happy event, was a sister of Sir Henry's; a fourth was the daughter of an old crony of Miss Baker's; and the other four were got to order—there being no doubt a repertory for articles so useful and so ornamental.

Old Mr Bertram behaved well on the occasion. He told Miss Baker that nothing was to be spared—in moderation; and he left her to be sole judge of what moderation meant. She, poor woman, knew well enough that she would have at some future day to fight over with him the battle of the bills. But for the moment he affected generosity, and so a fitting breakfast was prepared.

And then the bells were rung, the Hadley bells, the merry marriage-bells.

I know full well the tone with which they toll when the soul is ushered to its last long rest. I have stood in that green churchyard when earth has been laid to earth, ashes to ashes, dust to dust—the ashes and the dust that were loved so well.

But now the scene was of another sort. How merrily they rang, those joyous marriage-bells! Youth was now to know the full delight of matured happiness. Soul should be joined to soul, heart to heart, hand to hand, manly strength and vigour to all the grace and beauty of womanhood. The world was pleasant with its most joyous smile as it opened its embraces to the young pair—about to be two no longer—now to become one bone and one flesh. Out rung the Hadley bells, the happy marriage-bells.

And when should bells ring so joyously? Do they not give promise of all that this world knows of happiness? What is love, sweet pure love, but the anticipation of this, the natural longing for this, the consummation of our loving here? To neither man nor woman does the world fairly begin till seated together in their first mutual home they bethink themselves that the excitement of their honeymoon is over. It would seem that the full meaning of the word marriage can never be known by those who, at their first outspring into life, are surrounded by all that money can give. It requires the single sitting-room, the single fire, the necessary little efforts of self-devotion, the inward declaration that some struggle shall be made for that other one, some world's struggle of which wealth can know nothing. One would almost wish to be poor, that one might work for one's wife; almost wish to be ill used, that one might fight for her.

He, as he goes forth to his labour, swears within his heart that, by God's help on his endeavours, all shall go well with her. And she, as she stands musing alone in her young home, with a soft happy tear in her bright eye, she also swears in her heart that, by God's help, his home shall be to him the sweetest spot on the earth's surface. Then should not marriage-bells ring joyously? Ah, my friends, do not count too exactly your three hundreds a year—your four hundreds. Try the world. But try it with industry and truth, not with idleness and falsehood.

And now Sir Henry and Lady Harcourt were to try the world in sweet communion together. One may say that, as to doubt about the trial, there was need of none. He had more than won his spurs. He was already a practised knight in the highest flight of the world's tourneys. And for her, too, there was little cause of fear. They who saw her arrayed in that bright frosty marriage morning, and watched the majesty of her brow, the brilliancy of her eye, the grace and dignity of her step, all swore that the young lawyer had done well. He had found for himself a meet companion for his high career; a proper bride for his coming greatness. And so the marriage-bells rang on, with all their merriness, with all their joy.

And now the words have been said, the vows have been plighted, the magic circlet of pure gold has done its wondrous work. The priest smiles and grasps their hands as he gives them his parting friendly blessing. Laughing bridesmaids press in to sign the book, and all observe that no signature was ever written with more decision than that of Caroline Waddington.

Caroline Waddington now no longer! Yes; the deed had, in truth, been done. The vows had been plighted. She had taken this man to be her wedded husband, to live together with him after God's ordinance. She had sworn to obey him, and serve him, and—Ah! ah! ah! How had she lived while that word was uttered to her! how had she lived to swear that falsest oath!

But it was not then, while standing at the altar, that the struggle had been made. Then she did but act her part, as some stage-queen acts hers. She acted it well; that was all. There was no meaning in her words then. Though her lips moved, she swore no oath. Her oath had been sworn before that.

No educated woman, we may suppose, stands at the altar as a bride, without having read and re-read those words till they are closely fixed on her memory. It is a great oath, and a woman should know well what that is to which she is about to pledge herself. Caroline Waddington had studied them well. She would live with him after God's ordinance; that is, as his wife. Yes, she was prepared for that. She would obey him.

Yes; if obedience were required, she would give it. Serve him? oh, yes, certainly; to the best of her power of mind and body. Love him? No; she was bold, at least, if not righteous. No; she could not love him. But, then, how few who were married complied with all those behests? How many were undutiful, disobedient, careless? Might she not except for herself one point? be false on one article if she were true in so many? She would honour him, for honour was possible to her; she would keep him in sickness and health, and forsaking all other—yes, all other, in body certainly, in heart too if God would give her ease—and keep herself only to him, her husband. And so she swore to it all before she went there—all, with the one exception.

And Sir Henry swore too—with a light, indifferent oath, which, however, he had no intention of breaking in any part. He would live with her, and love her, and comfort her, and all that sort of thing;—and very well she would look at the top of his table, in black velvet.

And the merry bells went on ringing as they trooped back to the old man's house. They went in gay carriages though the distance was but some hundred yards. But brides and bridegrooms cannot walk on their wedding-days in all their gala garments, though it be but a few hundred yards.

And then, as they entered the breakfast-room, the old man met them, and blessed them. He was too infirm to go to church, and had seen none of them before the ceremony; but now that the deed was done, he also was there, dressed in his best, his last new coat, not more than twelve years old, his dress waistcoat, sent home before the Reform Bill,* his newest shoes, which creaked twice worse than any of their older brethren. But when a man can shower thousands on a wedded pair, what do they, or even the bridesmaids, care about his clothes?

And then after this fashion he blessed them—not holding each a hand as he might otherwise have done; for his infirmities compelled him to use two crutches.

'I wish you joy, Sir Henry—of your bride—with all my heart. And a bonny bride she is, and well able to take her place in the world. Though you'll be rich and well to do, you'll not find her over-extravagant. And though her fortune's not much for a man like you, perhaps, she might have had less, mightn't she? ha! ha! ha! Little as it is, it will help—it will help. And you'll not find debts coming home after her; I'm sure of that. She'll keep your house well together; and your money too—but I guess you'll not leave that to her keeping.

'And I wish you joy with all my heart, my Lady Harcourt. You've done very well—much better doubtless than we were thinking of; you and me too. And as for me, I was an old fool.' Mr Bertram was doubtless thinking of that interview with his nephew. 'Much better, much better. Your husband's a rising man, and he'll live to be a rich man. I have always thought a lawyer's profession very good for a man who would know how to make money at it. Sir Henry knows how to do that well. So I wish you joy with all my heart, Lady Bertram—Harcourt I mean. And now we'll sit down and have a bit of something to eat.' Such was the marriage-blessing of this old man, who knew and understood the world so well. To be Lady Harcourt, and have the spending of three or four thousand a year! What a destiny was that for his granddaughter! And to have achieved that without any large call upon his own purse!

It was not intended that Sir Henry and his bride were to sit down to the breakfast. That is, I believe, now voted to be a bore—and always should have been so voted. They had done, or were now to do their necessary eating in private, and the company was to see no more of them. An effort had been made to explain this to Mr Bertram, but it had not been successful. So when Caroline kissed him, and bade him adieu after his little speech, he expressed himself surprised.

'What, off before the breakfast! What's the good of the breakfast then?' His idea, in his extravagance, had been that he would give a last feed to the solicitor-general. But he had another piece of extravagance in his mind, which he had been unable to bring himself to perpetrate till the last moment; but which now he did perpetrate.

'Sir Henry, Sir Henry,' and he toddled to a window. 'Here; you'll be spending a lot of money on her in foreign parts, and

I think you have behaved well; here,' and he slipped a piece of paper into his hands. 'But, remember, it will be the last. And, Sir Henry, remember the interest of the three thousand—punctually—eh, Sir Henry?'

Sir Henry nodded—thanked him—slipped the bit of paper into his pocket, and followed his bride to the carriage.

'Your grandfather has just given me five hundred pounds,' was his first word in private to his wife.

'Has he?' said Lady Harcourt; 'I'm very glad of it; very.' And so she was. What else had she to be glad of now, except hundreds—and hundreds—and hundreds of pounds?

And so they were whisked away to London, to Dover, to Paris, to Nice.

'Sed post equitem sedet atra cura.'*

The care was very black that sat behind that female knight. But we will not now follow either her thoughts or her carriage-wheels.

CHAPTER XXXI

SIR LIONEL GOES TO HIS WOOING

YES, they were off. All the joys of that honeymoon shall be left to the imagination of the reader. Their first conversation, as it took place in the carriage which bore them from Mr Bertram's door, has been given. Those which followed were probably more or less of the same nature. Sir Henry, no doubt, did strive to give some touch of romance to the occasion; but in no such attempt would his wife assist him. To every material proposition that he made, she gave a ready assent; in everything she acceded to his views; she would dine at two or at eight, as he pleased; she was ready to stay two weeks or only two days in Paris, as best suited him; she would adapt herself to pictures, or to architecture, or to theatres, or to society, or to going on and seeing nothing, exactly as he adapted himself. She never frowned, or looked black, or had headaches, or couldn't go on, or wouldn't stay still, or turned herself into a Niobean deluge,* as some ladies, and very nice ladies too, will sometimes do on their travels. But she would not talk of love, or hold his hand, or turn her cheek to his. She had made her bargain, and would keep to it. Of that which she had promised him, she would give him full measure; of that which she had not promised him—of which she had explained to him that she had nothing to give—of that she would make no attempt to give anything.

So they spent their Christmas and opened the new year at Nice, and made an excursion along the Cornice road to Genoa, during which Lady Harcourt learned for the first time that the people of Italy are not so free from cold winds as is generally imagined; and then, early in February, they returned to their house in Eaton Square. How she soon became immersed in society, and he in Parliament and the County Courts, we may also leave to the imagination of the reader. In a month or two from that time, when the rigours of a London May shall have commenced, we will return to them again. In the meantime, we must go back to Hadley—the two old Bertrams, and dear Miss Baker.

The marriage feast, prepared by Miss Baker for the wedding guests, did not occupy very long; nor was there any great inducement for those assembled to remain with Mr Bertram. He and Miss Baker soon found themselves again alone; and were no sooner alone than the business of life recommenced.

'It's a very splendid match for her,' said Mr Bertram.

'Yes, I suppose it is,' said Miss Baker. Miss Baker in her heart of hearts had never quite approved of the marriage.

'And now, Mary, what do you mean to do?'

'Oh, I'll see and get these things taken away,' said she.

'Yes, yes; stop a minute; that's of course. But what I mean is, what do you mean to do with yourself? you can't go back and live at Littlebath all alone?'

If I were to use the word 'flabbergasted' as expressing Miss Baker's immediate state of mind, I should draw down on myself the just anger of the critics, in that I had condescended to the use of slang; but what other word will so well express what is meant? She had fully intended to go back to Littlebath, and had intended to do so at the earliest moment that would be possible. Was not Sir Lionel still at Littlebath? And, moreover, she fully intended to live there. That she would have some little difficulty in the matter, she had anticipated. Her own income—that which was indefeasibly her own—was very small; by far too small to admit of her permanently keeping on those rooms in Montpellier Terrace. Hitherto their income, her own and Caroline's put together, had been very comfortable; for Mr Bertram had annually paid to her a sum which of itself would have been sufficient for her own living. But she had not known what difference Caroline's marriage might make in this allowance. It had been given to herself without any specification that it had been so given for any purpose; but yet it had been an understood thing that Caroline was to live with her and be supported. And though Caroline's income had also been used, it had gone rather in luxurious enjoyments than in necessary expenses; in the keep of a horse, for instance, in a journey to Jerusalem, in a new grand piano, and such like. Now there might naturally be a doubt whether under altered circumstances this allowance from Mr Bertram would remain unaltered.

But it had never occurred to her that she would be asked to live at Hadley. That idea did now occur to her, and therefore she stood before her uncle hesitating in her answer, and—may my inability to select any better word be taken in excuse?—'flabbergasted' in her mind and feelings.

But her doom followed quickly on her hesitation. 'Because,' said Mr Bertram, 'there is plenty of room here. There can be no need of two houses and two establishments now; you had better send for your things and fix yourself here at once.'

'But I couldn't leave the rooms at Littlebath without a quarter's notice;'— the coward's plea; a long day, my lord—a long day—'that was particularly understood when I got them so cheap.'

'There will be no difficulty in reletting them at this time of the year,' growled Mr Bertram.

'Oh, no, I suppose not; one would have to pay something,

of course. But, dear me! one can hardly leave the place where one has lived so long all of a moment.'

'Why not?' demanded the tyrant.

'Well, I don't know. I can hardly say why not; but one has so many people to see, and so many things to do, and so much to pack up.'

It may be easily conceived that in such an encounter Miss Baker would not achieve victory. She had neither spirit for the fight, nor power to use it even had the spirit been there; but she effected a compromise by the very dint of her own weakness. 'Yes, certainly,' she said. 'As Mr Bertram thought it best, she would be very happy to live with him at Hadley—most happy, of course; but mightn't she go down and pack up her things, and settle with everybody, and say good-bye to her friends?' Oh, those friends! that horrible Miss Todd!

And thus she got a month of grace. She was to go down immediately after Christmas-day, and be up again at Hadley, and fixed there permanently, before the end of January.

She wrote to Caroline on the subject, rather plaintively; but owning that it was of course her duty to stay by her uncle now that he was so infirm. It would be very dull, of course, she said; but any place would be dull now that she, Caroline, was gone. And it would be sad giving up her old friends. She named one or two, and among them Sir Lionel. 'It would be a great pleasure to me,' she went on to say, 'if I could be the means of reconciling the two brothers—not but what Sir Henry Harcourt will always be Mr Bertram's favourite; I am sure of that. I don't think I shall mind leaving Miss Todd, though she does pretend to be so friendly; I was never quite sure she was sincere; and then she does talk so very loud; and, in spite of all she says, I am not sure she's not looking out for a husband.'

And then she went back to Littlebath, intent on enjoying her short reprieve. Something might happen; she did not ask herself what. The old gentleman might not last long; but she certainly did not speculate on his death. Or;—she had a sort of an idea that there might be an 'or,' though she never allowed herself to dwell on it as a reality. But on one point she did make up her mind, that if it should be her destiny to keep house for either of those two gentlemen, she would much rather keep house for Sir Lionel than for his brother.

Her absolute money-dealings had always been with Mr Pritchett; and as she passed through town, Mr Pritchett came to her and made her the usual quarterly payment.

'But, Mr Pritchett,' said she, 'I am going to live with Mr Bertram after another month or so.'

'Oh, ma'am; yes, ma'am; that will be very proper, ma'am. I always supposed it would be so when Miss Caroline was gone,' said Pritchett, in a melancholy tone.

'But will it be proper for me to have this money now?'

'Oh, yes, ma'am. It wouldn't be my duty to stop any payments till I get orders. Mr Bertram never forgets anything, ma'am. If he'd meant me to stop it, he wouldn't have forgot to say so.'

'Oh, very well, Mr Pritchett;' and Miss Baker was going away.

'But, one word, if you please, ma'am. I don't detain you, ma'am, do I?' and you might have guessed by Pritchett's voice that he was quite willing to let her go if she wished, even though his own death on the spot might be the instant result.

'Oh dear, no, Mr Pritchett,' said Miss Baker.

'We all see how things have gone, ma'am, now;—about Miss Caroline, I mean.'

'Yes, she is Lady Harcourt now.'

'Oh, yes, I know that, ma'am,' and Mr Pritchett here sank to the lowest bathos of misery. 'I know she's Lady Harcourt very well. I didn't mean her ladyship any disrespect.'

'Oh dear, no, of course not, Mr Pritchett. Who would think such a thing of you, who's known her from a baby?'

'Yes, I have know'd her from a babby, ma'am. That's just it; and I've know'd you from a'most a babby too, ma'am.'

'That was a very long time ago, Mr Pritchett.'

'Yes, it is some years now, certainly, Miss Baker. I'm not so young as I was; I know that.' Mr Pritchett's voice at this juncture would have softened the heart of any stone that had one. 'But this is what it is, ma'am; you're going to live with the old gentleman now.'

'Yes, I believe I am.'

'Well, now; about Mr George, ma'am.'

'Mr George!'

'Yes, Mr George, Miss Baker. It ain't of course for me to say anything of what goes on between young ladies and young gentlemen. I don't know anything about it, and never did; and I don't suppose I never shall now. But they two was to have been one, and now they're two.' Mr Pritchett could not get on any further without pausing for breath.

'The match was broken off, you know.'

'It was broke off. I say nothing about that, nor about them who did it. I know nothing, and therefore I say nothing; but this I do say: that it will be very hard—very hard, and very cruel if so that the old gentleman is set against Mr George because Sir Henry Harcourt has got a handle to his name for himself.'

The conference ended in a promise on Miss Baker's part that she, at least, would say nothing against Mr George; but with an assurance, also, that it was impossible for her to say anything in his favour.

'You may be sure of this, Mr Pritchett, that my uncle will never consult me about his money.'

'He'll never consult any human being, ma'am. He wouldn't consult Solomon if Solomon were to go to Hadley o' purpose. But you might slip in a word that Mr George was not in fault; mightn't you, ma'am?'

Miss Baker reiterated her promise that she would not at any rate say anything evil of George Bertram.

'He is such a foolish young man, ma'am; so like a baby about money. It's that's why I feel for him, because he is so foolish.'

And then Miss Baker prosecuted her journey, and reached Littlebath in safety.

She had not been long there before Sir Lionel had heard all the news. Miss Baker, without knowing that a process of pumping had been applied to her, soon made him understand that for the present Sir Henry had certainly not been received into the place of heir. It was clear that but a very moderate amount of the old gentleman's wealth—he was usually now called the old gentleman by them all; Sir Lionel, Miss Baker,

Mr Pritchett, and others—had been bestowed on the rising lawyer; and that, as far as that point was concerned, the game was still open. But then, if it was open to him, Sir Lionel, through Miss Baker, it was also open to his son George. And it appeared from Miss Baker's testimony that, during the whole period of these wedding doings, no word had escaped the mouth of the old gentleman in vituperation or anger against George. Perhaps George after all might be the best card. Oh, what an excellent card might he be if he would only consent to guide himself by the commonest rules of decent prudence! But then, as Mr Pritchett had truly observed, Mr George was so foolish! Moreover, Sir Lionel was not blind to the reflection that the old gentleman would never countenance his marriage with Miss Baker. Whatever Mr Bertram's good intentions Miss Baker-wards might be, they would undoubtedly be frustrated by such a marriage. If Sir Lionel decided on Miss Baker, things must be so arranged that the marriage should be postponed till that tedious old gentleman should move himself off the scene; and the tedious old gentleman, moreover, must not be allowed to know anything about it.

But with Miss Todd there need be no secrecy, no drawback, no delay—no drawback but that of doubtful reception; and after reception, of doubtful masterdom.

On thorough review of all the circumstances, much balancing them in his high mind, Sir Lionel at last thus resolved. He would throw himself, his heart, and his fortune at the feet of Miss Todd. If there accepted, he would struggle with every muscle of the manhood which was yet within him for that supremacy in purse and power which of law and of right* belongs to the man. He thought he knew himself, and that it would not be easy for a woman to get the better of him. But if there rejected—and he could not confess but what there was a doubt—he would immediately fall back upon Miss Baker. Whatever he did must be done immediately, for in less than a month's time Miss Baker would be out of his reach altogether. As to seeking Miss Baker at Hadley, that would be above even his courage. All must be done within the next month. If on Miss Baker was to fall the honour of being Lady Bertram, she must not only receive him within the month, but, having done so, must also agree to wear her vestal zone* yet a little longer, till that troublesome old gentleman should have departed.

Such being his month's work—he had not quite four weeks left when he came to this resolution—he wisely resolved to commence it at once.

So on one Monday morning he sallied out to the Paragon about two o'clock. At that hour he knew Miss Todd would be surely at home; for at half past one she ate her lunch. In the regularity of her eatings and her drinkings, Miss Todd might have been taken as an example by all the ladies of Littlebath. Sir Lionel's personal appearance has been already described. Considering his age, he was very well preserved. He was still straight; did not fumble much in his walk; and had that decent look of military decorum which, since the days of Cæsar and the duke,* has been always held to accompany a hook-nose. He had considered much about his toilet; indeed, he did that habitually; but on this occasion he had come to the conclusion that he had better make no unusual sacrifice to the Graces.* A touch of the curling-iron to his whiskers, or a surtout* that should be absolutely fresh from the tailor's hands, might have an effect with Miss Baker; but if any impression was to be made on Miss Todd, it would not be done by curled whiskers or a new coat. She must be won, if won at all, by the unsophisticated man.

So the unsophisticated man knocked at the door in the Paragon. Yes; Miss Todd was at home. Up he went, and found not only Miss Todd, but also with Miss Todd the venerable Mrs Shortpointz, settling all the details for a coming rubber of whist for that evening.

'Ah, Sir Lionel; how do? Sit down. Very well, my dear,'—Miss Todd called everybody my dear, even Sir Lionel himself sometimes; but on the present occasion she was addressing Mrs Shortpointz—'I'll be there at eight; but mind this, I won't sit down with Lady Ruth, nor yet with Miss Ruff.' So spoke Miss Todd, who, by dint of her suppers and voice, was becoming rather autocratic at Littlebath.

'You shan't, Miss Todd. Lady Ruth—'

'Very well; that's all I bargain for. And now here's Sir Lionel; how lucky! Sir Lionel, you can be so civil, and so useful. Do give Mrs Shortpointz your arm home. Her niece was to call; but there's been some mistake. And Mrs Shortpointz does not like walking alone. Come, Sir Lionel.'

Sir Lionel strove against the order; but it was in vain. He had to yield; and walked away with old Mrs Shortpointz on his arm. It was hard, we must acknowledge, that a man of Sir Lionel's age and standing should be so employed at such a moment, because that flirt, Maria Shortpointz, had gone out to see young Mr Garded ride by in his pink coat and spattered boots. He would have let her fall, and break her leg, only that by doing so he would have prolonged the time of his own attendance on her. She lived half across Littlebath; and her step, ordinarily slow, was slower than usual now that she was leaning on a knight's arm. At last she was deposited at home; and the gallant colonel, having scornfully repudiated her offer of cake and sherry, flew back to the Paragon on the wings of love—in a street cab, for which he had to pay eighteenpence.

But he was all too late. Miss Todd had gone out in her fly just three minutes since; and thus a whole day was lost.

On the Tuesday, in proper course, he was due at Miss Baker's. But for this turn, Miss Baker must be neglected. At the same hour he again knocked at the door of the Paragon, and was again admitted, and now Miss Todd was all alone. She was rarely left so very long, and the precious moments must be seized at once. Sir Lionel, with that military genius which was so peculiarly his own, determined to use his yesterday's defeat in aid of today's victory. He would make even Mrs Shortpointz serviceable.

When gentlemen past sixty make love to ladies past forty, it may be supposed that they are not so dilatory in their proceedings as younger swains and younger maidens. Time is then behind them, not before them; and urges them on to quick decisions. It may be presumed, moreover, that this pair knew their own minds.

'How cruel you were to me yesterday!' said Sir Lionel, seating himself not very close to her—nor yet very far from her.

'What! about poor Mrs Shortpointz? Ha! ha! ha! Poor old lady; she didn't think so, I am sure. One ought to be of use sometimes, you know, Sir Lionel.'

'True, true, Miss Todd; quite true. But I was particularly unfortunate yesterday. I wished that Mrs Shortpointz was hanging—anywhere except on my arm. I did, indeed.'

'Ha! ha! ha! Poor Mrs Shortpointz! And she was so full of you last night. The beau ideal of manly beauty! that was what she called you. She did indeed. Ha! ha! ha!'

'She was very kind.'

'And then we all quizzed her about you; and Miss Finesse called her Lady Bertram. You can't think how funny we old women are when we get together. There wasn't a gentleman in the room—except Mr Fuzzybell; and he never seems to make any difference. But I tell you what, Sir Lionel; a certain friend of yours didn't seem to like it when we called Mrs Shortpointz Lady Bertram.'

'And were you that friend, Miss Todd?'

'I! Ha! ha! ha! No; not I, but Miss Baker. And I'll tell you what, Sir Lionel,' said Miss Todd, intending to do a kinder act for Miss Baker than Miss Baker would have done for her. 'And I'll tell you what; Miss Baker is the nicest-looking woman of her time of life in Littlebath. I don't care who the other is. I never saw her look better than she did last night; never.' This was good-natured on the part of Miss Todd; but it sounded in Sir Lionel's ears as though it did not augur well for his hopes.

'Yes; she's very nice; very nice indeed. But I know one, Miss Todd, that's much nicer.' And Sir Lionel drew his chair a little nearer.

'What, Mrs Shortpointz, I suppose. Ha! ha! ha! Well, every man to his taste.'

'I wonder whether I may speak to you seriously, Miss Todd, for five minutes?'

'Oh laws, yes; why not? But don't tell me any secrets, Sir Lionel; for I shan't keep them.'

'I hope what I may say need not be kept a secret long. You

joke with me about Miss Baker; but you cannot really believe that my affections are placed there? You must, I think, have guessed by this time—'

'I am the worst hand in the world at guessing anything.'

'I am not a young man, Miss Todd—'

'No; and she isn't a young woman. She's fifty. It would all be very proper in that respect.'

'I'm not thinking of Miss Baker, Miss Todd.'

'Dear! well now, I really thought you were thinking of her. And I'll tell you this, Sir Lionel; if you want a wife to look after you, you couldn't do better than think of her—a nice, good-tempered, cheerful, easy, good-looking woman; with none of the Littlebathian nastiness about her;—and a little money too, I've no doubt. How could you do better than think of her?' Would it not have softened Miss Baker's heart towards her friend if she could have heard all this?

'Ah; you say this to try me. I know you do.'

'Try you! no; but I want you to try Miss Baker.'

'Well; I am going to make an attempt of that kind, certainly; certainly I am. But it is not with Miss Baker, as I cannot but think you know;' and then he paused to collect his ideas, and take in at a *coup d'œil* the weak point to which his attack should be turned. Meanwhile, Miss Todd sat silent. She knew by this time what was coming; and knew also, that in courtesy the gentleman should be allowed to have his say. Sir Lionel drew his chair again nearer—it was now very near—and thus began:—

'Dear Sarah!—' How he had found out that Miss Todd's name was Sarah it might be difficult to say. Her signature was S. Todd; and Sir Lionel had certainly never heard her called by her Christian name. But facts were with him. She undoubtedly had been christened Sarah.

'Dear Sarah!—'

'Ha! ha! ha! Ha! ha! ha!' laughed Miss Todd, with terrible loudness, with a shaking of her sides, throwing herself backwards and forwards in the corner of her sofa. It was not civil, and so Sir Lionel felt. When you first call your lady-love by her Christian name, you do not like to have the little liberty made a subject of ridicule—you feel it by far less if the matter be taken up seriously against you as a crime on your part.

'Ha! ha! ha!' continued Miss Todd, roaring in her laughter louder than ever; 'I don't think, Sir Lionel, I was ever called Sarah before since the day I was born; and it does sound so funny. Sarah. Ha! ha! ha!'

Sir Lionel was struck dumb. What could he say when his little tenderness was met in such a manner?

'Call me Sally, if you like, Sir Lionel. My brothers and sisters, and uncles and aunts, and all those sort of people, always called me Sally. But, Sarah! Ha! ha! ha! Suppose you call me Sally, Sir Lionel.'

Sir Lionel tried, but he could not call her Sally; his lips at that moment would not form the sound.

But the subject had now been introduced. If he should ever be able to claim her as his own, he might then call her Sarah, or Sally, or use any other term of endearment which the tenderness of the moment might suggest. When that day should come, perhaps he might have his own little joke; but, in the meantime, the plunge had been taken, and he could now swim on.

'Miss Todd, you now know what my feelings are, and I hope that you will at any rate not disapprove of them. We have known each other for some time, and have, I hope, enjoyed and valued each other's society.' Miss Todd here made a little bow, but she said nothing. She had a just perception that Sir Lionel should be permitted to have his say, and that, as matters had become serious, it would be well for her to wait till he had done, and then she might have her say. So she merely bowed, by way of giving a civil acquiescence in Sir Lionel's last little suggestion.

'I have hoped so, dear Miss Todd'—he had taken a moment to consider, and thought that he had better drop the Sarah altogether for the present. 'In myself, I can safely say that it has been so. With you, I feel that I am happy, and at my ease. Your modes of thought and way of life are all such as I admire and approve,'—Miss Todd again bowed—'and—and—what I mean is, that I think we both live very much after the same fashion.'

Miss Todd, who knew everything that went on in Littlebath, and was *au fait* at every bit of scandal and tittle-tattle in the place, had probably heard more of the fashion of Sir Lionel's life than he was aware. In places such as Littlebath, ladies such as Miss Todd do have sources of information which are almost miraculous. But still she said nothing. She merely thought that Sir Lionel was a good deal mistaken in the opinion which he had last expressed.

'I am not a young man,' continued Sir Lionel. 'My brother, you know, is a very old man, and there are but fifteen years' difference between us.' This was a mistake of Sir Lionel's; the real difference being ten years. 'And you, I know, are hardly yet past your youth.'

'I was forty-five last Guy Fawkes' day,' said Miss Todd.

'Then there are fifteen years' difference between us.' The reader will please to read 'twenty.' 'Can you look over that difference, and take me, old as I am, for your companion for life? Shall we not both be happier if we have such a companion? As to money—'

'Oh, Sir Lionel, don't trouble about that; nor yet about your age. If I wanted to marry, I'd as lief have an old man as a young one; perhaps liefer: and as to money, I've got enough for myself, and I have no doubt you have too'—nevertheless, Miss Todd did know of that heavy over-due bill at the livery stables, and had heard that the very natty groom who never left Sir Lionel's phaëton for a moment was a sworn bailiff; sworn to bring the carriage and horses back to the livery-stable yard—'but the fact is, I don't want to marry.'

'Do you mean, Miss Todd, that you will prefer to live in solitude for ever?'

'Oh, as for solitude, I'm not much of a Robinson Crusoe, nor yet an Alexander Selkirk.* I never found any of its charms. But, Lord bless you, Sir Lionel, people never leave me in solitude. I'm never alone. My sister Patty has fifteen children. I could have half of them to live with me if I liked it.' This view of the case did throw some cold water on Sir Lionel's ardour.

'And you are quite resolved on this?' he said, with a dash of expiring sentiment in his tone.

'What! to have Patty's children? No, I find it more convenient to pay for their schooling.'

'But you are quite resolved to—to—to give me no other, no more favourable answer?'

'Oh! about marrying. On that subject, Sir Lionel, my mind is altogether made up. Miss Todd I am, and Miss Todd I mean to remain. To tell the truth plainly, I like to be number one in my own house. Lady Bertram, I am quite sure, will be a fortunate and happy woman; but then, she'll be number two, I take it. Eh, Sir Lionel?'

Sir Lionel smiled and laughed, and looked at the ground, and then looked up again; but he did not deny the imputation. 'Well,' said he, 'I trust we shall still remain friends.'

'Oh, certainly; why not?' replied Miss Todd.

And so they parted. Sir Lionel took his hat and stick, and went his way.

CHAPTER XXXII

HE TRIES HIS HAND AGAIN

MISS TODD shook hands with him as he went, and then, putting on her bonnet and cloak, got into her fly.

She felt some little triumph at her heart in thinking that Sir Lionel had wished to marry her. Had she not, she would hardly have been a woman. But by far her strongest feeling was one of dislike to him for not having wished to marry Miss Baker. She had watched the gallant soldier closely for the last year, and well knew how tenderly he had been used to squeeze Miss Baker's hand. He had squeezed her own hand too; but what was that? She made others the subject of jokes, and was prepared to be joked upon herself. Whatever Oliver Sir Lionel, or other person, might give her, she would give back to him or to her—always excepting Mrs Leake—a Rowland* that should be quite as good. But Miss Baker was no subject for a joke, and Sir Lionel was in duty bound to have proposed to her.

It is perhaps almost true that no one can touch pitch and not be defiled. Miss Todd had been touching pitch for many years past, and was undoubtedly defiled to a certain extent. But the grime with her had never gone deep; it was not ingrained; it had not become an ineradicable stain; it was dirt on which soap-and-water might yet operate. May we not say that her truth and good-nature, and love of her fellow-creatures, would furnish her at last with the means whereby she might be cleansed?

She was of the world, worldly. It in no way disgusted her that Sir Lionel was an old rip, and that she knew him to be so. There were a great many old male rips at Littlebath and elsewhere. Miss Todd's path in life had brought her across more than one or two such. She encountered them without horror, welcomed them without shame, and spoke of them with a laugh rather than a shudder. Her idea was, that such a rip as Sir Lionel would best mend his manners by marriage; by marriage, but not with her. She knew better than trust herself to any Sir Lionel.

And she had encountered old female rips; that is, if dishonesty in money-dealings, selfishness, coarseness, vanity, absence of religion, and false pretences, when joined to age, may be held as constituting an old female rip. Many such had been around her frequently. She would laugh with them, feed them, call on them, lose her money to them, and feel herself no whit degraded. Such company brought on her no conviction of shame. But yet she was not of them. Coarse she was; but neither dishonest, nor selfish, nor vain, nor irreligious, nor false.

Such being the nature of the woman, she had not found it necessary to display any indignation when Sir Lionel made his offer; but she did feel angry with him on Miss Baker's behalf. Why had he deceived that woman, and made an ass of himself? Had he had any wit, any knowledge of character, he would have known what sort of an answer he was likely to get if he brought his vows and offers to the Paragon. There he had been received with no special favour. No lures had been there displayed to catch him. He had not been turned out of the house when he came there, and that was all. So now, as she put on her bonnet, she determined to punish Sir Lionel.

But in accusing her suitor of want of judgment, she was quite in the dark as to his real course of action. She little knew with how profound a judgment he was managing his affairs. Had she known, she would hardly have interfered as she now did. As she put her foot on the step of the fly she desired her servant to drive to Montpellier Terrace.

She was shown into the drawing-room, and there she found Miss Baker and Miss Gauntlet; not our friend Adela, but Miss Penelope Gauntlet, who was now again settled in Littlebath.

'Well, ladies,' said Miss Todd, walking up the room with well-assured foot and full comfortable presence, 'I've news to tell you.'

They both of them saw at a glance that she had news. Between Miss P. Gauntlet and Miss Todd there had never been cordiality. Miss Todd was, as we have said, of the world, worldly; whereas Miss Gauntlet was of Dr Snort, godly. She belonged plainly to the third set of which we have spoken; Miss Todd was an amalgamation of the two first. Miss Baker, however, was a point of union, a connecting rod. There was about her a savouring of the fragrance of Ebenezer,* but accompanied, it must be owned, by a whiff of brimstone. Thus these three ladies were brought together; and as it was manifest that Miss Todd had news to tell, the other two were prepared to listen.

'What do you think, ladies?' and she sat herself down, filling an arm-chair with her goodly person. 'What do you think has happened to me today?'

'Perhaps the doctor has been with you,' said Miss P. Gauntlet, not alluding to the Littlebath Galen,* but meaning to insinuate that Miss Todd might have come thither to tell them of her conversion from the world.

'Better than ten doctors, my dear,'—Miss Penelope drew herself up very stiffly—'or twenty! I've had an offer of marriage. What do you think of that?'

Miss P. Gauntlet looked as though she thought a great deal of it. She certainly did think that had such an accident happened to her, she would not have spoken of it with such a voice, or before such an audience. But now her face, which was always long and thin, became longer and thinner, and she sat with her mouth open, expecting further news.

Miss Baker became rather red, then rather pale, and then red again. She put out her hand, and took hold of the side of the chair in which she sat; but she said nothing. Her heart told her that that offer had been made by Sir Lionel.

'You don't wish me joy, ladies,' said Miss Todd.

'But you have not told us whether you accepted it,' said Miss Penelope.

'Ha! ha! ha! No, that's the worst of it. No, I didn't accept it. But, upon my word, it was made.'

Then it was not Sir Lionel, thought Miss Baker, releasing her hold of the chair, and feeling that the blood about her heart was again circulating.

'And is that all that we are to know?' asked Miss Penelope.

'Oh, my dears, you shall know it all. I told my lover that I should keep no secrets. But, come, you shall guess. Who was it, Miss Baker?'

'I couldn't say at all,' said Miss Baker, in a faint voice.

'Perhaps Mr O'Callaghan,' suggested Miss Penelope, conscious, probably, that an ardent young evangelical clergyman is generally in want of an income.

'Mr O'Callaghan!' shouted Miss Todd, throwing up her head with scorn. 'Pho! The gentleman I speak of would have made me a lady. Lady—! Now who do you think it was, Miss Baker?'

'Oh, I couldn't guess at all,' said poor Miss Baker. But she now knew that it was Sir Lionel. It might have been worse, however, and that she felt—much worse!

'Was it Sir Lionel Bertram?' asked the other.

'Ah! Miss Gauntlet, you know all about the gentlemen of Littlebath. I can see that. It was Sir Lionel. Wasn't that a triumph?'

'And you refused him?' asked Miss Penelope.

'Of course I did. You don't mean to say that you think I would have accepted him?'

To this Miss Penelope made no answer. Her opinions were of a mixed sort. She partly misbelieved Miss Todd—partly wondered at her. Unmarried ladies of a certain age, whatever may be their own feelings in regard to matrimony on their own behalf, seem always impressed with a conviction that other ladies in the same condition would certainly marry if they got an opportunity. Miss Penelope could not believe that Miss Todd had rejected Sir Lionel; but at the same time she could not but be startled also by the great fact of such a rejection. At any rate her course of duty was open. Littlebath should be enlightened on the subject before the drawing-room candles were lit that evening; or at any rate that set in Littlebath to which she belonged. So she rose from her chair, and, declaring that she had sat an unconscionable time with Miss Baker, departed, diligent, about her work.

'Well, what do you think of that, my dear?' said Miss Todd, as soon as the two of them were left alone.

It was strange that Miss Todd, who was ordinarily so good-natured, who was so especially intent on being good-natured to Miss Baker, should have thus roughly communicated to her friend tidings which were sure to wound. But she had omitted to look at it in this light. Her intention had been to punish Sir Lionel for having been so grossly false and grossly foolish. She had seen through him—at least, hardly through him; had seen at least that he must have been doubting between the two ladies, and that he had given up the one whom he believed to be the poorer. She did not imagine it possible that, after having offered to her, he should then go with a similar offer to Miss Baker. Had such an idea arisen in her mind, she would certainly have allowed Miss Baker to take her chance of promotion unmolested.

Miss Baker gave a long sigh. Now that Miss Gauntlet was gone, she felt herself better able to speak; but, nevertheless, any speech on the subject was difficult to her. Her kind heart at once forgave Miss Todd. There could now be no marriage between that false one and her friend; and therefore, if the ice would only get itself broken, she would not be unwilling to converse upon the subject. But how to break the ice!

'I always thought he would,' at last she said.

'Did you?' said Miss Todd. 'Well, he certainly used to come there, but I never knew why. Sometimes I thought it was to talk about you.'

'Oh, no!' said Miss Baker, plaintively.

'I gave him no encouragement—none whatever;—used to send him here and there—anything to get rid of him. Sometimes I thought—' and then Miss Todd hesitated.

'Thought what?' asked Miss Baker.

'Well, I don't want to be ill-natured; but sometimes I thought that he wanted to borrow money, and didn't exactly know how to begin.'

'To borrow money!' He had once borrowed money from Miss Baker.

'Well, I don't know; I only say I thought so. He never did.'

Miss Baker sighed again, and then there was a slight pause in the conversation.

'But, Miss Todd—'

'Well, my dear!'

'Do you think that—'

'Think what? Speak out, my dear; you may before me. If you've got any secret, I'll keep it.'

'Oh! I've got no secret; only this. Do you think that Sir Lionel is—is poor—that he should want to borrow money?'

'Well; poor! I hardly know what you call poor. But we all know that he is a distressed man. I suppose he has a good income, and a little ready money would, perhaps, set him up; but there's no doubt about his being over head and ears in debt, I suppose.'

This seemed to throw a new and unexpected light on Miss Baker's mind. 'I thought he was always so very respectable,' said she.

'Hum-m-m!' said Miss Todd, who knew the world.

'Eh?' said Miss Baker, who did not.

'It depends on what one means by respectable,' said Miss Todd.

'I really thought he was so very—'

'Hum-m-m-m,' repeated Miss Todd, shaking her head.

And then there was a little conversation carried on between these ladies so entirely *sotto voce* that the reporter of this scene was unable to hear a word of it. But this he could see, that Miss Todd bore by far the greater part in it.

At the end of it Miss Baker gave another, and a longer, and a deeper sigh. 'But you know, my dear,' said Miss Todd, in her most consolatory voice, and these words were distinctly audible, 'nothing does a man of that sort so much good as marrying.'

'Does it?' asked Miss Baker.

'Certainly; if his wife knows how to manage him.'

And then Miss Todd departed, leaving Miss Baker with much work for her thoughts. Her female friend Miss Baker had quite forgiven; but she felt that she could never quite forgive him. 'To have deceived me so!' she said to herself, recurring to her old idea of respectability. But, nevertheless, it was probably his other sin that rankled deepest in her mind.

Of Miss Baker, it may be said that she had hardly touched the pitch; at any rate, that it had not defiled her.

Sir Lionel was somewhat ill at ease as he walked from the Paragon to his livery stables. He had certainly looked upon success with Miss Todd as by no means sure; but, nevertheless, he was disappointed. Let any of us, in any attempt that we may make, convince ourselves with ever so much firmness that we shall fail, yet we are hardly the less down-hearted when the failure comes. We assure ourselves that we are not sanguine, but we assure ourselves falsely. It is man's nature to be sanguine; his nature, and perhaps his greatest privilege.

And Sir Lionel, as he walked along, began to fear that his own scruples would now stand in the way of that other marriage—of that second string to his bow. When, in making his little private arrangements within his own mind, he had decided that if Miss Todd rejected him he would forthwith walk off to Miss Baker, it never occurred to him that his own feelings would militate against such a proceeding. But such was now absolutely the fact. Having talked about 'dear Sarah,' he found that even he would have a difficulty in bringing himself to the utterance of 'dear Mary.'

He went to bed, however, that night with the comfortable reflection that any such nonsense would be dissipated by the morning. But when the morning came—his morning, one P.M.—his feeling he found was the same. He could not see Miss Baker that day.

He was disgusted and disappointed with himself. He had flattered himself that he was gifted with greater firmness; and now that he found himself so wanting in strength of character, he fretted and fumed, as men will do, even at their own faults. He swore to himself that he would go tomorrow, and that evening went to bed early, trying to persuade himself that indigestion had weakened him. He did great injustice, however, to as fine a set of internal organs as ever blessed a man of sixty.

At two o'clock next day he dressed himself for the campaign in Montpellier Terrace; but when dressed he was again disorganized. He found that he could not do it. He told himself over and over again that with Miss Baker there need be no doubt; she, at least, would accept him. He had only to smile there, and she would smile again. He had only to say 'dear Mary,' and those soft eyes would be turned to the ground and the battle would be won.

But still he could not do it. He was sick; he was ill; he could not eat his breakfast. He looked in the glass, and found himself to be yellow, and wrinkled, and wizened. He was not half himself. There were yet three weeks before Miss Baker would leave Littlebath. It was on the whole better that his little arrangements should be made immediately previous to her departure. He would leave Littlebath for ten days, and return a new man. So he went up to London, and bestowed his time upon his son.

At the end of the ten days much of his repugnance had worn off. But still the sound of that word 'Sarah,' and the peal of laughter which followed, rang in his ears. That utterance of the verbiage of love is a disagreeable task for a gentleman of his years. He had tried it, and found it very disagreeable. He would save himself a repetition of the nuisance and write to her.

He did so. His letter was not very long. He said nothing about 'Mary' in it, but contented himself by calling her his dearest friend. A few words were sufficient to make her understand what he meant, and those few words were there. He merely added a caution, that for both their sakes, the matter had better not at present be mentioned to anybody.

Miss Baker, when she received this letter, had almost recovered her equanimity. Hers had been a soft and gentle sorrow. She had had no fits of bursting grief; her wailings had been neither loud nor hysterical. A gentle, soft, faint tinge of melancholy had come upon her; so that she had sighed much as she sat at her solitary tea, and had allowed her novel to fall uncared for to the ground. 'Would it not be well for her,' she said to herself more than once, 'to go to Hadley? Would not any change be well for her?' She felt now that Caroline's absence was a heavy blow to her, and that it would be well that she should leave Littlebath. It was astonishing how this affair of Miss Todd's reconciled her to her future home.

And then, when she was thus tranquil, thus resigned, thus all but happy, came this tremendous letter, upsetting her peace of mind, and throwing her into a new maze of difficulties.

She had never said to herself at any time that if Sir Lionel did propose she would accept him. She had never questioned herself as to the probability of such an event. That she would have accepted him a fortnight ago, there can be no doubt; but what was she to do now?

It was not only that Sir Lionel had made another tender of his hand to another lady ten or twelve days since, but to this must be added the fact that all Littlebath knew that he had done so. Miss Todd, after the first ebullition of her comic spleen, had not said much about it; but Miss P. Gauntlet's tongue had not been idle. She, perhaps, had told it only to the godly; but the godly, let them be ever so exclusive, must have some intercourse with the wicked world; and thus every lady in Littlebath now knew all about it. And then there were other difficulties. That whispered conversation still rang in her ears. She was not quite sure how far it might be her mission to reclaim such a man as Sir Lionel—this new Sir Lionel whom Miss Todd had described. And then, too, he was in want of money. Why, she was in want of money herself!

But was there not something also to be said on the other side? It is reported that unmarried ladies such as Miss Baker generally regret the forlornness of their own condition. If so, the fault is not their own, but must be attributed to the social system to which they belong. The English world is pleased to say that an unmarried lady past forty has missed her hit in life—has omitted to take her tide at the ebb; and what can unmarried ladies do but yield to the world's dictum? That the English world may become better informed, and learn as speedily as may be to speak with more sense on the subject, let us all pray.

But, in the meantime, the world's dictum was strong at Littlebath, and did influence this dear lady. She would prefer the name of Lady Bertram to that of Miss Baker for the remainder of the term of years allotted to her. It would please her to walk into a room as a married woman, and to quit herself of that disgrace, which injustice and prejudice, and the folly of her own sex rather than of the other, had so cruelly attached to her present position. And then, to be *Lady* Bertram! There were but few angels at this time in Littlebath, and Miss Baker was not one of them: she had a taint of vanity in her composition; but we doubt if such female vanity could exist in any human breast in a more pardonable form than it did in hers.

And then, perhaps, this plan of marrying might have the wished-for effect on Sir Lionel's way of living;—and how desirable was this! Would it not be a splendid work for her to reclaim a lost colonel? Might it not be her duty to marry him with this special object?

There certainly did appear to be some difficulty as to money. If, as Miss Todd assured her, Sir Lionel were really in difficulties, her own present annuity—all that she could absolutely call her own—her one hundred and eighty-nine pounds, seventeen shillings and threepence per annum—would not help them much. Sir Lionel was at any rate disinterested in his offer; that at least was clear to her.

And then a sudden light broke in upon her meditations. Sir Lionel and the old gentleman were at variance. We allude to the old gentleman at Hadley: with the other old gentleman* of whom we wot, it may be presumed that Sir Lionel was on tolerably favourable terms. Might not she be the means of bringing the two brothers together? If she were Lady Bertram, would not the old gentleman receive Sir Lionel back to his bosom for her sake—to his bosom, and also to his purse? But before she took any step in the dark, she resolved to ask the old gentleman the question.

It is true that Sir Lionel had desired her to speak to no person on the subject; but that injunction of course referred to strangers. It could not but be expected that on such a matter she should consult her best friends. Sir Lionel had also enjoined a speedy answer; and in order that she might not disappoint him in this matter, she resolved to put the question at once to Mr Bertram. Great measures require great means. She would herself go to Hadley on the morrow—and so she wrote a letter that night, to beg that her uncle would expect her.

'So; you got tired of Littlebath before the month was out?' said he.

'Oh! but I am going back again.'

'Going back again! Then why the d— have you come up now?' Alas! it was too clear that the old gentleman was not in one of his more pacific moods.

As these words were spoken, Miss Baker was still standing in the passage, that she might see her box brought in from the fly. She of course had on her bonnet, and thickest shawl, and cloak. She had thick boots on also, and an umbrella in her hand. The maid was in the passage, and so was the man who had driven her. She was very cold, and her nose was blue, and her teeth chattered. She could not tell her tale of love in such guise, or to such audience.

'What the d— has brought you up?' repeated the old gentleman, standing with his two sticks at the sitting-room door. He did not care who heard him, or how cold it was, or of what nature might be her present mission. He knew that an extra journey from Littlebath to London and back, flys and porters included, would cost two pounds ten shillings. He knew, or thought that he knew, that this might have been avoided. He also knew that his rheumatism plagued him, that his old bones were sore, that he could not sleep at night, that he could not get into the City to see how things went, and that the game was coming to an end with him, and that the grave was claiming him. It was not surprising that the old gentleman should be cross.

'I'll tell you if you'll let me come into the room,' said Miss Baker. 'Take the box upstairs, Mary. Half-a-crown! oh, no, two shillings will be quite enough.' This economy was assumed to pacify the old gentleman; but it did not have the desired effect. 'One and sixpence,' he holloed out from his crutches. 'Don't give him a halfpenny more.'

'Please, sir, the luggage, sir,' said the fly driver.

'Luggage!' shouted the old man. His limbs were impotent, but his voice was not; and the fly-driver shook in his shoes.

'There,' said Miss Baker, insidiously giving the man two and threepence. 'I shall not give you a farthing more.' It is to be feared that she intended her uncle to think that his limit had not been exceeded.

And then she was alone with Mr Bertram. Her nose was still blue, and her toes still cold; but at any rate she was alone with him. It was hard for her to tell her tale; and she thoroughly wished herself back at Littlebath; but, nevertheless, she did tell it. The courage of women in some conditions of life surpasses anything that man can do.

'I want to consult you about that,' said she, producing Sir Lionel's letter.

The old gentleman took it, and looked at it, and turned it. 'What! it's from that swindler, is it?' said he.

'It's from Sir Lionel,' said Miss Baker, trembling. There were as yet no promising auspices for the fraternal reconciliation.

'Yes; I see who it's from—and what is it all about? I shan't read it. You can tell me, I suppose, what's in it.'

'I had hoped that perhaps, sir, you and he might—'

'Might what?'

'Be brought together as brothers and friends.'

'Brothers and friends! One can't choose one's brother; but who would choose to be the friend of a swindler? Is that what the letter is about?'

'Not exactly that, Mr Bertram.'

'Then, what the d— is it?'

'Sir Lionel, sir, has made me—'

'Made you what? Put your name to a bill, I suppose.'

'No; indeed he has not. Nothing of that kind.'

'Then what has he made you do?'

'He has not made me do anything; but he has sent me—an—an offer of marriage.' And poor Miss Baker, with her blue nose, looked up so innocently, so imploringly, so trustingly, that any one but Mr Bertram would have comforted her.

'An offer of marriage from Sir Lionel!' said he.

'Yes,' said Miss Baker, timidly. 'Here it is; and I have come up to consult you about the answer.' Mr Bertram now did take the letter and did read it through.

'Well!' he said, closing his eyes and shaking his head gently. 'Well!'

'I thought it better to do nothing without seeing you. And that is what has brought me to Hadley in such a hurry.'

'The audacious, impudent scoundrel!'

'You think, then, that I should refuse him?'

'You are a fool, an ass! a downright old soft-headed fool!' Such was the old gentleman's answer to her question.

'But I didn't know what to say without consulting you,' said Miss Baker, with her handkerchief to her face.

'Not know! Don't you know that he's a swindler, a reprobate, a penniless adventurer? Good heavens! And you are such a fool as that! It's well that you are not to be left at Littlebath by yourself.'

Miss Baker made no attempt to defend herself, but, bursting into tears, assured her uncle that she would be guided by him. Under his absolute dictation she wrote the enclosed short answer to Sir Lionel.

'Hadley, January—, 184—.

'Dear Sir,

'Mr Bertram says that it will be sufficient to let you know that he would not give me a penny during his life, or leave me a penny at his death, if I were to become your wife.

'Yours truly,

'MARY BAKER.'

That was all that the old gentleman would allow; but as she folded the letter, she surreptitiously added the slightest imaginable postscript to explain the matter—such words as occurred to her at the spur of the moment.

'He is so angry about it all!'

After that Miss Baker was not allowed back to Littlebath, even to pack up or pay her bills, or say good-bye to those she left behind. The servant had to do it all. Reflecting on the danger which had been surmounted, Mr Bertram determined that she should not again be put in the way of temptation.

And this was the end of Sir Lionel's wooing.

CHAPTER XXXIII

A QUIET LITTLE DINNER

SIR HENRY HARCOURT was married and took his bride to Paris and Nice; and Sir Lionel Bertram tried to get married, but his bride—bride as he hoped her to have been—ran away by herself to Hadley. In the meantime George Bertram lived alone in his dark dull chambers in London.

He would fain have been all alone; but at what was perhaps the worst moment of his misery, his father came to him. It may be remembered how anxiously he had longed to know his father when he first commenced that journey to Jerusalem, how soon he became attached to him, how fascinated he had been by Sir Lionel's manners, how easily he forgave the first little traits of unpaternal conduct on his father's part, how gradually the truth forced itself upon his mind. But now, at this time, the truth had forced itself on his mind. He knew his father for what he was.

And his mind was not one which could reject such knowledge, or alter the nature of it because the man was his father. There are those to whom a father's sins, or a husband's sins, or a brother's sins are no sins at all. And of such one may say, that though we must of compulsion find their judgment to be in some sort delinquent, that their hearts more than make up for such delinquency. One knows that they are wrong, but can hardly wish them to be less so.

But George Bertram was not one of them: he had been in no hurry to condemn his father; but, having seen his sins, he knew them for sins, and did condemn them. He found that his uncle had been right, and that Sir Lionel was a man whom he could in no wise respect, and could hardly love. Money he perceived was his father's desire. He would therefore give him what money he could spare; but he would not give him his society.

When, therefore, Sir Lionel announced his arrival in town and his intention to remain there some little time, George Bertram was by no means solaced in his misery. In those days he was very miserable. It was only now that he knew how thoroughly he loved this woman—now that she was so utterly beyond his reach. Weak and wavering as he was in many things, he was not weak enough to abandon himself altogether to unavailing sorrow. He knew that work alone could preserve him from sinking—hard, constant, unflinching work, that one great cure for all our sorrow, that only means of adapting ourselves to God's providences.

So he set himself to work—not a lazy, listless reading of counted pages; not history at two volumes a week, or science at a treatise a day; but to such true work as he found it in him to do, working with all his mind and all his strength. He had already written and was known as a writer; but he had written under impulse, carelessly, without due regard to his words or due thought as to his conclusions. He had written things of which he was already ashamed, and had put forth with the *ex cathedra* air of an established master ideas which had already ceased to be his own. But all that should be altered now. Then he had wanted a quick return for his writings. It had piqued him to think that the names of others, his contemporaries, were bruited about the world, but that the world knew nothing of his own. Harcourt was already a noted man, while he himself had done no more than attempted and abandoned a profession. Harcourt's early success had made him an early author; but he already felt that his authorship was unavailing. Harcourt's success had been solid, stable, such as men delight in; his had as yet resulted only in his all but forced withdrawal from the only respectable position which he had achieved.

And now Harcourt's success was again before him. Harcourt had now as his own that which he had looked to as the goal of all his success, the worldly reward for which he had been willing to work. And yet what was Harcourt as compared with him? He knew himself to be of a higher temperament, of a brighter genius, of greater powers. He would not condescend even to compare himself to this man who had so thoroughly distanced him in the world's race.

Thinking, and feeling, and suffering thus, he had begun to work with all the vehemence of which he was master. He would ask for no speedy return now. His first object was to deaden the present misery of his mind; and then, if it might be so, to vindicate his claim to be regarded as one of England's worthy children, letting such vindication come in its own time.

Such being the state of his mind, his father's arrival did not contribute much to his comfort. Sir Lionel was rather petulant when he was with him; objected to him that he had played his cards badly; would talk about Caroline, and, which was almost worse, about the solicitor-general; constantly urged him to make overtures of reconciliation to his uncle; and wanted one day five pounds, on another ten pounds, and again on a third fifteen pounds. At this moment George's fixed income was but two hundred pounds a year, and any other wealth of which he was possessed was the remainder of his uncle's thousand pounds. When that was gone, he must either live on his income, small as it was, or write for the booksellers. Such being the case, he felt himself obliged to decline when the fifteen pounds was mentioned.

'You can let me have it for a couple of months?' said Sir Lionel.

'Not conveniently,' said his son.

'I will sent it you back immediately on my return to Littlebath,' said the father; 'so if you have got it by you, pray oblige me.'

'I certainly have got it,' said the son—and he handed him the desired check; 'but I think you should remember, sir, how very small my income is, and that there is no prospect of its being increased.'

'It must be altogether your own fault then,' said the colonel, pocketing the money. 'I never knew a young man who had a finer hand of cards put into his hand—never; if you have played it badly, it is your own fault, altogether your own fault.' In truth, Sir Lionel did really feel that his son had used him badly, and owed him some amends. Had George done his duty, he might now have been the actual recognized heir of his uncle's wealth, and the actual possessor of as much as would have been allowed to a dutiful, obedient son. To a man of Sir Lionel's temperament, it was annoying that there should be so much wealth so near him, and yet absolutely, and, alas! probably for ever out of his reach.

Sir Lionel had resolved to wait in London for his answer, and there he received it. Short as was poor Miss Baker's letter, it was quite sufficiently explicit. She had betrayed him to the old gentleman, and after that all hopes of money from that source were over. It might still be possible for him to talk over Miss Baker, but such triumph would be but barren. Miss Baker with a transferred allegiance—transferred from the old gentleman to him—would be but a very indifferent helpmate. He learnt, however, from Littlebath that she was still away, and would probably not return. Then he went back in fancied security, and found himself the centre of all those amatory ovations which Miss Todd and Miss Gauntlet had prepared for him.

It was about two months after this that George Bertram saw Sir Henry Harcourt for the first time after the marriage. He had heard that Sir Henry was in town, had heard of the blaze of their new house in Eaton Square, had seen in the papers how magnificent Lady Harcourt had appeared at court, how well she graced her brilliant home, how fortunate the world esteemed that young lawyer who, having genius, industry, and position of his own, had now taken to himself in marriage beauty, wealth, and social charms. All this George Bertram heard and read, and hearing it and reading it had kept himself from the paths in which such petted children of fortune might probably be met.

Twice in the course of these two months did Sir Henry call at Bertram's chambers; but Bertram was now at home to no one. He lived in a great desert, in which was no living being but himself—in a huge desert without water and without grass, in which there was no green thing. He was alone; to one person only had he spoken of his misery; once only had he thought of escaping from it. That thought had been in vain: that companion was beyond his reach; and, therefore, living there in his London chambers, he had been all alone.

But at last they did meet. Sir Henry determined not to be beaten in his attempt to effect a reconciliation, wrote to him, saying that he would call, and naming an hour. 'Caroline and you,' he said, 'are cousins; there can be no reason why you should be enemies. For her sake, if not for mine, do oblige me in this.'

Bertram sat for hours with that note beneath his eyes before he could bring himself to answer it. Could it really be that she desired to see him again? That she, in her splendour and first glow of prosperous joy, would wish to encounter him in his dreary, sad, deserted misery? And why could she wish it? and, ah! how could she wish it?

And then he asked himself whether he also would wish to see her. That he still loved her, loved her as he never had done while she was yet his own, he had often told himself. That he could never be at rest till he had ceased to make her the first object of his thoughts he had said as often. That he ought not to see her, he knew full well. The controversy within his own bosom was carried on for two hours, and then he wrote to Sir Henry, saying that he would be at his chambers at the hour named. From that moment the salutary effort was discontinued, the work was put aside, and the good that had been done was all revoked.

Sir Henry came, true to his appointment. Whatever might be his object, he was energetic in it. He was now a man of many concernments; hours were scanty with him, and a day much too short. The calls of clients, and the calls of party, joined to those other calls which society makes upon men in such brilliant stations, hardly left him time for sleeping; but not the less urgent was he in his resolve to see his beaten rival who would so willingly have left him to his brilliant joy. But was not all this explained long even before Christianity was in vogue? 'Quos Deus vult perdere, prius dementat.'* Whom God will confound, those he first maddens.

Nothing could exceed the bland friendship, the winning manners, and the frank courtesy of Sir Henry. He said but little about what was past; but that little went to show that he had been blessed with the hand of Caroline Waddington only because Bertram had rejected that blessing as not worthy his acceptance. Great man as he was, he almost humbled himself before Bertram's talent. He spoke of their mutual connection at Hadley as though they two were his heirs of right, and as though their rights were equal; and then he ended by begging that they might still be friends.

'Our careers must be widely different,' said Bertram, somewhat touched by his tone; 'yours will be in the light; mine must be in the dark.'

'Most men who do any good live in the dark for some period of their lives,' said Harcourt. 'I, too, have had my dark days, and doubtless, shall have them again; but neither with you nor with me will they endure long.'

Bertram thought that Harcourt knew nothing about it, and sneered when the successful man talked of his dark days. What darkness had his mental eyesight ever known? We are all apt to think when our days are dark that there is no darkness so dark as our own.

'I know what your feelings are,' continued Sir Henry; 'and I hope you will forgive me if I speak openly. You have resolved not to meet Caroline. My object is to make you put aside that resolve. It is my object and hers also. It is out of the question that you should continue to avoid the world. Your walk in life will be that of a literary man; but nowadays literary men become senators and statesmen. They have high rank, are well paid, and hold their own boldly against men of meaner capacities. This is the career that we both foresee for you; and in that career we both hope to be your friends.'

So spoke the great advocate with suasive eloquence—with eloquence dangerously suasive as regarded his own happiness. But in truth this man knew not what love meant—not that love which those two wretched lovers understood so well. That his own wife was cold to him, cold as ice—that he well knew. That Bertram had flung her from him because she had been cold to him—that he believed. That he himself could live without any passionate love—that he acknowledged. His wife was graceful and very beautiful—all the world confessed that. And thus Sir Henry was contented. Those honeymoon days had indeed been rather dreary. Once or twice before that labour was over he had been almost tempted to tell her that he had paid too high for the privilege of pressing such an icicle to his bosom. But he had restrained himself; and now in the blaze of the London season, passing his mornings in courts of law and his evenings in the House of Parliament, he flattered himself that he was a happy man.

'Come and dine with us in a quiet way the day after tomorrow,' said Sir Henry, 'and then the ice will be broken.' George Bertram said that he would; and from that moment his studies were at an end.

This occurred on the Monday. The invitation was for the following Wednesday. Sir Henry explained that from some special cause he would be relieved from parliamentary attendance, at any rate till ten o'clock; that at the quiet dinner there would be no other guests except Mr and Mrs Stistick, and Baron Brawl, whose wife and family were not yet in town.

'You'll like the baron,' said Harcourt; 'he's loud and arrogant, no doubt; but he's not loud and arrogant about nothing, as some men are. Stistick is a bore. Of course you know him. He's member for Peterloo, and goes with us on condition that somebody listens to him about once a week. But the baron will put him down.'

'And Mrs Stistick?' said George.

'I never heard of her till yesterday, and Caroline has gone to call on her today. It's rather a bore for her, for they live somewhere half-way to Harrow, I believe. Half-past seven. Good-bye, old fellow. I ought to have been before Baron Brawl at Westminster twenty minutes since.' And so the solicitor-general, rushing out from the Temple, threw himself into a cab; and as the wheels rattled along the Strand, he made himself acquainted with the contents of his brief.

Why should Caroline have expressed a wish to see him? That was the thought that chiefly rested in Bertram's mind when Sir Henry left him. Why should it be an object of her to force a meeting between her and him? Would it not be better for them both that they should be far as the poles asunder.

'Well,' he said to himself, 'if it be no difficulty to her, neither shall it be a difficulty to me. She is strong-minded, and I will be so no less. I will go and meet her. It is but the first plunge that gives the shock.'

And thus he closed his work, and sat moodily thinking. He was angry with her in that she could endure to see him; but, alas! half-pleased also that she should wish to do so. He had no thought, no most distant thought, that she could ever now be more to him than the wife of an acquaintance whom he did not love too well. But yet there was in his heart some fragment of half-satisfied vanity at hearing that she did look forward to see him once again.

And how shall we speak of such a wish on her part? 'Caroline,' her husband had said to her at breakfast, 'it will be all nonsense for you and George Bertram to keep up any kind of quarrel. I hate nonsense of that sort.'

'There is no quarrel between us,' she replied.

'There ought to be none; and I shall get him to come here.'

The colour of her face became slightly heightened as she answered: 'If you wish it, Sir Henry, and he wishes it also, I shall not object.'

'I do wish it, certainly. I think it absolutely necessary as regards my position with your grandfather.'

'Do just as you think best,' said his wife. 'Twas thus that Lady Harcourt had expressed her desire to see George Bertram at her house. Had he known the truth, that fragment of half-satisfied vanity would have been but small.

In those early days of her marriage, Lady Harcourt bore her triumphs very placidly. She showed no great elation at the change that had come over her life. Her aunt from Hadley was frequently with her, and wondered to find her so little altered, or rather, in some respects, so much altered; for she was more considerate in her manner, more sparing of her speech, much less inclined to domineer now, as Lady Harcourt, than in former days she had ever been as Caroline Waddington. She went constantly into society, and was always much considered; but her triumphs were mainly of that quiet nature which one sometimes sees to be achieved with so little effort by beautiful women. It seemed but necessary that she should sit still, and sometimes smile, and the world was ready to throw itself at her feet. Nay, the smile was but too often omitted, and yet the world was there.

At home, though more employed, she was hardly more energetic. Her husband told her that he wished his house to be noted for the pleasantness of his dinner-parties, and, therefore, she studied the subject as a good child would study a lesson. She taught herself what the material of a dinner should be, she satisfied herself that her cook was good, she looked to the brilliancy of her appointments, and did her best to make the house shine brightly. The house did shine, and on the whole Sir Henry was contented. It was true that his wife did not talk much; but what little she did say was said with a sweet manner and with perfect grace. She was always dressed with care, was always beautiful, was always ladylike. Had not Sir Henry reason to be contented? As for talking, he could do that himself.

And now that she was told that George Bertram was to come to her house, she did not show much more excitement at the tidings than at the promised advent of Mr Baron Brawl. She took the matter with such indifference that Sir Henry, at least, had no cause for jealousy. But then she was indifferent about everything. Nothing seemed to wake her either to joy or sorrow. Sir Henry, perhaps, was contented; but lovely, ladylike, attractive as she was, he sometimes did feel almost curious to know whether it were possible to rouse this doll of his to any sense of life or animation. He had thought, nay, almost wished, that the name of her old lover would have moved her, that the idea of seeing him would have disturbed her. But, no; one name was the same to her as another. She had been told to go and call on Mrs Stistick, and she had gone. She was told to receive Mr Bertram, and she was quite ready to do so. Angels from heaven or spirits from below, could Sir Henry have summoned such to his table, would have been received by her with equal equanimity. This was dutiful on her part, and naturally satisfactory to a husband inclined to be somewhat exigeant. But even duty may pall on an exigeant husband, and a man may be brought to wish that his wife would cross him.

But on this occasion Sir Henry had no such pleasure. 'I saw Bertram this morning,' he said, when he went home for five minutes before taking his seat in the House for the night. 'He's to be here on Wednesday.'

'Oh, very well. There will be six, then.' She said no more. It was clear that the dinner, and that only, was on her mind. He had told her to be careful about his dinners, and therefore could not complain. But, nevertheless, he was almost vexed. Don't let any wife think that she will satisfy her husband by perfect obedience. Overmuch virtue in one's neighbours is never satisfactory to us sinners.

But there were moments in which Lady Harcourt could think of her present life, when no eye was by to watch her—no master there to wonder at her perfections. Moments! nay, but there were hours, and hours, and hours. There were crowds of hours; slow, dull, lingering hours, in which she had no choice but to think of it. A woman may see to her husband's dinners and her own toilet, and yet have too much time for thinking. It would almost have been a comfort to Lady Harcourt if Sir Henry could have had a dinner-party every day.

How should she bear herself; what should she say; how should she look when George Bertram came there as a guest to her house? How could he be so cruel, so heartless, so inhuman as to come there? Her path was difficult enough for her poor weary feet. He must know that—should, at any rate, have known it. How could he be so cruel as to add this great stumbling-block to her other perils?

The Wednesday came, and at half-past seven she was in her drawing-room as beautiful and as dignified as ever. She had a peculiar place of her own in the corner of a peculiar sofa, and there she lived. It was her goddess' shrine, and her worshippers came and did reverence before her. None came and sat beside her. Hers was not that gentle fascination which entices men, and women too, to a near proximity. Her bow was very gracious, and said much; but 'noli me tangere'* was part of its eloquence. And so Baron Brawl found, when on entering her drawing-room, he told her that the fame of her charms had reached his ears, and that he was delighted to have an opportunity of making her acquaintance.

Mr and Mrs Stistick were the next comers. Mrs Stistick sat herself down on an opposite sofa, and seemed to think that she did her duty to society by sitting there. And so she did. Only permit her so to sit, and there was no further labour in entertaining Mrs Stistick. She was a large, heavy woman, with a square forehead and a square chin, and she had brought up seven children most successfully. Now, in these days of her husband's parliamentary prosperity, she was carried about to dinners; and in her way she enjoyed them. She was not too shy to eat, and had no wish whatever either to be talked to or to talk. To sit easily on a sofa and listen to the buzz of voices was life and society to her. Perhaps in those long hours she was meditating on her children's frocks or her husband's linen. But they never seemed to belong to her.

Mr Stistick was standing on the rug before the fire, preparing for his first onslaught on Baron Brawl, when the servant announced Mr Bertram.

'Ah! Bertram, I'm delighted to see you,' said Sir Henry;—'doubly so, as dinner is ready. Judge, you know my friend Bertram, by name, at any rate?' and some sort of half introduction was performed.

'He who moved all Oxford from its propriety?' said the baron. But Bertram neither saw him nor heard him. Neither his eyes nor his ears were at his command.

As he took his host's proffered hand, he glanced his eyes for a moment round the room. There she sat, and he had to speak to her as best he might. At his last interview with her he had spoken freely enough, and it all rushed now upon his mind. Then how little he had made of her, how lightly he had esteemed her! Now, as she sat there before him his spirit acknowledged her as a goddess, and he all but feared to address her. His face, he knew, was hot and red; his manner, he felt, was awkward. He was not master of himself, and when such is the case with a man, the fact always betrays itself.

But he did speak to her. 'How do you do, Lady Harcourt?' he said, and he put his hand out, and he felt the ends of her fingers once more within his own.

And she spoke too, probably. But pretty women can say almost as much as is necessary on such occasions as this, without opening their lips. Whether she spoke, or whether she did not, it was the same to him. He certainly did not hear her. But her fingers did touch his hand, her eyes did rest upon his face; and then, in that moment of time, he thought of Jerusalem, of the Mount of Olives, of those rides at Littlebath, and of that last meeting, when all, all had been shattered to pieces.

'There are five hundred and fifty-five thousand male children between the ages of nine and twelve,' said Mr Stistick, pursuing some wondrous line of argument, as Bertram turned himself towards the fire.

'What a fine national family!' said the baron. 'And how ashamed I feel when I bethink myself that only one of them is mine!'

'Dinner is served,' said the butler.

'Mrs Stistick, will you allow me?' said Sir Henry. And then in half a minute Bertram found himself walking down to dinner with the member of Parliament. 'And we have school accommodation for just one hundred and fourteen,' continued that gentleman on the stairs. 'Now, will you tell me what becomes of the other four hundred and forty-one?'

Bertram was not at that moment in a condition to give him any information on the subject.

'I can tell you about the one,' said the baron, as Sir Henry began his grace.

'An odd thousand is nothing,' said Mr Stistick, pausing for a second till the grace was over.

The judge and Mr Stistick sat at Lady Harcourt's right and left, so that Bertram was not called upon to say much to her during dinner. The judge talked incessantly, and so did the member of Parliament, and so also did the solicitor-general.

A party of six is always a talking party. Men and women are not formed into pairs, and do not therefore become dumb. Each person's voice makes another person emulous, and the difficulty felt is not as to what one shall say, but how one shall get it in. Ten, and twelve, and fourteen are the silent numbers.

Every now and again Harcourt endeavoured to make Bertram join in the conversation; and Bertram did made some faint attempts. He essayed to answer some of Mr Stistick's very difficult inquiries, and was even roused to parry some raillery from the judge. But he was not himself; and Caroline, who could not but watch him narrowly as she sat there in her silent beauty, saw that he was not so. She arraigned him in her mind for want of courage; but had he been happy, and noisy, and light of heart, she would probably have arraigned him for some deeper sin.

'As long as the matter is left in the hands of the parents, nothing on earth will be done,' said Mr Stistick.

'That's what I have always said to Lady Brawl,' said the judge.

'And it's what I have said to Lord John;* and what I intend to say to him again. Lord John is all very well—'

'Thank you, Stistick. I am glad, at any rate, to get as much as that from you,' said the solicitor.

'Lord John is all very well,' continued the member, not altogether liking the interruption; 'but there is only one man in the country who thoroughly understands the subject, and who is able—'

'And I don't see the slightest probability of finding a second,' said the judge.

'And who is able to make himself heard.'

'What do you say, Lady Harcourt,' asked the baron, 'as to the management of a school with—how many millions of them, Mr Stistick?'

'Five hundred and fifty-five thousand male children—'

'Suppose we say boys,' said the judge.'

'Boys?' asked Mr Stistick, not quite understanding him, but rather disconcerted by the familiarity of the word.

'Well, I suppose they must be boys;—at least the most of them.'

'They are all from nine to twelve, I say,' continued Mr Stistick, completely bewildered.

'Oh, that alters the question,' said the judge.

'Not at all,' said Mr Stistick. 'There is accommodation for only—'

'Well, we'll ask Lady Harcourt. What do you say, Lady Harcourt?'

Lady Harcourt felt herself by no means inclined to enter into the joke on either side; so she said, with her gravest smile, 'I'm sure Mr Stistick understands very well what he's talking about.'

'What do you say, ma'am?' said the judge, turning round to the lady on his left.

'Mr Stistick is always right on such matters,' said the lady.

'See what it is to have a character. It absolutely enables one to upset the laws of human nature. But still I do say, Mr Solicitor, that the majority of them were probably boys.'

'Boys!' exclaimed the member of Parliament. 'Boys! I don't think you can have understood a word that we have been saying.'

'I don't think I have,' said the baron.

'There are five hundred and fifty-five thousand male children between—'

'Oh—h—h! male children! Ah—h—h! Now I see the difference; I beg your pardon, Mr Stistick, but I really was very stupid. And you mean to explain all this to Lord John in the present session?'

'But, Stistick, who is the one man?' said Sir Henry.

'The one man is Lord Boanerges. He, I believe, is the only man living who really understands the social wants of this kingdom.'

'And everything else also,' sneered the baron. The baron always sneered at cleverness that was external to his own profession, especially when exhibited by one who, like the noble lord named, should have confined his efforts to that profession.

'So Boanerges is to take in hand these male children? And very fitting, too; he was made to be a schoolmaster.'

'He is the first man of the age; don't you think so, Sir Henry?'

'He was, certainly, when he was on the woolsack,'* said Sir Henry. 'That is the normal position always assumed by the first man of his age in this country.'

'Though some of them when there do hide their lights under a bushel,' said the judge.

'He is the first law reformer that perhaps ever lived,' said Mr Stistick, enthusiastically.

'And I hope will be the last in my time,' said his enemy.

'I hope he will live to complete his work,' said the politician.

'Then Methuselah will be a child to him, and Jared and Lamech* little babies,' said the judge.

'In such case he has got his work before him, certainly,' said Mr Solicitor.

And so the battle was kept up between them, and George Bertram and Lady Harcourt sat by and listened; or more probably, perhaps, sat by and did not listen.

But when her ladyship and Mrs Stistick had retreated—Oh, my readers, fancy what that next hour must have been to Caroline Harcourt!—How Gothic, how barbarous are we still in our habits, in that we devote our wives to such wretchedness as that! O lady, has it ever been your lot to sit out such hour as that with some Mrs Stistick, who would neither talk, nor read, nor sleep; in whose company you could neither talk, nor read, nor yet sleep! And if such has been your lot, have you not asked yourself why in this civilized country, in this civilized century, you should be doomed to such a senseless, sleepless purgatory?—But when they were gone, and when the judge, radiant with fun and happiness, hastened to fill his claret beaker, then Bertram by degrees thawed, and began to feel that after all the world was perhaps not yet dead around him.

'Well, Mr Stistick,' said the baron; 'if Sir Henry will allow us, we'll drink Lord Boanerges.'

'With all my heart,' said Mr Stistick. 'He is a man of whom it may be said—'

'That no man knew better on which side his bread was buttered.'

'He is buttering the bread of millions upon millions,' said Mr Stistick.

'Or doing better still,' said Bertram; 'enabling them to butter their own. Lord Boanerges is probably the only public man of this day who will be greater in a hundred years than he is now.'

'Let us at any rate hope,' said the baron, 'that he will at that time be less truculent.'

'I can't agree with you, Bertram,' said Sir Henry. 'I consider we are fertile in statesmen. Do you think that Peel will be forgotten in a hundred years?' This was said with the usual candour of a modern turncoat. For Sir Henry had now deserted Peel.

'Almost, I should hope, by that time,' said Bertram. 'He will have a sort of a niche in history, no doubt; as has Mr Perceval,* who did so much to assist us in the war; and Lord Castlereagh, who carried the Union.* They also were heaven-sent ministers, whom Acheron has not as yet altogether swallowed up.'

'And Boanerges, you think, will escape Libitina?'*

'If the spirit of the age will allow immortality to any man of these days, I think he will. But I doubt whether public opinion, as now existing, will admit of hero-worship.'

'Public opinion is the best safeguard for a great man's great name,' said Mr Stistick, with intense reliance on the civilization of his own era.

'Quite true, sir; quite true,' said the baron,—'for the space of twenty-four hours.'

Then followed a calm, and then coffee. After that, the solicitor-general, looking at his watch, marched off impetuous to the House. 'Judge,' he said, 'I know you will excuse me; for you, too, have been a slave in your time; but you will go up to Lady Harcourt; Bertram, you will not be forgiven if you do not go upstairs.'

Bertram did go upstairs, that he might not appear to be unmanly, as he said to himself, in slinking out of the house. He did go upstairs, for one quarter of an hour.

But the baron did not. For him, it may be presumed, his club had charms. Mr Stistick, however, did do so; he had to hand Mrs Stistick down from that elysium which she had so exquisitely graced. He did hand her down; and then for five minutes George Bertram found himself once more alone with Caroline Waddington.

'Good-night, Lady Harcourt,' he said, again essaying to take her hand. This and his other customary greeting was all that he had yet spoken to her.

'Good-night, Mr Bertram.' At last her voice faltered, at last her eye fell to the ground, at last her hand trembled. Had she stood firm through this trial all might have been well; but though she could bear herself right manfully before stranger eyes, she could not alone support his gaze; one touch of tenderness, one sign of weakness was enough—and that touch was there, that sign she gave.

'We are cousins still, are we not?' said he.

'Yes, we are cousins—I suppose so.'

'And as cousins we need not hate each other?'

'Hate each other!' and she shuddered as she spoke; 'oh, no, I hope there is no hatred!'

He stood there silent for a moment, looking, not at her, but at the costly ornaments which stood at the foot of the huge pier-glass over the fireplace. Why did he not go now? why did he stand there silent and thoughtful? why—why was he so cruel to her?

'I hope you are happy, Lady Harcourt,' at last he said.

There was almost a savage sternness in her face as she made an effort to suppress her feelings. 'Thank you—yes,' she said; and then she added, 'I never was a believer in much happiness.'

And yet he did not go. 'We have met now,' he said, after another pause.

'Yes, we have met now;' and she even attempted to smile as she answered him.

'And we need not be strangers?' Then there was again a pause; for at first she had no answer ready. 'Is it needful that we should be strangers?' he asked.

'I suppose not; no; not if Sir Henry wishes it otherwise.'

And then he put out his hand, and wishing her good-night a second time, he went.

For the next hour, Lady Harcourt sat there looking at the smouldering fire. 'Quos Deus vult perdere, prius dementat.' Not in such language, but with some such thought, did she pass judgment on the wretched folly of her husband.

CHAPTER XXXIV

MRS MADDEN'S BALL

TWO days after the dinner, George Bertram called in Eaton Square and saw Lady Harcourt; but, as it happened, she was not alone. Their interview on this occasion was not in any great degree embarrassing to either of them. He did not stay long; and as strangers were present, he was able to talk freely on indifferent subjects. Lady Harcourt probably did not talk much, but she looked as though she did.

And then Adela Gauntlet came up to town for a month; and George, though he was on three or four occasions in Eaton Square, never saw Caroline alone; but he became used to seeing her and being with her. The strangeness of their meeting wore itself away: he could speak to her without reserve on the common matters of life, and found that he had intense delight in doing so.

Adela Gauntlet was present at all these interviews, and in her heart of hearts condemned them bitterly; but she could say nothing to Caroline. They had been friends—real friends; but Caroline was now almost like stone to her. This visit of Adela's had been a long promise—yes, very long; for the visit, when first promised, was to have been made to Mrs Bertram. One knows how these promises still live on. Caroline had pressed it even when she felt that Adela's presence could no longer be of comfort to her; and Adela would not now refuse, lest in doing so she might seem to condemn. But she felt that Caroline Harcourt could never be to her what Caroline Bertram would have been.

Lady Harcourt did whatever in her lay to amuse her guest; but Adela was one who did not require much amusing. Had there been friendship between her and her friend, the month would have run by all too quickly; but, as it was, before it was over she wished herself again even at Littlebath.

Bertram dined there twice, and once went with them to some concert. He met them in the Park, and called; and then there was a great evening gathering in Eaton Square, and he was there. Caroline was careful on all occasions to let her husband know when she met Bertram, and he as often, in some shape, expressed his satisfaction.

'He'll marry Adela Gauntlet; you'll see if he does not,' he said to her, after one of their dinners in Eaton Square. 'She is very pretty, very; and it will be all very nice; only I wish that one of them had a little money to go on with.'

Caroline answered nothing to this: she never did make him any answers; but she felt quite sure in her own heart that he would not marry Adela Gauntlet. And had she confessed the truth to herself, would she have wished him to do so?

Adela saw and disapproved; she saw much and could not but disapprove of all. She saw that there was very little sympathy between the husband and wife, and that that little was not on the increase.—Very little! nay, but was there any? Caroline did not say much of her lot in life; but the few words that did fall from her seemed to be full of scorn for all that she had around her, and for him who had given it all. She seemed to say, 'There—this is that for which I have striven—these ashes on which I now step, and sleep, and feed, which are gritty between my teeth, and foul to my touch! See, here is my reward! Do you not honour me for having won it?'

And then it appeared that Sir Henry Harcourt had already learned how to assume the cross brow of a captious husband; that the sharp word was already spoken on light occasions—spoken without cause and listened to with apparent indifference. Even before Adela such words were spoken, and then Caroline would smile bitterly, and turn her face towards her friend, as though she would say, 'See, see what it is to be the wife of so fine a man, so great a man! What a grand match have I not made for myself!' But though her looks spoke thus, no word of complaint fell from her lips—and no word of confidence.

We have said that Sir Henry seemed to encourage these visits which Bertram made to Eaton Square; and for a time he did so—up to the time of that large evening-party which was given just before Adela's return to Littlebath. But on that evening, Adela thought she saw a deeper frown than usual on the brows of the solicitor-general, as he turned his eyes to a couch on which his lovely wife was sitting, and behind which George Bertram was standing, but so standing that he could speak and she could hear.

And then Adela bethought herself, that though she could say nothing to Caroline, it might not be equally impossible to say something to Bertram. There had been between them a sort of confidence, and if there was any one to whom Adela could now speak freely, it was to him. They each knew something of each other's secrets, and each of them, at least, trusted the other.

But this, if it be done at all, must be done on that evening. There was no probability that they would meet again before her departure. This was the only house in which they did meet, and here Adela had no wish to see him more.

'I am come to say good-bye to you,' she said, the first moment she was able to speak to him alone.

To say good-bye! Is your visit over so soon?'

'I go on Thursday.'

'Well, I shall see you again, for I shall come on purpose to make my adieux.'

'No, Mr Bertram; do not do that.'

'But I certainly shall.'

'No;' and she put out her little hand, and gently—oh! so gently—touched his arm.

'And why not? Why should I not come to see you? I have not so many friends that I can afford to lose you.'

'You shall not lose me, nor would I willingly lose you. But, Mr Bertram—'

'Well, Miss Gauntlet?'

'Are you right to be here at all?'

The whole tone, and temper, and character of his face altered as he answered her quickly and sharply—'If not, the fault lies with Sir Henry Harcourt, who, with some pertinacity, induced me to come here. But why is it wrong that I should be here?—foolish it may be.'

'That is what I mean. I did not say wrong; did I? Do not think that I imagine evil.'

'It may be foolish,' continued Bertram, as though he had not heard her last words. 'But if so, the folly has been his.'

'If he is foolish, is that reason why you should not be wise?'

'And what is it you fear, Adela? What is the injury that will come? Will it be to me, or to her, or to Harcourt?'

'No injury, no real injury—I am sure of that. But may not unhappiness come of it? Does it seem to you that she is happy?'

'Happy! Which of us is happy? Which of us is not utterly wretched? She is as happy as you are, and Sir Henry, I have no doubt, is as happy as I am.'

'In what you say, Mr Bertram, you do me injustice; I am not unhappy.'

'Are you not? then I congratulate you on getting over the troubles consequent on a true heart.'

'I did not mean in any way to speak of myself; I have cares, regrets, and sorrows, as have most of us; but I have no cause of misery which I cannot assuage.'

'Well, you are fortunate; that is all I can say.'

'But Caroline I can see is not happy; and, Mr Bertram, I fear that your coming here will not make her more so.'

She had said her little word, meaning it so well. But perhaps she had done more harm than good. He did not come again to Eaton Square till after she was gone; but very shortly after that he did so.

Adela had seen that short, whispered conversation between Lady Harcourt and Bertram—that moment, as it were, of confidence; and so, also, had Sir Henry; and yet it had been but for a moment.

'Lady Harcourt,' Bertram had said, 'how well you do this sort of thing!'

'Do I?' she answered. 'Well, one ought to do something well.'

'Do you mean to say that your excellence is restricted to this?'

'Pretty nearly; such excellence as there is.'

'I should have thought—' and then he paused.

'You are not coming to reproach me, I hope,' she said.

'Reproach you, Lady Harcourt! No; my reproaches, silent or expressed, never fall on your head.'

'Then you must be much altered;' and as she said these last words, in what was hardly more than a whisper, she saw some lady in a distant part of the room to whom some attention might be considered to be due, and rising from her seat she walked away across the room. It was very shortly after that Adela had spoken to him.

For many a long and bitter day, Bertram had persuaded himself that she had not really loved him. He had doubted it when she had first told him so calmly that it was necessary that their marriage should be postponed for years; he had doubted it much when he found her, if not happy, at least contented under that postponement; doubt had become almost certainty when he learnt that she discussed his merits with such a one as Henry Harcourt; but on that day, at Richmond, when he discovered that the very secrets of his heart were made subject of confidential conversation with this man, he had doubted it no longer. Then he had gone to her, and his reception proved to him that his doubts had been too well founded—his certainty only too sure. And so he had parted with her—as we all know.

But now he began to doubt his doubts—to be less certain of his certainty. That she did not much love Sir Henry, that was very apparent; that she could not listen to his slightest word without emotion—that, too, he could perceive; that Adela conceived that she still loved him, and that his presence there was therefore dangerous—that also had been told to him. Was it then possible that he, loving this woman as he did—having never ceased in his love for one moment, having still loved her with his whole heart, his whole strength—that he had flung her from him while her heart was still his own? Could it be that she, during their courtship, should have seemed so cold and yet had loved him?

A thousand times he had reproached her in his heart for being worldly; but now the world seemed to have no charms for her. A thousand times he had declared that she cared only for the outward show of things, but these outward shows were now wholly indifferent to her. That they in no degree contributed to her happiness, or even to her contentment, that was made manifest enough to him.

And then these thoughts drove him wild, and he began to ask himself whether there could be yet any comfort in the fact that she had loved him, and perhaps loved him still. The motives by which men are actuated in their conduct are not only various, but mixed. As Bertram thought in this way concerning Lady Harcourt—the Caroline Waddington that had once belonged to himself—he proposed to himself no scheme of infamy, no indulgence of a disastrous love, no ruin for her whom the world now called so fortunate; but he did think that, if she still loved him, it would be pleasant to sit and talk with her; pleasant to feel some warmth in her hand; pleasant that there should be some confidence in her voice. And so he resolved—but, no, there was no resolve; but he allowed it to come to pass that his intimacy in Eaton Square should not be dropped.

And then he bethought himself of the part which his friend Harcourt had played in this matter, and speculated as to how that pleasant fellow had cheated him out of his wife. What Adela had said might be very true, but why should he regard Sir Henry's happiness? why regard any man's happiness, or any woman's? Who had regarded him? So he hired a horse, and rode in the Park when he knew Lady Harcourt would be there, dined with Baron Brawl because Lady Harcourt was to dine there, and went to a ball at Mrs Madden's for the same reason. All which the solicitor-general now saw, and did not press his friend to take a part at any more of his little dinners.

What may have passed on the subject between Sir Henry and his wife cannot be said. A man does not willingly accuse his wife of even the first germ of infidelity; does not willingly suggest to her that any one is of more moment to her than himself. It is probable that his brow became blacker than it had been, that his words were less courteous, and his manner less kind; but of Bertram himself, it may be presumed that he said nothing. It might, however, have been easy for Caroline to perceive that he no longer wished to have his old friend at his house.

At Mrs Madden's ball, Bertram asked her to dance with him, and she did stand up for a quadrille. Mr Madden was a rich young man, in Parliament, and an intimate friend both of Sir Henry's and of Bertram's. Caroline had danced with him—being her first performance of that nature since her marriage; and having done so, she could not, as she said to herself, refuse Mr Bertram. So they stood up; and the busy solicitor-general, who showed himself for five minutes in the room, saw them moving, hand-in-hand together, in the figure of the dance. And as he so moved, Bertram himself could hardly believe in the reality of his position. What if any one had prophesied to him three months since that he would be dancing with Caroline Harcourt!

'Adela did not stay with you long,' said he, as they were standing still.

'No, not very long. I do not think she is fond of London;' and then they were again silent till their turn for dancing was over.

'No; I don't think she is,' said Bertram, 'nor am I. I should not care if I were to leave it for ever. Do you like London, Lady Harcourt?'

'Oh, yes; as well as any other place. I don't think it much signifies—London, or Littlebath, or New Zealand.'

They were then both silent for a moment, till Bertram again spoke, with an effort that was evident in his voice.

'You used not to be so indifferent in such matters.'

'Used!'

'Has all the world so changed that nothing is any longer of any interest?'

'The world has changed, certainly—with me.'

'And with me also, Lady Harcourt. The world has changed with both of us. But Fortune, while she has been crushing me, has been very kind to you.'

'Has she? Well, perhaps she has—as kind, at any rate, as I deserve. But you may be sure of this—I do not complain of her.' And then they were again silent.

'I wonder whether you ever think of old days?' he said, after a pause.

'At any rate, I never talk of them, Mr Bertram.'

'No; I suppose not. One should not talk of them. But out of a full heart the mouth will speak. Constant thoughts will break forth in words. There is nothing else left to me of which I can think.'

Any one looking at her face as she answered him would have little dreamed how much was passing through her mind, how much was weighing on her heart. She commanded not only her features, but even her colour, and the motion of her eyes. No anger flashed from them; there was no blush of indignation as she answered him in that crowded room. And yet her words were indignant enough, and there was anger, too, in that low tone which reached his ear so plainly, but which reached no further.

'And whose doing has this been? Why is it that I may not think of past times? Why is it that all thought, all memories are denied to me? Who was it that broke the cup at the very fountain?'

'Was it I?'

'Did you ever think of your prayers? "Forgive us our trespasses." But you, in your pride—you could forgive nothing. And now you dare to twit me with my fortune!'

'Lady Harcourt!'

'I will sit down, if you please, now. I do not know why I speak thus.' And then, without further words, she caused herself to be led away, and sitting down between two old dowagers, debarred him absolutely from the power of another word.

Immediately after this he left the house; but she remained for another hour—remained and danced with young Lord Echo, who was a Whig lordling; and with Mr Twisleton, whose father was a Treasury secretary. They both talked to her about Harcourt, and the great speech he was making at that moment; and she smiled and looked so beautiful, that when they got together at the end of the supper-table, they declared that Harcourt was out-and-out the luckiest dog of his day; and questioned his right to monopolize such a treasure.

And had he been cruel? had he been unforgiving? had he denied to her that pardon which it behoved him so often to ask for himself? This was the question which Bertram was now forced to put to himself. And that other question, which he could now answer but in one way. Had he then been the cause of his own shipwreck? Had he driven his own bark on the rocks while the open channel was there clear before him? Had she not assured him of her love, though no word of tenderness had passed her lips? And whose doing had it been? Yes, certainly; it had been his own doing.

The conviction which thus came upon him did not add much to his comfort. There was but little consolation to him now in the assurance that she had loved, and did love him. He had hitherto felt himself to be an injured man; but now he had to feel that he himself had committed the injury. 'Whose doing has it been? You—you in your pride, could forgive nothing!' These words rang in his ears; his memory repeated to him hourly the tone in which they had been spoken. She had accused him of destroying all her hopes for this world—and he had answered not a word to the accusation.

On the morning after that ball at Mrs Madden's, Sir Henry came into his wife's room while she was still dressing. 'By-the-by,' said he, 'I saw you at Mrs Madden's last night.'

'Yes; I perceived that you were there for a moment,' Caroline answered.

'You were dancing. I don't know that I ever saw you dancing before.'

'I have not done so since I was married. In former days I used to be fond of it.'

'Ah, yes; when you were at Littlebath. It did not much matter then what you did in that way; but—'

'Does it matter more now, Sir Henry?'

'Well, if it would entail no great regret, I would rather that you did not dance. It is all very nice for girls.'

'You do not mean to say that married women—'

'I do not mean to say anything of the kind. One man has one idea, and another another. Some women are also not placed in so conspicuous a position as you are.'

'Why did you not tell me your wishes before?'

'It did not occur to me. I did not think it probable that you would dance. May I understand that you will give it up?'

'As you direct me to do so, of course I shall.'

'Direct! I do not direct, I only request.'

'It is the same thing, exactly. I will not dance again. I should have felt the prohibition less had I been aware of your wishes before I had offended.'

'Well, if you choose to take it in that light I cannot help it. Good-morning. I shall not dine at home today.'

And so the solicitor-general went his way, and his wife remained sitting motionless at her dressing-table. They had both of them already become aware that the bargain they had made was not a wise one.

CHAPTER XXXV

CAN I ESCAPE?

HAD not George Bertram been of all men the most infirm of purpose, he would have quitted London immediately after that ball—at any rate, for many months. But he was lamentably infirm of purpose. He said to himself over and over again, that it behoved him to go. What had either of them done for him that he should regard them? That had hitherto been the question within his own breast; but now it was changed. Had he not greatly injured her? Had she not herself told him that his want of mercy had caused all her misery? Ought he not, at any rate, to spare her now? But yet he remained. He must ask her pardon before he went; he would do that, and then he would go.

His object was to see her without going to Eaton Square. His instinct told him that Sir Henry no longer wished to see him there, and he was unwilling to enter the house of any one who did not wish his presence. For two weeks he failed in his object. He certainly did see Lady Harcourt, but not in such a way as to allow of conversation: but at last fortune was propitious,—or the reverse, and he found himself alone with her.

She was seated quite alone, turning over the engravings which lay in a portfolio before her, when he came up to her.

'Do not be angry,' he said, 'if I ask you to listen to me for a few moments.'

She still continued to move the engravings before her, but with a slower motion than before; and though her eye still rested on the plates, he might have seen, had he dared to look at her, that her mind was far away from them. He might have seen also that there was no flash of anger now in her countenance: her spirit was softer than on that evening when she had reproached him; for she had remembered that he also had been deeply injured. But she answered nothing to the request which he thus made.

'You told me that I was unforgiving,' he continued, 'I now come to beg that you will not be unforgiving also; that is, if I have done anything that has caused you—caused you to be less happy than you might have been.'

'Less happy!' she said; but not with that scorn with which she had before repeated his words.

'You believe, I hope, that I would wish you to be happy; that I would do anything in my power to make you so?'

'There can be nothing now in your power, Mr Bertram.' And as she spoke she involuntarily put an emphasis on the now, which made her words convey much more than she had intended.

'No,' he said. 'No. What can such a one as I do? What could I ever have done? But say that you forgive me, Lady Harcourt.'

'Let us both forgive,' she whispered, and as she did so, she put out her hand to him. 'Let us both forgive. It is all that we can do for each other.'

'Oh, Caroline, Caroline!' he said, speaking hardly above his breath, and with his eyes averted, but still holding her hand; or attempting to hold it, for as he spoke she withdrew it.

'I was unjust to you the other night. It is so hard to be just when one is so wretched. We have been like two children who have quarrelled over their plaything, and broken it in pieces while it was yet new. We cannot put the wheels again together, or make the broken reed produce sweet sounds.'

'No,' he said. 'No, no, no. No sounds are any longer sweet. There is no music now.'

'But as we have both sinned, Mr Bertram, so should we both forgive.'

'But I—I have nothing to forgive.'

'Alas, yes! and mine was the first fault. I knew that you really loved me, and—'

'Loved you! Oh, Caroline!'

'Hush, Mr Bertram; not so; do not speak so. I know that you would not wrong me; I know you would not lead me into trouble—not into further trouble; into worse misery.'

'And I, that might have led you—no; that might have been led to such happiness! Lady Harcourt, when I think of what I have thrown away—'

'Think of it not at all, Mr Bertram.'

'And you; can you command your thoughts?'

'Sometimes; and by practice I hope always; at any rate, I make an effort. And now, good-bye. It will be sweet to me to hear that you have forgiven me. You were very angry, you know, when you parted from me last at Littlebath.'

'If there be anything for me to forgive, I do forgive it with all my heart; with all my heart.'

'And now, God bless you, Mr Bertram. The thing that would most tend to make me contented would be to see you married to some one you could love; a weight would then be off my soul which now weighs on it very heavily.' And so saying, she rose from her seat, and left him standing over the engravings. He had thrown his pearl away; a pearl richer than all his tribe.* There was nothing for him now but to bear the loss.

There were other sources of unpleasantness between Sir Henry and his wife besides her inclination for dancing. Sir Henry had now paid one half-year's interest on the sum of money which had been lent to him by the old gentleman at Hadley, and had been rather disgusted at finding that it was taken as a matter of course. He was not at the present moment by any means overburdened with money. His constant devotion to politics interfered considerably with his practice. He was also perhaps better known as a party lawyer than as a practical or practising one; and thus, though his present career was very brilliant, it was not quite so profitable as he had hoped. Most lawyers when they begin to devote themselves to politics have secured, if not a fortune, at least the means of making it. And, even at his age, Sir Henry might have been said to have done this had his aspirations been in any way moderate. But they were not moderate. He wished to shine with extreme brilliancy; to live up to the character for wealth which the world gave him; and to give it out as a fact to be understood by all men that he was to be the heir of the Hadley Crœsus.

There was, perhaps, a certain wisdom in this, a wisdom of a dashing chancy nature. Fortune favours the brave; and the world certainly gives the most credit to those who are able to give an unlimited credit to themselves. But there was certainly risk in the life he led. The giving of elegant little dinners two or three times a week in London is an expensive amusement—and so he began to be very anxious about the old gentleman.

But what was he to do that he might get near those money-bags? There was the game. What best sportsman's dodge might he use so as to get it into his bag? Perhaps to do nothing, to use no sportsman's dodge would have been the best. But then it is so hard to do nothing when so much might be gained by doing something very well.

Sir Henry, duly instructed as to the weaknesses customary to old men, thought his wife would be his best weapon—his surest dodge. If she could be got to be attentive and affectionate to her grandfather, to visit him, and flatter him, and hover about him, much might be done. So thought Sir Henry. But do what he might, Lady Harcourt would not assist him. It was not part of her bargain that she should toady an old man who had never shown any special regard for her.

'I think you ought to go down to Hadley,' Sir Henry said to her one morning.

'What, to stay there?' said Caroline.

'Yes; for a fortnight or so. Parliament will be up now in three weeks, and I shall go to Scotland for a few days. Could not you make it out with the old gentleman till you go to the Grimsdales?'

'I would much rather remain at home, Sir Henry.'

'Ah, yes; that is just like you. And I would much rather that you went.'

'If you wish to shut the house up, I shall not object to go to Littlebath.'

'Very probably not. But I should object to you going there—exceedingly object to it. Of all places, it is the most vulgar, the most—'

'You forget that I have dear friends living there.'

'Dear friends! Yes; Miss Todd, I suppose. I think we may as well leave Miss Todd alone. At the present moment, I am particularly anxious that you should be attentive to your grandfather.'

'But I have never been in the habit of staying at Hadley.'

'Then the sooner you get into the habit the better.'

'I cannot think why you should wish me to trouble an old man who would not have the slightest pleasure in seeing me.'

'That is all nonsense. If you behave well to him, he would have pleasure. Do you ever write to him?'

'Never.'

'Write to him today then, and ask whether he would be glad to have you.'

Caroline did not answer her husband immediately, but went on buttering her toast, and sipping her tea. She had never yet disobeyed any positive order that he had given, and she was now thinking whether she could obey this order; or, if not, how she would explain to him that she could not do so.

'Well!' said he; 'why do you not answer me? Will you write to him today?'

'I had much rather not.'

'Does that mean that you won't?'

'I fear, Sir Henry, that it must mean it. I have not been on terms with my grandfather which would admit of my doing so.'

'Nonsense!' said her lord and master.

'You are not very civil to me this morning.'

'How can a man be civil when he hears such trash as that? You know how I am situated—how great the stake is; and you will do nothing to help me win it.' To this she made no answer. Of what use would it be for her to answer? She also had thrown away her pearl, and taken in exchange this piece of brass. There was nothing for her, too, but to bear her misery.

'Upon my word, you take it all very coolly,' he continued; 'you seem to think that houses, and furniture, and carriages, and horses are to grow up all round you without any effort on your own part. Does it ever strike you that these things cost money?'

'I will give them all up tomorrow if you wish it.'

'That you know is nonsense.'

'It was your doing to surround me with these things, and your reproach is not just. Nay, it is not manly.'

'A woman's idea of manliness is very extended. You expect to get everything, and to do nothing. You talk of justice! Do you not know that when I married you, I looked to your uncle's fortune?'

'Certainly not: had I known it, I should have told you how vain I believed any such hope to be.'

'Then, why on earth—?' But he refrained from finishing his question. Even he could not bring himself to tell her that he had married her with no other view. He merely slammed the door behind him as he left the room.

Yes; she had certainly thrown her pearl away. What a life was this to which she had doomed herself! what treatment was this for that Caroline Waddington, who had determined to win the world and wear it! She had given herself to a brute, who had taken her only because she might perhaps be the heiress of a rich old man.

And then she thought of that lost pearl. How could she do other than think of it? She thought of what her life would have been had she bravely committed herself to his hands, fearing nothing, trusting everything. She remembered his energy during those happy days in which he had looked forward to an early marriage. She remembered his tenderness of manner, the natural gallantry of his heart, the loving look of his bold eye; and then she thought of her husband.

Yes, she thought of him long and wildly. And as she did so, the indifference with which she had regarded him grew into hatred. She shuddered as her imagination made that frightful contrast between the picture which her eyes would have so loved to look on if it were only lawful, and that other picture to look on which was her legal doom. Her brow grew wildly black as she thought of his caresses, his love, which were more hateful to her even than his coarse ill-humour. She thought of all this; and, as she did so, she asked herself that question which comes first to the mind of all creatures when in misery: is there no means of release; no way of escape? was her bark utterly ruined, and for ever?

That marriage without love is a perilous step for any woman who has a heart within her bosom. For those who have none—or only so much as may be necessary for the ordinary blood-circulating department—such an arrangement may be convenient enough. Caroline Waddington had once flattered herself that that heart of hers was merely a blood-circulating instrument. But she had discovered her mistake, and learned the truth before it was too late. She had known what it was to love—and yet she had married Henry Harcourt! Seldom, indeed, will punishment be so lame of foot as to fail in catching such a criminal as she had been.

Punishment—bitter, cruel, remorseless punishment—had caught her now, and held her tight within its grasp. He, too, had said that he was wretched. But what could his wretchedness be to hers? He was not married to a creature that he hated: he was not bound in a foul Mezentian embrace* to a being against whom all his human gorge rose in violent disgust. Oh! if she could only be alone, as he was alone! If it could be granted to her to think of her love, to think of him in solitude and silence—in a solitude which no beast with a front of brass and feet of clay had a right to break, both by night and day! Ah! if her wretchedness might only be as his wretchedness! How blessed would she not think herself!

And then she again asked herself whether there might not be some escape. That women had separated themselves from their husbands she well knew. That pleas of ill-usage, of neglect, of harshness of temper, had been put forward and accepted by the world, to the partial enfranchisement of the unhappy wife, she had often heard. But she had also heard that in such cases cruelty must be proved. A hasty word, a cross look, a black brow would not suffice. Nor could she plead that she hated the man, that she had never loved him, that she had married him in wounded pique, because her lover—he whom she did love—had thrown her off. There was no ground, none as yet, on which she could claim her freedom. She had sold herself as a slave, and she must abide her slavery. She had given herself to this beast with the face of brass and the feet of clay, and she must endure the cold misery of his den. Separation—solitude—silence! He—that he whom her heart worshipped—he might enjoy such things; but for her there was no such relief within her reach.

She had gone up into her room when Sir Henry left her, in order that no one might see her wretchedness, and there she remained for hours. 'No!' at last she said aloud, lifting her head from the pillow on which her face had been all but hid, and standing erect in the room; 'no! I will not bear it. I will not endure it. He cannot make me.' And with quick steps she walked across and along the room, stretching forth her arms as though seeking aid from some one; ay, and as though she were prepared to fight the battle herself if no one would come to aid her.

At this moment there was a knock at her chamber-door, and her maid came in.

'Mr Bertram is in the drawing-room, my lady.'

'Mr Bertram! Which Mr Bertram?'

'Mr Bertram, my lady; the gentleman that comes here. Sir Henry's friend.'

'Oh, very well. Why did John say that I was at home.'

'Oh, my lady, I can't say that. Only he told me to tell your ladyship that Mr Bertram was in the drawing-room.'

Lady Harcourt paused for a moment. Then she said, 'I will be down directly;' and the Abigail retired. During that moment she had decided that, as he was there, she would meet him yet once again.

It has been said that Bertram was unwilling to go to Sir Henry's house. As long as he had thought of remaining in town he was so. But now he had resolved to fly, and had resolved also that before he did so he would call in the ordinary way and say one last farewell. John, the servant, admitted him at once; though he had on that same morning sent bootless away a score of other suppliants for the honour of being admitted to Lady Harcourt's presence.

Bertram was standing with his back to the door, looking into a small conservatory that opened from the drawing-room, when the mistress of the house entered. She walked straight up to him, after having carefully closed the door, and just touching his hand, she said, 'Mr Bertram, why are you here? You should be thousands and thousands of miles away if that were possible. Why are you here?'

'Lady Harcourt, I will divide myself from you by any distance you may demand. But may I not come to you to tell you that I am going?'

'To tell me that you are going!'

'Yes. I shall not trouble you much longer. I have become sure of this: that to remain near you and not to love you, to remain near you and not to say that I love you is impossible. And therefore I am going.' And he held out his hand, which she had as yet hardly taken—had barely touched.

He was going; but she was to remain. He would escape; but her prison bars could not be broken. Ah, that she could have gone with him! How little now would wealth have weighed with her; or high worldly hopes, or dreams of ambition! To have gone with him anywhere—honestly to have gone with him—trusting to honest love and a true heart. Ah! how much joy is there in this mortal, moribund world if one will but open one's arms to take it!

Ah! young ladies, sweet young ladies, dear embryo mothers of our England as it will be, think not overmuch of your lovers' incomes. He that is true and honest will not have to beg his bread—neither his nor yours. The true and honest do not beg their bread, though it may be that for awhile they eat it without much butter. But what then? If a wholesome loaf on your tables, and a strong arm round your waists, and a warm heart to lean on cannot make you happy, you are not the girls for whom I take you.

Caroline's bread was buttered, certainly; but the butter had been mixed with gall, and she could not bring herself to swallow it. And now he had come to tell her that he was going; he whose loaf, and arm, and heart she might have shared. What would the world say of her if she were to share his flight?

'Good-bye,' she said, as she took his proffered hand.

'And is that all?'

'What would you have, Mr Bertram?'

'What would I have? Ah, me! I would have that which is utterly—utterly—utterly beyond my reach.'

'Yes, utterly—utterly,' she repeated. And as she said so, she thought again, what would the world say of her if she were to share his flight?

'I suppose that now, for the last time, I may speak truly—as a man should speak. Lady Harcourt, I have never ceased to love you, never for one moment; never since that day when we walked together among those strange tombs. My love for you has been the dream of my life.'

'But, why—why—why?—' She could not speak further, for her voice was choked with tears.

'I know what you would say. Why was I so stern to you!'

'Why did you go away? Why did you not come to us?'

'Because you distrusted me; not as your lover, but as a man. But I did not come here to blame you, Caroline.'

'Nor to be blamed.'

'No, nor to be blamed. What good can come of reproaches? We now know each other's faults, if we never did before. And we know also each other's truth—' He paused a moment, and then added, 'For, Caroline, your heart has been true.'

She sat herself down upon a chair, and wept, with her face hidden within her hands. Yes, her heart had been true enough; if only her words, her deeds, her mind could have been true also.

He came up to her, and lightly put his hand upon her shoulder. His touch was very light, but yet she felt that there was love in it—illicit, dishonest love. There was treason in it to her lord's rights. Her lord! Yes, he was her lord, and it was treason. But it was very sweet that touch; it was as though a thrill of love passed across her and embraced her whole body. Treason to such a creature as that! a brute with a face of brass and feet of clay, who had got hold of her with a false idea that by her aid he could turn his base brass into gold as base! Could there be treason to such a one as he? Ah! what would the world say of her were she to share that flight?

'Caroline,' he murmured in her ear. 'Caroline; dearest Caroline!' Thus he murmured soft words into her ear, while his hand still rested gently on her shoulder—oh, so gently! And still she answered nothing, but the gurgling of her sobs was audible to him enough. 'Caroline,' he repeated; 'dearest, dearest Caroline.' And then he was on his knees beside her; and the hand which had touched her shoulder was now pressed upon her arm.

'Caroline, speak to me—say one word. I will go if you bid me. Yes, even alone. I will go alone if you have the heart to say so. Speak, Caroline.'

'What would you have me say?' and she looked at him through her tears, so haggard, so wild, so changed, that he was almost frightened at her countenance. 'What would you have me say? what would you have me do?'

'I will be your slave if you will let me,' said he.

'No, George—you mean that I might be your slave—for awhile, till you thought me too base even for that.'

'Ah! you little know me.'

'I should but little know you if I thought you could esteem me in that guise. There; God's mercy has not deserted me. It is over now. Go, George—go—go; thou, only love of my heart; my darling; mine that might have been; mine that never can be now—never—never—never. Go, George. It is over now. I have been base, and vile, and cowardly—unworthy of your dear memory. But it shall not be so again. You shall not blush that you have loved me.'

'But, ah! that I have lost your love.'

'You shall not blush that you have loved me, nor will I blush that I, too, have loved you. Go, George; and remember this, the farther, the longer, the more entirely we are apart, the better, the safer it will be. There; there. Go now. I can bear it now; dearest, dearest George.'

He took her outstretched hands in his, and stood for awhile gazing into her face. Then, with the strong motion of his arms, he drew her close to his breast, pressed her to his heart, and imprinted one warm kiss upon her brow. Then he left her, and got to the drawing-room door with his fleetest step.

'I beg your pardon, sir,' said John, who met him exactly on the landing; 'but I think my lady rang.'

'Lady Harcourt did not ring. She is not well, and you had better not disturb her,' said Bertram, trying to look as though he were no whit disconcerted.

'Oh, very well, sir; then I'll go down again;' and so saying John followed George Bertram into the hall, and opened the door for him very politely.

CHAPTER XXXVI

A MATRIMONIAL DIALOGUE

SIR HENRY had said also on this day that he would not dine at home; but he came home before dinner; and after being for a few minutes in his own study, he sent for his wife. Abigail, coming up to her, brought her Sir Henry's love, and would she be good enough to step downstairs for five minutes? This was very civil; so she did step down, and found Sir Henry alone in his study.

'George Bertram has been here today?' were the first words which the husband spoke when he saw that the door had been fairly closed behind his wife.

What communication there may have been between Sir Henry and his servant John is, O my reader, a matter too low for you and me. That there had been some communication we must both fear. Not that Sir Henry wished to find his wife guilty; not that he had at all suspected that he should find her guilty. But he did wish to have her entirely in his power; and he wished also that Bertram should be altogether banished from his house.

'George Bertram has been here today?' He did not look cruel, or violent, or threatening as he spoke; but yet there was that in his eye which was intended to make Caroline tremble. Caroline, however, did not tremble; but looking up into his face with calm dignity replied, that Mr Bertram had called that morning.

'And would you object to telling me what passed between you?'

Caroline still looked him full in the face. He was sitting, but she had not sat down. She was standing before him, faultless in demeanour, in posture, and in dress. If it had been his aim to confound her, he certainly had so far missed his object.

'Would I object to telling you what passed between us? The question is a very singular one;' and then she paused for a moment. 'Yes, Sir Henry, I should object.'

'I thought as much,' said he.

She still stood before him, perfectly silent, and he sat there, silent also. He hardly knew how to go on with the interview. He wanted her to defend herself, but this was the very thing which she did not intend to do. 'May I go now?' she asked, after awhile.

'No; not quite yet. Sit down, Caroline; sit down. I wish to speak to you. George Bertram has been here, and there has been that between you of which you are ashamed to speak!'

'I never said so, Sir Henry—nor will I allow you to say so. There has been that between us today which I would rather bury in silence. But if you command me, I will tell you all.'

'Command! you are always talking of commands.'

'I have to do so very often. In such marriages as ours they must be spoken of—must be thought of. If you command me, I will tell you. If you do not, I will be silent.'

Sir Henry hardly knew what answer to make to this. His object was to frighten his wife. That there had been words between her and George Bertram of which she, as his wife, would be afraid to tell, he had been thoroughly convinced. Yet she now offered to repeat to him everything if he would only desire her to do so; and in making this offer, she seemed to be anything but afraid.

'Sit down, Caroline.' She then sat down just opposite to him. 'I should have thought that you would have felt that, circumstanced as he, and you, and I are, the intercourse between you and him should have been of the most restrained kind—should have had in it nothing of the old familiarity.'

'Who brought us again together?'

'I did so; trusting to your judgment and good taste.'

'I did not wish to see him. I did not ask him here. I would have remained at home month after month rather than have met him, had I been allowed my own way.'

'Nonsense! Why should you have been so afraid to meet him?'

'Because I love him.'

As she said this she still looked into his face fearlessly—we may almost say boldly; so much so that Sir Henry's eyes almost quailed before hers. On this she had at any rate resolved, that she would never quail before him.

But by degrees there came across his brow a cloud that might have made her quail had she not been bold. He had come there determined not to quarrel with her. An absolute quarrel with her would not suit him—would not further his plans, as they were connected with Mr Bertram at Hadley. But it might be that he could not fail to quarrel with her. He was not a man without blood in his veins—without feelings at his heart. He could have loved her in his way, could she have been content to love him. Nay, he had loved her; and while she was the acknowledged possession of another, he had thought that to obtain her he would have been willing to give up many worldly goods. Now he had obtained her; and there she sat, avowing to him that she still loved his unsuccessful rival. It was no wonder that his brow grew black, despite his own policy.

'And he has been here today in order that you might tell him so?'

'He has been here today, and I did tell him so,' said Caroline, looking still full up into her husband's eyes. 'What brought him here I cannot say.'

'And you tell me this to my face?'

'Well; would you have me tell you a lie? Did I not tell you the same when you first asked me to marry you? Did I not repeat it to you again but a week before we were married? Do you think that a few months could make the difference? Do you think that such months as these have been could have effaced his memory?'

'And you mean, then, to entertain him as your lover?'

'I mean to entertain him not at all. I mean that he shall never again enter any house in which I may be doomed to live. You brought him here; and I—though I knew that the trial would be hard—I thought that I could bear it. I find that I cannot. My memory is too clear; my thoughts of other days too vivid; my remorse—'

'Go on, madam; pray go on.'

'No, I shall not go on. I have said enough.'

'Ah! you said more than that to him when he was here.'

'Not half so much.'

'Was he not kneeling at your feet?'

'Yes, sir, he did kneel at my feet;' and as she answered the question she rose up, as though it were impossible for her any longer to sit in the presence of a man who so evidently had set a spy upon her actions.

'Well, and what then? Since you are so little ashamed of the truth, tell it all.'

'I am not at all ashamed of the truth. He came to tell me that he was going—and I bade him go.'

'And you allowed him to embrace you—to hold you in his arms—to kiss you?'

'Ah me; yes—for the last time. He did kiss me. I feel his lips now upon my brow. And then I told him that I loved him; loved none but him; could love none other. Then I bade him begone; and he went. Now, sir, I think you know it all. You seem to have had two accounts of the interview; I hope they do not disagree?'

'Such audacious effrontery I never witnessed in my life—never heard of before!'

'What, sir, did you think that I should lie to you?'

'I thought there was some sense of shame left in you.'

'Too high a sense of shame for that. I wish you could know it all. I wish I could tell you the tone of his voice, and the look of his eye. I wish I could tell you how my heart drooped, and all but fainted, as I felt that he must leave me for ever. I am a married woman, and it was needful that he should go.'

After this there was a slight pause, and then she added: 'Now, Sir Henry, I think you know it all. Now may I go?'

He rose from his chair and began walking the length of the room, backwards and forwards, with quick step. As we have before said, he had a heart in his bosom; he had blood in his veins; he had those feelings of a man which make the scorn of a beautiful woman so intolerable. And then she was his wife, his property, his dependant, his own. For a moment he forgot the Hadley money-bags, sorely as he wanted them, and the true man spoke out with full, unabated anger.

'Brazen-faced harlot!' he exclaimed, as he passed her in his walk; 'unmitigated harlot!'

'Yes, sir,' she answered, in a low tone, coming up to him as she spoke, laying her hand upon his arm, and looking still full into his face—looking into it with such a gaze that even he cowered before her. 'Yes, sir, I was the thing you say. When I came to you, and sold my woman's purity for a name, a house, a place before the world—when I gave you my hand, but could not give my heart, I was—what you have said.'

'And were doubly so when he stood here slobbering on your neck.'

'No, Sir Henry, no. False to him I have been; false to my own sex; false, very false to my own inner self; but never false to you.'

'Madam, you have forgotten my honour.'

'I have at any rate been able to remember my own.'

They were now standing face to face; and as she said these last words, it struck Sir Henry that it might be well to take them as a sign of grace, and to commence from them that half-forgiveness which would be necessary to his projects.

'You have forgotten yourself, Caroline—'

'Stop a moment, Sir Henry, and let me finish, since you will not allow me to remain silent. I have never been false to you, I say; and, by God's help, I never will be—'

'Well, well.'

'Stop, sir, and let me speak. I have told you often that I did not love you. I tell you so now again. I have never loved you—never shall love you. You have called me now by a base name; and in that I have lived with you and have not loved you, I dare not say that you have called me falsely. But I will sin no more.'

'What is it you mean?'

'I will not deserve the name again—even from you.'

'Nonsense; I do not understand you. You do not know what you are saying.'

'Yes, Sir Henry, I do know well what I am saying. It may be that I have done you some injury; if so, I regret it. God knows that you have done me much. We can neither of us now add to each other's comfort, and it will be well that we should part.'

'Do you mean me to understand that you intend to leave me?'

'That is what I intend you to understand.'

'Nonsense; you will do no such thing.'

'What! would you have us remain together, hating each other, vilifying each other, calling each other base names as you just now called me? And do you think that we could still be man and wife? No, Sir Henry. I have made one great mistake—committed one wretched, fatal error. I have so placed myself that I must hear myself so called and bear it quietly; but I will not continue to be so used. Do you think he would have called me so?'

'Damn him!'

'That will not hurt him. Your words are impotent against him, though they may make me shudder.'

'Do not speak of him, then.'

'No, I will not. I will only think of him.'

'By heavens! Caroline, your only wish is to make me angry.'

'I may go now, I suppose?'

'Go—yes; you may go; I will speak to you tomorrow, when you will be more cool.'

'Tomorrow, Sir Henry, I will not speak to you; nor the day afterwards, nor the day after that. What you may wish to say now I will hear; but remember this—after what has passed today, no consideration on earth shall induce me to live with you again. In any other respect I will obey your orders—if I find it possible.'

She stayed yet a little while longer, leaning against the table, waiting to hear whether or no he would answer her; but as he sat silent, looking before him, but not at her, with his hands thrust deep into his pockets, she without further words withdrew, and quietly closed the door after her. As she did so, the faithful John was seen moving away to the top of the kitchen stairs. She would hardly have cared had the faithful John been present during the whole interview.

Sir Henry sat silent for a quarter of an hour, meditating how he would now play his game. As regarded merely personal considerations, he was beginning to hate Caroline almost as much as she hated him. A man does not like to be told by a beautiful woman that every hair of his head is odious to her, while the very footsteps of another are music in her ears. Perhaps it does not mend the matter when the hated man is the husband.

But still Sir Henry wished to keep his wife. It has been quite clear that Caroline had thrown up her game. She had flattered herself that she could play it; but the very moment the cards went against her she discovered her own weakness and threw them away. Sir Henry was of a stronger mind, and not so easily disgusted; he would try yet another deal. Indeed, his stakes were too high to allow of his abandoning them.

So arousing himself with some exertion, he dressed himself, went out to dine, hurried down to the House, and before the evening was over was again the happy, fortunate solicitor-general, fortune's pet, the Crichton* of the hour, the rising man of his day.

CHAPTER XXXVII

THE RETURN TO HADLEY

WE must now return for awhile to Hadley. Since the day on which Miss Baker had written that letter to Sir Lionel, she had expressed no wish to leave her uncle's house. Littlebath had no charms for her now. The colonel was still there, and so was the colonel's first love—Miss Todd: let them forgive and forget, and marry each other at last if they so pleased. Miss Baker's fit of ambition was over, and she was content to keep her uncle's house at Hadley, and to see Caroline whenever she could spare a day and get up to London for that purpose.

And the old gentleman was less bearish than she thought he would have been. He occasionally became rusty about shillings and sixpences, and scolded because his niece would have a second fire lighted; but by degrees he forgot even this grievance, and did not make himself more disagreeable or exacting than old age, wealth, and suffering generally are when they come together.

And then when Adela left London, Miss Baker was allowed to ask her to stop with them at Hadley—and Adela did as she was asked. She went direct from Eaton Square to Mr Bertram's house; and was still there at the time alluded to in the last chapter.

It was on the second morning after Sir Henry's visit to his wife that the postman brought to Miss Baker a letter from Lady Harcourt. The two ladies were sitting at the time over the breakfast-table, and old Mr Bertram propped up with pillows, with his crutches close to his hand, was sitting over the fire in his accustomed arm-chair. He did not often get out of it now, except when he was taken away to bed; but yet both his eye and his voice were as sharp as ever when he so pleased; and though he sat there paralyzed and all but motionless, he was still master of his house, and master also of his money.

'Good heavens!' exclaimed Miss Baker, with startled voice before her letter had been half read through.

'What's the matter?' demanded Mr Bertram sharply.

'Oh, Miss Baker! what is it?' asked Adela.

'Goodness gracious! Oh, dear! oh, dear! oh, dear!' And Miss Baker, with her handkerchief to her eyes, began to weep most bitterly.

'What ails you? Who is the letter from?' said Mr Bertram.

'Oh, dear! oh, dear! Read it, Adela. Oh, Mr Bertram, here is such a misfortune!'

'What is it, Miss Gauntlet? That fool will never tell me.'

Adela took the letter and read it through.

'Oh, sir,' she said, 'it is indeed a misfortune.'

'Devil take it! what misfortune?'

'Caroline has quarrelled with Sir Henry,' said Miss Baker.

'Oh, is that all?' said Mr Bertram.

'Ah, sir; I fear this quarrel will prove serious,' said Adela.

'Serious; nonsense; how serious? You never thought, did you, that he and she would live together like turtle doves? He married for money, and she for ambition; of course, they'll quarrel.' Such was the wisdom of Mr Bertram, and at any rate he had experience on his side.

'But, uncle; she wishes to leave him, and hopes that you'll let her come here.'

'Come here—fiddlestick! What should I do here with the wife of such a man as him?'

'She declares most positively that nothing shall induce her to live with him again.'

'Fiddlestick!'

'But, uncle—'

'Why, what on earth did she expect? She didn't think to have it all sunshine, did she? When she married the man, she knew she didn't care for him; and now she determines to leave him because he won't pick up her pocket-handkerchief! If she wanted that kind of thing, why did not she marry my nephew?'

This was the first time that Mr Bertram had been heard to speak of George in a tone of affection, and both Miss Baker and Miss Gauntlet were not a little surprised. They had never heard him speak of Caroline as his granddaughter.

During the whole of that day, Mr Bertram was obdurate; and he positively refused to receive Lady Harcourt at his house unless she came there with the full permission of her husband. Miss Baker, therefore, was obliged to write by the first post, asking for a day's delay before she sent her final answer. But on the next morning a letter reached the old gentleman himself, from Sir Henry. Sir Henry suggested that the loving grandchild should take the occasion of the season being so nearly over to pay a much-desired visit to her loving grandsire. He did not drop the quarrel altogether; but just alluded to it as a passing cloud—an unfortunate cloud certainly, but one that, without doubt, would soon pass away, and leave the horizon more bright than ever.

The matter was at last arranged by Mr Bertram giving the desired permission. He took no notice himself of Sir Henry's letter, but desired his niece to tell Caroline that she might come there if she liked. So Caroline did come; and Sir Henry gave it out that the London season had been too much for her, and that she, to her deep regret, had been forced to leave town before it was over.

'Sir Omicron was quite imperative,' said Sir Henry, speaking confidentially to his intimate parliamentary friend Mr Madden; 'and as she was to go, it was as well to do the civil to grandpapa Crœsus. I have no time myself; so I must do it by deputy.'

Now Sir Omicron in those days was a great physician.

And so Caroline returned to Hadley; but no bells rang now to greet her coming. Little more than six months had passed since those breakfast speeches had been spoken, in which so much golden prosperity had been promised to bride and bridegroom; and now that vision of gold was at an end; that solid, substantial prosperity had melted away. The bridal dresses of the maids had hardly lost their gloss, and yet all that well-grounded happiness was gone.

'So, you are come back,' said Mr Bertram.

'Yes, sir,' said Caroline, in a low voice. 'I have made a mistake in life, and I must hope that you will forgive me.'

'Such mistakes are very foolish. The sooner you unmake it the better.'

'There will be no unmaking this mistake, sir, never—never—never. But I blame no one but myself.'

'Nonsense! you will of course go back to your husband.'

'Never, Mr Bertram—never! I will obey him or you, or both, if that be possible, in all things but in that. But in that I can obey no one.'

'Psha!' said Mr Bertram. Such was Lady Harcourt's first greeting on her return to Hadley.

Neither Miss Baker nor Adela said much to her on the matter on the first day of her arrival. Her aunt, indeed, never spoke openly to her on the subject. It seemed to be understood between them that it should be dropped. And there was occasionally a weight of melancholy about Lady Harcourt, amounting in appearance almost to savage sternness, which kept all inquiry aloof. Even her grandfather hesitated to speak to her about her husband, and allowed her to live unmolested in the quiet, still, self-controlling mood which she seemed to have adopted with a determined purpose.

For the first fortnight she did not leave the house. At the expiration of that time, on one fine sunny Sunday morning she came down dressed for church. Miss Baker remarked that the very clothes she wore were things that had belonged to her before her marriage, and were all of them of the simplest that a woman can wear without making herself conspicuous before the world. All her jewellery she had laid aside, and every brooch and every ring that had come to her as a married woman, or as a girl about to be married—except that one ring from which an iron fate would not allow her to be parted. Ah, if she could but have laid aside that also!

And then she went to church. There were the same persons there to stare at her now, in her quiet wretchedness, who were there before staring at her in her—triumph may I say? No, there had been no triumph; little even then, except wretchedness; but that misery had not been so open to the public eye.

She went through it very well; and seemed to suffer even less than did her aunt. She had done nothing to spread abroad among the public of Hadley that fiction as to Sir Omicron's opinion which her lord had been sedulous to disseminate in London. She had said very little about herself, but she had at any rate said nothing false. Nor had she acted falsely; or so as to give false impressions. All that little world now around her knew that she had separated herself from her grand husband; and most of them had heard that she had no intention of returning to him.

She had something, therefore, to bear as she sat out that service; and she bore it well. She said her prayers, or seemed to say them, as though unconscious that she were in any way a mark for other women's eyes. And when the sermon was over, she walked home with a steady, even step; whereas Miss Baker trembled at every greeting she received, and at every step she heard.

On that afternoon, Caroline opened her heart to Adela. Hitherto little had passed between them, but those pressings of the hand, those mute marks of sympathy which we all know so well how to give when we long to lighten the sorrows which are too deep to be probed by words. But on this evening after their dinner, Caroline called Adela into her room, and then there was once more confidence between them.

'No, no, Adela, I will never go back to him.' Caroline went on protesting; 'you will not ask me to do that?'

'Those whom God has joined together, let not man put asunder,' said Adela, solemnly.

'Ah, yes; those whom God *has* joined. But did God join us?'

'Oh, Caroline; do not speak so.'

'But, Adela, do not misunderstand me. Do not think that I want to excuse what I have done; or even to escape the penalty. I have destroyed myself as regards this world. All is over for me here. When I brought myself to stand at that altar with a man I never loved; whom I knew I never could love—whom I never tried, and never would try to love—when I did that, I put myself beyond the pale of all happiness. Do not think that I hope for any release.' And Lady Harcourt looked stern enough in her resolution to bear all that fate could bring on her.

'Caroline, God will temper the wind to the shorn lamb, now as always, if you will ask Him.'

'I hope so; I hope so, Adela.'

'Say that you trust so.'

'I do trust. I trust in this—that He will do what is best. Oh, Adela! if you could know what the last month has been; since he came to the house!'

'Ah! why did he ever come?'

'Why, indeed! Did a man ever behave so madly?'

The man she alluded to here was Sir Henry Harcourt, not Mr Bertram.

'But I am glad of it, dearest; very glad. Is it not better so? The truth has been spoken now. I have told him all.'

'You mean Sir Henry?'

'Yes, I told him all before I left. But it was nothing new, Adela. He knew it before. He never dreamed that I loved him. He knew, he must have known that I hated him.'

'Oh, Caroline, Caroline! do not speak like that.'

'And would not you have hated him had you been tied to him? Now that sin will be over. I shall hate him no longer now.'

'Such hatred is a crime. Say what you will, he is still your husband.'

'I deny it. What! when he called me by that name, was he my husband then? Was that a husband's usage? I must carry his name, and wearily walk with that burden to the grave. Such is my penalty for that day's sin. I must abandon all hope of living as other women do. I shall have no shoulder on which to lean, hear no words of love when I am sick, have no child to comfort me. I shall be alone, and yet not master of myself. This I must bear because I was false to my own heart. But yet he is not my husband. Listen to me, Adela; sooner than return to him again, I would put an end to all this world's misery at once. That would be sinful, but the sin would be lighter than that other sin.'

When she spoke in this way, Adela no longer dared to suggest to her that she and Sir Henry might even yet again live together. In Adela's own mind, that course, and that alone, would have been the right one. She looked on such unions as being literally for better or for worse; and failing to reach the better, she would have done her best, with God's assistance, to bear the worst. But then Adela Gauntlet could never have placed herself in the position which Lady Harcourt now filled.

But greatly as they differed, still there was confidence between them. Caroline could talk to her, and to her only. To her grandfather she was all submission; to her aunt she was gentle and affectionate; but she never spoke of her fate with either of them. And so they went on till Adela left them in July; and then the three that were left behind lived together as quiet a household as might have been found in the parish of Hadley, or perhaps in the county of Middlesex.

During this time Lady Harcourt had received two letters from her husband, in both of which he urged her to return to him. In answer to the first, she assured him, in the civilest words which she knew how to use, that such a step was impossible; but, at the same time, she signified her willingness to obey him in any other particular, and suggested that as they must live apart, her present home with her grandfather would probably be thought to be the one most suitable for her. In answer to the second, she had simply told him that she must decline any further correspondence with him as to the possibility of her return.

His next letter was addressed to Mr Bertram. In this he did not go into the matter of their difference at all, but merely suggested that he should be allowed to call at Hadley—with the object of having an interview with Mr Bertram himself.

'There,' said the old man, when he found himself alone with his granddaughter; 'read that.' And Caroline did read it. 'What am I to say to that?'

'What do you think you ought to say, sir?'

'I suppose I must see him. He'll bring an action against me else, for keeping his wife from him. Mind, I tell you, you'll have to go back to him.'

'No, sir! I shall not do that,' said Caroline, very quietly, with something almost like a smile on her face. And then she left him, and he wrote his answer to Sir Henry.

And then Sir Henry came down to Hadley. A day had been named, and Caroline was sore put to it to know how she might best keep out of the way. At last she persuaded her aunt to go up to London with her for the day. This they did, both of them fearing, as they got out of the train, and returned to it, that they might unfortunately meet the man they so much dreaded. But fortune was not so malicious to them; and when they returned to Hadley they found that Sir Henry had also returned to London.

'He speaks very fair,' said Mr Bertram, who sent for Caroline to come to him alone in the dining-room.

'Does he, sir?'

'He is very anxious that you should go back.'

'Ah, sir, I cannot do that.'

'He says you shall have the house in Eaton Square to yourself for the next three months.'

'I shall never go back to Eaton Square, sir.'

'Or he will take a small place for you anywhere at the sea-side that you may choose.'

'I shall want no place if you will allow me to remain here.'

'But he has all your money, you know—your fortune is now his.'

'Well, sir!'

'And what do you mean to do?'

'I will do what you bid me—except going back to him.'

The old man sat silent for awhile, and then again he spoke.

'Well, I don't suppose you know your own mind, as yet.'

'Oh, sir! indeed I do.'

'I say I suppose you don't. Don't interrupt me—I have suggested this: that you should remain here six months, and that then he should come again and see—'

'You, sir.'

'Well—see me, if I'm alive: at the end of that time you'll have to go back to him. Now, good-night.'

And so it was settled; and for the next six months the same dull, dreary life went on in the old house at Hadley.

CHAPTER XXXVIII

CAIRO

MEN and women, or I should rather say ladies and gentlemen, used long ago, when they gave signs of weakness about the chest, to be sent to the south of Devonshire; after that, Madeira came into fashion; but now they are all despatched to Grand Cairo. Cairo has grown to be so near home, that it will soon cease to be beneficial, and then the only air capable of revigorating the English lungs will be that of Labuan or Jeddo.

But at the present moment, Grand Cairo has the vogue. Now it had so happened during the last winter, and especially in the drying month of March, that Arthur Wilkinson's voice had become weak; and he had a suspicious cough, and was occasionally feverish, and perspired o' nights; and on these accounts the Sir Omicron of the Hurst Staple district ordered him off to Grand Cairo.

This order was given in October, with reference to the coming winter, and in the latter end of November, Arthur Wilkinson started for the East. Two articles he had first to seek—the one being a necessary, and the other a luxury—and both he found. These were a curate and a companion. The Reverend Gabriel Gilliflower was his curate; and of him we need only hope that he prospered well, and lived happily under the somewhat stern surveillance of his clerical superior, Mrs Wilkinson. His companion was George Bertram.

About the end of November they started through France, and got on board the P. and O. Company's vessel at Marseilles. It is possible that there may be young ladies so ignorant as not to know that the P. and O. is the Peninsular and Oriental Steam Navigation Company, and therefore the matter is now explained. In France they did not stop long enough to do more than observe how much better the railway carriages are there than in England, how much dearer the hotels are in Paris than in London, and how much worse they are in Marseilles than in any other known town in the world.

Nor need much be said of their journey thence to Alexandria. Of Malta, I should like to write a book, and may perhaps do so some day; but I shall hardly have time to discuss its sunlight, and fortifications, and hospitality, and old magnificence, in the fag-end of a third volume; so we will pass on to Alexandria.

Oh, Alexandria! mother of sciences!* once the favoured seat of the earth's learning! Oh, Alexandria! beloved by the kings! It is of no use. No man who has seen the Alexandria of the present day can keep a seat on a high horse when he speaks of that most detestable of cities. How may it fitly be described? May we not say that it has all the filth of the East, without any of that picturesque beauty with which the East abounds; and that it has also the eternal, grasping, solemn love of lucre which pervades our western marts, but wholly unredeemed by the society, the science, and civilization of the West?

Alexandria is fast becoming a European city; but its Europeans are from Greece and the Levant! 'Auri sacra fames!'* is the motto of modern Greece. Of Alexandria it should be, 'Auri fames sacrissima!' Poor Arabs! poor Turks! giving way on all sides to wretches so much viler than yourselves, what a destiny is before you!

'What income,' I asked a resident in Alexandria, 'what income should an Englishman have to live here comfortably?' 'To live here *comfortably*, you should say ten thousand a year, and then let him cut his throat first!' Such was my friend's reply.

But God is good, and Alexandria will become a place less detestable than at present. Fate and circumstances must Anglicize it in spite of the huge French consulate, in spite of legions of greedy Greeks; in spite even of sand, mosquitoes, bugs, and dirt, of winds from India, and of thieves from Cyprus.

The P. and O. Company will yet be the lords of Egypt; either that or some other company or set of men banded together to make Egypt a highway. It is one stage on our road to the East; and the time will soon come when of all the stages it will neither be the slowest nor the least comfortable. The railway from Alexandria to Suez is now all opened within ten miles; will be all opened before these pages can be printed.

This railway belongs to the viceroy of Egypt; but his passengers are the Englishmen of India, and his paymaster is an English company.

But, for all that, I do not recommend any of my friends to make a long sojourn at Alexandria.

Bertram and Wilkinson did not do so, but passed on speedily to Cairo. They went to the Pharos and to Pompey's Pillar; inspected Cleopatra's Needle,* and the newly excavated so-called Greek church; watched the high spirits of one set of passengers going out to India—young men free of all encumbrances, and pretty girls full of life's brightest hopes—and watched also the morose, discontented faces of another set returning home burdened with babies and tawny-coloured nurses, with silver rings in their toes—and then they went off to Cairo.

There is no romance now, gentle readers, in this journey from Alexandria to Cairo; nor was there much when it was taken by our two friends. Men now go by railway, and then they went by the canal boat. It is very much like English travelling, with this exception, that men dismount from their seats, and cross the Nile in a ferry-boat, and that they pay five shillings for their luncheon instead of sixpence. This ferry does, perhaps, afford some remote chance of adventure, as was found the other day, when a carriage was allowed to run down the bank, in which was sitting a native prince, the heir to the pasha's throne. On that occasion the adventure was important, and the prince was drowned. But even this opportunity for incident will soon disappear; for Mr Brunel, or Mr Stephenson, or Mr Locke,* or some other British engineering celebrity, is building a railway bridge over the Nile, and then the modern traveller's heart will be contented, for he will be able to sleep all the way from Alexandria to Cairo.

Mr Shepheard's hotel at Cairo is to an Englishman the centre of Egypt, and there our two friends stopped. And certainly our countrymen have made this spot more English than England itself. If ever John Bull reigned triumphant anywhere; if he ever shows his nature plainly marked by rough plenty, coarseness, and good intention, he does so at Shepheard's hotel. If there be anywhere a genuine, old-fashioned John Bull landlord now living, the landlord of the hotel at Cairo is the man. So much for the strange new faces and outlandish characters which one meets with in one's travels.

I will not trouble my readers by a journey up the Nile; nor will I even taken them up a pyramid. For do not fitting books for such purposes abound at Mr Mudie's? Wilkinson and Bertram made both the large tour and the little one in proper style. They got at least as far as Thebes, and slept a night under the shade of King Cheops.*

One little episode on their road from Cairo to the Pyramids, I will tell. They had joined a party of which the conducting spirit was a missionary clergyman, who had been living in the country for some years, and therefore knew its ways. No better conducting spirit for such a journey could have been found; for he joined economy to enterprise, and was intent that everything should be seen, and that everything should be seen cheaply.

Old Cairo is a village some three miles from the city, higher up the river; and here, close to the Nilometer,* by which the golden increase of the river is measured, tourists going to the Pyramids are ferried over the river. The tourists are ferried over, as also are the donkeys on which the tourists ride. Now here arose a great financial question. The reis or master of the ferry-boat to which the clerical guide applied was a mighty man, some six feet high, graced with a turban, as Arabs are; erect in his bearing, with bold eye, and fine, free, supple limbs—a noble reis for that Nile ferry-boat. But, noble as he was, he wanted too many piastres—twopence-halfpenny a head too much for each donkey, with its rider.

And then there arose a great hubbub. The ordinary hubbub at this spot is worse than the worst confusion of any other Babel. For the traffic over the Nile is great, and for every man, woman, and child, for every horse and every ass, for every bundle of grass, for every cock and for every hen, a din of twenty tongues is put in motion, and a perpetual fury rages, as the fury of a hurricane. But the hubbub about the missionary's piastres rose higher than all the other hubbubs. Indeed, those who were quarrelling before about their own affairs came and stood round in a huge circle, anxious to know how the noble reis and his clerical opponent would ultimately settle this stiff financial difficulty.

In half an hour neither side would yield one point; but then at last the Egyptian began to show that, noble as he looked, he was made of stuff compressible. He gradually gave up, para* by para, till he allowed donkeys, men, and women to clamber over the sides of his boat at the exact price named by him of the black coat. Never did the church have a more perfect success.

But the battle was not yet over. No sooner was the vessel pushed off into the stream, than the noble reis declared that necessity compelled him to demand the number of piastres originally named by him. He regretted it, but he assured the clergyman that he had no other alternative.

And now how did it behove an ardent missionary to act in such a contest with a subtle Egyptian? How should the eloquence of the Church prevail over this Eastern Mammon? It did prevail very signally. The soldier of peace, scorning further argument in words with such a crafty reis, mindful of the lessons of his youth, raised his right hand, and with one blow between the eyes, laid the Arab captain prostrate on his own deck.

'There,' said he, turning to Wilkinson, 'that is what we call a pastoral visitation in this country. We can do nothing without it.'

The poor reis picked himself up, and picked up also his turban, which had been knocked off, and said not a word more about the piastres. All the crew worked with double diligence at their oars, and the party, as they disembarked from the boat, were treated with especial deference. Even the donkeys were respected. In Egypt the donkeys of a man are respected, ay, and even his donkey-boys, when he shows himself able and willing to knock down all those around him.

A great man there, a native, killed his cook one morning in a rage; and a dragoman, learned in languages, thus told the story to an Englishman:—'De sahib, him vera respecble man. Him kill him cook, Solyman, this morning. Oh, de sahib particklar respecble!' After all, it may be questioned whether this be not a truer criterion of respectability than that other one of keeping a gig.

Oh, those pyramid guides! foul, false, cowardly, bullying thieves! A man who goes to Cairo *must* see the Pyramids. Convention, and the laws of society as arranged on that point, of course require it. But let no man, and, above all, no woman, assume that the excursion will be in any way pleasurable. I have promised that I will not describe such a visit, but I must enter a loud, a screeching protest against the Arab brutes—the sheiks being the very worst of the brutes—who have these monuments in their hands. Their numbers, the filthiness of their dress—or one might almost say no dress—their stench, their obscene indecency, their clattering noise, their rapacity, exercised without a moment's intercession; their abuse, as in this wise: 'Very bad Englishman; dam bad; dam, dam, dam! Him want to take all him money to the grave; but no, no, no! Devil hab him, and money too!' This, be it remembered, from a ferocious, almost blackened Arab, with his face within an inch of your own. And then their flattery, as in this wise: 'Good Englishman—very good!'—and then a tawny hand pats your face, and your back, and the calves of your leg—'Him gib poor Arab one shilling for himself—yes, yes, yes! and then Arab no let him tumble down and break all him legs—yes, yes; break *all* him legs.' And then the patting goes on again. These things, I say, put together, make a visit to the Pyramids no delightful recreation. My advice to my countrymen who are so unfortunate as to visit them is this: let the ladies remain below—not that they ever will do so, if the gentlemen who are with them ascend—and let the men go armed with stout sticks, and mercilessly belabour any Arab who attempts either to bully or to wheedle.

Let every Englishman remember this also, that the ascent is not difficult, though so much noise is made about the difficulty as naturally to make a man think that it is so. And let this also be remembered, that nothing is to be gained by entering the pyramid except dirt, noise, stench, vermin, abuse, and want of air. Nothing is to be seen there—nothing to be heard. A man may sprain his ankle, and certainly will knock his head. He will encounter no other delights but these.

But he certainly will come out a wiser man than he went in. He will then be wise enough to know how wretched a place is the interior of a pyramid—an amount of wisdom with which no teaching of mine will imbue him.

Bertram and Wilkinson were sitting beneath the pyramid, with their faces toward the desert, enjoying the cool night air, when they first began to speak of Adela Gauntlet. Hitherto Arthur had hardly mentioned her name. They had spoken much of his mother, much of the house at Hurst Staple, and much also of Lady Harcourt, of whose separation from her husband they were of course aware; but Arthur had been shy of mentioning Adela's name.

They had been speaking of Mrs Wilkinson, and the disagreeable position in which the vicar found himself in his own house; when, after sitting silent for a moment, he said, 'After all, George, I sometimes think that it would have been better for me to have married.'

'Of course it would—or rather, I should say, will be better. It is what you will do when you return.'

'I don't know about my health now.'

'Your health will be right enough after this winter. I don't see much the matter with it.'

'I am better, certainly;' and then there was another pause.

'Arthur,' continued Bertram, 'I only wish that I had open before me the same chance in life that you have—the same chance of happiness.'

'Do not despair, George. A short time cures all our wounds.'

'Yes; a short time does cure them all—and then comes chaos.'

'I meant a short time in this world.'

'Well, all things are possible; but I do not understand how mine are to be cured. They have come too clearly from my own folly.'

'From such folly,' said Arthur, 'as always impedes the working of human prudence.'

'Do you remember, Arthur, my coming to you the morning after the degrees came down—when you were so low in spirits because you had broken down—when I was so full of triumph?'

'I remember the morning well; but I do not remember any triumph on your part.'

'Ah! I was triumphant—triumphant in my innermost heart. I thought then that all the world must give way to me, because I had taken a double-first. And now—I have given way before all the world. What have I done with all the jewels of my youth? Thrown them before swine!'*

'Come, George; you are hardly seven-and-twenty yet.'

'No, hardly; and I have no profession, no fortune, no pursuit, and no purpose. I am here, sitting on the broken stone of an old tomb, merely because it is as well for me to be here as elsewhere. I have made myself to be one as to whose whereabouts no man need make inquiry—and no woman. If that black, one-eyed brute, whom I thrashed a-top of the pyramid, had stuck his knife in me, who would have been the worse for it? You, perhaps—for six weeks or so.'

'You know there are many would have wept for you.'

'I know but one. She would have wept, while it would be ten times better that she should rejoice. Yes, she would weep; for I have marred her happiness as I have marred my own. But who cares for me, of whose care I can be proud? Who is anxious for me, whom I can dare to thank, whom I may dare to love?'

'Do we not love you at Hurst Staple?'

'I do not know. But I know this, that you ought to be ashamed of me. I think Adela Gauntlet is my friend; that is, if in our pig-headed country a modest girl may love a man who is neither her brother nor her lover.'

'I am sure she is,' said Arthur; and then there was another pause. 'Do you know,' he continued, 'I once thought—'

'Thought what?'

'That you were fond of Adela.'

'So I am, heartily fond of her.'

'But I mean more than that.'

'You once thought that I would have married her if I could. That is what you mean.'

'Yes,' said Wilkinson, blushing to his eyes. But it did not matter; for no one could see him.

'Well; I will make a clean breast of it, Arthur. Men can talk here, sitting in the desert, who would be as mute as death at home in England. Yes; there was once a moment, once *one* moment, in which I would have married her—a moment in which I flattered myself that I could forget Caroline Waddington. Ah! if I could tell you how Adela behaved!'

'How did she behave? Tell me—what did she say?' said Arthur, with almost feverish anxiety.

'She bade me remember, that those who dare to love must dare to suffer. She told me that the wounded stag, "that from the hunter's aim has ta'en a hurt," must endure to live, "left and abandoned of his velvet friends."—And she told me true. I have not all her courage; but I will take a lesson from her, and learn to suffer—quietly, without a word, if that be possible.'

'Then you did propose to her?'

'No; hardly that. I cannot tell what I said myself; but 'twas thus she answered me.'

'But what do you mean by taking a lesson from her? Has she any such suffering?'

'Nay! You may ask her. I did not.'

'But you said so just now; at any rate you left me to infer it. Is there any one whom Adela Gauntlet really loves?'

George Bertram did not answer the question at once. He had plighted his word to her as her friend that he would keep her secret; and then, moreover, that secret had become known to him by mere guesses. He had no right, by any law, to say it as a fact that Adela Gauntlet was not heart-whole. But still he thought that he would say so. Why should he not do something towards making these two people happy?

'Do you believe that Adela is really in love with any one?' repeated Arthur.

'If I tell you that, will you tell me this—Are you in love with any one—you yourself?'

The young clergyman was again ruby-red up to his forehead. He could dare to talk about Adela, but hardly about himself.

'I in love!' he said at last. 'You know that I have been obliged to keep out of that kind of thing. Circumstanced as I have been, I could not marry.'

'But that does not keep a man from falling in love.'

'Does it not?' said Arthur, rather innocently.

'That has not preserved me—nor, I presume, has it preserved you. Come, Arthur, be honest; if a man with thirty-nine articles round his neck can be honest. Out with the truth at once. Do you love Adela, or do you not?'

But the truth would not come out so easily. Whether it was the thirty-nine articles, or the natural modesty of the man's disposition, I will not say; but he did not find himself at the moment able to give a downright answer to this downright question. He would have been well pleased that Bertram should know the whole truth; but the task of telling it went against the grain with him.

'If you do, and do not tell her so,' continued Bertram, when he found that he got no immediate reply, 'I shall think you—. But no; a man must be his own judge in such matters, and of all men I am the least fit to be a judge of others. But I would that it might be so, for both your sakes.'

'Why, you say yourself that she likes some one else.'

'I have never said so. I have said nothing like it. There, when you get home do you yourself ask her whom she loves. But remember this—if it should chance that she should say that it is you, you must be prepared to bear the burden, whatever may be urged to the contrary at the vicarage. And now we will return to roost in this hole of ours.'

Arthur had as yet made no reply to Bertram's question; but as he crept along the base of the pyramid, feeling his steps among the sand and loose stones, he did manage to say a word or two of the truth.

'God bless you, George. I do love her—very dearly.' And then the two cousins understood each other.

It has been said that Alexandria has nothing of an Eastern town but its filth. This cannot at all be said of Cairo. It may be doubted whether Bagdad itself is more absolutely oriental in its appurtenances. When once the Englishman has removed himself five hundred yards from Shepheard's hotel, he begins to feel that he is really in the East. Within that circle, although it contains one of the numerous huge buildings appropriated to the viceroy's own purposes, he is still in Great Britain. The donkey-boys curse in English, instead of Arabic; the men you meet sauntering about, though they do wear red caps, have cheeks as red; and the road is broad and macadamized, and Britannic. But anywhere beyond that circle Lewis* might begin to paint.

Cairo is a beautiful old city; so old in the realities of age that it is crumbling into dust on every side. From time to time the houses are patched up, but only patched; and, except on the Britannic soil above alluded to, no new houses are built. It is full of romance, of picturesque oriental wonders, of strange sights, strange noises, and strange smells. When one is well in the town, every little narrow lane, every turn—and the turns are incessant—every mosque and every shop creates fresh surprise. But I cannot allow myself to write a description of Cairo.

How the dervishes there spun and shook, going through their holy exercises with admirable perseverance, that I must tell. This occurred towards the latter end of the winter, when Wilkinson and Bertram had nearly completed their sojourn in Cairo. Not but what the dervishes had roared out their monotonous prayer to Allah, duly every Friday, at 1 P.M., with as much precision as a service in one of your own cathedrals; but our friends had put the thing off, as hardly being of much interest, and at last went there when they had only one Friday left for the performance.

I believe that, as a rule, a Mahomedan hates a Christian: regarding him merely as Christian, he certainly does so. Had any tidings of confirmed success on the part of the rebels in India* reached the furthermost parts of the Turkish empire, no Christian life would have been safe there. The horrid outrage perpetrated at Jaffa, and the massacre at Jeddah, sufficiently show us what we might have expected. In Syria no Christian is admitted within a mosque, for his foot and touch are considered to carry pollution.

But in Egypt we have caused ourselves to be better respected: we thrash the Arabs and pay them, and therefore they are very glad to see us anywhere. And even the dervishes welcome us to their most sacred rites, with excellent coffee, and a loan of rush-bottomed chairs. Now, when it is remembered that a Mahomedan never uses a chair, it must be confessed that this is very civil. Moreover, let it be said to their immortal praise, that the dervishes of Cairo never ask for backsheish.* They are the only people in the country that do not.

So Bertram and Wilkinson had their coffee with sundry other travelling Britons who were there; and then each, with his chair in his hand, went into the dervishes' hall. This was a large, lofty, round room, the roof of which was in the shape of a cupola; on one side, that which pointed towards Mecca, and therefore nearly due east, there was an empty throne, or tribune, in which the head of the college, or dean of the chapter of dervishes, located himself on his haunches. He was a handsome, powerful man, of about forty, with a fine black beard, dressed in a flowing gown, and covered by a flat-topped black cap.

By degrees, and slowly, in came the college of the dervishes, and seated themselves as their dean was seated; but they sat on the floor in a circle, which spread away from the tribune, getting larger and larger in its dimensions as fresh dervishes came in. There was not much attention to regularity in their arrival, for some appeared barely in time for the closing scene.

The commencement was tame enough. Still seated, they shouted out a short prayer to Allah a certain number of times. The number was said to be ninety-nine. But they did not say the whole prayer at once, though it consisted of only three words. They took the first word ninety-nine times; and then the second; and then the third. The only sound to be recognized was that of Allah; but the deep guttural tone in which this was groaned out by all the voices together, made even that anything but a distinct word.

And so this was completed, the circle getting larger and larger. And it was remarked that men came in as dervishes who belonged to various ordinary pursuits and trades; there were soldiers in the circle, and, apparently, common labourers. Indeed, any one may join; though I presume he would do so with some danger were it discovered that he were not a Mahomedan.

Those who specially belonged to the college had peculiar gowns and caps, and herded together on one side of the circle; and it appeared to our friends, that throughout the entertainment they were by far the least enthusiastic of the performers.

When this round of groaning had been completed—and it occupied probably half an hour—a young lad, perhaps of seventeen years, very handsome, and handsomely dressed in a puce-coloured cloak, or rather petticoat, with a purple hat on his head, in shape like an inverted flower-pot, slipped forth from near the tribune into the middle of the circle, and began to twirl. After about five or six minutes, two other younger boys, somewhat similarly dressed, did the same, and twirled also; so that there were three twirling together.

But the twirling of the elder boy was by far the more graceful. Let any young lady put out both her hands, so as to bring the one to the level of her waist, and the other with the crown of her head, and then go round and round, as nearly as possible on the same spot; let her do this so that no raising of either foot shall ever be visible; and let her continue it for fifteen minutes, without any variation in the attitude of her arms, or any sign of fatigue,—and then she may go in for a twirling dervish. It is absurd to suppose that any male creature in England could perform the feat. During this twirling, a little black boy marked the time, by beating with two sticks on a rude gong.

This dance was kept up at first for fifteen minutes. Then there was another short spell of howling; then another dance, or twirl; and then the real game began.

The circle had now become so large as to occupy the greater part of the hall, and was especially swelled by sundry new arrivals at this moment. In particular, there came one swarthy, tall, wretched-looking creature, with wild eyes, wan face, and black hair of extraordinary length, who took up his position, standing immediately opposite to the tribune. Other new comers also stood near him, all of whom were remarkable for the length of their hair. Some of them had it tied up behind like women, and now proceeded to unloose it.

But at this period considerable toilet preparations were made for the coming work. All those in the circle who had not come in from the college with gowns and caps, and one or two even of them, deliberately took off their outer clothing, and tied it up in bundles. These bundles they removed to various corners, so that each might again find his own clothes. One or two put on calico dressing-gowns, which appeared to have been placed ready for the purpose; and among these was the cadaverous man of the black hair.

And then they all stood up, the dean standing also before his tribune, and a deep-toned murmur went round the circle. This also was the word Allah, as was duly explained to Bertram by his dragoman; but without such explanation it would have been impossible to detect that any word was pronounced. Indeed, the sound was of such nature as to make it altogether doubtful from whence it came. It was like no human voice, or amalgamation of voices; but appeared as though it came from the very bowels of the earth. At first it was exceedingly low, but it increased gradually, till at last one might have fancied that the legions of Lucifer were groaning within the very bowels of Pandemonium.*

And also, by slow degrees, a motion was seen to pervade the circle. The men, instead of standing fixedly on their legs, leaned over, first to the right and then to the left, all swaying backwards and forwards together in the same direction, so that both sound and motion were as though they came from one compact body.

And then, as the groan became louder, so did the motion become more violent, till the whole body heaved backwards and forwards with the regularity of a pendulum and the voice of a steam-engine. As the excitement became strong, the head of the dervishes walked along the inner circle, exciting those to more violence who already seemed the most violent. This he did, standing for a few minutes before each such man, bowing his own head rapidly and groaning deeply; and as he did so, the man before whom he stood would groan and swing himself with terrible energy. And the men with the long hair were especially selected.

And by degrees the lateral motion was abandoned, and the

dervishes bowed their heads forwards instead of sideways. No one who has not seen the operation can conceive what men may achieve in the way of bowing and groaning. They bowed till they swept the floor with their long hair, bending themselves double, and after each motion bringing themselves up again to an erect posture. And the dean went backwards and forwards from one to another, urging them on.

By this time the sight was terrible to behold. The perspiration streamed down them, the sounds came forth as though their very hearts were bursting, their faces hidden by their dishevelled locks, whatever clothes they wore were reeking wet. But still they flung themselves about, the motion becoming faster and faster; and still the sounds came forth as though from the very depths of Tartarus. And still the venerable dean went backwards and forwards slowly before them, urging them on, and still urging them on.

But at last, nature with the greater number of them had made her last effort; the dean retired to his tribune, and the circle was broken up. But those men with the long hair still persevered. It appeared, both to Bertram and Wilkinson, that with them the effort was now involuntary. They were carried on by an ecstatic frenzy; either that, or they were the best of actors. The circle had broken up, the dervishes were lying listlessly along the walls, panting with heat, and nearly lifeless with their exertions; but some four, remaining with their feet fixed in the old place, still bowed and still howled.

'They will die,' said Bertram.

'Will they not be stopped?' said Wilkinson to their dragoman.

'Five minutes, five minutes!' said the dragoman. 'Look at him—look at him with the black hair!' And they did look.

Three of them had now fallen, and the one remained still at his task. He swept the ground with his hair, absolutely striking it with his head; and the sounds came forth from him loudly, wildly, with broken gasps, with terrible exertion, as though each would be his last, and yet they did nothing to repress him.

At last it seemed as though the power of fully raising his head had left him, and also that of lowering it to the ground.

But still he made as it were a quarter-circle. His hands were clutched behind his back, and with this singular motion, and in this singular attitude, he began to move his feet; and still groaning and half bowing, he made a shuffling progress across the hall.

The dervishes themselves appeared to take no notice of him. The dean stood tranquil under his tribune; those who had recovered from their exertions were dressing themselves, the others lay about collecting their breath. But the eyes of every stranger were on the still moving black-haired devotee.

On he went, still howling and still swinging his head, right towards the wall of the temple. His pace was not fast, but it seemed as though he would inevitably knock his own brains out by the motion of his own head; and yet nobody stopped him.

'He'll kill himself,' said Wilkinson.

'No, no, no!' said the dragoman; 'him no kill—him head berry hard.'

Bertram rushed forward as though to stay the infuriate fanatic, but one or two of the dervishes who stood around gently prevented him, without speaking a word.

And then the finale came. Crack he went against the wall, rebounded off, and went at it again, and then again. They were no mock blows, but serious, heavy raps, as from a small battering-ram. But yet both Bertram and Wilkinson were able to observe that he did not strike the wall, as he would naturally have done had there been no precaution. Had he struck it with his head in motion, as was intended to be believed, the blow would have come upon his forehead and temples, and must probably have killed him; but instead of this, just as he approached the wall, he butted at it like a ram, and saved his forehead at the expense of his poll. It may probably be surmised, therefore, that he knew what he was about.

After these three raps, the man stood, still doubled up, but looking as though he were staggered. And then he went again with his head towards the wall. But the dean, satisfied with what had been done, now interposed, and this best of dervishes was gently laid on his back upon the floor, while his long matted hair was drawn from off his face. As he so lay, the sight was not agreeable to Christian eyes, whatever a true Mahomedan might think of it.

'Twas thus the dervishes practised their religious rites at Cairo. 'I wonder how much that black fellow gets paid every Friday,' said Bertram, as he mounted his donkey; 'it ought to be something very handsome.'

CHAPTER XXXIX

THE TWO WIDOWS

THE winter was now nearly over, and the travellers had determined to return to England. Whatever other good purpose the city of Cairo might or might not serve, it had restored Wilkinson to health. Bertram was sufficiently weary of living in a country in which the women go about with their faces hidden by long dirty stripes of calico, which they call veils, and in which that little which is seen of the ladies by no means creates a wish to see more. And Wilkinson, since the conversation which they had had at the Pyramids, was anxious to assume his own rights in the vicarage-house at Hurst Staple. So they decided on returning about the middle of March; but they decided also on visiting Suez before doing so.

In these days men go from Cairo to Suez as they do from London to Birmingham—by railway; in those days—some ten or twelve years back, that is—they went in wooden boxes, and were dragged by mules through the desert.

We cannot stay long at Suez, nor should I carry my reader there, even for a day, seeing how triste and dull the place is, had not our hero made an acquaintance there which for some time was likely to have a considerable effect on his future life.

Suez is indeed a triste, unhappy, wretched place. It is a small oriental town, now much be-Europeanized, and in the process of being be-Anglicized. It is not so Beelzebub-ridden a spot as Alexandria, nor falling to pieces like Cairo. But it has neither water, air, nor verdure. No trees grow there, no rivers flow there. Men drink brine and eat goats; and the thermometer stands at eighty in the shade in winter. The oranges are the only luxury. There is a huge hotel, which contains long rows of hot cells, and a vast cave in which people eat. The interest of the place consists in Pharoah's passage over the Red Sea; but its future prosperity will be caused by a transit of a different nature:—the passage of the English to and from India will turn even Suez into an important town.

Here the two travellers encountered a flood of Indians on their return home. The boat from Calcutta came in while they were there, and suddenly all the cells were tenanted, and the cave was full of spoiled children, tawny nurses, pale languid mothers, and dyspeptic fathers. These were to be fellow-travellers homewards with Bertram and Wilkinson.

Neither of our friends regarded with favour the crowd which made them even more uncomfortable than they had been before. As Englishmen in such positions generally do, they kept themselves aloof and scowled, frowned at the children who whined in the nearest neighbourhood to them, and listened in disgust to the continuous chatter about punkahs, tiffins, and bungalows.*

But close to them, at the end of the long table, at the common dinner, sat two ladies, on whom it was almost impossible for them to frown. For be it known that at these hotels in Egypt, a man cannot order his dinner when he pleases. He must breakfast at nine, and dine at six, as others do—or go without. And whether he dine, or whether he do not, he must pay. The Medes and Persians* were lax and pliable in their laws in comparison with these publicans.

Both George and Arthur would have frowned if they could have done so; but on these two ladies it was impossible to frown. They were both young, and both pretty. George's neighbour was uncommonly pretty—was, indeed, one of the prettiest women that he had ever seen;—that any man could see anywhere. She was full of smiles too, and her smile was heavenly;—was full of words, and her words were witty. She who sat next Arthur was perhaps less attractive; but she had large soft eyes, which ever and anon she would raise to his face, and then let fall again to her plate in a manner which made sparks fly round the heart even of our somewhat sombre young Hampshire vicar.

The four were soon in full conversation, apparently much to the disgust of two military-looking gentlemen who sat on the other side of the ladies. And it was evident that the military gentlemen and the ladies were, or ought to be, on terms of intimacy; for proffers of soup, and mutton, and wine were whispered low, and little attempts at confidential intercourse were made. But the proffers were rejected, and the attempts were in vain. The ladies preferred to have their plates and glasses filled by the strangers, turned their shoulders on their old friends with but scant courtesy, and were quite indifferent to the frowns which at last clouded those two military brows.

And the brows of Major Biffin and Captain M'Gramm were clouded. They had been filling the plates and glasses of these two ladies all the way from Calcutta; they had walked with them every day on deck, had fetched their chairs, picked up their handkerchiefs, and looked after their bottled beer at tiffin-time with an assiduity which is more commendable in such warm latitudes. And now to be thrown on one side for two travelling Englishmen, one in a brown coat and the other in a black one—for two muffs, who had never drunk sangaree* or sat under a punkah!

This was unpleasant to Major Biffin and Captain M'Gramm. But then why had the major and the captain boasted of the favours they had daily received, to that soft-looking, superannuated judge, and to their bilious friend, Dr O'Shaughnessy? The judge and the doctor had of course their female allies, and had of course repeated to them all the boasts of the fortunate major and of the fortunate captain. And was it not equally of course that these ladies should again repeat the same to Mrs Cox and Mrs Price? For she who was so divinely perfect was Mrs Cox, and she of the soft, lustrous eyes was Mrs Price. Those who think that such a course was not natural know little of voyages home from Calcutta to Southampton.

But the major, who had been the admirer of Mrs Cox, had done more than this—had done worse, we may say. The world of the good ship 'Lahore,' which was bringing them all home, had declared ever since they had left Point de Galle, that the major and Mrs Cox were engaged. Now, had the major, in boasting of his favours, boasted also of his engagement, no harm perhaps might have come of it. The sweet good-nature of the widow might have overlooked that offence. But he had boasted of the favours and pooh-poohed the engagement! 'Hinc illæ lacrymæ.'* And who shall say that the widow was wrong? And as to the other widow, Mrs Price, she was tired of Captain M'Gramm. A little fact had transpired about Captain M'Gramm, namely, that he was going home to his wife. And therefore the two ladies, who had conspired together to be civil to the two warriors, now conspired together to be uncivil to them. In England such things are done, as it were, behind the scenes: there these little quarrels are managed in private. But a passage home from India admits of but little privacy; there is no behind the scenes. The two widows were used to this, and quarrelled with their military admirers in public without any compunction.

'Hinc illæ lacrymæ.' But the major was not inclined to shed his tears without an effort. He had pooh-poohed the idea of marrying Mrs Cox; but like many another man in similar circumstances, he was probably willing enough to enter into such an arrangement now that the facility of doing so was taken from him. It is possible that Mrs Cox, when she turned her pretty shoulder on Major Biffin, may herself have understood this phasis of human nature.

The major was a handsome man, with well-brushed hair, well-trimmed whiskers, a forehead rather low, but very symmetrical, a well-shaped nose, and a small, pursy mouth. The worst of his face was that you could by no means remember it. But he knew himself to be a handsome man, and he could not understand how he could be laid aside for so ugly a lout as this stranger from England. Captain M'Gramm was not a handsome man, and he was aware that he fought his battle under the disadvantage of a wife. But he had impudence enough to compensate him for the double drawback.

During this first dinner, Arthur Wilkinson was not more than coldly civil to Mrs Price; but Bertram became after a while warmly civil to Mrs Cox. It is so very nice to be smiled on by the prettiest woman in the room; and it was long since he had seen the smile of any pretty woman! Indeed, for the last eighteen months he had had but little to do with such smiles.

Before dinner was over, Mrs Cox had explained to Bertram that both she and her friend Mrs Price were in deep affliction. They had recently lost their husbands—the one, by cholera; that was poor dear Cox, who had been collector of the Honourable Company's taxes at Panjabee. Whereas, Lieutenant Price, of the 71st Native Bengal Infantry, had succumbed to—here Mrs Cox shook her head, and whispered, and pointed to the champagne glass which Bertram was in the act of filling for her. Poor Cox had gone just eight months; but Price had taken his last glass within six. And so Bertram knew all about it.

And then there was a great fuss in packing the travellers into the wooden boxes. It seems that they had all made up their own parties by sixes, that being the number of which one box was supposed to be capable. But pretty women are capricious, and neither Mrs Price nor Mrs Cox were willing to abide by any such arrangement. When the time came for handing them in, they both objected to the box pointed out to them by Major Biffin—refused to be lifted in by the arms of Captain M'Gramm—got at last into another vacant box with the assistance of our friends—summoned their dingy nurses and babies into the same box (for each was so provided)—and then very prettily made way for Mr Bertram and Mr Wilkinson. And so they went across the desert.

Then they all stayed a night at Cairo, and then they went on to Alexandria. And by the time that they were embarked in a boat together, on their way to that gallant first-class steamer, the 'Cagliari,' they were as intimate as though they had travelled round the world together, and had been as long about it as Captain Cook.

'What will you take with you, Mrs Cox?' said Bertram, as he stood up in the boat with the baby on one arm, while with the other he handed the lady towards the ship's ladder.

'A good ducking,' said Mrs Cox, with a cheery laugh, as at the moment a dashing wave covered them with its spray. 'And I've got it too, with a vengeance. Ha! ha! Take care of the baby, whatever you do; and if she falls over, mind you go after her.' And with another little peal of silver ringing laughter, she tripped up the side of the ship, and Bertram, with the baby, followed after her.

'She is such a giddy thing,' said Mrs Price, turning her soft eyes on poor Arthur Wilkinson. 'Oh, laws! I know I shall be drowned. Do hold me.' And Arthur Wilkinson did hold her, and nearly carried her up into the ship. As he did so, his mind would fly off to Adela Gauntlet; but his arms and legs were not the less at the service of Mrs Price.

'And now look after the places,' said Mrs Cox; 'you haven't a moment to lose. And look here, Mr Bertram, mind, I won't sit next to Major Biffin. And, for heaven's sake, don't let us be near that fellow M'Gramm.' And so Bertram descended into the *salon* to place their cards in the places at which they were to sit for dinner. 'Two and two; opposite to each other,' sang out Mrs Cox, as he went. There was a sweetness in her voice, a low, mellow cheeriness in her tone, which, combined with her beauty, went far to atone for the nature of what she said; and Bertram not unwillingly obeyed her behests.

'Oh, my blessed baby!' said Mrs Price, as the nurse handed her the child—which, however, she immediately handed back. 'How can I thank you enough, Mr Wilkinson? What should we have done without you? I wonder whether it's near tiffin. I am so faint.'

'Shall I fetch you anything?' said he.

'If you could get me a glass of porter. But I don't think they'll give it you. They are so uncivil!'

Arthur went for the beer; but went in vain. The steward said that lunch would be ready at twelve o'clock.

'They are such brutes!' said Mrs Price. 'Well, I suppose I must wait.' And she again turned her eyes upon Arthur, and he again thought of Adela Gauntlet.

And then there was the ordinary confusion of a starting ship. Men and women were hurrying about after their luggage, asking all manner of unreasonable questions. Ladies were complaining of their berths, and servants asking where on *h*earth they were to sleep. Gentlemen were swearing that they had been shamefully doubled up—that is, made to lie with two or three men in the same cabin; and friends were contriving to get commodious seats for dinner. The officers of the ship were all busy, treating with apparent indifference the thousand questions that were asked them on every side; and all was bustle, confusion, hurry, and noise.

And then they were off. The pistons of the engine moved slowly up and down, the huge cranks revolved, and the waters under the bow rippled and gave way. They were off, and the business of the voyage commenced. The younger people prepared for their flirtations, the mothers unpacked their children's clothes, and the elderly gentlemen lighted their cigars.

'What very queer women they are!' said Arthur, walking the deck with his cousin.

'But very pretty, and very agreeable. I like them both.'

'Don't you think them too free and easy?'

'Ah, you must not judge of them by women who have lived in England, who have always had the comfort of well-arranged homes. They have been knocked about, ill-used, and forced to bear hardships as men bear them; but still there is about them so much that is charming. They are so frank!'

'Yes, very frank,' said Arthur.

'It is well to see the world on all sides,' said George. 'For myself, I think that we are lucky to have come across them—that is, if Major Biffin does not cut my throat.'

'I hope Captain M'Gramm won't cut mine. He looked as though he would.'

'Did you ever see such an ass as that Biffin? I don't wonder that she has become sick of him; and then he has behaved so very badly to her. I really do pity her. She has told me all about it.'

'And so has Mrs Price told me all about Captain M'Gramm.'

'Has she? Well! It seems that he, Biffin, has taken advantage of her frank, easy manner, and talked of her to every man in the ship. I think she has been quite right to cut him.' And so they discussed the two ladies.

And at last Mrs Price got her porter, and Mrs Cox got her pale ale. 'I do like pale ale,' said she; 'I suppose it's vulgar, but I can't help that. What amuses me is, that so many ladies drink it who are quite ashamed to say they like it.'

'They take it for their health's sake,' said Bertram.

'Oh, yes; of course they do. Mrs Bangster takes her half-pint of brandy every night for her health's sake, no doubt. Would you believe it, Mr Bertram, the doctor absolutely had to take her out of the saloon one night in the 'Lahore'? Didn't he, Mrs Price?'

'Indeed he did. I never was so shocked.—Just a little drop more to freshen it.' And Mr Wilkinson gave her another glass of porter.

Before they reached Malta, all the passengers from India had agreed that Mrs Cox and Bertram would certainly make a match of it, and that Wilkinson was also in danger.

'Did you ever see such flirts?' said Mrs Bangster to Dr O'Shaughnessy. 'What an escape Biffin has had!'

'She is a deuced pretty woman, Mrs Bangster; and I'll tell you what: Biffin would give one of his eyes to get her back again if he could.'

'Laws, doctor! You don't mean to tell me that he ever meant to marry that thing?'

'I don't know what he meant before; but he would mean it now, if he got the opportunity.'

Here Captain M'Gramm joined them. 'Well, Mac,' said the doctor, 'what news with the widow?'

'Widow! they'd all be widows if they could, I believe.'

'Indeed, I wouldn't, for one,' said Mrs Bangster. 'B. is a deal too well off where he is. Ha! ha! ha!'

'But what about Mrs Price—eh, Mac?' continued the doctor.

'There she is. You'd better go and ask her yourself. You don't suppose I ever cared about such a woman as that? Only I do say this: if she goes on behaving herself in that way, some one ought to speak to the captain.'

But Mrs Cox and Mrs Price went on their own way, heeding such menaces not at all; and by the time they had reached Malta, they had told the whole history of their lives to the two gentlemen—and perhaps something more.

At Malta they remained about six hours, and the four dined on shore together. Bertram bought for them Maltese veils and bad cameos; and Wilkinson, misled by such an example, was forced to do the same. These treasures were not hidden under a bushel when they returned to the ship; and Dr O'Shaughnessy, Mrs Bangster, the fat judge, and a host of others, were more sure than ever that both the widows were re-engaged.

And Arthur Wilkinson was becoming frightened in his mind. 'Upon my word,' said he, as he and George were walking the deck at sunrise the next morning, 'upon my word, I am getting very tired of this woman, and I really think we are making a show of ourselves.'

'Making a show of ourselves! What do you mean?'

'Why, walking with them every day, and always sitting next to them.'

'As to sitting next to them, we can't help that. Everybody always sits in the same place, and one must sit next some one; and it wouldn't be kind to leave them to walk alone.'

'I think we may overdo it, you know.'

'Ah, well,' said George, 'you have some one else to think about. I have no one, unless it be this widow. She is kind to me, and as to what the world says, I care nothing about it.'

On that day Wilkinson was busy with his books, and did not walk with Mrs Price—a piece of neglect which sat uneasily on that lady's mind. But at ten o'clock, as usual, Bertram was pacing the deck with Mrs Cox.

'What is the matter with your friend?' said she.

'Oh, nothing. He is home-sick, I suppose.'

'I hope he has not quarrelled with Minnie.' For the two ladies had come to call each other by their Christian names when they were in company with the gentlemen; and Bertram had once or twice used that of Mrs Cox, not exactly in speaking to her, but in speaking of her in her presence.

'Oh, dear, no,' said Bertram.

'Because it is so odd he should not give her his arm as usual. I suppose you will be treating me so as we draw nearer to Southampton?' And she looked up at him with a bewitching smile, and pressed gently on his arm, and then let her eyes fall upon the deck.

My brother, when you see these tricks played upon other men, the gall rises black within your breast, and you loudly condemn wiles which are so womanly, but which are so unworthy of women. But how do you feel when they are played upon yourself? The gall is not so black, the condemnation less loud; your own merit seems to excuse the preference which is shown you; your heart first forgives and then applauds. Is it not so, my brother, with you? So it was, at least, with George Bertram.

'What! treating you with neglect, because we are soon to part?'

'Yes, exactly so; just that: because we are soon to part. That is what makes it so bitter. We have been such good friends, haven't we?'

'And why should we not remain so? Why should we talk of parting? We are both going to England.'

'England! Yes, but England is a large place. Come, let us lean on the taffrail, and look at the dolphins. There is that horrid fellow eyeing me, as he always does; Major Biffin, I mean. Is he not exactly like a barber's block? I do so hate him!'

'But he doesn't hate you, Mrs Cox.'

'Doesn't he? Well then, he may if he likes. But don't let's talk of him. Talk to me about England, Mr Bertram. Sometimes I do so long to be there—and then sometimes I don't.'

'You don't—why not?'

'Do you?'

'No, I do not; I tell you frankly. I'd sooner be here with you to talk to, with you to look at.'

'Psha, Mr Bertram! what nonsense! I can't conceive that any woman can ever be worth looking at on board a ship—much less such a one as I! I know you're dying to get home.'

'I might be if I had a home.'

'Is your home with that uncle of yours?' She had heard so much of his family; but he had as yet spoken to her no word about Caroline. 'I wonder what he would say if he could see you now leaning here and talking to me.'

'If he has any knowledge of human nature, he would say that I was a very happy fellow.'

'And are you?' As she asked him, she looked up into his face with such an arch smile that he could not find it in his heart to condemn her.

'What will you think of my gallantry if I say no?'

'I hate gallantry; it is all bosh. I wish I were a man, and that I could call you Bertram, and that you would call me Cox.'

'I would sooner call you Annie.'

'Would you? But that wouldn't be right, would it?' And her hand, which was still within his arm, was pressed upon it with ever so light a pressure.

'I don't know why it should be wrong to call people by their Christian names. Should you be angry if I called you Annie?'

'That might depend—Tell me this, Mr Bertram; how many other ladies do you call by their Christian names?'

'A dozen or two.'

'I'll be bound you do.'

'And may I add you to the number?'

'No, Mr Bertram; certainly not.'

'May I not? So intimate as we have become, I thought—'

'I will not be one of a dozen or two.' And as she answered him, she dropped her tone of raillery, and spoke in a low, soft, sweet voice. It sounded so sweet on Bertram's ear.

'But if there be not one—not one other; not one other now—what then, Annie?'

'Not one other now?—Did you say now? Then there has been one.'

'Yes; there has been one.'

'And she—what of her?'

'It is a tale I cannot tell.'

'Not to me? I should not like you the less for telling me. Do tell me.' And she pressed her hand again upon his arm. 'I have known there was something that made you unhappy.'

'Have you?'

'Oh, yes. I have long known that. And I have so wished to be a comfort to you—if I could. I, too, have had great suffering.'

'I am sure you have.'

'Ah! yes. I did not suffer less because he had been unkind to me.' And she put her handkerchief to her eyes, and then brought her hand again upon his arm. 'But tell me of her—your one. She is not your one now—is she, Mr Bertram?'

'No, Annie; not now.'

'Is she—?' And she hesitated to ask whether the lady were dead, or married to some one else. It might, after all, only be a lovers' quarrel.

'I drove her from me—and now she is a wife.'

'Drove her from you! Alas! alas!' said Mrs Cox, with the sweetest emphasis of sympathy. But the result of her inquiries was not unsatisfactory to her.

'I don't know why I should have told you this,' said he.

'I am so glad you have,' she replied.

'But now that I have told you—'

'Well—'

'Now may I call you Annie?'

'You have done so two or three times.'

'But may I?'

'If it please you, you may.' And the words, though whispered very low, fell clearly upon his ear.

'Dearest Annie!'

'But I did not say you might call me that.'

'But you are.'

'Am I?'

'Dearest—all but she. Will that make you angry with me?'

'No, not angry; but—'

'But what?'

She looked up at him, pouting with her lip. There was a half-smile on her mouth, and half a tear in her eyes; and her shoulder leant against him, and her heart palpitated. She had never been so beautiful, never so attractive.

'But what—? What would you say, Annie?'

'I would say this.—But I know you will think me very bold.'

'I shall not think you too bold if you will say the truth.'

'Then I would say this—that if I loved a man, I could love him quite as fondly as she loved you.'

'Could you, Annie?'

'I could. But he should not drive me from him, as you say you did her; never—never—never. He might kill me if he would; but if I once had told him that I loved him, I would never leave him afterwards.'

'Tell me so, Annie.'

'No, Mr Bertram. We have not known each other long enough.' And now she took her hand from his arm, and let it drop by her side.

'Tell me so, dear Annie,' he repeated; and he tried to regain her hand.

'There is the luncheon-bell; and since Mr Wilkinson won't go to Mrs Price, I must do so.'

'Shall I go?' said he.

'Do; I will go down by myself.'

'But you love me, Annie?—say that you love me.'

'Nonsense. Here is that fellow, Biffin. Do you go for Mrs Price—leave me to myself.'

'Don't go downstairs with him.'

'You may be sure I won't—nor with you either this morning. I am half inclined to be angry with you.' And so saying, she moved away.

'Ah, me! what have I done!' said Bertram to himself, as he went upon his mission. 'But she is a sweet creature; as beautiful as Hebe; and why should I be wretched for ever?'

She had moved towards the companion-ladder, and as she did so, Major Biffin followed her.

'Will you not allow me to give you an arm downstairs?' said he.

'Thank you, Major Biffin. It is rather crowded, and I can go better alone.'

'You did not find the stairs in the 'Lahore' too crowded.'

'Oh, yes, I did; very often. And the 'Lahore' and the 'Cagliari' are different things.'

'Very different, it seems. But the sea itself is not so fickle as a woman.' And Major Biffin became a picture of injured innocence.

'And the land is not so dry as a man, Major Biffin; that is, some men. Ha! ha! ha! Good-morning, Major Biffin.' And so saying, she went down by herself.

On the next day, Arthur still preferred his book to walking with Mrs Price; and that lady was once again seen with her arm in that of Captain M'Gramm's. This made a considerable consternation in the ship; and in the afternoon there was a slight quarrel between the two ladies.

'And so, Minnie, you are going to take up with that fellow again?'

'No; I am not. But I don't choose to be left altogether to myself.'

'I never would have anything to say to a married man that drops his wife as he does.'

'I don't care two straws for him, or his wife. But I don't want to make myself conspicuous by a quarrel.'

'I'm sure Wilkinson will be annoyed,' said Mrs Cox.

'He's a muff,' said Mrs Price. 'And, if I am not mistaken, I know some one else who is another.'

'Who do you mean, Mrs Price?'

'I mean Mr Bertram, Mrs Cox.'

'Oh, I dare say he is a muff; that's because he's attentive to me instead of leaving me to myself, as somebody does to somebody else. I understand all about that, my dear.'

'You understand a great deal, I have no doubt,' said Mrs Price. 'I always heard as much.'

'It seems to me you understand nothing, or you wouldn't be walking about with Captain M'Gramm,' said Mrs Cox. And then they parted, before blood was absolutely drawn between them.

At dinner that day they were not very comfortable together. Mrs Price accepted Mr Wilkinson's ordinary courtesies in a stately way, thanking him for filling her glass and looking after her plate, in a tone and with a look which made it plain to all that things were not progressing well between them. George and his Annie did get on somewhat better; but even they were not quite at their ease. Mrs Cox had said, before luncheon, that she had not known Mr Bertram long enough to declare her love for him. But the hours between luncheon and dinner might have been a sufficient prolongation of the period of their acquaintance. George, however, had not repeated the question; and had, indeed, not been alone with her for five minutes during the afternoon.

That evening, Wilkinson again warned his friend that he might be going too far with Mrs Cox; that he might say that which he could neither fulfil nor retract. For Wilkinson clearly conceived it to be impossible that Bertram should really intend to marry this widow.

'And why should I not marry her?' said George.

'She would not suit you, nor make you happy.'

'What right have I to think that any woman will suit me? or what chance is there that any woman will make me happy? Is it not all leather and prunella?* She is pretty and clever, soft and feminine. Where shall I find a nicer toy to play with? You forget, Arthur, that I have had my day-dreams, and been roused from them somewhat roughly. With you, the pleasure is still to come.'

After this they turned in and went to bed.

CHAPTER XL

REACHING HOME

EARLY in their journeyings together, Mrs Cox had learned from George that he was possessed of an eccentric old uncle; and not long afterwards, she had learned from Arthur that this uncle was very rich, that he was also childless, and that he was supposed to be very fond of his nephew. Putting all these things together, knowing that Bertram had no profession, and thinking that therefore he must be a rich man, she had considered herself to be acting with becoming prudence in dropping Major Biffin for his sake.

But on the day after the love scene recorded in the last chapter, a strange change came over the spirit of her dream. 'I am a very poor man,' Bertram had said to her, after making some allusion to what had taken place.

'If that were all, that would make no difference with me,' said Mrs Cox, magnanimously.

'If that were all, Annie! What does that mean?'

'If I really loved a man, I should not care about his being poor. But your poverty is what I should call riches, I take it.'

'No, indeed. My poverty is absolute poverty. My own present income is about two hundred a year.'

'Oh, I don't understand the least about money myself. I never did. I was such a child when I was married to Cox. But I thought, Mr Bertram, your uncle was very rich.'

'So he is; as rich as a gold-mine. But we are not very good friends—at any rate, not such friends as to make it probable that he will leave me a farthing. He has a granddaughter of his own.'

This, and a little more of the same kind, taught Mrs Cox that it behoved her to be cautious. That Major Biffin had a snug little income over and above that derived from his profession was a fact that had been very well ascertained. That he was very dry, as dry as a barber's block, might be true. That George Bertram was an amusing fellow, and made love in much better style than the major, certainly was true. But little as she might know about money, Mrs Cox did know this—that when poverty comes in at the door, love flies out at the window,* that eating and drinking are stern necessities; that love in a cottage is supposed to be, what she would call, bosh; and that her own old home used to be very unpleasant when Cox was in debt, and those eastern Jewish harpies would come down upon him with his overdue bills. Considering all this, Mrs Cox thought it might be well not to ratify her engagement with Mr Bertram till after they should reach Southampton. What if Biffin—the respectable Biffin—should again come forward!

And so they went on for a few days longer. Bertram, when they were together, called her Annie, and once again asked her whether she loved him. 'Whether I do, or whether I do not, I shall give you no answer now,' she had said, half laughing. 'We have both been very foolish already, and it is time that we should begin to have our senses. Isn't it?' But still she sat next him at dinner, and still she walked with him. Once, indeed, he found her saying a word to Major Biffin, as that gentleman stood opposite to her chair upon the deck. But as soon as the major's back was turned, she said to Bertram, 'I think the barber's block wants to be new curled, doesn't it? I declare the barber's man has forgotten to comb out its whiskers.' So that Bertram had no ground for jealousy of the major.

Somewhere about this time, Mrs Price deserted them at dinner. She was going to sit, she said, with Mrs Bangster, and Dr O'Shaughnessy, and the judge. Mrs Bangster had made a promise to old Mr Price in England to look after her; and, therefore, she thought it better to go back to Mrs Bangster before they reached Southampton. They were now past Gibraltar. So on that day, Mrs Price's usual chair at dinner was vacant, and Wilkinson, looking down the tables, saw that room had been made for her next to Dr O'Shaughnessy. And on her other side, sat Captain M'Gramm, in despite of Mrs Bangster's motherly care and of his own wife at home. On the following morning, Mrs Price and Captain M'Gramm were walking the deck together just as they had been used to do on the other side of Suez.

And so things went on till the day before their arrival at Southampton. Mrs Cox still kept her seat next to Bertram, and opposite to Wilkinson, though no other lady remained to countenance her. She and Bertram still walked the deck arm in arm; but their whisperings were not so low as they had been, nor were their words so soft, nor, indeed, was the temper of the lady so sweet. What if she should have thrown away all the advantages of the voyage! What if she had fallen between two stools! She began to think that it would be better to close with one or with the other—with the one despite his poverty, or with the other despite his head.

And now it was the evening of the last day. They had sighted the coast of Devonshire, and the following morning would see them within the Southampton waters. Ladies had packed their luggage; subscriptions had been made for the band; the captain's health had been drunk at the last dinner; and the mail boxes were being piled between the decks.

'Well, it is nearly over,' said Mrs Cox, as she came upon deck after dinner, warmly cloaked. 'How cold we all are!'

Yes; it is nearly over,' answered Bertram. 'What an odd life of itself one of these voyages is! How intimate people are who will never see each other again!'

'Yes; that is the way, I suppose. Oh, Mr Bertram!'

'Well, what would you have?'

'Ah, me! I hardly know. Fate has ever been against me, and I know that it will be so to the last.'

'Is it not cold?' said Bertram, buttoning up a greatcoat as he spoke.

'Very cold! very cold!' said Mrs Cox. 'But there is something much colder than the weather—very much colder.'

'You are severe, Mrs Cox.'

'Yes. It is Mrs Cox here. It was Annie when we were off Gibraltar. That comes of being near home. But I knew that it would be so. I hate the very idea of home.' And she put her handkerchief to her eyes.

She had had her chance as far as Bertram was concerned, and had let it pass from her. He did not renew his protestations; but in lieu of doing so, lit a cigar, and walked away into the forepart of the vessel. 'After all, Arthur is right,' said he to himself; 'marriage is too serious a thing to be arranged in a voyage from Alexandria to Southampton.'

But luckily for Mrs Cox, everybody did not think as he did. He had gone from her ruthlessly, cruelly, falsely, with steps which sounded as though there were triumph in his escape, and left her seated alone near the skylights. But she was not long alone. As she looked after him along the deck, the head of Major Biffin appeared to her, emerging from the saloon stairs. She said nothing to herself now about barber's blocks or uncurled whiskers.

'Well, Mrs Cox,' said the major, accosting her.

'Well, Major Biffin;' and the major thought that he saw in her eye some glimpse of the smile as of old.

'We are very near home now, Mrs Cox,' said the major.

'Very near indeed,' said Mrs Cox. And then there was a slight pause, during which Major Biffin took an opportunity of sitting down not very far from his companion.

'I hope you have enjoyed your voyage,' said he.

'Which voyage?' she asked.

'Oh! your voyage home from Alexandria—your voyage since you made the acquaintance of Mr—what's his name, the parson's cousin?'

'Mr What's-his-name, as you call him, is nothing to me, I can assure you, Major Biffin. His real name, however, is Bertram. He has been very civil when some other people were not inclined to be so, that is all.'

'Is that all? The people here do say—'

'Then I tell you what, Major Biffin, I do not care one straw what the people say—not one straw. You know whose fault it has been if I have been thrown with this stranger. Nobody knows it as well. And mind this, Major Biffin, I shall always do as I like in such matters without reference to you or to any one else. I am my own mistress.'

'And do you mean to remain so?'

'Ask no questions, and then you'll be told no stories.'

'That's civil.'

'If you don't like it, you had better go, for there's more to follow of the same sort.'

'You are very sharp tonight.'

'Not a bit sharper than I shall be tomorrow.'

'One is afraid even to speak to you now.'

'Then one had better hold one's tongue.'

Mrs Cox was receiving her suitor rather sharply; but she probably knew his disposition. He did not answer her immediately, but sat biting the top of his cane. 'I'll tell you what it is, Mrs Cox,' he said at last, 'I don't like this kind of thing.'

'Don't you, Mr Biffin? And what kind of thing do you like?'

'I like you.'

'Psha! Tell me something new, if you must tell me anything.'

'Come, Annie; do be serious for a moment. There isn't much time left now, and I've come to you in order that I may get a plain answer.'

'If you want a plain answer, you'd better ask a plain question. I don't know what you mean.'

'Will you have me? That's a plain question, or the deuce is in it.'

'And what should I do with you?'

'Why, be Mrs Biffin, of course.'

'Ha! ha! ha! And it has come to that, has it? What was it you said to Dr O'Shaughnessy when we were off Point de Galle?'

'Well, what did I say?'

'I know what you said well enough. And so do you, too. If I served you right, I should never speak to you again.'

'A man doesn't like to be humbugged, you know, before a whole shipful of people,' said the major, defending himself.

'And a woman likes it just as little, Major Biffin, please to remember that.'

'Well; I'm sure you've been down upon me long enough.'

'Not a bit longer than you deserved. You told O'Shaughnessy, that it was all very well to amuse yourself, going home. I hope you like your amusement now. I have liked mine very well, I can assure you.'

'I don't think so bad of you as to believe you care for that fellow.'

'There are worse fellows than he is, Major Biffin. But there, I have had my revenge; and now if you have anything to say, I'll give you an answer.'

'I've only to say, Annie, that I love you better than any woman in the world.'

'I may believe as much of that as I like.'

'You may believe it all. Come, there's my hand.'

'Well, I suppose I must forgive you. There's mine. Will that please you?'

Major Biffin was the happiest man in the world, and Mrs Cox went to her berth that night not altogether dissatisfied. Before she did so, she had the major's offer in writing in her pocket; and had shown it to Mrs Price, with whom she was now altogether reconciled.

'I only wish, Minnie, that there was no Mrs M'Gramm,' said she.

'He wouldn't be the man for me at all, my dear; so don't let that fret you.'

'There's as good fish in the sea as ever were caught yet; eh, Minnie?'

'Of course there are. Though of course you think there never was such a fish as Biffin.'

'He'll do well enough for me, Minnie; and when you catch a bigger, and a better, I won't begrudge him you.'

That night Mrs Cox took her evening modicum of creature-comforts sitting next to her lover, the major; and our two friends were left alone by themselves. The news had soon spread about the ship, and to those ladies who spoke to her on the subject, Mrs Cox made no secret of the fact. Men in this world catch their fish by various devices; and it is necessary that these schemes should be much studied before a man can call himself a fisherman. It is the same with women; and Mrs Cox was an Izaak Walton* among her own sex. Had she not tied her fly with skill, and thrown her line with a steady hand, she would not have had her trout in her basket. There was a certain amount of honour due to her for her skill, and she was not ashamed to accept it.

'Good-night, Mrs Cox,' Bertram said to her that evening, with a good-humoured tone; 'I hear that I am to congratulate you.'

'Good-night,' said she, giving him her hand. 'And I'll say good-bye, too, for we shall all be in such a flurry tomorrow morning. I'm sure you think I've done the right thing—don't you? And, mind this, I shall hope to see you some day.' And so saying, she gave him a kindly grasp, and they parted. 'Done right!' said Bertram; 'yes, I suppose she has; right enough at least as far as I am concerned. After all, what husband is so convenient as a barber's block?'

On the following morning they steamed up the Southampton river, and at nine o'clock they were alongside the quay. All manner of people had come on board in boats, and the breakfast was eaten in great confusion. But few of the ladies were to be seen. They had tea and rolls in their own cabins, and did not appear till the last moment. Among these were Mrs Cox and Mrs Price.

These ladies during their journey home had certainly not been woe-begone, either in personal appearance or in manner. And who would have the heart to wish that they should be so? They had been dressed as young ladies on board ship usually do dress, so that their widowhood had been forgotten; and, but for their babies, their wifehood might have been forgotten also.

But now they were to be met by family friends—by friends who were thinking of nothing but their bereavements. Old Mr Price came to meet them on board, and Mrs Cox's uncle; old gentlemen with faces prepared for sadness, and young ladies with sympathetic handkerchiefs. How signally surprised the sad old gentlemen and the sympathetic young ladies must have been!

Not a whit! Just as our friends were about to leave the ship that morning, with all their luggage collected round them, they were startled by the apparition of two sombre female figures, buried in most sombre tokens of affliction. Under the deep crape of their heavy black bonnets was to be seen that chiefest sign of heavy female woe—a widow's cap. What signal of sorrow that grief holds out, ever moves so much as this? Their eyes were red with weeping, as could be seen when, for a moment, their deep-bordered handkerchiefs were allowed to fall from their faces. Their eyes were red with weeping, and the agonizing grief of domestic bereavement sat chiselled on every feature. If you stood near enough, your heart would melt at the sound of their sobs.

Alas! that forms so light, that creatures so young, should need to be shrouded in such vestments! They were all crape, that dull, weeping, widow's crape, from the deck up to their shoulders. There they stood, monuments of death, living tombs, whose only sign of life was in their tears. There they stood, till they might fall, vanquished by the pangs of memory, into the arms of their respective relations.

They were Mrs Cox and Mrs Price. Bertram and Wilkinson,

as they passed them, lifted their hats and bowed, and the two ladies, observing them, returned their salutation with the coldest propriety.

CHAPTER XLI

I COULD PUT A CODICIL

ON their journey up from Southampton, George and Arthur parted from each other. George went on direct to London, whereas Arthur turned off from Basingstoke towards his own home.

'Take my advice now, if you never do again,' said Bertram, as they parted; 'make yourself master of your own house, and as soon after as possible make her the mistress of it.'

'That's easily said, old fellow,' repeated the other.

'Make the attempt, at any rate. If I am anything of a prophet, it won't be in vain;' and so they parted.

At Southampton they had learnt that there had been a partial crash in the government. The prime minister had not absolutely walked forth, followed by all his satellites, as is the case when a successful turn in the wheel gives the outs a full whip-hand over the ins, but it had become necessary to throw overboard a brace or two of Jonahs,* so that the ship might be lightened to meet a coming storm; and among those so thrown over had been our unfortunate friend Sir Henry Harcourt.

And this, as regards him, had hardly been the worst of it. We all know that bigwigs are never dismissed. When it becomes necessary to get rid of them, they resign. Now resignation is clearly a voluntary act, and it seemed that Sir Henry, having no wish that way, had not at first performed this act of volition. His own particular friends in the cabinet, those to whom he had individually attached himself, were gone; but, nevertheless, he made no sign; he was still ready to support the government, and as the attorney-general was among those who had shaken the dust from their feet* and gone out, Sir Henry expected that he would, as a matter of course, walk into that gentleman's shoes.

But another learned gentleman was appointed, and then at last Sir Henry knew that he must go. He had resigned; but no resignation had ever appeared to have less of volition in it. And how could it be otherwise? Political success was everything to him; and, alas! he had so played his cards that it was necessary to him that that success should be immediate. He was not as those are who, in losing power, lose a costly plaything, which they love indeed over-well, but the loss of which hurts only their pride. Place to him was everything; and feeling this, he had committed that most grievous of political sins—he had endeavoured to hold his place longer than he was wanted. Now, however, he was out. So much, in some sort of way, Bertram had learnt before he left Southampton.

His first business in London was to call on Mr Pritchett.

'Oh, master George! oh, master George!' began that worthy man, as soon as he saw him. His tone had never been so lachrymose, nor his face so full of woe. 'Oh, master George!'

Bertram in his kindest way asked after his uncle.

'Oh, master George! you shouldn't be going to them furren parts—indeed you shouldn't; and he in such a state.'

'Is he worse than when I last saw him, Mr Pritchett?'

'Gentlemen at his time of life don't get much better, master George—nor yet at mine. It's half a million of money; half—a—million—of—money! But it's no use talking to you, sir—it never was.'

By degrees Bertram gathered from him that his uncle was much weaker, that he had had a second and a much more severe attack of paralysis, and that according to all the doctors, the old gentleman was not much longer for this world. Sir Omicron himself had been there. Miss Baker had insisted on it, much in opposition to her uncle's wishes. But Sir Omicron had shaken his head and declared that the fiat had gone forth.

Death had given his order; the heavy burden of the half-million must be left behind, and the soul must walk forth, free from all its toils, to meet such æthereal welcome as it could find.

Mr Bertram had been told, and had answered, that he supposed as much. 'A man when he was too old to live must die,' he had said, 'though all the Sir Omicrons in Europe should cluster round his bed. It was only throwing money away. What, twenty pounds!' And being too weak to scold, he had turned his face to the wall in sheer vexation of spirit. Death he could encounter like a man; but why should he be robbed in his last moments?

'You'll go down to him, master George,' wheezed out poor Pritchett. 'Though it's too late for any good. It's all arranged now, of course.'

Bertram said that he would go down immediately, irrespective of any such arrangements. And then, remembering of whom that Hadley household had consisted when he left England in the early winter, he asked as to the two ladies.

'Miss Baker is there, of course?'

'Oh, yes, Miss Baker is there. She doesn't go to any furren parts, master George.'

'And—and—'

'Yes, she's in the house, too—poor creature—poor creature!'

'Then how am I to go there?' said George, speaking rather to himself than to Mr Pritchett.

'What! you wouldn't stay away from him now because of that? You ought to go to him, master George, though there were ten Lady Harcourts there—or twenty.' This was said in a tone that was not only serious, but full of melancholy. Mr Pritchett had probably never joked in his life, and had certainly never been less inclined to do so than now, when his patron was dying, and all his patron's money was to go into other and into unknown hands.

Some other information Bertram received from his most faithful ally. Sir Henry had been three times to Hadley, but he had only once succeeded in seeing Mr Bertram, and then the interview had been short, and, as Mr Pritchett surmised, not very satisfactory. His last visit had been since that paid by Sir Omicron, and on that occasion the sick man had sent out to say that he could not see strangers. All this Mr Pritchett had learned from Miss Baker. Sir Henry had not seen his wife since that day—now nearly twelve months since—on which she had separated herself from him. He had made a formal application to her to return to him, but nothing had come of it; and Mr Pritchett took upon himself to surmise again, that Sir Henry was too anxious about the old gentleman's money to take any steps that could be considered severe, until—. And then Mr Pritchett wheezed so grievously that what he said was not audible.

George immediately wrote to Miss Baker, announcing his return, and expressing his wish to see his uncle. He did not mention Lady Harcourt's name; but he suggested that perhaps it would be better, under existing circumstances, that he should not remain at Hadley. He hoped, however, that his uncle would not refuse to see him, and that his coming to the house for an hour or so might not be felt to be an inconvenience. By return of post he got an answer from Miss Baker, in which she assured him that his uncle was most anxious for his presence, and had appeared to be more cheerful, since he had heard of his nephew's return, than he had been for the last two months. As for staying at Hadley, George could do as he liked, Miss Baker said. But it was but a sad household, and perhaps it would be more comfortable for him to go backwards and forwards by the railway.

This correspondence caused a delay of two days, and on one of them Bertram received a visit which he certainly did not expect. He was sitting in his chamber alone, and was sad enough, thinking now of Mrs Cox and his near escape, then of Adela and his cousin's possible happiness, and then of Caroline and the shipwreck of her hopes, when the door opened, and Sir Henry Harcourt was standing before him.

'How d'ye do, Bertram?' said the late solicitor-general, putting out his hand. The attitude and the words were those of friendship, but his countenance was anything but friendly. A great change had come over him. His look of youth had deserted him, and he might have been taken for a careworn, middle-aged man. He was thin, and haggard, and wan; and there was a stern, harsh frown upon his brow, as though he would wish to fight if he only dared. This was the successful man—fortune's pet, who had married the heiress of the millionaire, and risen to the top of his profession with unexampled rapidity.

'How are you, Harcourt?' said Bertram, taking the proffered hand. 'I had no idea that you had heard of my return.'

'Oh, yes; I heard of it. I supposed you'd be back quick enough when you knew that the old man was dying.'

'I am glad, at any rate, to be here in time to see him,' said George, disdaining to defend himself against the innuendo.

'When are you going down?'

'Tomorrow, I suppose. But I expect to have a line from Miss Baker in the morning.'

Sir Henry, who had not sat down, began walking up and down the room, while Bertram stood with his back to the fire watching him. The lawyer's brow became blacker and blacker, and as he rattled his half-crowns in his trousers-pocket, and kept his eyes fixed upon the floor, Bertram began to feel that the interview did not promise to be one of a very friendly character.

'I was sorry to hear, Harcourt, that you are among the lot that have left the Government,' said Bertram, hardly knowing what else to say.

'D— the Government! But I didn't come here to talk about the Government. That old man down there will be gone in less than a week's time. Do you know that?'

'I hear that in all probability he has not long to live.'

'Not a week. I have it from Sir Omicron himself. Now I think you will admit, Bertram, that I have been very badly used.'

'Upon my word, my dear fellow, I know nothing about it.'

'Nonsense.'

'But it isn't nonsense. I tell you that I know nothing about it. I suppose you are alluding to my uncle's money; and I tell you that I know nothing—and care nothing.'

'Psha! I hate to hear a man talk in that way. I hate such humbug.'

'Harcourt, my dear fellow—'

'It is humbug. I am not in a humour now to stand picking my words. I have been infernally badly used—badly used on every side.'

'By me, among others?'

Sir Henry, in his present moody mind, would have delighted to say, 'Yes,' by him, Bertram, worse, perhaps, than any other. But it did not suit him at the present moment to come to an open rupture with the man whom he had been in such a hurry to visit.

'I treated that old man with the most unbounded confidence when I married his granddaughter—'

'But how does that concern me? She was not my granddaughter. I, at least, had nothing to do with it. Excuse me, Harcourt, if I say that I, of all men, am the last to whom you should address yourself on such a subject.'

'I think differently. You are his nearest relative—next to her; next to her, mind—'

'Well! What matter is it whether I am near or distant? Lady Harcourt is staying with him. Did it suit her to do so, she could fight your battle, or her own battle, or any battle that she pleases.'

'Yours, for instance?'

'No, Sir Henry. That she could not do. From doing that she is utterly debarred. But I tell you once for all that I have no battle. You shall know more—if the knowledge will do you any good. Not very long since my uncle offered to settle on me half his fortune if I would oblige him in one particular. But I could not do the thing he wanted; and when we parted, I had his positive assurance that he would leave me nothing. That was the last time I saw him.' And as Bertram remembered what that request was to which he had refused to accede, his brow also grew black.

'Tell me honestly, then, if you can be honest in the matter, who is to have his money?'

'I can be very honest, for I know nothing. My belief is that neither you nor I will have a shilling of it.'

'Well, then; I'll tell you what. Of course you know that Lady Harcourt is down there?'

'Yes; I know that she is at Hadley.'

'I'll not submit to be treated in this way. I have been a deuced sight too quiet, because I have not chosen to disturb him in his illness. Now I will have an answer from him. I will know what he means to do; and if I do not know by tomorrow night, I will go down, and will, at any rate, bring my wife away with me. I wish you to tell him that I want to know what his intentions are. I have a right to demand as much.'

'Be that as it may, you have no right to demand anything through me.'

'I have ruined myself—or nearly so, for that woman.'

'I wonder, Harcourt, that you do not see that I am not the man you should select to speak to on such a subject.'

'You are the man, because you are her cousin. I went to enormous expense to give her a splendid home, knowing, of course, that his wealth would entitle her to it. I bought a house for her, and furnished it as though she were a duchess—'

'Good heavens, Harcourt! Is this anything to me? Did I bid you buy the house? If you had not given her a chair to sit on, should I have complained? I tell you fairly, I will have nothing to do with it.'

'Then it will be the worse for her—that's all.'

'May God help her! She must bear her lot, as must I mine, and you yours.'

'And you refuse to take my message to your uncle?'

'Certainly. Whether I shall see him or not I do not yet know. If I do, I certainly shall not speak to him about money unless he begins. Nor shall I speak about you, unless he shall seem to wish it. If he asks about you, I will tell him that you have been with me.'

After some further discussion, Harcourt left him. George Bertram found it difficult to understand what motive could have brought him there. But drowning men catch at straws. Sir Henry was painfully alive to the consideration, that if anything was to be done about the rich man's money, if any useful step could be taken, it must be done at once; the step must be taken now. In another week, perhaps in another day, Mr Bertram would be beyond the power of will-making. No bargain could then be driven in which it should be stipulated that after his death his grandchild should be left unmolested —for a consideration. The bargain, if made at all, must be made now—now at once.

It will be thought that Sir Henry would have played his game better by remaining quiet; that his chance of being remembered in that will would be greater if he did not now make himself disagreeable. Probably so. But men running hither and thither in distress do not well calculate their chances. They are too nervous, too excited to play their game with judgment. Sir Henry Harcourt had now great trouble on his shoulders: he was in debt, was pressed for money on every side, had brought his professional bark into great disasters—nearly to utter shipwreck—and was known to have been abandoned by his wife. The world was not smiling on him. His great hope, his once strong hope, was now buried in those Hadley coffers; and it was not surprising that he did not take the safest way in his endeavours to reach those treasures which he so coveted.

On the following morning, George received Miss Baker's letter, and very shortly afterwards he started for Hadley. Of course he could not but remember that Lady Harcourt was staying there; that she would naturally be attending upon her grandfather, and that it was all but impossible that he should not see her. How were they to meet now? When last they had been together, he had held her in his arms, had kissed her forehead, had heard the assurance of her undying love. How were they to meet now?

George was informed by the servant who came to the door that his uncle was very ill. 'Weaker today,' the girl said, 'than ever he had been.' 'Where was Miss Baker?' George asked. The girl said that Miss Baker was in the dining-room. He did not dare to ask any further question. 'And her ladyship is with her grandfather,' the girl added; upon hearing which George walked with quicker steps to the parlour door.

Miss Baker met him as though there had been no breach in their former intimacy. With her, for the moment, Lady Harcourt and her troubles were forgotten, and she thought only of the dying man upstairs.

'I am so glad you have come!' she said. 'He does not say much about it. You remember he never did talk about such things. But I know that he will be delighted to see you. Sometimes he has said that he thought you had been in Egypt quite long enough.'

'Is he so very ill, then?'

'Indeed he is; very ill. You'll be shocked when you see him: you'll find him so much altered. He knows that it cannot last long, and he is quite reconciled.'

'Will you send up to let him know that I am here?'

'Yes, now—immediately. Caroline is with him;' and then Miss Baker left the room.

Caroline is with him! It was so singular to hear her mentioned as one of the same family with himself; to have to meet her as one sharing the same interests with him, bound by the same bonds, anxious to relieve the same suffering. She had said that they ought to be as far as the poles asunder; and yet fortune, unkind fortune, would bring them together! As he was thinking of this, the door opened gently, and she was in the room with him.

She, too, was greatly altered. Not that her beauty had faded, or that the lines of her face were changed, but her gait and manners were more composed; her dress was so much more simple, that, though not less lovely, she certainly looked older than when he had last seen her. She was thinner too, and, in the light-grey silk which she wore, seemed to be taller, and to be paler too.

She walked up to him, and putting out her hand, said some word or two which he did not hear; and he uttered something which was quite as much lost on her, and so their greeting was over. Thus passed their first interview, of which he had thought so much in looking forward to it for the last few hours, that his mind had been estranged from his uncle.

'Does he know I am here?'

'Yes. You are to go up to him. You know the room?'

'The same he always had?'

'Oh, yes; the same.' And then creeping on tiptoe, as men do in such houses, to the infinite annoyance of the invalids whom they wish to spare, he went upstairs, and stood by his uncle's bed.

Miss Baker was on the other side, and the sick man's face was turned towards her. 'You had better come round here, George,' said she. 'It would trouble Mr Bertram to move.'

'She means that I can't stir,' said the old man, whose voice was still sharp, though no longer loud. 'I can't turn round that way. Come here.' And so George walked round the bed.

He literally would not have known his uncle, so completely changed was the face. It was not only that it was haggard, thin, unshorn, and grey with coming death; but the very position of the features had altered. His cheeks had fallen away; his nose was contracted; his mouth, which he could hardly close, was on one side. Miss Baker told George afterwards that the left side was altogether motionless. George certainly would not have known his uncle—not at the first glance. But yet there was a spark left in those eyes, of the old fire; such a spark as had never gleamed upon him from any other human head. That look of sharpness, which nothing could quench, was still there. It was not the love of lucre which was to be read in those eyes, so much as the possessor's power of acquiring it. It was as though they said, 'Look well to all you have; put lock and bar to your stores; set dragons to watch your choice gardens; fix what man-traps you will for your own protection. In spite of everything, I will have it all! When I go forth to rob, no one can stay me!' So had he looked upon men through all his long life, and so now did he look upon his nephew and his niece as they stood by to comfort him in his extremity.

'I am sorry to see you in this state,' said George, putting his hand on to that of his uncle's, which was resting on the bed.

'Thank'ee George, thank'ee. When men get to be as old as I am, they have nothing for it but to die. So you've been to Egypt, have you? What do you think about Egypt?'

'It is not a country I should like to live in, sir.'

'Nor I to die in, from all that I hear of it. Well, you're just in time to be in at the last gasp—that's all, my boy.'

'I hope it has not come to that yet, sir.'

'Ah, but it has. How long a time did that man give me,

Mary—he that got the twenty pounds? They gave a fellow twenty pounds to come and tell me that I was dying! as if I didn't know that without him.'

'We thought it right to get the best advice we could, George,' said poor Miss Baker.

'Nonsense!' said the old man, almost in his olden voice. 'You'll find by-and-by that twenty pounds are not so easy to come by. George, as you are here, I might as well tell you about my money.'

George begged him not to trouble himself about such a matter at present; but this was by no means the way in which to propitiate his uncle.

'And if I don't talk of it now, when am I to do it? Go away, Mary—and look here—come up again in about twenty minutes. What I have got to say won't take me long.' And so Miss Baker left the room.

'George,' said his uncle, 'I wonder whether you really care about money? sometimes I have almost thought that you don't.'

'I don't think I do very much, sir.'

'Then you must be a great fool.'

'I have often thought I am, lately.'

'A very great fool. People preach against it, and talk against it, and write against it, and tell lies against it; but don't you see that everybody is fighting for it? The parsons all abuse it; but did you ever know one who wouldn't go to law for his tithes? Did you ever hear of a bishop who didn't take his dues?'

'I am quite fond enough of it, sir, to take all that I can earn.'

'That does not seem to be much, George. You haven't played your cards well—have you, my boy?'

'No, uncle; not very well. I might have done better.'

'No man is respected without money—no man. A poor man is always thrust to the wall—always. Now you will be a poor man, I fear, all your life.'

'Then I must put up with the wall, sir.'

'But why were you so harsh with me when I wanted you to marry her? Do you see now what you have done? Look at her, and what she might have been. Look at yourself, and what you might have been. Had you done that, you might have been my heir in everything.'

'Well, sir, I have made my bed, and I must lie upon it. I have cause enough for regret—though, to tell the truth, it is not about your money.'

'Ah, I knew you would be stiff to the last,' said Mr Bertram, angry that he could not move his nephew to express some sorrow about the half-million.

'Am I stiff, sir? Indeed, I do not mean it.'

'No, it's your nature. But we will not quarrel at the last; will we, George?'

'I hope not, sir. I am not aware that we have ever quarrelled. You once asked me to do a thing which, had I done it, would have made me a happy man—'

'And a rich man also.'

'And I fairly tell you now, that I would I had done as you would have had me. That is not being stiff, sir.'

'It is too late now, George.'

'Oh, yes, it is too late now; indeed it is.'

'Not but that I could put a codicil.'

'Ah, sir, you can put no codicil that can do me a service. No codicil can make her a free woman. There are sorrows, sir, which no codicil can cure.'

'Psha!' said his uncle, trying in his anger to turn himself on his bed, but failing utterly. 'Psha! Then you may live a pauper.'

George remained standing at the bedside; but he knew not what to do, or what answer to make to this ebullition of anger.

'I have nothing further to say,' continued his uncle.

'But we shall part in friendship, shall we not?' said George. 'I have so much to thank you for, that I cannot bear that you should be angry with me now.'

'You are an ass—a fool!'

'You should look on that as my misfortune, sir.' And then he paused a moment. 'I will leave you now, shall I?'

'Yes, and send Mary up.'

'But I may come down again tomorrow?'

'What! haven't they a bed for you in the house?'

Bertram hummed and hawed, and said he did not know. But the conference ended in his promising to stay there. So he went up to town, and returned again bringing down his carpet bag, and preparing to remain till all should be over.

That was a strange household which was now collected together in the house at Hadley. The old man was lying upstairs, daily expecting his death; and he was attended, as it was seemly that he should be, by his nearest relatives. His brother's presence he would not have admitted; but his grandchild was there, and his nephew, and her whom he had always regarded as his niece. Nothing could be more fitting than this. But not the less did Caroline and George feel that it was not fitting that they should be together.

And yet the absolute awkwardness of the meeting was soon over. They soon found themselves able to sit in the same room, conversing on the one subject of interest which the circumstances of the moment gave, without any allusion to past times. They spoke only of the dying man, and asked each other questions only about him. Though they were frequently alone together while Miss Baker was with Mr Bertram, they never repeated the maddening folly of that last scene in Eaton Square.

'She has got over it now,' said Bertram to himself; and he thought that he rejoiced that it was so. But yet it made his heart sad.

It has passed away like a dream, thought Lady Harcourt; and now he will be happy again. And she, too, strove to comfort herself in thinking so; but the comfort was very cold.

And now George was constantly with his uncle. For the first two days nothing further was said about money. Mr Bertram seemed to be content that matters should rest as they were then settled, and his nephew certainly had no intention of recurring to the subject on his own behalf. The old man, however, had become much kinder in his manner to him—kinder to him than to any one else in the house; and exacted from him various little promises of things to be done—of last wishes to be fulfilled.

'Perhaps it is better as it is, George,' he said, as Bertram was sitting by his bedside late one night.

'I am sure it is, sir,' said George, not at all, however, knowing what was the state of things which his uncle described as being better.

'All men can't be made alike,' continued the uncle.

'No, uncle; there must be rich men and there must be poor men.'

'And you prefer the latter.'

Now George had never said this; and the assertion coming from his uncle at such a moment, when he could not contradict it, was rather hard on him. He had tried to prove to Mr Bertram, not so much then, as in their former intercourse, that he would in no way subject his feelings to the money-bags of any man; that he would make no sacrifice of his aspirations for the sake of wealth; that he would not, in fact, sell himself for gold. But he had never said, or intended to say, that money was indifferent to him. Much as his uncle understood, he had failed to understand his nephew's mind. But George could not explain it to him now;—so he merely smiled, and let the assertion pass.

'Well; be it so,' said Mr Bertram. 'But you will see, at any rate, that I have trusted you. Why father and son should be so much unlike, God only can understand.' And from that time he said little or nothing more about his will.

But Sir Omicron had been wrong. Mr Bertram overlived the week, and overlived the fortnight. We must now leave him and his relatives in the house of sickness, and return to Arthur Wilkinson.

CHAPTER XLII

MRS WILKINSON'S TROUBLES

ARTHUR WILKINSON was received at home with open arms and warm embraces. He was an only son, an only brother, the head and stay of his family; and of course he was beloved. His mother wept for joy as she saw the renewed plumpness of his cheeks, and declared that Egypt must indeed be a land of fatness; and his sisters surrounded him, smiling and kissing him, and asking questions, as though he were another Livingstone.* This was very delightful; but a cloud was soon to come across all this sunshine.

Mrs Wilkinson, always excepting what care she may have had for her son's ill health, had not been unhappy during his absence. She had reigned the female vicaress, without a drawback, praying daily, and in her heart almost hourly, for the continuance in the land of such excellent noblemen as Lord Stapledean. The curate who had taken Arthur's duty had been a very mild young man, and had been quite contented that Mrs Wilkinson should leave to him the pulpit and the reading-desk. In all other matters he had been satisfied not to interfere with her power, or to contradict her edicts.

'Mr Gilliflower has behaved excellently,' she said to her son, soon after his return; 'and has quite understood my position here. I only wish we could keep him in the parish; but that, of course, is impossible.'

'I shouldn't want him at all, mother,' Arthur had replied. 'I am as strong as a horse now.'

'All the same; I should like to have him here,' said Mrs Wilkinson, in a tone which was the beginning of the battle. How sweet it would have been to her if Arthur could have gone to some good neighbouring parish, leaving her, with Gabriel Gilliflower as her assistant, to manage the souls of Hurst Staple! And why, as she almost asked herself—why should she not be addressed as the Reverend Mrs Wilkinson?

But the battle had to be fought, and there was to be an end to these sweet dreams. Her son had been meek enough, but he was not as meek as Mr Gilliflower; and now he was sharpening his arrows, and looking to his bow, and preparing for the war.

'Is Adela at Littlebath?' he asked of one of his sisters, on the third or fourth day after his arrival.

'Yes,' said Mary. 'She is with her aunt. I had a letter from her yesterday.'

'I wonder whether she would come here if you were to ask her.'

'Oh, that she would,' said Mary.

'I doubt it very much,' said the more prudent Sophia.

Mrs Wilkinson heard the conversation, and pondered over it. At the moment she said nothing, pressing down her grief in her deep heart; but that evening, in the book-room, she found Arthur alone; and then she began.

'You were not in earnest just now about Adela, were you, Arthur?'

'Indeed I was, mother; quite in earnest.'

'She has been very much away from Littlebath since her aunt came back from Italy to make a home for her. She was with us; and with the Harcourts, in London; and, since the break-up there, she was at Hadley. It would not be right to Miss Gauntlet to ask her away so soon.'

'I don't think Miss Gauntlet would mind her coming here; and even if she does—'

'And then my time is so much taken up—what with the schools, and what with the parish visiting—'

'Adela will do the visiting with you.'

'I really had rather not have her just at present; that is, unless you have some very particular reason.'

'Well, mother, I have a particular reason. But if you had rather that she did not come here, I will go to Littlebath instead.'

There was nothing more said on this occasion; but that was the beginning of the battle. Mrs Wilkinson could not but know what her son meant; and she now knew that all that she dreaded was to come upon her. It was not that she did not wish to see her son happy, or that she did not think that his being married and settled would tend to his happiness; but she was angry, as other mothers are angry, when their foolish, calf-like boys will go and marry without any incomes on which to support a wife. She said to herself over and over again that night, 'I cannot have a second family here in the parsonage; that's certain. And where on earth they're to live, I don't know; and how they're to live when his fellowship is gone, I can't think.' And then she shook her head, clothed as it was in her nightcap, and reposing as it was on her pillow. 'Two thousand pounds is every shilling she has—every shilling.' And then she shook her head again. She knew that the ecclesiastical income was her own; for had not the good Lord Stapledean given it to her? But she had sad thoughts, and feared that even on this point there might be a contest between her and her son.

Two mornings after this the blow came very suddenly. It was now her habit to go into the book-room after breakfast, and set herself down to work—as her husband, the former vicar, had done in his time—and as Arthur, since his return, usually did the same, they naturally found themselves alone together. On the morning in question, she had no sooner seated herself, with her papers before her, than Arthur began. And, alas! he had to tell her, not what he was going to do, but what he had done.

'I spoke to you, mother, of going to Littlebath the other day.'

'Yes, Arthur,' said she, taking her spectacles off, and laying them beside her.

'I have written to her, instead.'

'And you have made her an offer of marriage!'

'Exactly so. I was sure you must have known how my heart stood towards her. It is many years now since I first thought of this; but I was deterred, because I feared that my income—our income, that is—was insufficient.'

'Oh, Arthur, and so it is. What will you do? How will you live? Adela has got just two thousand pounds—about seventy or eighty pounds a year. And your fellowship will be gone. Oh, Arthur, how will all the mouths be fed when you have six or seven children round you?'

'I'll tell you what my plans are. If Adela should accept me—'

'Oh, accept you! She'll accept you fast enough,' said Mrs Wilkinson, with the venom with which mothers will sometimes speak of the girls to whom their sons are attached.

'It makes me very happy to hear you say so. But I don't know. When I did hint at the matter once before, I got no encouragement.'

'Psha!' said Mrs Wilkinson.

This sound was music to her son's ears; so he went on with the more cheerfulness to describe his plans.

'You see, mother, situated as I am, I have no right to expect any increase of income, or to hope that I shall ever be better able to marry than I am now.'

'But you might marry a girl who had something to help. There is Miss Glunter—'

'But it so happens that I am attached to Adela, and not to Miss Glunter.'

'Attached! But, of course, you must have your own way. You are of age, and I cannot prevent your marrying the cook-maid if you like. What I want to know is, where do you mean to live?'

'Here, certainly.'

'What! in this house?'

'Certainly. I am bound to live here, as the clergyman of the parish.'

Mrs Wilkinson drew herself up to her full height, put her spectacles on, and looked at the papers before her; then put them off again, and fixed her eyes on her son. 'Do you think there will be room in the house?' she said. 'I fear you would be preparing great discomfort for Adela. Where on earth would she find room for a nursery? But, Arthur, you have not thought of these things.'

Arthur, however, had thought of them very often. He knew where to find the nursery, and the room for Adela. His difficulty was as to the rooms for his mother and sisters. It was necessary now that this difference of opinion should be explained.

'I suppose that my children, if I have any—'

'Clergymen always have large families,' said Mrs Wilkinson.

'Well, I suppose they'll have the same nursery that we had.'

'What, and turn Sophy and Mary out of it!' And then she paused, and began to re-arrange her papers. 'That will not do at all, Arthur,' she continued. 'It would be unjust in me to allow that; much as I think of your interests, I must of course think of theirs as well.'

How was he to tell her that the house was his own? It was essentially necessary that he should do so, and that he should do so now. If he gave up the point at the present moment, he might give it up for ever. His resolve was, that his mother and sisters should go elsewhere; but in what words could he explain this resolution to her?

'Dear mother, I think we should understand each other—'

'Certainly,' said Mrs Wilkinson, laying her hands across each other on the table, and preparing for the onslaught.

'It is clearly my duty, as clergyman, to live in this parish, and to live in this house.'

'And it is my duty also, as was excellently explained by Lord Stapledean after your poor father's death.'

'My idea is this—' and then he paused, for his heart misgave him when he attempted to tell his mother that she must pack up and turn out. His courage all but failed him. He felt that he was right, and yet he hardly knew how to explain that he was right without appearing to be unnatural.

'I do not know that Lord Stapledean said anything about the house; but if he did, it could make no difference.'

'Not the least, I should think,' said the lady. 'When he appointed me to the income of the parish, it could hardly be necessary that he should explain that I was to have the house also.'

'Mother, when I accepted the living, I promised him that I would give you three hundred and fifty pounds out of the proceeds; and so I will. Adela and I will be very poor, but I shall endeavour to eke out our income; that is, of course, if she consents to marry me—'

'Psha!'

'—To eke out our income by taking pupils. To do that, I must have the house at my own disposal.'

'And you mean to tell me,' said the female vicaress, rising to her feet in her wrath, 'that I—that I—am to go away?'

'I think it will be better, mother.'

'And the poor girls!'

'For one or two of them there would be room here,' said Arthur, trying to palliate the matter.

'One or two of them! Is that the way you would treat your sisters? I say nothing about myself, for I have long seen that you are tired of me. I know how jealous you are because Lord Stapledean has thought proper to—' she could not exactly remember what phrase would best suit her purpose—'to—to—to place me here, as he placed your poor father before. I have seen it all, Arthur. But I have my duty to do, and I shall do it. What I have undertaken in this parish I shall go through with, and if you oppose me I shall apply to his lordship.'

'I think you have misunderstood Lord Stapledean.'

'I have not misunderstood him at all. I know very well what he meant, and I quite appreciate his motives. I have endeavoured to act up to them, and shall continue to do so. I had thought that I had made the house as comfortable to you as any young man could wish.'

'And so you have.'

'And yet you want to turn me out of it—out of my own house!'

'Not to turn you out, mother. If it suits you to remain here for another year—'

'It will suit me to remain here for another ten years, if I am spared so long. Little viper! I suppose this comes from her. After warming her in my bosom when her father died!'

'It can hardly have come from her, seeing that there has never yet been a word spoken between us on the subject. I fear that you greatly mistake the footing on which we stand together. I have no reasonable ground for hoping for a favourable answer.'

'Psha! viper!' exclaimed Mrs Wilkinson, in dire wrath. Mothers are so angry when other girls, not their own, will get offers; so doubly angry when their own sons make them.

'You will make me very unhappy if you speak ill of her,' said Arthur.

'Has it ever come into your head to think where your mother and sisters are to live when you turn them out?' said she.

'Littlebath,' suggested Arthur.

'Littlebath!' said Mrs Wilkinson, with all the scorn that she could muster to the service. 'Littlebath! I am to put up with the aunt, I suppose, when you take the niece. But I shall not go to Littlebath at your bidding, sir.' And so saying, she gathered up her spectacles, and stalked out of the room.

Arthur was by no means satisfied with the interview, and

yet had he been wise he might have been. The subject had been broached, and that in itself was a great deal. And the victory had by no means been with Mrs Wilkinson. She had threatened, indeed, to appeal to Lord Stapledean; but that very threat showed how conscious she was that she had no power of her own to hold her place where she was. He ought to have been satisfied; but he was not so.

And now he had to wait for his answer from Adela. Gentlemen who make offers by letter must have a weary time of it, waiting for the return of post, or for the return of two posts, as was the case in this instance. And Arthur had a weary time of it. Two evenings he had to pass, after the conversation above recounted, before he got his letter; and dreadful evenings they were. His mother was majestic, glum, and cross; his sisters were silent and dignified. It was clear to him that they had all been told; and so told as to be leagued in enmity against him. What account their mother may have given to them of their future poverty, he knew not; but he felt certain that she had explained to them how cruelly he meant to turn them out on the wide world; unnatural ogre that he was.

Mary was his favourite, and to her he did say a few words. 'Mamma has told you what I have done, hasn't she?'

'Yes, Arthur,' said Mary, demurely.

'And what do you think about it?'

'Think about it?'

'Yes. Do you think she'll accept me?'

'Oh! she'll accept you. I don't doubt about that.' How cheap girls do make themselves when talking of each other!

'And will it not be an excellent thing for me?' said he.

'But about the house, Arthur!' And Mary looked very glum. So he said nothing further to any of them.

On the day after this he got his answer; and now we will give the two letters. Arthur's was not written without much trouble and various copies; but Adela's had come straight from her heart at once.

'My dear Adela, 'Hurst Staple, April, 184—.

'You will be surprised to receive a letter from me, and

more so, I am sure, when you read its contents. You have heard, I know, from Mary, of my return home. Thank God, I am quite strong again. I enjoyed my trip very much. I had feared that it would be very dull before I knew that George Bertram would go with me.

'I wonder whether you recollect the day when I drove you to Ripley Station! It is eighteen months ago now, I believe; and indeed the time seems much longer. I had thought then to have said to you what I have to say now; but I did not. Years ago I thought to do the same, and then also I did not. You will know what I mean. I did not like to ask you to share such poverty, such a troubled house as mine will be.

'But I have loved you, Adela, for years and years. Do you remember how you used to comfort me at that grievous time, when I disappointed them all so much about my degree? I remember it so well. It used to lie on my tongue then to tell you that I loved you; but that would have been folly. Then came my poor father's death, and the living which I had to take under such circumstances. I made up my mind then that it was my duty to live single. I think I told you, though I am sure you forget that.

'I am not richer now, but I am older. I seem to care less about poverty on my own behalf; and—though I don't know whether you will forgive me for this—I feel less compunction in asking you to be poor with me. Do not imagine from this that I feel confident as to your answer. I am very far from that. But I know that you used to love me as a friend—and I now venture to ask you to love me as my wife.

'Dearest Adela! I feel that I may call you so now, even if I am never to call you so again. If you will share the world with me, I will give you whatever love can give—though I can give but little more. I need not tell you how we should be circumstanced. My mother must have three hundred and fifty pounds out of the living as long as she lives; and should I survive her, I must, of course, maintain the girls. But I mean to explain to my mother that she had better live elsewhere. There will be trouble about this; but I am sure that it is right. I shall tell her of this letter tomorrow. I think she knows what my intention is, though I have not exactly told it to her.

'I need not say how anxious I shall be till I hear from you. I shall not expect a letter till Thursday morning; but, if possible, do let me have it then. Should it be favourable—though I do not allow myself to have any confidence—but should it be favourable, I shall be at Littlebath on Monday evening. Believe me, that I love you dearly.

'Yours, dear Adela,

'ARTHUR WILKINSON.'

Aunt Penelope was a lady addicted to very early habits, and consequently she and Adela had usually left the breakfast-table before the postman had visited them. From this it resulted that Adela received her letter by herself. The first words told her what it contained, and her eyes immediately became suffused with tears. After all, then, her patience was to be rewarded. But it had not been patience so much as love; love that admitted of no change; love on which absence had had no effect; love which had existed without any hope; which had been acknowledged by herself, and acknowledged as a sad misfortune. But now—. She took the letter up, but she could not read it. She turned it over, and at the end, through her tears, she saw those words—'Believe me, that I love you dearly.' They were not like the burning words, the sweet violent protestations of a passionate lover. But coming from him, they were enough. At last she was to be rewarded.

And then at length she read it. Ah, yes; she recollected the day well when he had driven her to Ripley Station, and asked her those questions as he was persuading Dumpling to mount the hill. The very words were still in her ears. 'Would *you* come to such a house, Adela?' Ay, indeed, would she—if only she were duly asked. But he—! Had it not seemed then as if he almost wished that the proffer should come from her? Not to that would she stoop. But as for sharing such a house as his—any house with him! What did true love mean, if she were not ready to do that?

And she remembered, too, that comforting of which he spoke. That had been the beginning of it all, when he took those walks along the river to West Putford; when she had learned to look for his figure coming through the little wicket at the bottom of their lawn. Then she had taxed her young heart with imprudence—but in doing so she had found that it was too late. She had soon told the truth—to herself that is; and throughout she had been true. Now she had her reward; there in her hands, pressing it to her heart. He had loved her for years and years, he said. Yes, and so had she loved him; and now he should know it. But not quite at once—in some sweet hour of fullest confidence she would whisper it all to him.

'I think I told you; though, I am sure, you have forgotten that.'

Forget it! no, not a word, not one of his tones, not a glance of his eyes, as he sat there in her father's drawing-room that morning, all but unable to express his sorrows. She could never forget the effort with which she had prevented the tell-tale blood from burning in her cheeks, or the difficulty with which she had endured his confidence. But she had endured it, and now had come her reward. Then he had come to tell her that he was too poor to marry. Much as she loved him, she had then almost despised him. But the world had told him to be wiser. The world, which makes so many niggards, had taught him to be freer of heart. Now he was worthy of her, now that he cared nothing for poverty. Yes, now she had her reward.

He had allowed her till the second post for her reply. That was so kind of him, as it was necessary that she should tell her aunt. As to the nature of her reply—as to that she never doubted for a moment. She would consult her aunt; but she would do so with her mind fully made up as to the future. No aunt, no Mrs Wilkinson, should rob her of her happiness now that he had spoken. No one should rob him of the comfort of her love!

In the evening, after thinking of it for hours, she told her aunt; or, rather, handed to her Arthur's letter, that she might read it. Miss Penelope's face grew very long as she did read it; and she made this remark—'Three hundred and fifty pounds! why, my dear, there will be only one hundred and fifty left.'

'We can't keep our carriage, certainly, aunt.'

'Then you mean to accept him?'

'Yes, aunt.'

'Oh, dear! oh, dear! What will you do when the children come?'

'We must make the best of it, aunt.'

'Oh, dear! oh, dear! And you will have his mother with you always.'

'If so, then we should not be so very poor; but I do not think that that is what Arthur means.'

There was not much more said about it between them; and at last, in the seclusion of her own bedroom, Adela wrote her letter.

'Dear Arthur, 'Littlebath, Tuesday night.

'I received your letter this morning! but as you were so kind as to give me a day to answer it, I have put off doing so till I could be quite alone. It will be a very simple answer. I value your love more than anything in the world. You have my whole heart. I hope, for your sake, that the troubles which you speak of will not be many; but whatever they may be, I will share them. If I can, I will lessen them.

'I hope it is not unmaidenly to say that I have received your dear letter with true delight; I do not know why it should be. We have known each other so long, that it is almost natural that I should love you. I do love you dearly, dearest Arthur, and with a heart thankful for God's goodness to me, I will put my hand in yours with perfect trust—fearing nothing, then, as far as this world is concerned.

'I do not regard the poverty of which you speak, at least not for my own sake. What I have of my own is, I know, very little. I wish now that I could make it more for you. But no; I will wish for nothing more, seeing that so much has been given to me. Everything has been given to me when I have your love.

'I hope that this will not interfere with your mother's comfort. If anything now could make me unhappy, it would be that she should not be pleased at our prospects. Give her my kindest, kindest love; and tell her that I hope she will let me look on her as a mother.

'I will write to Mary very soon; but bid her write to me

first. I cannot tell her how happy, how very happy I really am, till she has first wished me joy.

'I have, of course, told aunt Penelope. She, too, says something about poverty. I tell her it is croaking. The honest do not beg their bread; do they, Arthur? But in spite of her croaking, she will be very happy to see you on Monday, if it shall suit you to come. If so, let me have one other little line. But I am so contented now, that I shall hardly be more so even to have you here.

'God bless you, my own, own, own dearest.

'Ever yours with truest affection,

'ADELA.'

And I also hope that Adela's letter will not be considered unmaidenly; but I have my fears. There will be those who will say that it is sadly deficient in reserve. Ah! had she not been reserved enough for the last four or five years? Reserve is beautiful in a maiden if it be rightly timed. Sometimes one would fain have more of it. But when the heart is full, and when it may speak out; when time, and circumstances, and the world permit—then we should say that honesty is better than reserve. Adela's letter was honest on the spur of the moment. Her reserve had been the work of years.

Arthur, at any rate, was satisfied. Her letter seemed to him to be the very perfection of words. Armed with that he would face his mother, though she appeared armed from head to foot in the Stapledean panoply. While he was reading his letter he was at breakfast with them all; and when he had finished it for the second time, he handed it across the table to his mother.

'Oh! I suppose so,' was her only answer, as she gave it him back.

The curiosity of the girls was too great now for the composure of their silent dignity. 'It is from Adela,' said Mary; 'what does she say?'

'You may read it,' said Arthur, again handing the letter across the table.

'Well, I do wish you joy,' said Mary, 'though there will be so very little money.'

Seeing that Arthur, since his father's death, had, in fact, supported his mother and sisters out of his own income, this reception of his news was rather hard upon him. And so he felt it.

'You will not have to share the hardships,' he said, as he left the room; 'and so you need not complain.'

There was nothing more said about it that morning; but in the evening, when they were alone, he spoke to his sister again. 'You will write to her, Mary, I hope?'

'Yes, I will write to her,' said Mary, half ashamed of herself.

'Perhaps it is not surprising that my mother should be vexed, seeing the false position in which both she and I have been placed; partly by my fault, for I should not have accepted the living under such conditions.'

'Oh, Arthur, you would not have refused it?'

'I ought to have so. But, Mary, you and the girls should be ready to receive Adela with open arms. What other sister could I have given you that you would have loved better?'

'Oh, no one; not for her own sake—no one half so well.'

'Then tell her so, and do not cloud her prospects by writing about the house. You have all had shelter and comfort hitherto, and be trustful that it will be continued to you.'

This did very well with his sister; but the affair with his mother was much more serious. He began by telling her that he should go to Littlebath on Monday, and be back on Wednesday.

'Then I shall go to Bowes on Wednesday,' said Mrs Wilkinson. Now we all know that Bowes is a long way from Hurst Staple. The journey has already been made once in these pages. But Mrs Wilkinson was as good as her word.

'To Bowes!' said Arthur.

'Yes, to Bowes, sir; to Lord Stapledean. That is, if you hold to your scheme of turning me out of my own house.'

'I think it would be better, mother, that we should have two establishments.'

'And, therefore, I am to make way for you and that—' viper, she was going to say again; but looking into her son's face, she became somewhat more merciful—'for you,' she said, 'and that chit!'

'As clergyman of the parish, I think that I ought to live in the parsonage. You, mother, will have so much the larger portion of the income.'

'Very well. There need be no more words about it. I shall start for Bowes next Wednesday.' And so she did.

Arthur wrote his 'one other little line.' As it was three times as long as his first letter, it shall not be printed. And he did make his visit to Littlebath. How happy Adela was as she leant trustingly on his arm, and felt that it was her own! He stayed, however, but one night, and was back at Hurst Staple before his mother started for Bowes.

CHAPTER XLIII

ANOTHER JOURNEY TO BOWES

MRS WILKINSON did not leave her home for her long and tedious journey without considerable parade. Her best new black silk dress was packed up in order that due honour might be done to Lord Stapledean's hospitality, and so large a box was needed that Dumpling and the four-wheeled carriage were hardly able to take her to the railway-station. Then there arose the question who should drive her. Arthur offered to do so; but she was going on a journey of decided hostility as regarded him, and under such circumstances she could not bring herself to use his services even over a portion of the road. So the stable-boy was her charioteer.

She talked about Lord Stapledean the whole evening before she went. Arthur would have explained to her something of that nobleman's character if she would have permitted it. But she would not. When he hinted that she would find Lord Stapledean austere in his manner, she answered that his lordship no doubt had had his reasons for being austere with so very young a man as Arthur had been. When he told her about the Bowes hotel, she merely shook her head significantly. A nobleman who had been so generous to her and hers as Lord Stapledean would hardly allow her to remain at the inn.

'I am very sorry that the journey is forced upon me,' she said to Arthur, as she sat with her bonnet on, waiting for the vehicle.

'I am sorry that you are going, mother, certainly,' he had answered; 'because I know that it will lead to disappointment.'

'But I have no other course left open to me,' she continued. 'I cannot see my poor girls turned out houseless on the world.' And then, refusing even to lean on her son's arm, she stepped up heavily into the carriage, and seated herself beside the boy.

'When shall we expect you, mamma?' said Sophia.

'It will be impossible for me to say; but I shall be sure to write as soon as I have seen his lordship. Good-bye to you, girls.' And then she was driven away.

'It is a very foolish journey,' said Arthur.

'Mamma feels that she is driven to it,' said Sophia.

Mrs Wilkinson had written to Lord Stapledean two days before she started, informing his lordship that it had become very necessary that she should wait upon him on business connected with the living, and therefore she was aware that her coming would not be wholly unexpected. In due process of time she arrived at Bowes, very tired and not a little disgusted at the great expense of her journey. She had travelled but little alone, and knew nothing as to the cost of hotels, and not a great deal as to that of railways, coaches, and post-chaises.* But at last she found herself in the same little inn which had previously received Arthur when he made the same journey.

'The lady can have a post-chaise, of course,' said the landlady, speaking from the bar. 'Oh, yes, Lord Stapledean is at home, safe enough. He's never very far away from it to the best of my belief.'

'It's only a mile or so, is it?' said Mrs Wilkinson.

'Seven long miles, ma'am,' said the landlady.

'Seven miles! dear, dear. I declare I never was so tired in my life. You can put the box somewhere behind in the post-chaise, can't you?'

'Yes, ma'am; we can do that. Be you a-going to stay at his lordship's, then?'

To this question Mrs Wilkinson made an ambiguous answer. Her confidence was waning, now that she drew near to the centre of her aspirations. But at last she did exactly as her son had done before her. She said she would take her box; but that it was possible she might want a bed that evening. 'Very possible,' the landlady said to herself.

'And you'll take a bite of something before you start, ma'am,' she said, out loud. But, no; it was only now twelve o'clock, and she would be at Bowes Lodge a very little after one. She had still sufficient confidence in Lord Stapledean to feel sure of her lunch. When people reached Hurst Staple Vicarage about that hour, there was always something for them to eat. And so she started.

It was April now; but even in April that bleak northern fell was very cold. Nothing more inhospitable than that road could be seen. It was unsheltered, swept by every blast, very steep, and mercilessly oppressed by turnpikes. Twice in those seven miles one-and-sixpence was inexorably demanded from her.

'But I know one gate always clears the other, when they are so near,' she argued.

'Noa, they doant,' was all the answer she received from the turnpike woman, who held a baby under each arm.

'I am sure the woman is robbing me,' said poor Mrs Wilkinson.

'No, she beant,' said the post-boy. They are good hearty people in that part of the world; but they do not brook suspicion, and the courtesies of life are somewhat neglected. And then she arrived at Lord Stapledean's gate.

'Be you she what sent the letter?' said the woman at the lodge, holding it only half open.

'Yes, my good woman; yes,' said Mrs Wilkinson, thinking that her troubles were now nearly over. 'I am the lady; I am Mrs Wilkinson.'

'Then my lord says as how you're to send up word what you've got to say.' And the woman still stood in the gateway.

'Send up word!' said Mrs Wilkinson.

'Yees. Just send up word. Here's Jock can rin up.'

'But Jock can't tell his lordship what I have to say to him. I have to see his lordship on most important business,' said she, in her dismay.

'I'm telling you no more that what my lord said his ain sell. He just crawled down here his ain sell. "If a woman comes," said he, "don't let her through the gate till she sends up word what she's got to say to me." ' And the portress looked as though she were resolved to obey her master's orders.

'Good heavens! There must be some mistake in this, I'm sure. I am the clergyman of Hurst Staple—I mean his widow. Hurst Staple, you know; his lordship's property.'

'I didna know nothing aboot it.'

'Oh, drive on, post-boy. There must be some mistake. The woman must be making some dreadful mistake.'

At last the courage of the lodge-keeper gave way before the importance of the post-chaise, and she did permit Mrs Wilkinson to proceed.

'Mither,' said the woman's eldest hope, 'you'll cotch it noo.'

'Eh, lad; weel. He'll no hang me.' And so the woman consoled herself.

The house called Bowes Lodge looked damper and greener, more dull, silent, and melancholy, even than it had done when Arthur made his visit. The gravel sweep before the door was covered by weeds, and the shrubs looked as though they had known no gardener's care for years. The door itself did not even appear to be for purposes of ingress and egress, and the post-boy had to search among the boughs and foliage with which the place was overgrown before he could find the bell. When found, it sounded with a hoarse, rusty, jangling noise, as though angry at being disturbed in so unusual a manner.

But, rusty and angry as it was, it did evoke a servant—though not without considerable delay. A cross old man did come at last, and the door was slowly opened. 'Yes,' said the man. 'The marquis was at home, no doubt. He was in the study. But that was no rule why he should see folk.' And then he looked very suspiciously at the big trunk, and muttered something to the post-boy, which Mrs Wilkinson could not hear.

'Will you oblige me by giving my card to his lordship—Mrs Wilkinson? I want to see him on very particular business. I wrote to his lordship to say that I should be here.'

'Wrote to his lordship, did you? Then it's my opinion he won't see you at all.'

'Yes, he will. If you'll take him my card, I know he'll see me. Will you oblige me, sir, by taking it in to his lordship?' And she put on her most imperious look.

The man went, and Mrs Wilkinson sat silent in the post-chaise for a quarter of an hour. Then the servant returned, informing her that she was to send in her message. His lordship had given directions at the lodge that she was not to come up, and could not understand how it had come to pass that the lady had forced her way to the hall-door. At any rate, he would not see her till he knew what it was about.

Now it was impossible for Mrs Wilkinson to explain the exact nature of her very intricate case to Lord Stapledean's butler, and yet she could not bring herself to give up the battle without making some further effort. 'It is about the vicarage at Hurst Staple,' said she; 'the vicarage at Hurst Staple,' she repeated, impressing the words on the man's memory. 'Don't forget, now.' The man gave a look of ineffable scorn, and then walked away, leaving Mrs Wilkinson still in the post-chaise.

And now came on an April shower, such as April showers are on the borders of Westmorland. It rained and blew; and after awhile the rain turned to sleet. The post-boy buttoned up his coat, and got under the shelter of the portico; the horses drooped their heads, and shivered. Mrs Wilkinson wished herself back at Hurst Staple—or even comfortably settled at Littlebath, as her son had once suggested.

'His lordship don't know nothing about the vicarage,' bellowed out the butler, opening the hall-door only half way, so that his face just appeared above the lock.

'Oh, dear! oh, dear!' said Mrs Wilkinson. 'Just let me down into the hall, and then I will explain it to you.'

'Them 'orses 'll be foundered as sure as heggs,' said the post-boy.

Mrs Wilkinson at last succeeded in making her way into the hall, and the horses were allowed to go round to the yard. And then at last, after half a dozen more messages to and fro, she was informed that Lord Stapledean would see her. So dreadful had been the contest hitherto, that this amount of success was very grateful. Her feeling latterly had been one of intense hostility to the butler rather than to her son. Now that she had conquered that most savage Cerberus,* all would be pleasant with her. But, alas! she soon found that in passing Cerberus she had made good her footing in a region as little desirable as might be.

She was ushered into the same book-room in which Arthur had been received, and soon found herself seated in the same chair, and on the same spot. Lord Stapledean was thinner now, even than he had been then; he had a stoop in his shoulders, and his face and hair were more grey. His eyes seemed to his visitor to be as sharp and almost as red as those of ferrets. As she entered, he just rose from his seat and pointed to the chair on which she was to sit.

'Well, ma'am,' said he, 'what's all this about the clergyman's house at Hurst Staple? I don't understand it at all.'

'No, my lord; I'm sure your lordship can't understand. That's why I have thought it my duty to come all this way to explain it.'

'All what way?'

'All the way from Hurst Staple, in Hampshire, my lord. When your lordship was so considerate as to settle what my position in the parish was to be—'

'Settle your position in the parish!'

'Yes, my lord—as to my having the income and the house.'

'What does the woman mean?' said he, looking down towards the rug beneath his feet, but speaking quite out loud. 'Settle her position in the parish! Why, ma'am, I don't know who you are, and what your position is, or anything about you.'

'I am the widow of the late vicar, Lord Stapledean; and when he died—'

'I was fool enough to give the living to his son. I remember all about it. He was an imprudent man, and lived beyond his means, and there was nothing left for any of you—wasn't that it?'

'Yes, my lord,' said Mrs Wilkinson, who was so troubled in spirit that she hardly knew what to say. 'That is, we never lived beyond our means at all, my lord. There were seven children; and they were all educated most respectably. The only boy was sent to college; and I don't think there was any imprudence—indeed I don't, my lord. And there was something saved; and the insurance was always regularly paid; and—'

The marquis absolutely glared at her, as she went on with her domestic defence. The household at Hurst Staple had been creditably managed, considering the income; and it was natural that she should wish to set her patron right. But every word that she said carried her further away from her present object.

'And what on earth have you come to me for?' said Lord Stapledean.

'I'll tell your lordship, if you'll only allow me five minutes. Your lordship remembers when poor Mr Wilkinson died?'

'I don't remember anything about it.'

'Your lordship was good enough to send for Arthur.'

'Arthur!'

'Yes, my lord.'

'Who's Arthur?'

'My boy, my lord. Don't you remember? He was just in orders then, and so you were good enough to put him into the living; that is to say, not exactly into the living, but to make him curate, as it were; and you allocated the income to me; and—'

'Allocated the income!' said Lord Stapledean, putting up his hands in token of unlimited surprise.

'Yes, my lord. Your lordship saw just how it was; and, as I could not exactly hold the living myself—'

'Hold the living yourself! Why, are you not a woman, ma'am?'

'Yes, my lord, of course; that was the reason. So you put Arthur into the living, and you allocated the income to me. That is all settled. But now the question is about the house.'

'The woman's mad,' said Lord Stapledean, looking again to the carpet, but speaking quite out loud. 'Stark mad. I think you'd better go home, ma'am; a great deal better.'

'My lord, if you'd only give yourself the trouble to understand me—'

'I don't understand a word you say. I have nothing to do with the income, or the house, or with you, or with your son.'

'Oh, yes, my lord, indeed you have.'

'I tell you I haven't, ma'am; and what's more, I won't.'

'He's going to marry, my lord,' continued Mrs Wilkinson, beginning to whimper; 'and we are to be turned out of the house, unless you will interfere to prevent it. And he wants me to go and live at Littlebath. And I'm sure your lordship meant me to have the house when you allocated the income.'

'And you've come all the way to Bowes, have you, because your son wants to enjoy his own income?'

'No, my lord; he doesn't interfere about that. He knows he can't touch that, because your lordship allocated it to me—and, to do him justice, I don't think he would if he could. And he's not a bad boy, my lord; only mistaken about this.'

'Oh, he wants his own house, does he?'

'But it isn't his own house, you know. It has been my house ever since his father died. And if your lordship will remember—'

'I tell you what, Mrs Wilkinson; it seems to me that your son should not let you come out so far by yourself—'

'My lord!'

'And if you'll take my advice, you'll go home as fast as you can, and live wherever he bids you.'

'But, my lord—'

'At any rate, I must beg you not to trouble me any more about the matter. When I was a young man your husband read with me for a few months; and I really think that two presentations to the living have been a sufficient payment for that. I know nothing about your son, and I don't want to know anything. I dare say he's as good as most other clergymen—'

'Oh, yes; he is, my lord.'

'But I don't care a straw who lives in the house.'

'Don't you, my lord?' said Mrs Wilkinson, very despondently.

'Not one straw. I never heard such a proposition from a woman in my life—never. And now, if you'll allow me, I'll wish you good-morning, ma'am. Good-morning to you.' And the marquis made a slight feint, as though to raise himself from his chair.

Mrs Wilkinson got up, and stood upright before him, with her handkerchief to her eyes. It was very grievous to her to have failed so utterly. She still felt sure that if Lord Stapledean would only be made to understand the facts of the case, he would even yet take her part. She had come so far to fight her battle, that she could not bring herself to leave the ground as long as a chance of victory remained to her. How could she put the matter in the fewest words, so as to make the marquis understand the very—very truth?

'If your lordship would only allow me to recall to your memory the circumstances of the case,—how you, yourself, allocated—'

Lord Stapledean turned suddenly at the bellrope, and gave it a tremendous pull—then another—and then a third, harder than the others. Down came the rope about his ears, and the peal was heard ringing through the house.

'Thompson,' he said to the man, as he entered, 'show that lady the door.'

'Yes, my lord.'

'Show her the door immediately.'

'Yes, my lord,' said Thompson, standing irresolute. 'Now, ma'am, the post-chaise is waiting.'

Mrs Wilkinson had still strength enough to prevent collapse, and to gather herself together with some little feminine dignity. 'I think I have been very badly treated,' she said, as she prepared to move.

'Thompson,' shrieked the marquis, in his passion; 'show that lady the door.'

'Yes, my lord;' and Thompson gracefully waved his hand, pointing down the passage. It was the only way in which he could show Mrs Wilkinson the way out.

And then, obedient to necessity, she walked forth. Never had she held her head so high, or tossed her bonnet with so proud a shake, as she did in getting into that post-chaise. Thompson held the handle of the carriage-door; he also offered her his arm, but she despised any such aid. She climbed in unassisted; the post-boy mounted his jade; and so she was driven forth, not without titters from the woman at the lodge-gate. With heavy heart she reached the inn, and sat herself down to weep alone in her bedroom.

'So, you've come back?' said the landlady.

'Ugh!' exclaimed Mrs Wilkinson.

We will not dwell long on her painful journey back to Hurst Staple; nor on the wretched reflections with which her mind was laden. She sent on a line by post to her eldest daughter, so that she was expected; and Dumpling and the phaëton and the stable-boy were there to meet her. She had feared that Arthur would come: but Arthur had dreaded the meeting also; and, having talked the matter over with his sisters, had remained at home. He was in the book-room, and hearing the wheels, as the carriage drew up to the door, he went out to greet his mother on the steps.

At the first moment of meeting there was nothing said, but she warmly pressed the hand which he held out to her.

'What sort of a journey have you had?' said Sophia.

'Oh, it is a dreadful place!' said Mrs Wilkinson.

'It is not a nice country,' said Arthur.

By this time they were in the drawing-room, and the mother was seated on a sofa, with one of her girls on each side of her.

'Sophy,' she said, 'get up for a moment; I want Arthur to come here.' So Sophy did get up, and her son, immediately taking her place, put his arms round his mother's waist.

'Arthur,' she whispered to him, 'I fear I have been foolish about this.'

That was all that was ever said to him about the journey to Bowes. He was not the man to triumph over his mother's failure. He merely kissed her when her little confession was made, and pressed her slightly with his arm. From that time it was understood that Adela was to be brought thither, as soon as might be, to reign the mistress of the vicarage; and that then, what further arrangements might be necessary, were to be made by them all at their perfect leisure. That question of the nursery might, at any rate, remain in abeyance for twelve months.

Soon after that, it was decided in full conclave, that if Adela would consent, the marriage should take place in the summer. Very frequent letters passed between Hurst Staple and Littlebath, and Mrs Wilkinson no longer alluded to them with severity, or even with dislike. Lord Stapledean had, at any rate, thoroughly convinced her that the vicarage-house belonged to the vicar—to the vicar male, and not to the vicar female; and now that her eyes had been opened on this point, she found herself obliged to confess that Adela Gauntlet would not make a bad wife.

'Of course we shall be poor, mother; but we expect that.'

'I hope you will, at least, be happy,' said Mrs Wilkinson, not liking at present to dwell on the subject of their poverty, as her conscience began to admonish her with reference to the three hundred and fifty pounds per annum.

'I should think I might be able to get pupils,' continued Arthur. 'If I had two at one hundred and fifty pounds each, we might be comfortable enough.'

'Perhaps Adela would not like to have lads in the house.'

'Ah, mother, you don't know Adela. She will not object to anything because she does not herself like it.' And in this manner that affair was so far settled.

And then Adela was invited to Hurst Staple, and she accepted the invitation. She was not coy in declaring the pleasure with which she did so, nor was she bashful or shamefaced in the matter. She loved the man that she was to marry—had long loved him; and now it was permitted to her to declare her love. Now it was her duty to declare it, and to assure him, with all the pretty protestations in her power, that her best efforts should be given to sweeten his cup, and smooth his path. Her duty now was to seek his happiness, to share his troubles, to be one with him. In her mind it was not less her duty now than it would be when, by God's ordinance, they should be one bone and one flesh.

While their mother had held her seat on her high horse, with reference to that question of the house, Sophia and Mary had almost professed hostility to Adela. They had given in no cordial adherence to their brother's marriage; but now they were able to talk of their coming sister with interest and affection. 'I know that Adela would like this, Arthur;' and 'I'm sure that Adela would prefer that;' and 'when we're gone, you know, Adela will do so and so.' Arthur received all this with brotherly love and the kindest smiles, and thanked God in his heart that his mother had taken that blessed journey to Bowes Lodge.

'Adela,' he once said to her, as they were walking together, one lovely spring evening, along the reedy bank of that river, 'Adela, had I had your courage, all this would have been settled long since.'

'I don't know,' she said; 'but I am sure of this, that it is much better as it is. Now we may fairly trust that we do know our own minds. Love should be tried, perhaps, before it is trusted.'

'I should have trusted yours at the first word you could have spoken, the first look you would have given me.'

'And I should have done so too; and then we might have been wrong. Is it not well as it is, Arthur?'

And then he declared that it was very well; very well, indeed. Ah, yes! how could it have been better with him? He thought too of his past sorrows, his deep woes, his great disappointments; of that bitter day at Oxford when the lists came down; of the half-broken heart with which he had returned from Bowes; of the wretchedness of that visit to West Putford. He thought of the sad hours he had passed, seated idle and melancholy in the vicarage book-room, meditating on his forlorn condition. He had so often wailed over his own lot, droning out a dirge, a melancholy væ victis for himself! And now, for the first time, he could change the note. Now, his song was 'Io triumphe,'* as he walked along. He shouted out a joyful pæan with the voice of his heart. Had he taken the most double of all firsts, what more could fate have given to him? or, at any rate, what better could fate have done for him?

And to speak sooth, fate had certainly given to him quite as much as he had deserved.

And then it was settled that they should be married early in the ensuing June. 'On the first,' said Arthur. 'No; the thirtieth,' said Adela, laughing. And then, as women always give more than they claim, it was settled that they should be married on the eleventh. Let us trust that the day may always be regarded as propitious.

CHAPTER XLIV

MR BERTRAM'S DEATH

SIR HENRY HARCOURT had certainly played his hand badly, considering the number of trumps that he had held, and that he had turned up an honour in becoming solicitor-general. He was not now in a happy condition. He was living alone in his fine house in Eaton Square; he was out of office; he was looked on with an evil eye by his former friends, in that he had endeavoured to stick to office too long; he was deeply in debt, and his once golden hopes with reference to Mr Bertram were becoming fainter and fainter every day. Nor was this all. Not only did he himself fear that he should get but little of the Hadley money, but his creditors had begun to have the same fears. They had heard that he was not to be the heir, and were importunate accordingly. It might be easy to stave them off till Mr Bertram should be under the ground; but then—what then? His professional income might still be large, though not increasing as it should have done. And what lawyer can work well if his mind be encumbered by deep troubles of his own?

He had told George Bertram that he would go down to Hadley and claim his wife if he did not receive a favourable message from his wife's grandfather; and he now determined to take some such step. He felt himself driven to do something; to bring about some arrangement; to make some use of the few remaining grains of sand which were still to run through the glass that was measuring out the lees of life for that old man.

So thinking, but not quite resolved as to what he would do when he reached the house, he started for Hadley. He knew that George was still there, that his wife was there, and that Mr Bertram was there; and he trusted that he should not fail at any rate in seeing them. He was not by nature a timid man, and had certainly not become so by education; but, nevertheless, his heart did not beat quite equably within his bosom when he knocked at the rich man's door.

Of course he was well known to the servant. At first he asked after Mr Bertram, and was told that he was much the same—going very fast; the maid did not think that Sir Henry could see him. The poor girl, knowing that the gentleman before her was not a welcome visitor, stood in the doorway, as though to guard the ladies who were in the drawing-room.

'Who is here now?' said Sir Henry. 'Who is staying here?'

'Mr George,' said the girl, thinking that she would be safest in mentioning his name, 'and Miss Baker, sir.'

'Lady Harcourt is here, I suppose?'

'Yes, sir; her ladyship is in the drawing-room,' and she shook in her shoes before him as she made the announcement.

For a moment Sir Henry was inclined to force his way by the trembling young woman, and appear before the ladies. But then, what would he get by it? Angry as he was with all the Hadley people, he was still able to ask himself that question. Supposing that he were there, standing before his wife; supposing even that he were able to bring her to his feet by a glance, how much richer would that make him? What bills would that pay? He had loved his wife once with a sort of love; but that day was gone. When she had been at such pains to express her contempt for him, all tenderness had deserted him. It might be wise to make use of her—not to molest her, as long as her grandfather lived. When the old miser should have gone, it would be time for him to have his revenge. In the meantime, he could gain nothing by provoking her. So he told the servant that he wished to see Mr George Bertram.

As it happened, George and Lady Harcourt were together,

and Miss Baker was keeping watch with the sick man upstairs. The drawing-room was close to the hall, and Caroline's eager ear caught the tones of her husband's voice.

'It is Sir Henry,' she said, becoming suddenly pale, and rising to her feet, as though prepared to retreat to some protection. Bertram's duller ear could not hear him, but he also rose from his chair. 'Are you sure it is he?'

'I heard his voice plainly,' said Caroline, in a tremulous whisper. 'Do not leave me, George. Whatever happens, do not leave me.' They called each other now by their Christian names, as cousins should do; and their intercourse with each other had never been other than cousinly since that parting in Eaton Square.

And then the door was opened, and the maid-servant, in the glummest of voices, announced that Sir Henry wanted to see Mr George.

'Show him into the dining-room,' said George; and then following the girl after a minute's interval, he found himself once more in the presence of his old friend.

Sir Henry was even darker-looking, and his brow still more forbidding than at that last interview at George's chambers. He was worn and care-marked, and appeared to be ten years older than was really the case. He did not wait till George should address him, but began at once:—

'Bertram,' said he, with a voice intended to be stern, 'there are two persons here I want to see, your uncle and my wife.'

'I make no objection to your seeing either, if they are willing to see you.'

'Yes; but that won't do for me. My duty compels me to look after them both, and I mean to do so before I leave Hadley.'

'I will send your name to them at once,' said George; 'but it must depend on them whether they will see you.' And so saying, he rang the bell, and sent a message up to his uncle.

Nothing was said till the girl returned. Sir Henry paced the room backward and forward, and George stood leaning with his back against the chimney-piece. 'Mr Bertram says that he'll see Sir Henry, if he'll step upstairs,' said the girl.

'Very well. Am I to go up now?'

'If you please, sir.'

Bertram followed Sir Henry to the door, to show him the room; but the latter turned round on the stairs, and said that he would prefer to have no one present at the interview.

'I will only open the door for you,' said the other. This he did, and was preparing to return, when his uncle called him. 'Do not go away, George,' said he. 'Sir Henry will want you to show him down again.' And so they stood together at the bedside.

'Well, Sir Henry, this is kind of you,' said he, putting his thin, bony hand out upon the coverlid, by way of making an attempt at an Englishman's usual greeting.

Sir Henry took it gently in his, and found it cold and clammy. 'It is nearly all over now, Sir Henry,' said the old man.

'I hope not,' said the visitor, with the tone usual on such occasions. 'You may rally yet, Mr Bertram.'

'Rally!' And there was something in the old man's voice that faintly recalled the bitter railing sound of other days. 'No; I don't suppose I shall ever rally much more.'

'Well; we can only hope for the best. That's what I do, I can assure you.'

'That is true. We do hope for the best—all of us. I can still do that, if I do nothing else.'

'Of course,' said Sir Henry. And then he stood still for awhile, meditating how best he might make use of his present opportunity. What could he say to secure some fraction of the hundreds of thousands which belonged to the dying man? That he had a right to at least a moiety of them his inmost bosom told him; but how should he now plead his rights? Perhaps after all it would have been as well for him to have remained in London.

'Mr Bertram,' at last he said, 'I hope you won't think it unbecoming in me if I say one word about business in your present state?'

'No—no—no,' said the old man. 'I can't do much, as you see; but I'll endeavour to listen.'

'You can't be surprised that I should be anxious about my wife.'

'Umph!' said Mr Bertram. 'You haven't treated her very well, it seems.'

'Who says so?'

'A woman wouldn't leave a fine house in London, to shut herself up with a sick old man here, if she were well treated. I don't want any one to tell me that.'

'I can hardly explain all this to you now, sir; particularly—'

'Particularly as I am dying. No, you cannot. George, give me a glass of that stuff. I am very weak, Sir Henry, and can't say much more to you.'

'May I ask you this one question, sir? Have you provided for your grand-daughter?'

'Provided for her!' and the old man made a sadly futile attempt to utter the words with that ominous shriek which a few years since would have been sure to frighten any man who would have asked such a question. 'What sort of man can he be, George, to come to me now with such a question?' And so saying, he pulled the clothes over him as though resolved to hold no further conversation.

'He is very weak,' said George. 'I think you had better leave him.'

A hellish expression came across the lawyer's face. 'Yes,' he said to himself; 'go away, that I may leave you here to reap the harvest by yourself. Go away, and know myself to be a beggar.' He had married this man's grandchild, and yet he was to be driven from his bedside like a stranger.

'Tell him to go,' said Mr Bertram. 'He will know it all in a day or two.'

'You hear what he says,' whispered George.

'I do hear,' muttered the other, 'and I will remember.'

'He hardly thinks I would alter my will now, does he? Perhaps he has pen and ink in his pocket, ready to do it.'

'I have only spoken in anxiety about my wife,' said Sir Henry; 'and I thought you would remember that she was your child's daughter.'

'I do remember it. George, why doesn't he leave me?'

'Harcourt, it will be better that you should go,' said Bertram; 'you can have no idea how weak my uncle is;' and he gently opened the door.

'Good-bye, Mr Bertram. I had not intended to disturb you.' And so saying, Sir Henry slunk away.

'You know what his will is, of course,' said Sir Henry, when they were again in the dining-room.

'I have not the slightest idea on the subject,' said the other; 'not the remotest conception. He never speaks to me about it.'

'Well; and now for Lady Harcourt. Where shall I find her?'

To this question George gave no answer; nor was he able to give any. Caroline was no longer in the drawing-room. Sir Henry insisted that he would see her, and declared his intention of staying in the house till he did so. But Miss Baker at last persuaded him that all his efforts would be useless. Nothing but force would induce Lady Harcourt to meet him.

'Then force shall be used,' said Sir Henry.

'At any rate not now,' said George.

'What, sir! do you set yourself up as her protector? Is she base enough to allow you to interfere between her and her husband?'

'I am her protector at the present moment, Sir Henry. What passed between us long since has been now forgotten. But we are still cousins; and while she wants protection, I shall give it to her.'

'Oh, you will; will you?'

'Certainly. I look upon her as though she were my sister. She has no other brother.'

'That's very kind of you, and very complaisant of her. But what if I say that I don't choose that she should have any such brother? Perhaps you think that as I am only her husband, I ought not to have any voice in the matter?'

'I do not suppose that you can care for her much, after the word you once used to her.'

'And what the devil is it to you what word I used to her? That's the tack you go on, is it? Now, I'll tell you fairly what I shall do. I will wait till the breath is out of that old man's body, and then I shall take my wife out of this house—by force, if force be necessary.' And so saying, Sir Henry turned to the front door, and took his departure, without making any further adieu.

'What dreadful trouble we shall have!' whimpered Miss Baker, almost in tears.

Things went on at Hadley for three days longer without any change, except that Mr Bertram became weaker, and less inclined to speak. On the third morning, he did say a few words:—'George, I begin to think I have done wrong about you; but I fear it is too late.'

His nephew declared that he was sure that things would turn out well, muttering any platitude which might quiet the dying man.

'But it is too late, isn't it?'

'For any change in your will, sir? Yes, it is too late. Do not think of it.'

'Ah, yes; it would be very troublesome—very troublesome. Oh, me! It has nearly come now, George, very nearly.'

It had very nearly come. He did not again speak intelligibly to any of them. In his last hours he suffered considerably, and his own thoughts seemed to irritate him. But when he did mutter a few words, they seemed to refer to trivial matters—little plagues which dying men feel as keenly as those who are full of life. To the last he preferred George either to his niece or to his granddaughter; and was always best pleased when his nephew was by him. Once or twice he mentioned Mr Pritchett's name; but he showed his dissent when they proposed to send for his man of business.

On the afternoon of that day, he breathed his last in the presence of his three relatives. His nearest relative, indeed, was not there; nor did they dare to send for him. He had latterly expressed so strong a disgust at the very name of Sir Lionel, that they had ceased by common consent to mention Bertram's father. He seemed to be aware that his last moments were approaching, for he would every now and then raise his withered hand from off the bed, as though to give them warning. And so he died, and the eyes of the rich man were closed.

He died full of years, and perhaps in one, and that the most usual acceptation of the word, full of honour. He owed no man a shilling, had been true to all his engagements, had been kind to his relatives with a rough kindness: he had loved honesty and industry, and had hated falsehood and fraud: to him the herd, born only to consume the fruits, had ever been odious; that he could be generous, his conduct in his nephew's earliest years had plainly shown; he had carried, too, in his bosom a heart not altogether hardened against his kind, for he had loved his nephew, and, to a certain extent, his niece also, and his granddaughter.

But in spite of all this, he had been a bad man. He had opened his heart to that which should never find admittance to the heart of man. The iron of his wealth had entered into his very soul. He had made half a million of money, and that half-million had been his god—his only god—and, indeed, men have but one god. The true worship of the one loved shrine prevents all other worship. The records of his money had been his deity. There, in his solitude at Hadley, he had sat and counted them as they grew, mortgages and bonds, deeds and scrip, shares in this and shares in that, thousands in these funds and tens of thousands in those. To the last, he had gone on buying and selling, buying in the cheap market and selling in the dear; and everything had gone well with him.

Everything had gone well with him! Such was the City report of old Mr Bertram. But let the reader say how much, or rather how little, had gone well. Faustus-like,* he had sold himself to a golden Mephistopheles, and his Margaret had turned to stone within his embrace.

How many of us make Faust's bargain! The bodily attendance of the devil may be mythical; but in the spirit he is always with us. And how rarely have we the power to break the contract! The London merchant had so sold himself. He had given himself body and soul to a devil. The devil had promised him wealth, and had kept his word. And now the end had come, though the day of his happiness had not yet arrived.

But the end had come. All this was but the beginning. If we may believe that a future life is to be fitted to the desires and appetites as they are engendered here, what shall we think of the future of a man whose desire has been simply for riches, whose appetite has been for heaps of money? How miserably is such a poor wretch cheated! How he gropes about, making his bargain with blind eyes; thinking that he sees beyond his neighbours! Who is so green, so soft, so foolishly the victim of the sorriest sharper as this man? Weigh out all his past, and what has it been? Weigh out his future—if you can—and think what it must be. Poor, dull Faustus! What! thou hast lost everything among the thimble-riggers?* Poor, dull, stupid wretch!

Mr Bertram had not been a good man, nor had he been a wise man. But he had been highly respectable, and his memory is embalmed in tons of marble and heaps of monumental urns. Epitaphs, believed to be true, testify to his worth; and deeds, which are sometimes as false as epitaphs, do the same. He is a man of whom the world has agreed to say good things; to whom fame, that rich City fame, which speaks with a cornet-à-piston* made of gold, instead of a brazen trumpet, has been very kind.—But, nevertheless, he was not a good man. As regards him, it will only remain for us to declare what was his will, and that shall be done in the next chapter.

It was settled that he should be buried on the sixth day after his death, and that his will should be read after his funeral. George had now to manage everything, and to decide who should be summoned to the reading. There were two whom he felt bound to call thither, though to them the reading he knew would be a bitter grief. There was, in the first place, his father, Sir Lionel, whose calls for money had not of late decreased in urgency. It would be seemly that he should come; but the opening of the will would not be a pleasant hour for him. Then there would be Sir Henry. He also was, of course, summoned, painful as it was to his wife to have to leave the house at such a time. Nor, indeed, did he wait to be invited; for he had written to say that he should be there before he received George Bertram's note. Mr Pritchett also was sent for, and the old man's attorney.

And then, when these arrangements had been made, the thoughts of the living reverted from the dead to themselves. How should those three persons who now occupied that house so lovingly provide for themselves? and where should they fix their residence? George's brotherly love for his cousin was very well in theory: it was well to say that the past had been forgotten; but there are things for which no memory can lose its hold. He and Caroline had loved each other with other love than that of a brother and a sister; and each knew that they two might not dwell under the same roof. It was necessary to talk over these matters, and in doing so it was very hard not to touch on forbidden subjects.

Caroline had made up her mind to live again with her aunt—had made up her mind to do so, providing that her husband's power was not sufficient to prevent it. Miss Baker would often tell her that the law would compel her to return to her lord; that she would be forced to be again the mistress of the house in Eaton Square, and again live as the prosperous wife of the prosperous politician. To this Caroline had answered but little; but that little had been in a manner that had thoroughly frightened Miss Baker. Nothing, Lady Harcourt had said, nothing should induce her to do so.

'But if you cannot help yourself, Caroline?'

'I will help myself. I will find a way to prevent, at any rate, that—' So much she had said, but nothing further: and so much Miss Baker had repeated to George Bertram, fearing the worst.

It was not till the day before the funeral that Caroline spoke to her cousin on the subject.

'George,' she said to him, 'shall we be able to live here?—to keep on this house.'

'You and Miss Baker, you mean?'

'Yes; aunt and I. We should be as quiet here as anywhere,—and I am used to these people now.'

'It must depend on the will. The house was his own property; but, doubtless, Miss Baker could rent it.'

'We should have money enough for that, I suppose.'

'I should hope so. But we none of us know anything yet. All your own money—the income, at least, coming from it—is in Sir Henry's hands.'

'I will never condescend to ask for that,' she said. And then there was a pause in their conversation.

'George,' she continued, after a minute or two, 'you will not let me fall into his hands?'

He could not help remembering that his own mad anger had already thrown her into the hands which she now dreaded so terribly. Oh, if those two last years might but pass away as a dream, and leave him free to clasp her to his bosom as his own! But the errors of past years will not turn themselves to dreams. There is no more solid stuff in this material world than they are. They never melt away, or vanish into thin air.

'Not if it can be avoided,' he replied.

'Ah! but it can be avoided; can it not? Say that you know it can. Do not make me despair. It cannot be that he has a right to imprison me.'

'I hardly know what he has a right to do. But he is a stern man, and will not easily be set aside.'

'But you will not desert me?'

'No; I will not desert you. But—'

'But what?'

'For your sake, Caroline, we must regard what people will say. Our names have been mixed together; but not as cousins.'

'I know, I know. But, George, you do not suppose I intended you should live here? I was not thinking of that. I know that that may not be.'

'For myself, I shall keep my chambers in London. I shall just be able to starve on there; and then I shall make one more attempt at the bar.'

'And I know you will succeed. You are made for success at last; I have always felt that.'

'A man must live somehow. He must have some pursuit; and that is more within my reach than any other: otherwise I am not very anxious for success. What is the use of it all? Of what use will it be to me now?'

'Oh, George!'

'Well, is it not true?'

'Do not tell me that I have made shipwreck of all your fortune!'

'No; I do not say that you have done it. It was I that drove the bark upon the rocks; I myself. But the timbers on that account are not the less shattered.'

'You should strive to throw off that feeling. You have so much before you in the world.'

'I have striven. I have thought that I could love other women. I have told others that I did love them; but my words were false, and they and I knew that they were false. I have endeavoured to think of other things—of money, ambition, politics; but I can care for none of them. If ever a man cut his own throat, I have done so.'

She could not answer him at once, because she was now sobbing, and the tears were streaming from her eyes. 'And what have I done?' she said at last. 'If your happiness is shattered, what must mine be? I sometimes think that I cannot live and bear it. With him,' she added, after another pause, 'I will not live and bear it. If it comes to that, I will die, George;' and rising from her chair, she walked across the room, and took him sharply by the arm. 'George,' she said, 'you will protect me from that; I say that you will save me from that.'

'Protect you!' said he, repeating her words, and hardly daring to look into her face. How could he protect her? how save her from the lord she had chosen for herself? It might be easy enough for him to comfort her now with promises; but he could not find it in his heart to hold out promises which he could not fulfil. If, after the reading of the will, Sir Henry Harcourt should insist on taking his wife back with him, how could he protect her—he, of all men in the world?

'You will not give me up to him!' she said, wildly. 'If you do, any blood will lie upon your head. George! George! say that you will save me from that! To whom can I look now but to you?'

'I do not think he will force you away with him.'

'But if he does? Will you stand by and see me so used?'

'Certainly not; but, Caroline—'

'Well.'

'It will be better that I should not be driven to interfere. The world will forget that I am your cousin, but will remember that I was once to have been your husband.'

'The world! I am past caring for the world. It is nothing to me now if all London knows how it is with me. I have loved, and thrown away my love, and tied myself to a brute. I have loved, and do love; but my love can only be a sorrow to me. I do not fear the world; but God and my conscience I do fear. Once, for one moment, George, I thought that I would fear nothing. Once, for one moment, I was still willing to be yours; but I remembered what you would think of me if I should so fall, and I repented my baseness. May God preserve me from such sin! But, for the world—why should you or I fear the world?'

'It is for you that I fear it. It would grieve me to hear men speak lightly of your name.'

'Let them say what they please; the wretched are always trodden on. Let them say what they please. I deserved it all when I stood before the altar with that man; when I forbade my feet to run, or my mouth to speak, though I knew that I hated him, and owned it to my heart. What shall I do, George, to rid me of that sin?'

She had risen and taken hold of his arm when first she asked him to protect her, and she was still standing beside the chair on which he sat. He now rose also, and said a few gentle words, such as he thought might soothe her.

'Yes,' she continued, as though she did not heed him, 'I said to myself almost twenty times during that last night that I hated him in my very soul, that I was bound in honour even yet to leave him—in honour, and in truth, and in justice. But my pride forbade it—my pride and my anger against you.'

'It is useless to think of it now, dear.'

'Ah, yes! quite useless. Would that I had done it then—then, at the last moment. They asked me whether I would love that man. I whispered inwardly to myself that I loathed him; but my tongue said "Yes," out loud. Can such a lie as that, told in God's holy temple, sworn before his own altar—can such perjury as that ever be forgiven me?'

'But I shall sin worse still if I go back to him,' she continued, after awhile. 'I have no right, George, to ask anything from your kindness as a cousin; but for your love's sake, your old love, which you cannot forget, I do ask you to save me from this. But it is this rather that I ask, that you will save me from the need of saving myself.'

That evening George sat up late alone, preparing for the morrow's work, and trying to realize the position in which he found himself. Mr Pritchett, had he been there, would have whispered into his ears, again and again, those ominous and all-important words, 'Half a million of money, Mr George; half a million of money!' And, indeed, though Mr Pritchett was not there, the remembrance of those overflowing coffers did force themselves upon his mind. Who can say that he, if placed as Bertram then was, would not think of them?

He did think of them—not over-deeply, nor with much sadness. He knew that they were not to be his; neither the whole of them, nor any part of them. So much his uncle had told him with sufficient plainness. He knew also that they might all have been his: and then he thought of that interview in which Mr Bertram had endeavoured to beg from him a promise to do that for which his own heart so strongly yearned. Yes; he might have had the bride, and the money too. He might have been sitting at that moment with the wife of his bosom, laying out in gorgeous plans the splendour of their future life. It would be vain to say that there was no disappointment at his heart.

But yet there was within his breast a feeling of gratified independence which sufficed to support him. At least he might boast that he had not sold himself; not aloud, but with that inward boasting which is so common with most of us. There was a spirit within him endowed with a greater wealth than any which Mr Pritchett might be able to enumerate; and an inward love, the loss of which could hardly have been atoned for even by the possession of her whom he had lost. Nor was this the passion which men call self-love. It was rather a vigorous knowledge of his own worth as a man; a strong will, which taught him that no price was sufficient to buy his assent that black should be reckoned white, or white be reckoned black.

His uncle, he knew, had misunderstood him. In rejecting the old man's offers, he had expressed his contempt for riches—for riches, that is, as any counterbalance to independence. Mr Bertram had taken what he said for more than it was worth; and had supposed that his nephew, afflicted with some singular lunacy, disliked money for its own sake. George had never cared to disabuse his uncle's mind. Let him act as he will, he had said to himself, it is not for me to dictate to him, either on the one side or the other. And so the error had gone on.

Tomorrow morning the will would be read, and George would have to listen to the reading of it. He knew well enough that the world looked on him as his uncle's probable heir, and that he should have to bear Mr Pritchett's hardly expressed pity, Sir Henry's malignant pleasure, and Sir Lionel's loud disgust. All this was nearly as bad to him as the remembrance of what he had lost; but by degrees he screwed his courage up to the necessary point of endurance.

'What is Pritchett to me, with his kind, but burdensome solicitude? what Sir Henry's mad anger? How can they affect my soul? or what even is my father? Let him rave. I care not to have compassion on myself; why should his grief assail me—grief which is so vile, so base, so unworthy of compassion?'

And thus schooling himself for the morrow, he betook himself to bed.

CHAPTER XLV

THE WILL

THE only attendants at old Mr Bertram's funeral were his nephew, Mr Pritchett, and the Hadley doctor. The other gentlemen were to be present only at the more interesting ceremony of reading the will. Sir Lionel had written to say that he was rather unwell; that he certainly would come up from Littlebath so as to be present at the latter performance; but that the very precarious state of his health, and the very inconvenient hours of the trains, unhappily prevented him from paying the other last sad duty to his brother's remains. Sir Henry Harcourt had plainly demanded at what hour the will would be read; and Mr Stickatit, junior—Mr George

Stickatit—of the firm of Dry and Stickatit, had promised to be at Hadley punctually at two p.m. And he kept his word

Mr Pritchett came down by an early train, and, as was fit on such an occasion, was more melancholy than usual. He was very melancholy and very sad, for he felt that that half million of money was in a great jeopardy; and, perhaps, even the death of his old friend of forty years' standing may have had some effect on him. It was a mingled feeling that pervaded him. 'Oh, Mr George!' he said, just before they went to the churchyard, 'we are grass of the field, just grass of the field; here today, and gone tomorrow; flourishing in the morning, and cast into the oven* before night! It behoves such frail, impotent creatures to look close after their interests—half a million of money! I'm afraid you didn't think enough about it, Mr George.'

And then the Hadley bells were rung again; but they were not rung loudly. It seemed to Bertram that no one noticed that anything more than usually sad was going on. He could hardly realize it to himself that he was going to put under the ground almost his nearest relative. The bells rang out a dirge, but they did it hardly above their breath. There were but three boys gathered at the little gate before the door to see the body of the rich man carried to his last home. George stood with his back to the empty dining-room fireplace: on one side stood Mr Pritchett, and on the other the Hadley doctor. Very few words passed between them, but they were not in their nature peculiarly lugubrious. And then there was a scuffling heard on the stairs—a subdued, decent undertaker's scuffling—as some hour or two before had been heard the muffled click of a hammer. Feet scuffled down the stairs, outside the dining-room door, and along the passage. And then the door was opened, and in low, decent undertaker's voice, red-nosed, sombre, well-fed Mr Mortmain told them that they were ready.

'These are yours, sir,' and he handed a pair of black gloves to George. 'And these are yours, sir,' and he gave another pair to the doctor. But the doctor held them instead of putting them on; otherwise Mr Mortmain could not be expected to change them after the ceremony for a pair of lighter colour. They understood each other; and what could a country doctor do with twenty or thirty pairs of black gloves a year? 'And these yours, Mr Pritchett.'

'Oh, Mr George!' sighed Pritchett. 'To think it should come to this! But he was a good gentleman; and very successful—very successful.'

There were not ten people in the church or in the churchyard during the whole time of the funeral. To think that a man with half a million of money could die and be got rid of with so little parade! What money could do—in a moderate way—was done. The coffin was as heavy as lead could make it. The cloth of the best. The plate upon it was of silver, or looked like it. There was no room for an equipage of hearses and black coaches, the house was so unfortunately near to the churchyard. It was all done in a decent, sombre, useful, money-making way, as beseemed the remains of such a man.

But it was on 'Change that he was truly buried; in Capel Court that his funeral sermon was duly preached. These were the souls that knew him, the ears to which his name loomed large. He had been true and honest in all his dealings—there, at least. He had hurt nobody by word or deed—excepting in the way of trade. And had kept his hands from picking and stealing—from all picking, that is, not warranted by City usage, and from all stealing that the law regards as such. Therefore, there, on 'Change, they preached his funeral sermon loudly, and buried him with all due honours.

Two had been named for the reading of the will, seeing that a train arrived at 1.45 P.M. And, therefore, when the ceremony was over, George and Mr Pritchett had to sit together in the dining-room till that time arrived. The doctor, who did not expect much from the will, had gone away, perhaps to prepare other friends for similar occupation. It was a tedious hour that they so passed, certainly; but at last it did make itself away. Lunch was brought in; and the sherry, which had been handed round with biscuits before the funeral, was again put on the table. Mr Pritchett liked a glass of sherry, though it never seemed to have other effect on him than to make his sadness of a deeper dye. But at last, between this occupation and the muttering of a few scraps of a somewhat worldly morality, the hour did wear itself away, and the hand of the old clock pointed to two.

The three gentlemen had come down by the same train, and arrived in a fly together. Mr George Stickatit, junior, paid for the accommodation; which was no more than right, for he could put it in the bill, and Sir Lionel could not. The mind of Sir Henry was too much intent on other things to enable him to think about the fly.

'Well, George,' said Sir Lionel; 'so it's all over at last. My poor brother! I wish I could have been with you at the funeral; but it was impossible. The ladies are not here?'—This he added in a whisper. He could not well talk about Lady Harcourt, and he was not at the present moment anxious to see Miss Baker.

'They are not here today,' said George, as he pressed his father's hand. He did not think it necessary to explain that they were staying at good old Mrs Jones's, on the other side of the Green.

'I should have been down for the funeral,' said Mr Stickatit; 'but I have been kept going about the property, ever since the death, up to this moment, I may say. There's the document, gentlemen.' And the will was laid on the table. 'The personalty will be sworn under five. The real* will be about two more. Well, Pritchett, and how are you this morning?'

Sir Henry said but little to anybody. Bertram put out his hand to him as he entered, and he just took it, muttering something; and then, having done so, he sat himself down at the table. His face was not pleasant to be seen; his manner was ungracious, nay, more than that, uncourteous—almost brutal; and it seemed as though he were prepared to declare himself the enemy of all who were there assembled. To Sir Lionel he was known, and it may be presumed that some words had passed between them in the fly; but there in the room he said no word to any one, but sat leaning back in an arm-chair, with his hands in his pockets, scowling at the table before him.

'A beautiful day, is it not, Mr Pritchett?' said Sir Lionel, essaying to make things pleasant, after his fashion.

'A beautiful day—outwardly, Sir Lionel,' sighed Mr Pritchett. 'But the occasion is not comfortable. We must all die, though; all of us, Mr George.'

'But we shall not all of us leave such a will as that behind us,' said Mr Stickatit. 'Come, gentlemen, are we ready? Shall we sit down?'

George got a chair for his father, and put it down opposite to that of Sir Henry. Mr Pritchett humbly kept himself in one corner. The lawyer took the head of the table, and broke open the envelope which contained the will, with a degree of gusto which showed that the occupation was not disagreeable to him. 'Mr Bertram,' said he, 'will you not take a chair?'

'Thank you, no; I'll stand here, if you please,' said George. And so he kept his position with his back to the empty fireplace.

All of them, then, were somewhat afraid of having their disappointment read in their faces, and commented upon by the others. They were all of them schooling themselves to bear with an appearance of indifference the tidings which they dreaded to hear. All of them, that is, except the attorney. He hoped nothing, and feared nothing.

Mr Pritchett nearly closed his eyes, and almost opened his mouth, and sat with his hands resting on his stomach before him, as though he were much too humble to have any hopes of his own.

Sir Lionel was all smiles. What did he care? Not he. If that boy of his should get anything, he, as an affectionate father, would, of course, be glad. If not, why then his dear boy could do without it. That was the intended interpretation of his look. And judging of it altogether, he did not do it badly; only he deceived nobody. On such occasions, one's face, which is made up for deceit, never does deceive any one. But, in truth, Sir Lionel still entertained a higher hope than any other of the listeners there. He did not certainly expect a legacy for himself, but he did think that George might still be the heir. As Sir Henry was not to be, whose name was so likely? And, then, if his son, his dear son George, should be lord of two, nay, say only one, of those many hundred thousand pounds, what might not a fond father expect?

Sir Henry was all frowns; and yet he was not quite hopeless. The granddaughter, the only lineal descendant of the dead man, was still his wife. Anything left to her must in some sort be left to him, let it be tied up with ever so much care. It might still be probable that she might be named the heiress—perhaps the sole heiress. It might still be probable that the old man had made no new will since Caroline had left his home in Eaton Square. At any rate, there would still be a ground, on which to fight, within his reach, if Lady Harcourt should be in any way enriched under the will. And if so, no tenderness on his part should hinder him from fighting out that fight as long as he had an inch on which to stand.

Bertram neither hoped anything, nor feared anything, except this—that they would look at him as a disappointed man. He knew that he was to have nothing; and although, now that the moment had come, he felt that wealth might possibly have elated him, still the absence of it did not make him in any degree unhappy. But it did make him uncomfortable to think that he should be commiserated by Mr Pritchett, sneered at by Harcourt, and taunted by his father.

'Well, gentlemen, are we ready?' said Mr Stickatit again. They were all ready, and so Mr Stickatit began.

I will not give an acute critic any opportunity for telling me that the will, as detailed by me, was all illegal. I have not by me the ipsissima verba;* nor can I get them now, as I am very far from Doctors' Commons.* So I will give no verbal details at all.

The will, moreover, was very long—no less than fifteen folios. And that amount, though it might not be amiss in a three-volume edition, would be inconvenient when the book comes to be published for eighteen-pence. But the gist of the will was as follows.

It was dated in the October last gone by, at the time when George was about to start for Egypt, and when Lady Harcourt had already left her husband. It stated that he, George Bertram, senior, of Hadley, being in full use of all his mental faculties, made this as his last will and testament. And then he willed and devised—

Firstly, that George Stickatit, junior, of the firm of Dry and Stickatit, and George Bertram, junior, his nephew, should be his executors; and that a thousand pounds each should be given to them, provided they were pleased to act in that capacity.

When Sir Lionel heard that George was named as one of the executors, he looked up at his son triumphantly; but when the thousand pounds were named, his face became rather long, and less pleasant than usual. A man feels no need to leave a thousand pounds to an executor if he means to give him the bulk of his fortune.

Secondly, he left three hundred pounds a year for life to his dear, old, trusty servant, Samuel Pritchett. Mr Pritchett put his handkerchief up to his face, and sobbed audibly. But he would sooner have had two or three thousand pounds; for he also had an ambition to leave money behind him.

Thirdly, he bequeathed five hundred pounds a year for life to Mary Baker, late of Littlebath, and now of Hadley; and the use of the house at Hadley if she chose to occupy it. Otherwise, the house was to be sold, and the proceeds were to go to his estate.

Sir Lionel, when he heard this, made a short calculation in his mind whether it would now be worth his while to marry Miss Baker; and he decided that it would not be worth his while.

Fourthly, he gave to his executors above-named a sum of four thousand pounds, to be invested by them in the Three per Cent. Consols, for the sole use and benefit of his granddaughter, Caroline Harcourt. And the will went on to say, that he did this, although he was aware that sufficient provision had already been made for his granddaughter, because he feared that untoward events might make it expedient that she should have some income exclusively her own.

Sir Henry, when this paragraph was read—this paragraph from which his own name was carefully excluded—dashed his fist down upon the table, so that the ink leaped up out of the inkstand that stood before the lawyer, and fell in sundry blots upon the document. But no one said anything. There was blotting-paper at hand, and Mr Stickatit soon proceeded.

In its fifth proviso, the old man mentioned his nephew George. 'I wish it to be understood,' he said, 'that I love my nephew, George Bertram, and appreciate his honour, honesty, and truth.' Sir Lionel once more took heart of grace, and thought that it might still be all right. And George himself felt pleased; more pleased than he had thought it possible that he should have been at the reading of that will. 'But,' continued the will, 'I am not minded as he is himself aware, to put my money into his hands for his own purposes.' It then went on to say, that a further sum of four thousand pounds was given to him as a token of affection.

Sir Lionel drew a long breath. After all, five thousand pounds was the whole sum total that was rescued out of the fire. What was five thousand pounds? How much could he expect to get from such a sum as that? Perhaps, after all, he had better take Miss Baker. But then her pittance was only for her life. How he did hate his departed brother at that moment!

Poor Pritchett wheezed and sighed again. 'Ah!' said he to himself. 'Half a million of money gone; clean gone! But he never would take my advice!'

But George felt now that he did not care who looked at him, who commiserated him. The will was all right. He did not at that moment wish it to be other than that the old man had made it. After all their quarrels, all their hot words and perverse thoughts towards each other, it was clear to him now that his uncle had, at any rate, appreciated him. He could hear the remainder of it quite unmoved.

There were some other legacies to various people in the City, none of them considerable in amount. Five hundred pounds to one, one thousand pounds to another, fifty pounds to a third, and so on. And then came the body of the will—the very will indeed.

And so Mr George Bertram willed, that after the payment of all his just debts, and of the legacies above recapitulated, his whole property should be given to his executors, and by them expended in building and endowing a college and almshouse, to be called 'The Bertram College,' for the education of the children of London fishmongers, and for the maintenance of the widows of such fishmongers as had died in want. Now Mr Bertram had been a member of the Honourable Company of Fishmongers.

And that was the end of the will. And Mr Stickatit, having completed the reading, folded it up, and put it back into the envelope. Sir Henry, the moment the reading was over, again dashed his fist upon the table. 'As heir-at-law,' said he, 'I shall oppose that document.'

'I think you'll find it all correct,' said Mr Stickatit, with a little smile.

'And I think otherwise, sir,' said the late solicitor-general, in a voice that made them all start. 'Very much otherwise. That document is not worth the paper on which it is written. And now, I warn you two, who have been named as executors, that such is the fact.'

Sir Lionel began to consider whether it would be better for him that the will should be a will, or should not be a will. Till he had done so, he could not determine with which party he would side. If that were no will, there might be a previous one; and if so, Bertram might, according to that, be the heir. 'It is a very singular document,' said he; 'very singular.'

But Sir Henry wanted no allies—wanted no one in that room to side with him. Hostility to them all was his present desire; to them and to one other—that other one who had brought upon him all this misfortune; that wife of his bosom, who had betrayed his interests and shattered his hopes.

'I believe there is nothing further to detain us at the present moment,' said Mr Stickatit. 'Mr Bertram, perhaps you can allow me to speak to you somewhere for five minutes?'

'I shall act,' said George.

'Oh, of course. That's of course,' said Stickatit. 'And I also.'

'Stop one moment, gentlemen,' shouted Harcourt again. 'I hereby give you both warning that you have no power to act.'

'Perhaps, sir,' suggested Stickatit, 'your lawyer will take any steps he may think necessary?'

'My lawyer, sir, will do as I bid him, and will require no suggestion from you. And now I have another matter to treat of. Mr Bertram, where is Lady Harcourt?'

Bertram did not answer at once, but stood with his back still against the chimney-piece, thinking what answer he would give.

'Where, I say, is Lady Harcourt? Let us have no juggling, if you please. You will find that I am in earnest.'

'I am not Lady Harcourt's keeper,' said George, in a very low tone of voice.

'No, by G—! Nor shall you be. Where is she? If you do not answer my question, I shall have recourse to the police at once.'

Sir Lionel, meaning to make things pleasant, now got up, and went over to his son. He did not know on what footing, with reference to each other, his son and Lady Harcourt now stood; but he did know that they had loved each other, and been betrothed for years; he did know, also, that she had left her husband, and that that husband and his son had been the closest friends. It was a great opportunity for him to make things pleasant. He had not the slightest scruple as to sacrificing that 'dear Caroline' whom he had so loved as his future daughter-in-law.

'George,' said he, 'if you know where Lady Harcourt is, it will be better that you should tell Sir Henry. No properly-thinking man will countenance a wife in disobeying her husband.'

'Father,' said George, 'Lady Harcourt is not in my custody. She is the judge of her own actions in this matter.'

'Is she?' said Sir Henry. 'She must learn to know that she is not; and that very shortly. Do you mean to tell me where she is?'

'I mean to tell you nothing about her, Sir Henry.'

'George, you are wrong,' said Sir Lionel. 'If you know where Lady Harcourt is, you are bound to tell him. I really think you are.'

'I am bound to tell him nothing, father; nor will I. I will have no conversation with him about his wife. It is his affair and hers—and that, perhaps, of a hundred other people; but it certainly is not mine. Nor will I make it so.'

'Then you insist on concealing her?' said Sir Henry.

'I have nothing to do with her. I do not know that she is concealed at all.'

'You know where she is?'

'I do. But, believing as I do that she would rather not be disturbed, I shall not say where you would find her.'

'I think you ought, George.'

'Father, you do not understand this matter.'

'You will not escape in that way, sir. Here you are named as her trustee in this will—'

'I am glad that you acknowledge the will, at any rate,' said Mr Stickatit.

'Who says that I acknowledge it? I acknowledge nothing in the will. But it is clear, from that document, that she presumes herself to be under his protection. It is manifest that that silly fool intended that she should be so. Now I am not the man to put up with this. I ask you once more, Mr Bertram, will you tell me where I shall find Lady Harcourt?'

'No, I will not.'

'Very well; then I shall know how to act. Gentlemen, good-morning. Mr Stickatit, I caution you not to dispose, under that will, of anything of which Mr Bertram may have died possessed.' And so saying, he took up his hat, and left the house.

And what would he have done had Bertram told him that Lady Harcourt was staying at Mrs Jones's, in the red brick house on the other side of the Green? What can any man do with a recusant wife? We have often been told that we should build a golden bridge for a flying enemy.* And if any one can be regarded as a man's enemy, it is a wife who is not his friend.

After a little while, Sir Lionel went away with Mr Pritchett. Bertram asked them both to stay for dinner, but the invitation was not given in a very cordial manner. At any rate, it was not accepted.

'Good-bye, then, George,' said Sir Lionel. 'I suppose I shall see you before I leave town. I must say, you have made a bad affair of this will.'

'Good-bye, Mr George; good-bye,' said Mr Pritchett. 'Make my dutiful compliments to Miss Baker—and to the other lady.'

'Yes, I will, Mr Pritchett.'

'Ah, dear! well. You might have had it all, instead of the fishmongers' children, if you had chosen, Mr George.'

And we also will say good-bye to the two gentlemen, as we shall not see them again in these pages. That Mr Pritchett will live for the remainder of his days decently, if not happily, on his annuity, may be surmised. That Sir Lionel, without any annuity, but with a fair income paid from the country's taxes, and with such extra pecuniary aid as he may be able to extract from his son, will continue to live indecently at Littlebath—for he never again returned to active service—that also may be surmised. And thus we will make our bows to these old gentlemen—entertaining, however, very different feelings for them.

And soon afterwards Mr Stickatit also went. Some slight, necessary legal information as to the executorship was first imparted; Sir Henry's threats were ridiculed; the good fortune of the fishmongers was wondered at, and then Mr Stickatit took his hat. The four gentlemen no doubt went up to London by the same train.

In the evening, Miss Baker and Lady Harcourt came back to their own house. It was Miss Baker's own house now. When she heard what her old friend had done for her, she was bewildered by his generosity. She, at any rate, had received more than she had expected.

'And what does he mean to do?' said Caroline.

'He says that he will dispute the will. But that, I take it, is nonsense.'

'But about—you know what I mean, George?'

'He means to insist on your return. That, at least, is what he threatens.'

'He shall insist in vain. No law that man ever made shall force me to live with him again.'

Whether or no the husband was in earnest, it might clearly be judged, from the wife's face and tone, that she was so. On the next morning, George went up to London, and the two women were left alone in their dull house at Hadley.

CHAPTER XLVI

EATON SQUARE

SIR HENRY HARCOURT had walked forth first from that room in which the will had been read, and he had walked forth with a threat in his mouth. But he knew when making it that that threat was an empty bravado. The will was as valid as care and law could make it, and the ex-solicitor-general knew very well that it was valid.

He knew, moreover, that the assistance of no ordinary policeman would suffice to enable him to obtain possession of his wife's person; and he knew also that if he had such possession, it would avail him nothing. He could not pay his debts with her, nor could he make his home happy with her, nor could he compel her to be in any way of service to him. It had all been bravado. But when men are driven into corners—when they are hemmed in on all sides, so that they have no escape, to what else than bravado can they have recourse? With Sir Henry the game was up; and no one knew this better than himself.

He was walking up and down the platform, with his hat over his brows, and his hands in his trousers-pockets, when Mr Stickatit came up. 'We shall have a little rain this afternoon,' said Mr Stickatit, anxious to show that he had dropped the shop, and that having done so, he was ready for any of the world's ordinary converse.

Sir Henry scowled at him from under the pent-house lid* of his hat, and passed on in his walk, without answering a word. The thing had gone too far with him for affectation. He did not care to make sacrifice now to any of the world's graces. His inner mind was hostile to that attorney of Bucklersbury, and he could dare to show that it was so. After that, Mr Stickatit made no further remark to him.

Yes; he could afford now to be forgetful of the world's graces, for the world's heaviest cares were pressing very heavily on him. When a man finds himself compelled to wade through miles of mud, in which he sinks at every step up to his knees, he becomes forgetful of the blacking on his boots. Whether or no his very skin will hold out, is then his thought. And so it was now with Sir Henry. Or we may perhaps say that he had advanced a step beyond that. He was pretty well convinced now that his skin would not hold out.

He still owned his fine house in Eaton Square, and still kept his seat for the Battersea Hamlets. But Baron Brawl, and such like men, no longer came willingly to his call; and his voice was no longer musical to the occupants of the Treasury bench. His reign had been sweet, but it had been very short. Prosperity he had known how to enjoy, but adversity had been too much for him.

Since the day when he had hesitated to resign his high office, his popularity had gone down like a leaden plummet in the salt water. He had become cross-grained, ill-tempered, and morose. The world had spoken evil of him regarding his wife; and he had given the world the lie in a manner that had been petulant and injudicious. The world had rejoined, and Sir Henry had in every sense got the worst of it. Attorneys did not worship him as they had done, nor did vice-chancellors and lords-justices listen to him with such bland attention. No legal luminary in the memory of man had risen so quickly and fallen so suddenly. It had not been given to him to preserve an even mind when adversity came upon him.

But the worst of his immediate troubles were his debts. He had boldly resolved to take a high position in London; and he had taken it. It now remained that the piper should be paid, and the piper required payment not in the softest language. While that old man was still living, or rather still dying, he had had an answer to give to all pipers. Even that answer would suffice him no longer. Every clause in that will would be in the 'Daily Jupiter' of the day after tomorrow—the 'Daily Jupiter' which had already given a wonderfully correct biography of the deceased great man.

As soon as he reached the London station, he jumped into a cab, and was quickly whirled to Eaton Square. The house felt dull, and cold, and wretched to him. It was still the London season, and Parliament was sitting. After walking up and down his own dining-room for half an hour, he got into another cab, and was whirled down to the House of Commons. But there it seemed as though all the men round him already knew of his disappointment—as though Mr Bertram's will had been read in a Committee of the whole House. Men spoke coldly to him, and looked coldly at him; or at any rate, he thought that they did so. Some debate was going on about the Ballot, at which members were repeating their last year's speeches with new emphasis. Sir Henry twice attempted to get upon his legs, but the Speaker would not have his eye caught. Men right and left of him, who were minnows to him in success, found opportunities for delivering themselves; but the world of Parliament did not wish at present to hear anything further from Sir Henry. So he returned to his house in Eaton Square.

As soon as he found himself again in his own dining-room, he called for brandy, and drank off a brimming glass; he drank off one, and then another. The world and solitude together were too much for him, and he could not bear them without aid. Then, having done this, he threw himself into his arm-chair, and stared at the fireplace. How tenfold sorrowful are our sorrows when borne in solitude! Some one has said that grief is half removed when it is shared. How little that some one knew about it! Half removed! When it is duly shared between two loving hearts, does not love fly off with eight-tenths of it? There is but a small remainder left for the two to bear between them.

But there was no loving heart here. All alone he had to endure the crushing weight of his misfortunes. How often has a man said, when evil times have come upon him, that he could have borne it all without complaint, but for his wife and children? The truth, however, has been that, but for them, he could not have borne it at all. Why does any man suffer with patience 'the slings and arrows of outrageous fortune,' or put up with 'the whips and scorns of time,' but that he does so for others, not for himself? It is not that we should all be ready, each to make his own quietus with a bare bodkin;* but that we should run from wretchedness when it comes in our path. Who fights for himself alone? Who would not be a coward, if none but himself saw the battle—if none others were concerned in it?

With Sir Henry, there was none other to see the battle, none to take concern in it. If solitude be bad in times of misery, what shall we say of unoccupied solitude? of solitude, too, without employment, for the man who has been used to labour?

Such was the case with him. His whole mind was out of tune. There was nothing now that he could do; no work to which he could turn himself. He sat there gazing at the empty fireplace till the moment became unendurably long to him. At last his chief suffering arose, not from his shattered hopes and lost fortunes, but from the leaden weight of the existing hour.

What could he do to shake this off? How could he conquer the depression that was upon him? He reached his hand to the paper that was lying near him, and tried to read; but his mind would not answer to the call. He could not think of the right honourable gentleman's speech, or of the very able leading article in which it was discussed. Though the words were before his eyes, he still was harping back on the injustice of that will, or the iniquity of his wife; on the imperturbable serenity of George Bertram, or the false, fleeting friends who had fawned on him in his prosperity, and now threw him over, as a Jonah, with so little remorse.

He dropped the paper on the ground, and then again the feeling of solitude and of motionless time oppressed him with a weight as of tons of lead. He jumped from his chair, and paced up and down the room; but the room was too confined. He took his hat, and pressing it on his brow, walked out into the open air. It was a beautiful spring evening in May, and the twilight still lingered, though the hour was late. He paced three times round the square, regardless of the noise of carriages and the lights which flashed forth from the revelries of his neighbours. He went on and on, not thinking how he would stem the current that was running against him so strongly; hardly trying to think; but thinking that it would be well for him if he could make the endeavour. Alas! he could not make it!

And then again he returned to the house, and once more

sat himself down in the same arm-chair. Was it come to this, that the world was hopeless for him? One would have said not. He was in debt, it is true; had fallen somewhat from a high position; had lost the dearest treasure which a man can have; not only the treasure, but the power of obtaining such treasure; for the possession of a loving wife was no longer a possibility to him. But still he had much; his acknowledged capacity for law pleadings, his right to take high place among law pleaders, the trick of earning money in that fashion of life; all these were still his. He had his gown and wig, and forensic brow-beating, brazen scowl; nay, he still had his seat in Parliament. Why should he have despaired?

But he did despair—as men do when they have none to whom they can turn them trustingly in their miseries. This man had had friends by hundreds; good, serviceable, parliamentary, dinner-eating, dinner-giving friends; fine, pleasant friends, as such friends go. He had such friends by hundreds; but he had failed to prepare for stormy times a leash or so of true hearts on which, in stress of weather, he could throw himself with undoubting confidence. One such friend he may have had once; but he now was among his bitterest enemies. The horizon round him was all black, and he did despair.

How many a man lives and dies without giving any sign whether he be an arrant coward, or a true-hearted, brave hero! One would have said of this man, a year since, that he was brave enough. He would stand up before a bench of judges, with the bar of England round him, and shout forth, with brazen trumpet, things that were true, or things that were not true; striking down a foe here to the right, and slaughtering another there to the left, in a manner which, for so young a man, filled beholders with admiration. He could talk by the hour among the Commons of England, and no touch of modesty would ever encumber his speech. He could make himself great, by making others little, with a glance. But, for all that, he was a coward. Misfortune had come upon him, and he was conquered at once.

Misfortune had come upon him, and he found it unendurable—yes, utterly unendurable. The grit and substance of the man within were not sufficient to bear the load which fate had put upon them. As does a deal-table in similar case, they were crushed down, collapsed, and fell in. The stuff there was not good mahogany, or sufficient hard wood, but an unseasoned soft, porous, deal-board, utterly unfit to sustain such pressure. An unblushing, wordy barrister may be very full of brass and words, and yet be no better than an unseasoned porous deal-board, even though he have a seat in Parliament.

He rose from his chair, and again took a glass of brandy. How impossible it is to describe the workings of a mind in such a state of misery as that he then endured! What—what! was there no release for him? no way, spite of this black fit, to some sort of rest—to composure of the most ordinary kind? Was there nothing that he could do which would produce for him, if not gratification, then at least quiescence? To the generality of men of his age, there are resources in misfortune. Men go to billiard-tables, or to cards, or they seek relief in woman's society, from the smiles of beauty, or a laughter-moving tongue. But Sir Henry, very early in life, had thrown those things from him. He had discarded pleasure, and wedded himself to hard work at a very early age. If, at the same time, he had wedded himself to honesty also, and had not discarded his heart, it might have been well with him.

He again sat down, and then he remained all but motionless for some twenty minutes. It had now become dark, but he would have no lights lit. The room was very gloomy with its red embossed paper and dark ruby curtains. As his eye glanced round during the last few moments of the dusk, he remembered how he had inquired of his Caroline how many festive guests might sit at their ease in that room, and eat the dainties which he, with liberal hand, would put before them. Where was his Caroline now? where were his guests? what anxiety now had he that they should have room enough? what cared he now for their dainties?

It was not to be borne. He clasped his hand to his brow, and rising from his chair, he went upstairs to his dressing-room. For what purpose, he had not even asked himself. Of bed, and rest, and sleep he had had no thought. When there, he again sat down, and mechanically dressed himself—dressed himself as though he were going out to some gay evening-party—was even more than ordinarily particular about his toilet. One white handkerchief he threw aside as spoiled in the tying. He looked specially to his boots, and with scrupulous care brushed the specks of dust from the sleeve of his coat. It was a blessing, at any rate, to have something to do. He did this, and then—

When he commenced his work, he had, perhaps, some remote intention of going somewhere. If so, he had quickly changed his mind, for, having finished his dressing, he again sat himself down in an armchair. The gas in his dressing-room had been lighted, and here he was able to look around him and see what resources he had to his hand. One resource he did see.

Ah, me! Yes, he saw it, and his mind approved—such amount of mind as he had then left to him. But he waited patiently awhile—with greater patience than he had hitherto exhibited that day. He waited patiently, sitting in his chair for some hour or so; nay, it may have been for two hours, for the house was still, and the servants were in bed. Then, rising from his chair, he turned the lock of his dressing-room door. It was a futile precaution, if it meant anything, for the room had another door, which opened to his wife's chamber, and the access on that side was free and open.

Early on the following morning, George Bertram went up to town, and was driven directly from the station to his dull, dingy, dirty chambers in the Temple. His chambers were not as those of practising lawyers. He kept no desk there, and no servant peculiar to himself. It had suited him to have some resting-place for his foot, that he could call his home; and when he was there, he was waited upon by the old woman who called herself the laundress—probably from the fact of her never washing herself or anything else.

When he reached this sweet home on the morning in question, he was told by the old woman that a very express messenger had been there that morning, and that, failing to find him, the express messenger had gone down to Hadley. They had, therefore, passed each other upon the road. The express messenger had left no message, but the woman had learned that he had come from Eaton Square.

'And he left no letter?'

'No, sir; no letter. He had no letter; but he was very eager about it. It was something of importance sure—ly.'

It might have been natural that, under such circumstances, George should go off to Eaton Square; but it struck him as very probable that Sir Henry might desire to have some communication with him, but that he, when he should know what that communication was, would in no degree reciprocate that desire. The less that he had to say to Sir Henry Harcourt at present, perhaps, the better. So he made up his mind that he would not go to Eaton Square.

After he had been in his rooms for about half an hour, he was preparing to leave them, and had risen with that object, when he heard a knock at his door, and quickly following the knock, the young attorney who had read the will was in his room.

'You have heard the news, Mr Bertram?' said he.

'No, indeed! What news? I have just come up.'

'Sir Henry Harcourt has destroyed himself. He shot himself in his own house yesterday, late at night, after the servants had gone to bed!'

George Bertram fell back, speechless, on to the sofa behind him, and stared almost unconsciously at the lawyer.

'It is too true, sir. That will of Mr Bertram's was too much for him. His reason must have failed him, and now he is no more.' And so was made clear what were the tidings with which that express messenger had been laden.

There was little or nothing more to be said on the matter between George Bertram and Mr Stickatit. The latter declared that the fact had been communicated to him on authority which admitted of no doubt; and the other, when he did believe, was but little inclined to share his speculations on it with the lawyer.

Nor was there much for Bertram to do—not at once. The story had already gone down to Hadley—had already been told there to her to whom it most belonged; and Bertram felt that it was not at present his province to say kind things to her, or seek to soften the violence of the shock. No, not at present.

CHAPTER XLVII

CONCLUSION

METHINKS it is almost unnecessary to write this last chapter. The story, as I have had to tell it, is all told. The object has been made plain—or, if not, can certainly not be made plainer in these last six or seven pages. The results of weakness and folly—of such weakness and such folly as is too customary among us—have been declared. What further fortune fate had in store for those whose names have been familiar to us, might be guessed by all. But, nevertheless, custom, and the desire of making an end of the undertaken work, and in some sort completing it, compel me to this concluding chapter.

Within six weeks after the death of Sir Henry Harcourt, the vicar of Hurst Staple was married to Adela Gauntlet. Every critic who weighs the demerits of these pages—nay, every reader, indulgent or otherwise, who skims through them will declare that the gentleman was not worthy of the lady. I hope so, with all my heart. I do sincerely trust that they will think so. If not, my labour has been in vain.

Mr Arthur Wilkinson was not worthy of the wife with whom a kind Providence had blessed him—was not worthy of her in the usual acceptation of the word. He was not a bad man, as men go; but she was—I must not trust myself to praise her, or I shall be told, not altogether truly, that she was of my own creating.

He was not worthy of her. That is, the amount of wealth of character which he brought into that life-partnership was, when counted up, much less than her contribution. But that she was fully satisfied with her bargain—that she was so then and so continued—was a part of her worthiness. If ever she weighed herself against him, the scale in which he was placed never in her eyes showed itself to be light. She took him for her lord, and with a leal heart and a loving bosom she ever recognized him as her head and master, as the pole-star to which she must turn, compelled by laws of adamant.* Worthy or unworthy, he was all that she expected, all that she desired, bone of her bone, flesh of her flesh, the father of her bairns, the lord of her bosom, the staff of her maintenance, the prop of her house.

And what man was ever worthy, perfectly worthy, of a pure, true, and honest girl? Man's life admits not of such purity and honesty; rarely of such truth. But one would not choose that such flowers should remain unplucked because no hands are fit to touch them.

As to the future life of the vicar of Hurst Staple and his wife, it is surely unnecessary to say much—or perhaps anything. It cannot be told that they became suddenly rich. No prime minister, won by her beauty or virtue, placed him upon the bench, or even offered him a deanery. Vicar of Hurst Staple he is still, and he still pays the old allowance out of his well-earned income to his mother, who lives with her daughters at Littlebath. One young lad after another, or generally two at a time, share the frugal meals at the parsonage; and our friend is sometimes heard to boast that none of these guests of his have as yet been plucked. Of the good things of the world, there is quite enough for her; and we may perhaps say, nearly enough for him. Who, then, shall croak that they are poor?

And now and then they walk along the river to West Putford; for among their choicest blessings is that of having a good neighbour in the old rectory. And walking there, how can they but think of old sorrows and present joys?

'Ah!' she whispered to him one day, as they crept along the reedy margin in the summer evening, not long after their marriage. 'Ah! dearest, it is better now than it was when you came here once.'

'Is it, love?'

'Is it not? But you misbehaved then—you know you did. You would not trust me then.'

'I could not trust myself.'

'I should have trusted you;—in all things, in everything. As I do now.'

And then he cut at the rushes with his walking-stick, as he had done before; and bethought himself that in those days he had been an ass.

And so we will leave them. May they walk in those quiet paths for long days yet to come; and may he learn to know that God has given him an angel to watch at his side!

Of the rosy Miss Todd, there is nothing to be said but this, that she is still Miss Todd, and still rosy. Whether she be now at Littlebath, or Baden, or Dieppe, or Harrogate, at New York, Jerusalem, or Frazer's River, matters but little. Where she was last year, there she is not now. Where she is now, there she will not be next year. But she still increases the circle of her dearly-loved friends; and go where she will, she, at any rate, does more good to others than others do to her. And so we will make our last bow before her feet.

We have only now to speak of George Bertram and of Lady Harcourt—of them and of Miss Baker, who need hardly now be considered a personage apart from her niece. No sooner was the first shock of Sir Henry Harcourt's death past, than Bertram felt that it was impossible for him at the present moment to see the widow. It was but a few days since she had declared her abhorrence of the man to whom her fate was linked, apparently for life, and who was now gone. And that declaration had implied also that her heart still belonged to him—to him, George Bertram—him to whom it had first been given—to him, rather, who had first made himself master of it almost without gift on her part. Now, as regarded God's laws, her hand was free again, and might follow her heart.

But death closes many a long account, and settles many a bitter debt. She could remember now that she had sinned against her husband, as well as he against her; and she had sinned the first, and perhaps the deepest. He would have loved her, if she would have permitted it; have loved her with a cold, callous, worldly love; but still with such love as he had to give. But she had married him resolving to give no love at all, knowing that she could give none; almost boasting to herself that she had told him that she had none to give.

The man's blood was, in some sort, on her head, and she felt that the burden was very heavy. All this Bertram understood, more thoroughly, perhaps, than she did; and for many weeks he abstained altogether from going to Hadley. He met Miss Baker repeatedly in London, and learned from her how Lady Harcourt bore herself. How she bore herself outwardly, that is. The inward bearing of such a woman in such a condition it was hardly given to Miss Baker to read. She was well in health, Miss Baker said, but pale and silent, stricken, and for hours motionless. 'Very silent,' Miss Baker would say. 'She will sit for a whole morning without speaking a word; thinking—thinking—thinking.' Yes; she had something of which to think. It was no wonder that she should sit silent.

And then after awhile he went down to Hadley, and saw her.

'Caroline, my cousin,' he said to her.

'George, George.' And then she turned her face from him, and sobbed violently. They were the first tears she had shed since the news had reached her.

She did feel, in very deed, that the man's blood was on her head. But for her, would he not be sitting among the proud ones of the land? Had she permitted him to walk his own course by himself, would this utter destruction have come upon him? Or, having sworn to cherish him as his wife, had she softened her heart towards him, would this deed have been done? No; fifty times a day she would ask herself the question; and as often would she answer it by the same words. The man's blood was upon her head.

For many a long day Bertram said nothing to her of her actual state of existence. He spoke neither of her past life as a wife nor her present life as a widow. The name of that man, whom living they had both despised and hated, was never mentioned between them during all these months.

And yet he was frequently with her. He was with her aunt, rather, and thus she became used to have him sitting in the room beside her. When in her presence, he would talk of their money-matters, of the old man and his will, in which, luckily, the name of Sir Henry Harcourt was not mentioned;

and at last they brought themselves to better subjects, higher hopes—hopes that might yet be high, and solace that was trustworthy, in spite of all that was come and gone.

And she would talk to him of himself; of himself as divided from her in all things, except in cousinhood. And at her instigation, he again put himself to work in the dusky purlieus of Chancery Lane. Mr Die had now retired, and drank his port and counted his per-cents. in the blessed quiet of his evening days; but a Gamaliel was not wanting, and George sat himself down once more in the porch. We may be sure that he did not sit altogether in vain.

And then Adela—Mrs Wilkinson we should now call her—visited the two ladies in their silent retirement at Hadley. What words were uttered between her and Lady Harcourt were heard by no other human ear; but they were not uttered without effect. She who had been so stricken could dare again to walk to church, and bear the eyes of the little world around her. She would again walk forth and feel the sun, and know that the fields were green, and that the flowers were sweet, and that praises were to be sung to God.—For His mercy endureth for ever.

It was five years after that night in Eaton Square when George Bertram again asked her—her who had once been Caroline Waddington—to be his wife. But, sweet ladies, sweetest, fairest maidens, there were no soft, honey words of love then spoken; no happy, eager vows, which a novelist may repeat, hoping to move the soft sympathy of your bosoms. It was a cold, sad, dreary matter that offer of his; her melancholy, silent acquiescence, and that marriage in Hadley church, at which none were present but Adela and Arthur, and Miss Baker.

It was Adela who arranged it, and the result has shown that she was right. They now live together very quietly, very soberly, but yet happily. They have not Adela's blessings. No baby lies in Caroline's arms, no noisy boy climbs on the arm of George Bertram's chair. Their house is childless, and very, very quiet; but they are not unhappy.

Reader, can you call to mind what was the plan of life which Caroline Waddington had formed in the boldness of her young heart? Can you remember the aspirations of George Bertram, as he sat upon the Mount of Olives, watching the stones of the temple over against him?

EXPLANATORY NOTES

1 *Væ Victis!*: 'woe to the vanquished!', Plautus, *Pseudolus*, V. ii. 1317, a proverbial saying since *c.*390 BC, when it was uttered in Rome by Brennus, leader of the invading Gauls.

2 *To him that hath . . . which he hath*: see Matthew 25: 29, Mark 4: 25.

Occupet extremum scabies: 'plague seize the hindmost', Horace, *Ars Poetica*, 417.

grand competitive examination: proposed for the Civil Service by the Trevelyan–Northcote report in 1854, but not generally used in the Home Civil Service till after 1870. See Trollope's attack on competitive examinations in *The Three Clerks* (1858).

With us, let the race . . . to the strong: 'The race is not to the swift, nor the battle to the strong.' Ecclesiastes 9: 11.

Lord Derby . . . Lord Palmerston . . . Lord George Bentinck . . . Mr Scott: foremost Victorian statesmen, who were also noted owners of racehorses. John Scott, employed by Lord Derby, was the trainer of Toxophilite and a successful jockey.

family of the Days: John Barham Day, Lord Bentinck's trainer, won several major races as a jockey (Lester Piggott is a descendant); his son, John, trained horses for many of the nobility; and his brother, Samuel, was a well-known jockey, who also kept livery stables in London.

Crucifix . . . Iliona . . . Toxophilite: famous racehorses. Crucifix, owned by Lord Bentinck and ridden by John Barham Day, won the Oaks in 1840; Iliona, owned by Lord Palmerston and trained by Day, won the Cesarewitch in 1841; Toxophilite, one of the best horses of his generation, was owned by Lord Derby. I am indebted for information about Iliona to Racing Promotional Literature.

Leicestershire: well known as a hunting county.

3 *Iphigenia*: in Greek mythology a daughter sacrificed by Agamemnon.

4 *"Vox populi, vox Dei"*: 'the voice of the people is the voice of God.' Alcuin, *Epistle to Charlemagne*, *c.*800 (*Admonitio ad Carolum Magnum: Works*, Epis. 127).

5 *wranglers*: candidates who have been placed in the first class in the mathematical tripos at Cambridge University.

Amaryllis . . . Neæra: Amaryllis is the name of a country girl or shepherdess in classical pastoral poetry. Naæra, mentioned by Horace and Virgil, is the name given to any sweetheart. See Milton, *Lycidas*, 68: 'To sport with Amaryllis in the shade/ Or with the tangles of Neæra's hair.'

double first: the achievement of first-class honours in two subjects.

7 *Winchester*: Winchester College, an English public school, founded in 1382 by William of Wykeham, Chancellor of England and Bishop of Winchester, to prepare boys for study at New College, Oxford, which he also founded. Pupils were known as Wykehamists.

8 *commoner*: a student not on the foundation, who has to pay for his board.

9 *Latin hexameters*: a form of Latin verse.

10 *Tracts . . . Puseyism . . . Froude . . . Newman*: 'Tracts for the Times' was a series of conservative theological essays produced by distinguished men at Oriel College, which bitterly divided Oxford. The majority view among the Tractarians, which was traditionalist and ritualistic, was led by Edward Bouverie Pusey. Three of the Tracts were contributed by the intellectual, Richard Hurrell Froude. John Henry Newman was the author of Tract XC in 1841, which offered a reinterpretation of the 39 Articles. Four years after the controversy he entered the Roman Catholic Church, later becoming a cardinal.

11 *the 'Remains'*: the collected writings of Hurrell Froude, published in 1837 and 1839, after his death in 1836, and including a preface by Newman.

the Sewells: William Sewell, Fellow of Exeter College, and one of the most prominent men in Oxford, left the Tractarians after the publication of Tract XC. His sister, Elizabeth Sewell, was a well-known novelist, one brother became premier of New Zealand, and another Warden of New College.

the Newdigate: a prize for poetry, founded by Sir Roger Newdigate, open to undergraduates at Oxford.

Keble . . . Faber: John Keble was Professor of Poetry at Oxford. The Oxford Movement may be dated from his preaching a famous sermon on 14 July 1833 against 'National

Apostasy' before the assize judges at St Mary the Virgin, Oxford. Frederick William Faber, a Fellow of University College, was admitted into the Roman Catholic Church in 1845.

13 *boody*: sulk.

14 *Aristophanes*: considered to be the greatest poet of the Old Attic Comedy. Eleven of his plays survive.

15 *'Frogs'*: a play by Aristophanes concerning Dionysus's visit to Hades to bring back Euripides.

16 *plucked*: rejected in a university examination. (*OED*)

18 *'Sound the timbrels . . . hero comes'*: libretto for Handel's oratorio *Joshua* (1748), III.

19 *Temple*: two of the Inns of Court, the Inner and Middle Temple, stand on the site once occupied by the Templars, an ancient military and religious order devoted to the protection of the Holy Sepulchre.

"dura ilia": 'strong stomach'.

21 *two members*: university seats were not abolished until 1948. Members of Parliament were elected by graduates of the University.

proctors: at Oxford and Cambridge officers appointed annually to discharge various administrative functions, and to be responsible for undergraduate discipline.

23 *'There is a tide . . . to fortune'*: *Julius Caesar*, IV. iii. 218.

24 *'Change . . . Capel Court*: the Stock Exchange, to which Capel Court led until 1973.

thirty-nine articles: doctrinal statement of the Church of England, imposed on the clergy before a relaxation in 1865.

25 *Marryat's novel . . . "Peter Simple"*: Frederick Marryat was a captain in the Navy and a novelist, who published *Peter Simple* in 1834. Its hero is a naval officer.

that other one: *Japhet in Search of a Father* (1836), the story of the struggles of a foundling.

26 *a man without property*: until 1858 no one could be elected to Parliament unless he owned real estate or personal property to the value of £600 a year as a county member, or £300 as a member for a borough.

29 *Chancery wig*: a barrister in the Court of Chancery, which had

the principal administration of equity.

Lincoln's Inn: one of the Inns of Court, where Trollope's father, a Chancery barrister, once had chambers.

31 *gig*: a light two-wheeled one-horse carriage. (*OED*)

32 *Jehu*: a fast driver or coachman: see 2 Kings 9: 20.

36 *simony*: the practice of buying or selling ecclesiastical preferments, benefices, or emoluments.

37 *lay impropriator*: a layman in possession of a living.

50 *man-sworn*: sworn falsely.

54 *Crœsus*: the last king of Lydia, renowned for his great wealth.

Colonel Waugh: Colonel William Petrie Waugh was a founder and director of the London and Eastern Banking Corporation. He attracted the savings of Anglo-Indians, particularly military men, or their widows, appropriating them for himself. In 1857 he fled to Spain, ostensibly for the sake of his health. Returning to London, he was arrested in 1863 with liabilities of about £1 million. See *The Times*, 15 Dec. 1857, 8; 15 Sept. 1858, 8; 13 Apr. 1863, 11.

55 *'Daily Jupiter'*: Trollope is referring to *The Times*, known as 'The Thunderer'. In classical mythology Jupiter, the king of gods, hurled thunderbolts.

opposition line: the railway mania was at its height in the mid-1840s, with enormous speculation in new ventures. The Great Western felt its commercial safety threatened by a rival line.

56 *Independent ministers*: ministers of Nonconformist churches. At the beginning of the nineteenth century these were identified with Congregationalists.

57 *Grub Street*: originally the name of a street near Moorfields in London inhabited by writers. Today the term is applied to any form of literary hack-work.

62 *Coke and Blackstone*: Sir Edward Coke (1552–1634), a judge and law writer of vast reputation. His chief works are his *Reports* and his *Institutes*. Sir William Blackstone (1723–80), also a legal writer and judge, is best known for his *Commentaries on the Laws of England*.

65 *military frock*: a military coat with long skirts.

caravansary: an eastern inn with a spacious courtyard where caravans put up.

dragoman: in eastern countries a man who acts as an interpreter.

67 *casemated batteries*: concealed artillery.

Tartarus: in mythology the infernal regions.

68 *Righi*: Rigi, a mountain near Lake Lucerne.

72 *vicegerent*: the administrative agent of a king; here appointed by God.

miraculous flames: on the morning of Easter Eve the holy fire issued from an aperture, in the Church of the Holy Sepulchre, signifying the descent of God upon the holy tomb. The fire was then spread from hand to hand among the pilgrims.

77 *Byzantine Sophia*: the principal church of Byzantium (later Constantinople, now Istanbul) was dedicated to St Sophia, or the eternal wisdom.

'over the brook Cedron': John 18: 1.

'fifteen furlongs from Jerusalem': see John 11: 18.

'cried, saying, Hosanna to the son of David': Matthew 21: 9.

78 *Dr Stanley*: Arthur Penrhyn Stanley, Professor of Ecclesiastical History at Oxford and later Dean of Westminster, who toured Egypt and the Holy Land and published his popular *Sinai and Palestine* in 1856.

Pariahs: social outcasts.

'where the Lord appeared . . . Ornan the Jebusite': 2 Chronicles 3: 1.

79 *'exceeding magnificent . . . throughout all countries'*: see 1 Chronicles 22: 5.

80 *'sat upon the mount, over against the temple'*: see Mark 13: 3.

'And as he went . . . thrown down': see Mark 13: 1–2.

'And when he was come . . . wept over it': Luke 19: 41.

'If thou hadst known . . . thy peace!': Luke 19: 42.

81 *'O Jerusalem, Jerusalem . . . desolate'*: Matthew 23: 37–8.

82 *dervishes*: Muslim holy men, who have taken vows of poverty and sometimes engage in fantastic practices.

83 *'did Solomon build . . . before Jerusalem'*: 1 Kings 11: 7.

84 *the Duke . . . Sir Charles Napier*: famous commanders. The Duke of Wellington, victor of Waterloo and later Prime

Minister, was known as the 'Great Duke'. Sir Charles Napier, known as 'Mad Charley', was the controversial commander of the British Baltic Fleet during the Crimean War.

'ars celare artem': more fully 'Ars est celare artem', 'Art consists in concealing art'. It is thought that this epigram may have its origin in Ovid, *Ars Amatoria*, II. 313.

96 *Juno*: consort of Jupiter, she represented the female principle of life.

Venus: goddess of love and beauty, identified with the Greek Aphrodite.

Paris: in Greek legend the son of King Priam of Troy. His seduction of Helen, wife of Menelaus, king of Sparta, started the Trojan War.

descend . . . daughters of men: see Genesis 6: 4.

97 *'Vera incessu patuit Dea'*: 'one recognized the goddess by her gait', Virgil, *Aeneid*, I. 405.

100 *wide-awake hat*: a felt hat with a broad brim.

101 *Murray*: John Murray published a series for travellers in Europe known as Murray's 'handbooks', beginning with *Holland, Belgium, and the Rhine*, in 1836.

Lord Malmesbury or Lord Clarendon: both held the post of Secretary of State for Foreign Affairs; Lord Malmesbury briefly in 1852 and 1858–9, and Lord Clarendon 1853–8.

Aceldama, the field of blood: see Matthew 27: 7–8.

105 *Gaza as Samson had*: see Judges 16; also Milton's *Samson Agonistes*. Samson was captured by the Philistines, blinded, and imprisoned in Gaza.

107 *"Praise undeserved is satire in disguise"*: Broadhurst [?], *To the Celebrated Beauties of the British Court*. See Bell, *Fugitive Poetry*, III. 118.

112 *as Esther was fair*: see Esther 2: 7.

116 *Jupiter*: in Roman mythology the supreme deity, corresponding to Zeus.

Hebe: daughter of Hera and Zeus, the cup-bearer of the gods.

118 *piastre*: English name of a small Turkish coin which circulated in Egypt.

127 *summum bonum*: 'the highest good', Cicero, *De Officiis*, I. ii. 5.

129 *Vale Valete*: farewell.

144 *Medea's secret*: Medea boiled Aeson, the father of Jason, with virtuous herbs, thus renewing his youth.

146 *Men delighted him not; nor women either*: see *Hamlet*, II. ii. 317.

153 *Gamaliel*: a master of the Jewish law, leading member of the Sanhedrin, and St Paul's spiritual tutor.

154 *Æneas*: Virgil tells in the *Aeneid* of Aeneas's long voyage and many adventures before he found Lavinium, the parent town of Rome.

Styx: in Greek mythology one of the rivers of the underworld.

161 *murdering monk*: Ambrosio, the main character in *The Monk: A Romance* (1796), a Gothic horror novel by Matthew Gregory ('Monk') Lewis.

Mrs Radcliffe's time: Ann Radcliffe, another Gothic novelist, best known for *The Mysteries of Udolpho* (1794).

165 *myrmidons*: faithful followers.

167 *Terpsichore*: in Greek mythology one of the nine Muses and the patron of lyric poetry and dancing.

168 *stud*: a number of hunters.

174 *Coke upon Littleton*: Sir Thomas Littleton (1422–81), judge and legal author. His fame rests upon a short treatise on 'Tenures'. Coke wrote an elaborate commentary on it. Littleton's text with Coke's comment long remained the principal authority on English real property law.

181 *Hecate*: a witch. See *Macbeth*, III. v. 1.

194 *the god . . . upon the stage*: in classical drama the introduction of a god, often with the aid of machinery, to resolve the plot.

195 *a very telling tale*: Trollope is probably referring to Dickens's *Bleak House* (1852–3), which satirized the Court of Chancery and its notorious delays.

196 *repeal of the corn laws*: the Anti-Corn Law League, led by Richard Cobden, and founded in 1839, together with the failure of the Irish potato crop in 1845, convinced the Prime Minister, Sir Robert Peel, to support the repeal of all Corn Laws, regulating the import and export of grain, which was achieved in 1846.

Jew senators . . . vote by ballot . . . property qualification: before

1858 Jews were excluded from Parliament. Although secret voting was not introduced until the Ballot Act of 1872, it was a live political issue throughout the period. See the note to p. 26 about property qualifications.

197 *Tories*: Trollope seems to be making a distinction between the emerging conservatism of Sir Robert Peel and Benjamin Disraeli, and the Tory Party before about 1815, which had broadly represented the interests of the country gentry and the merchant class.

Lord Eldon: Lord Chancellor of England in the early years of the nineteenth century, he was an inflexible conservative, opposing Roman Catholic political emancipation, the abolition of imprisonment for debt, the abolition of the slave trade, and the reform of the House of Commons.

198 *Catholic emancipation . . . Parliamentary reform*: the movement to gain political and civil rights for Roman Catholics was finally successful in 1829. The movement for Parliamentary reform began in the 1830s, with as its aims the removal of pocket boroughs, the redistribution of seats, and the extension of the franchise.

Sir Robert: Sir Robert Peel, Prime Minister and founder of the Conservative Party. He resigned in 1846 following the repeal of the Corn Laws.

199 *Mr Dod*: Charles Dod compiled summaries of parliamentary debates for *The Times* and published *Parliamentary Pocket Companion*, 1833–42, and *Parliamentary Companion*, 1843–55.

220 *'Romance of Scripture'*: Bertram's book shares the approach of David Friedrich Strauss's *Das Leben Jesu* (*The Life of Jesus*), which George Eliot (then Mary Ann Evans) translated and published in 1846. It rejected supernaturalism, and subjected the myths of the New Testament to methodical analysis, creating a great stir in theological circles.

sun standing still upon Gibeon: Joshua asked the Lord that the sun should stand still upon Gibeon until the people of Israel had avenged themselves upon the Amorites. See Joshua 10: 12.

221 *Mr Mudie*: Charles Edward Mudie, founder of the famous Mudie's Lending Library, who exercised considerable influence over the sales of books.

228 *Walpole*: Horace Walpole, author of the Gothic novel *The Castle of Otranto* (1765) and an assiduous letter writer.

234 *fellowship . . . married*: college fellows had imposed on them a regulation that they could not retain their fellowship if they married.

236 *wind out of the sails of the Whigs*: Trollope refers to the repeal of the Corn Laws, essentially a Whig measure, which was passed by a Conservative administration.

237 *Cobden*: Richard Cobden, best known for his successful fight for the repeal of the Corn Laws, and his defence of free trade.

Garrick: David Garrick, a famous eighteenth-century actor and producer, who brought to the stage a more natural style of acting.

240 *'The woman cannot be . . . makes not kinder'*: in spite of extensive research, the source of this quotation remains unidentified.

260 *phaeton*: a four-wheeled open carriage.

'res angusta': more fully, 'Haud facile emergunt quorum virtutibus obstat / Res angusta domi.' 'It is not easy for people to rise out of obscurity when they have to face straitened circumstances at home.' Juvenal, *Satires*, III. 164.

270 *'lusus naturæ'*: 'a freak of nature'.

273 *brougham*: a one-horse closed carriage.

pump-room: the room at a spa where the mineral water is dispensed by pump.

275 *Calliope*: in Greek mythology the chief of the nine Muses, and patron of epic poetry.

278 *devil's books*: 'Kartenspiel ist des Teufels Gebetbuch', 'cards are the devil's prayer-book' (German proverb).

286 *double-dummy*: a game in which two 'hands' belonging to imaginary players are exposed, so that each of the two players manages two 'hands'. (*OED*)

Napoleon . . . Ulm . . . Mack: at the battle of Ulm in 1805 Napoleon's Grande Armée secured a famous victory over the Austrian Army under Baron Karl Mack von Leiberich, by cutting off his retreat eastward, driving the Austrians into the city of Ulm and to surrender, while their Russian reinforcements were still a hundred miles away.

288 *Sindbad*: Sindbad the Sailor, a hero in *The Thousand and One Nights*. The 'old man of the sea', on the fifth voyage, compels Sindbad to carry him.

305 *Louis Philippe*: king of France, who liked to be known as 'le roi citoyen' ('the citizen king'). During the Revolution he had been sympathetic to the reform movement, and he was popular for his affectation of simplicity and republican manners, but his reign was not liberal and in 1848, following a revolt in Paris, he abdicated, taking refuge in England.

306 *'Labor omnia vincit improbus'*: more usually, 'Labor omnia vincit', 'Persistent labour overcomes all things', Virgil, *Georgics*, I. 145.

315 *Mr Smith*: Trollope is referring to Louis Philippe, the 'citizen king'.

Panem et circenses: more fully, 'Duas tantum res anxius optat, / Panem et circenses.' 'Only two things the people anxiously desire, bread and circus games.' Juvenal, *Satires*, X. 80.

316 *Dubarry*: Trollope probably intends Comtesse Marie Jeanne du Barry, mistress of Louis XV, who exercised great political influence at court. During the Revolution she was accused of conspiring against the republic and was publicly executed in Paris.

320 *Plutus*: in Greek mythology the god of abundance or wealth.

Quidnuncs: inquisitive people.

327 *horn of the golden calf*: an idol made from the golden earrings of the Israelites while Moses was absent on Mount Sinai. See Exodus 32.

328 *the Scriptures moved him . . . his sins*: the Exhortation spoken by the minister at the beginning of Morning Prayer. See *Book of Common Prayer*.

fee-simple: absolute ownership of an estate or inheritance of land.

331 *Pecksniff*: Seth Pecksniff, arch-hypocrite, a character in Dickens's *Martin Chuzzlewit* (1844).

332 *Stylites*: St Simeon Stylites, a Christian ascetic, who lived standing on top of a pillar. See Tennyson's poem, 'St Simeon Stylites'.

Yet, in my flesh, shall I see God: Job 19: 26.

Nothing is impossible with God: see Luke 1: 37. The debate between Wilkinson and Bertram is between traditional belief and the new theology.

333 *"Not by confusion . . . unity of Person"*: part of the Athanasian

Creed, said upon certain Feasts at Morning Prayer. See *Book of Common Prayer*.

334 *certain doctors*: the Nicene Creed was promulgated in 325 by the Council of Nicaea. It was elaborated and defended against heresy by Athanasius, Bishop of Alexandria, who expounded the doctrine of the Trinity and the divine relationship.

Cæsar's tribute: see Matthew 22: 17–21, Mark 12: 14–17, Luke 20: 22–5.

338 *"Welcome the coming, speed the parting guest"*: Pope, *Odyssey* (1725–6), XV. 83.

344 *"poor sequestered stag . . . velvet friend"*: see *As You Like It*, II. i. 33–50.

345 *God still tempers the wind to the shorn lamb*: Laurence Sterne, *Sentimental Journey* (1768; Penguin edn., 1967, 139).

346 *in durance vile*: 'In durance vile here must I wake and weep / And all my frowsy couch in sorrow steep.' Burns, *Epistle from Esopus to Maria* (1794), 57.

354 *Lord Boanerges*: 'sons of thunder' (Greek). Christ's name for his disciples, James and John (see Mark 3: 17); subsequently used to refer to any vociferous preacher. Trollope habitually applied it to Lord Brougham, a noted orator and president of the National Association for the Promotion of Social Science.

357 *Tom Moore*: Thomas Moore enjoyed great popularity during the early years of the nineteenth century for his long oriental poem *Lalla Rookh*, and for his lyrics to fit traditional melodies.

358 *Elysium . . . houris . . . asphodel*: Elysium was the paradise in Greek mythology to which were sent heroes on whom the gods conferred immortality; while houris were nymphs of the Muslim paradise. Asphodel was the immortal flower said to cover the Elysian meads.

'Gin a body meet a body comin' through the rye': Burns, 'Coming Through the Rye', taken from an old song, 'The Bob-tailed Lass'.

Lord Liverpool: Trollope was born in 1815. Liverpool reluctantly replaced the Prime Minister, Spencer Perceval, after his assassination in 1812, and remained in office for nearly fifteen years.

Vixi puellis nuper idoneus, et militavi: 'My life as a ladies' man has ended, though till lately I soldiered on', Horace, *Odes*, III. xxvi. 1.

gittern: an old instrument of the guitar kind strung with wire. (*OED*)

359 *lustrums*: periods of five years. In Latin sometimes used for periods of four years, which is more likely here.

bills of mortality: the parishes in and around central London. Originally a periodically published official return of the deaths for the 109 parishes in and around London, commenced by the London Company of Parish Clerks in 1592. Hence this district became known as 'within the bills of mortality'.

367 *fly*: a light, one-horse covered carriage, usually for hire.

373 *Lucretias*: Lucretia was a beautiful and virtuous heroine of Roman legend, who after her rape exacted an oath of vengeance from her father and husband, and stabbed herself to death.

385 *Reform Bill*: this was passed in 1832.

387 *'Sed post equitem sedet atra cura'*: 'behind the horseman sits black care', Horace, *Odes*, III. i. 40.

388 *Niobean deluge*: in Greek mythology Niobe was the typical sorrowful woman, weeping for the loss of all her children, slain by Apollo and Artemis.

393 *of law and of right*: the Married Women's Property Act of 1881 finally gave married women legal rights to property.

394 *vestal zone*: girdle of chastity. (*OED*)

Cæsar and the duke: see note to p. 84.

the Graces: goddesses of charm or beauty.

surtout: a man's overcoat.

399 *Alexander Selkirk*: an eighteenth-century sailor, who spent five years on an uninhabited island, and served as the prototype for Defoe's Robinson Crusoe.

400 *Oliver . . . Rowland*: to have a Rowland for an Oliver, blow for blow, tit for tat. They were two of Charlemagne's Paladins, who fought for five days on an island in the Rhine, without either gaining the upper hand. See Edward Hall, *Chronicles* (1548), 266, and *1 Henry VI*, I. ii. 30, 'England all Rowlands and Olivers bred.'

402 *Ebenezer*: dissenting chapel.

Galen: one of the most distinguished physicians of antiquity.

409 *other old gentleman*: the devil.

418 *'Quos Deus vult perdere, prius dementat'*: thought to be the Latin version of a Greek maxim.

423 *'noli me tangere'*: 'Touch me not' (Vulgate). See John 20: 17.

425 *Lord John*: probably Lord John Russell, a prominent Whig, who came out as an advocate of total free trade in advance of the repeal of the Corn Laws, and who became Prime Minister following Peel's resignation.

427 *woolsack*: the seat of the Lord Chancellor in the House of Lords, made of a large square bag of wool covered with cloth.

Methuselah ... Jared ... Lamech: figures representing great age. See Genesis 5: 15–27.

428 *Mr Perceval*: became Chancellor of the Exchequer in 1807, and was Prime Minister from 1809 until his assassination in 1812.

Lord Castlereagh ... Union: Viscount Castlereagh, as chief secretary to England's Irish governor, suppressed the Irish rebellion in 1798, and pushed through Dublin's Parliament the Act of Union in 1800, joining Ireland with Britain.

Acheron ... Libitina: in Greek mythology Acheron was a river in Hades; while Libitina was a Roman goddess of burials.

441 *He had thrown ... tribe*: see *Othello*, V. ii. 348.

445 *Mezentian embrace*: Mezentius was a mythical Etruscan king, who caused the living to be bound face to face with corpses and left to die of starvation. See Virgil, *Aeneid*, VIII. 485–8.

456 *Crichton*: James Crichton, commonly called the 'admirable' Crichton, a sixteenth-century orator, linguist, debater, man of letters, and scholar.

466 *Alexandria! mother of sciences!*: founded by Alexander the Great, in less than a century it had become the focal point of the highest development of Greek scholarship and science, and the home of the most famous library of antiquity.

'Auri sacra fames!': more fully, 'Quid non mortalia pectora cogis, / Auri sacra fames!' 'To what do you not drive the hearts of men, O accursed lust for gold!', Virgil, *Aeneid*, III. 56.

467 *Pharos ... Pompey's Pillar ... Cleopatra's Needle*: the Pharos of Alexandria was the most famous lighthouse in antiquity and one of the seven wonders of the world. Pompey's pillar, a monument in Alexandria, was dedicated to Diocletian.

Cleopatra's Needle, one of a pair of obelisks, having in fact no historical connection with the Egyptian queen, now stands on the Thames embankment in London.

Mr Brunel . . . Mr Stephenson . . . Mr Locke: famous British engineers. Brunel solved the problem of underwater tunnelling, Stephenson invented the railway engine, and Locke built railways in Britain and France.

468 *King Cheops*: the Greek name for King Khufu, builder of the Great Pyramid at Giza.

Nilometer: a graduated pillar used to measure the height to which the Nile rises during its annual floods.

469 *para*: a small Turkish coin.

472 *jewels . . . before swine!*: see Matthew 7: 6.

475 *Lewis*: John Frederick Lewis was a painter of Spanish and oriental subjects, who travelled in the east between 1839 and 1851.

rebels in India: in 1857 a mutiny of native troops in northern India quickly became a popular revolt, which was crushed by the British in 1859. In 1858 the British government had assumed rule from the East India Company.

476 *backsheish*: a gratuity, or tip.

478 *Pandemonium*: the abode of all the demons, represented by Milton in *Paradise Lost* as the capital of Hell.

482 *punkahs, tiffins, and bungalows*: punkahs were large swinging fans suspended from the ceiling and kept in motion by servants; tiffins was an Anglo-Indian term for light midday meals; and bungalows were originally single-storey Indian dwellings.

Medes and Persians: 'Now, O king, establish the decree, and sign the writing, that it be not changed, according to the law of the Medes and Persians, which altereth not.' Daniel 6: 8.

483 *sangaree*: a cold drink composed of wine diluted and spiced.

484 *'Hinc illæ lacrimæ'*: 'hence all those tears', Terence, *Andria*, I. i. 126.

495 *leather and prunella*: 'worth makes the man, and want of it, the fellow; / The rest is all but leather or prunella.' Pope, *Essay on Man* (1733), IV. 203. The contrast is between the cobbler and the parson, 'leather' with 'prunella', the material of the parson's gown.

496 *poverty comes in ... at the window*: an old proverb.

501 *Izaak Walton*: author of *The Compleat Angler* (1653).

503 *Jonahs*: fleeing from the Lord, Jonah volunteered to be cast overboard in order to calm the tempest caused by his presence. He was saved by the Lord in the belly of a great fish, where he remained for three days and nights. See Jonah 1: 1–17.

shaken the dust from their feet: 'when ye depart out of that house or city, shake off the dust of your feet.' Matthew 10: 14.

517 *Livingstone*: David Livingstone, missionary and explorer, who discovered Victoria Falls and returned to England a national hero in 1856.

531 *post-chaises*: travelling carriages, either hired from stage to stage, or drawn by horses so hired. (*OED*)

535 *Cerberus*: the monstrous dog guarding the entrance to the lower world, most frequently mentioned in connection with the descent of Heracles to Hades. See Homer, *Iliad*, VIII. 367.

541 *'Io triumphe'*: exclamation of joy or triumph.

549 *Faustus-like*: Faust, who died *c.*1540, was a German magician. In legend and literature he sold his soul to the devil in exchange for knowledge and power. See Christopher Marlowe, *Doctor Faustus* (1604).

550 *thimble-riggers*: professional sharpers who cheat at thimblerig, a swindling game played with three thimbles and a pea, and involving betting on the position of the pea.

cornet-à-piston: cornet.

557 *grass of the field ... into the oven*: see Psalm 103: 15–16, Matthew 6: 30, Luke 12: 28.

559 *personalty ... real*: the distinction is essentially between personal goods and land.

561 *ipsissima verba*: the very words.

Doctors' Commons: formerly a self-governing teaching body in London, similar to the Inns of Court, of practitioners of canon and civil law, who held doctorates in law from Oxford or Cambridge.

566 *build a golden bridge for a flying enemy*: Louis II of France to Brantôme. See Brantôme, *Memoirs*, I. 83.

568 *pent-house lid*: a hat with a sloping brim.

570 *the slings and arrows . . . bare bodkin*: see *Hamlet*, III. i. 58–76.

577 *adamant*: loadstone, or magnet.

THE WORLD'S CLASSICS

A Select List

SERGEI AKSAKOV: A Russian Gentleman
Translated by J. D. Duff
Edited by Edward Crankshaw

HANS ANDERSEN: Fairy Tales
Translated by L. W. Kingsland
Introduction by Naomi Lewis
Illustrated by Vilhelm Pedersen and Lorenz Frølich

JANE AUSTEN: Emma
Edited by James Kinsley and David Lodge

Mansfield Park
Edited by James Kinsley and John Lucas

ROBERT BAGE: Hermsprong
Edited by Peter Faulkner

WILLIAM BECKFORD: Vathek
Edited by Roger Lonsdale

CHARLOTTE BRONTË: Jane Eyre
Edited by Margaret Smith

THOMAS CARLYLE: The French Revolution
Edited by K. J. Fielding and David Sorensen

LEWIS CARROLL: Alice's Adventures in Wonderland *and* Through the Looking Glass
Edited by Roger Lancelyn Green
Illustrated by John Tenniel

GEOFFREY CHAUCER: The Canterbury Tales
Translated by David Wright

ANTON CHEKHOV: The Russian Master and Other Stories
Translated by Ronald Hingley

JOSEPH CONRAD: Victory
Edited by John Batchelor
Introduction by Tony Tanner

CHARLES DICKENS: Christmas Books
Edited by Ruth Glancy

FËDOR DOSTOEVSKY: Crime and Punishment
Translated by Jessie Coulson
Introduction by John Jones

GEORGE ELIOT: Daniel Deronda
Edited by Graham Handley

SUSAN FERRIER: Marriage
Edited by Herbert Foltinek

SARAH FIELDING: The Adventures of David Simple
Edited by Malcolm Kelsall

ELIZABETH GASKELL: Cousin Phillis and Other Tales
Edited by Angus Easson

KENNETH GRAHAME: The Wind in the Willows
Edited by Peter Green

THOMAS HARDY: A Pair of Blue Eyes
Edited by Alan Manford

JAMES HOGG: The Private Memoirs and
Confessions of a Justified Sinner
Edited by John Carey

THOMAS HUGHES: Tom Brown's Schooldays
Edited by Andrew Sanders

HENRIK IBSEN: An Enemy of the People, The Wild Duck,
Rosmersholm
Edited and Translated by James McFarlane

HENRY JAMES: The Ambassadors
Edited by Christopher Butler

RICHARD JEFFERIES: After London or Wild England
Introduction by John Fowles

JOCELIN OF BRAKELOND:
Chronicle of the Abbey of Bury St. Edmunds
Translated by Diana Greenway and Jane Sayers

GWYN JONES (Transl.):
Eirik the Red and Other Icelandic Sagas

RUDYARD KIPLING: The Day's Work
Edited by Thomas Pinney

CHARLOTTE LENNOX: The Female Quixote
Edited by Margaret Dalziel
Introduction by Margaret Anne Doody

KATHERINE MANSFIELD: Selected Stories
Edited by D. M. Davin

HERMAN MELVILLE: The Confidence-Man
Edited by Tony Tanner

PROSPER MÉRIMÉE: Carmen and Other Stories
Translated by Nicholas Jotcham

MARGARET OLIPHANT:
A Beleaguered City and Other Stories
Edited by Merryn Williams

EDGAR ALLAN POE: Selected Tales
Edited by Julian Symons

PAUL SALZMAN (Ed.):
An Anthology of Elizabethan Prose Fiction

PERCY BYSSHE SHELLEY: Zastrozzi *and* St. Irvyne
Edited by Stephen Behrendt

TOBIAS SMOLLETT: The Expedition of Humphry Clinker
Edited by Lewis M. Knapp
Revised by Paul-Gabriel Boucé

ROBERT LOUIS STEVENSON: Kidnapped and Catriona
Edited by Emma Letley

The Strange Case of Dr. Jekyll and Mr. Hyde
and Weir of Hermiston
Edited by Emma Letley

BRAM STOKER: Dracula
Edited by A. N. Wilson

WILLIAM MAKEPEACE THACKERAY: Barry Lyndon
Edited by Andrew Sanders

LEO TOLSTOY: Anna Karenina
Translated by Louise and Aylmer Maude
Introduction by John Bayley

ANTHONY TROLLOPE: The American Senator
Edited by John Halperin

Dr. Wortle's School
Edited by John Halperin

Orley Farm
Edited by David Skilton

VILLIERS DE L'ISLE-ADAM: Cruel Tales
Translated by Robert Baldick
Edited by A. W. Raitt

VIRGIL: The Aeneid
Translated by C. Day Lewis
Edited by Jasper Griffin

HORACE WALPOLE: The Castle of Otranto
Edited by W. S. Lewis

IZAAK WALTON and CHARLES COTTON:
The Compleat Angler
Edited by John Buxton
Introduction by John Buchan

MRS HUMPHREY WARD: Robert Elsmere
Edited by Rosemary Ashton

OSCAR WILDE: Complete Shorter Fiction
Edited by Isobel Murray

The Picture of Dorian Gray
Edited by Isobel Murray

ÉMILE ZOLA:
The Attack on the Mill and other stories
Translated by Douglas Parmeé